THE CHURCH IN ANGLO-SAXON ENGLAND

BY

JOHN GODFREY

CAMBRIDGE

AT THE UNIVERSITY PRESS

1962

PUBLISHED BY

THE SYNDICS OF THE CAMBRIDGE UNIVERSITY PRESS

Bentley House, 200 Euston Road, London, N.W.1
American Branch: 32 East 57th Street, New York 22, N.Y.
West African Office: P.O. Box 33, Ibadan, Nigeria

©

CAMBRIDGE UNIVERSITY PRESS

1962

*Printed in Great Britain by Spottiswoode, Ballantyne and Company Ltd
London and Colchester*

CONTENTS

CONTENTS

LIST OF ILLUSTRATIONS

PLATES

(Between pp. 504 and 505)

MAPS

PREFACE

It is now more than sixty years since William Hunt wrote his *History of the English Church from its Foundation to the Norman Conquest*, which he claimed as the first attempt at such a history undertaken with any degree of fullness. Meanwhile, many valuable contributions to the subject have appeared in the shape of specialised articles, and Miss Margaret Deanesly's *The Pre-Conquest Church in England* has recently been published. It is the aim of the present work to present a general and fairly comprehensive account of the development of the Church, and its derivative culture, in England from the earliest times until the closing years of the eleventh century. Inevitably, the earlier chapters must deal with Celtic religion, which touched the Anglo-Saxon very closely at many points. At the other end, it was thought preferable to continue the story beyond 1066, as the real close of Anglo-Saxon religious history comes well on in the reign of the Conqueror. The subjects of Anglo-Saxon clerical celibacy, and the history and development of the parochial system, for example, cannot be adequately studied without reference to developments beyond the Conquest.

The aim of the notes has, in general, been threefold: to give references for important or controversial points, to serve as a running guide to further reading, and to include comments which might seem out of place in the text. In the general bibliography I have tried to indicate the broad nature of the material, both primary and secondary, upon which the book is based.

The present nature and circumstances of my life preclude much contact with persons of intellect and scholarship, and it is upon the written word that I have relied for almost the whole of my information. I must in particular thank Sir Frank Stenton for his book *Anglo-Saxon England*, and Miss Dorothy Whitelock, without whose monumental edition of *English Historical Documents, c. 500–1042* my own contribution could scarcely have been made. No new material will be found in this present work, the aim being to utilise as much as possible of the published studies by scholars in various fields. Older books have not been overlooked, particularly W. Bright's *Chapters of Early English Church History*, which is a classic, and J. Lingard's *History and Antiquities of the Anglo-Saxon Church*.

The collection of books on which I have chiefly drawn is that contained in Dr William's Library, Gordon Square, London, whose courteous and efficient staff have made research a real pleasure. My thanks are also due to Dr Elsie Smith, Librarian of Salisbury cathedral; and to Mr Hugh Short, F.S.A., Curator of the Salisbury Museum, for advice in connection with the hanging bowls, one of which (the possession of the Earl of Pembroke) is the most precious object at present in the archeological collection of which he has oversight. I have received general encouragement from my friend the Rev. R. L. Sharp. I was very grateful in the summer of 1960 to the Rev. T. J. Gray, rector of Tyrella, Downpatrick, for conducting me over some of the scenes traditionally associated with St Patrick. There are other good friends, who have shown interest in the progress of the work. To all these, and to the many authors whose writings I have used, I offer my thanks.

For help in the provision of photographs I am indebted to the Trustees of the British Museum, and to Mr D. M. Wilson, Assistant Keeper of the Department of British and Medieval Antiquities; to Dr Wilhelm Holmqvist of Statens Historiska Museum, Stockholm; to Dr Erich Steingreber of the Bayerisches Nationalmuseum, Munich; to Mr G. Lane-Fox Pitt-Rivers, of Pitt-Rivers Museum, Dorset; to the Verkehrsamt of Cologne; to the Trustees of the Victoria and Albert Museum; and to the National Buildings Record. I am grateful to Mr Mark Dineley of Berwick St John, Wilts., for allowing me to reproduce the photograph—made by Mr P. G. Pearce-Smith—of the Frankish brooch in his collection. Miss Carter and Miss Sydenham of Shaftesbury enabled me to include an illustration of a cross-fragment in the abbey ruins which they tend with devoted care. The two folios from Salisbury manuscripts are here reproduced by permission of the dean and chapter and with the help of Dr Smith and Mr H. Bailey. For the Winchester troper photograph I am grateful to the Librarian of Corpus Christi College, Cambridge; and for the photograph of Kirk Hammerton church, to Canon G. W. O. Addleshaw, and to St Anthony's Hall, York. Professor C. W. Kennedy's translations of Anglo-Saxon poetry are utilised in Chapter XII by kind permission of Messrs. Hollis and Carter.

I owe much to the advice and helpful suggestions of the syndics and staff of the Cambridge University Press; and finally, I must express my deepest gratitude to my wife, whose constant encouragement has made the work possible.

John Godfrey

DONHEAD ST ANDREW, WILTSHIRE
1961

ABBREVIATIONS

D.C.B.	*Dictionary of Christian Biography.*
E.E.T.S.	Early English Text Society.
E.H.R.	*English Historical Review.*
Eng. Hist. Doc.	English Historical Documents.
E.P.N.S.	English Place-Name Society Publications.
H.E.	Bede, *Historia Ecclesiastica.*
H. & S.	A. W. Haddon and W. Stubbs, *Councils and Ecclesiastical Documents.*
J.E.H.	*Journal of Ecclesiastical History.*
J.T.S.	*Journal of Theological Studies.*
M.G.H.	*Monumenta Germaniae Historica.*
M.H.B.	*Monumenta Historica Britannica.*
P.L.	J. P. Migne, *Patrologia Latina.*
P.G.	J. P. Migne, *Patrologia Graeca.*
R.S.	Rolls Series.
Trans. R.H.S.	*Transactions of the Royal Historical Society.*
V.C.H.	*Victoria County History.*

*The superior figures in the text refer to notes
that begin on p. 438*

CHAPTER I

PRE-CHRISTIAN RELIGION
IN ROMAN BRITAIN

In the first century B.C. Britain formed part of the Celtic world, which covered a wide area in central and western Europe, and was inhabited by peoples of marked intelligence. Anything but uncouth barbarians, by the time of their conquest at the hands of Rome the Celts had achieved a culture of no mean order. The Celtic peoples were not homogeneous racially, though they had (virtually) a common language and art. There was, however, at least one aspect of their civilisation which does not appear to have been universal amongst them, namely, the religious manifestation known as druidism. This cult has aroused an extraordinary, not to say somewhat undeserved interest in modern times. A voluminous literature has grown up around it, much of it profitless, and it is difficult to arrive at an island of hard facts which may, perhaps, exist in the ocean of romanticism.

The little that is known of the druids is derived from references and passages, largely of a casual nature, in classical authors, of which by far the most valuable is Caesar's description of the system as practised in Gaul.[1] He tells us that the druidic priesthood was held in high veneration. It was these men who officiated at the worship of the gods and supervised the sacrifices. They were the teachers of the young. They made decisions in disputes, such as those concerned with lawsuits or with contested boundaries. If men did not accept their award they were excommunicated, and their neighbours avoided them. The priests were a highly privileged class, organised under a single head elected by his fellows, and exempt from military service and the payment of taxes. They were the custodians of the poetic tradition, knowing great quantities of verse by heart. Their distinctive religious doctrine was the transmigration of souls after death.[2] The original home of druidism, says Caesar, was Britain, whither pupils in his day still went for training in the duties and beliefs of this religion. The druids were the 'professional men' of the Celts, practising the crafts of priest, lawyer, teacher, and administrator. This is clear from

I

Caesar's account, but we must beware of exaggerating the extent of their learning, which by Roman standards was low.

It is not known whether druidism existed elsewhere than in Gaul and Britain, and its real character in the latter country is uncertain. On the strength of Caesar's account, it may be accepted that it was Britain which saw the origin of this religious system.[3] This is not, however, the universal view, and Sir T. D. Kendrick has argued further that the druids, as an organised priesthood, were not a feature of British druidism at all, but only of the Gallic; that there is no satisfactory evidence of a corporation of druids in this country, where druidic worship was conducted probably by kings and tribal chieftains, acting in a priestly capacity; and that the celebrated picture of white-robed priests conducting their rites in great stone circles is a romantic creation, unsupported by concrete evidence. It was Gallic druidism in which the classical writers were apparently interested. In Gaul the druids were undoubtedly a powerful body, politically as well as in the field of religion, until Caesar's time, after which their influence declined. We are told directly of the British druids in only one connection, that of the invasion of Anglesey in A.D. 59, which was described by Tacitus.

There was much that was noble in this religion, such as its encouragement of poetry and its inculcation of the military virtues, but the good was combined with the basest superstition and cruelty. The druids taught that the propitiation of the divine power required the offering of human lives. It was the custom to place criminals alive in huge wicker baskets, made in the shape of images, and set them on fire. Not only the guilty, but sometimes also innocent victims were sacrificed in this way when the supply of criminals ran short. When Boudicca achieved her temporary triumph over the Romans in A.D. 61 she celebrated victory by the offering of human beings. According to Diodorus Siculus and Strabo, the druids had a habit of practising divination from the agonised contortions of the victims whom they stabbed.

The Romans, not a squeamish people, were taken aback by such atrocities. Normally tolerant of strange religions, they acted vigorously against druidism. Suetonius says that the emperor Claudius (41–54) suppressed in Gaul this barbarous religion, which in the time of Augustus had merely been forbidden to Roman citizens.[4] It is clear that in Gaul, following the Roman conquest, druidism was deprived of its power, and indeed was probably identified in the Roman view with the spirit of national resistance. During the reign of Nero (54–68), Suetonius Paulinus launched a determined assault on the isle of Anglesey across the Menai Strait.[5] During the battle the druids, who in this affair appear as fanatical dervishes rather than as enlightened leaders, offered sacrifices and raised their hands to heaven, calling down imprecations on the invaders. At first disconcerted, the Roman soldiers then overpowered their opponents, including the priests and the black-robed women who gave frenzied encouragement to the native warriors. The sacred groves were felled and the island garrisoned. The Romans were determined that there should be none of this dangerous religious fanaticism in the province which they were to govern for nearly four centuries.

Pliny, writing c. A.D. 77, has a certain amount to say of druidical cere-monial.[6] To him it is really a species of magic, practised mainly in Gaul but also in Britain. He informs us that the druids held nothing more sacred than mistletoe and the oak on which it grew. They performed their rites in groves of oak-trees, and wherever mistletoe was discovered on a hard oak, it was cut down with great ceremony by a priest in white vestments bearing a golden sickle. The ceremony included the sacrifice of two white bulls. The mistletoe when given in drink had healing properties, making barren animals fertile, and proving a remedy against poison. The normal places of druidical worship were in fact the woods, and a popular notion of modern times that the megalithic monuments, notably Stonehenge, were the work of druids or normally used by them, is without foundation.[7]

But though druidism, in its most dangerous and revolting aspects, was suppressed, Celtic religion as such survived. Indeed, apart from its strong emphasis on immortality, there seems to have been nothing in the druidical theology to differentiate it from Celtic belief in general. The deities which lay at the heart of Celtic worship were many and various, about forty in number, some of them general Celtic deities known also outside Britain, others tending to assume a local colour. It is this localisation which is the dominant characteristic of Celtic religion in Britain. The archeologist has brought to light the dedica-tions of many divinities, such as Ancasta, a war-goddess, who had an altar at Bitterne, near Southampton.[8] Many of these Celtic deities were adopted by the Romans, or identified by them with gods of their own. Thus Maponus,[9] a young god who delighted in music, was

THE CHURCH IN ANGLO-SAXON ENGLAND

identified with Apollo—he has many dedications at the military station of Corbridge and elsewhere in the north. Cocidius[10] was a popular god regarded by the Romans as equivalent to Mars; he is represented in silver plaques discovered at Bewcastle as a fully armed warrior. He was a common object of worship in the military forts of the north and along the Wall.

An interesting example of a Celtic deity who was taken over by the conquerors is Sul,[11] tutelary goddess who presided over the medicinal hot springs at Bath. Of purely local origin, she is encountered nowhere else in the Empire. The Romans so highly appreciated her qualities that they gave the name 'Waters of Sul' to the place where she was honoured. Aquae Sulis in Romano-British times was never a centre of military or administrative importance, and was indeed quite a small town. But the Romans developed it into a spa which attracted visitors from many quarters, as numerous inscriptions testify. The radioactive waters were genuinely helpful to the rheumatic sufferer. All this was combined or at least parallel with religious devotion, and the temple of the healing goddess became a centre of pilgrimage. The Romans identified Sul with Minerva, their own goddess of healing. The temple at Aquae Sulis was a fine one, constructed along classical lines; there were many altars, and apparently a hierarchy of priests. We know the name of one of the latter, Calpurnius Receptus, whose tombstone has survived.

The second century seems to have been a very fruitful time for Romano-British religion. There are many dedications to Cocidius, and there may also be mentioned (purely by way of example) a temple to two local gods Anociticus and Antenociticus at Benwell, on Hadrian's Wall near Newcastle.[12] In the following century other gods made their appearance, such as Matunus, to whom a temple was built near Elsdon on the Northumbrian moors, during the reign of Caracalla.

It may be that in the third century the official Roman deities were worshipped more widely than before, as a result of the granting of citizenship to all provincials in 213. The greatest of Roman gods was Juppiter Optimus Maximus, who had many altars in this country, most of them set up by army officers. The cult was largely an official one, practised by military units. Juppiter defied assimilation with any native deity. Only once did he assume a Celtic epithet, that of Tanarus, a thunder-god, which appears on an altar dedicated by a centurion at

4

Chester, while on a single known occasion he shared an altar with the native god Cocidius. Other gods, such as Mars, were less aloof, and were frequently equated with British deities. It was Mars, moreover, rather than Juppiter who appealed to the common soldier. Mercury was worshipped for good luck. Minerva was favoured by architects. Vulcan was patron of the smith. The worship of many of these official cults required the services of Roman citizens, acting as *flamines* or high-priests. These deities were mingled or equated with native ones in varying degrees, most commonly in the capitals of the country districts, such as Silchester, where Hercules was equated with a Celtic god Segomo.[13]

Of all subjects of the old Roman deities the soldiers were the most loyal, though their devotion has something of the air of a compulsory church parade. The cult of the *numen* or *numina* of the emperor and his household was popular with the three legions stationed at the fortresses of Caerleon, Chester, and York. The auxiliary regiments, drawn from the provincials, also practised the cult, and the shrine of a regiment would ordinarily contain the statue of the reigning monarch. Vows for the welfare of the emperor and the State were solemnly renewed at the beginning of each year. The soldiers had their official and complementary cults, and on the Wall and elsewhere many dedicated altars survive. At the festival of the Rosaliae the regimental standards, which were customarily kept in chapels for safekeeping, were garlanded with roses, as at Corbridge in Northumberland. The Roman officer stationed on his lonely outpost at Chester or York or on the Wall had a family likeness to his modern British counterpart on the north-west frontier of India. He was brave and conservative, devoted to duty, true to his sovereign, and a staunch supporter of the officially established religion.

The emperor-worship which helped to hold together the diverse Empire for so many centuries was no mere set of sentimental ideas, but a clearly-defined cult. At Colchester (Camulodunum) there was a large and well-equipped temple for the service of the imperial worship, built like the temple at Aquae Sulis along classical lines. It perished in the revolt of Boudicca, queen of the Iceni. It is interesting to notice that though this imperial cult at Colchester was a British one, it had as its object of devotion the emperor. Tribal leaders were elected to serve as priests in turn, paying for festivals and games as part of their service. We find similar groups of priests for the imperial cult at Lincoln and

York, drawn from well-to-do citizens, who as part of their duties were expected to keep in repair such public utility works as bridges and sewers. It was in the service of the imperial cult that the provincials showed their gratitude for the peace and security which Rome had brought them.

One aspect of the cult was the linking up of the worship of the emperor's *numen* with altar and temple dedications. Thus a temple at Chichester (Noviomagus) was dedicated to Neptune and Minerva on behalf of the imperial family. Chichester also had a statue dedicated to Nero. The imperial cult was widespread in Britain, whose inhabitants apparently found it congenial. The *numen* of the emperor could either be worshipped by itself, or, as was frequently the case, in association with gods of various kinds.

There was one department of Roman religion however which seems to have made little appeal to the provincial inhabitants of Britain. This consisted of the Eastern cults, which had a strong hold on many Romans during the closing centuries of the Empire of the West. The influence which they exercised was a personal one, and they fulfilled a need of the human soul which the official deities of the pantheon could not satisfy. They were emotional, and yet in a sense intellectual, offering answers to many perplexing questions. Despite their attractions, however, these cults were practised in Britain only by the soldiers and the more Romanised urban elements of the population.

Such a cult was that of Juppiter Dolichenus, which is known to have existed in this country, and whose oracles were helpful to many. His elaborate worship required an unusual type of temple, containing various compartments. The cult was at its strongest in Britain during the third century. The Egyptian divinities Serapis and Isis also had their devotees, and so had the Asian Cybele, whose worship is suggested by fragments of sculpture at Corbridge. But most important of these cults in Britain was that of Mithras, a god of Zoroastrian origin, who had arrived in Rome during the first century B.C. It was a secret cult, open only to men, and welcomed especially by the soldiers. It offered a unique knowledge of God and union with him, demanding in return a high standard of conduct. Members were introduced to the mysteries by graded stages, and exacting tests were imposed on candidates. It was a difficult religion to follow, and the evidence for Britain suggests that its adherents here were comparatively few in relation to the numbers of those practising other cults. Such Mithraic dedications as we possess are nearly always the work of army officers. The temples are invariably small, designed to accommodate a handful of worshippers. They are all in military areas, with the single known exception in London, which served the needs of merchants. The cult was at its height in the third and early fourth centuries. Temples have been excavated at Housesteads, Rudchester, and in recent years at Carrawburgh,[14] all on Hadrian's Wall. A Persian cult thus reached to the distant confines of the north-west—a remarkable testimony to the mobility of religious ideas possessing sufficient capacity to answer man's deepest needs. The three Wall temples, which were all of course dedicated by soldiers (in two cases by regimental commanders), had their vicissitudes, and the succession of worship was apparently not always maintained. It seems there were times when the number of worshippers on a station would sink to one or two. The Carrawburgh temple came to an end early in the fourth century, when it was destroyed and turned into a rubbish dump, which must surely be the most ignominious fate which could overtake a place of worship. This may well have been the work of a zealous Christian commanding officer, following the Edict of Milan in 313.

The ritual varied at these Mithraic shrines. But Mithras himself was common to them, along with his attendant gods of Light and Darkness. Mithras was a god of the sun, Sol Invictus, who always triumphed over darkness. There is evidence at Carrawburgh and Housesteads for a bull-killing relief, but no indication of a taurobolium or pit in which initiates stood while the blood of a slain bull was poured over them. Mithras himself certainly was a bull-slayer, but the nauseating ceremonies involving baptism in the blood of a bull belonged to the Mysteries of the Phrygian Cybele rather than to Mithraism.

Besides the three temples on Hadrian's Wall, there is other evidence for the existence of the cult, as at Carlisle, Newcastle, Wallsend, and elsewhere. A post-war discovery which aroused wide public interest was the Mithraic temple in London, which seems for the most part to have served the spiritual needs of merchants from the East.

Non-Christian religion during the Romano-British period thus presents a picture of almost bewildering variety. The Celtic form of religion, though under the druids (at any rate in Gaul) powerfully organised, was from a spiritual point of view never more than fragmentary. Numerous unconnected divinities, with diverse attributes and qualities, and with local significance, were scattered over the province in wood and stream and hill. The Roman religion with its Juppiter presiding loftily over the destinies of the State, and its worship of the deified emperors, had a stronger underlying reality and unity. But to a large extent it was an official faith, lacking warmth or depth; to many Romans it must have seemed that its demise could not be long delayed. The rise of the Mysteries indicated the need for a religion essentially more religious. The time was ripe, in Britain as elsewhere, for a new and altogether dynamic religion, which would be close to men's hearts and yet firmly based on the eternal Godhead; which would grapple with the fundamental problems of existence, and offer its adherents an attractive, if stern and exacting, way of life.

CHAPTER II

CHRISTIANITY IN ROMAN AND SUB-ROMAN BRITAIN

It is quite impossible to determine the exact origin of the Christian religion in Britain, though persistent attempts have been made to carry its beginning back to the very dawn of the Christian era. In this way some half-dozen apostles have been brought to these shores, notably St Paul. The earliest writer who has been held to state that the great Apostle of the Gentiles came to Britain is the Gallic poet and bishop Venantius Fortunatus, who wrote in the latter half of the sixth century. But this view is drawn from a faulty reading of his verse, and in any case a line or two of poetry is no firm foundation for a historical fact.[1] A much earlier writer, Clement of Rome, stated that Paul came to 'the boundary of the West',[2] but this could refer to Spain and not necessarily Britain, or could be a merely rhetorical designation of the western extremities of the Empire. Welsh legend tells how Bran the Blessed, father of the British hero Caratacus, went to Rome as a hostage for his son, became a Christian during his sojourn there, and brought the Faith back with him to Britain, early in the second half of the first century. But Tacitus, who gives an account of Caratacus, and mentions his wife, daughters, and brothers, says nothing of his father.[3] Indeed the latter must certainly have been dead at the time, to allow of his son's being possessed of the chieftainship.

The most famous and beautiful legend of all relating to the conversion of Britain is of course that of Joseph of Arimathea, who is said to have arrived in Britain with twelve companions in the year 63 at the bidding of the apostle Philip. According to this tradition Joseph brought with him the Holy Grail, and built at Glastonbury the first British church. The story first appears in the writings of the twelfth-century William of Malmesbury,[4] and probably had its origin amongst the Glastonbury monks. It was subsequently repeated by many medieval writers with sundry variations, and after surviving the Reformation period, was assailed by archbishop Ussher in the first half of the seventeenth century and finally demolished by Edward

9

Stillingfleet, bishop of Worcester, in 1685. The latter writer, however, made out a case for the coming of St Paul to Britain which convinced many historians until comparatively recent times.[5]

Controversialists of the Reformation period and beyond found in the theme of the arrival of Christianity in Britain a happy playground. Thus archbishop Ussher in his *Discourse of the Religion Anciently Professed by the Irish and the British*, published in 1631, was anxious to demonstrate the non-papal ancestry of the British Church. Writers belonging to the Reformed Churches tried hard to show that the earliest Church of these islands was actually a Protestant Church, which was a distortion of the truth. On the other hand Romanists sought to prove that the Church of Britain was a daughter of Rome, making much of the story of Lucius. According to this account, which apparently was a Roman tradition of sixth-century origin,[6] in 167 Lucius, king of the Britons, requested pope Eleutherus to send missionaries to his country. According to Bede,[7] the mission was a success, and the Britons preserved their new faith uncorrupted and entire, until the time of Diocletian (284–305). Lucius was certainly a historical figure, but Bede erred in thinking he had anything to do with Britain. There could have been no native British ruler at this time with the power of independent action which the story implies, especially when the object of Lucius' request was at variance with official Roman policy. Lucius was otherwise known as Agbarus IX, king of Edessa (or Britium). The story is not mentioned by the sixth-century writer Gildas, the usual authority for early Church history in Britain used by Bede, who has clearly adopted the Roman tradition. The ninth-century British writer Nennius repeats the story.[8]

Such legends, of great interest in themselves, have a historical value in that they indicate by implication the very early advent of Christianity to this country. It is perhaps an overstatement to say that the legends were invented to explain a fact, but there is at least this grain of truth or likelihood in the Lucius story—that the second half of the second century was probably the period during which the Faith was introduced to the province of Britain. There is no evidence however of any missionary activity, and we may suppose rather that there were individual contacts, commercial and military, between Britain and Gaul which resulted in a natural germination of Christianity in the former country. Even this is at best a supposition; to say more would be mere guesswork. But there is a small corpus of patristic evidence which suggests that there were Christians (though not necessarily an organised Church) in Britain by the late second century. Thus in a list of Christian lands, including the regions of the Celts, compiled by Irenaeus in about 176, no mention is made of Britain.[9] But by the beginning of the third century the Faith had made sufficient progress to attract the notice of two distant Fathers. Writing *c.* 200 or shortly afterwards, Tertullian includes the Britons in a list of peoples who have accepted Christ. Christianity, he says, has penetrated to the remote parts of Britain which the Romans have not been able to reach.[10] If this could be taken literally, and not as the rhetorical exaggeration which it probably is, it would be a significant statement, implying a widespread diffusion of Christianity in Britain. As it is, however, it is a valuable statement as being the first concrete reference to the existence of Christianity here. About a generation later, Origen makes a number of references to this country.[11] He says that the Christian religion has secured adherents in Britain, though most Britons have not yet heard the Gospel.

It is tempting to assume from the negative statement of Irenaeus *c.* 176 and the positive one of Tertullian *c.* 200, that it was definitely in the last quarter of the second century that Christianity was introduced to Britain. But the evidence is too slender to support so cut-and-dried a solution. Thus, Christians may well have existed as individuals in Britain at the time Irenaeus was writing, though not in sufficient numbers to attract the attention of outside observers. Again, the testimonies of Tertullian and Origen may be taken as proof that the Faith of Christ was being practised in the island as the third century opened. But the number of Christians must have been small, and as a Church they can have made no impact on society. The influential religious movements of the time were all non-Christian.

Eusebius, writing during the fourth century in defence of Christianity, amongst various arguments uses that of its success. If, he asks, the apostles were deceivers, how did they come to progress so widely through the world? The fact that they conquered Rome, Persia, Armenia, Scythia, and that some should have penetrated even to the land of the Indians on the one hand and crossed over to the British Isles on the other, is surely proof of divine aid.[12] Coming from one of the most reputable of early Church historians, this is an impressive testimony to the very early arrival of Christianity in Britain. But the passage in which it occurs is highly rhetorical and could hardly have been intended by the writer as a factual statement, except in the broadest terms. It would seem to prove no more than that by the time Eusebius wrote, the doctrine of the apostles was well established in Britain. Of a similar nature is the testimony of Theodoret, bishop of Cyrus, early in the fifth century; he states that the fishermen, publicans, and tent-makers (that is to say, the apostles and earliest disciples) successfully evangelised the Romans and other nations, including the Scythians, Persians, Britons, and Germans.

The Church in Britain probably made small but steady progress during the third century, and then there came a setback. According to Bede the persecution of Diocletian, the last great effort of the Empire to extirpate Christianity, reached Britain, and many persons died in the confession of their faith.[13] Amongst the martyrs were Alban, who suffered near Verulamium, and Aaron and Julius. It must be remembered however that Bede is less reliable for the earlier period than he is for the Anglo-Saxon period of Church history, and his account cannot be taken at its face value. Bede's authority for the British Church, as noted above, was Gildas, a rather vague writer who lived in the sixth century.

Gildas praises the courage in persecution of Alban of Verulam, Aaron and Julius—whom he calls citizens of Caerleon—and others, both men and women, in both places. He relates the famous story of Alban's hiding of the confessor who is being pursued by his persecutors and his exchange of clothes with him. He tells how the survivors of the persecution hid in woods, deserts, and caves, and how ten years after the upheaval the Christians repaired their churches, which had been levelled with the ground, and also founded new ones in memory of the martyrs.

But we cannot be sure that this disturbance in Britain was actually part of the Diocletianic persecution (303–5), and in fact Gildas himself confessed his uncertainty over the matter. After mentioning the perse-cution of Diocletian in other lands, he then comes to the British perse-cution, that in which Alban suffered, and in his own words, 'he con-cludes' that the latter was a part of the former persecution.[14] It is clear from his text that he had no precise or authentic authority for his state-ment. On this self-confessed conjecture of Gildas is ultimately based the whole tradition that Alban suffered during the persecution of Diocletian. We may perhaps feel more certain of the connection between Alban and Verulam, which is distinctly mentioned by Gildas, who as a writer usually avoided precise statements. But there is not a word of Verulam in the late fifth-century *Life of Germanus*, by Constantius, in which we find our earliest reference to Alban. According to this work, the Gallic bishops Germanus and Lupus, of whom we shall hear more later, came to Britain in 429 and during the course of their stay paid a visit to the tomb of Alban, where they offered prayers and relics. In the final analysis, therefore, we can be certain that in the earlier part of the fifth century Alban was being reverenced as a martyr in Britain.

A strong argument against our identifying the British persecution as part of the general one of 303–5 is that Britain belonged to that section of the Empire then under the caesar Constantius, who seems to have had some sympathy for Christians.[15] On the other hand, the reference of Gildas to the levelling of churches is entirely in line with what is known of Diocletian's campaign against Christianity, in which the destruction of churches and the sacred books played an exceptionally prominant part. If the persecution in Britain did not belong to the Diocletianic, it must have been part of the Decian (249–51), and it is doubtful whether there was really a Church worth the persecuting in Britain by that early date.

With the accession of Constantine to the imperial seat and the consequent Great Peace there was a general advance of the Church all over the Empire. The celebrated 'edict' of toleration at Milan in 313, probably a joint statement of the two Augusti, Constantine and Licinius, declared that those who wished to practise Christian worship might now do so without interference, and all confiscated Church property was to be restored to its rightful ownership. Licinius, whose sphere of responsibility was the East, failed to keep his word, but in the West the gain was permanent and persecution was not renewed. An important consequence of this unprecedented State patronage was that during the fourth century the bishops were able to deliberate in a series of Councils. The Church in Britain shared in the new life, and sent three bishops to the Council of Arles, in 314, which met to settle a dispute relating to the election of a bishop for the see of Carthage. The name and title of only one of the three bishops is certain—Restitutus, bishop of London. One was bishop of York, and called Eborius, which sounds more like his title than his name. The third was a bishop named Adelphius, possibly of Lincoln or Caerleon. They took a priest and deacon with them. The Council of Arles, amongst its canons, enjoined that clergy should remain in the places to which they were ordained, and that bishops should not invade dioceses not their own. Ordinations were to be performed by seven bishops acting together, or three at the least. It is clear from such provisions that the Churches represented at the Council were of the regular episcopal and diocesan type. At the close of the proceedings the Council sent a copy of its decisions to pope Sylvester.

Soon afterwards, in 325, the great Council of Nicaea was held, but there is no satisfactory evidence that it was attended by British representatives. The lists of bishops present at this first ecumenical gathering of ecclesiastics vary and are not too reliable.[16] Though the invitation to attend the Council was extended by Constantine to the whole Church, the West does not appear to have been interested in the points at issue, which were of a subtle theological character. The emperor's offer of a free journey failed to tempt the Western bishops, and even the bishop of Rome was only represented by two deacons. There was one bishop from Italy present, and one from Gaul. In these circumstances it is scarcely likely that there should have been any representation from Britain. The exact number of bishops attending is unknown, though it was probably in the region of two hundred and fifty, most of them from the Greek-speaking provinces. The Council drew up a statement of faith, and passed twenty canons concern- ing Church law and discipline. Its condemnation of Arianism was accepted by the British Church, of whose general orthodoxy at this time there can be no doubt.[17] By this time the island Church had a tradition of sound instruction behind it, as a result of which it was able to show a firm front towards current alternatives to Catholic Christianity.

In 343 a Council was held at Sardica, the modern Sophia, which again upheld the orthodox position, of which the champion was Athanasius. The lists of bishops present do not specify any from Britain,[18] but we do know that the Church of Britain again accepted the orthodox findings, as this is acknowledged by Athanasius himself.[19] It appears that many bishops sent in their adherence to the Council, though unable to attend. In general, the British Church at this time was apparently recognised for its soundness of belief. In 358 Hilary of Poitiers, while an exile in Phrygia, wrote to the bishops of Britain, amongst others, praising them for their freedom from heresy.[20] Besides its doctrinal affirmations, the Sardica Council marked an important step forward in the development of papal authority, as it appears to have accorded to Rome a primacy of jurisdiction, as distinct from the primacy of honour which it already possessed. At the close of the Council the bishops present sent an account of their deliberations to pope Julius, their reason for this action, as they said, being that it was meet that the bishops should make reference to their head, the see of St Peter.

Britain was definitely represented at the Council of Ariminum, which met in 360 and consisted of some four hundred bishops. It is known that three British bishops who attended took advantage of the offer of the emperor Constantius to draw their travelling expenses from imperial funds; the possibility is of course not excluded that there were other bishops from Britain present who made private arrangements over their expenses.[21] It is interesting in this connection to find a question being asked by fourth-century churchmen which is an issue in our own day. Should the clergy be dependent for their financial support on public funds, or on the generosity of their congregations? Sulpicius Severus says that these three British bishops, alone of the entire assembly, drew assistance from the State, preferring this course to accepting the charity of individuals. He defends their action, upon which, however, a certain bishop Gavidius pours contempt.[22]

It is clear from the above evidence that the Church was well established in fourth-century Britain, with a hierarchy of Catholic bishops, and accepted on the Continent as an integral part of the Church Universal. In the last quarter of the century this British membership of the whole Church is proved beyond question by the many references in the works of Chrysostom and Jerome. But it is probable that the British Church was quite small, consisting of local community-groups, with a total membership comprising a modest proportion of the population. Assuming the pattern followed to be that of Gaul and Italy, each community-group of any size—invariably situated in a town— would have its bishop. The later system whereby dioceses were comparatively few, the bishop ruling a large territorial area, grew up amongst the Germanic peoples. During the first four centuries the Church generally was an urban institution, and there is no reason whatever for supposing that unique conditions prevailed in Britain. While the conciliar and patristic evidence, therefore, definitely establishes that the episcopal system was at work in Britain during the fourth century, it may mislead us (by the paucity of specific references) into thinking that there were fewer bishops than there actually were.

There may have been many bishops, their relationships with their flocks being pastoral and personal, similar to those between the incumbent and congregation of a large town parish today. Such churchmen would be far removed in character from the monarchical prelates of the middle ages and perhaps even more from the committee bishops of modern times. The British bishops, it may be further remarked, do not seem to have been mere attached functionaries, as in the Celtic Churches later on; we find them referred to by the names of their sees. The organisation was not tribal, but diocesan.

Very few material objects survive from the Romano-British Church. In 1892 there were discovered at Silchester (Calleva Atrebatum) in Hampshire, near Basingstoke, the remains of a building which would seem to have been a church, situated in the vicinity of the forum of the Roman town. There is no inscription or monogram to indicate definitely that it was a Christian building, but its plan, conforming to the basilican type common in the Empire during the fourth century, can leave us in little doubt. The building, which is orientated, contains a central portion thirty feet long by ten feet wide, with a western apse. There are aisles on either side. At the east end is a narthex seven feet deep, extending the whole width of the building. Some mosaic paving in the apse seems to mark the site of the altar. A very small building is thus suggested, which served the needs of the Christian community in a town of two thousand inhabitants or more. A Christian gold ring found in Silchester doubtless belonged to some member of this church's congregation. The Christians were clearly a minority, and in the same town there was a temple of Mars, used apparently until the end of the Roman period, in addition to three other temples.[23]

The poverty and minority-status of the Romano-British Church are apparent from the circumstance that there was no Christian style as such in the art of Roman Britain. Amongst the few surviving material objects there is nothing except the subject-matter and one or two signs to indicate that the owners were, or seem to have been, Christian. In Cumberland and Westmorland there are a few Christian tombstones, as also in the extreme south-west, particularly Cornwall. The sacred monogram for the name of Christ has been found in villas, worked into mosaics, as at Chedworth in Gloucestershire. A mosaic at Frampton, Dorset, also has the Chi-Rho, worked into a general pavement-pattern which includes a representation of Neptune and an inscription dedicated to him. Artistic eclecticism of this kind proves nothing. It may indicate that the owner was a pagan at heart, but not unwilling to give a cautious welcome to the religion favoured by the imperial court; it may, on the other hand, suggest a Christian of convinced beliefs compelled to accept a decoration of pagan motifs because of the traditional atmosphere still prevailing in art, yet determined to include some small symbol of his own religious convictions. The same Christian emblem of the Chi-Rho was found on pewter plate at Appleshaw, Hants. It is also seen, along with the fish symbol, on finger-rings and other objects, and the fact that examples tend to multiply towards the close of the fourth century is held to suggest that Christianity gradually found acceptance amongst the richer classes. Earlier in this century it appears to have been chiefly a religion of the poor, from which the wealthy and educated kept aloof, even for a considerable period after Milan in 313. The indigent bishops of 360, who alone in the whole Catholic Church had to accept government charity, were probably the leaders of a Church which was economically poor.

It is hazardous to speculate on the nature of church decoration and furnishings during this period. There has been some discussion over the function of a series of bowls, of which there are examples at Faversham, Lullingstone, Salisbury, and elsewhere.[24] The presence of the cross and the fish amongst their decorative motifs suggests Christian workmanship, and it may well be that these bowls, which were suspended by chains, served some ecclesiastical purpose. Their use as church lamps seems to be ruled out by the frequent occurrence of intricate carving in the interior. Perhaps they were used as washing basins, or even as pyxes for the reserved sacrament. They may of course have been purely domestic. There is a similar ambiguity in a fine repoussé silver flagon, of the late Romano-British period, part of the treasure discovered on Traprain Law in East Lothian in 1919, a frieze of which depicts the Temptation of Eve, the striking of the Rock by Moses, and the Adoration of the Magi. Though there is nothing to suggest that this flagon was necessarily an ecclesiastical vessel, it is a good example of the type of thing which may have been in use in some churches. In the same treasure was a *colatorium*, or strainer for the wine used in the Eucharist. That Christianity was still not fully sure of its position, even as late as the early fifth century, is shown by the fact of the adaptation of a villa for use as a church. In the villa discovered at Lullingstone in Kent two rooms had been adapted for Christian worship; one room had a scheme of coloured frescoes, with the Chi-Rho set within a wreath of leaves and buds, while the other was decorated with a row of *orante* figures within a portico on the west wall, and a Chi-Rho, also within a wreath.[25]

The Church in Britain being generally urban, its churches would be sited in places subsequently built over and difficult to excavate. This possibility must be allowed for in any assessment of the incidence of Christian archeological remains. There must have been a good many churches such as that of St Martin, Canterbury, built during the Roman period, and where queen Bertha later worshipped. Bede explicitly states that Ethelbert gave permission in 597 to Augustine and his companions to build or repair churches.[26]

Throughout the fourth century, however, Christianity had still to compete with pagan rivals. In spite of the adoption of the Faith by Constantine, it was by no means taken for granted that the Church had triumphed. Nobody could have foretold the glorious victories which yet awaited her, and it would have been madness even to suggest that a Christian civilisation would replace that of Rome, which her citizens still regarded as eternal. After Milan most citizens of the Empire remained non-Christians. In Britain, Romano-Celtic temples were being built during the fourth century. There was a widespread, lingering regard for the old religion. Julian the Apostate, emperor from 361 to 363, openly repudiated Christ and made a bold attempt to restore paganism along new lines, borrowing several features from Christianity. He realised the strength and appeal of the Church, and tried to make paganism equally attractive. Thus he imitated the charitable work of the Church, and adopted Christian ecclesiastical organisation at certain points. He did not revive persecution, though if he had reigned longer he would probably have been driven to do so eventually in order to maintain his policy. His chance death in an expedition on the Persian frontier ended this rather bizarre experiment.

It is tempting to ascribe to the reactionary reign of Julian a Juppiter column which once stood on a stone pedestal seventeen inches wide and high, inscribed on three sides, found in 1891 at Cirencester (Corinium), where it may still be seen.[27] The inscription records that L. Septimius, governor of Britannia Prima, restored this monument to Juppiter; on the top of the pedestal is a hole for the tenon of the actual column, which has disappeared. This appears to be the re-erection, by a man with nostalgic feelings for the old religion, of an old heathen monument which had been neglected through the growth of a new faith. It is an indication that here in Cirencester, as in Silchester, Christianity had a firm (if only a limited) hold in the fourth century.

It has been thought that a similar pagan revival can be inferred from a group of altars concentrated for the most part in the central area of Hadrian's Wall. The value of their inscriptions is seriously weakened by reason of their inconsistent spelling, though it seems clear that the deity to whom the altars are dedicated was Hvitir, who (to judge from the initial aspirate) may have been a German god. But the plural is often used, and it is possible to argue that the dedicators may have had in mind the *di veteres*, the 'old gods'.[28]

There can be no doubt however about a temple to the Celtic deity Nodens, at Lydney in the Severn valley. We have here a substantial and thriving heathen establishment constructed a half-century or more after Milan. The whole, built within an earthwork on a hill-top, contains elaborate arrangements for the convenience of the numerous pilgrims who visited the shrine. The eight thousand Roman coins, mostly of the fourth century, discovered in the neighbourhood, are clear enough evidence of the number of those pilgrims. There are bathrooms and a guesthouse. The construction of the building is solid. There is no indication here that the local inhabitants regarded the old religion as worn out and Christianity as necessarily the universal religion of the not too distant future.

At the beginning of the fifth century a great darkness falls upon Britain as elsewhere in the Empire of the west. So it must assuredly seem to the historian today, though the citizen of *c.* 400 or for many years after would have been puzzled by any suggestion that the old order had commenced its decline. To the average man a world without the Empire was scarcely conceivable. The great new fact of the time, little did he know it, was the emergence of the Church as a power in the affairs of men. Even Christians themselves probably did not realise the greatness which was becoming theirs through the agency of the Holy Spirit and the march of events. Content to argue over abstruse theological dogmas, they had little sense of their destiny to dominate public life in the secular world. In general, they were satisfied with the luxury of their newly found peace and security. On the other hand, there was beginning to appear that missionary spirit which would transform the face of Europe and carry the name of Christ to outlying regions. By about the middle of the fourth century a brave attempt had already been made to convert the Goths by an evangelist of unorthodox views but outstanding character. This was Ulfilas, who amongst other labours translated the scriptures into Gothic. New energies and enthusiasms were stirring the hearts of many Christians. The long struggle with a persecuting State had kindled a martial, not to say intolerant, spirit in the heart of the Church.

In spite of the shadows, and perhaps because of them, the Church in Britain now begins to emerge more clearly, and recognisably great Christians make their appearance. Of such was St Patrick, the Apostle of Ireland, and the first considerable missionary to leave the shores of Britain. The exact details of his career are tantalisingly uncertain, though a clear impression of a great man may be obtained from two primary authorities, the *Confessio* found amongst other material in the illuminated manuscript in the library of Trinity College Dublin known as the Book of Armagh, and an epistle to the subjects of a British prince Coroticus which is contained in later manuscripts.[29] Both these works are accepted with confidence as Patrick's own, probably written towards the close of his life. Subsequently, Patrick is not mentioned until a letter of Cummian, abbot of Durrow, *c.* 630, in which he is referred to as 'Patricius, papa noster'. Bede does not allude to him, but that writer was not especially interested in Ireland and had no love for the ways of Celtic Christians. Two documents of the second half of the seventh century, an incomplete memoir of the saint by Tirechán, and a Life by Muirchú, contain material which is probably a compound of legends and genuine traditions.

Many theories have been put forward by modern scholars, and the situation is still far too fluid for a general work to offer other than the traditional view of Patrick's life and career, expounded as it was, for example, by Professor J. B. Bury in his classic treatment of the subject.[30]

According to this view, which hitherto has been regarded as sufficiently convincing but which may in the light of future research have to be revised at various points, Patrick had a church upbringing, he himself being a Christian of the third or fourth generation. So he informs us in his autobiographical *Confessio*, where he writes that his grandfather Potitus was a priest and his father Calpurnius a deacon.[31] One notes the existence of a married clergy, but even as early as the fourth century efforts were being made to enforce celibacy. In 385, a few years before Patrick's birth, pope Siricius had expressed his disapproval of married priests.[32] Patrick's mother was called Concessa; his own Romanic name Patricius was apparently combined with the native one of Sucat. The adoption of Roman names was but one way by which British Celts expressed their confidence in the Empire. Calpurnius, Patrick's father, was a man of some small property, owning a farm, and performing the unpopular duties of *decurio* or town-councillor.[33] As Constantine had exempted the clergy from the civic obligations of the *curia*, with its ruinous financial responsibilities, it may be that Calpurnius was rendering these services voluntarily. His son Patrick was born *c.* 389, at Bannavem Taberniae, the site of which is unknown, though it was probably somewhere near the western coasts of Britain, as the family were the victims of an Irish raid *c.* 405.[34] Possibly the site was in the vicinity of the Severn mouth, in which case the family would be living not very far from the temple at Lydney. Certainly there must have been many instances about this time of Christian families living alongside a still vigorous paganism. Perhaps many Christians were not uninfluenced by the attempts of the traditional religion to reassert itself. Some Britons may have been sceptical altogether. Patrick himself informs us that when he was carried off he was an unbeliever, though the Lord enlightened him in captivity.

As a result of the raid the young Patrick was taken to Ireland with many other captives. The episode illustrates the insecurity in which Romano-Britons now increasingly passed their lives. At the opening of the fifth century the raids of the Scots (Irish) were increasing, with the decline of the Roman power.

There followed six years of slavery for Patrick in Connaught, in the servitude of one Milchu, during which time the lad's faith as a Christian was aroused. He says that 'the Lord opened the perception of his unbelief'. As he tended the cattle of his master, he found solace in frequent prayers. He would rise in the middle of the night, in frost, cold, or rain, to seek his God. One night he had a dream, which led him to forsake his bonds. He heard a voice telling him that he would soon depart for his native land, and that a ship was ready for him. Escaping, he crossed the sea in a merchant-vessel laden with a cargo of the Irish wolf-hounds highly prized in Europe. He landed with the crew in a desolate tract of country, where they wandered for a month. This was probably Gaul, much of which was a wilderness following the devastations of the invading Vandals, Alans, and Sueves from c. 407 onwards. He made his way, it seems, to the small island of Lérins off the coast of Provence, where a monastic community had recently been founded by St Honoratus. His vocation was stirring within him, and after preliminary training at Lérins he proceeded to Auxerre, where according to a strong Irish tradition he was a pupil of St Germanus. At about the time of his vocation there probably occurred the visit which he is known to have made to his home and family in Britain, whom he found safe and well. They did their best to persuade him to remain with them, but his resolution was fixed. In 432 he was consecrated, following years of preparation in which he never became an accomplished scholar but which gave him the orthodox basis of belief on which his missionary labours in Ireland were to meet with considerable success.

Patrick was not the first in the field in Ireland. Christians from that country were already making their mark on the Continent in the fourth century, judging from the instance of Mansuetus, first bishop of Toul, who was said to be an Irishman. According to the tenth-century poet Adso, writing in his Life of Mansuetus, Ireland had Christians in that bishop's time. Jerome c. 416 wrote contemptuously of a certain ignorant Irishman who was a Christian. Fragmentary evidence of this sort, however, indicates no more than that there were individual Irishmen who were eager for the truth, but had to leave their native country to find it.[35] We are on firmer ground with a statement of Prosper of Aquitaine that in 431 pope Celestine sent Palladius to be the first bishop to those Irishmen who believed in Christ.[36] But the existence of individual believers in Ireland does not necessitate the presupposition of an established Irish Church. Indeed, Prosper elsewhere writes that while Celestine endeavoured to keep Britain Catholic, his concern with Ireland was to make it Christian.[37] The statement of this chronicler, writing in the fifth century almost contemporaneously with the events which he is recounting, that the episcopacy was given to Ireland initially by the papacy has been accorded its due meed of importance. It places the apparent indifference of Patrick himself to the Roman see in a somewhat puzzling light, though it must be remembered that at this early stage Rome had not yet become the arbiter and mistress of the Churches, and it was by no means considered necessary to make constant reference to Rome.

In the event, the mission of Palladius was short-lived, terminated probably by his death a few months after its commencement. It was then, according to the traditional view, that Patrick, by this time a man of some forty-three years, arrived to begin his renowned apostolate.

The Ireland to which he came was agricultural and rural, quite devoid of urban life. This fact must be borne in mind when we consider the subsequent development of church organisation in that country. In Gaul and Roman Britain the civic arrangements for government affected the ecclesiastical, being intrinsically conducive to the diocesan system. Ireland was tribal, ruled by a multitude of small kings, their subjects living mostly in villages or isolated farmsteads. The unit of society was the *tuarth* or tribe, and it is not difficult to envisage the evolution of religious tribal communities against such a background. This actually transpired after Patrick's death, though he himself was not a protagonist of that monastic organisation which was to become so marked a feature of Celtic Christianity.

One of Patrick's objectives on his arrival in Ireland was the conversion of Milchu, his old master, who, however, on the advice of his druids shut himself up in his house, which he then set on fire, and perished in the flames rather than risk being caught in the Christian spell. The druids, Patrick's main adversaries, were indeed a great influence in Ireland, though little is known about them, since all reference to them was deliberately excluded from the early laws of the country when these came to be revised under Christian influence. There were points of difference between the druids of Gaul and those of Ireland. It is clear, however, that the latter were the scholars and teachers, and regarded by the people as sorcerers and magicians. They would naturally see in Christianity a threat to their position. Akin to them were the bards, who were the poets and historians—men greatly in demand, but resented for their mercenary attitude. Attempts were sometimes made to suppress them, as later at a great gathering at Drumceatt in 575. The bards, however, were not specifically heathen, and readily adapted themselves to the new religion, in which indeed they found much scope for their musical and poetical talents. The account of Patrick's contest with the druids at the court of Loiguire the High King at Tara is legendary, but it helps to explain the nature of the opposition which the missionary-saint encountered. It is clear that in the course of his mission he broke the power of heathenism, and came to exercise much influence over the tribal kings. The latter in their acceptance of Christianity would be invariably followed by their subjects. Patrick adopted the practice, essential to missionaries in the Dark Ages following the imperial collapse, of attempting above all the conversion of the nobility. Once this was accomplished the battle was won.

But Patrick had a lively care for all members of his flock, as is shown by the episode of Coroticus. This prince was the ruler of Strathclyde, one of those local potentates who maintained order after the withdrawal of the Romans. He was himself a baptised Christian, but of barbarous manner of life. On a certain occasion his soldiers carried out a marauding raid on the Irish coast, as a result of which they took captive some recently baptised converts, and put others to the sword. Patrick acted promptly. He sent a letter by trusted messengers to Strathclyde, in which he laid the responsibility for the outrage on Coroticus, and demanded the release of the captives.

Whether or not Patrick's letter had any beneficial outcome is unknown, but it survives as one of our best authorities for the character of Patrick himself. Written like the *Confessio* in an uncultivated style, it is proof enough of the lack of learning of which the writer himself was fully conscious, and which apparently brought upon him contempt from some of his contemporaries in Britain. Both works however reveal a truly great Christian, capable and enthusiastic, inspired by a lofty sense of vocation.

Patrick was also the probable author of the justly famous 'Lorica', popularly known as St Patrick's Breastplate, and associated in modern hymnology with Trinity Sunday. It is contained in a manuscript book of hymns in the possession of Trinity College, ascribed to the eleventh or twelfth centuries. Composed in an ancient dialect, the 'Lorica' is evidently the production of a time when paganism was still a powerful force in Ireland. It breathes the spirit of early Irish Christianity. In our own day this hymn is a favourite with young people and can be heard at its best in a public-school chapel.[38] It echoes the enthusiasm which the great apostle enkindled in the hearts of his converts. This magnificent hymn, regarded by the early Irish Christians as a strong shield against natural and supernatural terrors, also illustrates the legendary power of Patrick against demons, serpents, and toads. The well-known immunity of Ireland from snakes and other loathsome creatures has been attributed to the beneficent influence of the saint.[39] The legend of the shamrock, however, though the most popular of the many associated with his life, cannot be traced back earlier than

1600. It is not mentioned in any of the early or medieval lives of the saint.

Patrick laboured long in Ireland, and though he did not complete the conversion of this country, he is the true founder of the Irish Church. There is some evidence that in 441 he may have visited Rome, at the beginning of the pontificate of Leo I, who is said to have confirmed him in the Catholic Faith.[40] Of greater certainty is the foundation of the primatial see of Armagh in 444, Patrick's most important ecclesiastical act. It seems that some four years before his death, Patrick resigned the see of Armagh, and spent the closing stages of his life in retirement. He died in 461 at Saul (where he is reputed to have built his first church), on Strangford Lough in the modern County Down, hard by Downpatrick. In the traditions which grew up, these places disputed with Armagh the honour of holding his grave.

There are no visible remains of the churches founded by Patrick, and indeed the average contemporary Irish church with its attendant buildings must have been crude and simple, built invariably of wood and essentially functional. Little is known of the course of Church history in Ireland in the decades following Patrick's death, though according to the eighth-century *Catalogue of the Irish Saints* the Irish Church remained for a considerable period episcopal and not monastic in its organisation. The Christian religion seems to have finally triumphed over heathenism during the reign of the High King Diarmait, about a century after Patrick's death. It was a great and signal achievement. Patrick, brought up a member of a clerical family in the Romano-British Church with its tradition of membership in the Church Universal, and spending a large part of his life in the bosom of the Gallic Church, must have been thoroughly imbued with the principles of the continental Church order. There is no reason whatever for supposing that he intended the Irish Church to follow the insular and particularist road which it eventually took. With his predecessor Palladius, he was instrumental in drawing Ireland within the unity and brotherhood of Western Churches. In a happy phrase the conversion of Ireland has been called 'the last and strangest conquest of Imperial Rome'.[41] Ireland might also be regarded as the earliest outright conquest for militant and expansionist Christianity, the first non-Romanised country to surrender to the Catholic Church.

Amongst the contemporaries or immediate successors of St Patrick may be mentioned St Bridget (not to be confused of course with the

Swedish fourteenth-century saint of that name). She was founder and first abbess of the double monastery at Kildare—a type of institution which was to have great influence in the early Anglo-Saxon Church. Legend relates how she foretold the birth of St Columba, who would become a great tree overshadowing both Ireland and Scotland. She died c. 523. St Mochta, a contemporary of hers, is also said to have uttered prophecies concerning Columba; a redoubtable missionary, he came over to Ireland and preached in County Louth.

Another Briton of late Romano-British times whose sphere of labour lay beyond his native shores was Pelagius. In its own way his influence on the development of British Christianity has been as important as that of the Apostle of Ireland, and he has his followers to our own day. Though we know nothing of his earlier years, he is a clearly defined figure from c. 400 to 418, the mature and controversial period of his life.

Arriving in Rome c. 400, he was repelled by the low moral standards of many Christians there, and proceeded to expound a doctrine according to which a sinful man should exert himself on his own behalf and not merely sit back and await salvation through the grace of God. He taught at Rome during the pontificate of Anastasius (398–402). Denying the existence of original sin, or the essential corruption of human nature (which he regarded as a doctrine conducive to moral laxity), he maintained the necessity of will-power in the improvement of individual character. Pelagius himself was a man of blameless and austere life, held in the highest esteem by those who knew him. He revolted from the idea of hereditary sin, and declared that each new individual soul was a pure creation of God.

After the sack of Rome in 410 Pelagius came with his chief disciple Coelestius, who was an Irishman and far more disposed to controversy than was his gentle master, to seek refuge in Carthage. Here he continued his teaching, but was confronted by St Augustine, who declared that sin was transmitted by generation and that man could be saved only by God's grace. The Fall was complete, a fact of universal application, and all mankind infected with the sin of Adam, in whom all men existed potentially. Man may be able to help himself, but he cannot take the initiative; prevenient grace must help him on to the road of salvation in the first place, and must be supplemented by continual supplies of grace. Man is helpless to save himself, because of his inherited depravity. Only grace, the free gift of God, can avail him, and grace moreover is irresistible, in the sense that once the will comes beneath its impact it has no desire to resist the good. All this constituted a very powerful doctrine, and it was additionally fortified by the theory of predestination. By God's decree, some men are elected to salvation (*praedestinatio*), while others are assigned to condemnation (*reprobatio*)—the question of right conduct does not affect the issue either way. Pelagius could hardly be blamed for thinking that such a theological doctrine was not the handmaid of ethics.

Each of the two schools of thought had its protagonists, and there was much controversy. The teaching of Pelagius could not be squared with the belief that Christ died for all men, but many Christians found it attractive and it was widely accepted, in Britain as elsewhere. It is quite unfair to the British Church to speak of Pelagianism as a British heresy.[42] Though the heresiarch himself was a native of the British Isles[43] (probably of the mainland, though not necessarily so), it was abroad that his views came to be developed and expounded, especially in Rome. The introduction of the heresy into Britain may be attributed to the expulsion of Pelagians from Rome during the pontificate of Celestine (422–32). One of the exiles, Agricola, himself the son of a Pelagian bishop Severianus, found his way to Britain, where he proceeded to corrupt the churches by his doctrine.[44] When handled by a devout and learned man like Pelagius himself, Pelagianism may seem an attractive doctrine; when expounded by second-rate persons, it becomes merely plausible. Its dangers were soon apparent, and the Catholic Church acted energetically.

In 416 Pelagianism was condemned by two African synods, at Carthage and Mileve respectively, Augustine being present at the latter. The excommunication of Pelagius and Coelestius was upheld by Innocent I. The next pope, Zosimus, wavered in his attitude and tended to favour the views of Pelagius. The African bishops protested, and persisted on Pelagius being compelled to acknowledge that for every single good action the grace of God through Christ is required. It was the authentic voice of Catholic and Evangelical Christianity. Pressure was put upon the pope by the emperor Honorius, and Pelagius was forced into exile in 418. Little hereafter is known of him. Pelagianism was formally condemned by the general Council of Ephesus in 431.

The condemned doctrines lingered on in the attenuated form known as semi-Pelagianism, which found its main champions amongst the monks of the new monasteries coming to life in the south of Gaul, notably Lérins. Thus John Cassian, an influential figure in the history of Western monasticism, whilst he refused to accept the doctrine of Pelagius that human nature is essentially uncorrupted, maintained the freedom of the human will and the non-irresistibility of Divine grace. It is not possible, he thought, to define exactly the relation between free will and grace—both are necessary in the work of salvation. Cassian denied the Augustinian doctrines of prevenient grace and predestination, and declared that man himself could take the first step in procuring his salvation without awaiting the motive power of grace.[45] Catholic Christianity has subsequently upheld the doctrine of prevenient, though not that of irresistible grace.

A British bishop who has been accused of falling under the influence of Pelagianism or at least semi-Pelagianism is Fastidius, who probably wrote between 420 and 430, at a time when Agricola was importing the heresy into Britain. But a close examination of his work yields no evidence of the taint. His attractive book, *On the Christian Life*, addressed to a Christian widow Fatalis, presents a picture of widowhood as a noble vocation and helps us incidentally to appreciate the esteem with which widows were regarded in the early Church. He advises Fatalis to be humble and quiet, to perform deeds of mercy and righteousness unceasingly, and to be occupied with reading and prayer. Though the book is orthodox, it yet paints the background against which the doctrines of Pelagius achieved their popularity. According to Fastidius no man could be accounted a Christian unless he imitated the example of Christ. 'A Christian is he who shows pity to all, who is not in any way troubled by injury, who does not allow a poor man to be oppressed if he be present.'[46]

The book is free of fanaticism or rancour, and with its humane, pious, and cultured tone, represents a type of Christianity which may well have been common in Britain at this time, and which has much to commend it.

However, a more adventurous type of Christianity also existed in Britain during the closing decades of the Roman period. In St Ninian[47] (*c.* mid fourth century to 432) we have a Romano-Briton who was not content to lead a pious, gentle existence at home, but found his vocation as a warrior of Christ, like St Patrick extending the frontiers of the Faith at a time when the Empire was struggling to hold what it possessed. Born in Galloway or Cumberland, he was (according to Ailred of

Rievaulx) the son of a Christian. The same writer informs us that he visited St Martin of Tours, by whom he appears to have been greatly influenced. On the authority of Bede, we learn that he was trained at Rome.[48] Proceeding on a mission to preach to the Picts of Galloway, he built a church near the present town of Whithorn c. 400, and a monastery in connection with it. The church was built of stone, which Bede remarks was not usual among the Britons, and was known as Candida Casa because of its whitewashed walls. It is in this remote region that Scotland's earliest known Christian archeological remains have been found, the stones of Kirkmadrine, in Wigtownshire, which may date from about Ninian's time.[49] A few miles from Whithorn is 'St Ninian's cave' (where the saint traditionally prayed), facing the sea, with a cross scratched on the walls. Later in his career Ninian established churches elsewhere in Scotland. A large number of inscriptions suggests his widespread activity, and three islands bear his name, though such inscriptions and dedications do not necessarily indicate his presence. Scotland at this time was inhabited by two great groups of Picts, separated by the Grampian mountains. It seems to have been the southern group which Ninian evangelised; the northern group would receive the Gospel from Columba in the following century. Despite the comparatively limited sphere of his operations, however, Ninian may be claimed as the first recognisable missionary to Scotland. He was also a pioneer of monasticism in Britain, and the monastery which he established at Whithorn subsequently developed into an important centre for the training of missionaries. After Ninian's death, his Pictish converts unfortunately fell away from the Faith, and Patrick in his Coroticus letter refers to them as apostates.

Another Briton who made progress in the monastic life, outside his native land, was Faustus. He became abbot of Lérins in 433, where he remained for twenty-seven years. He was then promoted to the bishopric of Riez (Rhegium) in the province of Aix, and in 462 was taking part in a council at Rome. Like Patrick, and (possibly) Ninian, he had a Christian family background, his mother being an exceptionally devout woman. In southern Gaul he came under the influence of semi-Pelagianism, and Sidonius Apollinaris, in the course of a cordial letter to him, refers in discreet and polite language to his somewhat unsound views.[50] Like John Cassian, Faustus insisted on the need for human effort in co-operation with divine grace. He had a wide reputation for learning, but after his death c. 490 came to be regarded as heretical.

For the fourth and early fifth centuries the documentary evidence is often confusing and uncertain, and it will perhaps never be possible to arrive at a thoroughly reliable chronology. But in connection with the Church of Britain two broad facts appear to stand out. One is its membership of what was virtually a federation of Western Churches, which regarded the Roman see as the model and accorded to it a unique prestige. The British Church was no more independent of Rome than was, for example, its neighbour the Church of Gaul. Relations may have been more intermittent, but this was not through any matter of principle, but because of geography. Secondly, the British Church was conspicuously orthodox. In 325 it gave its adherence to the decrees of Nicaea against Arianism, in 343 it accepted the Council of Sardica's acquittal of Athanasius, and in 418 the anti-Pelagian decrees of the Council of Carthage. Hilary of Poitiers, as we have observed, praised the Britons for their freedom from the taint of Arianism, and Athanasius mentioned them as amongst his orthodox supporters. Chrysostom wrote of the British Isles as professing the Christian religion. Jerome also spoke well of the Britons, who with other Christians 'worship the one Christ, and observe the same rule of truth'.[51]

Though Pelagius himself was a Briton, his heresy was not of British origin, and he is said by Marius Mercator to have first acquired his views on grace from the Syrian, Rufinus. Neither does the heresy appear to have made the headway in this country which it made amongst the monks of south Gaul. It may be that some individuals were attracted to it, but certainly the British Church had no champions of semi-Pelagianism such as the early fifth-century scholars John Cassian, Vincent of Lérins, and Hilary of Arles. In 421 or soon after, however, Britain inaugurated her long tradition of the granting of asylum to nonconformists, when exiled Pelagians from Rome came hither. Not satisfied with obtaining refuge, they proceeded to propagate their views. The Britons, fearful for the purity of their faith, appealed to Rome for help. The result was the two famous missions of Germanus, in 429 and 447.[52]

Two sources give us most of our knowledge of this commanding figure, who was bishop of Auxerre from c. 418 until his death c. 450. The earlier of these is the Chronicle of the contemporary Prosper of Aquitaine; the other, the *Vita Germani* of Constantius, was written c. 480. According to the latter, an embassy arrived in Gaul from Britain, asking help against the Pelagians, who were endangering the Catholic Faith.[53] A council was held, and Germanus went in answer to the appeal. He took with him a young bishop called Lupus, who had recently been consecrated bishop of Troyes.

The earlier authority, Prosper, agrees on the fact of this mission, and gives us the date, 429. But it also introduces the important detail that Germanus was sent by the pope, Celestine, at the request of a deacon Palladius. There is no reason whatever to doubt this, particularly as Prosper, besides being contemporary with Germanus, is more formal and historical in his account than the later writer Constantius, who is romantic and less factual. It is not difficult to square the holding of the Gallic council with direct papal action. It should be noted incidentally that the miraculous element looms large in Constantius, though he was an accomplished Latin writer and the fact that Germanus remains a living figure is largely due to him.

The two visiting champions duly vindicated the orthodox faith. They then offered thanks at the tomb of St Alban, and deposited relics of the apostles there, taking in exchange a handful of the earth upon which the martyr had suffered. The celebrated episode of the Alleluia victory followed. The Picts and Saxons had joined forces, and were harassing the Britons, who appealed for help to Germanus, no doubt in the knowledge of his youthful experience as a military officer. He led the army on Easter Day into a valley surrounded by hills, with the order that the troops were to shout at his command. The Britons were placed in ambush at strategic points. As the enemy approached, the whole army revealed itself with the cry of 'Alleluia'. The startled enemy fled, and a bloodless victory was gained. The site of this unique battle has been placed not very probably at Maes Garmon (the field of Garmon) in Flintshire, which seems to be too far to the west.

The two prelates returned to Gaul. But after several years the help of Germanus was again called for. The heresy was still troublesome in the island. He came back, accompanied once more by a newly consecrated prelate, this time Severus, bishop of Trier. Prosper does not mention this second visit, and in fact he had left Gaul in 440 and was out of touch with developments in that country. But Constantius records it, informing us that miracles were performed for the sick, conversions were multiplied, and the heretics confounded. The reference to conversions is interesting—the Church in Britain still apparently did not include the entire population. The visit probably occurred c. 447.[54]

Shortly before this, in 446, an appeal had also been made by the Britons for military aid to the consul Aetius. The Saxons were pressing them hard: 'the barbarians drive us to the sea—the sea throws us back to the barbarians.' The threat was far graver than that from the Picts and Saxons seventeen years before. It is possible that the Britons were hoping for another mighty work on their behalf by the militant bishop of Auxerre. If so, they were disappointed; the flood of Germanic invasion could not now be stayed.

This second mission, however, was more successful than the first theologically, and according to Constantius the Faith in Britain endured undefiled to his own day (c. 480). There can be no doubt that the impact which Germanus made on the fifth-century Church of Britain was considerable. His name was long gratefully remembered.[55]

A point which emerges from these comings and goings between Britain and Gaul is the close relationship existing between their respective Churches, almost that of daughter and mother. It is not insignificant that Constantius (who was a priest of the church of Lyons) devotes a large proportion of his Life of St Germanus to the latter's visits to Britain. The traffic was a two-way one. Thus, a British bishop, Riocatus, visited first of all Faustus, bishop of Riez, and then Sidonius Apollinaris, the Gallic prelate and man of letters, on his way home. He stayed in the latter's villa in the Auvergne for some time, as the barbarians were at large. This must have been before 475, by which year Sidonius was an exile and Auvergne in the hands of Euric the Visigoth.[56] Sidonius calls Riocatus 'bishop and monk'.

The debt which the Church of Britain owed to that of Gaul was considerable. Germanus, besides his exertions on behalf of orthodox religion in Britain, was also (in the opinion of many) probably a teacher of Patrick, who did so much for Ireland. Yet another pupil of his at Auxerre was Illtud, himself perhaps the teacher of David and Gildas, and of great influence in the Welsh Church. Our knowledge of Illtud is unfortunately small. But it is clear that he was the founder of the first great British monastery known to us, that of Llan-Illtud, which became a flourishing educational centre. With Illtud, and his reputed pupil David, we enter the field of Celtic Christianity proper.

Until about the end of the fourth century and for some indefinite period beyond, the Church of Britain appears as a constituent and participating member of the Church Universal. During the latter half of the fifth century the connection between Britain and Gaul lessens. As the Angles and Saxons enter the country, the Christian communities become consolidated in the west. And then for a century or more the British Church, by this time more correctly designated the Welsh Church, is in isolation, separated from the main currents of Christianity abroad. It develops some strongly marked characteristics of its own. It retains the Easter date prescribed by the Council of Arles, but altered by the Roman Church in 455. The Welsh Church, however, is in a line of unbroken continuity with the Church of Roman Britain, and its members are the spiritual and ecclesiastical descendants of the Christians noted by Tertullian and Origen. The Welsh Church is more than something of purely native growth. It has been assisted in its development by influences from the main centres of Western Christianity. The isolation which overtook it in the sixth century was unnatural and forced upon it by special circumstances, the result of geography and the Teutonic migrations. The mission of Augustine in 597 would prepare the way towards what was largely the restoration of a previously existing situation.

CHAPTER III

CHRISTIANITY
AMONGST THE CELTS

What caused the outlying, though sound and orthodox, British Church to wither away from the parts of Britain later known as England as though it had never been? It is difficult to deny the completeness of its eclipse in the century or more preceding the arrival of Augustine in 597, during which period it consolidated itself in the west of the island, changing in character to a great extent, and becoming a predominantly monastic Church.

Until about the middle of the fourth century, Roman Britain was reasonably safe and secure, guarded from the north by Hadrian's Wall, which stretched from the Tyne to the Solway Firth, and from Channel pirates by a series of fortifications found at intervals from the Wash to Southampton Water. Then in 360 the Picts and Scots ravaged the northern frontier. They were joined by the Saxons seven years later, and the combined force broke through the Wall and proceeded to subject the country to a series of marauding raids. The situation was restored by Theodosius, who also repaired the Wall. From now on the security of Britain was more or less uncertain. The position was still further aggravated in 401, when the Roman general Stilicho withdrew troops from the island for more urgent defence operations on the mainland. In 409 the emperor Honorius told the Britons to take care of their own defence. It is not clear whether or not Roman troops subsequently returned. If they did, it is probable that there were only limited numbers of them for a few years, in the south-east parts of the island.

Romano-Britain during its closing decades was thus heavily under attack, which moreover came from several quarters. The pressure of the Picts, inhabiting north Britain (Scotland), against the Hadrianic Wall, was supplemented by the raids of the Scots of Ireland against the western coasts, from the Channel of the Severn northwards to the Clyde. The Romans towards the close of the occupation period built fortifications at Cardiff, Carnarvon, and Holyhead. The most interesting affair in this connection is of course the raid of the Scots in which Patrick, with thousands of other Britons, was carried off. It was probably only typical of many such raids during these years when the Roman power was in decline.

But though the Irish were thus causing difficulty for Britain, from this time they were beginning to come under Christian influences, and there was in fact no serious threat of obliteration to the churches of western Britain from this source. For the Christian communities of the centre, south, and east, however, along with Romano-British civilisation as a whole, the situation was serious. The Teutonic raiders who threatened them were a destructive force, and particularly so because they were thoroughly heathen.

From the third century German marauders had troubled the eastern and southern shores of Britain, and it was to counter their attacks that the elaborate defences of the 'Saxon Shore' had been organised by the Roman authorities. The ruins of the fort at Richborough (Rutupiae), for example, are an impressive indication of the seriousness with which the Romans regarded the threat. The first attack known to us took place in the last quarter of the third century, when the imperial fleet inflicted a defeat on the raiders. The engagement may have been a considerable one, as the victory went to the head of the Roman commander Carausius, who declared himself emperor of Britain and ruled independently of Rome for seven years.

The Germanic invasion and settlement of Britain however, as is common knowledge, began seriously in the fifth century. Crossing the North Sea in their open boats from about the beginning of the fifth century onwards, these German tribesmen moved up the rivers of eastern and southern Britain. Later they brought their families with them, and took advantage of the collapse of the Roman power to make a permanent home for themselves. The same German migration occurred elsewhere into the Empire, but it was nowhere so thorough as in Britain. There have been attempts in recent years to minimise the completeness of the Anglo-Saxon conquest, and there is a danger that our view may veer from one extreme to the other. It is important that we avoid the error of regarding the Anglo-Saxons as essentially a military aristocracy lording it over a large subject native population as was the case with the Teutonic conquerors elsewhere in the Empire.[1] The north Germans who occupied Britain were far more than this. Along with other lines of argument, such as those of language and place-names, which among the English were largely free of Celtic influence, there should be mentioned the virtual disappearance of the Christian religion from the territories now known as England. This disaster did not occur in Gaul or Lombardy, where the Church maintained its succession unbroken. The fate of the Romano-Britons is a historical mystery. Arguments will continue concerning the proportions in which they were slaughtered by the Germans, took refuge in the west or over the sea in Armorica (the later Brittany), survived in isolated pockets, or were retained as wives or slaves of the conquerors.[2] In a confusing situation all these elements doubtless existed. But it is not easy to agree with the late R. G. Collingwood, who argued that the greater part of the natives were probably absorbed into the population of the new settlements. If this was so, what happened to their religion, with its properly constituted bishoprics and churches? Why did they so easily abandon it? It may be, of course, that the proportion of Christians was still small by the second half of the fifth century, and that these were the Britons who fled, rather than consent to live with the heathen Germans. But it is more likely that most Britons were Christians by this time—and it is not usual for the Christian Church to surrender so readily as Collingwood's view seems to infer. What is beyond dispute is that the British Church, as an ecclesiastical institution with hierarchical organisation, ceased to exist in the most populous parts of the island, and continued only in the west of Britain. A Christian Church which had maintained close connections with Gaul was now circumscribed and isolated from the rest of the Catholic community.

The British monk Gildas, writing in the middle of the sixth century, describes the invasion in rhetorical language.[3] The conflagration 'blazed over cities and regions, and did not cease until after almost the entire island had been devastated, it licking the western seas with its ruddy tongue'. He compares the assault with that of the Assyrians on Judaea. He tells how the people were slain along with their priests, and the altars polluted. Some fugitives reached the hills, only to be overtaken and slain in heaps. Others gave themselves up as slaves, overcome with hunger. A few managed to hold out in woods and mountains until the invasion had spent its initial force, and then found a champion around whom they could rally, Ambrosius Aurelianus.

Others found a refuge overseas, chanting in their misery beneath the swelling sails, 'Thou hast given us as sheep to the slaughter and scattered us among the Gentiles'. This is probably a reference to a large-scale emigration of Christian Britons about the middle of the fifth century, who found refuge in Armorica. It is an aspect of the conquest which may be more important than has hitherto been realised. Indeed, Britons in large numbers may have already been in Armorica, having fled there from the raids of Picts and Scots, and some may even have found refuge further afield. In this way some seem to have made their passage to Galicia in northern Spain, and British bishops there in the sixth and seventh centuries are referred to by Spanish councils. The see of Britonia in Galicia was still in existence in 900.

The first actual mention of a British bishop in Armorica occurs in 461, when Mansuetus, 'episcopus Brittonum', was present at the council of Tours in that year. Brittany was reckoned as being within the province of Tours, whose metropolitan at this time was Perpetuus, who presided over this Tours council, as well as over one at Vannes in 463, at which a Briton, named Paternus, was consecrated bishop. This latter council passed a canon ordering a uniform liturgical use within the province, which suggests a large-scale influx of Christians from elsewhere, bringing foreign customs with them. Sidonius Apollinaris writes in 468 of the Britons 'north of the Loire'.[4] According to another writer[5] the Britons on the continental mainland were numerous enough to furnish an army of twelve thousand men, under their king Riothimus, to assist the struggling imperial forces against the advancing Visigoths. This is no doubt an exaggeration. But it is clear that there were substantial settlements on the peninsula which as a result came to be known as Brittany and the inhabitants as Bretons. This view is supported by the occurrence of regional names such as Cornouailles and Domnonie. To this day a form of the old British language is spoken in parts of the peninsula; it is closely similar to the now extinct Cornish.[6]

The immigrations seem to have proceeded steadily over many years, with a particularly strong ecclesiastical element. It is possible that here is much of the answer to the problem of the disappearance of the British Church in England. The immigrants brought their peculiar practices with them, and Gregory of Tours speaks of differences concerning the Easter date in his day (d. 594).[7] Celtic customs were to continue in Brittany until they were put down by Louis the Pious in 818.

The most impressive testimony, however, to British influence in

Brittany is the hagiographical tradition. There are many legendary lives of Breton saints of the period roughly 450–800, most of whom came from Great Britain or Ireland. Of such was St Brioc, a Briton who is said to have founded monasteries in Brittany before he died *c.* 500. Contemporary with him was St Winwalocus, son of a British prince who fled to Brittany; he founded the monastery of Landevenech. There is much to be said for the view[8] that a main reason of the migrations was a purely religious one, namely the sudden emergence of a new approach to Christianity in Britain in the fifth century. Men had become fired with the vision of leaving all for Christ, of devoting their lives to Him in the monastic life. There was more scope for this in an entirely new setting. Thus St Samson came to Brittany and settled at Dol, 'forsaking native land and parents for the love of God'. Also came Maclovius, or St Malo, who founded the see of Aleth; and Paul Aurelian, a native of Glamorgan, who migrated to Brittany after some years as a recluse in wild country. The immigrant Britons do not seem to have been particularly grateful for the refuge given to them. Not content with making the peninsula virtually their own, they oppressed the natives, and the Breton Church was for centuries a thorn in the flesh of the metropolitan of Tours.[9]

We shall now consider the British Church during its second, that is, the post-Roman period, during which it appears in connection with Wales and Ireland respectively.

The Church of Wales was all that remained of the British Church on the mainland of Britain, and the Church of Ireland may be regarded as essentially an offshoot of the Church of Wales. But in character both of these Churches developed along different lines from those of the Church of the Romano-Britons. The first Church of Britain was diocesan and congregational, monasticism being unknown at any rate until the closing stages, as of course it was also unknown in the Christian Church at large during the first two or three centuries of our era. But during the fourth century, if not before, there had been an exodus to the Egyptian deserts, where solitary and sensitive souls sought refuge from persecution, urban wickedness, and the worldliness attendant upon State patronage of Christianity. When these individuals proceeded to join themselves together for mutual encouragement and support, the Christian monastic movement had begun. It spread northwards to places like Lérins, the island near Marseilles which became a nursery of monks and missionaries. From here it extended westwards, where its fervent spirit was welcomed by the defeated and displaced Britons, who found in specialised 'religion' a compensation for their temporal losses. The first monk actually known to have been resident in Britain was Riocatus, who was an acquaintance of Sidonius Apollinaris in the second half of the fifth century, as we have seen. The first really important name, however, in the history of British monasticism is that of Illtud.

The details of Illtud's life are legendary, though it seems that he may have been a Briton born in Brittany. Crossing to Britain he settled as a monk at Hodnant, later known as Llanilltud, where he was joined by disciples. The site may have been the present Llantwit Major, in Glamorganshire, some miles west of Cardiff; or, as some think, on Caldy Island, off the Pembrokeshire coast. The 'llan', or monastic church and enclosure, of Illtud, probably founded c. 500, became a centre of renowned spiritual and educational activity. The school which Illtud founded in connection with it was no doubt intended, in practice, to train men for the religious life, but it appears also to have offered a liberal education. Illtud stands out as the first important teacher in British monasticism, and with him that indispensable feature in religion and civilised life, namely organised education, appears to take its rise in the history of Christianity in these islands.

It is in fact because of his pupils that Illtud, early known as 'teacher of the Britons', is chiefly remembered as one of the makers of Celtic Christianity. Amongst his reputed pupils were Paul Aurelian and Samson, mentioned above, who carried his influence with them on their migration to Armorica, the little Britain beyond the seas. Samson was one of the most considerable figures in Celtic Christianity. Born in Pembrokeshire, he was dedicated as a child to God by his devout parents, who brought him to Illtud to be trained in the religious life. He succumbed to the wanderlust which was to become so marked a characteristic of the Celtic spirit, and visiting first Dumnonia, the south-west peninsula of Britain, he afterwards sailed for Brittany. Dedications as far removed from each other as the Scilly Isles, Dorset, and Guernsey, are a testimony to his widespread influence.

Another possible product of Llanilltud was Gildas, best known as the author of *The Overthrow of Britain*, one of our main authorities for the Anglo-Saxon conquest. In this work, unflattering in its portrayal of the British, the author declaims against their temporal and spiritual rulers, at whose feet he places the blame for the ruin of Britain. The princes, he says, are steeped in immorality and debauchery, and the clergy are wolves rather than pastors. The rhetorical and exaggerated style of Gildas has long been admitted, but it would be unjust to him to dismiss his book as of no account. Though not an exact historical work, when read discriminately it can at least supply valuable evidence relating to the climate of contemporary opinion. Moreover, from various allusions and notices it is possible to form a picture of the general nature of church doctrine and life. Thus we see a Church firmly based on belief in the Trinity, with churches dedicated to the martyrs in which the Eucharistic sacrifice was offered and the service sweetly chanted. Gildas himself had the roving Celtic spirit, and visited Ireland and perhaps Brittany.

The most celebrated however of those who are said to have received their early training under Illtud was St David (c. 520–88), the Dewi Sant beloved of all Welshmen. Unfortunately, our earliest life of him, written by Rhigyfarch,[10] is as late as the eleventh century, though there is no reason to doubt the substantial truth of the account of monastic austerity which it contains.

David, we are told, built his monastery at Menevia (St David's), where many postulants came to join him, including kings and princes, Constantine king of Cornwall amongst them. A hard life awaited them. In the description of austerities practised at the monastery we clearly see the mark of Orientalism, and indeed Rhigyfarch explicitly says that David took the Egyptian monks as his model.

David thought idleness to be the mother of vices. His monks worked in the fields with the yoke on their shoulders, disdaining the aid of oxen in ploughing. They produced with their own hands everything necessary for the needs of the community. There was no needless conversation. When the day's labour was over, they went to their cells, to read, write, or pray, until the bell for vespers called them together again. There was then an evening meal of bread and herbs, seasoned with salt, though the aged and weak were allowed something more agreeable. The meal was followed by three hours in church, for a service which seems to be nocturns (matins). After some hours of sleep, the monks rose for prayer at cock-crow.

All things were held in common, and any monk who referred to a book or some such article as his own possession was subject to harsh penance. There was unquestioned obedience to the abbot. Clothing was of the roughest material, made of skins. An applicant for admission was required to stay at the gate for ten days, after which, if he survived this preliminary ordeal, he was admitted and placed under the care of a senior monk. His soul was then broken in with many adversities. A new monk brought nothing with him, but was received naked as one escaping from shipwreck.

David himself exceeded his monks in the life of austerity. After nocturns, when his family had retired to their slumber, he would stay behind in church to hold converse with the angels. His entire day was spent in teaching and prayer, and in care for the brethren, for the orphans and widows, and the needy. He is said to have lived continually on bread and water. Sometimes, as an act of self-inflicted discipline, he would stand frozen in cold water. In all this we see monastic self-abnegation in its extremist form. It was an unrealistic way of life, and could not endure long in the history of monachism. There is no reason for believing that such austerity was usual in those earliest British monasteries, and Gildas doubtless expressed the feelings of many beside himself when he criticised the wisdom of such self-inflicted miseries.

Roughly contemporary with David, and also the founder of a monastery, was St Cadoc. Like many other Celtic saints, he was nurtured in a Christian home, after which he fell under the influence of an Irish hermit, Meuthi, who was then in Wales. Cadoc founded the monastery of Llancarvon, which as a religious and educational centre rivalled Llanilltud. He travelled widely, to Ireland, to Brittany (where there are many dedications to St Cadoc), and to Rome and Jerusalem.

Another British saint of this period was Kentigern, also known as St Mungo, founder of the city of Glasgow. Few clear facts emerge concerning him, though enough to form a convincing impression of an adventurous personality.[11] Born about the end of the first quarter of the sixth century, he was, it seems, the son of a British prince and a Christian mother. He became in due course a missionary in Strathclyde, where Ninian had laboured many years previously. He gathered disciples around him, his 'family', and fixed his centre on a site which acquired the name Glasgu (Dear Family). Travelling south, he preached around Carlisle. He came to Wales, where he was cordially welcomed by David. He established a monastery at Llanelwy, the later St Asaph. Returning subsequently to Strathclyde, he evangelised for a while amongst the heathen of Dumfriesshire. He spent his closing years at Glasgow, where he died in 612.

Largely parallel with the history of the Welsh Church, whose great age was the sixth century, is that of the Church of Cornwall. Every visitor to this westerly region of Great Britain has been struck by the prevalence of place-names which in village after village indicate the presence of a local saint. It must not of course be assumed that these 'saints' were usually canonised Christians in the medieval sense. Many undoubtedly were local Christians who impressed their personality on a particular district, and left a name behind them, in some cases founding the church. We have a remarkable instance of this, probably not untypical, in the graveyard of Llansadurn ('the church —or religious settlement—of Saturninus'), where there is actually a very early tombstone commemorating Beatus Saturninus and his wife.[12]

A monument of this age, almost unique, is the romantically situated church on the sands near Perranporth, on the north Cornish coast. Of its great antiquity and its Celtic foundation there can be no doubt, though Piran himself, the reputed founder, is a shadowy figure. He is said to have arrived in Cornwall about the close of the fifth century. This church was long buried in the sands, until discovered by chance at the beginning of the nineteenth century. It has been made secure for the future by a concrete covering of extraordinary incongruity. Though altered in Norman times, as the chevron moulding of the south doorway indicates, a sixth- or seventh-century date is probable for the four walls of unhewn stone. These walls are not built perpendicularly, but incline inwards. This is an indication of very early date, for the stress of the roof was a problem for primitive builders, who adopted the device of making the walls incline inwards to take the outward thrust of the roof.[13]

Also excavated in the last century was the Cornish oratory of Gwithian, a building similarly devoid of architectural embellishment. It is now reburied by the sands.

Of even greater interest are the dry-built walls of a Celtic monastery at Tintagel, in the same county, excavated in 1933 and the following year.[14] The monastery, founded c. 500, is on an exposed and rocky island, on the ledges of which are several cells cut out of the rock. Here the monks said their orisons, to the ceaseless sound of the breakers and the seagull's cry, and in the contemplation of a view of almost unparalleled splendour. Roman or sub-Roman pottery found on the site is apparently of southern manufacture and suggests connections between the monks and south Gaul.

At about this time Cornwall and Wales seem to have owed much to missionaries from Ireland, already late in the fifth century consumed with evangelistic fervour. Thus, existing churches in Britain would be strengthened with a fresh infusion, and entirely new churches would be founded. St Piran is claimed as an Irishman, and others who may have arrived in Cornwall early in the sixth century were St Fingar and St Ia. The actual foundation of Glastonbury is sometimes attributed to this Irish influx.

During the sixth century the Celtic Christian world of western Britain was certainly anything but stagnant. We gain an impression of a Church centred to an increasing extent on monasteries, and looking for leadership to 'specialised' Christians. There was a ferment of activity. The later Romano-British Church had been a 'safe' Church, commendably careful for its orthodoxy, but lacking in that adventurous and outward spirit without which the Christian Faith withers and dies. It had, moreover, been somewhat lacking in self-reliance, and too readily inclined to appeal for outside help in its difficulties. The advent of the Teutonic invaders, though it robbed the British Christians of their property and drove them from their shrines, infused a new character into them. We now find a constant coming and going, a multitude of 'saints' crossing the seas hither and thither, with an interchange of personalities between Wales, Cornwall, Ireland and Brittany. A vigorous and highly characterised Celtic Christianity of the West matured. But there is nothing more remarkable than the absolute exclusion of England from the sphere of its operations during this period. The absence of Celtic personalities or activity from the eastern half of Britain during the great Celtic age, when there is a large accumulation of evidence for their existence in the West, would read strangely if we were to believe that the Anglo-Saxon kingdoms were inhabited largely by the original, that is a Celtic, population. There is virtually no evidence that these kingdoms were even partly within the Celtic world, or regarded as being so by the Celts themselves. The English considered themselves Germanic, and the Welsh looked upon them as a wholly alien people.

So far as the Christianisation of the English, the main theme of this book, was concerned, the Church of Wales (and of Cornwall) represented what is virtually a dead-end. To this extent, after the heroisms of the sixth century have been considered, this Church passes out of the main stream of the history of religion and culture in England. The Welsh were great adventurers. They were missionaries, with an unquenchable thirst for travel. But they could be good haters of their enemies, as well as enthusiastic warriors of Christ. It is clear that they never forgave the English for the crime of dispossession. When Augustine came to Kent at the end of this century of Celtic achievement he looked for aid, as was only natural, from the Welsh. It seemed for a moment that the Welsh Christians might be prepared to co-operate with him in evangelistic work amongst the Anglo-Saxons. But they could not rise to it. The English deserved only perdition. Augustine had to go it alone, as we shall see, and he did not get very far.

It is clear that on the mainland of Britain a Church, which had at first been episcopal and congregational became in the sixth century increasingly monastic, a development which also took place in Ireland.

According to the document known as the *Catalogue of the Irish Saints*,[15] the Irish Church during its first period (*c*. 430–544) was essentially episcopal in organisation, having no fewer than three hundred and fifty bishops. The immediate reaction of the modern English reader is to suspect an exaggeration here. It is difficult for him to grasp the idea of a multitude of bishops in one Church, especially in a country but recently converted, so accustomed is he to thinking of a bishop as monarchical and magnificent, ruling over a wide territorial area. But it is not necessary to assume that the *Catalogue* is seriously exaggerating. Irish society was arranged on a tribal basis, and as each group was Christianised, Patrick seems to have consecrated a bishop for it.[16] Just as there were numerous kings, so were there numerous bishops, with an authority very real though circumscribed in extent.

The second period of the Irish Church (544–99), according to the *Catalogue*, is primarily monastic. There are now only a few bishops but many priests.[17] They observe the Celtic Easter, on the fourteenth moon after the vernal equinox, and tonsure the head from ear to ear, two practices which had been carried over from the first period. There is great variety in worship, and liturgical usages are being received from David, Gildas, and Cadoc. Monastic influences were in fact coming in from abroad, and great monasteries now arose in Ireland, such as those of Bangor, Clonard, Clonfert, and Clonmacnoise, which became in due course centres of intellectual activity. This passion for study was combined with an asceticism derived from Egyptian models, probably by way of the more severe monasticism of Wales. The Irish monasteries, moreover, it is essential to bear in mind, were quite unlike the later Benedictine abbeys with their complex and highly ordered system of offices and buildings. The Irish monks lived in huts and worshipped in oratories rather than in a large, central church. The whole was surrounded by an earthwork, within which large numbers of highly individualistic 'religious' maintained a communal and brotherly existence.

We have already noticed the propensity of the Celt towards travel. He must be ever on the move. This characteristic appears very strongly amongst the Irish, whose monks we find setting out as pioneers and pilgrims of Christ, impelled by some indefinable quality almost unknown elsewhere. Such splendid and well-appointed ships as those of the vikings in a later age were not for them. With slender equipment they set sail onto unknown seas. There must have been many tragedies, countless monks of whom no more was heard. But it was this urge which was to make the Irish the greatest missionaries of the Dark Ages.

Such a missionary was St Columbanus. Born in Leinster c. 543, he was trained at the northern Irish monastery of Bangor.[18] Landing in Gaul, he proceeded to Burgundy, where he founded Luxeuil, which became the greatest monastery of contemporary western Europe, with six hundred monks. There were also other communities, such as Anegray and Fontaines, throughout the Frankish domains, founded by him, and based on Irish ascetic principles. In spite of being so far distant from his native land he maintained Celtic ideas relating to organisation, and would not submit to the diocesan bishops around him. Trouble was caused when he brought in an Irish bishop to consecrate the altar at Luxeuil. His attacks on royal immorality earned him the enmity of Theoderic king of Burgundy and his formidable grandmother Brunhildis. Banished in 610, Columbanus set out on his wanderings again and eventually arrived in Italy, where he established his last monastery, the famous house of Bobbio. He died there in 615. Amongst his companions was St Gall, who has left his name in Switzerland.

It was a time of decadence for the Roman Church, which found a rival in the vigorous, learned, and expansionist Irish Church. From Iceland to Lombardy Irish monks and influence were to be encountered. It is not widely enough known that Iceland was discovered by them two generations before the arrival of the Northmen there. For sheer adventure in Christ's service nothing in the Dark Ages can exceed the story of St Brendan, a half-historical, half-legendary person who with a few companions set sail in search of the Promised Land. It seems certain that their voyages took them to the Scottish northern isles, and perhaps included more besides. Carrying their culture with them, the Irish established numerous monastic centres in Europe in which Christianity became entrenched and the flame of learning kept alight.[19]

The Irish were in fact the main agents during this period for the preservation and transmission of classical culture. Without the Irish Church, it is hard to see how the tradition of classical education, supreme in Europe until only yesterday, could have survived. The old Roman schools had perished in the barbarian invasions, and the Church on the Continent showed no particular anxiety to preserve the old learning. The great founder of the western monks, Benedict of Nursia, did not encourage scholarship; Gregory the Great actively discouraged it. To such men the Latin classical writers were indissolubly connected with paganism. An honourable exception must be made in favour of Cassiodorus, who founded the monastery of Viviers in 540, and who intended his monks not only to love God but also to be the servants of intellectual enlightenment. He prescribed for them a scheme of studies in which both Christian and pagan literature had a place. He drew up a classification of the liberal arts which became standardised and the basis of all study throughout the middle ages, comprising the trivium (grammar, rhetoric, dialectic), and the quadrivium (arithmetic, geometry, music, astronomy). He collected ancient manuscripts and established a scriptorium.

It was mainly, however, the British Isles which fostered the liberal arts throughout this period and for a considerable time beyond. First the Irish, and then the Anglo-Saxons (following upon their conversion) were Europe's leading scholars. The contents of Irish learning were not necessarily very wide or varied, but there was an unparalleled enthusiasm for study along familiar lines. There was Latin, always indispensable to the Christian scholar. The writings of Columbanus, who studied at Bangor under its abbot Comgall, reveal a facile style, though with a tendency to pedantry, and he often quotes or echoes Virgil, Ovid, Persius, Horace, and Sallust. Mathematics and astronomy were necessary for churchmen setting great importance on the right calculation of the calendar. Whether the Irish knew Greek during this period is doubtful;[20] the introduction of Greek into the British Isles was probably due in the first instance to Theodore and Hadrian in the latter half of the seventh century, but it is noteworthy that they were to include eager Irishmen amongst their pupils at Canterbury.

As a result of the adoption of Latin culture, Latin became the language of the Celtic Churches. One of the marked differences between the Western and Eastern Churches was the failure (if such a term may be used) of the former to exploit the vernacular tongues. In the East, during and after the time that Patrick was preaching in Ireland, there were vigorous vernacular Christian literatures in such languages as Armenian and Coptic, Syriac and Ethiopic. Patrick and his successors, however, made Latin the language of the Irish Church. In this they doubtless took their cue from Britain, where Latin was both the official language during the imperial age and colloquially spoken. Indeed it is likely that Patrick, as the son of a Roman town-councillor, knew Latin equally well with his native British tongue. Notwithstanding, Patrick might well have started off with Gaelic as the liturgical and ecclesiastical linguistic medium. If he had done so, there would probably have been in existence today a vast corpus of native literature to delight the Celtic scholar. To his momentous choice of Latin, on the other hand, it is perhaps no exaggeration to ascribe the preservation and transcription of classical literature and culture. Further, if the Irish Church had adopted Gaelic, those separatist tendencies which became so pronounced after Patrick's time might have been irresistible, and Celtic Christianity may well have remained permanently in schism.[21]

It is often forgotten that learning and culture never simply fall from the skies or grow out of the soil, but are invariably based on a competent system of education. The larger Irish monasteries had their schools (following the practice of Illtud of Wales),[22] which came to be thronged with students, including (from the seventh century onwards) many from foreign lands. At Armagh there was a 'Saxon quarter' of students, comprising a third part of the city. According to Aldhelm, English students went to Ireland in fleets, swarming to the Irish schools like bees gathering honey. Bede mentions the warm and friendly welcome which the foreigners received.[23] Amongst those who came to these Irish schools for instruction were men whom we shall encounter in the course of this history, such as Dagobert king of the Franks, Agilbert bishop of Dorchester, Aldfrith the Northumbrian king,

Willibrord the apostle of the Frisians, and Chad the saint of the midlands. Prominent amongst these schools may be mentioned Clonard, founded *c.* 520 by St Finian, a pupil of David; Moville, founded by another St Finian; Clonfert, which owed its existence to St Brendan, who often visited monasteries other than his own; Clonmacnoise, which was founded by Ciaran Mac, who, however, died early, not living to rule for any length of time a monastery and school which acquired a wide reputation; and Aran, established by St Enda on one of a group of islands off Galway bay, a nursery of many Irish saints. All these schools were founded during the first half of the sixth century or very shortly afterwards. They were the foundations of that tradition of Irish culture which was to influence so profoundly the course of Anglo-Saxon Christianity.

The greatest product of these schools was a missionary and saint whose career must now be reviewed at some length, both because he was the founder of the Church of northern Britain to which the English Church was to owe so much, and also as the outstanding representative of the Celtic version of Christianity—as seen in his own personality.

St Columba[24] was born at Gartan, a village amongst the hills of Donegal, in the year 521, of royal parentage. His father was a great-grandson of Niall of the Nine Hostages, High King of All Ireland, who had conducted a heavy raid on western Britain *c.* 400, possibly the one in which the young Patrick was carried off. Columba's mother also was descended from a line of kings. His royal extraction was to be of great service to him in his missionary labours later on, enabling him to exert a strong influence on contemporary affairs, political no less than religious. He was born into a Christian home, and owed much, it seems, in the early fostering of his vocation, to his mother Aethne. In a vision she had been told by an angel that she was to bring forth a son who would be the means of leading numberless souls to heaven.

Columba received his education at various centres, including the monastery of Clonard, where he studied under St Finian, as also under St Finian of Moville, besides owing much to an old Irish bard named Gemman. He was ordained deacon and priest, after which he returned to his native Ulster. He founded a monastery first at Derry, for which he ever after retained a strong affection. Other foundations followed, two of which have given their names to the well-known examples of Irish illumination, the Book of Durrow and the Book of Kells. The former book, which is preserved at Trinity College, Dublin, has a note in the first person to the effect that it was copied by Columba himself in twelve days. However, this note is not above suspicion, and it is thought that the book is about a century later than Columba's time, and of Northumbrian workmanship though under Irish influence. The Book of Kells, though of about the same date as that of Durrow, is probably Irish.[25]

Columba, who was in all respects a typical Irish Celt, doubtless long cherished the ambition to 'go on pilgrimage for the sake of Christ'. But it was not until reaching his early forties that he set out on the mission by which he has since been known and which carried with it such consequences for the religious and cultural future of England.

There is no reason to suppose that the traditional, and picturesque, causes of the saint's departure from Ireland are not substantially true. It seems that the impetuous and strong-minded Columba had quarrelled with Diarmait, High King of Ireland. A certain young man, son of the king of Connaught, had committed murder at Tara, court of the High King. He took refuge with Columba, but was dragged out and put to death by Diarmait. A reasonable enough action, it may appear, but taken as a personal affront by Columba. At about the same time, in 561, Columba coveted a beautiful psalter which his old teacher, St Finian of Moville, had brought back with him from a pilgrimage to Rome. He asked his permission to copy it. This was refused. Columba thereupon stole by night into the church where the book was kept, and copied it secretly. He was surprised at his work, and ordered by Finian to surrender the copy. On his refusal the matter was referred to king Diarmait for judgment. He decided in favour of Finian: 'To every cow her calf, to every book its offspring book.'

It is difficult for modern Christians to believe the traditional story that because of these two grievances Columba, now a responsible and matured monk of forty, deliberately stirred up war against Diarmait. But it must be remembered that the Irish were anything but pacifists. Even monastic communities were known on occasion to take up arms against each other. Physical fighting was regarded as a natural way of settling a quarrel. It is certain that a battle was now fought between the High King and the O'Donnells, Columba's own clan, and that Columba actively encouraged the latter. He spent the night preceding the battle in fasting and prayer. St Michael the Archangel appeared to him and promised him victory, but pronounced sentence of exile upon him for his worldliness. A battle was fought at Cooladrummon, near Sligo, to the accompaniment of the prayers of St Finian on the one side and those of St Columba on the other. King Diarmait was defeated, but three thousand dead lay on the field. Columba was held to share a high measure of responsibility for the slaughter, and he was excommunicated by a Church synod convened soon afterwards. The upshot was his departure from his native land, overcome, it is said, with remorse, and resolved to convert one heathen soul for each life that had been lost in the battle.

It so happened that there was a colony of his own countrymen settled under their king Conall, himself a kinsman of Columba, in Dalriada on the western coast of northern Britain, and thither the exile went. He would therefore not be friendless in this distant region, and there he could establish a base for his project of missionary work amongst the Picts. In 563 Columba set sail from Derry with twelve disciples. On the eve of Pentecost he landed at Iona, a small island some three miles long by a mile or so wide, separated by a narrow strait from the coast of Mull.

It was an ideal place for a settlement of monks, dedicated to prayer and missionary labour. The land was good for farming, and the neighbouring seas teemed with fish. Within reasonable distance were three groups of people: Columba's countrymen the Scots of Dalriada, the Britons of Strathclyde and Galloway who already had memories of St Ninian and were now being cared for by St Kentigern, and the vast virgin territory inhabited by the Picts. Northwards lay the numerous islands of the Hebrides, eastwards the mountains of the Grampian range. There was much scope here for a group of dedicated men.

Columba at once recognised in Iona his future base, and he secured the gift of the island from his kinsman king Conall. He then set about building the monastery which was to become in the intensity of its spiritual influence almost another Rome.

Nothing now remains of its original buildings, which according to Adamnan, Columba's biographer, were of wood or wattle. The whole was surrounded in the Celtic fashion by a vallum or cashel, which may still be detected. Within this enclosure were huts, refectory, guest-house, and church. Columba's own hut was slightly separate, on a small eminence.

The original band of brethren increased in numbers, until there were enough to be classified in three groups. These were the 'seniors', engaged in intellectual labour such as that of the scriptorium; the 'working brothers', who did the manual work; and the 'juniors', or novices. All wore the cowl, a white tunic and leathern sandals, and were tonsured in the Celtic fashion from ear to ear. The threefold vow of poverty, celibacy, and obedience was the rule.

The great work to which Columba had set himself was the conversion of the Picts, and not long after founding his monastery he visited their king, Brude, who kept his seat near the modern Inverness, some one hundred and fifty miles from Iona. After completing their journey through a wild and inhospitable country, Columba and the few companions he took with him arrived at the king's fortress, where they found the gates closed against them. Adamnan relates how the gates opened miraculously to Columba on his making the sign of the cross over them, and the overawed king Brude greeted him.

There followed what was virtually a competition in the power of working miracles between Columba on the one hand, and the chief druid of Brude's court, Broichan, on the other. Thus on one occasion, as Columba was embarking on Loch Ness, Broichan raised a storm against him, but the saint sailed away against the wind. As a result of his superior powers, Columba asserted his authority over the court, druidism was overthrown, and the way was open for the spread of the Christian religion throughout northern Britain. In 575 Columba paid a return visit to Ireland, accompanied by the king of the Dalriadic Scots, Aidan, who had succeeded Conall after being consecrated at Iona by Columba. Back in his native land, Columba was received with great reverence, and the fact of his exile was forgiven or forgotten. While in Ireland on this occasion he attended an important synod at Drumceatt, in county Londonderry, at which kings and ecclesiastics from all over the island were present. At this assembly Columba interceded successfully on behalf of the order of bards, which it was proposed should be suppressed.

He lived a further twenty-two years, spent mostly at Iona, but including some additional visits to Ireland, and evangelistic voyages to the Hebrides. Columba was visited himself at Iona by various founders of Irish monasteries. In 579 he had a dispute concerning a church with one of these founders, St Comgall; the result was an armed battle between the two sides, though the outcome is not known.

In 584 king Brude died and was succeeded by Gartnaidh, a southern Pict. The result was a union of the northern and southern Pictish kingdoms. The new king was a Christian, and anxious to co-operate with Columba, whose sphere of influence from now on was greatly widened. Iona became the spiritual capital of practically the whole of modern Scotland, though it naturally was in the western Isles and along the western coast that its influence was most felt.

Columba died in Iona on 6 June 597. He retained his vigour until the end. On his last day he made his round of the monastery and blessed the brethren. Even a white horse which served the community by carrying milk came to him for his blessing. Climbing the hill of more than three hundred feet from which a splendid view is to be obtained, the saint stretched out his hands over the monastery lying beneath and commended it to God's care. Returning to his cell, he continued with the transcription of a psalter on which he was engaged. Finally, at vespers he enjoined his monks to love one another, and promised to pray for them in heaven. When they arrived in church at midnight for nocturns they found him already there, kneeling in prayer beside the altar. Making over them the sign of blessing, he passed away.[26]

Though there is much of the miraculous in Adamnan's *Life of Columba*, it would be a hopeless task to attempt to disentangle it from what some would call the hard facts.[27] And indeed it is a task which no one who has grown to love Celtic Christianity would wish to undertake. Columba's life was a romance. His personality was rooted in the poetical view of life. In his impetuosity, his patriotism, his intensity of religion, he was a true Irishman. He had, it seems, a genuine gift of second sight. His character had its shadows too, but only such as to make the man himself all the more lovable. It is because of his imperfections that his sanctity is so clearly marked.

Columba was succeeded as abbot of Iona by his cousin Baithene, who had come with him as one of his twelve disciples years before. He was so devout that it was said of him that at meals he repeated the opening versicle of the office, 'Deus in adjutorium meum intende', between every two mouthfuls of food. He was followed in 600 by Laisren, at the time abbot of Durrow. The next two abbots were Fergna Brit (605–23) and Seghine (623–52). The latter was a noted champion of the Celtic Easter. It was during his abbacy that the Columban Church sent Aidan, a monk of Iona, as missionary to the Northumbrians, in response to the request of king Oswald. Next in the abbacy came Suibhne (652–7), who was followed by Cuimine

Ailbhe (657–69), whose book *De virtutibus Sancti Columbae* was used by Adamnan in his Life of the saint. For the next ten years Failbhe was abbot, and then Adamnan (679–704), author of the Life which ranks as one of the best medieval biographies. Adamnan became converted to the Roman manner of observing Easter, but he scarcely refers to it in the Life. He shocked the brethren at Iona by adopting the Roman tonsure.

After Adamnan's death there was a division between the monks over the Roman question, until in 717 the Celtic observant monks were expelled from the Pictish kingdom. In 794 Iona had its first visitation from the vikings, who about that time started showing an interest in the island monastic centres of Britain. The abbey was rebuilt and refounded more than once subsequently in the middle ages, and in our own day continues to attract men of spiritual vision.

All of the abbots from Columba to Adamnan with one exception (Suibhne) were descendants of Niall of the Nine Hostages, king of All Ireland (379–405). This royal and aristocratic strain was very marked in the leadership of the Celtic Churches, and may account to a great extent for their proud and independent spirit.[28]

The Church which Columba founded in northern Britain was a direct offshoot of the Irish Church, and reproduced its distinctively Celtic characteristics. These must now be briefly outlined, as they form much of the background against which the conversion of the English took place.

Most remarkable of these characteristics was the universality of the monastery as the central ecclesiastical unit.[29] The mother-house was Iona, to whom the Columban Church as a whole looked as the Head. In Wales and Cornwall the situation was more obscure. Though there are instances of Welsh abbots having been consecrated bishops without being appointed to sees, there were also definite bishoprics (established, however, in monasteries).[30] Such were Menevia (St David's), Bangor, St Asaph, and Llandaff. In Cornwall there appear to have been episcopal sees at Padstow and St German's.[31] Both Wales and Cornwall had known the imperial civil organisation, which was conducive to the establishment of dioceses. No such organisation ever existed in Ireland, whose conquest had not been attempted by the Romans. There was apparently no diocesan system as such in the Irish Church and bishops were retained mainly, if not entirely, for the exercise of functions peculiar to the episcopal office, such as the conferring of holy orders. A bishop would be part of the complement of the ordinary monastic household. It is true that the abbot of a Celtic monastery was sometimes in episcopal orders, but he would rule his ecclesiastical subjects not as bishop, but as abbot. The effective government of the Irish and Columban Churches was by abbots, who normally or at least very often were in priestly orders only. It must not, however, be thought that the episcopal office was in any way despised. On one occasion, when a certain bishop was visiting Iona, Columba gave precedence to him at mass. The point is that in the Celtic Churches ecclesiastical government was exercised from monasteries, not from episcopal households.[32] One result of the unsettled nature of the episcopal office was the growth of a class of unemployed, wandering bishops (*episcopi vagantes*), who sought their fortune where they could.

The worship of the Celts followed the normal Catholic pattern,[33] though it had several distinctive features. The canonical offices were sung daily, with an arrangement of psalmody differing from that of the Benedictine Office. Thus vespers had twelve psalms, and at Bangor the *Gloria in excelsis* was sung at vespers and matins.

The traditional final hour of the day, compline, does not seem to have been used in Celtic worship until at least the ninth century.[34] Compline amongst the Celts probably grew into a distinct office out of the informal night prayers of the community. During the psalmody of the Office great reverence was enjoined—coughing, sneezing, and yawning, were forbidden. The Eucharist was celebrated on Sundays and holy-days,[35] and included the mixed chalice, unleavened wafer-bread, and communion in both kinds. There was apparently no definite rule about the time of day when it should be celebrated, and one reference in Adamnan suggests that evening masses may have been known.[36] The mass was sacrificial in character,[37] and it was believed that the bread and wine after consecration became the Body and Blood of Christ.[38]

The liturgy was not of the Roman family, and it is probable that in the Columban and Irish Churches the Gallican rite was used.[39] There are various lines of evidence to suggest this, notably three liturgical fragments of the Scoto-Irish Church, known as the Books of Dimma, of Mulling, and of Deer. The first two of these are of the seventh or eighth century, the Book of Deer rather later. Each consists of a service for the communion of the sick, approximating in form to that of the Gallican rite rather than to that of the Roman. We are fortunate in possessing a complete Celtic liturgy in the Stowe Missal, an Irish manuscript of the eighth century or later.[40] Distinctive features of this rite are the litany between the epistle and gospel (a Gallican feature), the absence of the 'filioque' clause from the Creed, and an unvarying epistle and gospel. The mass as a whole is different from the Roman, though it contains the Roman canon. It has much of the well-known Eastern prolixity, and it must have given considerable scope to the choral abilities of the Celts, with their bardic tradition. We are told that the Picts of king Brude were greatly impressed by the singing of Columba and his monks.[41] But the Celts did not use the Gregorian chant, which according to Bede was introduced into Britain as a result of the Roman mission.[42] The Irish were skilled harpists, though it is not known that they used this instrument in divine service.

Holy orders were always conferred by a bishop, though the abbot might join in the act by laying his hand on the candidate's head. The canonical rule requiring three bishops to be present at the consecration of a bishop was not invariably followed in the Irish and Columban Churches.[43] In the Anglo-Saxon Church, Celtic orders came to be dubiously regarded. It was because of this suspicion that Theodore ordered Chad, two of whose consecrators had been Celtic bishops, to be reconsecrated.[44] According to the canons of Theodore all priests ordained by Celtic bishops were to be ordained afresh by a Catholic bishop.[45]

The Celtic monks were pre-eminently men of prayer and fasting. Their prayer was natural, spontaneous, and boundless in its scope. Thus both prayer for the dead, and to the dead, were used. The writers of manuscripts request their readers to pray for them. The disciples of Columba invoked their master for help in difficult times when he was absent from them during his lifetime on his various journeys, and they continued to invoke him after his death. There seems to be little evidence in the Columban Church, however, for invocation of the Blessed Virgin Mary, though litanies of the saints were a prominent feature of its worship. Fasting was observed on Wednesdays and Fridays, except during Paschaltide. Every day in Lent, with the exception of Sundays, was a fast-day. A peculiar practice of the Columban Church was to consecrate the site of a proposed new monastery or church by a period of fasting on the spot.

Both public and private confession were part of the Church's life.[46]

An individual often had a soul-friend, some holy priest to whom he was especially attached, who heard his confession and gave him absolution. Thus Columba in Ireland had as his soul-friend St Laisren, to whom he confessed his sin in connection with the sanguinary battle which lay on his conscience, and who assigned to him as penance lasting exile from his homeland. It may be taken as established that the penitential code was a Celtic invention, to be transmitted to England and the Continent from the seventh century onwards.[47] There were detailed attempts to provide penances for specific offences. The actual origin of private confession is obscure, and it was maintained by E. Loening that it spread outwards to the lay membership of the Church from the monastery.[48] It is certainly the case that St Columbanus was a zealous advocate of sacramental confession,[49] and that this was practised in the Irish Church, probably on a voluntary basis, by laymen as well as religious.[50]

The sign of the cross, as in the Anglo-Saxon Church subsequently, was invested with quasi-miraculous powers, able to ward off demons and confer protection in battle. A cross would be erected to mark a specially sacred spot or to commemorate a noteworthy event. The numerous standing crosses which survive from Celtic times are evidence of the reverence paid during this early period to the symbol of our redemption.

Concerning the general orthodoxy of the Celtic Churches there can be no doubt. This was to become evident later on when the question of their relations to the new Roman Church in Britain arose. Bede, who upbraids the Celtic Churchmen over such matters as the date of Easter, commends them for their firm and orthodox faith in the weightier content of the Christian religion such as the Redemption of mankind through the Passion, Resurrection, and Ascension of Jesus Christ, God and Man. At the conference of Whitby in 663, no complaint was made by the Roman party that the Scottish Church was unsound in belief; the burden of its argument was that by stubbornly adhering to such practices as the Celtic tonsure and Easter, the British Christians were keeping themselves aloof from the main body of Christendom.

The independence of the Scoto-Irish Church from Rome for a considerable period must be conceded, though its significance should not be exaggerated. This Church was after all further removed from Rome than was any other. The barbarian invasions, which drove a barrier between Rome and the Celtic West, covered a crucial period when important liturgical and disciplinary changes were being made by the papacy. In any case all Churches at this time exercised their everyday government in practical independence of the pope, though much reverence was paid to him and his see, by the Celts as by everyone else. As we have seen, the codex coveted by Columba had been brought back from Rome. There were doubtless many contacts of this nature with Rome.

The historical facts concerning the main issue are, however, clear. Though Palladius was sent to Ireland by Rome, and there is no evidence that Patrick was ill-disposed towards the source of his predecessor's authority, yet in the post-Patrician period the Irish Church steadily drifted away from its continental connections. In the story of Columba's mission to Scotland the existence of the pope is virtually ignored. Adamnan does not even refer to him, though he himself had become a convert to the Roman methods. It might be argued that the absence of any mention of hostility or resistance to the bishop of Rome does not preclude the existence of an unspoken, underlying loyalty. This is of course true. But we must not forget the fact of Columbanus's mission on the Continent. On the very doorstep of Rome he maintained his Celtic independence.[51] And when at Whitby the Columban monks were explicitly called upon to accept Rome by abandoning their traditional customs, the acceptance was by no means general. By that time one can speak of a definite schism, which was to last for over a century afterwards. Writing c. 731, Bede stated it to be still the custom of the Britons, at that time, to ignore the faith and religion of the English, i.e. the Roman.[52] Gregory III in 739 warned the bishops of Bavaria and Alemannia against false and heretical priests from Britain.[53] But the Celts were losing the battle, no matter how stubbornly fought, and by the close of the eighth century the Roman Easter was adopted by all the British bishops. It was the victory of common sense against ecclesiastical pride and insular tradition; whether it was a victory of the truth must remain a matter of opinion.

On the whole, Rome had little to do with the remarkable achievement of the conversion of the Celtic peoples. To a great extent this was a conversion of Celts by Celts, and it is therefore scarcely surprising that the resultant Christianity developed along idiosyncratic lines. Though Celtic missionaries drove deep into the heart of the Continent, they never acquired a love for Roman method and organisation. Celtic Christianity was unique in the entire Christian world.

According to Renan, 'no race took over Christianity with so much originality'.[54] The Celts are a striking example of a race dedicating its peculiar qualities, its instincts, its imagination, to the service of Christ. Their conversion is all the more remarkable in view of the thorough insistence of the saints and apostles at work amongst them that idolatry be abandoned. The acceptance of the Faith by the Celts was as full-blooded as by any other people, but nowhere else was the pre-Christian ethos retained in so attractive a form.

CHAPTER IV

THE HEATHEN ANGLO-SAXONS

The beginnings of the English people, it appears from Bede,[1] are to be seen in the arrival half-way through the fifth century of the Saxons, Angles, and Jutes, 'three most formidable German races'. It was during the reign of Marcian (450–7), who ruled jointly with Valentinian (425–55), that three ship-loads of Teutons came at the invitation of Vortigern, and were granted lands in the east of Britain in return for the protection which they provided against the Picts. They sent a report back to Germany that the country was fertile and the Britons cowards in war. A larger fleet followed, with a substantial body of troops, who also received land, and money, from the hard-pressed inhabitants. Great authority has always been attached to this information, which, however, suggests a classification more tidy and exact than was probably the case. The origin of the three races is by no means clear. Tacitus, writing in the first century A.D.,[2] includes the Angles in a group of strong tribes, who are generally held to have inhabited the present-day eastern Schleswig. In the same group he places the Eudoses, who have been taken to be the Jutes, but he does not refer to the Saxons. In the second century, Ptolemy in his *Geography* places the Saxons in the modern Holstein. According to the same writer the Angles lived further inland, west of the Elbe, but early English tradition strongly supports the view that their home was the modern Danish peninsula. It seems that by the fifth century the Jutes had moved from their original home southwards, across the Elbe, and in the direction of the Rhineland. It was from the latter region, not from the northern peninsula, that they are believed to have made the crossing to Britain.

The Jutes who occupied Kent, however (beside the Isle of Wight and part of Hampshire), making the first German settlement in this country, may well have been a mixed race of freebooters and mercenaries under Jutish leadership. Invited by a native chieftain to aid him as *foederati*, a common enough practice in later imperial times, they proceeded in due course to appropriate the land for themselves. It is thought, on archeological and other grounds, that they adopted much of the Romano-British way of life. They became the most civilised of the heathen English kingdoms, with strong continental connections. The boundaries of their south-east kingdom were probably not very different from those of the modern county of Kent. By the close of the sixth century it had attained its greatest power.

The Saxons prior to their invasion of Britain probably inhabited the lands reaching from their original home in the district around Kiel westwards perhaps as far as the Ems. At no very late date in Anglo-Saxon history the terms Angle and Saxon seem to have been regarded in some measure as interchangeable. Thus the Northumbrians, called Angles by Bede, are elsewhere referred to as Saxons, and conversely the entire race of the English are in the eighth century known as Angles.[3] This was, however, three centuries after the migration, when the English had acquired a broad national consciousness, and there is no reason to reject the traditional view that the invading Saxons and Angles were of distinct groups. The Saxons began the settlement of Sussex in the last quarter of the fifth century, after perhaps trying their fortune unsuccessfully in Gaul, and men of the same group may have occupied Surrey by way of the Thames. Aelle, conqueror of Sussex, was according to Bede the first Saxon king to establish an *imperium* over all the kings south of the Humber. Clearly, however, it could have been an influence of only limited character. About the same time, Anglian groups crossed the North Sea and penetrated from the Wash into the valley of the upper Thames. Early in the sixth century, more Saxons arrived, under Cedric, in Southampton Water. The mid-sixth-century writer Procopius informs us that in his day Britain was inhabited by three peoples—the British, Frisians, and Angles.[4] This suggests that many Frisians had made the crossing in company with the main Germanic groups. It is a fact that the Frisian dialect is the most closely related to Old English, and that the Anglo-Saxon missionaries in the seventh and eighth centuries were to show a special regard for the Frisians.

The broad certainty is that large areas of south and east Britain were successfully invaded by groups or tribes from north and north-western Germany.[5] It is probable that by *c.* 550 the inhabitants of the south, from Kent westwards to Hampshire, and the fen-dwellers of the large East Anglian region, were mostly German. There were scattered groups of them elsewhere, and on the whole they seem to have settled on the heavy, well-watered soil, similar to that which they had left behind them on the Continent, and suitable to their heavy type of plough. The whole character of their settlement suggests that they did not come only as military adventurers and conquerors, but seeking a place in the sun as farmers and family-men, bringing their wives and children with them. Out of the Anglo-Saxon settlements in the Trent valley developed the kingdom of Mercia. With the strengthening of the Wessex kingdom and its expansion westward, and the development of the northern kingdoms of Deira and Bernicia, the permanent occupation of the eastern half of Britain by Teutonic peoples was assured. The issue was finally settled by two important victories, that of Ceawlin and his West Saxons at Deorham, Gloucestershire, in 577, and that of the Northumbrians under Aethelfrith at Chester in 615. From this time on, the British were divided virtually into three nations—those of Wales, Strathclyde, and Devon and Cornwall.

By now the Anglo-Saxons, organised into some eight kingdoms or more,[6] had settled down to enjoy the fertile land which their fathers and they had conquered. They were for the most part an uncivilised people, doubtless regarded as barbarians by the dispossessed British, and living almost wholly in villages and farmsteads.[7] The towns of Romano-Britain largely disappeared, and there were neither schools nor literature. All men from the kings downwards lived in buildings of wood. Though there were easily-worked, well-stocked quarries all around in the form of ruined towns, fortifications, and roads, the Anglo-Saxons seem to have made no attempt to build in stone during their heathen period, though the ruins themselves probably impressed their imagination, as certain of their later poets testified. Thus in the elegy on a ruined city (possibly Bath) known as 'The Ruin', the poet speaks of the broken walls and the crumbling castles—roofs are falling in, frost is getting into the cement of buildings undermined by age.[8] Men of the forest clearing, the Anglo-Saxons used wood as their native material. There was an abundant supply in a land of forests, such as Selwood, Savernake, Sherwood, and Epping. Their dress was simple and not unattractive, set off with the bright colours and jewellery of which the Saxons, like other Germanic folk, were fond. A largely blonde people,[9] they loved to display their hair, which they grew long, unlike the close-cut, clean-shaven Romans.

Much has been written concerning their primitive institutions (a happy playground for the democratic Victorians), and the bonds which held their society together.[10] It may suffice here to mention two of their fundamental principles—kinship, and loyalty to one's lord.

There was no clan system as amongst the Celts, and yet there existed a strong sense of family interdependence. This found its most characteristic expression in the *wergeld*, the money compensation due to an injured family. The fear of vengeance by kinsfolk was an effective deterrent, more so perhaps than the modern, degrading system of imprisonment.

In some ways even more important was the comitatus-principle, by which a leader relied on the allegiance of a band of followers. It was a Germanic principle which Tacitus had noticed. He said that the Germans counted it lasting shame to leave a battle alive after their chief had fallen.[11] 'The chiefs fight for victory, the companions for their chief.' At the same time, this allegiance is not given for nothing. An open-handed generosity on the part of their chief is expected by his followers;[12] and to keep the latter adequately supplied in food and gifts, constant resort to war is necessary. This bond between a man and his lord was brought over by the Saxons to England, and remained a basic principle of society throughout the entire Anglo-Saxon period. It figures prominently in Old English literature, where we repeatedly meet with the devoted band of companions, the *gesithas*, who stand fast by their leader. The earlier conception of companionship evolved into one of service, but the tradition of personal loyalty remained unchanged. The principle was to be taken over by the Church. St Wilfred would have his devoted followers, such as his biographer Eddius. The attitude of the missionary St Boniface towards the pope was essentially that of an Anglo-Saxon thegn to his king. The principle came to be sublimated by countless Saxons into a noble devotion to Christ, 'the young hero'. The loyalty of man for lord is the key to much that might otherwise seem surprising in the history of the Anglo-Saxon Church.[13]

The Anglo-Saxons of the fifth and sixth centuries were entirely heathen. Tacitus has something to say concerning the heathen sites of the north German tribes, including the Angles. He describes the sanctuary of a goddess Nerthus, or Mother Earth, which was situated on an island in the ocean.[14] The sanctuary took the form of a sacred grove, with a carriage which none but the priest might touch and containing the presence of the goddess. At festivals the carriage was first drawn by cows through the people, and then washed in a lake, after which the slaves performing this office were drowned. 'Thus mystery creates fear, and an unwillingness to be curious about that sight which may only be viewed by those about to die.' The Angles, however, are not known to have brought this cult with them to Britain, and in fact our knowledge of Anglo-Saxon religion is disappointingly meagre.[15] This is of course due to the avoidance of reference to the old religion by our earliest, and Christian, writers. Students in the past were tempted to repair the deficiency by enlarging on certain obvious affinities between Old English heathenism and Scandinavian mythology, but the dangers inherent in this approach have become apparent.[16] In his *De Temporum Ratione* Bede offers a certain amount of information in a description of the heathen significance of the names of the months.[17] Thus February was Sol-monath, when cakes were offered to the gods. March and April were devoted to two obscure goddesses, Hretha and Eostre respectively. The Christian festival of Easter is apparently named after the latter. The autumn months September and November were known as Halig-monath and Blot-monath, with religious rites and sacrifices which included the slaughter of cattle. The winter feast of Yule occurred during December and January, and included some ceremony associated with 'mothers'.

The attributes of the most important deities of our distant ancestors, Tiw, Woden, and Thunor, whose names are perpetuated in those of three of our weekdays, are by no means clearly defined. It is not to be assumed that Woden and Thunor were identical with the Norse Odin and Thor, about whom more is known. It is clear, however, that Tiw was a Germanic war-god, equated by the Romans with Mars. His name is found in some early Anglo-Saxon personal names, such as Tiowulf. Thunor, the thunder-god, equated with Juppiter, was more widely worshipped. He was one of the gods whom the continental Saxons were to be specifically called on to renounce by the missionaries who approached them in due course. Woden, regarded by the Romans as equivalent to their Mercury, was in the opinion of Tacitus the most worshipped of German gods. He was a war-god who could bring victory, an aristocratic god whom kings claimed as their ancestor. A sure defence against one's enemies, it was a wise precaution to name after him a great earthwork, such as the Wansdyke—Wodnes dic.

Place-names indeed have long been recognised as a useful source of information about Old English heathenism,[18] and an impetus has been given to this study by the investigations of the English Place-Name Society.[19] That the gods had localised cult-centres is proved by such names as Tuesley in Surrey; Woodnesborough in Kent; Wensley in

Derbyshire; the field-names Wodnesfeld and Wedynsfeld in Essex; Thunderley and Thundersley in Essex, Thursley and Thunderfield in Surrey, and the boundary-names Thunresfeld and Thunres leah in Wiltshire and Hampshire respectively. A significant feature of the heathen place-names is the nature of their distribution. This is by no means general, and it has been pointed out[20] that their incidence tends to be greatest just where Bede specifically refers to particularly strong heathen resistance. Thus in Essex, where the old religion was to react more strongly than elsewhere, surviving place-names indicate many instances of heathen centres. In East Anglia, on the other hand, where the Christian Church established itself very smoothly, there is not a single proved example of a heathen place-name. The inference clearly is that the East Saxons were more firmly attached to their traditional gods than were their neighbours to the north. Similarly in Northumbria, where the Church had an enthusiastic welcome, there is no evidence of heathenism from place-names.

In addition to the place-names compounded with the name of a god, there are others which suggest the presence of a heathen site more generally. Thus some are compounded with the Old English 'ealh', temple, 'hearh', hill sanctuary, and 'weoh', shrine. We thus get Ealhfleot, a channel from Faversham to the sea; a number of Harrowdens; and Wye in Kent. There are a few names which are a compound of both 'weoh' and 'leah' (probably a forest clearing),[21] e.g. Willey in Surrey, Whyly in Sussex, Wheely Down in Hampshire, Wylye in Wiltshire. Rare but interesting examples are Peper Harow, Cusanweoh, both in Surrey, and Patchway in Sussex. Each of these indicates the shrine or sanctuary of a specific individual, Peper, Cusa, and Paeccel respectively. That a tribal group of settlers might combine to establish a holy place is shown by the original name of Harrow-on-the-Hill, Gumeninga hearh, 'sanctuary of the Gumeningas', and Basingahearh, a place in Surrey long vanished.

An interesting feature of these place-names is the absence of any attempt to replace them with Christian names after the Conversion. Such a place as Tisbury, Wiltshire, a fairly important Christian centre in the eighth century, continued to be known as 'Tiw's stronghold'. In a sense, this was in line with pope Gregory's recommendation to Augustine that the English should not be deprived too ruthlessly of the memorials of their old religion.[22] The Christian element in English place-names is far less pronounced than it is in those of Cornwall and

Wales. But on the other hand, an enthusiasm for place-name study should not lead us into an exaggerated view of its importance for the diffusion of heathenism amongst the sixth-century Anglo-Saxons. Out of the many thousands of place-names, the actual percentage of those compounded in this way is small, and it would be perilous to argue from this evidence alone that heathenism in the pre-Christian period was vigorously alive in Anglo-Saxon England.

In view of the comparative ease with which Augustine and the other missionaries were to carry through the Conversion, it is difficult to resist the conclusion that in the course of the migration and conquest the Germanic heathenism of the invaders had been considerably weakened. We will not find in any of the English kingdoms except Essex anything approaching the stubborn adherence to heathenism in the face of Christian pressure which would later be found in Frisia, or amongst the continental Saxons, or to an even greater extent amongst the Scandinavians. No other Germanic people was converted so easily and rapidly as the English. The survival of a very high proportion of the British population, with their Christian religion, may be suggested as the reason for this.[23] But it must be re-emphasized that in sixth-century England there is no concrete evidence of the survival of the Romano-British Church. The Saxons doubtless knew of the Christian religion, but that they were actually rubbing shoulders with baptised Christians and familiar with the sight of bishops and monks (except in the most westerly areas and in special circumstances such as those of Ethelbert's court where the queen was a Christian) is mere surmise.

Our general picture of Anglo-Saxon religion is of a faith which has diverged somewhat from Teutonic mythology as known on the Continent, and weakened in intensity of conviction, and yet remains thoroughly Germanic. The offering of human beings has disappeared, but animal sacrifice is known, if only in the expedient form of the disposal of surplus livestock with the approach of winter. Belief in Woden and the other great gods of the Teutonic pantheon is probably weaker than elsewhere in the Germanic world. But men still erect their temples and shrines, and in them they are known to have placed images and altars.[24] There are priests whom we shall encounter in the course of the Conversion, such as Coifi of Northumbria, and others more loyal to their profession, like the Sussex priest who attempted to bind the hands of St Wilfred by magic, and the London priests around whom the East Saxons rallied. More significant than these manifestations of organised religion, however, was the widespread belief in charms and incantations, in the spiritual potency of trees and wells, in a whole army of elves, dragons, and nightmares. To this latter category belong the 'waelcyrian', ghoulish females of a type decidedly more degenerate than the northern Valkyries. The Anglo-Saxons never lost their love of Germanic legends, and retained a place in their thoughts for such figures as Weland the Smith, maker of trusty swords, and Egil the Archer. Both of these have left their traces in English place-names, as in the case of the megalithic sarsens on the Berkshire Downs which came to be known as Wayland's Smithy, and in Aylesbury, Bucks, and Aylesford in Kent. Many of these beliefs and traditions would survive the introduction of Christianity, and to a great extent it would be true that the triumph of the Church entailed not an uprooting but a reinterpretation of existing processes of thought.

CHAPTER V

THE MISSION OF ST AUGUSTINE

It was to these Anglo-Saxon peoples that the blessings of the Gospel were now to be made available. Neglected by their Celtic neighbours, the salvation of their souls would be undertaken by the greatest figure of the sixth century, pope Gregory the Great. It is to this man, more than to any other single person, that the English people owe the Christian religion—an ironical distinction for one who never set foot on English soil.

Gregory, the first great medieval pope, was born in Rome *c.* 540, during the reign of Justinian.[1] He was of aristocratic origin, his father Gordianus being a member of the official ruling class, and possessed of much landed property in Sicily, besides a mansion on the Caelian Hill in Rome. There is no definite proof that Gordianus held office in the Church, though it is thought that he was in orders. There can be no doubt, however, about the piety of Gregory's mother Silvia, of whom it is said that after the death of her husband she embraced a life of devout seclusion.[2] One of the most significant features of the story of the conversion of Britain is the frequency with which its outstanding personalities are the sons of devout, Christian mothers. This has emerged time and again in connection with the Celtic saints. By birth and early environment Gregory was a Roman and a Christian, and throughout his life this double influence was present in his character. He experienced no dramatic conversion. In him there was no embracing of a new ideal or faith, no vigorous casting away of the old man. We find combined in him, almost naturally, the spirit and obligations of ancient Rome along with the faith and asceticism of the middle ages. He is the key to the true understanding of the medieval Church.

About the middle of the sixth century classical Rome had at last reached the end of the road. The popular view that Rome died with the coming of Alaric in 410 has long been abandoned by scholars, who are more inclined to see in the imperialist ambitions of Justinian the real cause of Rome's final ruin. The wars which that emperor unleashed for the conquest or recovery of the Italian peninsula, and in which the generals Belisarius, Narses, and Totila played so notable a part, left Rome in an unenviable position. Aqueducts and public buildings were reduced to ruins, while famine and pestilence became the lot of the wretched inhabitants. The old pagan worship was suppressed, but Christianity had not as yet gained enough strength to fill the spiritual vacuum thus created. The architectural and artistic glories of classical Rome were sadly diminished, through war and neglect. It is true that the temples, closed since 394, had been replaced by Christian basilicas, such as St John Lateran and St Maria Maggiore. But in the opinion of many contemporaries the world held no future, and the end of all things could not be long delayed. It was out of the faith and piety generated by such fears that a new western Europe was constructed of which the Church was the chief architect.

Gregory as a young man joined the imperial civil service, and in 573 became the prefect of Rome. It was soon after this that he found his true vocation, and as a preliminary exercise expended his patrimony on the poor and the founding of monasteries, the family home on the Caelian becoming a monastery for himself and some companions, which he dedicated to St Andrew. In 579 pope Pelagius II sent him as his *apocrisiarius*[3] to Constantinople, charged with the duty of obtaining help from the emperor against the ravages of the Lombards in Italy. It was on his return to Rome a few years later that he encountered the sight in the Roman slave-market which in the expressive words of a late Anglo-Saxon writer stirred in him the desire to convert a people 'well worth winning to God'.[4]

There is no need to question the authenticity of the famous story of the slave-boys, told by Bede,[5] and found also in an earlier work, an eighth-century Life of Gregory written in Northumbria.[6] It is not difficult to see how the tale may have reached the northern kingdom. Possibly it was told by Gregory to Augustine, preserved in the common talk of St Augustine's monastery at Canterbury, and ultimately arrived in Northumbria through the agency of the abbot Albinus and the priest Nothelm,[7] along with other traditions. Gregory himself, however, does not mention the incident in any of his surviving writings. The scene was probably the Roman Forum, and the date *c.* 585 or soon after.

It appears that Gregory after the incident went almost at once to Pelagius II (578–90), a strong pope zealous for the prestige and authority of the Roman see. He was urged to send missionaries to the English by Gregory, who declared himself ready to go. But the authority of the pope was overruled. What Pelagius may have been willing, the Roman people were unwilling to grant. With a sure instinct they saw in Gregory their future protector, and he was pursued and brought back. This was to prove fortunate not only for the Romans but also ultimately for the English, for Gregory now had the advantage of a number of years during which the original idea could expand into a plan.

In 590 the bubonic plague was ravaging Rome, one of its victims being Pelagius.[8] Gregory, at this time abbot of his own monastery on the Caelian and secretary to Pelagius, was chosen by the clergy and people to succeed his master. Anxious to avoid the promotion, he wrote to the emperor Maurice, begging him to withhold confirmation. But the letter was intercepted. It was a terrible time for the Romans, afflicted not only by external foes but by the ravages of disease. Gregory's first important task as pope was the organising of a penitential procession, and in the inspiration and comfort which he brought as a whole to the Romans he revealed himself a leader of the highest order. The official seal was soon set upon his leadership. Confirmation of the election arrived towards the end of the summer, and on 3 September Gregory was consecrated in St Peter's, being at the time about fifty years old.

Gregory now had to abandon all intention which he may have had of personally visiting Britain, and in fact for the remaining fourteen years of his life he stayed in Rome. He was troubled during this period by the encroaching Lombards from the north and by the Donatist heresy in Africa. He had much literary work on hand, and displayed an unceasing care for the Roman people. Ill-health was a constant hindrance to him. But the idea of converting the English was still not only very much in his mind—it was broadening into a far-reaching conception. It seems clear enough that Gregory in the first instance was moved by pure evangelistic fervour. But is it fanciful to think that to this motive was now added a wider one? Gregory was a Roman, and while contemplating the ruins of the city may have dreamed of a restoration of its glories, the memory of which was still fresh in men's minds. The wars of Justinian which had reduced the city of Rome to its existing sad state were comparatively recent. Britain, as Gregory knew, was a province of the old Empire. It had been lost during the troubles of the fifth century, but there was no reason why it should not be regained. Britain might once more receive Roman civilisation and march behind Roman banners, though in place of the eagles there was now the cross. This was a far-sighted view which in time was to bring ardent adherents to the papacy. Before many generations were passed the successors of the converted English would themselves evangelise successfully their heathen kinsfolk on the Continent, and they would be the most loyal of all subjects of the papacy. On the other hand, it might be maintained that there was nothing consciously far-seeing in Gregory's mind. His writings suggest that along with many of his contemporaries he believed the end of the world to be imminent. In this case, although it is possible to read an imperialist motive into Gregory's plans, evangelism would still seem to have been the prime motive in his project for the conversion of the English.

In or about 595 Gregory sent a certain priest Candidus to Gaul to help in the management of his estates in that country. While on his way Candidus received a letter from his master, instructing him to buy English boys of the age of seventeen or eighteen with the money he would receive from the revenue of the estates.[9] The boys were to be placed in monasteries, and it was Gregory's hope that they would prove profitable in God's service. Gregory clearly has in mind here the purchase of slaves, and one wonders what English boys were doing in Gaul. Perhaps they had been captured in war and bartered to the Franks. The beautiful objects found in Jutish graves in Kent are evidence of trade with the Franks. Yet though Gregory wished the boys to be trained as monks, he can scarcely have envisaged a missionary role for them. We read nowhere that they were ever used as such. Gregory would never have entrusted so important a work to recent converts, and enforced ones at that. But they might be valuable in a few years' time as interpreters or general assistants to the mature men trained in Roman discipline to whom the mission was to be entrusted.

It should be noted that though slave-boys in the market had aroused Gregory's pity, and Candidus had been told to purchase slaves, we have no evidence that Gregory disapproved of slavery as such. The Church officially accepted the institution, though under her influence steps of a humanitarian nature were being taken. In Constantine's reign it had been enacted that the ceremony of manumission should take place in church. As this imparted a sacred character to the act of enfranchisement it represented a solid advance. Manumission by

Gregory's day had come to be looked on as an act of mercy, which benefited one's own soul. Large numbers of freed slaves became monks and priests, despite the efforts of Leo the Great to stop the practice. An unsympathetic historian has admitted that the action of the Church in working for the freedom of the slave was unceasing.[10] But the Church was on its guard against an indiscriminate acceptance of slaves wishing to enter holy orders. Gregory insisted that a slave admitted to a monastery should be carefully tested, and returned to servitude if his vocation proved mistaken.[11]

It was not Northumbria, the home of the slave-boys on sale in the Forum, that Gregory chose as the sphere of his English mission. The most civilised of the English kingdoms at this time was Kent, and this was the obvious region for the start of operations. According to the explicit statement of Bede,[12] its king Ethelbert (c. 560–616) exercised a general 'imperium' as far north as the Humber. From the fact that he was later to be able to arrange a conference between Augustine and the British bishops on the borders of England and Wales, it appears likely that his authority extended also far to the west. Kent was in itself only a small kingdom, but the nearest to Gaul and therefore the most accessible to continental culture. The Merovingian kings were in close contact with the royal house of Ethelbert. Kentish culture was comparatively high, though the Sutton Hoo ship-find in East Anglia is an impressive warning against any assumption that other English kingdoms were sunk in ignorance and barbarism. It is unlikely however that Gregory selected Kent because of its relatively high cultural level. To him any English kingdom must have seemed little more than outlandish. Indeed Kent probably appeared in this light also to the Franks, who must have regarded Ethelbert as a petty king. His wife Bertha was a Frank, daughter of Charibert, king of Paris, but it is likely that in bestowing one of their princesses on a heathen island kinglet the Merovingians were acting condescendingly. The contemporary Frankish historian Gregory of Tours does not take much notice of the marriage. He says that Charibert had by his wife Ingoberg a daughter who was afterwards taken as a bride to Kent. In recording the death of Ingoberg he states that she left a daughter married to the son of 'a certain king of Kent'.[13] It has in fact been suggested that the marriage made Ethelbert into a kind of vassal of the Merovingians, and that it was in this light that the pope regarded him.[14] In a commendatory letter to the brothers Theodoric and Theodebert, kings of

Burgundy and Austrasia respectively, requesting their support of Augustine who was shortly to pass through their territories on his way to Kent, Gregory expresses the hope that they desire all their subjects to become Christians.[15] On the other hand, it does not seem likely that Ethelbert was ever a formal vassal of the Franks. Gregory may have been merely flattering the youthful kings.

The man whom Gregory selected as leader for the expedition was in 596 the *praepositus* or prior of the monastery on the Caelian. Concerning Augustine's earlier life little is known. He had been a pupil of Felix, bishop of Messana, and at some time or other a fellow-pupil with Gregory.[16] He was a trusted intimate of the latter and experienced in monastic discipline. Gregory still held the abbot's office formally in his own hands, though the effective government of the house was exercised by Augustine.

It was in the fourteenth year of the emperor Maurice that Augustine set out from Rome with several companions.[17] The fourteenth year ran from August 595 to August 596, and we may take it that the expedition started in the spring of 596. Sailing from Italy to Provence, they were welcomed there by the provincial governor Arigius, by Protasius, bishop of Aix, and by Stephen, abbot of Lérins. It seems that they rested a while in the island-monastery, a congenial spot, but one where they were more than likely to become unnerved. The monastic life was visible there in a most attractive form, a reminder of the life they were leaving behind for unknown perils. Moreover, Celtic monks from the British Isles had visited Lérins, where they had doubtless left tales of the hateful Saxons. Immediately ahead of Augustine and his band lay Gaul—and a cursory perusal of the pages of Gregory of Tours is sufficient indication of the barbarism of that land in the sixth century. If such a state of affairs was possible in a country which had accepted Christianity, what was to be expected at the hands of untamed heathens? Conferring together, the monks lost courage. They longed to resume their monastic routine. They sent Augustine back to Gregory with a request to relieve them of their task.

Gregory's answer was a foregone conclusion. He would not hear of the mission being abandoned through rumoured dangers, and Augustine returned with a letter containing a characteristic combination of firmness and gentleness. 'It is better not to begin a good work at all, than to begin it and then turn back.' The same letter announced the appointment of Augustine as abbot, with the instruction that he was to be obeyed implicitly. So far as we know, in fact, Augustine himself had not lost courage, but had rather been prevailed upon by the fears of his companions. It may well be that he had asked the pope to strengthen his hands. Gregory concluded the letter by commending his beloved sons to the grace of God. He himself longed to be with them in this great work, but failing that he hoped to share the reward of their labours in heaven.

At the same time, in July 596, Gregory dispatched a number of letters to prominent persons whom Augustine was likely to meet on his way through Gaul.[18] The writing of these letters suggests it was the turbulent state of Gaul as much as rumoured dangers in Britain which had frightened the missionaries. Letters were received by the bishops of Marseilles, Arles, Vienne, Lyons, Autun, and Tours, who were asked to help Augustine by providing him with necessities on his journey. The agent Candidus is incidentally remembered; the bishops must ensure that he is not obstructed in his work of estate-management. In a different category, though written at the same time, are the letters to Protasius, bishop of Aix, and Stephen, abbot of Lérins. Gregory does not ask help of these men, because Augustine has already given a good report of them, and their good offices can apparently be taken for granted. In his letter to Protasius, the pope is more concerned with the revenues of his Gallic estates; Stephen is congratulated for the harmony which prevails in the Lérins community, but warned against the snares of the devil.

The letters which Gregory addressed to prominent lay persons are more guarded and flattering in their tone. He tells the provincial governor Arigius that he has heard of his charity, and hopes he will help Augustine. In his letter to the young kings Theodoric and Theodebert he refers to their kingdoms as outstanding for Christian integrity, and expresses the high hopes he holds of them. It has come to his notice that the English wish to be Christians, but that the neighbouring clergy hang back.[19] He has therefore sent Augustine, with other monks, and advised him to take some priests from the neighbourhood as interpreters. The two kings must do all they can to help. The most important of this group of letters, however, is one to Brunhildis, the terrible and yet not ignoble grandmother of Theodoric and Theodebert, and the effective ruler of Burgundy and Austrasia. Gregory informs her that the English have expressed a desire for Christianity, but that the bishops 'in the neighbourhood' are not very helpful in the matter. He has therefore sent Augustine, a tried and trusted monk, who with the help and co-operation of Brunhildis will attempt the conversion.

These letters to Brunhildis and her grandsons are our only evidence that the English themselves had expressed a wish for the Christian religion. Bede does not refer to any such request, but it seems inconceivable that Gregory would have said so much without factual grounds. When Augustine and his band landed in Kent they were to encounter no opposition, let alone suffer any martyrdoms, and Ethelbert's behaviour would strongly suggest he had sent out a discreet hint, designed to reach the ears of the pope, that he might be willing to receive the Faith. By the bishops of the neighbourhood Gregory undoubtedly means those of Gaul. He did not know sufficient concerning the British bishops either to censure or to praise them. But in his letters to the Gallic bishops—Virgilius bishop of Arles and Protasius excepted—he hints that they have hitherto been lukewarm. They will hear from Augustine a full account of the project, which they must support whole-heartedly.

A comparatively smooth journey across Gaul was now assured. Leaving the Lérins and Marseilles region the missionaries arrived at Arles. They passed up the valley of the Rhone to Lyons and Chalons, where Theodoric kept his court. Journeying westwards they came to Tours, too late to meet Gregory, the historian-bishop, who had recently died. Perhaps they saw something of Venantius Fortunatus, now nearing the end of his life at Poitiers, some miles south of Tours. An utterly different type from either Augustine or the pope, this man was the outstanding literary figure of Gaul, remembered in our own day by his hymnology, of which the *Vexilla regis* (the hymn for Passion Sunday) is a conspicuous example. Augustine and his companions seem to have passed most of the winter at Paris, where they were hospitably entertained by Clothair II, king of Neustria, and his mother Fredegund, the implacable enemy of Brunhildis. They then prepared, soon after Easter, for the final stage of their journey.

We are impressed by the spirit of caution which characterised this journey through Gaul. Every care was taken to make the way as smooth as possible. The support of rulers was constantly solicited. This rather unadventurous yet disciplined spirit was to remain throughout a characteristic of the Roman mission to Canterbury. It is in marked contrast to the enthusiastic and abandoned heroism of the Celtic missionaries.

The Channel crossing was uneventful. With his band of about forty followers Augustine landed in the Isle of Thanet, at that period separated from the mainland by the Wantsum. The precise landing-place has been much debated, but it was probably Richborough, the natural port in this neighbourhood towards which an important ship would sail.[20] Without losing time Augustine sent messengers to Ethelbert informing him of his arrival and the purpose of his mission. He had come from Rome, and brought the 'best of messages, which assured to those who would receive it eternal joys in heaven and an everlasting kingdom with the true and living God'. The following course of events makes it reasonably certain that the king was prepared for Augustine's coming and had already decided his attitude. His Christian wife Bertha may have predisposed him in favour of the new religion, though Gregory's correspondence suggests that she made no serious effort to convert him. Perhaps Gregory was rather unjust to Bertha in this respect, as for all we know she may have been unobtrusively commending her religion to her husband in a more effective way than that of argument. She had become his queen on the express condition that no hindrance be presented to the practice of her faith, and had brought with her a Frankish bishop Liudhard as chaplain. She used as her private chapel the old Roman church of St Martin, a little to the east of Canterbury.[21] It is likely that Ethelbert, in view of the ease with which he was now converted, was sometimes present at mass in this church, if only in the capacity of curious spectator. About Liudhard we know nothing.

An easy victory followed, and so far were the English from roughly repelling Augustine, that they even extended to him the greatest courtesy.[22] There seem to be two reasons for Augustine's quick success. Firstly, English heathenism was on the way out. This was certainly so in Kent, though elsewhere, as in Essex and Sussex, the old religion would reassert itself vigorously, and later on Penda of Mercia was to adopt the role of heathen champion. Secondly, as we have seen, the Kentish court was already half-committed to Christianity. The king was interested, at least from a worldly point of view, in the religion of his powerful Frankish neighbours. And once he was won over, his thegns would not be slow to follow, for the comitatus-principle would weigh heavily with them. In the entire history of the English conversion, the missionaries were to follow an invariable policy of making a direct approach to the ruler in the first instance.

Ethelbert moved cautiously, ordering the missionaries to remain in the Isle of Thanet, though meanwhile he kept them supplied with provisions. After some days he arrived in the island and commanded Augustine and his companions to appear before him in the open air. There was an old belief that a man could get the better of an opponent by magical means if he encountered him under a roof. Belief in magic was general, and would remain so under Christian influence. Bede himself does not discountenance it. He tells a curious tale of a prisoner-of-war named Imma, whose bonds were in the habit of falling off at nine in the morning. This was the hour at which his brother Tunna, an abbot, said mass for him.[23]

When the king and his thegns were ready to receive the mission Augustine with his monks advanced towards him, singing litanies, and carrying a silver cross and a picture of the Saviour painted on a board. We have no trustworthy record of the sermon which followed, but it is clear that it was concerned with the heart of the gospel. Bede says that Augustine preached 'the word of life'.[24] According to a much later writer, the homilist Aelfric, Augustine preached the redemption of the world by Christ and the opening of the heavenly kingdom to the faithful.[25] The solemn aspect of the monks, probably dark-haired men with black robes—in contrast with the English arrayed in bright clothes and jewels—the cadences of the Roman chant, and the charm of the leader's fresh and simple message, must have combined to make a strong impression on the audience. In his reply the king acknowledged the beauty of what he had heard, but refused to adopt something new and untried. It was asking a great deal of him to abandon the usages of his ancestors. The messengers however had come a long way and were clearly sincere; he would not hinder them in their preaching, and promised to supply them with necessities.

The meeting broke up and the missionaries made their way to the Kentish capital, where the king had assigned to them a lodging. As they approached the city they sang the antiphon, 'We beseech thee, O Lord, in all thy mercy, that thy anger and wrath be turned away from this city and from thy holy house, for we have sinned. Alleluia.'[26] Arriving at their lodging, they 'began to follow the apostolic life after the way of the primitive church'. From the outset they used St Martin's church, where they recited their offices, preached, and baptised.[27] Impressed by the charm of their doctrine and the simplicity of their lives, many became converts, though meanwhile the king restricted christian activities to St Martin's.

The conversion of Ethelbert himself however soon followed, and he was baptised, according to a late authority, on the feast of Pentecost.[28] From now on there was a steady flow of recruits, and in the phrase of John Lingard, 'the priests of Woden began to lament the solitude of their altars'.[29] No compulsion was brought to bear, though the king showed special favour to those who became Christians. Soon he granted to Augustine a house more in keeping with his status, and conferred on the mission possessions of various kinds—an important step, marking the beginning of English church endowment. It is tempting to think Ethelbert had in mind the example of Constantine in handing over the palace of the Lateran to pope Sylvester. There is a later story, scarcely credible, that Ethelbert gave his Canterbury palace to Augustine, he himself going to live in a new one in Reculver. On the contrary, the subsequent history of the relations between Augustine and Ethelbert suggests that the two men remained close together in Canterbury. The king would hardly vacate his capital to make way for a newly arrived missionary, however much he favoured him.

The mission now prospered so rapidly that at Christmas Augustine was in a position to baptise ten thousand converts. His next step was to obtain episcopal orders, so that a priestly succession might be maintained. He therefore repaired to Arles, where he was consecrated by Virgilius its bishop.[30] On his return he sent two of his companions, Laurentius and Peter, to tell Gregory of the success achieved, and to ask his advice on some difficult problems. Augustine also now set about building new churches and restoring old ones, thus providing the Faith with visible centres. He rebuilt a church which had been in Canterbury since Romano-British times, and consecrated it in the name of the Saviour Jesus Christ, making there a home for himself and his successors. This church was finally completed in 602 or the following year. Not far from the city, on the east side, he founded a monastery, known in his day as St Peter's but to subsequent generations as St Augustine's. Within its precincts Ethelbert built and endowed the church of SS. Peter and Paul as a burying-place for Augustine and his successors and the kings of Kent. This church was completed after Augustine's death. The first abbot of St Peter's was Peter, afterwards drowned while crossing the Channel.

Also on the east side of the city, about midway between St Martin's and the city walls, was a temple which it is said Ethelbert had used for heathen sacrifice.[31] This was purified by Augustine and dedicated to St Pancras. Pancras was a Roman boy of noble family who had suffered martyrdom under Diocletian, and whose family had owned the land on which the Caelian monastery of St Andrew was built. It is possible then that in choosing the dedication of this church, thoughts of his old monastery came into Augustine's mind. They were to enter his mind later, when he dedicated the cathedral of Rochester to St Andrew. The adaptation of heathen temples as Christian churches was a noteworthy characteristic of the Roman mission in England, a practice hitherto rare in western Christendom. The Pantheon in Rome, which became the church of All Saints, is an exception helping to prove the rule, and even this dedication did not occur until four years after Gregory's death. The popularisation of the practice is usually ascribed to Gregory, but he may well have been given the idea by Augustine's purification of Ethelbert's temple. Augustine showed enterprise and originality in this matter at least.

Laurentius and Peter duly arrived in Rome, in the early summer of 598, and informed the pope of Augustine's opening successes. Gregory at once wrote to Eulogius, bishop of Alexandria, who had promised to pray for the mission, with the good news that his prayers had been effective.[32] The two messengers from Augustine also handed to the pope the request for advice and reinforcements. The delay which followed is one of the puzzles of the whole story. The two men stayed in Rome for no less than three years. Why was Gregory so long in letting them go? Gregory's ill-health is often suggested, and indeed it is the excuse put forward by Gregory himself. In the preface to his replies to Augustine's questions he states that Laurentius and Peter had asked to be dismissed as soon as possible, but unfortunately he is in pain because of the gout. He apologises for not answering each point as carefully as he might otherwise have done. But though the fact of Gregory's ill-health is certain, it hardly seems likely that this alone could have held up for three years the reply to an important document. It was certainly a contributory reason, as also was Gregory's preoccupation with affairs of Church and State. But it is a well-known fact that busy men are the most to be trusted for prompt and methodical attention to business. The root reason for the delay was probably the shortage of suitable man-power. Augustine had asked for more helpers, and first-class men are simply not to be produced by a mere nod of the head. In fact this, rather than the request for advice, may well have been the real reason for the visit of Laurentius and Peter to Rome. And the pope was just not going to be hurried over the problem of finding the right men for Kent. The English mission was one of his most cherished projects, and he did not intend to ruin it now, after so promising a start, by a hasty choice. Subsequent events were to show how justified were his fears. He hesitated until 601, when Laurentius and Peter set out from Rome, accompanied by the welcome reinforcements. The most prominent of these were Mellitus, apparently the leader of this second expedition from Rome to Kent, and Justus, Paulinus, and Rufinianus. The first three of these were to become the first bishops of London, Rochester, and York respectively. The very fact that Augustine was to choose his first bishops from these new-comers and not from the original band, indicates that during his earlier years in Kent he was handicapped by a lack of outstanding men. Even so, the pope did not succeed in providing just the men who were needed. When the inevitable heathen reaction came a few years later, all three of these new bishops were to show a discreet caution in retreating at the first sight of danger.

The second expedition, like the first, took with it commendatory letters from the pope.[33] Gregory thanks Brunhildis for her kindness to Augustine on his way through Gaul, and indeed the formidable Frankish queen appears in a favourable light in Gregory's correspondence. There were letters for Theodoric king of Burgundy, for several bishops, for Theodebert king of Austrasia, and Clothair of Neustria. There were gifts for Ethelbert, besides vessels, ornaments, relics, and books for use in the English Church. Two manuscript copies of the gospels, now in the Bodleian and at Corpus Christi College, Cambridge, are often assigned to this parcel of gifts. Of greater interest to the historian than either the commendatory letters or the gifts are the letters which Gregory addressed to the king and queen of Kent and to Augustine. In a vigorous letter to Ethelbert he calls on him to make greater efforts against heathenism, to destroy the temples and the worship of idols.[34] With his characteristic flattery he reminds Ethelbert of Constantine. He advises him to pay deferential attention to Augustine, whom he warmly praises for his training in monastic discipline and his knowledge of the scriptures. Gregory harps on one of his favourite themes when he reminds Ethelbert of the approaching end of the world. If any signs of the end—such as plagues, famines, wars, earthquakes—should appear in Ethelbert's kingdom, he is not to be alarmed.

Gregory's letter to Bertha is particularly interesting.[35] He begins by remarking that those who desire the reward of heaven must work hard to make gains for God. Laurentius and Peter have told him of her helpfulness to Augustine, but this is not enough on her part. She has been too slow in commending her religion to her husband, and must now make up for her past neglect with interest. He reminds her how Constantine's mother Helena drew the hearts of the Romans to the Christian religion, and she can do the same for the English. The letter combines exceptional frankness with characteristic flattery. The pope says that Bertha's fine qualities are known not only at Rome, but even by the emperor at Constantinople. This letter, by its vigour and earnestness of tone, reveals the importance which the pope placed on the influence of a queen over her husband, and through him over the nation.

Before we consider in detail the celebrated *responsa* of Gregory to Augustine, it may be remarked that after Laurentius and Peter had left Rome Gregory sent a messenger after them, with a letter for Mellitus.[36] The pope had reconsidered his advice to Ethelbert concerning the destruction of heathen temples; Mellitus is to tell Augustine that the temples should not be destroyed, but only the idols within them. The temples are to be sprinkled with holy water and furnished with altars and relics. The transition of the people from heathenism to Christianity will in this way be facilitated, if they do not have to forsake their accustomed places of worship. Gregory goes even further than this, as he expressly sanctions in his letter the adaptation of the heathen practice of sacrificing slaughtered cattle to devils. On dedication festivals, or at the festivals of martyrs whose relics are in a specific temple concerned, the worshippers may hold religious feasts, involving the slaughter of animals. If a man wishes to climb, says Gregory, he should do so by steps and not by leaps.

We now come to the important correspondence of Gregory with Augustine, the *responsa*.[37] In addition to the replies to particular questions, it includes two letters to the archbishop. A lengthy communication, of a private yet hortatory character, the first is not of any great historical importance. God is thanked for the initial successes, though at the same time Augustine is warned against pride, such as may well result from the miracles which the pope hears have been accomplished. Gregory, as an old fellow-monk of Augustine's, was apparently aware of a strain of arrogance in the latter's character, which in fact was shortly to be revealed in the archbishop's dealings with the British churchmen. The second letter is more important.[38] Gregory sends a pallium to Augustine, with the customary direction that it is to be worn only at mass. He is to consecrate twelve bishops, who will be subject to his jurisdiction, and it is implied in the letter, though not stated explicitly, that as soon as possible Augustine will remove his seat from Canterbury to London. He should send a bishop to York, the choice of person being left in Augustine's hands, and this prelate may in turn consecrate twelve bishops if there is sufficient progress in the area to justify it. He too will receive the pallium, but will be subject to the jurisdiction of Augustine. He will be independent of the see of London after Augustine's death, when the senior of the two by consecration will take precedence. They will confer together in ecclesiastical planning. Meanwhile Augustine shall exercise authority over his own bishops, those of the bishop of York, and also over all the bishops of Britain. The last-named are to accept their standards of belief and conduct from Augustine. Gregory's scheme of two provinces was clearly based on the old Roman division of the country into Upper and Lower Britain, of which London and York were the principal cities. The scheme was never fully realised. Augustine consecrated only two suffragans for the south, and in the north he accomplished nothing at all. His own metropolitical see remained fixed at Canterbury. It would not have been feasible to place it in London, which was a pagan stronghold—far better and more cautious to remain in the shadow of Ethelbert's protection. Afterwards, when the Church was well established in the south-east, and the removal to London could have been safely made, sentiment and tradition forbad the change.[39] The twelfth suffragan for the southern province was not established until 737, at Leicester. There was no fully established archbishopric at York until about the same time, and its only suffragan sees then were Hexham, Lindisfarne, and Whithorn; in later medieval times even this number was to be reduced. Gregory's plan for the division of honour and authority between the north and south was the cause of the independent spirit so long shown by York. It is only in the recent history of the Church of England, with the growth of the northern population through industrial development, that Gregory's scheme has at last been realised.

We shall now consider the advice offered to Augustine in his various problems by the pope, taking the *responsa* in order.[40]

(1) Augustine asks—how are the bishops to conduct themselves in relation to their clergy, how are the offerings of the faithful to be divided, and how is the bishop to comport himself in church?

Gregory replies that the custom of the Apostolic see is for offerings to be divided into four portions—one for the bishop and his *familia* to enable them fulfil their duty of hospitality, and the other three parts for the clergy, the poor, and the repair of churches. In Augustine's case however, Gregory points out, this scheme will not entirely apply, as he is living under monastic rule and should therefore hold property in common with others. Clergy below the rank of subdeacon may marry,[41] and in that case will receive separate stipends, though they will remain under ecclesiastical rule. The pope, it appears, is somewhat impatient with Augustine. It should not be necessary, he goes on, to remind those living the common life that the dividing of portions is irrelevant in their case. The pope is rather hard on the archbishop here, who after all was not now the prior of a Roman monastery but had the oversight of an infant Church. But the question concerning the demeanour of a bishop in church, truly puerile, Gregory refuses even to discuss; he simply advises Augustine to read the scriptures, particularly the epistles to Timothy.[42]

(2) Augustine is puzzled at the divergences between the liturgical practices of Rome and Gaul. Should there be different customs in the Church which professes the one Faith? In Rome he would of course be familiar with the Roman liturgy. But in the fifth and sixth centuries the liturgical situation in the Church of the west was altogether more fluid than that which later came to prevail.[43] The concept of an imposed book was a development of the medieval and modern Churches. At this early time the bishop and even the priest had a wide measure of discretion in the prayers which he used at the altar. But in the minds of men like Augustine the idea of a rigid uniformity was beginning to take shape. On his way through Gaul Augustine would be introduced to the Gallican liturgy, which was probably celebrated also by Liudhard in St Martin's Canterbury. Augustine was now saying mass in this church, doubtless according to the Roman rite as contained in the Gelasian sacramentary. There was thus a state of confusion which could not continue indefinitely, and intolerable to Augustine with his

habits of Roman order and discipline.[44]   Gregory's answer is a model of good sense and moderation.

Augustine should select with care whatever in the Roman, Gallican, or any other Church is likely to be pleasing to God, and introduce the same into the use of the English Church. The pope points out that the new Church in Kent is untrammelled by tradition and offers a fair field for experiment. It is an opportunity which Augustine should exploit while it lasts. In spite of the undoubted excellence of both the Roman and the Gallican liturgies, Augustine need not feel bound to accept all that is in them. The new Church should have the best possible liturgy. Augustine should gather together the best features of the various Churches, and thus form a distinctive use. It was sound advice, which apparently Augustine did not follow. The Roman mass came to prevail in the Church of the English. Later, in 747, the council of Cloveshoe accepted as the right standard that which had been received from the Church of Rome.[45]

(3) The archbishop asks—what should be done to a man who has stolen from a church?

In his reply, marked by charity and moderation, Gregory draws a distinction between those who steal, though they are in profitable employment, and those who steal through want. The punishment is varied accordingly. The stolen goods must certainly be restored, but it will be enough if exact restitution is made. This provision, even if satisfactory to Augustine, would not suit Germanic laws of compensation, and Ethelbert in his laws was to go much further. In due course the king would decree a twelve-fold restoration of stolen church property—a bishop's property to be restored eleven-fold, a priest's nine-fold, a deacon's six-fold, a clerk's three-fold. The Church was an unarmed institution, and had to be guarded by powerful deterrents.

(4) May two brothers marry two sisters?

Gregory dismisses the question briefly, emphatically, almost contemptuously. Of course they may marry—scripture has nothing to the contrary. For the second time Gregory pointedly reminds Augustine of the authority of the Bible.

(5) This question, also concerned with the marriage-laws, is more worthy of a reasoned answer. Within what decrees may relatives marry—may a man marry his stepmother or sister-in-law?

It is clear that Augustine had encountered the prevalent Anglo-Saxon custom of marriage with one's stepmother, a notable instance of which later on was the marriage of Ethelbert's son Eadbald with his father's widow (not Bertha, but a second wife). Gregory in his reply states that such unions are abominable; marriage with a sister-in-law is also wrong, because she has become one flesh with the brother. But those who contract such unions are not to be excommunicated unless their sin is committed after their baptism. As for the marriage of first cousins, Gregory points out that this is permitted by Roman law, though he himself prefers to follow holy scripture, which forbids the practice. The third or fourth generation should be reached before marriage is undertaken.[46]

(6) May a bishop be consecrated by a single bishop, difficulties of distance preventing the presence of other bishops?

There is again a note of sarcasm in Gregory's reply. 'As you are at present the only bishop in the English Church, you can hardly help consecrating another bishop single-handed.' He also has a tilt at the bishops of Gaul, of whom he holds no high opinion. He implies that they would be too indolent to cross the Channel to help consecrate bishops even if invited. Augustine's policy should be to create bishops according to an arrangement whereby their sees will be close together and difficulties of travel thus lessened, so that irregularities in the consecration of bishops may in future be avoided. When in due course the entire country has been covered by dioceses, it should then be the rule for three or four bishops to meet for a consecration.[47]

(7) How, asks Augustine, is he to deal with the bishops of Gaul and Britain?

In his reply, Gregory confers no authority upon Augustine over the Gallic bishops. The bishop of Arles has possessed the pallium[48] from ancient times, and cannot be deprived of his authority. If Augustine should happen to visit Gaul, he may co-operate with the bishop of Arles in the administration of church discipline, and should that bishop be lukewarm urge him on. Gregory quotes the law, 'When a man passeth through another man's corn, he may not put a sickle thereto, but may rub the ears with his hand and eat'. Gregory writes separately to the bishop of Arles explaining the position.[49] And then, after thus dealing at comparative length with the bishops of Gaul, the pope in one short sentence commits the bishops of Britain to Augustine.

This famous answer is the most puzzling thing in the whole of Gregory's English correspondence. It is inconceivable that Augustine was claiming jurisdiction over the old established dioceses of Gaul, and yet this is how Gregory seems to have read his question. A possible explanation, put forward many years ago by A. J. Mason,[50] is that Augustine was referring to Gaulish ecclesiastics in Kent. Liudhard doubtless resented Augustine's intrusion into St Martin's church, and may have been causing difficulty. We know virtually nothing of Liudhard, but it is possible that he was more important than we think. Augustine's second question implies that there was a sufficient Gaulish element in Kent to cause friction; if there was confusion in liturgical observance, there may well also have been some unfriendly argument over matters of jurisdiction. Who was spiritual leader in the royal household, Augustine or Liudhard? Augustine may well be requesting guidance in connection with his dealings with Liudhard and his Frankish entourage. The Gaulish church in Kent was small and had made no attempt at missionary work, but it had royal patronage from the queen. Augustine is anxious for his position in relation to this church to be clearly defined. At the same time his question is a wide one. The form of the question suggests[51] that he was thinking of more than one Gallic bishop. So far as we know, Liudhard was the only one in Kent, in which case Augustine must have had the bishops of Gaul itself also in mind. Though he could not possibly claim any authority over them, he might have feared their claiming authority over him. It is possible, as we have noticed, that Ethelbert himself was an informal vassal of the Merovingians.

By the 'bishops of Britain' Augustine could not have meant any others than the Celtic bishops in the west of the island. He himself was as yet the only bishop for the English, and it was obvious he would exercise authority over those whom he would shortly consecrate. But whom did Gregory understand him to mean? A. J. Mason was quite off the rails here: 'It looks as if Gregory knew nothing of these Celtic bishops, so that the last sentence of his reply had no direct reference to them, but meant the bishops whom Augustine himself would appoint.'[52] This view is put out of court by Gregory's separate letter to Augustine,[53] in which it is explicitly stated that Augustine is to hold authority not only over the bishops whom he would consecrate, and those who would be consecrated by the bishop of York, 'but even all the priests of Britain'.[54] Mason admitted the common view to be that the British bishops are intended here. But he countered with the incredibly vague reply: 'It is doubtful whether Gregory was aware of their existence. He probably wished to make his statement as large as possible, without exactly analysing its contents.'[55] We must consider Laurentius and Peter to have been extremely reticent if they did not mention the existence of a native British Church to Gregory during their three years in Rome. That Gregory was in fact referring to the British bishops of Wales and the other western parts is clear from the full text of the single sentence which concluded his reply. 'But we commit all the bishops of Britain to you, brother, that the unlearned may be taught, the weak made strong by advice, the perverse corrected with authority.' One could hardly describe as unlearned, weak, and perverse, English bishops soon to be consecrated, but not yet in existence.

It is nevertheless clear that Gregory had but a small knowledge of the Celtic bishops. He was unaware of their independent spirit, their traditions, their long roll of saints. They were an outlandish group of Christians on the edge of the world. We may be sure that if he had known the facts, he would have treated the question at greater length, and defined Augustine's relations to the Celts with his customary care and moderation.

(8, 9) Both of these questions are concerned with the subject of ritual defilement, and though the answers are of considerable length, they are of no importance to the modern reader.[56]

How are we to sum up this celebrated document? Unfortunately it throws scarcely any light on the subject of Anglo-Saxon heathenism. Augustine does not ask for advice in connection with heathen beliefs and practices. It seems that these beliefs were now so lightly held that they were not worth bothering about. At any rate this is the inference we draw from Augustine's lack of interest in them. Augustine's main concern seems to have been in the sphere of church government, ceremonial regulation, and liturgical observance. We should beware of making too much of this apparent pre-occupation with the externals of religion. It is the Roman love of order and discipline which the archbishop is revealing, and this may not be such a bad thing. In any case it is unfair to assume that Augustine did not care for weightier matters. Before Ethelbert's court he preached 'the word of life'. Now that he had secured the initial successes, he was concerned to establish the ecclesiastical framework within which the gospel could grow. He nevertheless reveals an aridity of mind which evokes Gregory's impatience. It is clear throughout that Gregory was conversant with both the faults and excellences of Augustine.

In the whole story of the early Conversion the pope stands out as a truly great figure. His answers are a model of moderation, states-manship, and charity, erring only over the question of the Celtic bishops, where he was inadequately informed. Indeed, in favour of the general authenticity of the *responsa*, it might be argued that they reveal the impact of a single dominating mind. After the dispatch of this advice and the second group of missionaries, we hear no more of Gregory in connection with England, though he lived for another three years. So far as we know, he held no further communication with the archbishop. Without his support and guidance in the early years, however, Augustine would have accomplished little. It is Gregory whom Bede affectionately calls 'our apostle', who brought the English from Satan's power to the faith of Christ.

With the papal mandate giving him jurisdiction over all Britain, Augustine was now in a position to establish contact with the Christians of the west. It was plain to him that he had no hope of converting the Anglo-Saxons unaided, and the obvious allies were the British. With Ethelbert's help he invited the Britons, represented by their bishops and scholars, to a place which in Bede's day was still known as Augustine's Oak, on the borders of the Hwicci (roughly our Worcestershire) and West Saxony. Aust, near the left bank of the Channel, is often identified as the place of meeting. It might be asked whether Augustine would have travelled so far to meet the Britons. But any locality near the borders of the Hwicci and Wessex would be a long way from Kent. That Augustine was prepared to make so long a journey to meet the Celtic delegates, shows that he fully realised the importance of the Welsh Church.

At the meeting Augustine asked the Celts to keep Catholic peace with him and to co-operate in preaching to the heathen. This proposal presupposed a reasonable amount of doctrinal unity, and the most serious divergence in fact was the dating of Easter.[57] After a protracted discussion, the Britons refused to give way. To end the deadlock, Augustine proposed a trial of strength—a sick man would be intro-duced and the side by whose prayers he was healed considered the victors. The Celts reluctantly agreed, and a blind Englishman was brought forward. The British bishops could not heal him, whereas when Augustine prayed the sufferer at once received his sight. There was a fleeting moment of unity, and Augustine was acclaimed by both sides. The Britons acknowledged that Augustine preached the true way of righteousness. They must first, however, consult their brethren before their immemorial customs could be abandoned. They therefore requested a further conference, at which a larger number of representatives would be present.

Bede does not say where the second conference was held, though presumably it was at the same place. Seven British bishops and many scholars attended, notably from the great monastery of Bangor-is-coed, near Chester, ruled at the time by the abbot Dinoot. Before their arrival they resorted to a recluse renowned for his wisdom, and sought his advice touching the advisability of surrendering their traditions. He said, 'If he is a man of God, follow him.' Their natural rejoinder to this rather vague advice was, 'How shall we be able to prove this?' The hermit replied, 'The Lord said, "Take my yoke upon you and learn of me, for I am meek and lowly of heart". If therefore this Augustine is meek and humble of heart, we may believe that he himself bears the yoke of Christ, and is presenting it to you to bear. But if he is hard and proud, it is plain that he is not of God, and we need not mind what he says.' They asked again, 'And how shall we tell this?' 'Arrange', he said, 'that he with his followers arrives first at the place of meeting. If he arises at your approach, you will hear him with deference, knowing him to be a servant of Christ. But if he make light of you, and will not rise in your presence, even though you are the greater in number, then make light of him also.'

This story is as inherently probable as that of the slave-boys in the Forum. The advice of the hermit agrees well with the spirit of Celtic Christianity. Augustine acted as foreseen by the recluse. On the approach of the Britons he remained seated. It is easy to censure him for his lack of courtesy, and tactless he certainly was. But he was after all the representative of Rome, and there are greater faults than pride in one's mission. Unfortunately the Britons drew the obvious inference of arrogance, and from henceforth were at pains to contradict all that Augustine said. The incident is an admirable illustration of the grave harm which can be caused by thoughtlessness in small matters.

The archbishop was not unreasonable in his demands. Would the Britons keep Easter at the Roman time and baptise in the Roman manner, and agreeing on these two points, join with him in the English mission? Other points of difference would be overlooked, though Augustine's authority must be recognised. There was no suggestion to the British that they would be required to give up their Celtic liturgy. But their minds were made up. The miraculous healing of the blind man was forgotten. Their resolution had been stiffened by conversation with their brethren at Bangor. We may be certain that it was hatred of the Saxons, no less than love of their own peculiar traditions, which made them choose the course they did. And this is how Augustine himself read their minds. In a heated moment he half lost his temper, and exclaimed that if they would not preach life to the English, the English would bring death to them. It seemed to later English churchmen that Augustine's prediction was fulfilled at the battle of Chester in 615, when British clergy were massacred by the savage Aethelfrith.[58]

The two conferences cannot be precisely dated, but they seem to have taken place in 602 or the following year. In 604 Augustine consecrated Mellitus and Justus to the sees of London and Rochester respectively. The consecration of a bishop for London is interesting; it shows that from the outset Augustine had no intention of obeying Gregory's instruction to remove his see from Canterbury to London. He would have had ample justification for doing so, as London, the capital of the East Saxons, was an important city—as it had been in Roman times, and 'a centre of trade for many peoples, who came to it by land and sea'.[59] The East Saxon king was Saebert, a nephew of Ethelbert through his sister Ricula, and subject to his uncle.[60] It was a difficult task for Mellitus to undertake, as Essex was a stronghold of heathenism. But he 'preached the word of truth', and when it was clear that success was possible, Ethelbert built for him the church of St Paul in London to contain his episcopal seat. Justus was consecrated in Rochester as bishop for that city. Canterbury, London, and Rochester were within easy reach of each other, and we thus see the archbishop beginning to implement Gregory's plan for a number of adjacent bishoprics, so that in future three or four bishops might assemble for consecrations. Ethelbert endowed both of the new bishoprics with lands and other properties.

It may have been about this time that Augustine consecrated Laurentius as his own successor, an uncanonical act. It had sometimes been done before, as when Athanasius consecrated his successor shortly before his death. When in the eighth century Boniface of Germany wished to do the same, permission was refused by pope Zacharius. There was something to be said for the practice, which helped to secure a smooth succession. In later times the kings of France were to arrange for their heirs to be crowned in advance, to lessen the chances of disturbances after their deaths. In Augustine's case the action was doubtless justified; it was a wise precautionary measure, ensuring that the infant English Church should not be endangered even for an hour through want of leadership. Bede cites the example of St Peter, who was commonly supposed to have consecrated his successor Clement.[61]

The consecrations were Augustine's last recorded acts. Unfortunately the year of his death is unknown. In the lengthy epitaph on the archbishop's tomb, as cited by Bede, only the day and month are mentioned.[62] 'Here rests the lord Augustine, first archbishop of Canterbury, who was sent here by the blessed Gregory, bishop of the city of Rome. Supported by God and the working of miracles, he led king Ethelbert and his people away from the worship of idols to the faith of Christ. The course of his ministry having been fulfilled he died on 26 May, in the reign of that king.' The king himself died in 616 (after a reign of fifty-six years), but Augustine almost certainly predeceased him by many years.

Augustine was buried in the open, alongside the church of SS. Peter and Paul, still in course of erection. As soon as the church was completed and consecrated, the archbishop's body was brought inside and interred in the north aisle, where subsequent archbishops of Canterbury were also buried. Ethelbert, Bertha, and Liudhard were likewise buried in this church; there is much to be said for the idea that this church was built primarily to serve as a royal and episcopal mausoleum. It was not long before the aurora of sainthood gathered round the archbishop's name, and in Bede's day masses in his honour were being said each Saturday in the church of SS. Peter and Paul. At the synod of Cloveshoe in 747 it was decreed that the days of Augustine and Gregory should be officially observed in the English Church.

St Augustine is almost a text-book example of the type of man who has greatness thrust upon him. He has attained his immortality in the annals of the English people not by his personal character and achievements, but as the chosen instrument for the accomplishment of a design quite beyond his capacity and which had matured in the mind of a far greater man. He himself was a legalist rather than an evangelist, a priest rather than a prophet. In his favour must be remembered his loyalty, his perseverance in what may well have been an irksome and unwelcome task—undertaken through a sense of duty rather than in a spirit of missionary zeal. He was a model of caution, and cannot be accused of attempting the impossible. In confining his activities to a small geographical area it might indeed be maintained that he the more firmly laid the foundations of an archiepiscopal see which has enjoyed an unbroken succession to the present day. The presumed shortness of his apostolate in this country must also be taken into account before a harsh judgment is passed upon him. There are few instances in history of missionaries accomplishing much in the space of a few years. If Augustine had lived longer, and been given time to learn the lessons of his mistakes, his archiepiscopate might well have been a notable one. As it was, he restored the lost connection with Rome, and brought the race of the Saxons for the first time into the orbit of ecclesiastical civilisation. For them, the mission of Augustine was the beginning of order and discipline, and of those processes of written law and centralisation which were to lead them to national unity.

By no stretch of imagination can Augustine be called a great man. It has been common in the past to attribute his deficiencies to the fact of his monastic training. But this cannot be maintained. The Church has a long roll of successful missionaries who were men of religious profession. The tendency of Augustine to be preoccupied with sacred trivialities cannot be traced to the influences of his early environment. He did however have a lack of sympathy with non-Roman Christians which was fraught with unfortunate consequences. His character is starkly revealed in the pages of Bede and the correspondence of Gregory. He was a man of narrow views who could not adjust his perception to penetrate to the true significance of things. History has been kind to St Augustine, but he himself exercised a disproportionately small influence on the course of historical events.

And yet despite Augustine's only too obvious failings, it is ungenerous of Englishmen to be hard towards him. Though his achievement was limited and prosaic, it was enduring. Those who denigrate St Augustine often forget that his mission was specifically to Kent, not to England, which politically did not yet exist. In the professed purpose of his mission he actually succeeded, and he did so in spite of his lack of really good helpers. In the latter connection, the long delay of Gregory in sending the second group of missionaries is really the key to the problem. It was through the dearth of first-class assistants, and because of the continual strife between the English kings, that the wider scheme for two metropolitans each with twelve diocesan bishops came to nothing. The refusal of the Celtic bishops to co-operate was a severe blow to Augustine. But though he showed lack of understanding in his dealings with them, they were not ready for joint operations with Rome anyhow. They preferred to go their own way, and Celtic missionaries from the north would in due course make their distinctive contribution. Meanwhile in Kent the work of Augustine would never be undone. In the Augustinian succession itself, no fewer than eleven bishops (six Italians, five Englishmen) would be consecrated; they covered a period of about two generations, until succeeded by the more dynamic leadership of Theodore of Tarsus.

CHAPTER VI

FURTHER STAGES
IN THE ROMAN MISSION

Laurentius, who succeeded Augustine, made a renewed effort towards union with the Celtic Christians of the west. Bede records the letter which he addressed in his own name and in that of his fellow-bishops Mellitus and Justus to the Scots.[1] The archbishop also wrote to the British bishops. He upbraids the Scots, saying that he had mistakenly thought them to be worthier Christians than the British. He has gathered, however, from the example of Columbanus in Gaul that the Scots are no different from the Britons. This impression has been confirmed by the visit to Britain of a certain Irish bishop Dagan, who refused to eat in company with Laurentius.[2]

Meanwhile, Mellitus went to Rome to discuss with Boniface IV certain matters relating to the English Church. While he was there, the pope held a synod of Italian bishops in which Mellitus also took part, and which drew up regulations for the monastic life.

Ethelbert was succeeded in 616 by his son Eadbald, under whom there was a heathen reaction. Eadbald not only refused to be a Christian, but disgraced himself in the eyes of churchmen by marrying his father's widow (Ethelbert's second wife).[3] Bede relates with some relish that as a result the new king was smitten with intermittent insanity.

In Essex the heathen reaction was more serious. It followed the death of the Christian king Saebert, whose three sons had remained heathen. During their father's lifetime they had held their peace, but now openly advocated the old religion. Bede says that according to the popular story they would attend church and when they saw the bishop administering holy communion demanded that he give them also some of the 'pretty bread' to eat. He refused, demanding first their baptism. The upshot was the expulsion of Mellitus, who made his way to Laurentius and Justus. The three bishops took counsel together, and decided there was no point in staying amongst such inveterate heathens. Mellitus and Justus withdrew to Gaul, where they intended to await the course of events. Laurentius also was on the point of

93

departing. On his last night in Britain he ordered his bed to be made up in the church of SS. Peter and Paul. But the apostle Peter appeared to him in a vision and scourged him, upbraiding him for his desertion of his flock. In the morning the archbishop went to Eadbald and showed to him the marks of his scourging. The king took alarm, forsook his heathen worship, renounced his unlawful marriage, and was baptised.[4] He also recalled the two runaway bishops from Gaul. Justus duly returned to Rochester, but Mellitus found that the Londoners would not have him back, preferring to remain under their heathen priests. The penitent Eadbald did his best to help the restored bishops, but his influence was far below that of his father Ethelbert.

Meanwhile, Laurentius died, and was succeeded as archbishop of Canterbury by Mellitus, who ruled for five years. He died in 624, when he was buried like his predecessors in the monastery of St Peter. Bede speaks well of him as one who, though crippled by gout, kept his mind alert. Noble by birth, he was even nobler in his thoughts. He was succeeded by Justus, who consecrated Romanus as his successor at Rochester. Justus received the pallium from Boniface V, along with a vigorous letter in which the pontiff exhorted the archbishop to press on with missionary work. A quarter of a century had elapsed since the original dispatch of Augustine, and it may well have been felt in Rome that the mission was showing a tendency to stand still.[5]

Fortunately there now developed a set of circumstances which made an extension of the Roman mission possible. At this time the Northumbrian kingdom was ruled by Edwin, who sent suitors to Eadbald of Kent, asking the hand of his sister Ethelburga in marriage. The Northumbrian king was told it was not lawful for a Christian bride to be given to a heathen, whereupon he promised not to interfere in any way with the practice of her religion. Moreover, he would become a Christian himself should the new religion obtain a favourable report from his advisers. The maiden was accordingly sent to Edwin, accompanied by Paulinus, who was to strengthen her and her companions with daily exhortation and the sacraments.

It is clear that Paulinus, who had been one of the second group of missionaries who came over in 601, was sent north in the capacity of missionary as much as that of domestic chaplain. Before his departure he was consecrated bishop by Justus, in July 625. He travelled north, 'intent upon calling the nation whither he was bound to the acknowledgement of the truth'.[6] For a year his labours were fruitless.

Then at Eastertide in 626 an attempt was made on Edwin's life by an assassin from Wessex. The plot was thwarted, and in gratitude the king allowed his newly-born daughter Eanfled to be baptised. She was the first Northumbrian to be made a Christian, along with eleven others of the royal household. The king himself promised to receive baptism if there was a successful outcome to the expedition which he was now planning against Cuichelm, the Wessex king who had plotted the attempted murder. Returning home a conqueror, he still refused to hurry the matter of his conversion, though he never again served idols. Meanwhile he received instruction in Christian doctrine from Paulinus. A thoughtful man, he was accustomed to sit for long periods in silence, holding conversation with himself.

It so happened that many years previously, in 616, Edwin had been an exile at the court of Raedwald, king of the East Angles, who was strongly tempted at the time by Aethelfrith of Northumbria through means of bribes and threats to betray his guest. One night a stranger had appeared to Edwin while the latter was brooding over the dangers of his position, and promised to deliver him should he on his part undertake to follow the stranger's advice on being given a sign on some future occasion. The sign would be the laying of the stranger's hand upon his head. Deliverance duly came, and Edwin entered his kingdom of Northumbria. As he now sat in deep thought on a certain occasion, Paulinus approached and laid his hand upon his head, inquiring whether he recognised the sign. He called on him to embrace the Faith, and follow the precepts of Him who years before had delivered him from his enemies.

It has been surmised that Paulinus himself was the stranger at Raedwald's court, and this is not unlikely. There is a blank of a quarter of a century in Paulinus's life of which we know nothing, and it may well be that he worked in East Anglia during this time. It is difficult to believe that a man like Paulinus was idle, or virtually so, during this lengthy period.

Edwin insisted that before he took the final step he must first consult his witan. In the debate which followed, Edwin's chief priest Coifi frankly acknowledged his lack of personal profit in the practice of his religion. None had been more diligent in its service than he, and yet he had been ill rewarded. The thegn who followed him in the discussion showed more spirituality, in the famous speech concerning the sparrow flying through the hall in winter.[7] Coifi then proposed the immediate destruction of the heathen temples and altars. The king renounced idolatry and adopted Christianity. The high priest mounted a horse and took a spear in his hand, flinging it as an act of defiance at the temple of Goodmanham. But apart from this support, it is clear that in his decision to accept Christianity, Edwin had been influenced by a letter from pope Boniface.[8] In this fine epistle, firm in its tone and respectful though without the fulsomeness which often marks the letters of Gregory the Great to secular rulers, Edwin is reminded how the Holy Spirit can warm the frozen hearts of even the most distant peoples. He is urged to reject fortune-tellers and idolatry, and receive the sign of the holy Cross, by which the whole world has been redeemed.

The king was duly baptised at York, on Easter Day 627, in St Peter's, a temporary wooden church which he built while he was under instruction. Paulinus was established in the city as bishop, and the building of a stone church commenced. There followed six years of intensive evangelisation. At one time, on the royal estate of Yeavering in Northumberland, the bishop was fully occupied for thirty-six days teaching and baptising. This was in Bernicia, the northern province of the Northumbrian kingdom. In the southern province, Deira, Paulinus baptised many Christians in the river Swale, near Catterick. In all this, Paulinus owed much of his success to the ready support of the ruler. For many years, indeed, Edwin's reign was gratefully remembered in Northumbria. Its effectiveness was summed up in the proverb that a woman could cross with her new-born babe from sea to sea with no fear of molestation; its humanity in the king's practice of erecting posts with brass bowls near springs close to highways. Edwin moreover understood the importance of kingly dignity, and on his progresses caused a standard, in imitation of the Roman *tufa*, to be borne before him.

Paulinus also preached in Lindsey, the province south of the Humber, where Blaecca, the *praefectus* or reeve of the city of Lincoln, was converted. In the same city Paulinus built a stone church, which in Bede's day was still standing, though badly damaged through neglect and war.[9] It is in connection with the conversion of Lindsey that we have an interesting description of Paulinus's personal appearance. Bede says that a certain priest Deda, whom he describes as a man of great accuracy, informed him how he himself had been told by an elderly man that he had been baptised by Paulinus in the river Trent along with numerous other people, in the presence of king Edwin.[10]

This old man had described Paulinus as tall, somewhat bent, with black hair, a spare face, and a thin hooked nose, looking at the same time venerable and formidable. It is probably on oral transmission of this sort that most of the knowledge of our early history which we possess is ultimately based. It represents an authority which cannot be despised.

With such excellent progress in the north, Gregory's scheme for a second archbishopric seemed to be maturing, and Honorius I sent a pallium to Paulinus. About the same time Justus, archbishop of Canterbury, died, and was succeeded by a churchman bearing the same name as the pope. He was consecrated by Paulinus. But before Paulinus received his own pallium, his archbishopric was overthrown by the defeat and death of Edwin at the battle of Hatfield Chase near Doncaster in 632, where the king was overcome by the combined forces of the heathen Penda, king of Mercia, and Cadwallon, Christian king of Gwynedd. The Welshman in his little hour of triumph was pitiless to the Englishman. He spread destruction and slaughter, sparing neither sex nor age, declaring as his intention the extermination of the English race. In the face of this disaster Paulinus took to flight, returning by sea to Kent, taking with him the widowed queen and her infant daughter, and other members of the royal household. It would be easy to condemn hastily this apparent desertion by Paulinus of his flock, forgetting that the queen was his primary charge. However, the devoted and indefatigable assistant of Paulinus, James the deacon, stayed behind, and continued to teach and baptise, establishing his headquarters near Catterick. He was a skilful singer, and later on, with the restoration of peaceful conditions, played a notable part in the introduction of Gregorian chant to this country. Paulinus on his return to Kent became bishop of Rochester, in succession to Romanus who had been drowned on a voyage to Rome,[11] and he remained in this see until his death in 643. The widowed queen on her arrival back in Kent founded the monastery of Lyminge, the first English religious house for women.

Not long before Paulinus's death Eadbald had died, and was succeeded in the Kentish kingdom by his son Eorconbert, who ordered that all idols in his kingdom should be destroyed. He was the earliest English king to prescribe the observance of Lent.[12]

Meanwhile the conversion of East Anglia was also in progress. Raedwald, king of the peoples in this region from the late sixth century to about 616 or later, had received baptism during a visit to Kent. On his return home, however, his heathen wife and others weakened his faith, and he compromised by having both Christian and heathen altars in his temple. Aldwulf, king of the East Angles in Bede's day, remembered having seen this temple in his boyhood.[13] It was Raedwald's heathen wife who had persuaded him as a man of honour not to betray his guest Edwin. Perhaps she pointed out to him now that it was dishonourable to desert his ancestral gods—king Ethelbert's mind had been uneasy on this score in 597. More practically, the motive of Raedwald's wife in persuading her husband to abandon Christianity might have been a fear that baptism was a sign and symbol of submission to the Kentish king. Throughout the episode, Raedwald's wife appears as a strong character, in the true tradition of Teutonic women. Raedwald was a powerful king, who has sometimes been considered the same commemorated by the ship-burial at Sutton Hoo, near Woodbridge.[14] His principal seat may well have been at Rendlesham nearby. He defeated and slew Aethelfrith king of Northumbria at the battle of the river Idle in 616, his own son Regnhere being killed in the fight. We hear no more of Raedwald after this.

About 628 king Edwin urged Eorpwald, son and successor of Raedwald, to adopt Christianity. He did so, but was soon afterwards murdered, after which there was an interval of three years' heathenism. His half-brother Sigbert, who had received Christianity as an exile in Gaul, where he was well instructed in church schools, then became ruler.[15] He proceeded to introduce the Faith, and was aided in this move by archbishop Honorius, who sent to him a bishop by the name of Felix, a Burgundian. The labours of this missionary were most fruitful, and the whole kingdom was brought 'to the gifts of heavenly felicity'. Sigbert founded a school for boys on the model of those he had seen in Gaul, Felix supplying it with teachers 'after the Roman manner'. Dunwich became the latter's episcopal seat, and it was here that he died after an able episcopate of seventeen years. The place-name Felixstowe, near Ipswich, perpetuates his memory. Though the East Anglian mission stemmed from Canterbury, its continental connection should be noted, and it may be surmised that it had a Gallic character. There were, moreover, other influences at work in East Anglia. No special significance should be attached to Bede's statement that Felix had a high regard for Aidan.[16] But an Irish ascetic Fursa with some companions was welcomed by Sigbert, who gave them a derelict castle (possibly that of Burgh in Suffolk) in which to settle.[17] Fursa was a missionary, and converted many unbelievers to Christ, besides strengthening the faith of those who already believed. Within the bounds of the castle he built a monastery, pleasantly situated in the woods, close by the sea. A later king Anna enriched this monastery with fine buildings and many gifts. Fursa, however, was a visionary —liable to fall into states of trance—rather than a practical man. Wishing to rid himself of the tiresome business of governing his monastery, he handed its care over to his brother, Foilan, and departed for Gaul, where he spent his remaining years.[18] The story is of interest as showing that by this time at least, towards the middle of the seventh century, there were Celts who did not disdain to live and work amongst the English. But Fursa was of course an Irishman, not a Welshman.

Sigbert was the first Anglo-Saxon prince to enter religion. After reigning some years, he received the tonsure, and joined a monastery of his own foundation. He was succeeded as king by his kinsman Ecgric. Subsequently, when Penda attacked the East Angles, Sigbert was dragged from his monastery by his former subjects in the hope that his presence would improve the morale of the troops. He refused to go armed into the battle, which was a victory for Penda, both Ecgric and Sigbert being killed.

Ecgric was succeeded by Anna, who ruled the East Angles from c. 635 to 654. A nephew of Raedwald, he was a Christian king whose main significance was in the devout children whom he produced. At this time there was little opportunity for the religious life in England, and those who wished to adopt this vocation often crossed to Gaul, to such houses as Faremoutiers-on-Brie and Chelles. Anna's sister-in-law Hereswid became a nun at the latter house. Her sister St Hild also contemplated going to Gaul. Anna had four daughters. One was Sexburga, wife of Eorconbert king of Kent; in her widowhood she became abbess of a convent which she founded in the Isle of Sheppey, and subsequently abbess of Ely. Of the others, Ethelburga became abbess of Faremoutiers; Ethelthryth (St Etheldreda) founded the church of Ely, of which she was the first abbess; and Witburga was a recluse at Dereham. The two daughters of Sexburga also entered religion. Eorcongota became a nun at Faremoutiers, and her sister Ermenild—who was previously queen of the Mercians—became a nun under her mother at Sheppey, and succeeded her at Ely.

A monastic saint of the East Anglian Church of whom scarcely anything is known, though he was highly regarded by his contemporaries, was Botolf. He founded in 654[19] a monastery at Icanhoh, a place which has not been identified satisfactorily. He gathered a community around him, to whom he gave a rule compiled from various authorities, and was visited *c.* 670 by Ceolfrith, subsequently abbot of Jarrow, who had heard of his fame.

The Church of East Anglia seems to have been built upon a firm foundation, and its line of bishops centred on Dunwich endured well into the ninth century. The conversion of East Anglia was a solid achievement, and suggests that a mixture of influences in a Church's life does not make for instability.

The foundation of the Church in Wessex proceeded concurrently with that of East Anglia, but under different auspices and with less favourable results. The initiative was taken by pope Honorius I, apparently without reference to the archbishop of Canterbury. The missionary chosen for this work was Birinus, consecrated bishop by Asterius, archbishop of Milan. The original intention was for him to go to the midlands, and it is quite possible that the pope envisaged here a future archbishopric. But when Birinus landed in Wessex, he was so startled by the heathenism of the folk he met, that he stayed and preached the Word to them, without troubling to travel further inland. He secured an outstanding success with the baptism of Cynegils, the West Saxon king, in 635. Oswald, who had followed Edwin as king of Northumbria, and was prospective son-in-law to Cynegils, was present at the time and doubtless had something to do with the conversion. He stood as godfather to the Wessex king. The two kings gave the 'civitas' of Dorchester-on-Thames to Birinus as his episcopal seat, and here he settled, secure in his royal patronage for a few years. There was difficulty after the death of Cynegils in 643, and there is no indication that Birinus made much impression on the West Saxon people as a whole. He cannot be credited with the foundation of a line of bishops, and the diocese of Dorchester did not really settle down until the beginning of the tenth century. Birinus certainly appears an attractive figure, but what little we know of him does not impress us with the conviction that he was one of the great men of the Conversion.[20]

Cenwalh, Cynegils's successor and second son, refused to accept Christianity. He waged war in 645 with Penda, king of Mercia, who expelled him from his kingdom. He then lived as an exile for three years with Anna, by whom he was persuaded to accept baptism. The weakness of the foundations laid by Birinus is apparent from the sequel. On returning to his Wessex kingdom, Cenwalh secured as his bishop a certain Frank named Agilbert, who had come over to Wessex following a course of study in Ireland. But after several years as bishop of the West Saxons, Agilbert still had not mastered their dialect, to Cenwalh's annoyance. He accordingly introduced another bishop, Wini, a Saxon, who had received his orders in Gaul. Dividing his territory into two dioceses, the king appointed Wini to that of Winchester, c. 661. In high dudgeon, Agilbert withdrew to Gaul, where he became in due course bishop of Paris. It was not long before the native bishop Wini proved unsatisfactory, and was deprived of his see. Taking refuge with Wulfhere, king of the Mercians, he purchased from him the see of London, of which he remained bishop until his death. It is curious and indeed humbling to find the famous see of Winchester being founded under such sordid influences, and a man of dubious type its first incumbent. The king afterwards pleaded with Agilbert to return. He refused, but sent in his stead his nephew Leuthere, who was duly consecrated bishop of Winchester by archbishop Theodore, and proved a satisfactory prelate.

The closing stages of the Roman mission to England are soon told. On the death of Felix, bishop of the East Anglians, archbishop Honorius consecrated Thomas, a native of the fens, as his successor; Thomas in turn was succeeded by a Kentishman Bertgils. Honorius himself died in 652, and after a vacancy of a year and a half, a Wessex man Deusdedit (his native name was Frithonas)[21] became sixth archbishop of Canterbury. Nothing is known further of Deusdedit except that he consecrated Damian, a native of Sussex, to the bishopric of Rochester, and himself died in 663. His death marked the end of the Augustinian succession, and the appointment of his successor Theodore the opening of a new phase in English Church history. The most interesting feature in the final stages of the Canterbury mission is the elevation of native Englishmen to the episcopate. This is a sure sign that the Church was taking root. The progress made by the Roman mission in the south-east over a period of some sixty-five years had on the whole been solid and substantial. In the north, however, it was a failure. The lasting conversion of the important kingdom of Northumbria was the work of Celtic missionaries, who brought with them influences and traditions of great consequence for the development of culture and religion in England.

CHAPTER VII

THE CELTIC MISSION
TO ENGLAND

The triumph of the Welsh king Cadwallon over the Northumbrians, during which he devastated their lands and put warrior and civilian alike to the sword, was fortunately brief. When Edwin fell at Hatfield Chase in 632, it must have seemed that the north-eastern kingdom had suffered an almost irretrievable disaster. But in the following year the tables were turned over Cadwallon by the victory of Oswald at Heavenfield.

Edwin and Oswald, two of the most attractive of the early English kings, were sprung of separate lines of the Northumbrian royal house. Edwin, the son of Aelle, came of the Deiran branch; Oswald was great-grandson of Ida, first of the kings of Bernicia.[1] Oswald's father was that Aethelfrith who, it will be remembered, massacred the monks of the Welsh monastery of Bangor near Chester. Though the two houses were in a state of almost constant rivalry, they were united by the marriage of Aethelfrith to Acha, the sister of Edwin. Oswald was the offspring of this union. It was by the championship of this young prince that the Church was now to take firm root in Northumbria.

The decisive victory at Heavenfield, a few miles from Hexham, has been described by Bede.[2] The army of Oswald, he says, was small in numbers, but strengthened by Christ. At dawn on the day of battle, Oswald caused a wooden cross to be made and placed in a hole in the ground, he himself holding it erect while the soil was heaped around it. He then ordered his soldiers to kneel down with him, and ask God's aid, he himself invoking St Columba. In the following battle the physically superior forces of Cadwallon were defeated, and the Welsh king himself slain. Thus was his short reign of exultant ferocity in England ended. The political significance of the victory was the end of any possibility of the reconquest of Britain by the Welsh. From the religious viewpoint it entailed the triumph of Christianity in Northumbria, ironically enough, the defeated army being composed of Christians with centuries of Church influence behind them, while the followers of Oswald, on the other hand, were just beginning to find their way to the profession of the Faith. Thus Anglians recently heathen set up the cross as their standard against a host of barbarous Christians.

Oswald reigned as king over all Northumbria for the next eight years (633–41), and as overlord over the English kingdoms south of the Humber. It was doubtless in the latter capacity that he confirmed the grant by the Wessex king Cynegils of Dorchester-on-Thames to Birinus. Bede says that he was overlord also over all the nations of Britain, but this was probably exaggerated praise on behalf of a king on whom the mantle of sainthood was in due course to descend. St Oswald was the first really devout English king. He had habits of prayer which would have been praiseworthy even in a monk, sometimes spending a large part of the night over his devotions. He was as kind and generous as he was pious, and a good friend to the poor and stranger. His manliness was proved by his victory over Cadwallon; his zeal for the Faith by his sponsorship of Cynegil's baptism, and above all by his reintroduction of Christianity to Northumbria.

Many years previously he and his brother Oswy had fled from the reigning king Edwin, and found asylum with the monks of Iona.[3] The opposition between Oswald and Edwin, it need hardly be said, had dynastic and political causes. It was the same dynastic feud between the houses of Deira and Bernicia which had led years before to the exile of Edwin, who fled from the wrath of Oswald's father to seek refuge with Raedwald. It was during this period of East Anglian exile that Edwin had made contact with Christianity. Similarly, Oswald and Oswy were introduced to the new religion during their stay with the Celtic monks, with whom they spent much of their seventeen years of exile. But whereas Edwin, like Ethelbert of Kent, seems to have adopted the Faith for reasons of expediency, Oswald was so thoroughly instructed by the monks of Iona that he became a Christian by genuine conviction.

In his decision to re-establish Christianity in Northumbria Oswald now naturally turned to his former tutors, at this time under the abbacy of Seghine, who though only in priest's orders was exercising supreme authority over the province with all its bishops—'a strange arrangement', comments Bede.[4] In response to the king's request, a missionary was sent. A man of austere manner, he was repelled by the barbarous ways of the Northumbrians and their stubborn disposition. Returning to Iona, he reported to the community the futility of attempting the conversion of such a people. The voice of one of the monks was raised in remonstrance. 'You expected too much to begin with, brother. You should have fed them with the milk of easy doctrine and led them by stages to the harder and more sublime precepts of God's word.' The name of the speaker was Aidan. The counsel of the brethren was that he himself should go to Northumbria. He was consecrated bishop, and dispatched to Oswald, in the year 634.

Practical considerations would normally have indicated York as the centre of the missionary work which was now to commence. It had been the seat of a British bishopric, and Paulinus had baptised Edwin there. It was a central place, but this was not likely to be an over-riding consideration to a man of Celtic religious temperament. Aidan found in the island of Lindisfarne a far more congenial headquarters, an almost perfect counterpart to the beloved home which he had left. Here there could be seclusion, while at low tide the strait separating the island from the mainland was readily passable. It is a place which may still be visited under the original conditions. Though there are no surviving traces of the church and monastery built by Aidan, Lindisfarne retains its character and is little changed, though there are disturbing signs that its age-long immunity may not last much longer. In its simplicity combined with an indefinable romanticism, in its isolation and its accessibility to the storms of nature, it is an epitome of the spirit of Celtic Christianity. The modern traveller can still feel, as Alcuin felt in the ninth century, that there is no more venerable spot in Britain.[5] Here time is stationary, and one has the sense of contact with eternity. The sanctity of the place, moreover, is not derived from beautiful legends, as at Glastonbury, but from incontrovertible his-torical facts. Even today the island defies the spirit of restlessness and speed. Though a modern causeway has within recent years been thrown across the wet sands, it can still only be traversed at low-tide, and the motorist must frequently wait patiently before crossing to set foot on the holiest of English soil. It was here that Aidan established a see and monastery which endured for 241 years.

It must not, however, be thought that Aidan was a mere visionary devoid of worldly wisdom. The island, as the saint would be well aware, was within sight of Bamburgh, where king Oswald had his prin-cipal vill. The monastery would be within reach of royal protection.

York had been the civil and ecclesiastical capital of Northumbria under Edwin, a position which it would later regain under Oswy, brother and successor of Oswald. Meanwhile Aidan and Oswald were able to work together, in close proximity, towards their ends. It was a remarkable partnership, drawing forth the admiration of Bede, who praises the Celtic missionary as 'a man of singular meekness, piety, and moderation', zealous in God's service, if not entirely 'according to knowledge'. 'He practised what he preached; he neither sought nor loved anything worldly, and what the rich or kings gave him he distributed immediately to the poor. He traversed the countryside on foot, never on horseback, unless absolutely necessary.'[6]

At Lindisfarne Aidan lived the ordinary life of a monk, bringing fellow-Celts over from Iona to help launch the community. With an eye to its continuance he started a school for twelve English boys, two of whom, Cedd and his brother Chad, subsequently came to play an influential part in the conversion of the Anglo-Saxons. For greater seclusion in his devotional exercises Aidan would sometimes sail over to the neighbouring Farne islands, and in Bede's day the spot where he was accustomed to sit was still pointed out. From time to time he set out from his monastery, crossing the sands at low-tide, to evangelise the Northumbrian villages on the mainland. Places like Etal and Ford, Wooler and Chillingham, Lucker and Alnmouth, must all have heard the gentle voice of Aidan. He would penetrate into the Cheviots, and southwards across the Tyne. He normally traversed this enchanting countryside on foot. This was a practice fully in accord with apostolic ways, and moreover made it easier for Aidan to converse with those whom he encountered on the road. That the work of Paulinus had not been entirely in vain is shown by Bede's statement that some of those whom Aidan met were already believers, whom he encouraged to stand fast in their faith. In fairness to the Roman missionary from Kent, it should be remembered that to a great extent Aidan entered into his labours.

Like Columba, Aidan could never be idle, and while on his preaching circuits would meditate and recite the offices. Sometimes Oswald accompanied him and acted as interpreter—'a most beautiful sight', remarks Bede. Their co-operation reminds us of that of king Sigbert and bishop Felix in East Anglia. Oswald, however, found his bishop an unconvivial guest at Bamburgh; Aidan, as soon as he had satisfied his modest needs, would retire from the company to read or pray. On one Easter Day a large silver dish filled with delicacies was brought to the table. The king ordered it to be distributed to the poor at his gate, and the silver dish broken up and divided amongst them. Moved with admiration, Aidan exclaimed, taking hold of the king's right hand, 'May this hand never decay'. It was long afterwards believed that Oswald's uncorrupted hand was preserved in a silver casket in Bamburgh church, though the twelfth-century William of Malmesbury was sceptical about it.[7]

Aidan never showed undue favour to the rich and powerful, and would not accept presents from them, except to hand over to the poor or to redeem captives. The Deiran king Oswine later on persuaded him to accept a fine horse for his journeys, apparently when Aidan was becoming older and physically weaker, but he soon gave it away to a beggar, to the not unnatural annoyance of the donor. Throughout Northumbria the work of God prospered. Churches were built, and the people gladly assembled to hear God's word. Lands and gifts were secured for the endowment of religious houses. English boys were taught by Celtic teachers not only the rudiments of knowledge but also advanced learning. Aidan was not alone in his task. Many Scottish missionaries followed him, and with great devotion preached throughout Northumbria.

Aidan was a true Celt, and the Christianity introduced by him was essentially identical with that of Columba, with the exception that he himself, the abbot, was in episcopal orders. He observed the Celtic Easter, to the great sorrow of Bede, and practised the Celtic custom of consecrating land intended for sacred purposes by a long process of fasting and prayer. The life was simple, and there was no beautiful art or architecture.[8] As usual amongst the Celts, church life found its most characteristic expression in monasticism. The Columban Church was ruled from the island monastery of Iona; the Northumbrian Church now came to be governed by the religious community on Holy Island. During Aidan's episcopate, moreover, communities for women made their appearance. The first Northumbrian woman to follow the vocation of a nun was Heiu, of Hartlepool, who was dedicated to the life by Aidan. The most famous was Hild, who received from him encouragement and direction.

In 641 Oswald, still a young man not yet forty, was defeated and slain by the heathen Penda, king of Mercia, at the battle of Maserfield, usually identified with Oswestry in Shropshire. This was undoubtedly a severe blow to Aidan. The king was a great champion of the Church, in the true tradition of the numerous earthly rulers whose history teaches us that Christianity could have accomplished little on behalf of civilisation and culture in the world without the assistance of temporal power. The Christian instinct assigned to Oswald the title of saint. His mortal remains rapidly acquired sanctity.[9] The Church which, with his great bishop and advisor, he had fostered, had been built upon a sound foundation, and maintained a vitality which was to raise it to a leading position in Anglo-Saxon England.

Oswald was succeeded by his younger brother Oswy, who for the first part of his long reign of twenty-nine years failed to hold Deira and Bernicia together. The victory of Maserfield had left Penda the most powerful king in England. Conscious of his relatively weak position, Oswy in 651 made an attempt to reunite the two Northumbrian kingdoms. He invaded Deira, and connived at the murder of its king Oswine, whose successor (a son of Oswald) nevertheless looked not to Oswy but to Penda as his overlord. The murder of Oswine is one of the tragedies of Northumbrian history—a most disgraceful deed—a reminder that baptism and the profession of Christianity did not always change the hearts of barbarian kings. Like Oswald and Oswy, Oswine was a Christian ruler, as simple and gentle in manner as he was handsome in appearance. He won everyone's love by his dignity of conduct, men from afar vying with each other to enter his service. His outstanding characteristic was his humility. He worked well with Aidan, who had continued to evangelise in the kingdom of Deira as well as in Bernicia after Oswald's death. The quarrel between Oswy and Oswine was clearly a great grief to Aidan. Shortly after receiving news of the murder, he had a stroke. He died leaning against a wooden buttress at the west end of Bamburgh church, on 31 August, ever since known as 'Aidan's rest', in the year 650.

St Aidan was succeeded at Lindisfarne by another product of Iona, Finan, under whom the Celtic mission extended the area of its operations.[10] It will be recalled that Birinus had in the first instance been sent into this country to evangelise the midlands, though he had actually settled down at Dorchester-on-Thames and limited his work to Wessex. The conversion of Mercia, the midland kingdom, was now seriously commenced by four missionaries sent thither by Finan. The old king of Mercia, Penda, was as inveterate a heathen as ever. Better disposed towards Christianity was his son Peada, to whom he had committed the sub-government of the Middle-Angles, inhabiting the region between the Trent and Bedfordshire. He was a worthy young man highly praised by Bede.[11] He visited Northumbria, and married Alhflaed, daughter of Oswy, a condition of the union being his acceptance of baptism. Meanwhile Oswy's son Alchfrith had married Peada's sister Kyniburga, who became a devout Christian, and subsequently in her widowhood an abbess. Nearly all the children and grandchildren of Penda, in fact, became convinced Christians. His son Peada was so impressed by the Christian message, during his visit to the north, that he declared he would be a Christian whether he obtained the lady's hand or not. In this he was greatly influenced by his brother-in-law Alchfrid.

The baptism of Peada with all his retinue by Finan duly followed. It took place at At-the-Wall, which lay probably somewhere within the bounds of the modern Newcastle—according to Bede it was near the Roman Wall, twelve miles inland from the east coast.[12] The young convert returned home accompanied by four priests, chosen for their learning and good life. The old king Penda did not oppose this move, which marked the beginning of the conversion of central England. The year was 653, not long before Penda's death. Unfortunately we know little about this mission, apart from the names of the four missionaries. Three of them, Cedd, Adda, and Betti, were Englishmen, and one, Diuma, an Irishman. Arriving in Mercia, they 'preached the word, and were gladly heard; and many, both nobles and common people, renounced the evils of idolatry, and daily were baptised'. Though Penda put no obstacles in their way, he voiced his contempt for those who accepted Christ and did not obey His precepts. It is impossible not to admire this king, who was true to his convictions until the end. He had the good sense to see that the future lay with Christianity, yet he was too honest to become a trimmer. He apparently realised the futility of persecution. The deaths or sufferings of a few individual Christians could not hinder the spread of the doctrines which they held. We would gladly know more of this king, who in spite of his bellicosity had no crimes to his account like the 'murder most foul' which stained the Christian hands of Oswy.

In 654 war broke out between Penda and Oswy. The Mercian king set out with a large force, accompanied by a number of Welsh chieftains, determined to conquer Oswy, for whom he had a personal dislike.[13] In desperation the Northumbrian tried in vain to buy off

Penda with gifts. On the eve of the battle Oswy promised his infant daughter to God should the victory be his. In the fight which followed, on the banks of the Winwaed, near Leeds, Penda was defeated and killed, and Oswy became the greatest of the English kings. The royal child was duly placed as an oblate with Hild, abbess of Hartlepool, and twelve monasteries were founded, estates being assigned to their endowment. The victory was a great event in the history of English Christianity. It marked the end of the heathen power, and since the death of Penda no secular ruler has openly identified himself with an anti-Christian policy in this country.

Oswy confirmed Peada in his rule over the Middle-Angles, and according to the Chronicle the two rulers acted jointly to found a monastery in honour of St Peter at Medeshamstede, later known as Peterborough, one of the greatest of medieval abbeys.[14] Peada had a brief career. A year or two after the foundation of the monastery, he was murdered, according to common report by the treachery of his wife Alhflaed. For some three years all Mercia was under the direct rule of Oswy, and then following a Mercian rebellion Wulfhere, a younger brother of Peada, became king. During his reign of seventeen years the Church made much progress in the midlands. Bede, though a Northumbrian, praises the independent spirit of the Mercians,[15] who recovered their freedom after driving out the representatives of a king whom they refused to recognise. Free men under their own king, he says, they are now willing servants of Christ, the true King. Wulfhere proved himself a Christian ruler, and he was of considerable help to Wilfred and Chad.

The first bishop for the midlands was the Irishman Diuma, who was consecrated by Finan. Within a decade Diuma was followed by three bishops in rapid succession—Ceollach, Trumhere, and Jaruman—two of whom were of Irish birth or training. In the establishment of this midlands see there is no evidence of any influence on the part of Rome or Canterbury, or that its earliest bishops showed any concrete allegiance to the Roman Church or had any connections with it. Their spiritual capital was Lindisfarne, and there is nothing to suggest otherwise than that they were followers of the Celtic form of Christianity. It is not known where, if anywhere, these first four bishops of the midlands diocese had their seat. But in the general reorganisation of the English dioceses during the primacy of Theodore the see was to be established at Lichfield, which for a brief period at the end of the eighth century acquired metropolitical rank, and in course of time became one of the most enduring centres of English ecclesiastical life. Thus the first preaching of the Celtic priests introduced by Peada laid a firm foundation in the midlands, and the work there never receded. Between the earliest bishop Diuma and Peter, who occupied the see under archbishop Lanfranc in 1072, there were some three dozen holders of the see, and there seems to have been no break in the succession.

The only member of the original band of four priests of whom we know much was Cedd. He was now to lead another mission in which Celtic Christianity was the driving force.

Many years previously, the Roman mission had introduced the Church to the East Saxons, but an upsurge of heathenism had forced Mellitus to withdraw in 616. There is evidence that Essex was something of a stronghold of the old religion,[16] and for a generation after the initial setback no attempt seems to have been made to reintroduce the Gospel to that region. But as in Northumbria, so also in Essex, Iona succeeded where Rome failed. Soon after the middle of the century the Essex king Sigbert, who used to pay friendly visits to Oswy, was persuaded by the latter to adopt Christianity. It will be noted how potent a feature in the conversion of England was this commendation of Christ by one king to another. In this as in much else the fortunes of the Anglo-Saxon Church were closely bound up with the desires and convictions of the kings. In a noble passage[17] Bede tells how Oswy convinced Sigbert in brotherly argument of the futility of idolatry, and demonstrated to him the majesty of God, Creator of heaven and earth, governing the world in righteousness.

Sigbert consequently became a 'citizen of the eternal kingdom', and requested Oswy to send him Christian teachers. The Northumbrian king recalled Cedd from Mercia, and directed him to Essex, accompanied by a single priest. Their work was eminently successful, so that they 'gathered together a numerous Church' to the Lord. Encouraged by this success, Cedd, in the expressive phrase of Bede, 'returned home to Lindisfarne' to confer with Finan, who along with two other bishops raised him to episcopal orders. Returning to Essex with a more ample authority, he built churches in several places, and ordained deacons and priests. Like the earliest bishops of Mercia, Cedd had no fixed seat, and is not known to have had any connection with London. But Bede mentions two places which were used as missionary centres, Tilbury and Ythancaestir. In each of these places Cedd established monks, whom he instructed in the regular life. It was clearly the Celtic monastic, rather than the Roman diocesan, system of organisation which was followed. The church which Cedd built at Ythancaestir, within the old Roman fort of Othona, survives in a remote spot by the mud flats and marshes of Bradwell as one of our earliest memorials of the Conversion.

Cedd remained bishop of the East Saxons until his death, but his work amongst them was broken by visits to the north. On one of these he acquired of Aethelwald, king of Deira, a piece of land at Lastingham, a desolate place on the Yorkshire moors, where he built a monastery. It is in connection with this foundation that Bede records a valuable description of the Celtic custom of dedicating a sacred site by a long fast.[18] Cedd intended to remain on the spot a whole Lent, fasting severely. When there were still ten days of Lent left, he was summoned to the king, whereupon one of his three brothers took over from him and completed the fast. It was to Lastingham that Cedd came to die in 664, soon after the conference of Whitby, in which he took part.

CHAPTER VIII

THE TRIUMPH OF ROME

By the middle of the seventh century it must have been clear that two distinct forms of the Christian religion were competing for the spiritual allegiance of the Anglo-Saxon peoples. There could have been no doubt by now of the ultimate triumph of Christianity itself. Heathenism, though it was to linger on in the life of the people for generations, was as a living force perceptibly waning. By *c.* 660 all England except Sussex and the Isle of Wight had formally adopted the Faith. The Conversion was an achievement all the more notable in that it was carried through in a remarkably short period of time, and it is not to be belittled because of the absence of persecution. The success of the Christian preaching in the English kingdoms is still more marked in view of the diverse and uncoordinated efforts by which it was carried into effect.

There has been too strong a tendency in the past to assign definite spheres of success, as it were, to the Celtic and Roman missions respectively, as well as puerile, not to say unworthy, attempts to determine whether Rome or Iona played the greater part in bringing our forefathers to the light of the Gospel.[1] It is as futile to call Lindisfarne the cradle of Christianity in England as it would be to regard the Conversion as centred round Augustine. The chief credit can be assigned to no single agency or person.

In Kent the Roman Church was stronger than elsewhere in England, but even here other influences may have been operative. The existence of bishop Liudhard must not be forgotten, nor Augustine's anxiety over the confusing situation caused by a worship apparently carried on in two liturgies, Roman and Gallican, side by side. It is possible too that the presence of the Irish Dagan was not without some significance. On the whole, however, we are justified in regarding the mission to Canterbury as a solid piece of work on the part of Rome, and that famous diocese as a child of the papacy.

Rome was also responsible for the foundation of the Church in Wessex, but (so far as we know) acting independently of Canterbury. The failure of the first, that is, the Augustinian, line of archbishops to establish a commanding position over the other Churches in England is noticeable. None of these bishops were in themselves really outstanding men. Much depended too on the support which the king was able to give to his bishop. After Ethelbert's death the kings of Kent dropped into a relatively unimportant position. It is therefore not surprising perhaps that Birinus saw no need to seek direction from Canterbury, and that his king Cenwalh, the successor of Cynegils, though an adherent to Roman ways, made no move to place the infant Church of his realm in subordination to the Church of a king whom he did not regard as a superior. Moreover, we again find evidence of Irish influence. An Irishman Maildubh founded at Malmesbury a monastery which was from the first a centre for Irish scholars; and the second bishop of the West Saxons, Agilbert, though a Frank by race, had been educated in Ireland.

In Essex the Canterbury mission overreached itself, and so violent was the heathen reaction to its preaching in this kingdom that it must be assumed that Cedd, an Englishman but of Celtic religious training, had a fair field when he resumed the work there a generation later. Further north, in East Anglia, the achievement was predominantly Roman, but again the all-pervading Irishman is on the scene. It was under the auspices of the archbishop of Canterbury that Felix, a Burgundian missionary who received his episcopal orders in Gaul, founded the see of Dunwich. But his king Sigbert, who had taken the initiative in approaching the archbishop for help, was also well disposed to the Irishman Fursa, whom he introduced and supported.

Mercia owed nothing in the matter of its Church's foundation to Rome or Canterbury, though three of its original four missionary priests, as we have seen, were English. The Church of the midlands was derived in the first instance from Lindisfarne.

The great importance of Celtic Christianity in the history of the Conversion derives to a considerable extent from its influence in Northumbria, destined for a time to hold a commanding place amongst the English kingdoms, and in the age of Bede the centre of a brilliant Christian culture. But Aidan and his fellows were probably indebted in some degree to their Roman predecessors. It is difficult to find evidence for the conjecture[2] that many of those who heard Paulinus preach and were baptised in such large numbers by him were survivors of the old British population and already Christian. On the other hand, it is probably true that Aidan sowed and reaped the land which Paulinus had ploughed.

There was thus an intricate intermingling of the Irish and Roman strands in the Conversion, and it is likely that the adherents of the two traditions were on the whole on good terms with each other. But it must have appeared to many that the Anglo-Saxons would soon have to choose the way in which they were going to continue. The decision to be made would be a momentous one, whose importance it is hard to overestimate. There is no denying the great strength of the Scottish Church, especially in the currently influential Northumbrian kingdom. The Church in England, if the decision had gone the way of the Celts, might have become permanently part of Celtic Christianity as a whole. In this case there might have developed in the British Isles, with branches on the Continent, a great and singular Confession, independent of Rome and with its distinctive liturgy and customs. It would have been a Church of the Catholic type. At the same time it might well have avoided the pitfalls of that clerical arrogance which was to be so characteristic of Rome and was the root cause of the Reformation. Britain might have been practising today a religion not unlike that of the Orthodox Churches of eastern Europe.

On the other hand, it must be remembered that the Roman Church was firmly entrenched in parts of England, and possessed strong continental connections. It would never have been easy for the Scottish Church to supplant it, even if the decision of the Whitby conference had been in its favour. Anglo-Saxon Christianity might well have chrystallised into two separate Churches. When one bears in mind the unifying influence politically which the Church was to exert on the English kingdoms, it is not difficult to envisage, by a parallel reasoning, what might have become a permanent division of England into two countries.

It was in Northumbria that the crisis came to a head. During the episcopate of Finan, Aidan's successor at Lindisfarne, there was a steady growth in Roman sentiment and the emergence of a definite Roman party. It had the good fortune to secure a champion in Oswy's son Alchfrith, sub-king of Deira, who was a friend of Cenwalh, the Romanising Wessex king, and who also came under the influence of Wilfred, who epitomised the new spirit which was developing amongst the younger Northumbrian nobles and churchmen. The earlier career of this ecclesiastic, who was to exercise so great an influence on the affairs of the Anglo-Saxon Church, may be conveniently sketched at this point.

Wilfred,[3] born in 634 of a devout mother, left his home at the age of fourteen, goaded apparently by the cruelty of his stepmother—his own mother was dead—and eager to seek the Kingdom of Heaven. 'Comely in appearance and exceedingly sharp of wit', he secured an introduction to Eanfled, Oswy's queen. After a few years he was moved by the Holy Spirit (says his biographer Eddius) to visit the see of the chief of apostles St Peter, a feat which no Northumbrian had yet attempted. He arrived in Rome in 654, after dallying at Lyons on the way, and while in the holy city visited the shrines of the saints daily. He met a certain archdeacon Boniface,[4] a papal advisor, who acquainted him with the true Easter rule, not observed by 'the British and Scottish schismatics', and many other ecclesiastical rules, besides instructing him in the four gospels. The archdeacon also introduced him to the pope, who gave him his blessing.

Wilfred returned, calling again at Lyons, where Dalfinus,[5] the brother of the archbishop, Annemundus, adopted him as his spiritual son. The old Gallic city had clearly cast a spell on Wilfred. Here there was the ruined grandeur of ancient Rome, side by side with the rising splendour of the Church. Lyons moreover was a long-standing centre of Christian influence, where many martyrs, including the slave-girl Blandina and the bishop Pothinus, had died in the persecution of 177,[6] and where St Irenaeus had been bishop. The young man remained here for three years, during which time he received the Roman tonsure, in the shape of Our Lord's crown of thorns (unlike the Celtic tonsure, which was shaved straight across the head from ear to ear). After Annemundus had been put to death by the secular authorities, in somewhat obscure circumstances, Wilfred returned to his native Northumbria.

On his journey to Rome he had been accompanied by another young man of good birth, a few years older than himself. This was Biscop Baducing, known in religion subsequently as Benedict Biscop, of whom we shall hear more. At this time he was twenty-five years old, and beginning to develop an enthusiasm for Roman culture which was to be the great interest of his life. This journey was the first of six which he would make to Rome. Young ecclesiastics like Wilfred and Biscop represented the tide which was starting to flow in Northumbrian church affairs. Of noble birth, they understood the importance of dignity. The wet sands of Holy Island, which when crossed barefoot brought one to an isolated collection of rude buildings, were not their line of country. They were impressed far more by the majesty of Rome, whose traditions moreover were even greater than those of Iona. They were apparently genuinely alarmed at the prospect of their Church becoming marooned in the mists of the western seas.

Arriving in Northumbria, Wilfred was greeted by Alchfrith, who granted him an estate of ten hides at Stamford[7] near York for religious purposes. He also conferred on him a monastery at Ripon which had been occupied for a brief period by some monks of the Celtic persuasion and who had departed rather than change their views. As abbot of Ripon Wilfred became widely respected, and charitable to the poor. At Alchfrith's request he was ordained priest by Agilbert, formerly bishop of Dorchester and at this time visiting the north. This was, at least by modern standards, a presumptuous and uncanonical act on the part of Agilbert—to ordain a man in another's diocese, without so much as asking leave of the reigning bishop. The diocesan at this time was Colman, a monk from Iona who had succeeded Finan as bishop of Lindisfarne in 660. It is likely anyhow that the young Wilfred was so contemptuous of Lindisfarne and its ways after seeing the grandeur of Rome at close quarters, that he would never have consented to submit to ordination at the hands of a Celtic bishop. This dissatisfaction of the rising generation with the outlandish ways of Iona and Lindisfarne was the main cause of the crisis which now arose.

It was the Paschal question which precipitated the famous 'synod' of Streoneshalh, generally identified with Whitby, held in the autumn of 663.[8] Here the abbess Hild now ruled over a double monastery, one of the twelve monasteries founded by Oswy after his victory over Penda. The complicated mathematics of the controversy, which was a very old one in the Christian Church, are probably of little interest, and certainly of no importance, to most modern readers.[9] It should, however, be noted that in calculating the exact date of Easter various cycles were used from time to time, of which an eighty-four-year cycle was used by the Celts, and a nineteen-year cycle, the more accurate, by the Roman Church. The latter cycle had been adopted by Rome after much discussion and study in 455, but the Scots refused to conform, save in southern Ireland, where the more accurate cycle was adopted in 633. The question was less academic than it may seem, as there were years when the rival cycles decreed different Sundays for the observance of Easter.

Oswy, the Northumbrian king, as an adherent to the Scottish Church, observed the more venerable but less accurate Easter. His queen, that daughter of Edwin who had been escorted as a child by Paulinus to Kent and there reared in the Roman ways, kept the Paschal feast according to the revised reckoning. In 663 the king foresaw that in the following year it would so happen that the festival would be celebrated on different Sundays by the contending parties. This would be a matter of considerable inconvenience in the life of the court, not sufficiently serious to cause undue anxiety to Oswy if he had been a thoroughly convinced Celt in his religious views, but enough perhaps to make him wonder whether now was the time to make a prudent change. As in the case of Bertha and Ethelbert, it is possible that Oswy's queen had been quietly exerting her influence on him. He decided to call a conference at which the Paschal controversy could be discussed by representatives of both sides.[10]

Besides the king himself, who presided, the Celtic delegates included Cedd, bishop of the East Saxons, the abbess Hild, and Colman, bishop of Lindisfarne. The Roman representatives were Oswy's son Alchfrith, bishop Agilbert, Wilfred, and James the deacon (by this time probably an old man); also a priest Agatho, and a Kentish priest Romanus, chaplain to the queen. One important figure who had played no small part in the controversy leading to the crisis was absent. This was Ronan, an Irishman who had studied in Gaul and Italy, was an ardent supporter of the Roman cause, and had tried hard but unavailingly to convert Finan.

Oswy opened the controversy by saying that those who served the one God should follow one rule of life, and that just as they looked forward to the same heavenly kingdom so they should not differ in their manner of worship. He then invited Colman to state the case for the Celtic Easter. Colman argued that they dared not change it, the same as that observed by St John the Evangelist, the beloved of the Lord, as well as by Polycarp, Columba, and their fathers and predecessors. The argument was one of loyalty to a long tradition.

The king next called upon Agilbert to present the Roman case. Distrusting his command of the English tongue, which was still inadequate, he begged leave that his disciple Wilfred might speak for him. Wilfred proceeded to state that in his travels he had seen the Roman

Easter celebrated not only at Rome, where the apostles Peter and Paul were buried, but also in Italy and Gaul. It was practised moreover in Africa, Asia, Egypt, Greece, and in fact all over the world, except by the obstinate inhabitants of two remote islands, and even here the observance was not unanimous. Wilfred's argument was essentially one of universality.

Colman protested that they followed the example of a great apostle, who was considered worthy to lay his head on the Lord's breast. In a long and elaborate reply Wilfred maintained that the situation had been changed by the decrees of the apostolic see, which it was a sin not to accept. In a slighting reference to Columba, he asked Colman whether the Celtic saint was to be preferred before the blessed Peter, who held the heavenly keys.

This decided the issue. Oswy intervened and asked whether it was true that Christ really gave the keys of heaven to St Peter? Colman answered in the affirmative; according to Eddius the conference unanimously declared Peter to be the holder of the keys, and the rock on which the Church was built. The king thereupon refused to oppose the doorkeeper of heaven. He could scarcely have realised that he had made one of the most crucial decisions in English history.

The conference broke up. Cedd, who listened to both sides most carefully during the debate, abandoned the Celtic Easter. Agilbert departed and became bishop of Paris. Alchfrith, the prince to whom the initiative was really due in getting the conference together, is heard of no more. His disappearance is one of the mysteries of Anglo-Saxon history. It is thought by many that the celebrated and beautiful cross at Bewcastle was erected to the memory of him and his wife Cuniburga, Penda's daughter, possibly by Wilfred.

Colman was given the option of conforming to Rome or surrendering his see. He chose the latter. Accompanied by his Irish monks and about thirty English members of the community who stood by him, he left Holy Island, carrying some of the bones of St Aidan with him. A number of the brethren chose to remain; on Colman's request the king appointed Eata, one of Aidan's original pupils and now abbot of Melrose, to be abbot of Lindisfarne. Eata now observed the Roman Easter, but he did not actually come to Holy Island for the time being, preferring to rule the two monasteries from Melrose in plurality. Colman and his company went on to Iona, where Cuimine was at this time abbot. They then journeyed to Innisboffin, off the coast of Mayo, where they founded a monastery. The Irish and English monks, however, could not agree together, and in one of his most delightful sketches Bede describes how at harvest time the Irish monks were wont to wander round the countryside, leaving their English brethren to bear the burden and heat of the day, and then return in winter expecting to enjoy the provisions gathered in. The incident is a revealing one, indicating that the differences between Celt and Roman were far deeper than is suggested by arguments about the Easter date and the shape of the tonsure, and were rooted in temperament and character. Colman wisely separated the English into a monastery of their own. He himself died on Innisboffin twelve years after Whitby.

He had been succeeded as bishop of Lindisfarne by Tuda, a member of the Roman party, who died shortly afterwards. The see was then vacant for some years. Northumbria was divided into two dioceses, one under Wilfred, who had his seat at Ripon, and the other under Ceadda (St Chad), brother of Cedd, centred on York. Ceadda was consecrated by Wini, bishop of Winchester, assisted by two Celtic bishops. Wilfred was more cautious, having some doubts concerning the validity of Celtic consecrations, and went over to Gaul, where he was consecrated in grand style by twelve Catholic bishops, of whom one was Agilbert.[11] According to Gallic custom the newly-consecrated sat in a golden chair, and was carried aloft by the bishops into the church while the choir chanted hymns and canticles. They then ordered him back to his see in York, bidding him stand firm in the Catholic Faith. All this was doubtless very pleasing to the young man. He was so delighted with his present surroundings that he dallied there for two years, leaving his diocese to take care of itself.

The future of English Christianity was now clearly marked. For close on nine hundred years the Church in England would be in communion with the Holy See, a constituent and integral part of undivided western Christendom. The civilisation which Rome represented and transmitted would now be more easily attainable by the Anglo-Saxons. From a merely domestic point of view, life in the English Church would tend to be more harmonious. The recent controversies were consuming energies which should have been used to further the work of the Conversion, not yet complete. There had been a real danger that the English Church might split into two distinct communions. This danger was past, and though it would be several years before the Church was effectively united and organised, the ecclesiastical and spiritual forces of the Anglo-Saxon kingdoms were now able to go forward with renewed confidence. The prestige of the Church and her ministers was high. Bede writes of this time that 'wherever any clerk or monk happened to come, he was received with joy by all, as the servant of God; and any who happened to meet him on their journeys, hastened forward to him with reverence, eager for his blessing. Great attention was paid to sermons, and the people came crowding into the churches or monasteries on Sundays, not for material benefit, but to hear God's word. If a priest chanced to enter a village, the inhabitants gathered together to hear the word of life from him. Priests and clerks went about for no other purpose but to preach, baptise, and visit the sick—in short, to care for souls.'[12] It is a fine picture of a people accepting the gospel with the eagerness of a newly found faith, taught by pastors with a lofty sense of vocation. We are a long way here from the angry anticlericalism of the later middle ages, from the seeking after benefices, the pluralism and non-residence, that marred the witness of the Church when it was raised to a position of wealth and power—a long way too from that pall of indifference to spiritual affairs which has descended upon the English people in the twentieth century, and which must surely bring an element of frustration into the work of modern ministers of religion.

Though with regard to its long-term results the conference of Whitby was decisive, its immediate effects were limited, applying only to the northern kingdom. English Christianity remained for some time unorganised as one Church. Though the Roman Easter was enforced, at any rate increasingly, other Celtic customs continued. There was a residue of ill-feeling, and the ostentatious ways of Wilfred were resented by lovers of Celtic simplicity such as Hild. On Lindisfarne the monastic community, though they had accepted the Roman Easter, followed Celtic customs until well into the eighth century. The refractory Celtic Christians long continued to make their influence felt in the English Church, and as late as 816 a council at Chelsea had to enact that no ecclesiastic of Irish race should exercise spiritual functions in England.[13]

It is in the life and character of St Cuthbert[14] that we best view the process whereby the Celtic and Roman strands in Anglo-Saxon Christianity gradually coalesced. This great saint, whose name has meant so much in northern tradition, might be held by some to hold an undeservedly high reputation. In his lifetime, however, he exerted a singular influence over his contemporaries, and for long after his death his bones were invested with a wonder-working power.

As a boy he was brought up by a widow whom he regarded with the affection due to a mother. He tended sheep on the hills above Leader Water, and it was during these years that he saw a vision, occurring on the night of Aidan's death, in which he saw angels bearing a holy soul to heaven. This determined his vocation, and he forsook his sheep for the life of a monk. Early in the winter of 651 he rode to the monastery of Melrose, whose prior was Boisil, a man with a reputation for sanctity. As the young postulant approached the gate, Boisil—who was standing by—was at once struck by his appearance, and exclaimed, 'Behold a servant of God'. Cuthbert remained here for thirteen years, a model Celtic monk, diligent in study, prayer, and manual labour. This period was broken towards the end by a short spell at Ripon, whither he was sent with other monks to colonise a new monastery on land given by Oswy's son Alchfrith. The prince, however, ordered the adoption of Roman ways, whereupon the monks returned to Melrose, and Wilfred was installed as abbot of Ripon, as we have seen.

Meanwhile Boisil died, after spending the last few days of his life in the study of the fourth gospel with Cuthbert, who succeeded him as prior. During his Melrose days Cuthbert showed himself an ardent evangelist in the neighbouring districts. He would set out periodically on preaching tours, traversing valleys, climbing steep hills, and visiting the smallest hamlets. His hearers loved and trusted him, and were accustomed to pour out to him in confession the secrets of their hearts. At a time when sacramental confession was not yet general and compulsory, this was a sure sign of trust and love.

In 664 Eata, abbot of Melrose, to whom had been handed the oversight of Lindisfarne monastery on Colman's departure, sent Cuthbert thither as prior. It is clear that Cuthbert by this time had become an adherent to the Roman party, and during this period of office at Lindisfarne he gradually brought the monks round to his point of view. Although the more inveterate of the Celtic monks of Holy Island had departed with Colman, those left behind were still largely Celtic in sentiment and spirit. They showed rough opposition to their prior from Melrose, but by his calm patience he won their allegiance and love. During his years as prior on the island he was a true example of the monastic life. Constant in his prayers and psalms, he was so fervent in the life of devotion that he invariably shed tears at the celebration of the Eucharist. In his dress he was neither fussy nor slovenly, and he prescribed clothes of undyed wool for his monks. He continued his Melrose practice of frequent evangelistic visits to the neighbouring country folk, as Aidan had done before him. After several years on Lindisfarne he also emulated Aidan in departing for the nearby Farne islands, but whereas his predecessor had merely made periodic visits there for the purpose of retreat, Cuthbert surrendered his duties as prior and settled down as a hermit. Love of the solitary life seems to have been deeply rooted in his nature, and before leaving for Farne he spent a period of retirement in a secluded spot just outside the monastery. On the islet whither he went he raised with his own hands a circular hut of stones and turf, divided into two compartments, one of which served as an oratory. The wall was higher than human height, and the floor sunk deep, so that the occupant might see nothing but the sky. The Lindisfarne monks helped Cuthbert to dig a well. The saint never anticipated at this stage that his life on Farne would be entirely uninterrupted, and he was not so discourteous as to forbid the approach of his fellow-men. During his brief period at Ripon he had been guest-master or hospitaller, an office which would tend to school him against unsocial behaviour. He now built a second hut, larger than his own, where visitors might be accommodated.

At first the brethren were accustomed to come over from Lindisfarne with supplies of food, but not wishing to saddle them with this burden, Cuthbert was before long growing his own barley. He received visitors, such as Herbert, a hermit on an island on Derwentwater, who came to him annually for spiritual counsel. From the far parts of Britain strangers arrived, and it is said that none ever went away with the sorrow which he brought. He comforted the afflicted, strengthened the souls of the tempted, reconciled those at enmity, instructed the ignorant, and exhibited to all the love of Christ.

His solitary life and austerities undoubtedly affected his mental and spiritual outlook as time went on. Like St Anthony in the desert and St Guthlac in the fens, St Cuthbert was attacked by fiends. His devotional life became morbid. He began to be impatient of guests, and would not come forth to greet them, but merely looked at them through the window. Finally even this was shut, and the saint would not reveal himself save to give an urgently requested blessing. His contemporaries did not think the less of him for this, perhaps even more. But many will feel today that there was a deterioration here from the earlier Cuthbert, amongst his brethren, 'living according to holy scripture, practising a life of contemplation within the active life'.[15]

By this time in St Cuthbert's life we are of course well beyond the year of the Whitby conference. Oswy had been succeeded by Ecgfrith, a warlike king whose ambitions were to lead him to defeat and death at the hands of the Picts at Nectansmere near Forfar in 685. A year previously he had concurred with Theodore, archbishop of Canterbury, to make Cuthbert bishop of Hexham in succession to Tunbert, who had been deposed. Messengers were sent to Farne to inform Cuthbert of his election. He ignored the tidings, and refused to leave his cell. The king, accompanied by Trumwine, a missionary bishop working amongst the Picts at Abercorn, on the Firth of Forth, with several monks and nobles crossed over to Farne. Weeping and kneeling at his feet, they pleaded with the hermit to accept the honour to which he was called. Overcome by their entreaties, and perhaps by a sudden sense of responsibility towards his fellow-men, he 'bent his neck to the yoke of the episcopate'. He was consecrated on Easter Day 685 by Theodore and six other bishops at York. But, as it so happened, he never ruled Hexham. His old superior Eata, now bishop of Lindisfarne, was prevailed upon by Cuthbert to come to Hexham, while he himself returned as bishop to his old beloved island community.

Before setting out for Lindisfarne he paid a visit to Carlisle, which had been given to him by Ecgfrith, and whither the queen had gone to sojourn while her husband was away campaigning against the Picts. Cuthbert and others had pleaded with the king not to go, and to forget his dream of subduing the northern people. A gloomy foreboding filled their minds. The townsfolk were displaying to Cuthbert a fountain, an interesting piece of old Roman work, when suddenly his face became overcast. He muttered, 'Oh, I think the battle is over.' A priest standing by asked what he meant. It was 3 p.m. on 20 May. He evaded the question, made straightway for the queen, who was staying in a religious house of which her sister was abbess, and advised her to proceed as soon as possible to York. Soon afterwards tidings arrived of the annihilation of the Northumbrian host at Nectansmere, at the very time when Cuthbert had received his second sight.

This battle marked the virtual end of Northumbria as a great political power. Anglian influence in Pictland, which had been considerable, now ceased. Trumwine and his monks had to abandon their missionary work at Abercorn. The dead king himself was buried at Iona by abbot Adamnan. His widow Iurminburg took the veil, and according to Eddius was changed from a she-wolf 'into a lamb of God, a perfect abbess'. Ecgfrith was succeeded by Aldfrith, an apparently natural son of Oswy by a British princess. He must not be confused with Alchfrith, who seems now to have been dead. The new king, an interesting figure, was the first English secular ruler with scholarly inclinations. He had studied under Irish teachers, possibly at Malmesbury, and also in Ireland itself. He wrote Gaelic verse, and was skilled both in the scriptures and in general knowledge.[16] His learning was later to call forth the praise of Alcuin.[17] Bede praises him, moreover, for his qualities as a ruler who retrieved the kingdom from its ruined state, though within narrower bounds. He ruled well for twenty years, and made no attempt to renew the disastrous wars of his predecessor and half-brother. His reign is important in ecclesiastical history as establishing exceptionally peaceful conditions, within which the Northumbrian Church could quietly make progress towards its most brilliant period.[18] To him the pen was greater than the sword, and it was largely his influence which made possible the wonderful flowering of Northumbrian learning in the age of Bede. After his death in 704 there followed a long period of dynastic feuds, from which the Northumbrian kingdom never recovered.

For a short time of less than two years Cuthbert was a diligent bishop of Lindisfarne. He continued his ascetic habits, and kept his mind fixed on heavenly things. His sermons were distinguished by their clarity, and were informed with gentleness and dignity. He had the mark of a true teacher, in that he practised what he taught. He regarded helping the weak as equivalent to an act of prayer. He fed the hungry and clothed the naked, protected widows and orphans, and redeemed captives. He perambulated his diocese with energy. We are told how once he was occupied in confirming for two days in a clearing of the woods where a tent had been put up to serve as a church, on which occasion he restored to health a youth suffering with fever. Cuthbert comforted the people during an outbreak of pestilence. He visited Carlisle again, to ordain priests and to dedicate to the religious life Ecgfrith's widow. While there he was visited by Herbert, the hermit of Derwentwater, who declared his hope that they might both die together when the time came.

But though Cuthbert proved himself a true father in God during his short active episcopate, his heart was not in public affairs. For the closing weeks of his life he retired to his hermitage of Farne, arriving there shortly after Christmas 686. Towards the end of February his last illness overtook him. Herefrith, abbot of Lindisfarne, visited him. A storm blew up after he had gone back to the monastery, and raged for five days. It was impossible to cross the tempestuous seas. When the winds had fallen, Herefrith returned with some of the monks, and found Cuthbert in the guesthouse, whither he had managed to crawl from his cell. He was worn out with exhaustion and an ulcerated foot. He produced five onions from beneath his bed, of which half a one had been eaten. He consented that some of the monks should stay behind to nurse him. Though he agreed reluctantly to the request of the community that his body should be buried at Lindisfarne, he himself would have preferred the little island where, as he put it, 'he had fought for the Lord'. On 19 March Herefrith and some others carried him back to his own cell. There Cuthbert gave his last message to the abbot for transmission to the brethren. They were to be charitable amongst themselves, hospitable to strangers, and must avoid all communion with those who departed from catholic unity, whether by keeping Easter at the wrong time or by the perversity of their life. Soon after midnight he received the Eucharist, and passed away in a sitting posture, peacefully and without a groan. Herefrith gave the tidings to the brethren, who were outside the cell singing the psalm 'Deus repulisti nos'. One of them went to a slight eminence and held two torches aloft, the agreed signal. The monks in Lindisfarne, also at this moment engaged in nocturns, knew by the twin lights over the midnight waters that their master was taken from them.

His body was buried, in accordance with the wishes of the community, in the church at Lindisfarne, and there remained for nearly two centuries. Removed in 875, it found its final rest in 999 on the spot over which arose Europe's most majestic mausoleum, the cathedral church of Durham.

From his early days as a shepherd-boy on the Lammermuir Hills until his death on a sea-girt rock, Cuthbert was a thorough-going Celt in his approach to life and religion. He was Celtic in his love of solitude. It should not be supposed that he was urged by any sentimental regard for that wild nature of which there is abundance in Northumbria. On Farne he deliberately constructed his hut so that he should see nothing but the heavens, and it may be inferred that he was either impervious to the splendid prospect around him or excluded it purposely from his attention. Neither does he seem to have been a mystic. He was content to fight his solitary battles against the demons who barred his way to the heavenly kingdom. He was Celtic also in his extreme asceticism, derived ultimately from the Christian East and which Benedict of Nursia in his rule for western monks studiously avoided. Most characteristic of all perhaps was his love of animals and his care for their needs. The seals who crawled out of the waves to kiss the feet of Cuthbert kneeling on the sands at dawn are of the same picture as the faithful old horse coming up to Columba for a last blessing. This Celtic love for animals was to constitute an attractive feature of Northumbrian art, where in sculpture and illumination a host of creatures are intertwined intricately in vine and scroll.

And yet this fervid Celt, as a dying injunction, would have his disciples avoid the fellowship of those who refused to conform to Rome. It is true that this was in connection with the principle of the Easter date. But this principle was fundamental, signifying Catholic unity. The fact that Cuthbert was on the winning side in the controversy without doubt accounts for much of his subsequent popularity. But he was nevertheless a truly holy man, who lived close to his Master Christ. He may have had faults, but they were not recognised as such by his contemporaries. His self-renunciation and his calling as a 'warrior of Christ' were such as to endear him to the Anglo-Saxons with their tradition of heroism.

This account of the saint has taken us beyond the general course of history which immediately followed Whitby. Retracing our path, we must now consider the process of reorganisation and consolidation which is associated above all with the name of archbishop Theodore.

CHAPTER IX

THEODORE AND WILFRED

For five years after Whitby the English Church, though it had now received a clear direction, was virtually a ship without a captain. Near disaster was caused by a plague in which the clergy suffered severely. In the consequent shortage of leaders, there was something approaching a restoration of heathenism. Amongst the many victims of the pestilential outbreak was Cedd, bishop of the East Saxons. In Essex, still apparently a stronghold of the old religion despite the labours of Cedd, there was a strong reaction. Under king Sighere a widespread apostasy resulted in a restoration of temples and idolatry, as a protection against the mortality. His co-regent Sebbi, however, stood firm in the Faith along with his people.[1] The overlord of Essex, Wulfhere king of the Mercians, sent his bishop Jaruman to restore the situation. Sebbi himself subsequently ended his days as a monk. Throughout his reign of thirty years, he had always preferred the life of devotion to that of public affairs.

Deusdedit, archbishop of Canterbury since 654, died of the pestilence shortly after the Whitby council. A man of mediocre qualities, he does not seem to have exercised any authority outside his own diocese. But the importance with which the Canterbury see was regarded in the ecclesiastical life of the whole country is shown by the joint action of Egbert, king of Kent, and Oswy, king of Northumbria, in proceeding to choose a new archbishop, after a vacancy of some length.[2] 'With the election and consent of the church of the English', their choice fell on Wighard, a good and suitable candidate, a Canterbury priest who had been a member of Deusdedit's *familia*. He was sent to Rome for consecration, so that on his return he might create Catholic bishops for the English Church. The episcopate had been virtually wiped out in the pestilence.[3] Wighard duly reached Rome and presented himself before pope Vitalian (657–72). But shortly afterwards he also, with most of his party, succumbed to the plague. The pope now himself proceeded to choose an archbishop for Canterbury, to the lasting benefit of the English Church and nation. His ultimate choice was an old man, but as with Lanfranc four centuries later, it was to be demonstrated that for a long, vigorous, and enlightened rule a person ripe with experience is sometimes to be preferred before youth.

In the first instance the pope invited Hadrian, an African with a reputation for learning and at the same time abbot of a monastery near Naples, to accept the appointment. Feeling himself insufficiently experienced for the office of archbishop, Hadrian suggested instead an older monk Andrew. The latter, however, was in ill-health at the time. Hadrian thereupon proposed to the pope another monk, Theodore, as a suitable person to fill the vacancy.

Theodore was born c. 602 at Tarsus in Cilicia, though the details of his earlier life are unknown.[4] It seems that he may have left his native land, which was being overrun by Persian invaders, and found his way to Athens. Both Tarsus and Athens, notable centres of learning, thus shared the distinction of producing one who came to hold a great reputation as a Greek and Latin scholar and philosopher. The first clear fact in his life is his appearance at Rome in 667.

Theodore was by training an Orthodox of the East. The remarkable circumstance that the first great primate of the English Church was taken from the Orthodox communion has been insufficiently realised. There is still a popular tendency to look upon the latter as a creation of the mid-eleventh century—a travesty of the real situation. The difference between East and West had crystallized long before, and at the stage in Church history which we have reached all was not well between pope and patriarch. The seventh century was a period of bitter controversy concerning the will of Christ, in which the popes had to fight hard against the emperors and patriarchs. Pope Martin I (649–53) maintained the doctrine of two wills in the One Christ and formally broke off communion with Constantinople. Imperial forces were sent against him, and he subsequently died in circumstances of great suffering in the Crimea. He was succeeded in the papal chair by Eugenius I, who was more compliant with the emperor, and accepted a theological formula which recognised three wills in Christ. His successor Vitalian forwarded a profession of faith to the emperor, and was on good terms with the patriarch Peter, though a subsequent patriarch Theodore removed Vitalian's name from the diptychs.[5]

It is therefore clear that relations both theologically and politically were anything but smooth in the seventh century between East and West. There were also many refugees in Rome to complicate the situation. It is possible, moreover, to argue that the popes may have had something of an inferiority complex in their relations with Constantinople, as is suggested by their constant assertion of themselves. Generally, they came to hold suspicions concerning the right belief of Eastern Christians. When Vitalian appointed the Eastern monk Theodore to Canterbury, it was on condition that he took as his companion Hadrian, who besides knowing the route across Gaul, would ensure that the new archbishop introduced no erroneous doctrine.

Before they could set out, it was necessary to wait four months for Theodore's hair to grow, that it might be shorn afresh into the Roman shape. As Theodore was not yet in holy orders, he was now ordained, and finally consecrated by the pope himself on 26 March 668. In May he commenced his journey to England, accompanied by Hadrian and also by Benedict Biscop, at this time in Rome on one of his frequent visits. He consented to instruct the new archbishop in the English tongue during the journey, and to act as his interpreter.

There were many delays. Ebroin, mayor of the palace in Neustria, suspected Hadrian as really on a political errand from the emperor Constantine IV, to the English kings, in conspiracy against himself.[6] He therefore detained Hadrian, while Theodore went on to Paris. There the archbishop stayed for some time with Agilbert, former bishop to the West Saxons, who would doubtless acquaint him with the state of affairs in England. Egbert of Kent sent his reeve over to Gaul to hasten matters, and escorted the archbishop to Étaples where, however, he was detained for a while by illness. On his recovery he crossed the Channel, and arrived at his church in Canterbury in May 669, after a journey of nearly a year.

His first act was to appoint Benedict Biscop to the abbacy of SS. Peter and Paul in Canterbury. After two years Biscop was succeeded by Hadrian, who had arrived in England soon after Theodore.

The English Churches were in a sorry state. For five years there had been no archbishop, and there were only three bishops at the time of Theodore's arrival. Of these one was Wini, the simoniacal bishop of London; the others were Wilfred and Chad—the former had returned from his consecration in Gaul after a protracted stay, to find that his diocese, weary of waiting for him, now had the latter as its bishop. It was not a promising situation. So far as there was a diocesan system at all, it was in a state of hopeless confusion. Yet it was the muddle created by a welter of vacant sees and conflicting interests which offered practically a clear field in the work of reorganisation to Theodore, which he was not slow to exploit.

He commenced his primacy with a progress through the Anglo-Saxon parts of the island, teaching the right rule of life and the correct way of observing Easter. He was everywhere well received, though the Irish clergy were a little sullen.[7] His first objective was to get the episcopate into action again. He consecrated Putta for Rochester, and Bisi—a man of great spirituality—for Dunwich. Wini was left undisturbed in his see of London. Chad was removed from York, which he had been ruling excellently, but to which he had no canonical title. The rightful bishop Wilfred was placed in his see. Chad humbly stood down, with the observation that he had never thought himself worthy of the office anyhow, and retired to the monastery of Lastingham. But Wulfhere the Mercian king asked Theodore for a bishop, and with the consent of Oswy, Theodore sent Chad. As it was essential that there should be no doubt concerning his position as bishop—he had received his episcopal orders from a simoniacal English bishop and two schismatic British bishops—Theodore reconsecrated him conditionally.[8] He admired Chad for his humility. But at the same time he was insistent that he should now rule his new diocese according to Roman ideas of practical efficiency. He must abandon the Celtic custom of visiting his diocese on foot. When Chad remonstrated, the archbishop himself forcibly lifted him on to a horse, and virtually ordered him to do as he was told.

Chad now became bishop of the Mercians and the first bishop of Lichfield, holding the see until his death two and a half years later. Near the church he built a house, where with his *familia* of seven or eight brethren he was accustomed to pray and read when not engaged in pastoral duties. One interesting member of the *familia* was Owini, who had forsaken the life of a steward at the East Anglian court for monastic life at Lastingham. He had presented himself as a postulant holding an axe and hatchet in his hands. He now accompanied Chad from Lastingham to Lichfield. Having no aptitude for study, he made himself useful to the brethren as a manual worker and handyman.

Chad was a man who lived close to heaven, in daily expectation of death. He heard the voice of God in the wind. Angels were his familiar companions. Bede praises him for his merits as a teacher, for his humility, prayer, and poverty, and speaks well of his episcopate.[9] It does not, however, seem that Chad perambulated his large diocese (which included Lindisfarne as well as Mercia) after the manner of Aidan or Cuthbert. He died on 2 March 672, and was buried in St Mary's church. His remains were afterwards removed to a new church of St Peter, where his shrine became the basis of the prosperity of the medieval cathedral of Lichfield.

Bede is full of praise for these opening years of Theodore's archiepiscopate.[10] Theodore was the first archbishop whom the whole English Church obeyed. From him and Hadrian there flowed rivers of learning which watered the hearts of their hearers. There were never happier times since the Angles first arrived in Britain. An important development of these years was the beginning of the adoption of Gregorian chant by all the English Churches. It was an art which the Anglo-Saxons found hard to master. Until this time it had been known thoroughly only in Kent, though James the Deacon had introduced it into Northumbria. Wilfred now determined that it should be more widely known in his diocese, and sent to Kent for Eddius, his future biographer and an expert in chant. Putta, the new bishop of Rochester, was exceedingly skilful in Gregorian music, which he had learned from the disciples of Gregory I. He was a man of simple life, but out of his depth in worldly affairs. Later, in 676, when Aethelred king of the Mercians ravaged Kent and destroyed Rochester, Putta was to take refuge with Seaxwulf, then the Mercian bishop, who gave him a church and a parcel of land. Here he spent the rest of his life in peace, and made no attempt to restore his former shattered diocese. In his retirement he was always most ready to go and help those, however, who wished to learn church music.[11] It was about this time, in 670, that Theodore consecrated to the see of Winchester Agilbert's nephew Leuthere. There had been no bishop in Wessex since Wini had left Winchester four years before. In 670 and 673 respectively Theodore lost his two chief supporters by the deaths of Oswy and Egbert. But there was now the embryo of something which looked like a bench of bishops, and in 672 the primate was in a position to take the momentous step of convening the first general council of the English Church.

It was a very small assembly, more like a modern committee, which met on 26 September at Hertford. Only four bishops besides Theodore were present—Bisi, Putta, Leuthere, and Winfrith (who had recently succeeded Chad at Lichfield). Wini of London was absent,[12] and Wilfred was represented by a proctor. The council confirmed the Roman calculation of Easter. Bishops, monks, and priests were not to wander about, but must stay in the particular spheres to which they were called. This actually was quite an important measure, as marking the end of the migratory stage in the Conversion, and the inauguration of an established diocesan system. The bishops were not to interfere with monasteries. Their order of precedence was to be determined by the dates of consecration. Some discussion ensued over the question of increasing the number of dioceses as the faithful multiplied, but it was decided to defer this for the time being. Matrimonial legislation was touched upon. It was enacted that the bishops should meet in synod twice a year if possible, but annually at least, at a place known as Cloveshoe, which is unidentified. In the event even this minimum provision was found impossible of realisation.[13]

The real significance of the synod was twofold. In the first place it marked the introduction into the English Church of the forms of synodical government, long observed on the Continent, and with which Theodore was undoubtedly familiar. The bishops met on this occasion 'according to the prescription of the venerable canons, to treat of the necessary affairs of the Church'. According to the fifth canon of Nicaea, holy synod was an essential part of ecclesiastical life and organisation, as expressing the mind of the Church. Like the Council of Chalcedon later, Nicaea decreed that a provincial synod should meet twice yearly. The Council of Arles had laid down that a bishop bidden to a synod was obliged to attend, unless ill, in which case he might send a proctor. In correct synodical form, the meeting at Hertford opened solemnly 'in the name of God and the Saviour Jesus Christ'. The bishops were reminded of the need for observing the canonical decrees of the Fathers. Theodore produced a collection of canons, from which he selected the ten subjects which were discussed as particularly applicable to the needs of the English Church at this time.

With his practical frame of mind, Theodore did not allow the assembly to end in mere discussion, but secured the passing of nine clear resolutions. Much of the importance of this synod indeed lay in its sheer formality, something quite unlike the improvised (though none the less effectual) proceedings at Whitby. There were to be no vague misunderstandings as to what the synod had decided. A record of the proceedings was written down by the synodical clerk Titillus, each bishop appending his signature.

Secondly, the Hertford synod is memorable—indeed a milestone in our national history—as marking the first occasion on which representatives of the English met together for common discussion and decision. From 672 onwards we are justified in speaking of the English Church, whereas previously there were, rather, several regional Churches. Hertford, moreover, is the ultimate precursor of our parliamentary system. The Anglo-Saxons would continue for a considerable period to be organised politically in separate kingdoms, but their Church was now legislating as one body under the presidency of the archbishop, and the way towards national unification had been shown.[14]

Theodore's progress through the kingdoms had convinced him that there should be more dioceses, and he had tentatively, it seems, raised the matter at Hertford. Self-interest on the part of one or more of the bishops brought the proposal to nothing, but Theodore did not disguise his intention of implementing his plans as opportunities arose. Kent was adequately supplied with its two bishoprics, at Canterbury and Rochester. But Mercia and Northumbria especially were far too large to be cared for adequately by a single bishop in each case. Theodore's first opportunity came in East Anglia, whose bishop Bisi was old and ill. After his death his diocese was divided into two, centred on Dunwich and North Elmham, for the South-folk and North-folk respectively. Thus were launched two dioceses which had a lengthy career; the former endured until its annihilation by the vikings in the latter half of the ninth century, the latter until nearly the close of the eleventh.

Not long afterwards, c. 675, Winfrith, the successor of Chad at Lichfield, was deposed for disobedience, probably for resisting the division of his large diocese. This gave Theodore the chance to carry out a radical reorganisation of the ecclesiastical arrangements for Mercia, with the assistance of king Aethelred and his witan. The actual dating and sequence of this reorganisation are, however, by no means clear.[15]

The diocese of Lichfield was hopelessly unwieldy, reaching from the Wash to the hills of Wales, from the Humber to the Thames. On some occasion prior to 680 the dioceses of Worcester and Hereford were formed out of it. The first bishop of Hereford is thought to have been that same Putta, bishop of Rochester, who after the Mercian King's devastation of Kent found refuge with Aethelred's own bishop and was given some land and a church, which may well have been at Hereford.[16] This diocese was almost certainly founded about this time, to embrace the tribes of settlers, known as the Magonsaetan, across the Severn, inhabiting what must have been a very indeterminate area, with much admixture of the Celtic and Germanic racial stocks. The diocese of Worcester was created for the Hwicci, who occupied the Severn valley, in the country roughly represented by the modern Worcestershire and Gloucestershire. These were a distinct people, of mixed Anglian and Saxon race, comprising some seven thousand households.[17] Thus originated the two famous West midland dioceses, which have had an unbroken continuity to our own day.

About this time Aetla became bishop of Dorchester-on-Thames. The people of this region were West Saxons who seem to have fallen under the domination of Mercia. Birinus and Agilbert had been bishops here, but the see had apparently petered out. Theodore did not succeed in really reviving the see, and the diocese of Dorchester was not firmly founded until 909.

It was during this phase in his episcopate also that Theodore founded the diocese of Leicester for the Middle Angles, though there was some confusion in the succession of bishops until it settled down in 737. Meanwhile the bishopric of Lichfield continued, though in a much reduced form. Its bishop from c. 675 for some sixteen years was Seaxwulf, who had been the first abbot of Medeshamstede. About 675 Theodore appointed Eorcenwald to the bishopric of London. By the time of Bede his memory was held in such veneration that the litter in which he was carried about in his diocese while sick was credited with miraculous properties. He founded two monasteries, Chertsey in Surrey for himself, and Barking in Essex for his sister Ethelburga. According to William of Malmesbury, Eorcenwald was so renowned a saint that his successors in the see were dwarfed by comparison, scarcely even their names being remembered. He died c. 693.[18]

The most difficult problem, however, was Northumbria. From 669 to 677 the whole of Northumbria was governed as a single diocese by Wilfred, until he fell foul of king Ecgfrith. Wilfred was spiritual adviser to the queen, Ethelthryth, one of Anna's daughters, who on his encouragement forsook her husband and took the veil.[19] It was she who give him the site on which he built the monastery of Hexham. The king not unnaturally became ill-disposed to Wilfred, and his unfriendly feelings were now fanned into enmity by his second wife Iurminburg (whom he married during the lifetime of the first—a lawful marriage in the circumstances). She played on the king's jealousy by reminding him of the earthly magnificence of Wilfred, his wealth and princely retinues, the many monasteries which had placed themselves under his protection.[20] Not only Ecgfrith, but apparently Theodore also, was alarmed at Wilfred's love of power, and it may well be that Theodore was fearful of Wilfred establishing a second archbishopric. Of our two authorities for the protracted and discreditable controversy which followed, Bede has little to say in the matter, and Eddius, while he narrates it at length, does so with obvious bias, even going so far as to make the fantastic charge that Theodore was bribed by Ecgfrith to help him get rid of Wilfred.[21] All that we know of Theodore's character makes this more than unlikely. Eddius apparently realises he is raising an accusation which will hardly be believed, as he moreover observes that even wise men may be blinded by bribery.

The sequence of following events is not exactly clear. But it is certain that the primate visited Northumbria and carved up Wilfred's see. Eddius says slightingly that Theodore 'picked up' three bishops from elsewhere and consecrated them over parts of Wilfred's diocese. This is certainly an unjust statement, as the three bishops had all been closely connected with Northumbria. Bosa, a man of 'great sanctity and humility', whom Theodore consecrated bishop of Deira with his seat at York, was trained under Hild at Whitby. Eata, who became bishop for the Bernician territory, was one of Aidan's original twelve pupils; he was at the time prior of Lindisfarne, from which he seems to have administered his diocese (with Hexham as a twin see-centre). Eadhaeth, bishop of the new diocese of Lindsey, composed of territory lately conquered by Ecgfrith from Mercia, had accompanied Chad from Northumbria to Mercia;[22] the regions of this diocese had not been under Wilfred's jurisdiction.

In fairness to Theodore one would like to think that Wilfred was left in control of at least some of his diocese under this new arrangement.[23] But there is no first-hand evidence that this was so, and it seems that by an exceedingly presumptuous action Wilfrid was deprived of his see, without even being consulted. He made his way to the court, where he asked the king and archbishop for an explanation, but was merely told that though they found no fault in him, what had been done was necessary and could not be altered. Theodore's motive was probably two-fold. Besides the strictly practical one that the huge Northumbrian diocese needed dividing, he seems to have considered it politic that

Wilfred himself should be deflated. By his earlier deposition of Chad, and more recently of Winfrith, he had shown that he was quite prepared to take strong measures against individual prelates. This time, however, he misjudged his opponent. Wilfred decided to appeal to Rome. It was the first of such appeals in the history of the English Church. Meanwhile Ecgfrith confiscated Wilfred's property.

There followed an adventurous episode in Wilfred's career. While crossing the Channel, on his way to Rome, he was driven by rough weather on to the Frisian coast. He spent the winter of 677–8[24] as a missionary amongst the inhabitants of the interior, thus inaugurating the great tradition to be taken up in due course by Willibrord, Boniface, and many other Englishmen, on the Continent. He can be claimed as the first Englishman to preach the Gospel outside his native land. He instructed the Frisians diligently in the main articles of the Creed, and baptised many thousands under their king Aldgisl, including most of the chiefs. About this time there occurred an unusually prosperous fishing season, attributed by the people to the Christian missionary, and which was a main cause of his success. But any ideas of settling down to pioneering work of this sort were far from Wilfred's thoughts, and in the event the work in Frisia soon collapsed. Only a decade later, a missionary named Wictbert was to preach for two years in this country to no avail, and not long afterwards Willibrord found an almost entirely heathen people. The Frisians were in fact to prove one of the most intractable of non-Christian peoples, and it was at their hands that Boniface suffered martyrdom more than two generations after the first preaching amongst them by Wilfred.

Continuing his journey in the spring of 678, Wilfred probably spent a considerable time first with king Dagobert II of Austrasia, and then with Perctarit king of the Lombards. The former tried hard to persuade him to accept the bishopric of Strasbourg. The latter told Wilfred that he had received offers of bribes from Britain if he would detain him on his journey, which he had contemptuously refused. Wilfred arrived in Rome in the summer of 679, a quarter of a century after his first visit. He obtained an audience of pope Agatho, whom he found already acquainted with his case by a messenger sent ahead by Theodore. In October a council of more than fifty bishops met in the Lateran basilica, when the matter was considered. After reading the memorandum sent by Theodore, they invited Wilfred to state his case. The burden of his argument was that he had by uncanonical means been deprived of his see and others intruded into it. The council upheld him, but it also tried to appease Theodore. Wilfred was to be restored to his bishopric, and the intruding bishops deprived; Wilfred was then to choose coadjutor bishops, with the help of a council at York, who were to be consecrated by Theodore.

Besides dealing with Wilfred's appeal, the Lateran council of 679 also seems to have given attention to the question of the relations between Theodore and his bishops, which apparently were not too good. Wilfred was the third bishop to be roughly treated by the primate. Before leaving for Rome, he had taken counsel with the other bishops, according to his biographer, though there is no evidence that they supported him. But it does seem probable that the bishops were restive about their primate's policy of diocesan division. The 679 council now decreed that the maximum number of bishops in England was to be twelve, including the archbishop. This was in fact the number of bishoprics in England at this time, including the newly created sees in Northumbria. In other words, the pope accepted the Northumbrian action as a *fait accompli*, but warned Theodore not to cause similar disturbance in future.

While Wilfred was away, the English Church held its second synod under Theodore, that of Hatfield, in 679.[25] The object of the synod was doctrinal. It was convened so that the English Church might declare its adherence to the Catholic Faith, at present in danger through the Monothelite heresy.[26] A general appeal had gone forth from pope Agatho, who was anxious for declarations of orthodoxy from the various national Churches in support of the council which he was planning to hold in Rome to consider the problem, and in preparation for a forthcoming ecumenical council in Constantinople. The adherence of the Church of the English was particularly valuable, as its metropolitan was personally acquainted with this theological controversy through his life-long residence in the East. The council duly met in Rome in the spring of 680, and one notes with satisfaction that Wilfred was apparently the official representative of the Church in England to attend and declare the English adherence.

As soon as this council was over Wilfred returned home. He bore with him a copy of the findings of the 679 council, and also a papal document confirming him in his possession of his monasteries of Hexham and Ripon. His reception in Northumbria probably surprised him. He appeared before a council, produced his documents, and was thrown into prison by Ecgfrith. The council did not question the right of Rome to give a judgment in such a case—it asserted that Wilfred must have obtained the judgment by bribery. The conditions of his imprisonment were harsh. For the whole of a northern winter he was confined in a dark cell. His only solace was the recitation of the psalter, which he would of course know by heart. The king offered him the return of his old see if he would admit his document from Rome to be fraudulent. He refused, and by way of additional punishment was put in chains. According to Eddius, queen Iurminburg now fell into convulsive fits, and in alarm the king let Wilfred go free, whereupon his queen recovered. The biographer tells of the miraculous aid which sustained his hero in prison—how an unearthly light pierced the darkness, how the chains fell from his hands.[27]

Wilfred again embarked on a period of wanderings, during which he was to accomplish some valuable missionary work in the remaining heathen parts of England. It must be remembered, however, that Wilfred was never a missionary by choice or vocation, but rather by accident; the consuming interest of his life was the maintenance or recovery of his own ecclesiastical interests in Northumbria.

Wilfred now proceeded to Mercia, where a friendly donor gave him some land on which to build a monastery. It seemed that here he might find peace, but it was short-lived. At the instigation of the Mercian queen, who was Ecgfrith's sister, he was ordered to depart, and accompanied by a retinue of priests and attendants he crossed over into Wessex. Even here the hatred of the Northumbrian royal house pursued him. The Wessex queen was sister to Iurminburg, the 'she-wolf' of Eddius's narrative. Continuing his journey, he found sure refuge with Aethelwalh, king of the South Saxons.

Though Aethelwalh was himself a Christian, his people were still heathen, and during the next five years Wilfred applied himself zealously to their conversion. Sussex was a small kingdom, which had remained largely outside the main stream of Anglo-Saxon life, separated as it was from Kent and the north-east by the dense forest of Andredsweald. It seems that Aethelwalh (whose kingdom included the Isle of Wight and the area of Hampshire known as Meonware, besides Sussex) had made an attempt to convert his people which, however, came to little or nothing. Half-a-dozen monks, under their abbot Dicul, an Irishman, who had built themselves a small monastery at Bosham,[28] on the Sussex coast near Chichester, were probably introduced by the king, possibly from Mercia where he himself had received his Christianity at the hands of king Wulfhere, who was his godfather at baptism. Aethelwalh's queen Eaba, a native of the Hwicci, was already a Christian at the time of her marriage. There would seem to have been at least a certain amount of success for Christian missions in Sussex, as we find a South Saxon, Damian, becoming bishop of Rochester in 655.[29] But the main body of the people were clearly heathen on Wilfred's arrival. Bede is explicit that the inhabitants of the surrounding districts were quite indifferent to the preaching of Dicul, to whom they would not even listen.

Some fifteen years previously Wilfred had been crossing the Channel on his way back from his consecration in Gaul. Eddius, with a vivid touch, relates how the clergy on the boat were by their chanting of the psalmody giving the time to the rowers, when a violent wind arose from the south-east, and forced them on to the unknown coast of Sussex. On landing they were met by a crowd of heathen wreckers, headed by their chief priest, who tried by magical cursing to bind their hands. One of Wilfred's men thereupon slew him with a stone from his sling—an interesting piece of evidence that Christians did not despise the power of heathen magical art. A battle ensued, in which the South Saxons were put to flight. Meanwhile the tide, which was out, miraculously came back before its time in answer to Wilfred's prayer, and the company was able to get the ship floated and out to sea before the heathens returned to renew the assault with a larger force, this time under the command of their king. The vessel was also favoured by the wind, which veered and carried it safely to Sandwich.[30]

After a lapse of many years Wilfred was now back amongst the South Saxons, whom he evangelised with enthusiasm and success. A disastrous drought gave him his opportunity. Famine was sore in the land, and so intolerable was the misery that starving men were throwing themselves in batches over the cliffs into the sea. Strangely enough they had never seriously learnt the art of fishing, which Wilfred now taught them through the use of nets.[31] Their hunger appeased, they listened attentively to the spiritual message of the man who had won their confidence by his care for their material needs. As previously to the Frisians, Wilfred now taught the South Saxons the basic doctrines of the Faith, his method being one of teaching rather than exhortation. Four priests who had accompanied him loyally assisted him in this work, as a result of which the ealdormen and thegns were baptised. The rest of the people shortly followed. On the day of the general baptism, a gentle but steady rain ended the three-year drought, and the earth revived.[32]

The king granted to Wilfred the Selsea peninsula, consisting of eighty-seven hides, where he established his episcopal seat. Here, on a spot since submerged by the sea, he raised a minster, where the regular monastic life was followed. He remained bishop of the South Saxons for five years. The king also presented him with two hundred and fifty slaves, whom Wilfred baptised and set at liberty. Unfortunately the dreaded pestilence invaded the settlement, and secured many victims.

The apostolate of Wilfred in Sussex (681–6) is the finest period in his life, and one of the best pieces of work in the whole history of the Conversion, which it virtually completed. Only the Isle of Wight remained. But in 685 king Aethelwalh was slain by a daring young adventurer, Caedwalla,[33] who on being expelled from his native Wessex had come with a military force to try his fortune against Sussex. Wilfred prudently sought Caedwalla's friendship, and obtained from him a quarter of the Isle of Wight. The savage young man vowed to massacre the entire population of the island, with the intention of bringing in his own people. The islanders were the last of the English to remain heathen. But before Wilfred could set himself to the task of their conversion, the way was opened for him to return to his native Northumbria. He placed his nephew Beornwine in supervision of his newly acquired properties on the island, along with a priest Hiddila to prosecute mission work, and made his departure.

The conversion of the Isle of Wight was complete within a few years. Bede places on record that two young men, brothers of Arwald, king of the island, became believers before their execution by Caedwalla. They had managed to flee the island, but were betrayed and captured. A certain abbot and priest, Cynebert, asked permission of Caedwalla to instruct the youths in Christianity before they died. They were duly baptised, and went to their deaths with joy, not doubting that they would pass into everlasting life.

During Wilfred's absence in the south, Theodore made an extension to the diocesan arrangements of Northumbria, by establishing a see for the Picts in Galloway, who had come under the rule of Ecgfrith by conquest. Thus Trumwine became bishop of Abercorn on the

Firth of Forth in 680, and held this outpost until it collapsed with the defeat and death of Ecgfrith at Nectansmere in 685.

The death of the Northumbrian king, Wilfred's implacable enemy, opened the way for his return to Northumbria and his reconciliation with Theodore. There is no doubt that this was anxiously desired by the latter. The two men met by appointment in London. According to Eddius, Theodore was troubled in his conscience, especially as he was now very old and tending to illness, at having agreed to the spoliation of Wilfred's property and his exile. He confessed his sin to God and St Peter, and declared his wish to appoint Wilfred as his successor. Such self-humiliation on Theodore's part is not in the least likely from what we know of his character, though he does seem to have exerted himself on Wilfred's behalf. He was perhaps impressed with reports of the mission in Sussex, and wished to reward the bishop by making amends in some degree. He wrote to Ecgfrith's successor Aldfrith, urging him to come to an agreement with Wilfred, and also to Aelfled, abbess of Whitby, and to Aethelred, king of Mercia. As a result of the approach to the midland king, Wilfred during the course of his journey northwards secured the restoration of his Mercian properties. Aldfrith received him kindly when he arrived in Northumbria in 686.

According to the Roman decree, he was to be restored to his diocese of York, and a council convened at which new bishops were to be chosen. The actual result was different. Eddius says that Wilfred recovered from Aldfrith his see of York, together with his monasteries of Hexham and Ripon, and that the king moreover drove out the intruding bishops.[34] These latter were Bosa of York and Eadhaeth of Ripon. The old view was to accept this statement that Wilfred now recovered York.[35] But more recent studies have demonstrated its unlikelihood. Bosa is still found as bishop of York in subsequent years and continued to hold the see until his death in 705. It is true Bede says that Wilfred recovered his own see.[36] He could, however, have scarcely meant by this the whole diocese originally held in Northumbria, for he also states that Hexham, vacated by Eata's death shortly before Wilfred's return, was occupied by John of Beverley,[37] who stayed there until he became bishop of York in 705. Moreover, the Lindisfarne diocese continued in existence after the return of Wilfred, who, however, administered it for a year following the death of its bishop Cuthbert in 687. The truth probably is that Wilfred merely recovered Ripon, his first see, to which he had been consecrated after the conference of Whitby.[38]

The reconciliation with Wilfred was the last recorded act of Theodore, who died on 19 September 690, at the age of eighty-eight. His great achievement was his diocesan reorganisation. In the face of much opposition he had managed, on the whole successfully, to divide the two great dioceses of Mercia and Northumbria, though the division of Wessex was not to come until after his death. He had, moreover, welded into a single Church an assortment of provincial Churches, themselves the result of the work of various agencies. Many generations would elapse before the English came to be ruled by one king, but the unifying work of Theodore in the ecclesiastical sphere pointed the way and set the example to what was possible politically.

Theodore was not concerned only with the external framework of religion. He was undoubtedly active during his primacy trying to enforce Christian standards of morality and decency amongst clergy and laity. This is clear from the penances which he prescribed for numerous specified offences, and which form the nucleus of the collection which after his death came to be gathered together under the name of Theodore's *Penitentiale*.[39] In two books, it is a compilation by a certain priest Eoda of answers made in response to questions put to Theodore. The subject-matter includes much that is repellant. It shows that heathenism was still very much a power in the land, and some of the disgusting practices mentioned are an indication of what the Church was trying to combat.[40] The longest and most interesting passages, however, relate to divorce, which for certain causes Theodore permits. A man deserted by his wife, who refuses to return, may remarry after five years. The archbishop liberally recognised the circumstances of the times, and allowed remarriage if a partner had been carried off into captivity with little or no hope of return. A person whose husband or wife entered religion also seems to have been permitted to marry again. If a man was condemned to slavery for life, his wife may remarry after waiting a year. Theodore was a disciplinarian and an autocrat, but in these provisions we discern the workings of a humane mind which could not be confined to over rigid conceptions. The same mental fluidity is noticeable in the fact that although he was a devoted disciple of Rome, he would not consent to an implementation of the papal decrees relating to Wilfred's restoration. Again, though convinced that his policy of diocesan division was right, he did not precipitately enforce it upon an unwilling episcopate, but at Hertford was prepared to bow before current opinion, and await his time patiently. It was probably Theodore's cosmopolitanism which largely accounted for his flexibility and receptivity of mind. Having known the Church in many lands, he had all the more to offer to the particular Church over which he was set. It was his readiness to tread a pliant path which brought him to the acceptance of private confession as a usage of the Church, taking this over from the Celts.[41] This was one of his most important innovations, destined to affect profoundly the development of the Western Church's inner life.

There is little to indicate the nature of Theodore's own personality. Though his work stands massively, the man himself curiously eludes us. It seems that he did not possess those winning graces which make such attractive figures out of many of his contemporaries. His Feast subsequently came to be observed on 19 September, but there has long been doubt over his sainthood. It was as an administrator and organiser that he made his mark, and the instinct of the Church has never recognised in such men the true life-blood of Christianity.

Theodore was succeeded in July 692 after a vacancy of nearly two years by Berhtwald, abbot of Reculver,[42] a capable prelate who seems to have maintained his authority over the other bishops. In this connection we possess the first letter known to have been written by one Englishman to another.[43] It is from Waldhere, bishop of London, to Berhtwald, in 704 or 705. Waldhere says he is due to attend a council for the settlement of differences between the kings of Essex and Wessex, involving clerics, and he asks the primate's permission to go. The authority built up by Theodore was still a reality. During Berhtwald's primacy the number of bishops was increased. Two dioceses were founded which would endure until the Norman Conquest—Sherborne in 705 and Selsey in 709.[44] But according to Bede, although Berhtwald was a very learned man, he was not comparable with his predecessor.[45]

Meanwhile on Theodore's death Wilfred had reasserted his claims. He could not have been happy about the settlement of 686, though he again demanded the whole of his former diocese, but Aldfrith insisted that he must observe the terms of its division. There followed in 691 Wilfred's second expulsion. It was perhaps on this occasion that Aldhelm, the great scholar of whom we shall be hearing more, wrote a letter to the abbots of Wilfred's monasteries which has been preserved by William of Malmesbury, calling on Wilfred's clergy to support their master in his exile, and reminding them of the contempt deserved by those who were unfaithful to their lord.[46] For eleven years Wilfred was in Mercia, where king Aethelred welcomed him 'with great honour on account of his reverence for the Apostolic see'.[47] He was given episcopal work, apparently as bishop of Leicester, and was particularly active in the founding of monasteries.[48]

But he was still determined on a restoration to his Northumbrian properties, and about the end of the seventh century he again brought the matter to the notice of Rome, though he did not himself journey thither. Sergius I referred the question back to the English Church, and the result was a council at Austerfield, on the southern Northumbrian borders, in 702, convened by Aldfrith. Wilfred attended in company with several abbots of his monasteries, and archbishop Berhtwald was himself present, with most of the bishops. There was a sharp debate, in which Wilfred upbraided his opponents for contentiously standing out against the decrees of three popes, Agatho, Benedict, and Sergius.

According to Eddius, the archbishop and the king proposed that Wilfred should surrender every item of his property in Northumbria and Mercia. But there was opposition to this harsh move, directed towards an eminent man against whom after all no crime was alleged. It is clear that Wilfred's opponents had been goaded beyond measure by his unreasonable persistence in demanding the restoration of the old situation, and by preferring his own interests to the general good of the Church. But they relaxed a little, and agreed that he should retain the monastery of St Peter at Ripon, provided that he solemnly agreed in writing to confine himself to the abbey precincts and abandon all episcopal functions. Wilfred indignantly protested, pointing out that it was he who had taken the initiative in rooting out Celtic errors, in converting Northumbria to the true Easter and tonsure, in introducing the method of two choirs chanting alternately, in establishing the Benedictine rule. He might with justice have reminded his hearers of his missionary labours also, and of his achievements in building great churches. He again appealed to Rome. Both the king and primate considered that he had made his fault all the greater in thus preferring Rome's judgement to theirs. Aldfrith wished to put him under arrest, but this would have been a violation of the safe-conduct under which he had come to the council. The bishops refused to be party to such action, and instead he was deposed from his episcopal office and allowed to depart. He made his way again to the friendly Mercian court.

After a solemn preparation of fasting and prayer by his monastic communities, Wilfred set out on his third and final visit to Rome. Amongst his companions was Acca, subsequently bishop of Hexham. Eddius says that Wilfred made the journey on foot, though he was by now seventy years old. Soon after landing on the Continent he called on Willibrord, working as a missionary at this time in Frisia, a visit which must have been of great interest to Wilfred with his early memories of this region. The party arrived in Rome early in 704.

Wilfred was kindly received by John VI,[49] to whom meanwhile had been forwarded messengers from archbishop Berhtwald, with a written statement of the charges against Wilfred. A synod of neighbouring bishops was called to judge the case. Wilfred asked it to confirm previous papal decrees in his favour, to the effect that his old see of York should be restored to him, or at least his monasteries of Hexham and Ripon. The counter-charge against him was that he contumaciously refused to accept the synodical decrees of the English Church. The synod in Rome dragged on for four months, consisting of no less than seventy sittings; the protracted proceedings are evidence of the importance with which the case was regarded in Roman eyes. It seemed that deadlock had been reached, when it was recalled that twenty-five years previously Wilfred had supported the Roman Church over the Monothelite question. This offered a welcome way out of the impasse, and the pope declared Wilfred innocent of the charges against him, affirming the decrees of his predecessors on his behalf. Berhtwald was ordered to call a synod in England to settle the matter, and kings Aethelred and Aldfrith to implement the papal decrees. It was a skilful move on the part of the papacy. Rome had avoided having to make a definite award in a difficult case, it had placated Wilfred by formally confirming previous decrees, and had been politic in referring to Canterbury the final decision. It is a classic example of the art of evading responsibility, in which ecclesiastics were to become supreme masters.

Wilfred set out on his return journey, bearing with him as usual relics and rich vestments of silk and purple for his churches, along with the papal letters for the archbishop and the two kings.[50] On the way home he fell ill, and during four days and nights lay in a trance at Meaux, receiving a vision of St Michael, who told him that through the

Blessed Virgin's intercession he would live a further four years. The archangel assured him that on his return to England his most valued possessions were to be restored to him, and he would end his days in peace. He was reminded that though he had built churches in honour of St Peter and St Andrew, he had raised no edifice to St Mary, an omission which he must put right. Wilfred related the dream to his faithful priest Acca, who in turn later told it to Eddius.

On his return Wilfred found that his good friend Aethelred was king of Mercia no longer. He had resigned his crown for the life of religion, and was now abbot of Bardney, in Lindsey. The two men met, kissed each other, and wept for joy. Aldfrith of Northumbria was so weary of Wilfred's importunate pleadings that he refused even to discuss anything further relating to him. Not long afterwards, towards the end of 705, the scholarly king died, at Driffield in the East Riding. According to the record of Eddius, the death of Aldfrith was the result of divine vengeance, and the king was truly penitent before the end, realising his error in opposing the judgements of the Apostolic see. His death was a sad event for Northumbria. He was succeeded by Eadwulf, the first of many weak kings who ruined the fortunes of the northern kingdom.

Meanwhile, in obedience to the pope, Berhtwald called a synod, held by the river Nidd. The episcopate was not so well represented as at Austerfield, and the archbishop was the only southern prelate to make the journey. It is probable that most men were by now somewhat bored with Wilfred. A final compromise was reached, in which the decrees of Agatho, Benedict, and Sergius, were once more ignored. Though it might have been possible, through a vacancy caused by the death of bishop Bosa about this time, to have restored Wilfred to the York see, this was not done, and Wilfred's last opportunity to satisfy his ambition was gone. John of Beverley was translated from Hexham to York, and Wilfred was given the see of Hexham. He also recovered the monastery of Ripon, besides all his possessions in Mercia and Northumbria. The reconciliation was sealed by a Eucharist in which the bishops joined in the breaking of bread, after which they 'returned to their homes in the peace of Christ'.

Wilfred spent the next three or four years in peace. Then, feeling the approach of death, he made his final arrangements. In the presence of some of his monks at Ripon, he opened his hoard of gold, silver, and jewels, which he bade them divide in four parts: the first and second for the churches of SS. Mary and Paul at Rome, and for the poor, respectively, the third for the abbots of Hexham and Ripon to enable them to 'purchase the friendship of kings and bishops', and the fourth part to his faithful companions who had shared his exile with him. After further business, the bishop gave the monks his blessing, and thereafter, as a community, 'they saw his face no more'. He proceeded southwards and made a final visitation of his Mercian monasteries, taking care to increase their endowments, and 'gladden their hearts with money'. Finally, he reached his monastery of St Andrew at Oundle, where his last illness overtook him. Here the great Christian warrior died peacefully, without a groan or murmur. His body was carried in solemn procession to Ripon, where it was interred on the south side of the altar. The year of his death was 709, and he was about seventy-five years of age.

Wilfred was without question the greatest personality in the English Church of the seventh century, but it is difficult to form a true and satisfying estimate of him. Though he was a champion of the Roman Church, it is probable that even those who had the Roman cause most at heart found him sometimes a source of embarrassment. Nothing is more significant than the sparseness with which Bede treats him, though he must have been fully acquainted with the details of his career. Very damaging also to Wilfred's reputation is the steady opposition shown to him by some of the finest characters of the time, such as Theodore, the abbess Hild, the scholarly and able king Aldfrith, all of whom had the best interests of the Church in England at heart. There can be no doubt that in everyday life his personal character was a winning one, and he gathered a party round him which loved him to the end. The converts of Frisia and especially Sussex had good cause to reverence him, though his greatness as a missionary should not be exaggerated. His missionary tours were but episodes in his career, the grand aim of which was far removed from pure evangelistic zeal. Almost to the end of his life he pursued with striking persistence the goal of episcopal oversight of all Northumbria, even when it had become clear to all fairminded observers in England that the public well-being of the Church required otherwise. His zeal for his own rights and position was as keen as his devotion to the Apostolic see, and it is possible to argue that in his own lifetime he did as much harm as good to the Roman cause in England. The repeated rejection of papal decrees in Wilfred's favour is very striking. The case of Wilfred taught men to be cautious of Roman intervention. On the other hand, after the time of Wilfred there were no further cases of arbitrary deposition of Anglo-Saxon prelates by the king or metropolitan, and his appeal to Rome had set a precedent which would be taken up in later generations by men with a grievance.

In his character and outlook Wilfred was ahead of his time, pointing the way forward to the Church of the middle ages, the proudest institution in human history. Spirituality was present in him, but joined with a sense of the importance of grandeur in temporal affairs. It was his ostentatious ways, his splendid retinue, his many possessions, which produced much of the opposition from a generation which remembered the simple ways of Aidan and heard daily of the austerities of Cuthbert. It could scarcely be said of him that he was a despiser of wealth. He was far-seeing, however, in his realisation that rich possessions are necessary for a Church which is to do its work effectively in the world. The opprobrium which was his lot was such as will inevitably be experienced by any Christian body which possesses wealth.

In positive favour of Wilfred we have his introduction of the Benedictine Rule to his native land, and his advocacy of Roman ways. The last, it should hardly be necessary to point out, was no mere matter of the shape of the tonsure and the date of Easter. Romanism brought with it amongst other things a dignified and beautiful architecture, to provide a worthy setting for the grave and decorous manner of singing the mass and office known as Gregorian chant. Wilfred was in fact one of the pioneers of that wonderful development, medieval worship, in which mind and heart are at rest with eternal verities. It was largely through Wilfred that the Catholic and Roman culture which has meant so much in the formation of Western civilisation was first made part of the English religious tradition.

Though not a scholar like his contemporary and sympathiser Aldhelm, Wilfred was skilful in debate. He had a sense of the dramatic, as when at the dedication of his Ripon minster he stood before the altar in the presence of kings, and facing the congregation read aloud a catalogue of lands given to him, along with a list of churches which the British clergy had deserted when fleeing before the English warriors.

It must be remembered, finally, that not all of Wilfred's life was spent in contentions. His faults rivet themselves so firmly on one's consciousness, and indeed are so disingenuously inserted into the narrative of his life by the admiring Eddius, that it is easy to overlook the long periods when he was patient under rebuffs. Despite his undoubtedly rough treatment by Theodore, we see him quietly at work in the midland countryside and elsewhere for years on end, building minsters and instructing the people. He was of the type which can inspire both love and hate. He had his bitter enemies, particularly in the Northumbrian royal house, but there can be no denying the affection in which he was held by those who lived closest to him, who believed him to be 'a great man and faithful servant' who after death found a home with God and His saints.[51]

CHAPTER X

MONKS AND NUNS
IN EARLY ENGLAND

During the century or two after the coming of Augustine monasticism occupied a more important part in relation to the whole life of the English Church than it has done at any time since. This was particularly so in those parts of the country most deeply influenced by the Celtic missions, in which the monastery was the primary unit; but in the dioceses of the Roman mission the monastic institute was also regarded with the highest reverence. There was scarcely a time in the whole history of the Anglo-Saxon Church, except perhaps during the years immediately following the Danish invasions of the ninth century, when it would have occurred to men that Christian life and culture could even exist without the monastic profession. The monk was the most highly regarded of men, and he was the prime mover in virtually all Christian enterprise.

Christian monasticism was born in the Middle East. The Greek word 'monos' ('alone') in itself indicates the nature of the first stage of the movement, during which individuals separated themselves from society and lived as solitaries. The earliest known Christian hermit seems to have been Paul of Thebes,[1] who lived in a grotto on the Red Sea coast, where amongst his visitors was Anthony, a Copt who lived from c. 251 to 356.[2] The latter adopted the life of asceticism, and in 285 established himself in a solitary fastness in the Thebaid.[3] This eremitical type of the religious life spread rapidly in Egypt, and also in Syria—where it developed along extremely austere lines.[4]

Solitariness is contrary to human nature, however, and it was not long before hermits were drawing together in a manner of life best described as semi-eremetical. Each would have his own cell, but the cells would be contiguous, the members of the 'community' meeting only on Saturday and Sunday for the Liturgy. This intermediate stage (which in later times was to be revived by the Carthusian and other orders) prepared the way for the coenobitic type of monasticism, which was generally to prevail both in East and West. Its founder was

Pachomius (*c.* 290–345),[5] who founded a monastery on an island of the Upper Nile. All the brethren lived under a common roof, and were subject to organised discipline. Pachomius founded eight monasteries for men, and possibly also some houses for women. Extreme austerity remained a feature of his system, but it was considerably modified by Basil of Caesarea, who developed a coenobitic way of life in which all the monks ate, slept, and worshipped together.

In 360 Martin founded a monastery in the neighbourhood of Poitiers, soon removed to Marmoutier near Tours. This was followed in the course of half a century by the famous house of Lérins, founded by Honoratus,[6] and two monasteries of Cassian near Marseilles. In his *Institutes* and *Collations* Cassian describes a system which is deeply influenced by the monasticism of Egypt. This same Eastern influence is discernible in the Celtic monasteries of Wales and Ireland, which, however, had highly distinctive features.

The repugnance towards the monastic life which is widespread in our own day amongst Protestants would scarcely have been understood by Christians of the fourth and fifth centuries, to whom the 'religious' were men and women making a serious attempt to obey the command of Christ that all should be forsaken. Monasticism was not unnatural or irresponsible. On the contrary, it was scriptural. The monks were the professional soldiers of the Christian army, highly disciplined and under constant training for warfare against the world, the flesh, and the devil. The end of persecutions heralded by the Edict of Milan in 313 also gave an impetus to the monastic life. Heroic and fanatical Christians, deprived of the State as their natural enemy, directed their spiritual weapons against the demons of the deserts, rocks, and caves.

When St Benedict of Nursia (died *c.* 547) founded his monastery at Monte Cassino and drew up his Rule, he had no intention of founding an Order. His Rule was designed for one house or group of houses, and did not at first spread widely. The ultimate triumph of the Rule was, however, secured by its inherent excellence, its freedom from trivialities, and its firm foundation upon rational principles.

Though Benedict was conversant with the Eastern type of monasticism, he debarred extreme asceticism from his scheme, which was intended to be something possible for the average devout man. The monastery was 'a school for the service of God'. A postulant was required to promise not only celibacy and poverty, but also obedience to the abbot and life-long membership of the house which he proposed to enter ('stability'). There were no private cells, and the monastic property was corporately held. Each monk was required to share in the agricultural and domestic work of the community, which so far as possible should be self-sufficient, with its own water, mill, gardens, and bakery. The life was simple and hard, probably differing little as far as its material standards were concerned from that of the contemporary Italian peasant. No attempt was made to design specifically conventual buildings, and probably for most of Benedict's monasteries an ordinary Italian dwelling-house was used, its open court becoming the prototype of the medieval cloister. The most important function of the monks was the recitation of the *opus Dei*, which took precedence of all other activities. An hour or two after midnight there was sung the night office of nocturns (now more generally known as matins), in accordance with the example of the psalmist, 'At midnight I will rise to give thanks unto thee.'[7] This was followed by reading and meditation. Labour in the fields occupied the daytime, with the lesser 'hours' of prayer at three-hourly intervals. Vespers was sung at the close of the day's work, and the day itself closed with night prayers, after the 'collation' or reading from sacred books.[8] Strict silence was then observed, and the monks retired to bed very early, thus ensuring their full quota of sleep. Mass was not said daily, but was sung on Sundays and holy-days. The plainest of clothes were worn, but its actual character was decided by the abbot, according to the nature of the climate. Normally, however, a cowl and tunic would suffice, with boots and stockings for the feet. For bedding a monk was permitted a mattress, two woollen blankets, and a pillow. A monk's bed was regularly searched for private property, which was strictly forbidden. Besides his clothes, the only articles a monk was allowed to have about him were a knife, pen and tablets, and a needle and handkerchief. The executive officers of the monastery were known as *decani*—one for every ten brethren. The abbot was elected by the whole house, and held office for life. He was to be obeyed without question, but at the same time must act with the counsel of his brethren, the advice of the entire community being sought in grave problems.

It was essentially the life of a Christian community living very plainly, from which both luxury and extreme austerity were debarred. Absent too was scholarship. We find no trace in St Benedict's Rule of that passion for learning which was to become so marked a feature of the life of the Benedictine Order in later centuries. Moreover, it was not usual for the monk at this stage to be in holy orders. The earliest brethren were laymen, following a vocation of prayer and humility.

Monte Cassino survived the death of its founder about fifty years. It then became the victim of Lombard raids, and was not restored until the early years of the eighth century. Despite this violent interruption, however, the Rule survived; its great rival in the sixth and seventh centuries, the Celtic system, gradually gave way before it, and St Benedict was increasingly recognised as the Father of western monks.

In the sixth century it would certainly not have been possible to speak of a Benedictine Order, and Benedict's Rule was one amongst many guides to the religious life. Several houses no doubt based their lives on the Rule, while others adapted certain of its features along with those of other rules. Even Benedict himself had acknowledged his debt to Basil. There must certainly have been a good deal of eclecticism on the part of monastic communities at this time. Nevertheless, the Benedictine type of monasticism steadily became more widely known, and received a strong encouragement from the patronage of Gregory the Great. It is reasonably certain that the Rule was observed in the monastery of St Andrew on the Caelian, and that a knowledge of it was introduced into Kent by Augustine and his band in 597. They are only known to have founded one monastery, that of SS. Peter and Paul[9]—the later St Augustine's—and we have no explicit evidence that the Rule was introduced at this time. But it is almost inconceivable that it was not used at least as a basic guide for the general life of the community, and in this sense we may perhaps justifiably regard this house as the first Benedictine house in England, and indeed the earliest to be established outside Italy.[10]

In the Anglo-Saxon kingdoms as a whole, however, it was the Celtic form of the monastic institute which made the greatest progress in the immediate future. In the north especially its influence was far reaching. The midlands saw the foundation of monasteries whose general type is uncertain, but which do not seem to have been Benedictine houses in the usually accepted sense. In Northumbria Benedictinism was first introduced by Wilfred, as he himself explicitly claims in the catalogue of personal achievements which he listed in his self-defence before king Aldfrith. 'Did not I arrange the life of the monks according to the rule of the holy father Benedict which none had introduced there before?'[11] It was, however, Benedict Biscop who was chiefly responsible for the firm establishment of the monastic life according to the Benedictine Rule in the northern kingdom.

Biscop Baducing (to give him his natural name) was born c. 628 into a noble family, in course of time entering the service of Oswy king of Northumbria.[12] But receiving a call to 'take service under the true King', in 653 he made the first of his many visits to Rome,[13] having been selected as companion for Wilfred, then a youth of nineteen. He made his second visit to Rome in 665, and then spent some two years at the island monastery of Lérins, where he was professed and probably received the name in religion by which he has since been known. Returning to Rome in 667, he was requested by Vitalian to accompany Theodore to England as general guide and interpreter. On arrival in Kent he was appointed temporary abbot of SS. Peter and Paul, holding the office for two years. He was then succeeded by Hadrian, who meanwhile (it appears) had been mastering the native language. Biscop's fourth visit to Rome followed in 671.

Thus far Biscop appears as an indefatigable traveller and as a guide and helper to other men. His great creative work now followed. On his return from his fourth Rome visit, he was given some land on the north bank of the Wear by king Ecgfrith, with the instruction to build a monastery in honour of St Peter. This was in 674. The monastery of Wearmouth was to prove a foundation of incalculable importance in the history of English religion and culture. It was scarcely founded when Benedict was again on his journeys, this time to Gaul in search of masons to build for the monastery a church 'according to his beloved Roman manner'.[14] The resultant church still stands, containing much of the original work, a priceless jewel in a setting of dreary nineteenth-century industrialism. Glaziers were also imported, who made windows for the church, and taught their craft to the English. Vestments and church furniture were procured. When all was ready, the church was consecrated with the solemn celebration of mass. Books which Biscop had purchased at Rome and Vienne in the course of his travels were deposited in the monastery—a simple enough act in itself, but destined to have momentous consequences. The founder drew up a rule for the brethren, based certainly on that of St Benedict, but drawing also on the customs of the seventeen monasteries which Biscop had visited.[15] The Wearmouth foundation had its teething troubles, some of the more aristocratic monks rebelling against the discipline imposed. But Biscop had a good and loyal prior in Ceolfrith, a pupil of Wilfred's at Ripon, who had studied monasticism at various houses. Some five years after the foundation of Wearmouth, Benedict Biscop again set out for Rome, accompanied by Ceolfrith, who was anxious to learn the rules of the monastic life as observed at the centre of western Christendom. Pope Agatho received Biscop favourably, and granted him a bull of privilege for his monastery. During this visit he obtained the services of John,[16] precentor of St Peter's and abbot of St Martin's, the latter being one of the various 'basilical' monasteries of Rome whose functions were primarily liturgical. The acquisition of a liturgical and musical expert was the chief significance of this fifth visit to Rome. The pope, however, used the occasion to secure the Anglo-Saxon Church against the Monothelite heresy, at this time very troublesome, especially in the Church of Constantinople. John was instructed to take with him to Northumbria a copy of the decrees against the heresy recently promulgated at a synod in Rome, and on his return was to report on the orthodoxy of the English Church. In 680 Biscop returned home to Wearmouth, with Ceolfrith and John. A period of intensive instruction in Gregorian chant followed, monks from most of the Northumbrian monasteries visiting Wearmouth to benefit from the presence there of the master from Rome. John moreover not only taught singing, but also committed to writing for the use of the Wearmouth monks a description of the whole course of religious festivals as observed in the Roman Church. On his way back to Rome, John the Chanter died. But the testimony of the faith of the English which he carried with him was conveyed to Rome, and received with much satisfaction by the pope.

Meanwhile king Ecgfrith, seeing that his donation of land to Benedict had been put to profitable use, presented him with a second estate, at Jarrow a few miles south of Wearmouth. In the autumn of 681, twenty-two of the Wearmouth brethren were led by Ceolfrith to occupy the conventual buildings of the new monastery. Dedicated to St Paul, it was constituted a joint foundation with that of St Peter at Wearmouth. A church was commenced of which much, as in the case of Wearmouth, survives in the present parish church.[17] Of the first band of brothers twelve were novices still awaiting the tonsure. One of these twelve was a small boy aged eight who had recently been given to Benedict Biscop as a child-oblate. His name was Bede.

In 685 Biscop made his sixth and final journey to Rome. On his return he found the Jarrow community stricken with disaster. Plague had carried off all the monks who were able to sing the office, excepting abbot Ceolfrith and one small boy, who can have been none other than Bede. The two had attempted to sing the psalmody without the antiphons, but after a week of the maimed rite, Ceolfrith could bear it no longer, and the singing of the full office had been resumed, while new choir monks were being trained.

Soon after his return Biscop was laid low by a paralytic disease, and his end was certain. He exhorted the brethren to observe the rule he had compiled for them, based on his wide experience; to preserve carefully the library which he had established; and especially to choose a successor on grounds of personal merit and not of noble birth. He would rather, he declared, his monastery became a wilderness than that his own brother, who was unfit for the office, should succeed him.[18] In the event he left the brethren little choice. On his sick-bed he sent for Ceolfrith, abbot of Jarrow, and with the approval of all, made him abbot of the joint foundation. Benedict survived for a few more months, dying on 12 January 689.

Though the monasteries of Wearmouth and Jarrow owed so much to the personality and individuality of their founder, they were fundamentally Benedictine houses, and have always been recognised as such.[19] On the whole, however, the Rule was not strictly observed in England at this time. The founder of a house was free to enjoin any rule or combination of rules he chose, and there was therefore much variety. It seems, for example, to have been a frequent practice—though not at the monasteries of Biscop—for monks to occupy their own cells, in contradiction to the strict requirement of a common dormitory. Again, Anglo-Saxon monks did not always observe St Benedict's injunction concerning the democratic election of the abbot. The aristocratic spirit was strong in Anglo-Saxon monasteries. Abbots and abbesses were repeatedly succeeded by their blood relations, as when Wilfred carefully arranged for his nephew to succeed him at Ripon. On the whole, however, we are probably justified in believing that by c. 700 at most houses, the Benedictine Rule influenced the character of the life.

Monasteries were recruited partly through genuine vocations of adult men and women, and partly by the system of child-oblation. Though the practice of offering small children for life-long service in religion has long been discontinued by the Church—indeed for some centuries before the Reformation—there is little or no evidence that it was repugnant to the Anglo-Saxon religious consciousness. It had Biblical precedence, as in the case of Samuel.[20] Bede is an instance of a child-oblate who made an excellent monk and who so far as we know never wished to change his station. There is no reason for supposing that in his contentment he was exceptional. Amongst other religious dedicated at an early age may be mentioned the infant daughter whom Oswy offered to God on the eve of the battle of the Winwaed, who eventually became a most worthy abbess, successor of Hild at Whitby.[21] The irrevocable character of the act of child-oblation is shown by the case of an infant who was restored to life by Wilfred and offered to him by the grateful parents. The latter subsequently repented of their generosity, and wished to keep their son, but the saint insisted on receiving him to be trained in the monastic life. It would be unjust to censure Wilfred for harshness in this respect—the principle involved was that of the sanctity of an oath, a matter of more concern in a primitive and loosely bound society than any considerations of human happiness.

The most interesting feature of Anglo-Saxon monasticism during this early period was the institution of the double monastery.[22] Such a house, it is important to remember, was not a mixed community of men and women, but really two closely adjacent monasteries under a single head. Double monasteries were not unknown elsewhere in the western world of the seventh and eighth centuries, and the English institution was essentially an importation. Such houses existed in the earliest days of monasticism in the East, and arose from the purely practical need of a convent of women for the services of priests. Thus the sister of St Pachomius established a house for women close by her brother's monasteries; and St Basil's monks were within easy reach of the community ruled by his sister. Double communities became common in the East, but were proscribed by Justinian.[23]

There were double houses in Ireland, as at Kildare, and doubtless the institution in England owed something to Irish influence.[24] But it probably owed more to Gaul. In the sixth century and later there were Gallic double monasteries, as at Faremoutiers-en-Brie,[25] a nunnery where there were men living in separate buildings—and Poitiers, where a community for women apparently had a close association with a male house in the vicinity. When Theodore arrived in England he condemned the principle of double monasteries, which indicates that they certainly existed here and probably from as early as the middle of the seventh century. He did not, however, attempt to suppress them. Amongst monasteries which followed the double system were Bardney, Much Wenlock, Repton, and Ely, and the two famous houses of Whitby and Wimborne. The last named was founded by two sisters of Ine, king of Wessex, who ruled it in succession. We know something of its life and organisation from the account given by Rudolf of Fulda, the German biographer of Leoba, one of its nuns, who went out to help Boniface.[26] Rudolf says that in ancient times two monasteries were established in Wimborne, for men and women respectively, each enclosed by strong and lofty walls. It was strictly enjoined from the outset that entrance to each house be barred to persons of the opposite sex. The only exceptions made were in favour of the priests who said mass, and even they were required to depart from the women's house immediately their function was ended. So strict was the seclusion of the women that the abbess conducted business with her monks through a window. According to Rudolf, one abbess named Tetta was so anxious to isolate her nuns from the company of men, that the very bishops were denied admission. At Barking, another double house, the separation between the men's and women's quarters was so complete that when plague carried off the men it seems to have been some time before any of the women fell victims.[27] Bede's text makes it probable, too, that the men and women had separate churches. But it is pleasing to find a certain amount of affection existing between the sexes, as when the nuns, after singing their matins, left their church to visit the graves of their stricken brethren.

The segregation in fact was not equally strict everywhere, and there is evidence that at some monasteries the monks and nuns may have seen something of each other. Thus Aldhelm writes in one of his poems of monks and nuns singing the office antiphonally. 'Let us all with triumph celebrate this day, and sing to Christ the God alternate hymns. . . . Let antiphons with sweet accents strike the ear, and the ode of psalms clang with the double trumpet. . . . Let us, brothers, praise the Almighty with accordant voice, and the band of sisters join us in frequent song. Let us give forth under the vault of the temple hymns and psalms and festal responsaries, making melody with the modulations of the psaltery, and strike as the psalmist bids the ten-stringed lyre. Let each one adorn the new shrine with voice, and the brother or sister who reads, the lector, or lectrix, untie the sacred volumes.'[28] The repute of the double monasteries was high, only

Coldingham in Bernicia giving cause for anxiety. Here both brethren and sisters were idle and fond of gossip, and moreover much addicted (in the case of the nuns) to extravagance in dress. A fire which destroyed the Coldingham house was held by contemporaries to be divine vengeance for its prevailing laxity.[29] It was by reason of the Coldingham case that St Cuthbert was said to have ordered all females to be excluded from his church at Lindisfarne, a rule which was long obeyed in any churches where his body had rested.

Though there were many houses exclusively for men, it appears that double monasteries were the only institutions providing for nuns. These were invariably ruled by women, and the double arrangement was apparently simply dictated by practical necessity. The services of men were needed in the general life of any community which aimed at self-sufficiency.[30] They were required not only for the administration of the sacraments, but also for heavy field labour and the indispensable hunting of game.

The double monastery was at its zenith in the seventh century, and exercised great influence on the religious life of the nation particularly through a number of outstanding abbesses. Afterwards it fell slowly into disfavour,[31] and passed out of existence during the general eclipse of monasticism in the course of the disturbed ninth century. In the second phase of Anglo-Saxon monasticism, associated with the tenth-century revival, double monasteries played no part. The sheer necessity for nuns of the co-partnership of men in those troublous times is shown by the insignificance into which nunneries fell with the disappearance of the double monastery. At the time of the Norman Conquest there were only nine nunneries in the whole of England.

Abbesses were frequently of royal or aristocratic blood. The most celebrated, and one of the most influential women in English history, was Hild.[32] Daughter of Hereric, a nephew of king Edwin, she was reared in heathenism, but became a Christian at the age of thirteen, being amongst the converts baptised along with Edwin on Easter Eve 627. We next hear of her spending a year in East Anglia with the intention of crossing over to Gaul to join the monastic community at Chelles. But she was invited by Aidan to return to Northumbria, and in 649 became abbess of a house near Hartlepool. Here she succeeded Heiu, the first Northumbrian woman to become a nun. At Hartlepool—where the graves of her nuns were discovered during the course of excavations in 1833—she was frequently visited by Aidan, who held her in the highest regard, and by other discreet men. It was while at Hartlepool that she received into her care the infant Aelfled, daughter of Oswy. In 657 she founded the monastery at Streoneshalh, better known by its later Danish name of Whitby. Here the woman whom all came to revere as 'mother' established a community in which, after the manner of the infant Church, there were neither rich nor poor but where everything was held in common. Princes came to seek her counsel. The study of scripture was strictly enjoined on the monks, and Whitby indeed came to be regarded as in some sense a training ground for priests. No fewer than five of Hild's pupils became bishops —Bosa, Hedda, Oftfor, John of Beverley, and Wilfred II. In the personality of this great woman, instructed and baptised by Paulinus and later strengthened in the Faith by Aidan, we see a meeting of Roman and Celtic Christianity. We also recognise in her the type of woman held in high honour amongst the Germanic peoples, the woman whose *rede* or counsel was universally respected, in whom (according to Tacitus) resided 'a holy and prophetic sense'.[33] The last years of Hild's life were clouded with illness, until she died in 680.

St Hild was by no means exceptional amongst Anglo-Saxon religious women. There was, for example, the notable abbess Etheldreda, one of the four daughters of Anna king of the East Angles who all became heads of nunneries. Born *c.* 630 in Suffolk, she married Tonbert, a fenland chieftain, from whom she received as a wedding-gift the isle of Ely, comprising an area of six hundred hides surrounded by marsh. Subsequently, after the death of her first husband, she married Ecgfrith of Northumbria. Marriage, however, was distasteful to her, and she eventually managed to persuade Ecgfrith to allow her take the veil at Coldingham, where her husband's aunt was abbess. After a time Ecgfrith relented and came to reclaim her. She fled from Coldingham, and with miraculous assistance made good her escape to her territory in the fens. Here she founded a double monastery, the ancestor of the great medieval abbey and cathedral of Ely. She was supported in this enterprise by her cousin king Aldwulf, and was joined shortly by her sister Sexburga, previously queen to Eorconbert, king of Kent. After an abbacy of six years, marked by considerable austerity, she died of the plague in 679. She was succeeded in the headship of the house by Sexburga, who was in turn followed by her daughter and her granddaughter successively. The royal foundation of Ely is very clearly marked.

Scarcely less important perhaps in the life of the times was her near contemporary Mildred, daughter of a Herefordshire under-king, though little is known of her. She was closely associated with the foundation of the nunnery of Minster-in-Thanet, of which she became abbess. She seems to have been the one considerable saint of the Kentish Church. Her early background and training lay elsewhere, however, in the border country of the west where her father founded a double house at Leominster and her sister Milburga was abbess of Much Wenlock. Both St Etheldreda (also known as St Audry) and St Mildred became popular saints in the medieval English calendars.

It is hard to exaggerate the influence of the abbesses in seventh-century English Church history, an influence which may well have been as great as that of the abbots. One may search in vain the later history of the English Church for such an incident as that of Aldfrith, king of Northumbria, choosing two abbesses to whom to convey his last words and instructions—a trust and responsibility which one would have thought to attach rather to the bishop's office. These two particular women were Aelfled, abbess of Whitby, and Oedilburga, abbess of Hackness, whose monument amongst the fragments of Hackness church speaks of her as 'mater amantissima'.

Nuns made diligent students, and were particularly useful in helping to provide the raw material for scholarship through their patience in writing and copying. Until there were adequate facilities in England, it was customary for English ladies and girls to receive their education in Gallic convents, such as Faremoutiers-en-Brie, near Meaux, which was one of the most celebrated houses, founded in the seventh century by Fara under the influence of the Columban monasticism in the first instance, and much helped economically by an Englishwoman, Bathildis, queen of Clovis II.[34] Amongst its nuns was Eorcongota, daughter of Eorconbert, king of Kent. Its earliest abbesses included both a daughter and a step-daughter of Anna, king of the East Angles.[35] Other monasteries which seem to have made a speciality of educating girls from England were Andeley on the Seine, and Chelles on the outskirts of Paris.[36] We can be sure also that women of the cloister made their contribution to the beauty of Catholic worship by producing vestments and church embroidery, and in so doing laid the foundations of an art in which the Anglo-Saxons were in due course to achieve a continental reputation. Neither did they lack the brave and adventurous spirit, and in the great Age of Missions in the eighth century the nunneries of England were to provide helpers for Boniface and his companions in Germany.

Although there was much royal support for monasticism, it must not be forgotten that its growth was popular and spontaneous and in the final analysis not due to official encouragement, whether royal or ecclesiastical. The establishment of a religious house became an act of the commonest piety. Each had its founder, who might in fact have several houses under his ultimate control; thus Wilfred possessed several monasteries in scattered parts of England, ruled by abbots responsible to himself. Sometimes a mother-house sent out colonies, and the result was a family of monasteries. We see a free and natural urge to the religious life on the part of the Anglo-Saxons steadily acquiring discipline and organisation, and there can be no doubt that it was the monasteries, not the parishes, which were the backbone of the seventh- and eighth-century English Church.

The founder of a house assumed direct lordship over both the abbot of his house and all its properties. This was in full accord with Germanic ideas of proprietorship, and was a conception and practice making impossible a strict observance of the Rule of St Benedict. Thus, the founder of a monastery would claim, at least in some cases, the right of appointing its abbot. An interesting example of monastic ownership is the house founded by the father of St Willibrord on the mouth of the Humber, the ownership of which was still in the hands of his descendant Alcuin more than a century later. Probably the founding of a monastery was in most cases a pious act (or at least piety was an element in an amalgam of mixed motives), but its possession was sure to become a valuable perquisite. The monks were good agriculturists, and often succeeded by their patient labour in transforming barren heath or waste fen into productive land. Monasteries thus frequently became the object of aristocratic greed.

During this period of Anglo-Saxon monasticism we see the beginning of many houses which were to play a notable part in our religious and social history, though it must be remembered that direct continuity was broken in all, or almost all, cases by the invasions of the Northmen in the ninth century. Some of these houses have already been mentioned. Of others, we see Glastonbury, already a centre of Celtic Christianity, taken over by Saxon monks following the conquests of Ine, king of Wessex. The monastery of Evesham dates from c. 700. It is related how a herdsman of Egwin, bishop of Worcester,[37] called Eoves, claimed to have seen a vision of Our Lady, in which she appeared to him chanting heavenly songs. He reported the matter to his master, who visited the spot and likewise saw the vision.

More famous as a man than any of the individuals connected with the foundation of Glastonbury or Evesham was Guthlac (674–714).[38] Born of royal Mercian stock, in his early youth he took to the sport of private warfare, leading a band of comrades in a career of robbery with violence. After about nine years he conceived a loathing for this manner of life, and resolved to become a servant of Christ. Entering the double monastery of Repton, ruled over at this time by abbess Elfrida, he received the tonsure and was instructed in the mysteries of the ecclesiastical life. Here he remained for two years, and then decided to become a hermit, making his way to the fens. It is hard for the modern visitor to this highly cultivated if monotonous region to realise its character before the great draining operations of comparatively recent generations. In this strange and eerie region nature ran riot, and there was plenty of encouragement for a disordered human imagination.[39]

Here and there in the morass there were islands of firm land, and to one of these, called Crowland, Guthlac was guided in a fishing-boat by a fen-dweller Tatwine, who assured the young monk that it was devoid of human habitation though haunted by awesome creatures. Guthlac could wish for nothing better, and here he settled in 699. It was here that he fought his demons and made friends with the animals. His austerities became famous, and he received numerous visitors, including many of high degree. Amongst those who visited Crowland were Hedda, bishop of Lichfield, who admitted the hermit to the priesthood, and Aethelbald, future king of Mercia. No one, said Guthlac's biographer, ever saw him angry, excited, or sad. He died in early middle-age, but not before he had established a reputation for sanctity which in years to come would form the nucleus of the prosperity of one of the greatest medieval abbeys.[40]

The number of religious houses founded in the course of the seventh and eighth centuries must have been very large. Some of them doubtless came early to grief and died out through lack of postulants. Besides the substantial foundations with ample endowments and many inmates, there were great numbers of *monasteriola*, petty houses which could never have had more than a limited existence. It must have seemed to many of the more rationally minded churchmen that the monastic movement was over-reaching itself, that far too many of the best men and women were entering the religious life, while a dangerously high proportion of the land was securing exemption from the burden of secular service through being donated to monasteries.

Towards the close of his life Bede was acutely conscious of the danger, and in November 734 wrote to Egbert, a former pupil of his and now bishop of York. Bede recommended him to secure from Rome his see's promotion to an archbishopric, which was duly done in the following year. But Bede's main concern in his letter[41] lay in the falling standards of church life which he observed all around him. This letter is a clear indication that the original missionary impulse had slackened. Bede thinks there should be more parish priests and bishops to shepherd the people. He complains that according to common report many small villages and farmsteads in remote districts have not seen a bishop for years.[42] Confirmations are not being held,[43] and teachers are not available to instruct the people in their moral duties. The holy communion is neglected. Bede recommends daily communion, which, he says, is the constant practice throughout Italy and Gaul, Africa, Greece, and the East. In England, however, because of the carelessness of teachers, this devotion has so declined amongst the laity that even the more devout only communicate at Christmas, Epiphany, and Easter. Bede goes on to say that there are numerous folk, including young people, who might be brought to communicate each Sunday.

With the help of his kinsman king Ceolwulf, Egbert should try to implement pope Gregory's scheme for twelve northern bishops. Priests and teachers should be appointed to the villages, so that the holy mysteries might be celebrated, the gospel preached, baptism administered, and the Catholic Faith (as contained in the Apostles' Creed and the Lord's Prayer) be taught in the vernacular. Amongst the ignorant who only know their native tongue, Bede includes clergy and monks—he has often, he says, had occasion to provide Anglo-Saxon versions of the Creed and Lord's Prayer for priests devoid of Latin.

Basically, the letter is a plea for more sees, which Bede seems to think would go a long way towards solving the religious deficiencies of the north. At the time the only Northumbrian bishoprics were those of York, Lindisfarne, Hexham, and Whithorn. Bede recognises that the founding of new sees might prove difficult, as so much of the wealth that would have been useful for this purpose has been made over to the monasteries. A way out of the difficulty would be for new sees to be established in religious houses, and their bishops elected by the monks. Such episcopal monasteries would of course need increased revenues, and Bede suggests that institutions which were monasteries only in name might be annexed to them. There were many such places, he writes, which served no useful purpose to anyone. They neither benefited religion, nor provided soldiers towards meeting the menace of the barbarians (no doubt the Picts, following their victory at Nectansmere). Such pseudo-monasteries were simply places of refuge for renegade monks and for members of society who sought to evade all responsibility. We must make allowances for Bede's high standards, and for his love of order and discipline. The actual state of affairs may have been less degenerate than he infers. One would gladly know more of the system of family-monasteries, which he condemns out of hand. For some thirty years there had been a widespread practice whereby a man would found a monastery and rule it as abbot though continuing to live in it with wife and family. Amidst much abuse, there may well have been instances of devout families living a corporate life of devotion without the severance of natural ties.[44] But about the positively bad character of some houses Bede has no doubt whatever. He advises Egbert to look into the condition of all monasteries in his diocese. Some monasteries do not even have a priest, he complains, and the worship of God is shamefully neglected, though secular poetry and minstrelsy are given a ready welcome.[45]

That Bede's advice with regard to the suppression of useless monasteries was followed at least to some extent seems likely from a letter of pope Paul I to archbishop Egbert and his brother the king of Northumbria in 757–8. The pope mentioned the arrival in Rome of an abbot Forthred with a complaint that three monasteries granted to him by a certain abbess had been forcibly taken away from him and given to a layman.[46] The king was ordered to restore the monasteries to the abbot, and to ensure that laymen were not allowed to take over the properties of religious persons. It was always the orthodox ecclesiastical view that land and revenues granted to religion should remain so dedicated for ever, but Bede was sufficiently a patriot to realise that this would inevitably entail a material weakening of the realm in the long run. In the course of this century two powerful kings, Aethelbald of Mercia and Charles Martel on the Continent, were active in reclaiming from the Church material possessions urgently needed for secular purposes.[47]

That the monastic institute in England declined in fervour and efficiency during the eighth century seems undeniable, though the actual causes of the decline are not easy to recognise. The remorseless operation of human frailty must probably be taken into account. The high esteem in which monks and nuns were held had led to their enrichment, and this in turn to a growth of comfort and luxury with a parallel decay of spirituality. The best men and women of Anglo-Saxon cloisters, as we shall see, departed for sterner fields of service overseas. Religion in England, now a century and a half old, was no longer an adventure.

It was not primarily, however, decay from within, but rather external pressure which occasioned the collapse of the first line of Anglo-Saxon monasteries. In 793 the Northmen sacked Lindisfarne. The turn of Jarrow came in 794. Two or three generations of Englishmen were to live under the constant dread of heathen raids. The Church was brought to the verge of ruin. Christian civilisation hung in the balance. The monasteries, as the main depositories of the nation's wealth and art, were an obvious target. By the time of the settlement between Alfred and Guthrum in 878 the monastic institute in England had virtually ceased to exist.

CHAPTER XI

ARCHITECTURE AND ART
IN PRE-DANISH ENGLAND

The architectural history of Christian England begins with the mission of Augustine to Kent, where in the remains of a group of churches at Canterbury and elsewhere we have the means for a comparative study which can scarcely be rivalled in contemporary Europe. The Augustinian mission marked the resumption of solid building in this country. The group comprises some half-dozen or more churches in the southeast, with features of marked consistency. They have been discussed by several writers,[1] and the following account can do little more than underline knowledge which is already well known, but which can scarcely be omitted from a general survey of the Church and its culture in Anglo-Saxon times.

On his arrival in Kent in 597, Augustine used St Martin's for a while, until the church of SS. Peter and Paul was begun in the same year. At Augustine's death seven or more years later, the building of this church was still in progress. It was consecrated by archbishop Laurentius in 613.[2] What survives suggests a building twenty-seven feet wide, but the disappearance of the east end rules out the possibility of ascertaining the length. The church consisted of a nave, with a rectangular narthex eleven feet wide at the west end, and almost certainly a chancel at the east end. There was a chamber or porticus flanking the nave to the north-east, and a somewhat smaller one on the south-east, both serving as tomb-chapels. The larger one, known as St Gregory's, contained the tombs of the archbishops from Augustine to Deusdedit, six in all. The next two archbishops, Berhtwald and Theodore, were buried in the nave just outside the chamber, which was full by the time of their deaths. The smaller porticus, dedicated to St Martin, contained the graves of Ethelbert, Bertha, and the Frankish bishop Liudhard. In the extreme north-west corner of the church there is a further tomb, which contained the body of some unidentified person. Outside was a bench. The church was very small, and could clearly have played little part in the popular life of the Kentish Church. Its royal and episcopal character is pronounced.[3]

Very close geographically to SS. Peter and Paul, and indeed probably constituent parts of the same monastery, were the churches of St Mary and St Pancras. The former, which stood only a few yards to the east of SS. Peter and Paul, was founded c. 620 by Eadbald of Kent. Nothing remains except portions of the west wall. The surviving fragments of St Pancras, some eighty yards further to the east, are more substantial.

About the time of Augustine's death, Ethelbert founded a church at Rochester dedicated to St Andrew, whose rubble foundations still exist. A generation later, soon after 633, St Ethelburga founded St Mary's church at Lyminge, of which (as at Rochester) the foundations reveal the existence of an apse. Perhaps the most interesting, however, of this Kentish group of churches was one which was unfortunately dismantled in 1805, though not before it had been sketched by an obliging artist. This was the Reculver church of St Mary, which may reasonably be dated by an entry for 669 in the Chronicle informing us that king Egbert gave Reculver to his mass-priest Bassa, to enable him to build a church there. This church housed one of the finest pieces of Anglo-Saxon sculpture, carved on a cross which stood at the east end of the nave.

St Martin's church, a little to the east of the city of Canterbury, was already in use at the time of Augustine's arrival, as indeed it still is. It is probable that uninterrupted Christian worship has been maintained here for a longer period than in any other English church. Of the original building the chancel survives. The only church of the south-east group which is outside Kent is St Peter's, Bradwell-on-Sea, in Essex. Largely intact, it is almost certainly the church founded here in 653 by Cedd.

When we turn to consider the distinguishing characteristics of this group, we notice in the first place their small dimensions. None of these churches could ever have accommodated more than a comparative handful of worshippers at one time. They were missionary churches, whose founders held a position of which they were uncertain. Their structure not surprisingly was plain, devoid of costly ornament so far as we know, though of competent workmanship. It is clear that the architects and builders were imported from the Continent. The Anglo-Saxons constructed their buildings of wood, and though they were doubtless skilled carpenters, masonry and bricklaying must have been at this stage beyond them. The walls of the Augustinian churches were constructed of Roman brick, and the floors of mortar mixed with the dust of pounded brick—known technically as *opus signinum*. The most characteristic feature of these churches was the provision of chambers leading off from the nave. It seems that all churches of the group, except perhaps St Andrew's, Rochester, had one such porticus or more. At SS. Peter and Paul, and Reculver, the two most substantial of the churches, there was apparently something like a complete range of chambers around the north, west, and south sides of the nave. The western porticus of SS. Peter and Paul takes the form of a narthex, as we have seen, and while it is probably going too far to suggest[4] that this indicates the continued survival of the practice of separating the catechumens from the main body of worshippers in Augustine's time, it does at least show that the practice may not have been left so very far behind. It is not the least interesting and significant feature of English Church history that it begins in the deep twilight stage of Early Christianity, at the point where the latter was passing imperceptibly into the age of the Medieval Church.

Granted that there are traces of primitive Christianity in the Anglo-Saxon Church during its earliest stages, and in view of the fact that it was the Mediterranean lands which nurtured this early Faith, a brief consideration of the Christian architecture of the Middle East forms a helpful background to our studies.

It is in Syria that early Christian architecture may best be viewed, as there are in this region numerous church ruins of the fourth, fifth, and sixth centuries. Even so soon after the Peace of the Church as about the middle of the fourth century, there was a splendid edifice of the 'hall' type, with ten bays—the church of Julianos at Umm idj-Djimâl, whose piers and arches are of the highest workmanship.[5] Extremely beautiful too is the fifth-century church of St Mary, Shêkh Slemân,[6] of which the east end survives almost entirely, with much of the west end. There was a nave of six bays, with Ionic columns; the narthex consisted of a porch with four columns, to the west of which was an atrium. One more outstanding church may be mentioned here, that of Kalb Lauzeh, of *c.* 480 or perhaps later, which is largely intact.[7] It clearly foreshadows the Romanesque churches which in due course were to distinguish the architecture of Europe, and of which there are many imposing examples in England, France, Germany (especially the Rhineland), and northern Italy.

The churches of Syria contain many variations of the basilican style and of centrally planned buildings, and formed part of a civilisation of no mean order. During a period when Italy was being overrun by Germanic invaders, Syria enjoyed peace and prosperity, and produced not only churches but other public buildings of considerable dignity, besides private villas. This civilisation collapsed suddenly with the arrival of the Persians in 610–12 and the Arabs 633–8, and was never restored. So thoroughly had Syria been Christianised that even the smallest villages had their churches, and yet the Church's collapse early in the seventh century was final. There has been no revival of Christianity, and the churches have remained in ruins throughout medieval and modern times, serving for shelter to the shepherd and the nomad and as a sober lesson to those complacent optimists who may imagine that a Christian civilisation and culture is by its very nature eternal and indestructible.

Syrian architecture was 'one of the earliest expressions in stone of the new faith',[8] and its influence was great elsewhere in the Middle East and also in the West. Syrian churches had a number of common features. Thus, all were orientated, with a sanctuary at the east end. All had the two main divisions of nave and sanctuary. A very common arrangement was the provision of chambers on either side of the sanctuary. The chamber on the north side, known as the diaconicon, was the vestry or sacristy, where the sacred vessels were kept and the clergy robed; on the south side (as a rule) was the prothesis, where the deacon prepared the offerings of the congregation. The prevailing arrangement was for the diaconicon to open into the sanctuary, the prothesis into the south aisle, though there were many variations in this scheme. Where there was an opening between the diaconicon and the nave, it was usually a square-headed doorway; but the general tendency was for the prothesis to open into the nave through an open arch. The sanctuary itself might be either apsidal or rectangular in form.

The altar, at least in many cases, seems to have stood beneath a canopy or ciborium supported by columns, on a floor which was somewhat higher than the level of the nave. In many churches, as in that of St George at Zor'ah, there was apparently a ledge of solid stone around the curve of the apse, doubtless the bench for the clergy. There were other ceremonial arrangements, like the enclosed space at the east end of the central aisle, with an ornamented stone parapet, in the basilica at Zebed.[9] But this seems to have been unusual. More common was an interior semicircular wall situated directly opposite the apse, somewhat to the west of the middle of the church, as at Kharab Shems.[10] It indicates an enclosure with a low wall, possibly to accommodate a women's choir.

It is clear from surviving ruins that Syrian church architecture was a notable achievement and archeological evidence elsewhere suggests that it was influential in the development of Western culture. At the time when Syrian culture was at its zenith, numerous Syrian merchants and ecclesiastics were visiting Gaul and Italy.[11] Syrian influence in the West would certainly increase after the beginning of the seventh century,[7] with the conquest of the country by Persia and Islam, and an exodus westwards of Christian craftsmen.

The use of the diaconicon and prothesis was not generally adopted in the West, though it became normal in the Eastern Church. It spread to North Africa, Spain, and in some way difficult to understand also reached England. The use of subsidiary chambers was not adopted in Rome, and yet it is one of the most marked characteristics of the early Kentish churches. An apartment at the east end, overlapping the sanctuary and nave, is common, and in the Essex church of Bradwell the Syrian arrangement seems to have been almost exactly reproduced— here there was a north porticus opening into the chancel, and one on the south opening into the nave. It is not likely that the Eastern ceremonial, with its offertory procession from the prothesis round into the sanctuary, was ever carried out at Bradwell. But it is striking to find here the architectural plan which was created for that ceremonial, some fifteen or twenty years after the final collapse of the Syrian Church. It may be going too far to say that a Syrian refugee craftsman had something to do with the building of Bradwell. But the general adoption of side chambers by the architects of the early churches of south-eastern England—it is almost unique in the Western world—certainly points to Eastern influence, possibly by way of the Adriatic littoral.

Of similar type to the churches of the south-eastern group is that of Brixworth, Northamptonshire, probably the work of the monks of Medehamstede (the later Peterborough) c. 670.[12] It had a triple arcade, with porticus at the west end, and a semi-polygonal apse. The arches of the nave are of Roman brick. But the size of this church differentiates it from the Canterbury group. It is a spacious building, and even in its present contracted condition, with the arches walled in, there is an impression of great dignity. In the course of a generation the Christian community in England had grown, and the Church become more confident. Moreover, the work is inferior technically to that of the Canterbury churches, and this seems to point to the employment of English masons. The natives were beginning to learn the civilised arts, under the tutelage of the Church.

It is known that a considerable church was also built about this time at Abingdon.[13] But though we have a description of it, no traces have been found. It had the interesting feature of an apse at both the east and west ends, the earliest known example in the architecture of the West. The suggestion has been made[14] that this may have been a ritual arrangement for a double monastery, after the analogy of the Syrian churches, some of which have enclosures with low walls and a western apse towards the west end of the nave.

When we turn to Northumbria we find another group of seventh-century churches, from which, however, any trace of Eastern influence is absent. The two best known are those at Monkwearmouth, founded by Benedict Biscop c. 675, and Jarrow, whose chancel has been ascribed to this period, largely on the strength of the dedication stone now inside the church over the western tower-arch. This states that the church was dedicated in the fifteenth year of king Ecgfrith, which we know from Bede to have been in 685. Unfortunately, this is not positive proof that the chancel, the oldest part of the existing church, is of the original foundation, though there is a strong presumption in its favour as it is clearly very early Anglo-Saxon work. This chancel, 41 feet by $15\frac{3}{4}$ feet, is inferred to have been originally the nave. The oldest part of Monkwearmouth church is the west wall and the two-storied porch leading out from it, and is usually identified as Biscop's work. The tower is later, of the tenth or eleventh century. The plinth of the porch is an extremely early example of Anglo-Saxon Christian art, effective in its simplicity. Animals with their intertwined beaks support two balusters, on which in turn is an impost with another animal, perhaps a dog. A large figure in relief in the gable of the porch is so badly worn by the weather as to be unrecognisable.

Of about the same size as the original Jarrow church is the church of Escomb, also in County Durham. It is almost intact, and the best preserved of all churches of the post-Conversion period. The excellence of the radiated voussoirs of the tall chancel arch has led experts to think that the latter must be a re-erected Roman arch.[15] There was a fort close by at Binchester, as also at Corstopitum, which in turn provided material for the church of Corbridge, Northumberland, whose large and splendid western arch survives. The visible remains of Roman Britain must have been a marked feature of the seventh-century countryside. Their value as a quarry would be immediate and practical. But they may have been more than this, serving as a spur to the English to restore what their heathen forefathers had overthrown, and to show themselves worthy of the spiritual Rome which had brought them, in a sense, into the imperial fold.

Though it is clear that the Northumbrian group is later than the south-eastern, Monkwearmouth is the only example which can be dated with some certainty. The characteristics of these Northumbrian churches are markedly different from the Kentish. They are rectangular buildings, with high walls and small chancels. Such evidence as we have suggests a Gaulish influence, which is indeed what we would expect in view of Bede's express statement that Biscop imported masons from Gaul.[16] The proportions of the churches of Northumbria have been compared with those of a small church excavated at St Similien, Nantes, and with St Christophe de Suevres, a church probably founded c. 675.[17] The crude character of angels carved on stone slabs in the Poitiers Hypogeum, a building of the early seventh century, is also very similar to that of the angels on St Cuthbert's coffin at Durham. Finally, it is significant that the church of St Martin, Canterbury, where the Gallic ecclesiastic Liudhard ministered on behalf of Bertha, herself a Frank, is the only member of the English south-eastern group which reveals the Northumbrian characteristics. The evidence is somewhat fragmentary, but has a cumulative effect, suggesting the earliest church building in Northumbria to have been carried out under Gallic influence.

Wilfred is said to have built four churches at Hexham,[18] and one each at Ripon and York. Nothing survives save the crypt of St Andrew's Hexham, and that of Ripon. In addition, a little was learnt of the plan of St Andrew's when the modern nave was built. Fortunately we have the description by Eddius of his hero's churches. He cannot conceal his enthusiasm for the splendour of St Andrew's, extolling 'its crypts of wonderfully dressed stone, and the manifold building above ground, supported by various columns and many side aisles, and adorned with walls of notable length and height, surrounded by various winding passages with spiral stairs leading up and down'.[19] Eddius makes the bold claim that there is no other church north of the Alps built on such a scale. Bishop Acca subsequently enriched it with ornaments of precious metal, and provided altar frontals of purple silk.

Writing of the church at Ripon, Eddius says it was of polished stone, with columns and side aisles.[20] The church at York was essentially a restoration. Finding the existing building in a ruinous state, Wilfred renewed the roof with lead, and put glass into the windows to keep out the birds.[21] Towards the close of his life he erected a church at Hexham which he dedicated to St Mary. According to prior Richard it was almost round, with a porticus on each of the four sides.[22] It is the first instance in England of the centrally planned church. This ancient architectural form is Syrian and Byzantine, and there are five such churches by Constantine, in Jerusalem, Antioch, and Rome. Normally, however, such churches were intended as baptisteries or tomb-chapels rather than as public places of worship. The most notable example in the West, the church of St Vitale, Ravenna, was begun in 526, and carried out under distinctly Byzantine inspiration.[23]

After these examples there is a virtual gap in the history of English church architecture. For the eighth century and well into the ninth little is known to survive, though there may be fragments in village churches, belonging to this period, which it is difficult or impossible now to identify. Large churches are known to have been built, as by Ine (689–728) at Glastonbury, where excavations suggest a church with the Kentish characteristics, with flanking porticus and pink *opus signinum* floor. At York, archbishop Albert (767–80) built a church with columns and surrounded by chambers. It had no fewer than thirty altars, and was equipped with many upper compartments.[24] There is evidence that the Anglo-Saxons were fond of upstair chapels. In some cases, as at the later churches of Headbourne Worthy (near Winchester) and Bradford-on-Avon, it seems that surviving sculpture high up on interior walls may have formed part of the reredos of such chapels. Another known example of the eighth century was a church remarkable for its beauty which Offa built at St Albans.[25]

Of smaller churches containing portions in the present fabrics ascribed with some confidence to the eighth or earlier ninth century, we have Kirby Hill, Yorkshire, which has early vine-scroll ornament, and Britford near Salisbury, where the nave and two fine arches with vine-scroll are probably of this period. The ruined chapel at Heysham overlooking Morecombe Bay, Lancashire, and Somerford Keynes, Wiltshire, have early doorways, and there are indications that the latter was the work of Aldhelm.[26]

Of greater significance in the history of art are the sculptured stone crosses found throughout England, with a particularly high incidence in Northumbria and Mercia. For the seventh and eighth centuries there is nothing comparable with them elsewhere in Western Europe. So high is the excellence of much of the carving that some students have been unable to accept its early date. Mr W. G. Collingwood's theory[27] that the series began c. 740 with the Acca cross has, however, failed to gain general acceptance, and it is more probable that the beginnings of this art are to be ascribed to the last quarter of the seventh century.

It is not always remembered that by this time the English had been subject to Christian and civilising influences for almost a century, which is after all no mean span of time. A people unable to learn something from its teachers in two generations or more would be exceedingly boorish. It is likely, as we have seen, that by the time of the building of Brixworth c. 670 the English had learnt the art of masonry. Meanwhile, of course, the general building of stone churches was still a long way off. Perhaps the erection of a wooden cross in some convenient spot was the first intimation that the Church had arrived to proclaim its message to the inhabitants of an average village. Many of these crosses would be carved, and in course of time stone crosses would replace them. On the building of the first church, the cross would become superfluous, although in some cases it might be enshrined inside the building, as possibly at Reculver. There can be little doubt that the practical requirement of a focus for worship, during the preliminary stages when a village was dependent on occasional visits from the clergy of a neighbouring minster for its pastoral ministrations, was a primary cause of the initial erection of the standing crosses. This is the most satisfactory explanation of a phenomenon whose wide diffusion is by no means its least significant characteristic. The fact that there is seldom more than one cross, or its fragments, in one place is suggestive.

On the other hand, it is certain that many crosses were intended purely as memorials to the departed. Such is the case with the Acca cross. The twelfth-century writer Simeon of Durham informs us[28] that when Acca was buried outside the east end of Hexham church, two splendid crosses were placed on his grave, at the head and the feet. The present Acca cross consists of fragments which were discovered in scattered spots, one of which was near the east end of Hexham priory church, during restoration work in 1858. The celebrated cross at Bewcastle, Cumberland, is inscribed with the name of Cuniburga, daughter of Penda and wife of that Alchfrith (son of Oswy) who was closely associated with Wilfred. A less legible inscription seems to be a dedication to Alchfrith himself. This cross may well have been erected by Wilfred—it would be his way to do such a work in the grand manner such as we find at Bewcastle, and not by halves—as a memorial to Alchfrith, who disappears from history sometime between the Whitby conference in 663, at which he was present, and the death of his father in 670. In this case, the cross would probably be raised c. 670 and in any case not later than 709, the year of Wilfred's own death.

Of the same general type are the crosses which we are told were raised to mark the resting-places of Aldhelm's body on its journey from Doulting, where he died, to Malmesbury—as Edward I was to do centuries afterwards for his deceased queen Eleanor. On the route from Doulting to Malmesbury there was one cross every seven miles.[29]

Further, William of Malmesbury relates that in his day, in the earlier half of the twelfth century, there were two stone crosses ('pyramids'), sculptured and inscribed with names, including those of Kentwin, king of Wessex (676–85), and Hedda, bishop of Winchester (676–705). These crosses were 28 feet and 26 feet high respectively.[30]

Besides such outstanding examples of memorial sculpture, there exist also many small stone slabs usually bearing the name of the deceased. Formerly known as 'pillow-stones', it is now, however, agreed that their purpose was not to prop up the head of the body, but to serve as flat grave-stones. They are to be seen in large numbers at Lindisfarne and Hartlepool.

It is apparent that by about the close of the seventh century the practice of setting up sculptured crosses was well established. The important question is—did it merely grow out of the native soil, or was there some wider inspiration encouraging the Anglo-Saxons in the production of this art? It should be conceded, in the first place, that the initial idea of erecting stone crosses was Irish. Standing crosses were erected in Ireland from the earliest period of the Faith in that country, and when Irish missionaries arrived in Northumbria they raised wooden crosses as a symbol of the cause for which they laboured. The practice itself was adopted by the English, but the broad conception lying behind their crosses was drawn from the Eastern empire. In fact, Northumbrian art as a whole can scarcely be understood save as part of the great movement of Byzantine culture, though Celtic influences were interwoven into it. More particularly, in the present connection, it was the Byzantine devotion of the Veneration of the Cross which seems to have been the underlying inspiration of the erection of the crosses.[31]

The discovery of the True Cross in Jerusalem by Helena, mother of Constantine, in 327, led to the erection of the church of the Holy Sepulchre there to enshrine the relic. The liturgical worship of the cross was first practised in 335, in this church, and later on spread to Constantinople. When in 614 the Persians under Chosroes captured Jerusalem they carried off the precious relic, but it was recovered by the emperor Heraclius, who restored it to Jerusalem after it had been in captivity for fourteen years.[32] Meanwhile, the Veneration of the Cross had spread to the West, and the two famous hymns of Venantius Fortunatus, *Pange lingua* and *Vexilla regis*, are amongst its most noble fruits. Fortunatus was himself a lover of the sweet things of life, and something of a dilettante. But the arrival of a relic of the True Cross at Poitiers in 569, whither it had been sent to the devout queen Radegunde by the emperor Justin II, aroused the literary greatness which was in him. The same theme also inspired the poets of England, having doubtless been brought here by travellers such as Wilfred and Benedict Biscop. The poem 'Elene' includes a narrative of the discovery of the True Cross. But in one of the supreme masterpieces of Old English literature, the 'Dream of the Rood', the lyrical poet expresses his devotion to the instrument of our Redemption in language of haunting beauty. And it was not only on the poet that the Cross laid its spell, but on the minds of Anglo-Saxons in general, who now began to cover the land with those crosses of which so many fragments survive.[33]

Byzantium was the great arbiter of civilisation and culture, and its influence widespread throughout Europe. This was so much the case, that the differences between Byzantine and early Western art were not so pronounced as might be supposed. Thus the vine-scroll, the most persistent and attractive motive in Anglo-Saxon art, has similarities with Byzantine work which are too striking to be ignored. The motive is derived ultimately from classical art—it was much used in late Roman times, and subsequently made a great appeal to Christian artists, who doubtless connected it with the theme of feeding on Christ in the Eucharist.

There is an early example of the vine-scroll ornament on the silver dish, now in the Hermitage Museum, Leningrad, and shown at the Exhibition of Byzantine Art in Edinburgh and London in 1958.

Around the rim is a vine-scroll with various animals, such as the stag, sheep, and birds, pecking at grapes. An inscription reveals that the dish belonged to Paternus, who was bishop of Tomi, in the Black Sea region, from c. 517 to 520. It seems that he may have brought the dish home from Constantinople (after purchasing it there), and made various alterations to it in a more barbaric style.[34] It represents an art-relation which probably existed also between the Byzantine world and England. Throughout the Anglo-Saxon period, from c. 600 onwards, there was a constant trickle of ideas from Byzantium to this country. Travellers came home laden with purchased goods, like Aldhelm, who brought back from Italy a white marble altar. There was a steady stream of merchants and returning pilgrims. Such influences did not necessarily come directly from Byzantium itself, but probably in most cases intermediately through Italy. There is thus a similarity between the patterns on the Otley shaft and those on the posts of the ivory throne at Ravenna, which was virtually a Byzantine city. Further, there can be no doubt that with the ideas came many Eastern craftsmen, who found in the Anglo-Saxons apt and willing pupils. During the disturbed times of the Islamic conquests, many Eastern artists sought new homes. Again, the outbreak of the Iconoclastic controversy in 726, occasioned by the emperor Leo III's edict against images, rendered the figural artist superfluous for a long period in the East, and it is likely that there were many Byzantine artists and craftsmen who sought and obtained an entry into Western countries.

The Anglo-Saxons learnt quickly, and yet they developed a style of their own. Whereas, for example, in the Byzantine ivories there is a sophisticated economy, the natural result of a long experience, in the Anglian crosses every available square-inch is crowded with carving, the craftsmen in the enthusiasm of their newly found art wasting no opportunity to exercise their skill. Again, in Byzantine art the animal motive is largely missing, at any rate until the later periods; the art is essentially humanistic, and the significant relationships are those between man and man, and man with God. There is little feeling for nature as such. In the art of the Anglo-Saxons, on the other hand, there is a constant love of birds and beasts, which are intertwined in patterns of marvellous complexity.

With their characteristic and exuberant carving of vine-scroll, as well as of other motives such as the interlace and fret, the crosses are found in great numbers in Northumbria in the late seventh and the eighth centuries. With the decline of the northern kingdom there was a degeneracy in its art, but there are many fine examples in the midlands which are assigned to the eighth century, as at Sandbach in Cheshire and Eyam in Derbyshire.

The starting-point, however, of Anglo-Saxon sculpture is the carving on the cross now at Canterbury but originally in the church of Re-culver. It seems to be of seventh-century date, and the work of an imported craftsman who came in the wake either of Augustine's mission or that of Theodore.[35] It is in the classical tradition, and no English carvings of the pre-Danish period can rival its grace. Later work often shows its vitality, but never its vivacity. It is the work of a craftsman quite sure of his art.

Though the Reculver carving stands alone, it heralds a period of sculpture in England which has been regarded with justice as the golden age of Anglo-Saxon art. Between the coming of Theodore in 669 and the death of Bede in 735, English art attained a position which was unrivalled in the civilisation of the West. In the art of this time we see the traditions of the classical world combining with those of an essentially Teutonic people. ‚

This is illustrated admirably by the whalebone casket, a Northumbrian work of *c.* 700, which was acquired by Sir Augustus Franks in France and has been in the British Museum since 1867. Its panels contain not only representations of the capture of Jerusalem by Titus and the specifically Christian theme of the Adoration of the Magi, but also the Germanic Weland the Smith defending his home. We may gather the artist to have been detached in his spiritual allegiance, trying to please all his compatriots, whom he knows are not entirely surrendering their pagan traditions and mythology to the conquering Christ. Artistically, the work is vigorous, but lacks the restraint and discipline of an experienced art.

By far the greatest of the crosses are those of Ruthwell, in Dumfriesshire, now standing in the parish church there, and of Bewcastle, Cumberland. The former, over seventeen feet high, has in its finest panel an upright figure of Our Lord, carved in deep relief, with his hand raised in blessing. Mary Magdalene is wiping his feet with her hair, a crude piece of work which could have been executed only by a craftsman still learning his art. The heavy drapery is in contrast with the delicacy of that of Reculver. Other panels represent Christ in Majesty treading on the heads of beasts, evangelists with their symbols,

SS. Paul and Anthony (a clear suggestion here of Eastern influence), and various scriptural subjects. What the figure-sculpture may sometimes lack in delicacy, it amply makes up for in a truly monumental dignity. On the sides we have the vine-scroll, with birds and beasts pecking at grapes. Upon this cross are extracts from the 'Dream of the Rood', carved in runic letters.[36] The Bewcastle cross still stands in its native open air, nearly fifteen feet high, though the shaft unfortunately is gone. On the front are sculptured figures of John the Baptist, Christ in Majesty, and a falconer (perhaps a native rendering of John the Evangelist). On the rear is a rather stylised vine-scroll with birds and beasts. The sides are devoted to panels of interlace and chequer-work. Both crosses have inscriptions, that of Bewcastle being entirely of runes.

The Acca cross (for long at Durham, but now happily back in Hexham where it belongs), besides being a splendid artistic creation in itself, is the only cross which it seems possible to date fairly precisely, to c. 740 or soon after. Other examples of probable eighth-century work which may be mentioned as typical of a numerous class are those at Rothbury in Northumberland, Masham in Yorkshire, and Newent in Gloucestershire. The crosses of Abercorn and Aberlady are of interest as indicating that the Anglo-Saxon Church carried with it, wherever it went, not only the preaching of the gospel but also its art. These two crosses may conceivably be a product of the missionary diocese of Whithorn in Galloway, which existed from 681 to 686. They more probably, however, are a later product of this diocese, which was revived c. 730 and endured until the close of the century.[37]

During the later decades of the eighth century sculpture was at its best in the midlands. This at least seems to be indicated by the surviving examples, such as the Hedda stone in Peterborough cathedral and the carvings in the Leicestershire church of Breedon-on-the-Hill. The former is a block of stone, the two rectangular sides having arcades with figures of the apostles standing between, while the gabled roof contains an interlace design of paired animals. But this sculpture is in no way to be compared for excellence with the series of carved friezes in the interior of Breedon church. These latter are a survival of that church decoration which is known to have been of no mean order in the English Church during the late seventh and eighth centuries. We are told that Wilfred decorated the walls of his principal church at Hexham, as well as its pier-capitals and the sanctuary arch, with sculptured figures and coloured pictures.[38] According to Bede the pictures were of scriptural subjects, and procured in Rome. Though Wilfred's pictures themselves have disappeared, Roman church paintings of his time can still be seen on the walls of S. Maria Antiqua, the work of Greek artists. There were paintings at Benedict's church of Monkwearmouth.[39] It is known that on festivals the walls of the church at York were hung with silk and lights were suspended from the ceiling. But though the interiors of English churches were thus being adorned with sculpture, paintings, and embroidery, there is no evidence of the use of Byzantine mosaic.

The carved friezes around the walls of the church at Breedon are the best of what survives of this internal decoration.[40] Some sixty feet in length and comprising the vine-scroll and varied geometrical designs, they are a pointer to the capabilities of an important church of the Mercian period. A certain amount of similar carved frieze exists at Fletton near Peterborough, and at South Kyme, Lincolnshire. It is an attractive conjecture that such friezes may have served to embellish the low screens or 'cancelli' which probably partitioned off the singers' apartment in the church.[41] During this earlier period the clergy in the large churches probably sat on stone benches around the apse in the Syrian manner, and there is clear evidence that this was so at Reculver. In such cases the bishop or abbot would occupy the central place looking due west, and the well-known 'frith stool' at Hexham may have served this purpose. In the small village churches, of which Escomb is our earliest surviving example, accommodation was provided only for a celebrating priest with his server and the congregation —hence a small chancel entered by a narrow arch, and a nave. The same arrangement was adopted at the later church of Bradford-on-Avon.

Not only in the field of architecture and stone sculpture, but in that of manuscript-illumination, did the English of this period attain eminence. Books were a practical necessity in the services of the Church, besides being required for purposes of devotion and study, and artists were not slow to produce them with a beauty which has never been surpassed. From c. 650 the so-called Hiberno-Saxon school made its contributions to Christian culture until it expired, with so much else in Anglo-Saxon life, in the ninth century.

The only book, thought to be of the late seventh century, which survives complete in its original binding, is the Gospel of St John now in the possession of the Jesuit public school of Stonyhurst, Lancashire. The binding is of red leather, bearing a vine-scroll pattern with inter-lace on the front and cruciform ornament on the back. It was found in St Cuthbert's coffin in 1104. But though the binding is local Northum-brian work, the manuscript itself is more probably Italian. It is possible that it was imported, perhaps by Biscop, its binding being damaged in transit, necessitating a complete renewal. Nevertheless, the vine-scroll pattern shows unusually strong signs of foreign influence, and the leather is of an imported material.

Probably not long after this, *c.* 700, abbot Ceolfrith ordered the production of three copies of a Vulgate Bible which had been brought by Biscop from Rome. Two were intended for the use of the monks of Jarrow and Wearmouth. One of these has disappeared completely, and of the other a few leaves survive at Durham and in the British Museum. The third was a present for the pope, and Ceolfrith intended to convey it to him personally. He died, however, in 716 while on his way through Gaul, though the book was taken on by other members of his party. It was discovered in modern times in a monastery near Sienna, and is now at Florence. It is the book known as *Codex Amiatinus*, of considerable importance for the textual criticism of the Bible.[42] Though sparsely ornamented, its full-page Christ in Majesty is of great interest.

The earliest, however, of the great series of Hiberno-Saxon manu-scripts is that now at Trinity College, Dublin, a copy of the Latin gospels long thought to have been produced at the monastery whose name it bears, Durrow in County Offaly. It belongs to the period when the Columban mission was exerting its strongest influence in Northumbria. The work is barbaric in character, and apparently devoid of classical influence, as is well shown in the 'Lion of St Mark' illumination.[43] Amongst modern scholars, Sir T. D. Kendrick upholds its Irish origin.[44] He claims it to be the work of one of the greatest illuminators of the time, and that, in connection with one particular pattern, a considerable period of apprenticeship undoubtedly lies behind it. The Durrow style is bold—intricate patterns being con-ceived as part of a broad scheme—and in fact a page of Durrow in-evitably suggests a modern carpet design. Sir T. D. Kendrick thinks that the origin of the style is to be sought in the decorative schemes of Roman mosaic pavements, as seen for instance in Dorset and Somerset, and that this art may have found its way into Ireland with the retreat of the British Church westwards. He dates the manuscript *c.* 650.

A strong school of thought, however, attributes the Durrow book to Northumbria, even though it has certainly been in Ireland for the greater part of its life. Indeed, the Hiberno-Saxon style of which Durrow is an outstanding example is assigned a predominantly Northumbrian origin. The text of Durrow, too, is a good Vulgate one, which would be less likely to be found in Ireland than Northumbria at this time. The similarity of some of the zoomorphic patterns on the Sutton Hoo jewellery, moreover, to patterns found in the Durrow manuscript, suggests a common English origin.[45]

In this Hiberno-Saxon group of manuscripts the Lindisfarne Gospels, now one of the greatest treasures of the British Museum, stand supreme. They can be fairly accurately dated by a tenth-century note, of whose authenticity there is no question, on a blank page of the manuscript. This informs us that the book was written by Eadfrith, bishop of Lindisfarne, that Aethelwald—a later bishop of the same see—bound it, and that the ornamentation was the work of an anchorite named Billfrith. Eadfrith was bishop from 698 until his death in 721; the *terminus ad quem* for the writing of the manuscript is therefore the latter year. It should not necessarily be assumed, however, that Eadfrith wrote it during his tenure of episcopal office; nor, on the other hand, that he would be too busy as a bishop for such artistic labours (of just the kind to make a delightful relaxation for an occupied public man). We can, however, believe with confidence that the book was written during the closing years of the seventh or the opening years of the eighth century. The book was undoubtedly regarded by the monks of Holy Island as a proud possession, and the tradition of its authorship would be faithfully preserved.

The information concerning the book's origin is given by a priest Aldred, who during the tenth century glossed the Latin text in Old English. The three men specifically stated to have produced the book were non-Celtic, and the immediate influences under which they worked were Roman. The text, written in a half-uncial script, is that of the Vulgate, and the calendar is after the use of Naples—a probable influence here of abbot Hadrian, who was a Neapolitan. The miniatures of the four Evangelists are based on Italian originals, such as the picture of St Luke, which is thoroughly Byzantine in manner. There is a classical influence which is absent from the Book of Durrow. But the dexterity and wealth of the designs of the Lindisfarne Gospels display the Celtic influences which were also strong over the illuminator. The love of animals which characterised the Celtic saints is present in the patterns of birds and beasts, which intertwine their necks and elongate their bodies in a bewildering way. And yet despite these evidences of the hold which the Roman and the Celt had over the Northumbrian Christian, the latter's art, as revealed in these Gospels, remains native and Germanic, in its strength of purpose, its vitality, its constancy of design. Over the maze and the bewilderment stands the cross, as on the great 'carpet' pattern of folio 94^b, imposing upon it a fundamental unity.[46]

A product of the same Northumbrian school is the book known as the Echternach Gospels, associated with St Willibrord, and now in the Bibliothèque Nationale of Paris. There are two possible views concerning its origin. It may have emanated from the scriptorium of the monastery of Echternach (in the modern Luxembourg), founded by the Northumbrian missionary, thus making it rather later in date than the Lindisfarne Gospels. On the other hand, Willibrord may have taken the manuscript with him when he left Northumbria, in which case it is probably of about the same date as Lindisfarne, or even earlier. Lacking the Lindisfarne classicism, the Echternach figures are of an essentially barbaric design. Yet there is a refined sense of economy in the use of ornament, and great exactitude in line drawing.

Similar in style to the Echternach book are the Gospels of St Chad, now preserved at Lichfield cathedral. The figure-work is barbaric and hard, totally lacking the humane qualities of the figures of the Evangelists in the Lindisfarne Gospels. It is not easy to assign to it a correct place in the sequence, but it is possible that both it and the Echternach figures represent a progressive moving away from the Italian style of human portraiture.[47]

In these various manifestations of art the Anglo-Saxon found an expression of himself which he could scarcely have even imagined in heathen times. He made his priceless contributions to Western culture. It should hardly be necessary to labour the point that this art was carried out under the auspices of the Church and in her practical service. In stone architecture, in sculpture, in painting, the original inspiration and the constant encouragement came from Christianity. The Conversion found the Saxon a barbarian and left him a man of accomplished attainments. The power of the Christian Faith to transform a people is nowhere more clearly demonstrated. And yet the English remained English. Despite the many influences from Ireland, Rome, and the East, the Anglo-Saxons never lost the character of a Germanic people. In their art, as in much else concerning them, it is impossible to arrive at the full truth unless we bear in mind that the English were essentially a people of the North. It is an art in which is found constancy rather than waywardness, native exuberance rather than classical refinement.

With the destructive raids of the vikings in the ninth century this art suffered a violent interruption. It would be renewed along somewhat varying lines with the ecclesiastical and cultural revival which characterised the century and a half preceding the Norman Conquest.

CHAPTER XII

CHRISTIAN POETRY
IN ANGLO-SAXON ENGLAND

The Anglo-Saxons were a naturally poetical people, and one of the joys of winter was listening to the minstrel as he touched his harp and poured forth his verse. It is quite likely that much preaching was of this character, and many of the vernacular homilies produced in a later age were in a loose form of alliterative verse. There was probably many a preacher who rhetorically 'unlocked his word-hoard' to display to his hearers the treasures of the heavenly kingdom. At Cloveshoe in 747 clergy were explicitly forbidden to declaim dramatically in church like secular poets.[1] Bede in his account of Caedmon writes of men singing by turn at a feast, the harp going round from hand to hand. Many ordinary Englishmen were probably skilled at impromptu verse-making, and many others would have a stock of memorised poetry in their minds.

But there was also the professional minstrel, who was part of the accepted way of life amongst Germanic peoples. There would normally be one attached to the household of a king or important thegn. A harp was found, significantly, amongst the treasures of the Sutton Hoo ship-burial. It is possible that in these minstrels, improvising their lays with harp in hand and recounting semi-historical deeds before a relaxed and delighted audience, the origin of English poetry is to be sought.

The great bulk of Old English poetry is of the pre-Danish period. The vernacular literature of the tenth and eleventh centuries consists predominantly of prose, and will be considered in a later chapter. Most of the surviving poetry is preserved in four manuscripts which are themselves probably part of the fruit of the pre-Conquest age of book production. These are the Beowulf MS. in the British Museum, the Junius MS. in the Bodleian, the Exeter book which for nearly nine centuries has lain in the library of the dean and chapter of Exeter, and the MS. in the library of Vercelli cathedral, whither it found its way by some means impossible to determine. Of the small amount of vernacular verse which is not contained in any of these four collections may be mentioned the ' Be Domes Daege', and the 'Menologium' (a versified calendar of the ecclesiastical year), though these belong to the post-Danish period.

The Beowulf MS., which was formerly part of the collection of Sir Robert Cotton, and narrowly escaped destruction by fire in 1731, contains the 'Beowulf' itself, and the 'Judith'. The Junius MS. has four poems, the 'Genesis', 'Exodus', 'Daniel', and ' Christ and Satan'. It is illustrated with forty-nine drawings, possibly the work of abbot Aelfwine of Newminster near Winchester. The Exeter Book was amongst a collection of volumes presented to the south-western cathedral by bishop Leofric in 1046; unfortunately it is somewhat damaged. It contains the 'Ascension' and 'Juliana', and 'Advent Lyrics', as well as two poems on Judgment Day, the 'Life and Death of St Guthlac', and the 'Phoenix'. The Vercelli Book includes in addition to some prose homilies two outstanding poems inspired by devotion to the Cross, the 'Elene' and the 'Dream of the Rood', besides the 'Fates of the Apostles', the 'Address of the Soul to the Body', and the fine poem known as 'Andreas'.

Broadly speaking, this poetry is in two moods. The one is heathen, leading by stages to a poetry which is dogmatically Christian in character. It is seldom possible to draw the lines clearly. Thus, in 'Beowulf', Christian and heathen ideas are interwoven: the hero, though he is accorded a heathen funeral by cremation, complete with war-gear, goes after death to seek 'the splendour of the saints'. The poem was apparently issued in its present form for a Christian audience, yet it has a fundamentally heathen ethos. We find here that love of treasure and gaudy trinkets which characterised the German peoples, revealed to the modern eye so vividly by the discovery of Sutton Hoo. The dying Beowulf gloats over the jewels and costly ornaments which he has won from the dragon, just as St Wilfred on his death-bed ordered his treasurer to lay out his silver and gold in his sight. This passion for costly finery was a characteristic of the Anglo-Saxons right through their history. It was the riches of the monasteries which especially attracted the vikings. Later, in the years preceding the Norman Conquest, English embroidery had a continental reputation. In 'Beowulf', while the sentiments ascribed to the characters are apparently Christian, the outward form and ceremonies are heathen. It might well be that the epic was composed in substance before the Conversion, but revised later in the light of the new religion. It should be noted, however, that the Christian elements in the poem are vague, and a long way removed from convinced dogmatic belief.

Besides 'Beowulf', only fragments or short pieces remain of heathen poetry. In the fragments 'Finnsburh' and 'Waldhere' there is apparent the delight which the Teutons found in battle or at any rate in listening to tales about it. 'The Seafarer' contains some of the sea-descriptions at which Anglo-Saxon poets excelled. In this poem, as also in the 'Wanderer', we have a glimpse of that roving spirit which brought the English to these shores in the first instance, and later led them to Germany and the Scandinavian lands as missionaries. One of the finest of this group of poems is the 'Ruin', an elegy on the broken walls of what seems to be the Roman city of Bath.

Later, the subject-matter of poetry is drawn not from Teutonic mythology and half-history, but from the scenes and characters of the Bible and the themes of the Liturgy. The main inspiration is Christian, emanating from a Church with an established position and clearly defined beliefs. Yet even then the heathen spirit persists. Old Testament heroes are typical Teutonic warriors. In the 'Andreas', the apostle Andrew is in effect a northern sea-faring adventurer seeking conquests on behalf of his lord Jesus Christ.

When we turn to the more specifically Christian poetry, which is one of the outstanding manifestations of Anglo-Saxon culture, we are at the outset confronted with Caedmon. There is no need to question the historicity or the versifying ability of this celebrated cowherd turned monk, featured in one of Bede's best-loved passages, in which the origin of English Christian poetry is described.[2] We are told that he wrote of the Creation, the Exodus, the Incarnation, Passion, and Glory of Christ, the Coming of the Holy Ghost, the Apostles' teaching, and the Day of Doom. On the strength of this account, it was long usual to attribute to Caedmon the poems 'Genesis', 'Exodus', and 'Daniel', contained in the Junius MS. But critical study suggests different authors as responsible for this body of verse. This is particularly true of the 'Genesis', which it has been convincingly demonstrated is a combination of two poems, if not more. Lines 1–234 and 852 to the end of the entire work of nearly 3000 lines are known as 'Genesis A', and are assigned to the end of the seventh or the beginning of the eighth century. It describes the war in heaven and paraphrases Genesis chapters 1–22, following the Biblical narrative closely. 'Genesis B' consists of lines 235–851, and is assigned to the ninth century. It deals with the Fall of Man, in a distinctly more dramatic style than the earlier work. In 1875 the German scholar Sievers argued that it was really a translation of an Old Saxon original. A few years later the theory was satisfactorily proved by the discovery in the Vatican library of a few lines of Old Saxon verse which corresponded exactly to lines 791–817 of the Junius 'Genesis'. It is clear on stylistic grounds alone that Caedmon did not write the whole of this 'Genesis', though the possibility of his having written some of 'Genesis A' should not be excluded.

The similarity in treatment and style between 'Genesis B' and 'Paradise Lost' inevitably suggests that Milton made use of the former, and it is not unlikely that he knew the poem from the edition which was printed (for the first time) in Amsterdam in 1655. The publication of the text followed its acquisition by Francis Dujon (known in literature as Junius), librarian to Lord Arundel, in 1651 from James Ussher, archbishop of Armagh. If it could be proved that Milton personally met Junius—the two men were in London at the same time—the conclusion would be almost irresistible that the great portrait of Satan, defiant and unyielding, was actually borrowed from 'Genesis B', and thus ultimately from a German original.

The Germanic character of Lucifer in 'Genesis B' is unmistakable. He is an arrogant thegn guilty of disloyalty to his lord:

> Why must I slave?   What need (quoth he)
> That I serve a master?   My hands have might
> To work many wonders.   I have strength to rear
> A goodlier throne,   a higher in heaven.
> Why must I yield   or fawn for his favour
> Or bow in submission?   I may be God
> As well as He.   Brave comrades stand by me,
> Stout-hearted heroes   unfailing in strife.[3]

When bound in hell he appeals to his own *comitatus* to support him, reminding them of the gifts of treasure with which he rewarded them in the old days.

But though this early Christian poetry in England is deeply imbued with the Teutonic spirit, it leans heavily on scripture. Of perhaps greater interest is the extent to which it is influenced by the Liturgy. This is shown in the 'Exodus', a stirring martial poem describing the coming out of Egypt, the crossing of the Red Sea, and the defeat of the

Egyptian forces. The hearts of the pursued were low when they saw the enemy host approaching, with shining shields and banners held aloft. Birds of prey hovered above, and the wolves sang their dread evensong. Under Moses' leadership, however, the Lord's people were victorious, the trumpets of victory sounded, and men and women together sang their hymn of battle, while treasure of shields and apparel, cast up on the shore, was divided out.

Here the subject-matter is Biblical, and its treatment Germanic. But the immediate derivation of the themes is from the Holy Saturday Liturgy.[4] In fact only Exodus chapter 13 verse 17 to chapter 14 verse 31 and Exodus chapter 15 verses 1 to 21 of the actual Bible text seem to have been used. The main source was the twelve prophetic lections appointed to be read during the beautiful and expressive Ceremonies of Easter Eve. Thus the occurrence in the poem of the episodes of Noah's Flood and the Sacrifice of Isaac, absent from the Biblical Exodus narrative but an integral part of the old Holy Saturday rite, is incongruous and inexplicable unless we regard the liturgical text as the poet's source. In another poem of the so-called Caedmonian school, the 'Daniel', we have further evidence of liturgical influence in the inclusion of the Song of the Three Children, the canticle for Sunday at Lauds.

The fourth part of the Junius collection, known as 'Christ and Satan', really consists of three distinct poems, the 'Lamentations of the Fallen Angels', 'Christ's Harrowing of Hell', and the 'Temptation of Christ'. In these, as also in 'Daniel', there is a tendency to moralise. The ecclesiastic is beginning to exert his influence in poetry.

Cynewulf, who apparently flourished in the second half of the eighth century, is a more certain author than Caedmon, though we know nothing of the man himself. He wrote four poems, 'Ascension', 'Juliana', 'Elene', and the 'Fates of the Apostles', recognised as his by the inserted runes which spell his name towards the end of each poem. He was probably Northumbrian or Mercian, and may well have been identical with a Cynewulf who was bishop of Lindisfarne from 740 to 780 and died three years after his retirement. The nature of the verse, with its emphasis on Christian dogma, suggests a professional churchman as its author. We find here that stress on Trinitarian doctrine which is a marked feature of the homilist Aelfric two hundred and fifty years afterwards. 'Let us pray the Father that he grant us peace, the Son of God and the blithe Spirit.'[5] There are references to fundamental doctrines like the Incarnation and Passion, and the thought of Doomsday is never far away. 'The Judgment is near; we shall know reward according as we have won it.'[6] Men will be divided into three groups, as is declared in a passage illuminating for the study of doctrinal history:

Uppermost in the fire   shall be faithful souls,
The army of blessed ones   eager for glory:
But this they may sustain,   suffering lightly
Free from torture,   a valiant train.
For them the flame   of the fire shall be tempered
As may be mildest   and most easy to bear.
But sinful souls   soiled with evil,
Sorrowful spirits,   in the middle shall be chastened
In the hot surges   compassed with smoke.
And those of the third group,   accursed transgressors,
False foes of mankind,   a criminal host,
Shall be in the abyss   of blazing fire,
In the grip of the gleeds,   made fast in flame
For their former deeds.[7]

The increasing stress on Christian dogma which we find in this second mainstream of early English Christian poetry is in contrast with the character of the Caedmonian poems, where the Germanic spirit is written large on almost every page. But both the Caedmonian and the Cynewulfian poetry are the work of Christians who seriously accepted their Faith. It has been pointed out that sometimes the very structure and sequence of the poems are based on that of the Apostles' Creed.[8]

When we turn to consider some of the poems individually, we find 'Juliana' to be straightforward hagiography in the conventional manner, in which the saint bravely wins the crown of martyrdom. In the 'Fates of the Apostles' the apostles go out to evangelise in obedience to their Lord's command. The latter is in the Vercelli Book, which also contains three of the greatest Old English poems, 'Andreas', 'Elene', and the 'Dream of the Rood'.

'Andreas', which shows St Andrew at work as a missionary amongst cannibals in Scythia, whither he has gone to the assistance of St Matthew, has a northern and heroic mood which is struck in the opening lines. Speaking of the apostles, the poet declares:

Lo, we have heard   of twelve mighty heroes
Honoured under heaven   in days of old,

Thanes of God.   Their glory failed not
In the clash of banners,   the brunt of war,
After they were scattered   and spread abroad
As their lots were cast   by the Lord of heaven.
Famous these heroes,   foremost on earth,
Brave-hearted leaders   and bold in strife
When hand and buckler   defended the helm
On the plain of war   on the field of fate.[9]

In these lines the poet at once catches the ears of his listeners, whose outlook and ethos are still fundamentally Teutonic. As he proceeds he appeals also to their maritime instincts, and the poem is memorable for its description of storms at sea. The narrative of the voyage of St Andrew to Mermedonia, where his brother apostle is in dire straits, is a masterpiece of Anglo-Saxon verse:

Then the depths were troubled.   The horn-fish darted
Gliding through ocean;   the gray gull wheeled
Searching for carrion.   The sun grew dark.
A gale arose   and great waves broke;
The sea-streams were stirred.   Halyards were humming,
Sails were drenched.   Sea-terror grew
In the welter of waves.   The thanes were adread
Who sailed with Andrew   on the ocean-stream,
Nor hoped with life   ever to come to land.
Nor yet was it known   Who steered their ship
Through the breaking seas.
                              Then again the saint
As a loyal thane   thanked his great Leader
On the ocean-highway,   the oar-stirred sea,
Because his strength   had been stayed with food.[10]

The Master Mariner in command of the ship is the Lord Himself, the 'Warden of the wave'. At the height of the storm, He offers to put Andrew's companions ashore. But in the true spirit of the *comitatus* they refuse to desert their leader. To a remarkable extent, this poem represents the blending of the Germanic and Christian characters which was now taking place in England. The concluding lines express this with an almost startling directness:

There is One Eternal Lord   of all things living!
His might and power   upon all the earth
Are famous and blessed.   His bliss over all

In heavenly splendour   shines on the saints,
Gleaming in glory   for ever and ever,
With angels eternal.   He is True King![11]

The 'Elene' and 'Dream of the Rood' are inspired by the cult of the Veneration of the Cross, by this time exerting strong influence on the liturgical practice of the Western Churches. The cult had its origin in Constantine's vision of a flaming cross in the sky, as a result of which he defeated Maxentius and obtained the mastery of the Empire, and the subsequent journey of his mother Helena to Jerusalem, where she discovered the True Cross and the nails.

The 'Elene', a signed poem of Cynewulf, is based on this twin story of Constantine and Helena. Like the 'Andreas' it appeals to the martial sentiments of the Anglo-Saxons. Constantine is a 'mighty war-lord'. In the battle scenes we have the usual Germanic references to clamouring ravens and wailing wolves. After victory, the 'warden of armies' returns laden with booty to his stately seat accompanied by his thegns. Again the sea is a vivid theme, and Helena delights in her voyage to Jerusalem, as the 'Sea-steeds plunge and break through the billows'. The poem ends with the expressed hope that heaven may be the reward, in the company of the Lady Mary, of every man who keeps the Feast of the Cross which the Great Lord 'clasped with his arms'.

Of even higher poetic merit, and the most attractive of all Old English poems, is the famous 'Dream of the Rood'. Nowhere else do we find so lofty and lyrical an expression of devotion to the Cross. It is possible that there were two recensions of the poem, the runic inscriptions on the Ruthwell cross being extracts from the earlier one. The poem as we have it in the Vercelli Book seems to belong stylistically to the Cynewulfian school, in which case it might be a revised version of the earlier poem. In the poem the Cross is personified and tells the story of the Crucifixion to the dreaming poet, who sees at midnight a wondrous Tree in the sky, adorned with jewels and blazing in splendour. The Cross speaks to the sadly gazing poet:

Long years ago   (well yet I remember)
They hewed me down   on the edge of the holt,
Severed my trunk;   strong foemen took me,
For a spectacle wrought me,   a gallows for rogues.
High on their shoulders   they bore me to hill-top,
Fastened me firmly,   an army of foes!
Then I saw the King   of all mankind

In brave mood hasting   to mount upon me.
Refuse I dared not,   nor bow nor break,
Though I felt earth's confines   shudder in fear;
All foes I might fell,   yet still I stood fast.
   Then the young Warrior,   God, the All-Wielder,
Put off his raiment,   steadfast and strong;
With lordly mood   in the sight of many
He mounted the Cross   to redeem mankind.
When the Hero clasped me   I trembled in terror,
But I dared not bow me   nor bend to earth;
I must needs stand fast.[12]

It is a memorable work, one of the few truly great religious poems in the whole range of English literature. Its vision of Christ as the young Hero is Germanic, but the poem is inspired by faith in the Cross and Passion and is rooted in Christian dogma. The Saviour arose by virtue of His great might, ascended into heaven, and will return to earth with His angels on Judgment Day, when each man will receive his reward.

The vision gone, the poet prays to the Cross in his loneliness, longing for the day when It will take him to glory and the bliss of the saints.

These two poems were inspired to a great extent by the Feasts of the Invention and the Exaltation of the Cross, both of which were observed in the Anglo-Saxon Church. Of a more direct liturgical inspiration were the 'Advent Lyrics', contained in the Exeter Book.[13] These are based on eleven antiphons used during Advent, while one lyric is a development of two antiphons for Trinity Sunday Lauds. The poet elaborates the phrases of invocation and petition found in the liturgical O antiphons, sometimes adding an additional doctrinal element from the Bible or Fathers.

As an example we may take the antiphon: 'O mistress of the world sprung of royal seed: from thy womb Christ went forth as a bride-groom from his chamber: here in a manger lies He who rules the stars.' In the poet's development of this theme, Mary is not only Mistress of the world, but also Bride of the King of glory. The thegns of Christ in heaven carol and sing her Lady of the heavenly legions and of the hosts of hell.[14]

Closely associated with the 'Advent Lyrics' is a dialogue between Mary and Joseph which is the earliest piece of drama in our literature, and following the Lyrics in the Exeter Book is the 'Ascension'. In the case of this work, it is not the Liturgy, but a Latin homily of Gregory the Great which is the inspirational source.[15] The poem ends with a characteristic sea-description, in which is elaborated Gregory's metaphor of the mind being tossed hither and thither and its need to be fixed in heaven by the anchor of hope.

Also of the Cynewulfian school is the 'Life and Death of Saint Guthlac'. Of greater interest are the allegorical poems, the 'Panther' and 'Whale', which along with some lines dealing with a bird, apparently a partridge, constituted an Old English 'Physiologus'. The use of the figure of animals for didactic purposes was to become a favourite method of medieval writers, in the form known as 'Bestiaries'. The panther, says the Old English poet, is kind and friendly to all except the dragon, and thus is a symbol of Christ, who loves all save the ancient Foe. As the panther sleeps for three days after eating and then arises refreshed, so Christ arose from the grave on the third day. The whale is a type of Satan, snapping his grim jaws upon the unwary.

Of the same literary genre is the 'Phoenix', one of the most polished of Old English poems, which has been attributed to Cynewulf himself. It is largely a paraphrase of a Latin poem by Lactantius. The earthly paradise where the phoenix lives is described as a fertile land with sweet fountains, green trees, and unchanging weather. In this allegorical poem the phoenix is taken as the loss of Eden. The tree in which the creature rests is God's grace to man. The fire in which it is consumed is the fire of Judgment. Its rebirth is the resurrection to eternal life.

The greater part of the surviving Old English poetry is Christian. But during the seventh and eighth centuries there may well have been in circulation more non-Christian or even specifically heathen poetry than the small amount of extant fragments suggests. The hand of the ecclesiastic lay heavily on all literature, and it is likely that much work of the heathen poet was deliberately allowed to perish. This is as unfortunate for the historian as for the student and lover of literature, as a substantial body of heathen verse would have been of great value in his attempt to assess the strength and nature of heathenism as it grappled with the nascent Faith.

The Christian poetry was Mercian or Northumbrian, and dependent for its production on the fine northern schools such as York and

Jarrow. With the collapse of this educational system during the Danish incursions of the ninth century, the poetical tradition came to an end. When religion and culture revived under Alfred and his successors, vernacular writers found their medium in prose rather than verse, and its home was in Wessex rather than the midlands or the north. In literature, the Danish war marked the Great Divide, as in so much else in Anglo-Saxon history.

CHAPTER XIII

SCHOLARSHIP AND LEARNING
IN EARLY ENGLAND

The conversion of England, the art and the poetry which were amongst its fruits, and the missions to Frisia and Germany (to be recounted in the following chapter) would all have been impossible without a system of organised education and study in early Anglo-Saxon times. So much is certain, though perhaps less generally recognised than the virtual truism according to which the origins of English education lie with the arrival of Christianity, and the great flowering of learning and culture in the seventh and eighth centuries in England was a Christian one, inspired by the Church and in her services.

It is often conveniently forgotten, however, that the education imported into Kent with the Augustinian mission was not a Christian invention, but derived from pagan models. It is well therefore to preface a consideration of the Anglo-Saxon achievement in scholarship and learning with some remarks on the educational system of imperial Rome. On the whole, the early Church was not a promoter of schools, and seems to have regarded learning with some distrust. The reason for this antipathy lay in the contents of the normal school curriculum, which was based on the Latin poets, who used as their subject-matter the pagan mythology. There does not appear to have been a Christian system of formal education, apart from the catechetical schools, and these did not aim at imparting a liberal training. Most of the great Fathers of the early Church received their own education in the grammar and rhetoric schools of the pagan world. Clement of Alexandria was a student of the philosophy schools of Greece; Origen studied under the Neo-Platonist philosopher Ammonius Saccas. Even Basil and Gregory of Nazianzus, who were born in Christian families, were educated in pagan schools.[1] When Julian the Apostate in 362 closed the schools to Christian teachers, the move was regarded as a severe blow. Ultimately, it was these pagan schools which were the precursors of the schools of England. Moreover, the Roman schools themselves were greatly indebted to those of Greece.

At first the Roman schools were managed under private auspices,

197

but as they increased in number they became more highly organised. Vespasian (69–79) endowed teachers with stipends, and from about the second century the teachers generally were paid by the public authorities. Constantine in 321 excused them from municipal and military service. The educational system spread into the provinces, and there were schools even as far afield as Britain. Thus Agricola established Roman schools for the sons of British chieftains, as part of a general scheme for the encouragement here of Roman culture and civilisation.[2] Bonosus, an adventurer of the later Empire of the West who tried to set up his authority at Cologne, was the son of a British schoolmaster.[3] The schools were doubtless an important part of the cultural life of Romano-Britain, but were swept away by the Anglo-Saxon invasion. This is in contrast with the course of affairs on the Continent, where the schools continued despite the German inroads.

Everywhere in the Empire grammar schools were to be found, and rhetoric schools in the more important centres. The curriculum of the grammar school was often wide, but it was always based on grammar, which included not only the technical study of language as such, but also aimed at training the pupil's judgment concerning the books he read. He was therefore taken through many poets and other authors. Greek was taught as well as Latin. At about the age of fourteen the more able boys of the grammar school passed into the rhetoric school, where advanced instruction was given in the art of expression, which to the Roman was the highest accomplishment of the gentleman. Every Christian who had any education at all had it in these schools. The system remained pagan down to the fall of the western Empire, long after the time of Constantine. The absence of a Christian educational system during these vital formative years of the Church entailed that the Christian obtained his religious knowledge from the teachings of the clergy, in sermons and catechism. This helped to establish the prestige of the priesthood, and probably contributed in no small way to its authority and pride, which became a permanent feature of the Catholic Church.

In the earlier years of the sixth century, Priscian, a teacher at Constantinople, produced his famous Latin grammar, which remained a standard text for generations following. About the same time Cassiodorus wrote to the Roman Senate, exhorting it to maintain the claims of the grammar schools, and to see that the masters duly received their stipends. Public entertainers (actors and such like), he wrote, are well rewarded—how much more should the State remunerate the men who inculcate morals and intelligence into the future citizens of the Empire.[4]

Until about this time it is fair to regard education as a secular institution, but in the sixth century the Church began to take over its control. Gregory of Tours is the earliest prominent man of letters who is known to have been educated under definitely ecclesiastical auspices. By the close of the sixth century the Church was firmly established in the educational field in its own right, and there is strong evidence that the Roman mission to Kent in 597 brought teaching with it as well as preaching.[5]

There is no direct indication that Augustine himself founded a school at Canterbury, though this is highly probable. It is clear that there was a school settled in that city at least sometime during the first quarter of the seventh century. In 631 Sigbert, king of the East Angles, wishing to follow the excellent example of Gaul where he had been living in exile, founded a school for boys (undoubtedly at Dunwich, the seat of the see), where they might be taught grammar.[6] This is the first explicit reference to the establishment of a school in Anglo-Saxon England, but Bede makes it clear that it was founded on the model of a school already existing in Kent. He states that Sigbert was assisted in his scheme by bishop Felix, who came to him from that kingdom, and who provided him with masters after the manner of the school which had already been established at Canterbury. If a school was sufficiently settled to be able to furnish masters and teachers for another school, it must obviously have been in existence for a number of years.

In default of definite proof that this Kent school petered out during the generation or so following Augustine's death in 604 or soon after, it must surely be accepted as likely that it continued as a constituent part of the ecclesiastical arrangements in Canterbury, and that when Theodore arrived in 669 he found there at least the nucleus of a school. 'Both he and Hadrian were learned in sacred and secular letters, and attracted a great many students, into whose minds they poured streams of healthy knowledge. They not only taught them the scriptures, but also metre, astronomy, and arithmetic necessary for the calculation of the calendar.' So thorough was their teaching, Bede goes on to say, that in his days (c. 731) there were still alive some of their students who knew Greek and Latin equally well with their native tongue.[7]

In those happiest of times, he claims, anyone who wished to learn holy writ had teachers readily available. This famous passage in no way suggests that Theodore founded a new school, but rather that he infused new life into an institution already or but recently there. The most interesting point about the statement, perhaps, or at least its implication, is that the archbishop himself, along with Hadrian, took part in the teaching.

Amongst those who studied at the school of Theodore and Hadrian were Oftfor, who became bishop of Worcester; Tobias, bishop of Rochester, to whom Greek and Latin were as familiar as his own tongue; and John of Beverley, who in later life (in connection with his healing ministry) remembered medical instruction given by Theodore.[8] Another notable student was Albinus, who succeeded Hadrian in the abbacy of St Augustine's. He was so thoroughly instructed in the Canterbury school that he knew Latin like his native language and much Greek also. Aldhelm has usually been claimed as a pupil of Theodore and Hadrian, but his actual status as such is by no means certain. Bede, who praises Aldhelm's literary abilities and learning, does not say that he studied under Theodore and Hadrian, though he is careful to specify this in the case of Albinus and Tobias.

Aldhelm, however, had a high opinion of the Canterbury school directed by the archbishop and his abbot, and he apparently knew it well. It was no longer necessary to go to Ireland for classical learning. Greek and Latin masters were to be found on English soil. Indeed, so great is the fame of this school, that even the Irish flocked to it. Theodore, surrounded by a pack of Irish students, 'would scatter them with ease, rending them with the tusk of grammar, like a ferocious boar set upon by snarling Molossian hounds'.[9]

Meanwhile, apart from grammar, church music was being taught, and we see the germ of those song schools which were to form a feature of the educational life of the middle ages.[10] England was the first country outside Rome itself to receive the Gregorian chant.[11] Limited in the beginning to Kent, it now spread to the other churches.[12] After the defeat of Edwin at Hatfield in October 632 and the flight of Paulinus, the deacon James remained in the north, and with the restoration of peace became a teacher of church music, of which he had a considerable knowledge.[13] Later on, this work was continued by Stephanus Eddius, who also came from Kent. Theodore appointed to the see of Rochester Putta, an expert in Roman chant, which he had learned from the pupils of Gregory, doubtless at Canterbury.[14] In 678 John, the arch-chanter of St Peter's, Rome, was introduced to Northumbria by Benedict Biscop, to teach Gregorian music to his monks.

The greatest scholar of the seventh century in England, and indeed perhaps in western Europe, was Aldhelm. The main facts and influences in his life are clear, though there are some puzzling features chronologically. If William of Malmesbury's statement that he died at the age of seventy is correct, then he would be born c. 639, which is the usually accepted date.[15]

From about the beginning of the seventh century the whole of Wiltshire had probably been under West Saxon domination, and two important victories over the Welsh of Somerset, at Bradford-on-Avon in 652 and Penselwood in 658, drove the Celts further into the south-western peninsula, and made the countryside adjacent to the Bristol Channel really accessible to the English. It may have been some time after the former victory that Kenten, a member of the Wessex royal house, sent his young son Aldhelm to study under an Irishman Maildubh,[16] who had by his knowledge and sanctity gathered followers around him at the spot which subsequently came to be known as Malmesbury.

The Irish of the seventh century were continuing the tradition of learning developed earlier in the schools of their island. Their range of reading was wide, and they knew the Vulgate in Old Latin texts,[17] as well as apocryphal books such as the 'Gospel of Nicodemus' and the 'Acts of Pilate', which at this time were proscribed in the Roman Church, though still read by the Irish. They read the Greek Fathers in Latin translation, and the great Latin Fathers such as Ambrose and Augustine. About the time of Maildubh, in 655, an Irish scholar known as 'Augustine' wrote *Of the Wonders of Sacred Scripture*. There were other scholarly writers, such as Laidcend, who made a study of the writings of Gregory the Great; and Aileran the Wise, a spiritual writer of a fanciful turn of mind. The Irish were exceedingly fond of hymns, and it was in the seventh century that the *Bangor Antiphonary* was compiled. It is a collection of Latin hymns and prayers for the use of the monks of Bangor, drawn from various sources, continental and Irish.

Aldhelm, it seems, settled down as a monk under Maildubh, and it was probably under his influence that he developed the fanciful language for which his writings are well known. Irish scholars delighted in bizarre language, in the intricate manipulation of words for its own sake, and Ireland indeed seems to have been the place of origin of the literary game of words, put together mysteriously in accordance with rules known to the initiated.[18] The style might be said to resemble a combination of the crossword puzzle and certain types of modern poetry. It was a temporary fashion, a cult, incomprehensible to the ordinary man and not intended for him. Under the influence of this school Aldhelm advanced in classical and rhetorical learning, an erudite man of the times. He was also apparently affected by the works of Virgilius Maro Grammaticus, who had flourished in Gaul some years previously, a mammoth of erudition who was capable of keeping an argument going for a fortnight on the unpromising subject of the vocative case of 'ego'. It was from his Irish environment that Aldhelm doubtless contracted his passion for bookish learning, exemplified well by the pleasant tale told of him haggling over the price of a book with some shipmen who had beached at Dover.[19]

It was a time, however, when the rising young men of Saxon race were looking to Rome rather than to Ireland for spiritual and intellectual enlightenment. By 671 the school of Theodore and Hadrian at Canterbury was established, and, attracted by its high repute, Aldhelm thither made his way.[20] Here he was able to study Greek and Latin under teachers who really knew their subject. By this time he was, if the usually accepted chronology is correct, almost middle-aged, and it is not easy to regard him as a pupil in the commonly accepted sense of the term. He was rather a man who regarded the pursuit of knowledge as the main aim of his life, and could not miss this opportunity of benefiting from the lectures of scholars the like of whom England had not known before. It was perhaps while at Canterbury that he wrote the extant letter, important for our knowledge of contemporary studies, to Hlothere, bishop of Winchester.[21] He would gladly spend the coming Christmas dancing with the brethren, he writes, but study holds him back. He is busy learning Roman Law. There is also verse, with its hundred different metres, and the technique of setting it to music—a congenial intellectual exercise for an Anglo-Saxon. Astronomy and astrology hold his attention. He is occupied with mathematics, which he finds by no means an easy subject. It was difficult at this time, of course, because Arabic numerals were still unknown to Christians, who were compelled to use the cumbersome Roman characters.

Aldhelm visited Canterbury twice, before he succeeded Maildubh as abbot of Malmesbury on the latter's death. He remained in the abbey there for some thirty years, from 675 to 705. His diocesan bishop Hlothere died in 676, and was followed by Hedda, who remained occupant of the Winchester see until 705. Highly regarded as a good and just man, Hedda was distinguished by his natural clemency of character rather than by a devotion to scholarship.[22]

Aldhelm founded a monastery at Frome, which he dedicated to St John Baptist, and one at Bradford-on-Avon. William of Malmesbury wrote[23] that in his day there was in the latter place a small church dedicated to St Laurence, reputed to be the work of Aldhelm. The church known to William was surely the same which still exists, one of the best preserved of Saxon monuments. But the twelfth-century belief that it was Aldhelm's actual foundation was probably incorrect, and opinion in our own day assigns it to the tenth century.[24] Sometime between the foundation of these two monasteries Aldhelm visited Rome. He took ship at Wareham, Dorset, but pending a favourable wind and while his companions were collecting provisions for the voyage, he built a church, on whose site the present St Martin's church probably stands.[25] In Rome he was courteously received by Sergius I (687–701), and accorded the privilege of saying mass in the Lateran, an occasion which he marked by wearing a chasuble of red silk with designs of peacocks. He brought back with him a marble altar-stone so heavy that the unfortunate beast carrying it died under the burden while crossing the Alps. He also brought a letter of privilege from the pope, exempting Malmesbury and Frome from episcopal oversight.

In 705 Aldhelm was consecrated first bishop of the newly created diocese of Sherborne, which he ruled for four years. 'He constantly preached by night and day, diligently travelled throughout his diocese, and was faithful in fasting and good works, as in his prime.'[26] Apart from this general statement we know little of his episcopate, with which he continued to hold the abbacies of Malmesbury, Frome, and Bradford. He died in the spring of 709, in the wooden church of Doulting, Somerset, and was buried at Malmesbury. His relics were held there in the highest reverence, and in due course archbishop Lanfranc decreed that he be numbered amongst the saints.[27]

Aldhelm exercised a considerable influence in his day as a correspondent, and amongst those to whom he wrote was the cultured king Aldfrith, of Northumbria. Like that of Aldhelm, the scholarship of the king was deeply imbued with Irish influences, and the two may well have been fellow-students at Malmesbury. It was probably during the early years of his reign (685–705) that Aldfrith received a lengthy communication from Aldhelm in which the latter displayed his passion (typically Anglo-Saxon) for the construction of riddles—which reveal a love of nature and an eagerness to delve into the mysteries of ordinary daily life.[28] There are enigmas here upon such subjects as wind, fire, the rainbow, silkworms, and the dove; upon the organ and the lighthouse, and, characteristically, the library shelf and the writer's pen.

About the same time Aldhelm also wrote, in Latin prose, to the community of nuns at Barking, ruled by abbess Hildilith, who had succeeded the first abbess Ethelburga, sister of the founder Eorcenwald, bishop of London. The letter was entitled 'De Laudibus Virginitatis'. The nuns to whom the epistle is addressed are mentioned by name; besides Hildilith herself there are Justina, Cuthburga, Osburga, Aldgitha, Scholastica, Hidburga, Berngitha, Eulalia, and Tecla.[29] Aldhelm praises their study of holy books, their cultural attainments. The letter offers a revealing insight into the range of studies attempted by Anglo-Saxon nuns at this time. These ladies have studied the Bible and Fathers and tackled problems of history and allegory, besides dealing with the intricacies of grammar and metre.

He praises the celibate life. In Old Testament times marriage was very honourable, but under the new dispensation its relation to celibacy is that of silver to gold, or wool to silk. He recommends the nuns to include in their reading the *Collations* of Cassian and the *Morals* of pope Gregory. He condemns the fine dress which is fashionable amongst men and women of the cloister and indeed with the clergy generally—the scarlet tunics, the sleeves striped with silk, the shoes of red fur. Hair is being curled, and in place of the seemly dark veils there are coloured headdresses with flowing ribbons. It would seem that in general the austerity and plainness of monastic dress was being abandoned in England towards the close of the seventh century, in accordance with the well-known propensity of the Anglo-Saxons towards colourful clothing.[30]

But whatever the warning strictures of the letter, it leaves us with a feeling of respect for the women of at least one late seventh-century cloister. Let the bodily attire be what it may, here indeed was a grave learning. The letter was well received, and carefully preserved to become a standard text for medieval nuns.[31] Aldhelm followed it up with a work in Latin hexameters, *De Laudibus Virginum*, which he also dispatched to Hildilith and her nuns.

Aldhelm also wrote to Eahfrid,[32] a Saxon compatriot who had recently come home from Ireland after a six-year course of study there. In this letter he refers to the constant coming and going of students between the two islands. He calls on Eahfrid to use for the enlightenment of others the knowledge which he has acquired. Why, he asks somewhat ironically, do so many English students have to flock to Ireland? He is sure teachers of Greek and Latin are available in England. Why go to Ireland when it is possible to study under Theodore and Hadrian at Canterbury?

As a result of his literary reputation, Aldhelm received letters requesting aid. Artwil, an Irish prince,[33] asked him to polish some specimens of his written work which he sent to him. A letter arrived from an Irishman Cellanus, abbot of Peronne on the Somme, where Fursa was buried and which was a centre of Celtic learning.[34] Cellanus says that he has not had the privilege of meeting Aldhelm, but he has read his delightful treatises, and would be pleased to receive from Aldhelm some sermons for his own use. A young man Aethelwald, a former pupil (who has not very probably been identified with Aethelbald, king of Mercia 716–57), sent his first poems with a request for criticism. Two of them survive; they are good examples of Hisperic incomprehensibility.[35]

Aldhelm's well-known letter to the Welsh king Geraint is clear proof of his Roman loyalties, and marked a decisive stage in the triumph of the Catholic cause. Though educated under Celtic auspices, and highly regarded by Celtic scholars later in his life, Aldhelm was a Roman—as evinced by his support of Wilfred, and by the poem *O Roma nobilis* which he composed to mark the occasion of his pilgrimage to Rome.[36] In his own day and for long afterwards he was a popular vernacular poet, though none of this work survives. King Alfred greatly admired his verses. Aldhelm's flair for popular minstrelsy is exemplified by the story of his standing on the bridge at Malmesbury singing secular songs to attract an audience, and then leading his hearers on to weightier matters.

Though undoubtedly a man of much learning, Aldhelm has left curiously little to scholarship and culture in general, and his historical influence is in no way to be compared with that of Bede and Alcuin.

He was essentially a man of his own time. In his passion for technical learning he was characteristic of the seventh century. He understood his contemporaries well, and they in turn placed great confidence in him. A generation after his death his works were still in demand, as when Lull wrote from the Continent to his former master Dealwine, with the request for some prose or verse writings of Aldhelm to comfort him in his exile.[37] Above all, in Aldhelm more than in any other personality the Celtic zeal for letters is married to the Saxon temperament with its tradition of steadfast loyalty.

Until Hadrian was ready to assume the oversight of the Canterbury school, it was ruled by Benedict Biscop, who on being released from this duty made his fourth journey to Rome. It was as a result of these journeys, from which he came back laden with books, that he was able to lay the foundations of a great tradition of learning in Northumbria. On returning from his final visit to Rome, in 686, when he brought home with him a splendid addition to the resources he had already collected—numerous books and other treasures[38]—he was welcomed by Aldfrith, who had recently become king. In his farewell words to his monks, Biscop on his death-bed urged them to care for the library which he had assembled, a trust they worthily fulfilled. On the two monasteries of Biscop, according to William Stubbs, 'the civilisation and the learning of the eighth century rested'.[39] Biscop's successor Ceolfrith shared his interest in books, and he added many more volumes to the already large collection, before his own death c. 716 on the way to Rome with the gift of *Codex Amiatinus* for the pope.[40]

The Irish meanwhile had made their contributions to the beginnings of Northumbrian learning, and Bede tells us that English boys were taught by Celtic teachers the observance of regular discipline, along with more advanced studies. Aidan had twelve boys around him, whom he educated in the Christian way of life. In a later generation, Acca, who succeeded Wilfred at Hexham in 709, established there a full and excellent library,[41] a move which supports the general impression that his predecessor had not been greatly interested in scholarship. At the same time Acca invited Maban, a celebrated singer, who had been taught by the successors of Gregory's disciples in Kent, to instruct his clergy in church music and restore the chant to its original purity. He stayed with Acca twelve years.

At the time of Ceolfrith's death there were nearly six hundred monks in the joint foundation of Wearmouth-Jarrow. The most illustrious member of what must have been a veritable hive of industry was Bede, whose uneventful career is soon told. He was born a year or two after 670 on what afterwards became one of the estates of Jarrow,[42] and at the age of seven was given by relatives to be brought up by Benedict Biscop.[43] Concerning his parents we know nothing. He appears to have been early transferred from Wearmouth to Jarrow, and is traditionally identified with the choirboy who struggled to maintain the offices with abbot Ceolfrith after the choir-monks had been carried off by plague in 686.[44] In Jarrow he spent the whole of his life, broken so far as we know only by isolated visits to Lindisfarne and York. He applied himself wholly to the study of the scriptures, and in the intervals between the offices in church it was his constant delight to learn and teach and write.[45] He was ordained deacon at the age of nineteen, priest at thirty, receiving both these orders at the hands of John of Beverley.[46] His admission to the diaconate several years before the canonical age of twenty-five may probably be taken as a measure of rapid progress in his studies, his teachers including Trumbert, himself a pupil of Chad. This unexciting career, devoid of worldly ambition, was ended by his death at Jarrow in 735.

The literary work of Bede was made possible by the library assembled by Biscop and supplemented by Ceolfrith. Though he is remembered by posterity as the author of the *Ecclesiastical History*, this work was actually not written until towards the close of his life. Meanwhile he was a voluminous and encyclopaedic writer, and it is a remarkable fact, and not very creditable to English professional scholarship, that although a large corpus of his work is extant in numerous manuscripts, a full critical modern edition is still to be undertaken.[47] He himself gives a list of his writings at the end of the *Ecclesiastical History*. These include many commentaries on the books of the Old and New Testaments, which he probably regarded as the important part of his work. Other works include the *De natura rerum*, Histories of the Saints, Lives of Cuthbert in verse[48] and prose, and the History of the abbots Benedict, Ceolfrith, and Huebert.[49] The *Ecclesiastical History* was completed in 731. In 703 he produced a manual of chronology, the *De Temporibus*,[50] and in 725 a more advanced work on the same subject, *De Temporum Ratione*. It is this latter work which appears to have made popular in England the method of Dionysius Exiguus whereby the years are reckoned from the Incarnation of Our Lord. The interest of Bede and his fellow-countrymen in physical science appears in general to be underestimated. More particularly, the phenomena of the heavens fascinated the Anglo-Saxons (Aldhelm included such studies in his curriculum at Canterbury). There was a current liking for astrology, though Bede would have none of it, and later archbishop Egbert of York prescribed penances for those who put their trust in the courses of the stars and the movements of tides. The three works which Bede cites at the close of his list were probably actually his earliest, bearing as they do the stamp of school textbooks. Of these, the *De Orthographia*[51] is an elementary book, put together informally, with grammatical notes on an alphabetical list of words. The *De arte metrica* and *De schematibus et tropis* were dedicated to a 'fellow-deacon' named Cuthbert, from which it is clear that they were written before 702 or 703, when Bede was ordained priest. They consist of passages to illustrate form in poetry and prose.

It will be possible to answer the intriguing question as to the extent of Bede's own reading when there is a complete and analytical edition of all his works. Professor M. L. W. Laistner meanwhile has tackled the problem in an important article,[52] from which it is clear that above all Bede knew his Bible, which he quotes constantly and spontaneously. His knowledge of the pagan literature of classical antiquity was smaller, certainly less than that of Aldhelm. There are quotations from such authors as Lucretius, Terence, Horace, and Sallust, but apparently taken by Bede at second-hand from grammars which he used. The only classical poet whom he can be safely considered to have known by direct study was Virgil, a favourite author at the time. Of classical prose-writers Bede seems clearly to have known only Pliny. With Christian poets he was more familiar, constantly quoting from Ambrose, Prudentius, Sedulius, Fortunatus, and others.

Bede was first and foremost a theological student, widely read in patristic authors. Thus Professor Laistner's study established that in his commentary on Acts, Bede consulted Gregory's Homilies on the Gospels and on Ezekiel, and the same writer's *Pastoral Care* and *Morals*. He knew Ambrose, Augustine, and above all Jerome, whose commentaries he constantly used. In his *Retractations on Acts*, Bede revealed himself a sound textual critic, comparing the Greek text with the Latin versions. It is clear he had some acquaintance with New Testament Greek at the mature stage of his life during which he wrote this work, but it is doubtful whether his knowledge of Greek extended further than this, or even any further than the Greek of the Acts.[53]

He does not name many Greek Fathers, save those writing on the problems of the Easter date. He occasionally mentions Origen as a heretical writer, Basil the Great, and Clement of Alexandria, but he only knew them in translations. Professor Laistner does not know of a single passage of which we could be certain that Bede had made use of the Greek original, though on the other hand there are several instances where he clearly used a translation.[54]

Bede's attainments as a scholar must therefore not be exaggerated or misunderstood. He was not an original thinker, but rather an industrious and patient student making the fullest use of the fine library of Christian Latin writings established by Biscop and Ceolfrith. He states that from the time of his ordination to the priesthood until his fifty-ninth year, he has endeavoured, for his own benefit and that of his brethren, to compile extracts from the works of the Fathers on the Bible, and to comment on them.[55] This was a useful and necessary labour, as the original authorities were difficult of access to the ordinary reader. Bede was, however, no mere scissors-and-paste student, but a fine Biblical and patristic teacher, who in due course came to be regarded virtually as one of the Fathers of the Church, and his popularity is proved by the numerous surviving manuscripts of his works in the great European libraries. Thus there are seventy-seven manuscripts of the commentary on Acts still extant, and at least sixty-one manuscripts of the *De Temporum Ratione*. Perhaps the most significant point which has emerged from a closer study of Bede's works is his comparative ignorance of Greek, a deficiency all the more surprising in view of the fact that Greek was taught at Canterbury and Bede's own statement that in his day there were still alive pupils of that school who were as conversant with Latin and Greek as with their mother tongue.[56]

In his historical work Bede essentially fulfilled a contemporary popular demand. The deeds of the past formed a favourite subject of reading in the earlier years of the eighth century. After more than a century of Christianity, the Anglo-Saxons had acquired a sense of ecclesiastical history and tradition, and the general need was supplied by the writing of saints' lives, of which several were produced in Northumbria at this time. In the early years of the eighth century an anonymous monk of Lindisfarne wrote a Life of St Cuthbert, in which the personality of that saint is effectively depicted. The Life impressed Bede, who used it as the basic authority for his own two Lives of St

Cuthbert, one in verse and the other in prose.[57] Of less value is the Life of Gregory the Great by a Whitby monk. The valuable though tendentious Life of Wilfred by Eddius Stephanus had already been written years before. An excellent effort was a biography of abbot Ceolfrith by a monk of Wearmouth, as a result of which Bede was again inspired to attempt something along similar lines, which he did with his *History of the Abbots of Wearmouth and Jarrow*, containing an account of the first three rulers of the joint foundation. Meanwhile further south Felix had written the *Life of Guthlac*, and other biographical work is known to have been undertaken.

The crown of this hagiographical succession was the *Ecclesiastical History*. In this work Bede set himself to relate the history of Christianity in eastern Britain from the time of the Roman occupation until 731. It was a period, at any rate so far as the seventh century was concerned, rich in personalities, and Bede made the most of the opportunities presented to him. The great men and women of the Conversion are vivid characters to us, for which we must be grateful largely to the hagiographical background against which Bede wrote. Yet it would be unjust to say that the *History* is a mere string of saints' lives. The conception of history dominates the work. Facts and personalities, incidents and their causes, are woven together skilfully to illustrate a noble theme, the conversion of the German tribes settled in Britain from heathenism to the worship of the true and living God. Though the general reliability of the work is well known, it would be idle to pretend that it possesses the bleak objectivity cultivated by many modern historical writers. It is anything but plain fact-collecting, and the author writes with a clear purpose in mind. In his preface, dedicated to king Ceolwulf (who resigned his throne soon afterwards to become a monk at Lindisfarne), he claims that reading the deeds of good men is an encouragement to morals. Bede too was a thorough Romanist, strongly opposed to Iona, and it is probable that his work set the seal on the triumph of the Roman Church in England. Yet he was gentle to Aidan, whose memory he loved, and he hesitated to dwell for long on the tale of discord associated with Wilfred.

Attempts have been made recently to cast doubts on the accuracy of Bede,[58] and indeed no one will claim to exempt him from the close criticism which our early medieval sources must receive. But in the final analysis Bede's historical writings are as reliable, on the whole, as anything available for the period.[59] It has become almost a commonplace to point to the modern methods by which he worked, and it might be said that his concern for the truth is as evident as is the biased character of much work of our own day. For the avoidance of doubts concerning the accuracy of his narrative (as he himself expressly states), he lists in the Preface the authorities upon which the *Ecclesiastical History* is based. One is impressed by the broadly based character of this authority, and the care with which it was chosen. The most important element in it was abbot Albinus, whom Bede describes as a fine scholar, trained in the Canterbury school by Theodore and Hadrian, themselves learned men. Either verbally or in writing this man transmitted to Bede, through the medium of a London priest Nothelm, all that he considered worthy of recording from the history of the Gregorian mission to Kent—a good example of the rule that history is the record not of what happened but of what mattered. Albinus himself derived his information from written records and well-established traditions. Like an industrious research student, Nothelm visited Rome, where he examined the papal archives and made copies of letters of Gregory I and other popes.[60] On the advice of Albinus, he brought these to Bede. Albinus and Nothelm also helped Bede with a certain amount of information relative to the conversion of the East and West Saxons, the East Angles, and the Northumbrians. The West Saxon bishop Daniel forwarded him information in writing concerning church history in Wessex, Sussex, and the Isle of Wight. For the conversion of Mercia Bede's authority was the monks of Lastingham, who also helped him with the history of the Essex apostasy and the subsequent recovery of the Church in that territory. For the East Angles he was indebted partly to traditions, partly to information supplied by abbot Esi, who is otherwise unknown to us. He ascertained the development of Christianity in Lindsey from the correspondence of bishop Cynebert, and from the oral testimony of various trustworthy persons. For his own Northumbria Bede drew on first-hand knowledge, and on the evidence of numerous witnesses, who remembered the facts.

The weakest part of the *History*, as Bede himself appears to recognise, lies in the earlier chapters, dealing with the period from Caesar's invasion in 55 B.C. to the mission of Augustine. For this he used previous written authorities, notably Orosius, Gildas, and Constantius. But Bede's main concern was the conversion of the English, as indeed the title of his work indicates; in the doings of the British he was less interested. Having completed the *History*, he sent it to Ceolwulf for him to read and criticise, and then a second time submitted it to him for his considered views.

Bede's careful and critical approach to the writing of history is perhaps even more evident in the Preface to the prose *Life of Cuthbert*, addressed to the monks of Lindisfarne and bishop Eadfrith. Bede states that his work is the result of minute investigation. Reliable witnesses have been closely questioned. Information has been obtained from those who knew the saint personally, and to give a more precise authority to his narrative Bede mentions some of these witnesses by name. The work completed, he still hesitated to release it for general circulation, but repeatedly submitted it for personal perusal and correction to a priest Herefrith and others who had been well acquainted with the great saint. At their suggestion, a number of corrections were made. He finally sent the manuscript to the brethren of Lindisfarne, asking them to scrutinise it for any remaining errors. They declared the Life fully accurate, though Bede agreed to the addition of more facts to make it complete.

During the earlier part of the eighth century, it is clear, Jarrow held the intellectual pre-eminence in the English Church. But Bede's Preface to the *Ecclesiastical History* implicitly makes it certain that there was a wide diffusion of scholarship and learning throughout the country. Albinus, abbot of St Augustine's, was a trained scholar, and it was actually by his persuasion that Bede undertook the *History*. There was a ready audience for such a work. Moreover, an excellent knowledge of Latin was characteristic of the English Church about this time, as is evident from the correspondence of many men and women with Boniface. This correspondence was a product of the instruction which was apparently being given in the schools of Wessex. Boniface himself had the makings of a great scholar, but he chose to exercise his gifts in the world of men and affairs. The midlands also seem to have made their contribution, and produced at least one good scholar in Tatwine, who was abbot of Breedon-on-the-Hill, author of a grammar and Latin riddles, and archbishop of Canterbury 731–4.

The story of Bede's last days was told by Cuthbert, afterwards abbot of Wearmouth-Jarrow, in a letter to Cuthwin,[61] an old fellow-student of his who was at the time a member of some other monastery than Jarrow. During the spring of 735[62] Bede was ailing, though he continued to join in the Hours and teach daily in the school. In the intervals he was much occupied in recalling passages from Scripture, in preparation for his last moments. He also repeated passages from Anglo-Saxon poetry, besides composing a few vernacular lines himself in which is expressed the solemnity of rendering one's account at death. He found solace in chanting the antiphons, particularly the one still used at second vespers for the Feast of the Ascension at Magnificat, in the Roman rite—'O King of glory, Lord of hosts, who on this day didst ascend in triumph.' He kept in hand a translation into the vernacular of the first few chapters of the Fourth Gospel, and a compilation of some selections from Isidore. On the Tuesday before Ascension Day his health markedly deteriorated, his breathing becoming difficult and a tumour appearing on his feet. The following day the community set out on its Rogationtide procession, leaving behind a boy Wilbert as Bede's amanuensis. There remained one chapter to translate. Bede told the boy to write quickly. In the afternoon Cuthbert joined the dying man, and soon afterwards the priests of the community were called in, Bede distributing amongst them his small possessions— pepper, handkerchiefs, incense. He spoke separately to each priest, asking him to offer masses and prayers for his soul. As evening drew near, he worked on at his translation. His task completed, he passed away with the *Gloria patri* on his lips, his mind fully at rest with God.

The relics of Bede remained at Jarrow until the eleventh century, when they were transferred to Durham cathedral along with those of St Cuthbert. They rest today in the beautiful Galilee chapel at the west end, cresting the wooded slopes of the Wear. The great scholar was never formally canonised. He was reverenced, however, at many altars in the middle ages, particularly in the north, and his name was included in the York calendars.[63] To his contemporaries and fellow-countrymen Bede was the supreme scholar and teacher, 'the candle of the Lord' by whose writings the light of God was made manifest.

A year or two before he died Bede had visited York, whose newly elected bishop, Egbert, was one of his former pupils. It was following this visit, and some six months prior to his own death, that Bede wrote to him the famous letter in which he offered advice on ecclesiastical matters. Egbert was the virtual founder of the school at York, which during the second half of the eighth century became the centre of English education and learning.[64] It was hither that a small boy Alcuin was brought to learn his letters, some years after his birth in 730 (or soon afterwards) in Northumbria.[65]

In due course Egbert handed over the care of his school to Albert, one of his old pupils. The fame of the school spread, and Albert's advice was widely sought in educational affairs. In 767 he was promoted to the archbishopric of York, from which time onwards he delegated the headship of the school to Alcuin. On Albert's retirement in 778 (he died two years later), the archbishopric was formally separated from the mastership of the school—Eanbald succeeding to the see, Alcuin to the school. It was as a schoolmaster that Alcuin found his vocation, and he may be claimed as the first Englishman to be fully conscious of the call of teaching as the avenue to satisfaction in life. Though he was ordained deacon, he was never admitted to the priesthood, and there is no clear evidence that he was a professed monk.[66] To the school over which he presided came pupils from far afield, such as Joseph, an Irishman, and from Frisia Liudger, who subsequently became the first bishop of Munster.

In later years Alcuin described the wide and liberal instruction available at the York school under Albert, in his poem, 'Verses on the Saints of the Church of York',[67] one of our most important documents for the history of English education. It is clear that the trivium and quadrivium formed the basis of the curriculum. Albert taught grammar and rhetoric, law and chant, astronomy, and also it seems some biology and arithmetic. Scripture was a pre-eminent subject. It appears, however, that a pupil would not study all of these subjects, but only such as appealed to him or for which he had aptitude, the implication being that Albert had assistant masters skilled in the various branches of knowledge. Albert kept a look-out for youths of special promise, whom he took as boarders into his own household. He collected a splendid library, with a comprehensive range of authors, including Fathers like Jerome, Ambrose, Augustine, and Athanasius, and the writings of Aldhelm and Bede, besides classical writers such as Virgil, Cicero, and Aristotle, and the Christian poets Sedulius and Juvencus.

At York, in fact, there was a school organised along rational and formal lines. In a letter from the Continent to archbishop Eanbald, Alcuin advised the separation of the teaching of reading, singing, and writing, with special masters for each.[68] But Alcuin's concern for administrative detail did not preclude on his part a loftiness of ideal, evident in another letter, to Ethelbert bishop of Hexham, in which the supreme importance of education is urged. Salvation without teachers, he says, is scarcely possible. It is certainly a charitable work to feed the poor with earthly food—but an even greater to fill the hungry soul with spiritual learning. In a multitude of learned men lies the world's well-being.[69]

Three years after his elevation to the absolute mastership of the school Alcuin went to Rome to collect the pallium on behalf of Eanbald. On his return he met Charlemagne, whom he had already encountered on a previous occasion, and who now persuaded him to stay with him. From now on until the close of his life he was a member of that king's liberal and energetic court. The teaching of the palace school at Aachen on Alcuin's arrival in 782 tended to be in the hands of Italians, such as Peter, a deacon from Pisa, who taught grammar, as also did Paul, another deacon, who in addition wrote history and poetry. Alcuin praises the welcome which Charlemagne gave to scholars from all quarters. There was an urbane atmosphere about the court, exemplified in such men as Angilbert, a poet and lay abbot of St Riquier near Amiens, and Theodulf a Goth from Spain, a man of considerable culture who eventually became bishop of Orleans, remembered today as the reputed author of the Palm Sunday hymn, *Gloria, laus, et honor*.[70]

As master of the palace school Alcuin had ample opportunity for the exercise of his genius for teaching and educational administration. Under his direction the school increased its efficiency, but it is important to remember that there was not only an establishment for the instruction of youth as part of the educational arrangements of the court. Such indeed was the basis of Alcuin's work there, but the conception of education prevailing at Aachen was far wider. An intellectual atmosphere pervaded the whole place, and people of all ages were eager to acquire knowledge by formal and informal means, the method of discussion being used along with that of lectures. In his design for the diffusion of education amongst his people Charlemagne had a ready helper in Alcuin, who served him with the unswerving loyalty characteristic of the Anglo-Saxon.

It was this deep-rooted sense of loyalty which was probably the main cause of the steady English devotion to the cause of orthodoxy. The English Church on the whole did not produce philosophers or original thinkers, still less heretics, but rather guardians of a tradition, a sacred trust to be maintained for future generations. Bede himself was essentially a traditionalist, and even more so was Alcuin. The corpus of his extant works contains few signs of originality. His skill lay rather in the use of standard writings for the benefit of students. At the same time his contributions to learning, within the broad line of these conditions, were considerable, and written in lucid Latin, if not always free of grammatical errors. He wrote many Biblical commentaries, and to him, as to Bede, theology was the end of knowledge. His most important biography was that of his kinsman Willibrord, an indispensable work for the life of the Apostle to the Frisians, though unfortunately too concerned with miracles to be of outstanding value. He rewrote in an improved style earlier Lives, those of St Vedast and St Riquier. Though he lacked the true mind of a poet, he was a competent writer of verse.[71] He produced works on grammar and orthography. He did much to encourage the dialectical method, which constitutes the beginning of medieval scholastic philosophy, and on which in turn the fruitful investigations of modern science are ultimately based.[72]

Alcuin's gift for editorial scholarship produced two results of abiding importance. In the first place, he is generally credited with an influential share in Charlemagne's scheme for an emended Biblical text.[73] Secondly, in the liturgical field he supported the king's determination to have a uniform Use throughout his dominions. Alcuin edited the Gregorian Sacramentary, which Charlemagne had received from pope Hadrian, and combined with it a supplement drawn from various sources. The completed work forms the foundation of the modern Roman Missal.[74]

Heresies troubled him. In 793 he was called by the king to take up his pen against Adoptionism, which had spread from Spain into the Frankish realm. Alcuin shared the persistent Anglo-Saxon horror of false doctrine. In 795 he wrote home to England complaining of those who tore apart the seamless robe of Christ, something which 'even the soldiers at the Cross did not dare to do'.[75] The singing of the Creed at mass has been ascribed to his influence.[76] Of Eastern origin, this usage spread to Spain, thence by way of Ireland to Northumbria. It was now introduced into the Frankish Church as a move against Adoptionism, and before long would be an established feature of the Roman Liturgy. Far more troublesome, however, than Adoptionism was Iconoclasm. The death in 780 of Leo IV, the third Iconoclast emperor, meant a change in ecclesiastical policy on the part of Constantinople. His infant son Constantine VI succeeded him, though the affairs of government passed to his widow Irene, who ruled as regent, and proceeded to reverse the image-breaking programme of the Isaurian emperors. In 787 the Seventh General Council was held at Nicaea, attended by three hundred and fifty bishops and two papal legates, at which the veneration (προσκύνησις) of images was vindicated, though their worship and adoration (λατρέια) was forbidden as due to God alone. The Acts of this Council were endorsed by Irene, but were badly received in the West by Charlemagne. Unfortunately a faulty translation into Latin gave the impression that the Acts denounced those who would not adore the images of God Himself. The result was the treatise known as the *Caroline Books*,[77] inspired by the Frankish king, in which image-worship was condemned. The same misleading translation made its way to England, where Alcuin was at the time. He composed a letter on behalf of the English Church, strongly condemning the Nicene Acts.[78] At the council of Frankfurt in 794, attended by Alcuin and English delegates, the supposed decree of Nicaea 787 enjoining the adoration of images was condemned.

Alcuin had a considerable correspondence, wider in its scope than that of Boniface, the Apostle of Germany, though like the latter he was inclined in his later years to moralise and give advice. His contacts with England were better maintained than those of Willibrord and Boniface, but the turbulent state of affairs in his native Northumbria precluded any temptation on his part to return for more than occasional visits, fairly prolonged though these visits may on occasion have been. He appears to have grown weary, after some years, of Charlemagne's court, with its excess of energy and business, but his native soil offered him no prospect of the peace for which he craved. A favourite retreat to which he sometimes repaired was Echternach, the spiritual base of Willibrord, where another Anglo-Saxon, Beornred (afterwards archbishop of Sens), was at this time abbot. It was at the request of Beornred, a cousin of his, that he undertook his biography of Willibrord.

In 796 Charlemagne appointed Alcuin, already abbot of Ferrières and of St Lupus, Troyes, to the abbacy of St Martin, Tours.[79] He also possessed the small monastery of St Josse, near Etaples, whose importance lay in the convenient facilities for hospitality which it offered to English pilgrims and travellers to the mainland of Europe. Alcuin had wished to retire for his last years to York, but permission was refused by Charlemagne. He had then had the idea of retiring to Fulda, there to become a monk. It was following this, that he was appointed to Tours, though it was perhaps only during the last three or four years of his life that he was really able to settle down here. He died in the spring of 804, predeceasing by ten years the king whom he had so faithfully served, and was succeeded as abbot of St Martin's by an Englishman Fridugis, one of his old pupils. This man later became the head of the Imperial Chancery of Louis the Pious, Charles' son and successor.

Alcuin is the last great name in the history of Anglo-Saxon scholarship during its pre-Danish phase. His significance is essentially that of a transmitter, and he forms the bridge between the Golden Age of his own country and the Carolingian renaissance. His greatness emphasises the importance of York, with which his name has always been associated, but it would be dangerous to assume that the cultural heritage which distinguished England in the latter half of the eighth century was centred round the northern city alone, or concerned only with Northumbria as a whole. Though it is clear that Bede and Alcuin surpassed all their contemporaries in learning, the widely diffused character of eighth-century correspondence is proof enough of the good level of general education prevailing in the Anglo-Saxon kingdoms. This could scarcely have been the product of one or two centres of learning only. There is increasing evidence that Worcester and Lichfield may have possessed influential schools. Moreover, the tradition continued, so far as we know, into the ninth century.

But the fact that after Alcuin no giants were produced is fair evidence that there was some decay in efficiency and zeal, and the drying up of the Anglo-Saxon stream of evangelisation and teaching abroad in the earliest decades of the ninth century is significant. There was apparently an appreciable number of English monks and nuns on the Continent during the Carolingian Age, though it seems that the all pervading influence of Anglo-Saxons and British was by this time beginning to be resented in some quarters.[80] After the death of Alcuin the great tradition began to die, and Fridugis (who died in 834) was the last of the line. By the middle of the century the English Church was definitely in the grip of adversity, and could hardly afford to send abroad her best sons and daughters. It is possible to argue that the overseas enthusiasm of English Christians during their golden period had gravely weakened the Church at home, and had helped to bring it to the undefended state in which the invading Danes found it. On the other hand, largely as a result of the work of Anglo-Saxons, the Church in the northern lands of the Continent was well established, and it would not be long before Alfred the Great was inviting scholars from abroad to assist in the restoration of learning and religion in England.

CHAPTER XIV

THE ANGLO-SAXON MISSION TO THE CONTINENT (I)

One of the most remarkable manifestations of religion amongst Englishmen and Englishwomen of the late seventh and the eighth centuries was the urge to evangelise beyond these shores. The missionary activities of our forefathers during this period constitute a noble chapter of European history, and are in themselves a convincing proof of the thoroughness of the English Conversion. The Roman and the Celt had done their work well. The seed sown by Augustine, Aidan, and others, would produce a rich harvest, and the influence of the Anglo-Saxon missionaries in the Germanic lands of the Continent was to be immeasurable, forming much of the basis of medieval culture and civilisation. The history of these missions might seem on a superficial view to lie outside that of the English Church itself, belonging rather to that of Germany and the Lowlands. But so great was the interest shown in the missions by Anglo-Saxon Christians who remained at home, and so much were the missions an outpouring of the faith and energy of the English, that some account of their development must inevitably be included in a history of Anglo-Saxon Christianity.[1]

We have already considered the career of Wilfred, the first English missionary to leave his native land, who preached in Frisia during the winter of 677–8. But though it is likely that his work there had the effect of opening his fellow-countrymen's minds to the possibilities of aggressive evangelism abroad, he was not himself a missionary by vocation, and the results of his preaching in the Lowlands lacked immediate permanence.

The next name in the history of Anglo-Saxon missions is that of Egbert, a Northumbrian who may with greater justice be claimed as the real founder of the Frisian mission. An inmate or pupil of an Irish monastery as a young man, on surviving an outbreak of plague he made a vow never to return to his native England—this of course was an act of self-renunciation as a way of expressing his gratitude to God, and is in no way to be construed as a spurning of his motherland. He heard a call to missionary work amongst the continental peoples kindred to the English; the peoples from whom, according to Bede, the Angles and Saxons—in the eighth century still known as Germans by the Britons—had derived their origin.[2] Egbert made his preparations, choosing companions suitable by their learning and courage for the task. There appeared to him one morning, however, a certain brother, formerly a disciple of Boisil at Melrose, who told him of a vision which he had seen in the night. After his retirement to bed, his former master had appeared to him with a message from Egbert. It was Christ's will that Egbert should not go to the Continent. His duty was rather to instruct the monasteries of St Columba.

On considering the matter carefully, Egbert did not dispute the genuineness of the vision, though he decided all the same to go ahead with his preparations for the voyage. Some days later, the same brother returned to him with a second message from Boisil, insisting that he proceed to Columba's monastery (i.e. Iona). The ploughs of the Celtic monks were crooked, and Egbert must straighten them. Egbert persisted in his original plans, but before the ship could sail it was run aground by a violent storm. He was at last convinced, and decided to stay at home.

Such is the tradition recorded by Bede. Instead of himself embarking on the enterprise which he had planned, Egbert sent Wictbert, one of his companions. But on arriving in Frisia, Wictbert discovered circumstances less favourable than those enjoyed by Wilfred years before. The friendly king Aldgisl had been succeeded by the heathen Radbod. After two years of fruitless labour the missionary returned to Ireland, and like Wesley of a later age sensibly decided that he could be of more use to God by serving his own people. Once more it had been shown that without the support of the secular ruler, the missionary of the Dark Ages could accomplish little.

However, Egbert did not lose heart, and in 690 dispatched to Frisia a second mission, consisting of twelve disciples, of whom one was a priest named Willibrord. Subsequently, in 716, Egbert fulfilled the supernatural command laid upon him to convert the monks of Iona to the Roman usages.[3] He died in 729, at the age of ninety.

Willibrord[4] was born in November 658 of devout parents in Deira, his father Wilgils sending him in due course to be educated at Ripon. Growing steadily in grace and intelligence, at about the age of fifteen he made his religious profession. Wilgils himself in later life became a solitary on the headlands near the Humber mouth, many folk resorting to him, anxious to hear the word of God from his lips. Here he was given some land by the king and nobility to enable him build a church, which became the centre of a small religious community dedicated to St Andrew. In due course this church descended by lawful succession to Alcuin, apparently a member of the family.

At Ripon Willibrord would be one of Wilfred's spiritual sons, and it must have been here that he became imbued with that spirit of loyalty to Rome which was to be a major factor in his life. In 677 Wilfred was deprived of his see following the partition of the Northumbrian diocese by Theodore, and this seems to have led to the departure of Willibrord from Ripon. His biographer Alcuin tells us that on attaining his twentieth year the young man felt an urge to travel. Many of Wilfred's disciples exiled themselves at this time, in a kind of sympathy for their discomfited master. Willibrord like all Anglo-Saxons had heard of the flourishing schools of Ireland. Hastening overseas, he joined the community of Rathmelsigi, ruled by Egbert, where he made the acquaintance of Wictbert. In this holy and dedicated company the second stage of the future missionary's apprenticeship was passed. He remained here for twelve years. It will be noticed that Willibrord's training was Roman throughout, received under two men (Wilfred and Egbert) who were protagonists of Catholic ways. But we can be certain that during these years in Ireland Willibrord also caught much of the Celtic spirit, with its zeal and love of adventure in Christ's service.

By the time he had reached the age of thirty-two he was determined to preach to the northern peoples, and it is reasonable to suppose that he was encouraged to take up the work in Frisia by the example of his former master Wilfred in that region. In 690 he set out as one of the group of twelve, the second mission sent by Egbert, though there is nothing to suggest clearly that he was the initial leader. The expedition successfully crossed the Channel, and landed at the mouth of the Rhine. The company's immediate objective was the castle at Utrecht, the old Roman city of Trajectum, where Willibrord was in due course to establish his see.

Frisia had suffered much in the struggles for power which attended the decline of the Merovingian royal house, and had passed through an unsettled period. But with his decisive victory at Tertry in 687, Pippin II (of Heristal)—mayor of the palace in Austrasia—ousted his

Neustrian rivals and secured the predominance in the Frankish lands. The Frisians were troublesome neighbours of the Franks, and Pippin carried his arms against them until Frisia south and west of the Yssel was subdued. The Frisian king Radbod, an inveterate heathen who was to declare with some spirit that he would rather spend eternity in hell with his forefathers than in heaven without them, was a formidable adversary of the same stamp as Penda of Mercia.[5] At the time Willibrord arrived however (in 690), conditions were favourable, and the missionaries were able to begin their work with the support of Pippin. The latter well understood the value of Christianising his newly acquired territories, and indeed the Frisians, as later the Saxons further to the east, regarded baptism as in large measure a sign and symbol of subjection to the Franks.

But Willibrord was not content with obtaining the most powerful secular support available. He made his way to Rome to secure the approval of Sergius I—the same pope who had warmly received Aldhelm. Willibrord's departure raises one of the puzzling features of the Frisian mission. There seems to have been some doubt, perhaps amounting even to dissension, amongst the brethren as to who was to be accounted their leader. The fact of Willibrord's journey to secure the papal blessing suggests that it was in his hands that the leadership lay. But during his absence, the brethren elected as bishop another of their number, a modest and unassuming man named Suidbert, and sent him to England for consecration. This was during the vacancy in the metropolitan see which followed the death of Theodore in 690, and Suidbert's consecrator was Wilfred, at the time an exile in Mercia.[6]

The answer to the problem may lie in the fact that about this time the mission was tending to split up and overreach itself. The securing of Pippin's approval had possibly gone to the heads of the English missionaries. They may have thought that not only Frisian heathendom was well within their control, but that they could afford to send out subsidiary missions elsewhere. It was actually about this time that two English priests who had long lived in Ireland, and who were probably members of the band or followed shortly in its wake, set out as evangelists to the Saxons.[7] It should be remembered that the conversion of the continental Saxons, whom the English regarded as their next of kin, was the ultimate aim of all Anglo-Saxon missionary work during the seventh and eighth centuries. These two priests, who both bore the name of Hewald but should not be assumed therefrom to have been brothers, were too impetuous to wait. According to Bede, the one was dark and the other fair—both very pious, but the brunette the more learned of the two. On arriving amongst the Old Saxons they sought an audience of the nearest lord, occupying themselves meanwhile in prayer, the recitation of the offices, and the daily celebration of mass. The Saxons, however, fearful of the influence which the missionaries might exert over their chief, fell on them and put them to death before the audience was obtained. There was thus no popular desire to change the existing heathen worship for the religion of the Church. On hearing of the incident, the lord was furious that his subjects had taken matters into their own hands, and executed the murderers. The bodies of the Hewalds were subsequently found, and conveyed by Pippin's order to Cologne, where their relics are reverently preserved to this day in the church of St Cunibert on the banks of the Rhine hard by the Cathedral. Badly damaged by British bombers during the war, this small church is now being carefully restored.

Like the Hewalds, bishop Suidbert went beyond the Frisian borders in the execution of his missionary labours. On returning from his consecration in England he was established for a while at Wijk bij Duurstede, but soon set out to evangelise the Bructeri of Westphalia. He had some preliminary successes, but they were undone by a Saxon invasion of the region. He thereon retired to an island on the Rhine called In Litore and later known as Kaiserswerth, given to him by Pippin and his wife Plectrudis.[8] Here he founded a monastery, where he remained until his death in 713.

These brave but rash adventures must have convinced the Anglo-Saxon missionaries that their only practical policy was to consolidate a sound position in Frisia. This they proceeded to do, now under the firm leadership of Willibrord, returned from Rome. His visit to the pope was very significant. The English Church herself was in large measure the result of a papal mission; and now from the outset her first overseas daughter was brought by a deliberate action into the Roman fold.

Many years before this time bishop Eligius of Noyon and Tournai (641–60) had carried out missionary work in Flanders, and almost contemporaneously St Amandus, an Aquitanian (assisted by an Italian monk Jonas), worked amongst the Franks in the region of the Schelde. A missionary of irrepressible energy, Amandus had constantly to be attempting new conquests, rather than consolidating one small field.

He is said to have laboured amongst peoples as diverse and scattered as the Basques of the Pyrenees and the Slavs near the Danube. He established a church in the castle of Antwerp, which lay somewhat to the south of Frisia. Similarly, there had been a church in the castle of Utrecht from the earliest years of the seventh century, conferred on the bishop of Cologne by Dagobert I, as a base for missionary work amongst the Frisians. Nothing, however, had come of this latter project, and the pagans had destroyed the church.

Now Willibrord, as we have seen, had made for the castle of Utrecht on his initial entry into Frisia. It would be his work to prosecute the mission from which the bishops of Cologne had shrunk. About the time of his return from Rome he was also given Amandus's church in Antwerp, which in its position just without the Frisian borders would form a safe yet convenient base.

He now settled down to the work of evangelism, visiting many places systematically. It became clear that a Frisian Church was a possibility. The importance of the work was perceived by Pippin, who in 695 sent Willibrord to Rome for consecration as archbishop.[9] It is clear that in this the initiative was taken by Pippin, and not by Willibrord, who at first opposed the plan. It is the earliest known case of co-operation between a Carolingian ruler and the pope. For the first time we have a meeting of the three forces which were to affect so profoundly the course of European history—the papacy, the Carolingians, and the Anglo-Saxon missionary.

Willibrord, now a man in his late thirties, proceeded to Rome for the second time, with appropriate gifts from the secular ruler. He was consecrated on St Cecilia's day (22 November) 695, in the church of St Cecilia, Trastevere, by Sergius himself, and invested with the pallium as a symbol of his metropolitan oversight over the Frisian people and his authority to ordain bishops. The pope assigned to him the name of Clemens, after the saint whose feast began at vespers of the day of the consecration. Later on, Winfrith also when he received his missionary mandate would be given the name of the saint whose feast was being observed at the time, that is, Bonifatius. But Willibrord, unlike the Apostle of Germany, has always been known by his English name. After staying in Rome for a fortnight, Willibrord returned to Frisia, laden with relics and gifts.

On his return he received from Pippin the castle at Utrecht as the seat of his archbishopric. The situation was a strategic one. Utrecht was within that region of Friesland, west of the river Yssel and south of the Zuyder Zee, which had been subdued by Pippin. Yet only a few miles from the castle was the country of the heathen Frisians, between the Yssel and the Ems, under their king Radbod. Willibrord would be near a port, and thus well placed for receiving reinforcements from England. At Utrecht Willibrord built a church which he dedicated to the Saviour, as Augustine had done at Canterbury. Over the foundations of the church which the heathens had ruined years before he built a new church in honour of St Martin. There is an obvious, if only a partial, analogy here with Augustine and his arrival in Canterbury. To Willibrord, reared in the school of Wilfred, the Roman mission to Canterbury had meant the virtual origin of Christianity amongst the English, and it was under similar auspices that he was undertaking his own mission.

Willibrord now seriously commenced the apostolate which virtually inaugurated the great era of Anglo-Saxon influence on the Continent, an influence which would endure throughout the eighth century and beyond. He vigorously preached the Word, founded churches, and established communities of monks and nuns. His compatriots on the other side of the Channel followed his work with interest. Eddius, claiming that it was his own master Wilfred who had laid the foundation of the Faith in Frisia, says that Willibrord is building upon it with untiring energy.[10] Unfortunately, the total loss of the missionary's correspondence precludes any such knowledge of personal relationships as are revealed by the letters of Boniface. Englishmen, however, are known to have joined his mission. Wilfred interrupted his last journey to Rome, c. 703, to stay for a while with Willibrord, who told his old master (and Acca his companion) of miracles that were being wrought by some relics of St Oswald which he had with him (apparently brought from Ireland).[11] But though the first missionaries in Frisia were all foreigners, it was not long before Willibrord was ordaining to the priesthood converts of native stock.

Willibrord consecrated some of his Anglo-Saxon companions to the episcopate, though we do not know the names of any of them. Neither do we know whether a regular diocesan system was instituted, or whether, as is more likely, these bishops simply assisted Willibrord in a general way. In conferring upon Willibrord the pallium, Sergius had been over-optimistic. The time was not ripe for Frisia to become a province of the Church. In the event, the Frisian Church did not retain its provincial status after Willibrord's death, and in course of time Utrecht became an ordinary diocese in the province of Cologne.[12]

Willibrord made some heroic attempts to advance into the dangerous areas outside Frankish protection. After realising the futility of attempting the conversion of the heathen Frisians, he pushed north-eastwards to the Danish tribes, who were ruled by Ongendus, a man said to be more ferocious than a wild beast.[13] Though he received Willibrord honourably, his attitude was firm enough for the Englishman to be persuaded that here also heathenism was too strongly rooted to be replaced by Christianity for the present. He returned, though he brought with him thirty Danish youths, whom he instructed and baptised on the journey. Once again there is a parallel with Augustine, who trained Frankish lads in the hope that they might be of use to him in Kent. It was doubtless the intention of Willibrord that the young Danes should one day form the nucleus of a mission to their own country. Meanwhile an Englishman had struck the first blow in the Danish peninsula on behalf of Christ.

On the way home by sea, Willibrord was driven by a storm onto Heligoland, where he was forced to remain for some days. He baptised three persons here in a sacred spring, and also slaughtered for eating purposes some cattle considered sacred by the inhabitants, who worshipped a god Fosite. He was threatened by the king of the island, but retaliated by calling on him to renounce his ancestral errors and believe in the Lord Jesus Christ, accepting baptism in the waters of life. Though the king made no response to this appeal, he did not detain Willibrord, in spite of the provocation which the latter must have caused him.

Willibrord arrived safely home with his party from his Danish expedition, which so far as we know he never repeated. During this same general period, when he worked beneath the protection of Pippin, he came to Walcheren, where he was bold enough to smash an idol to pieces. He nearly paid with his life for this action. The heathen custodian struck him on the head with a sword in understandable anger, though no harm apparently came of the blow.

So long as he had the secular power behind him, Willibrord's work was a success in Frankish Frisia. But when shortly before Christmas in 714 Pippin of Heristal died, leaving Plectrudis as his widow with a child grandson as his heir, there was a general insurrection of the Frisians against Frankish domination, resulting in the capture of Utrecht. An interruption of some three or four years in Willibrord's work followed. But Charles Martel, the famous 'hammer', son of Pippin by an irregular union, restored the situation. In a series of battles he overcame the Neustrians, and the Burgundians and Aquitanians also acknowledged his authority. Though he continued to rule as mayor of the palace, he was the effective founder of the Carolingian house. He forced back the Frisians, who were besieging Cologne. Radbod, the unrelenting enemy of the Church, died in 719.

The stage was now set for the final scenes of Willibrord's labours, but again his success was confined to Frankish Frisia. The Frisians east of the Zuyder Zee remained stubbornly heathen. It was not until the reign of Charlemagne, grandson of Charles Martel, that they accepted baptism, and then only at the point of the sword.

In his later years Willibrord was closely associated with Echternach, in modern times a quiet, secluded town just inside the eastern borders of Luxembourg, with a fine basilica which has been completely rebuilt following extensive damage in the second World War. Lands had been given to Willibrord in this place c. 700 by Pippin and Plectrudis, and by Irmina, abbess of a convent at the ancient city of Trier nearby.[14] Here, in Echternach, he founded a monastery which became to him a safe retreat and a haven of rest, especially during the troubled times which followed Pippin's death. Doubtless for its greater security, Willibrord placed the monastery under the protection of Pippin, whose proprietary house it became. It is possible that the well-known illuminated manuscript called the Echternach Gospels, now in the Bibliothèque Nationale, Paris, may be a product of the monastery during its period of rule by Willibrord. Also at Paris is 'Willibrord's Calendar', an early eighth-century manuscript in an Anglo-Saxon hand; it is a calendar of the saints significant in Willibrord's career, such as Suidbert and Amandus.

During the closing years of his life Willibrord lived quietly, taking no further part in missionary or active episcopal duties. Like many Anglo-Saxon prelates, he had the good sense to acknowledge the decline in energy which usually accompanies old age. There is a marginal entry in the Calendar in the hand of the archbishop himself, which he appears to have inserted to mark the close of his career.[15] In this he refers to himself as Clemens Willibrordus and mentions his arrival on the Continent in 690 and his consecration by the pope in 695, which he clearly regards as the two great events of his life. The entry indicates that it was made in 728, when he was seventy years old.

Bede, writing at Jarrow *c.* 731, commented that Willibrord was still alive, though longing for the heavenly life after a career of spiritual warfare.[16] From other sources we know that during his closing years he had an assistant bishop to perform his duties for him.[17] After his probable retirement in 728 he survived for a further eleven years, dying on 7 November 739 at Echternach, where his memory is still revered and his mortal remains entombed in a worthy sarcophagus.

CHAPTER XV

THE ANGLO-SAXON MISSION
TO THE CONTINENT (II)

The Frisian mission, a notable achievement on the part of the Northumbrian Church, was the prelude, and yet more, to the even greater deeds that were to follow in central Europe on the part of West Saxons. This second missionary period is better documented, and as a result appears to us as richer in personalities. In particular, there can be no disputing the supreme greatness of Winfrith, or Boniface, probably the most able missionary ever produced by a north European country.

Winfrith, around whose career the history of the conversion of Germany is largely written, was born near Exeter of a good family c. 675 or shortly before. There is no need to dispute the traditional location of the actual birthplace at Crediton, but it should be borne in mind that there is no earlier authority for this tradition than the liturgical books of John Grandisson (1327–69),[1] though Crediton itself is mentioned in a charter as early as 739. According to his biographer Willibald,[2] Winfrith was a child with a precocious spiritual sense, receiving his monastic vocation at the age of four or five. He was encouraged in his religious bent by clergy making their evangelistic rounds, apparently from a neighbouring minster. On their arrival in his village, where they seem to have been given hospitality by his father, the boy would seek their company and ask their advice on spiritual matters.

At length he opened his heart to his father, who made no attempt to conceal his displeasure at the prospect of his son entering religion. But parental opposition only increased the ardour of the boy's wishes. He was accordingly sent as an oblate to the monastery of Adescancastre (the modern Exeter), ruled over at the time by abbot Wulfhard. Little if anything is known of Winfrith's life at this small house, though it is clear he was a hard student, making such progress that eventually there was nothing further his teachers could offer him. With his abbot's consent, therefore, he moved to the larger monastery of Nursling, near Southampton, which was under the care of abbot Winbert, a teacher whom Winfrith was to remember with affection in his old age.[3] The young monk progressed in the spiritual life, and in secular and sacred studies. He became skilled in grammar and rhetoric, and in

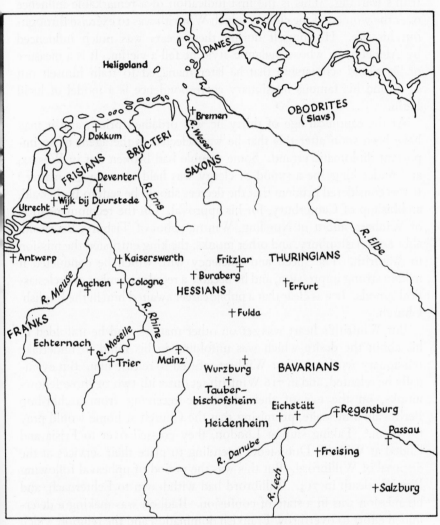

Map 1. Missions to the Continent: main ecclesiastical centres.

the making of verses,[4] meanwhile not neglecting the regular duty of manual labour. He was promoted to the office of teacher within the monastery, and his reputation spread, many monks from other houses arriving to benefit from his lectures on holy scripture. In some manner unspecified by the biographer (doubtless by correspondence) nuns as well as monks studied the sacred texts under the stimulation of Winfrith's learning. This is the first indication of a remarkable influence over the women of the cloister which Winfrith was to exercise throughout his life. He himself during these years was much influenced by Aldhelm, to whose pedantic style he fell a victim. It is a measure of his sound scholarship that he later managed to train himself out of it, and his famous missionary correspondence is a model of lucid Latin.

At the canonical age of thirty he was ordained priest, and it may have been soon after this that he was selected as the agent of an important diplomatic errand. Some trouble had broken out in Wessex, and under king Ine a synod of clergy was held to settle the matter.[5] It was considered prudent that the decrees should be sent to Berhtwald, archbishop of Canterbury, for his approval. On the recommendation of Winbert, abbot of Nursling, Wintra, abbot of Tisbury, Beorwald, abbot of Glastonbury, and other monks, the king entrusted the mission to Winfrith. The speed and efficiency with which he conducted it made a strong impression, and he became a regular member of ecclesiastical synods. It was clear that a public career awaited him in the English Church.

But Winfrith's heart was set on other matters, and he unfolded to his abbot the desire which was unfolding in his mind to undertake missionary work. At first Winbert refused to release him. But eventually he relented, and in 716 Winfrith set out with two or three fellow-monks, on the eve of their departure receiving from archbishop Berhtwald a message, promising that the Church at home would pray for them.[6] Taking ship at London, they crossed over to Frisia and landed at Wijk bij Duurstede, intending to place their services at the disposal of Willibrord. But this was the period of upheaval following Pippin's death in 714. Willibrord had withdrawn to Echternach, and his mission was in a state of confusion. Radbod was making a determined effort to overthrow Frankish domination and the religion which in his view was identified with it. Most of the churches had been destroyed and the idolatrous shrines restored. Winfrith made his way to Utrecht, where after being kept waiting for some days he secured a fruitless interview with Radbod. He had the good sense to recognise the futility of remaining in Frisia in the existing circumstances, and returned home to Nursling, having spent the entire summer and most of the autumn of 716 in this enterprise.[7]

He remained at Nursling for another year or two. During this time Winbert died, and it was the wish of the community to promote Winfrith to the abbacy. But other plans were crystallizing in his mind. Irrevocably set on becoming a missionary, he decided to go to Rome and place himself at the pope's disposal. Owing to the vacancy in the abbacy his immediate spiritual superior was Daniel, bishop of Winchester, whose approval he obtained and who helped the Nursling brethren in their choice of a superior.[8] He provided letters of introduction for Winfrith, who in the autumn of 718 again set sail from London, arriving in Gaul after a swift and uneventful voyage. He never saw his native land again. With his party he made the perilous crossing of the Alps, hastening before the full rigour of winter should overtake them. They reached Rome, and presented the customary offerings at St Peter's. Winfrith then obtained an audience of Gregory II (715–31), who listened with interest and had many subsequent discussions with him concerning his proposals. The pope was in no way hurried. He fully realised the calibre of the man before him, and the importance of the work contemplated. It seems to have been many weeks, even months, before Gregory made up his mind concerning Winfrith.

On 15 May 719 Gregory II formally commissioned Winfrith as a missionary in the papal service. The mandate, which is the earliest of its kind that we possess,[9] is addressed to Boniface, the name by which the great West Saxon missionary subsequently described himself, and by which he has ever since been known. The commission itself is general in its terms. Boniface is to preach God's Word to those bound fast in paganism, though he must use Roman rites and formularies, and according to the biographer Willibald[10] is to make a report on the peoples of Germany and ascertain whether their hearts and minds are yet ready for the Gospel. Any difficulties which may arise are to be referred to the Apostolic see.

Proceeding northwards, Boniface toured Thuringia, the region east of the Rhine, bordered by the Harz mountains to the north and the Danube to the south. Here the ground had been prepared by Frankish clergy, and by Irish missionaries such as St Kilian (who died c. 688),[11] but the churches as a whole were in an undisciplined state. In the eighth century the Church in Thuringia was failing, and many Christians lapsing into heathenism.[12] Meanwhile, Boniface received news that the formidable Radbod was dead, and he decided to go to Frisia. This is rather a surprising action, but in thus changing his ground he was quite within the terms of his roving commission. It was, moreover, the Frisian mission which had first stirred his mind towards missionary work. Taking ship down the Rhine, he reached Utrecht, where he joined forces with Willibrord, now back on the scene of his missionary labours, secure once again in the protection of the Frankish power. Boniface remained with the archbishop from 719 to 722, and the importance of this period should be recognised as one of training in missionary methods. It may be, moreover, that Boniface was hoping that Willibrord would provide help for him in Thuringia.[13] During this time pagan shrines were destroyed and churches built or restored. As a result of his service under Willibrord Boniface became familiar with the system of assistant or 'country' bishops (chorepiscopi), anomalous according to strict canon law, which decreed that there could be only one bishop to each diocese.[14] The employment of assistant bishops without title or see of their own was a characteristic of Anglo-Saxon Christianity at this time, and Boniface himself was in due course to adopt the practice.

During this Frisian period Boniface received letters from two English abbesses—Bugga and Eangyth.[15] The former, otherwise known as St Eadburga, daughter of the Wessex king Centwin and abbess of Minster-in-Thanet, was very helpful to Boniface by sending him books. She wrote to him in 720 asking for advice in her scriptural studies, and forwarding him money and an altar cloth as gifts. Eangyth in her letter poured out her depression, complaining of the worry which was her lot as abbess of a double monastery. She longed to get away from it by going on pilgrimage to Rome, and she asked Boniface's advice. We do not know his reply.

Feeling the approach of old age, Willibrord wished to make Boniface his coadjutor in the Utrecht see, but the latter begged to be excused, on the ground that he was below the canonical age of fifty. There was no small argument over this matter. According to Willibald, 'on the one hand the saint, deterred by a sense of humility, declined so great an honour; Willibrord, on the other, eager for spiritual gain, had in mind only the salvation of souls'.[16] This was a clash of the worthiest of motives. But Boniface's real reason for refusing consecration in Frisia arose perhaps from an uneasy feeling that by settling down as Willibrord's lieutenant for three years he had wandered too far from the terms of the apostolic commission. He reminded Willibrord that he had given him his services without consulting his master the pope. Without papal consent he dare not accept episcopal office. He must now make his way to the lands which Gregory really had in mind on the granting of the general commission.

Boniface set out for Amoeneburg, in Hesse, west of Thuringia. This was a region where the traditional Germanic heathenism was strong. It was theoretically within the diocese of Mainz, but the Frankish bishops had made no efforts to convert it. Boniface had an initial success with the conversion of two chiefs, the brothers Dettic and Deorwulf, and this was inevitably followed by the conversion of many Germans. There were soon enough Christians to call for the erection of a small church. The work promised so well that Boniface sent a messenger to Rome to report on what had been done and to ask the pope's advice. Gregory replied summoning Boniface to Rome.

Gregory met Boniface in the basilica of St Peter, where he examined him concerning his orthodoxy. The West Saxon, however, did not trust his skill in the colloquial Latin spoken in Italy at this time, and was allowed to submit his profession of faith in writing. At a second interview the pope and Boniface spent almost a whole day in each other's company discussing theological questions and the needs of the mission field. It is clear that Gregory was aware of the immense possibilities of the plan which Boniface must have unfolded to him at this time, but was making sure of his man. Fully satisfied, he consecrated him on 30 November 722.[17] There was never a clearer case of an Englishman dedicating himself to the service of the Holy See. Boniface took the oath of loyalty to the papacy which was customary with newly consecrated suburbicarian bishops. In place of the usual clause of loyalty to the emperor at Constantinople, however, there was substituted a promise to avoid communion with bishops who erred from the doctrine of the Fathers, and an undertaking to report such miscreants to Rome. The pope guaranteed Boniface his patronage and friendship, and gave him letters of commendation, particularly to Charles Martel, whom Boniface next visited, securing his approval.

There followed ten years of missionary work in Hesse and Thuringia, inaugurated by the famous felling of the sacred oak at Geismar, from whose timber he built a church in honour of St Peter.[18] The usual missionary technique was adopted of approaching in the first place the chieftains. To the early years of this period belongs a letter from

Daniel bishop of Winchester, written probably between 723 and 725, advising him on missionary methods.[19] He says that Boniface should aim at convincing his heathen opponents intellectually, a recommendation in line with the high scholarly level which prevailed in the Anglo-Saxon Church at this time. Perhaps Boniface's old diocesan distrusted spectacular affairs like the felling of sacred trees. About the same time Boniface received a letter of encouragement from Gregory II, who had been informed of the successful opening stages of the German mission.[20] We learn from this letter that a certain Frankish bishop, who had not himself bothered to preach in Thuringia, was now claiming jurisdiction over some of Boniface's territory. The pope assures Boniface that he has written to Charles requesting him to keep this bishop in order.

Missionary advance brought its problems, necessarily attendant upon the arrival of a new religion amongst a heathen folk. Boniface wrote for advice to the pope upon sundry items, as Augustine of Canterbury had done years before. The replies of Gregory II contain the remarkable provision that a man may divorce a partner in a state of ill-health disabling her from fulfilling her duties as a wife.[21] Another instance, in the same document, of seemingly harsh indifference to elementary human kindness occurs in the pope's reply concerning child oblates. Boniface was apparently perturbed over the problem of children given in their infancy to the cloister, but who on growing up wished to enter secular life and marry. Gregory will in no circumstances allow such an impiety. The document in fact is marked by that legality which has always been such a distinctive feature of the Church of Rome.

Boniface had to contend not only with heathenism, but also with perverse and heretical priests, like the wandering Celtic preachers whose system was inimical to the order and discipline dear to the Roman's heart. We know the names of some of these undisciplined churchmen —Torchtwine, Berthere, Eanbert, and Hunred. Moreover, the support of Charles Martel, who was not an enthusiastic adherent of the Church, had failed to come up to Boniface's expectations.

The report of Boniface's work spread widely, and the result was a welcome increase in the number of volunteers from England. It is apparent that for many years from c. 725–30 onwards the German mission was an absorbing subject of interest in the English Church. It came to bear the character of a great national enterprise, almost the satisfaction of a debt of honour—the conversion by the Anglo (or English) Saxons of their kinsmen on the Continent. The mission appealed especially to English writers and scholars, and intellectual men figured prominently amongst the first volunteers.[22] This was a fortunate circumstance for the young German Church, as it was thus enabled to be established on a rational basis. It is interesting also to find the Anglo-Saxon minster system, the precursor of the later parochial form of ecclesiastical division in England, being now introduced into Germany. The new missionaries from England were organised in scattered groups, from which went out the clergy to preach in the villages and country districts of Hesse and Thuringia. Amongst the many who joined Boniface at this stage or later were Wigbert, who became the first abbot of Fritzlar;[23] Burchard, a monk from Malmesbury who was afterwards bishop of Wurzburg; a priest named Denehard, apparently a sort of chaplain and right-hand man to Boniface, who employed him on embassies to Rome; and greatest of all, Lull.[24] Educated first at Malmesbury and later at Nursling by Boniface, Lull was destined to succeed his master in the leadership of the mission. Amongst nuns there was Leoba (or Leobgyth), a relative of Boniface on his mother's side, a learned woman of strong character in the true Anglo-Saxon tradition. After early training at Minster-in-Thanet, she went to Wimborne, then under a very strict regime conducted by the abbess Tetta. She was a correspondent of Boniface, sending him specimens of her verse with a request that he correct her literary style and send her an example of his own writing. She has studied, she says, under abbess Eadburga, whom she describes as a laborious student of holy scripture.[25] Leoba was accompanied to Germany by her relative Thecla, also of the Wimborne community, and by other nuns, including Chunihildt (Lull's aunt) and her daughter Berthgit—who were set over a school in Thuringia. Leoba herself became abbess of Tauberbischofsheim. As a whole, however, nuns did not come over with the first waves of missionaries, but from about fifteen to twenty years after 730, when the German mission was more firmly established. Walpurgis, well known in German medieval folklore, was the sister of the two brothers Winnibald and Willibald (not to be confused with the biographer) who joined the mission. Nearly all the missionaries were professed religious, and almost from the start the backbone of the mission consisted of Benedictine communities, such as those of Ohrdruf, Amoeneburg, and Fritzlar.

Boniface was active as a correspondent during this period, and *c*. 735 wrote two letters to abbess Eadburga, expressing gratitude for gifts of books and clothes. He also asked her to write out for him the Epistles of St Peter, in letters of gold.[26] He wrote *c*. 735, also, to Pecthelm, first bishop of Whithorn, who died about this time; to Nothelm, archbishop of Canterbury (735–39); and to an abbot Duddo, requesting from him commentaries on the writings of St Paul.[27]

Gregory II, to whom Boniface owed so much, died early in 731, and was succeeded by Gregory III, who continued his predecessor's support of the German mission. Boniface sent his greetings to the new pope, along with a report on the progress of the mission. The year 732 marked the third landmark in Boniface's career as a missionary in the papal service. The first was the original commissioning in 719, the second his consecration of 722. Now after the ten great years of evangelistic work in Hesse and Thuringia, he was granted metropolitan rank, with power to consecrate other bishops.[28] He remained, however, without an episcopal seat, and would be without one until 747, when Mainz became the formal centre of his see. Besides conferring the pallium upon him, Gregory gave him advice on a variety of topics, such as second marriage by widowers (of which Gregory disapproved), the eating of horseflesh (connected with heathen sacrifice), the sale by Christians of their slaves for sacrifice in heathen rites, and rebaptism— Boniface is to rebaptise Christians baptised by priests who at the same time were sacrificing to heathen gods. It is interesting to come across this reference to members even of the priesthood who, like the East Anglian king Raedwald a century earlier, tried to keep a foot in each camp.

The year 732 also marked an important event in general European history. The Arabs, having conquered Spain, had for some time been across the Pyrenees, and were devastating Septimania and Provence. They now advanced into Aquitaine, whose ruler duke Eudes called for aid to Charles Martel. For several days the Franks withstood the Arabs, led by Abd-ar-Rahman, at Tours, until the invaders were forced to withdraw. It was a memorable victory for Christian civilisation. Without it, Boniface could hardly have continued his work, and the subsequent history of Europe as a whole would have been vastly different.[29]

From about this time Boniface seems to have been much pre-occupied with the idea of converting the heathen Saxons, and it is clear that he was contemplating a mission amongst them. In 738 he wrote home to England, calling on all ranks of the Church to join in prayer for this great undertaking, in which would be attempted the conversion of the continental blood-brothers of the Anglo-Saxons.[30] The political conditions were favourable. Charles Martel had recently defeated the Saxons, and the way lay open, it seemed, to their Christianisation. In 738 Boniface paid his third visit to Rome, and we cannot doubt that it was with the object of securing papal approval of his Saxon project. While he was in Rome his preaching attracted many hearers, including the brothers Winnibald and Willibald[31]—it was as a result of this contact that they joined his mission. This Willibald is one of the most colourful figures in early English history. Reared at Waltham abbey, he became the most celebrated of Anglo-Saxon travellers, visiting the Holy Land as a pilgrim. His many adventures, which inaugurate the long history of English interest in the Middle East, took him to Sicily and Cyprus, to Syria and Constantinople. After returning, he settled down as a monk at Monte Cassino in 729. His travels are famous through the account of them written down by an Anglo-Saxon nun of Heidenheim, but there is no reason for assuming that they were unique. There were surely many pilgrims who had adventures of which to tell, and it seems that travel and geographical books were read by the missionaries in Germany, and indeed may have been part of the spur urging them to go abroad in the first instance. Cosmography was a favourite study of the Anglo-Saxons, who delighted to learn of the inhabitants of distant lands. Thus, Benedict Biscop had brought back from Rome a volume of cosmography, to be much admired by king Aldfrith. Bede mentions a Gallic bishop Arculf, who had toured Jerusalem, Damascus, Constantinople, Alexandria, and several islands, but during his return voyage was wrecked on the west coast of Britain. He found hospitality with Adamnan, abbot of Iona, who listened eagerly to his tales and committed them to writing, subsequently presenting the book to Aldfrith. The king made it generally available, and Bede included extracts from it in the closing chapters of the *Ecclesiastical History*.

However, Boniface's scheme for converting the Old Saxons was premature, as was also Charles Martel's victory over them. In the event Boniface never worked amongst the Saxons. Instead of securing the desired commission to attempt their conversion, he returned from

Rome with papal authority to organise the Church of southern Germany on a diocesan basis. He was now an old man, but the most enduring part of his work still lay ahead of him.

Boniface had already, in 735, visited Bavaria in his general capacity as regional archbishop with legatine powers for all Germany east of the Rhine. Bavaria, ruled since 736 by duke Odilo, had for many years been basically a Christianised country. In southern Germany there were monasteries like Reichenau, on an island in lake Constance, founded in 724 by a missionary of uncertain nationality by the name of Pirmin.[32] It is likely that Christianity had been known in Bavaria and Alamannia since Roman times. Frankish preachers had been active here. Of such were Rupert, who came originally from Worms and evangelised Bavaria and Austria, using as his centre the later Salzburg; Emmeram, who was associated with Regensburg; and Corbinian, who worked from Freising. Theodo I, duke of Bavaria, had tried hard to promote Christianity amongst his subjects, even visiting Gregory II in 716 in search of advice. As a result, a delegation had come to Bavaria in that year from Rome to help the Bavarian Church. After Theodo's death there was a period of confusion politically, still existing when Boniface visited Bavaria in 735. Odilo (who was probably Theodo's grandson) became duke in 736 with Charles Martel as his overlord. On the whole, Bavarian Christianity was undisciplined. Though there were some definite ecclesiastical centres such as Regensburg and Salzburg, bishops did not have settled seats, and the characteristic cleric of the region was nomadic. Contact with Rome was intermittent, and diocesan organisation virtually non-existent.

Boniface arrived in the duchy in 739 and at once settled down to work with the support of duke Odilo. He divided the country into four dioceses—Salzburg, Regensburg, Freising, and Passau—consecrating bishops for the first three. Vivilo, who had already been consecrated by Gregory III, and was at the time the only Bavarian bishop with a settled see, was confirmed in his possession of Passau. These four bishops were the first to serve under Boniface actually as diocesan bishops. Another see was established two years later at Eichstätt, serving a half-Christianised countryside in a wild region which had been assigned to Willibald as his sphere of labour.

On hearing of Boniface's achievements, Gregory III wrote in October 739 with congratulations and words of encouragement. He must persevere in his teaching of the Catholic and Roman faith.

Priests who had been ordained by bishops whose own consecration was dubious, were to be reordained; but Christians who had been baptised in the name of the Trinity need only be confirmed. The pope mentions a council which will be held shortly on the banks of the Danube, and which Boniface should attend. The archbishop is reminded of his own roving commission. He must not remain in one region once his task there is completed, and not shrink from difficult journeys in the service of Christianity.[33]

After the organising of the Church of Bavaria came that of the Church of Hesse and Thuringia. In 741 Boniface founded the sees of Buraburg, Wurzburg, and Erfurt, appointing Anglo-Saxons (Witta and Burchard) to open the episcopal lines of the first two. Boniface therefore now had eight diocesan bishops within the orbit of his authority. In addition, he had assistant bishops, who included Anglo-Saxons, without specified areas of their own. There were also some bishops of established dioceses in Alamannia who acknowledged his metropolitan authority.

During these years there was also a remarkable growth in the monastic life of Germany, numerous houses being founded in the generation from c. 740. Besides the thriving communities at Amoeneburg, Fritzlar, and Ohrdruf, there was founded c. 741 in the Passau diocese a house at Altaich, a daughter of Reichenau, and Benediktbeuern in the Bavarian Alps. The monastery at Eichstätt, north of the Danube, became the centre of Willibald's see. A few miles away was Heidenheim, the only known instance of a double monastery in eighth-century Germany, and clearly modelled on the English institution. It was ruled over by Willibald's brother Winnibald, who was succeeded by their sister Walpurgis on his death in 761. Another nun at Heidenheim was one whose name until recently was unknown—this was Huneberc, the English nun who wrote the account of Willibald's travels. Greatest of all these monasteries was Fulda, on whose foundation Boniface lavished a considerable amount of care, and to which he came repeatedly in his closing years for peace and refreshment. The buildings were commenced in 744 on land given by Carloman, and a Bavarian named Sturm,[34] who as a child had been offered to Boniface by Christian parents, was selected as first abbot. Four years later Sturm went to Monte Cassino to make a first-hand study of Benedictinism, returning in 750. By the time of his death in 779 there were over four hundred monks in his monastic family. Boniface meanwhile loved this place with much the same affection which Willibrord had felt for Echternach. In 751, at the petition of Boniface, the monastery was placed under the specific protection of the Holy See by pope Zacharias. It is clear that the founder was not prepared to leave this monastery, which he cherished above all others, to the mercy of Frankish bishops.

Charles Martel died in 741, and the ten years which followed were a period of co-operation between his sons Carloman and Pippin, and Boniface, in the task of reforming the Frankish Church. The death of Charles was a considerable loss to Boniface. The great Frankish ruler, though a 'hammer' of the Church no less than of the heathen forces which during his time pressed heavily on the borders of Christendom, had provided the settled conditions necessary for Boniface's work. It had been the practice of Charles to seize the properties of monasteries and churches to provide revenues for his mounted soldiers. He was cool in his relations with the papacy. But in the final analysis he must be counted as one of the champions of Christianity—carrying his sword against the heathen Frisians and Saxons, stemming the tide of Moslem invasion at Tours in 732, and protecting both Willibrord and Boniface in their missionary labours. He was succeeded in the mayoralty by his sons, Carloman, who assumed the government of Austrasia, and Pippin (the 'Short'), who took Neustria and Burgundy. Their father had been first and foremost a warrior. The sons (at least Carloman) were more peacefully inclined, and showed a greater enthusiasm in the practice of their church membership.

The new phase, however, opened badly. Gregory III died almost simultaneously with Charles Martel, and was succeeded by Zacharias (741–52), whose relations with Boniface were never so cordial as those which had prevailed during the pontificates of his predecessors. There was, moreover, an upheaval in the south, duke Odilo of Bavaria, who had always chaffed under Frankish overlordship, taking advantage of the change-over in secular government and its division. In his bid for independence he had a certain amount of support from the new pope, who saw in him a possible ally against the Lombards in Italy, a role which Charles had declined to fulfil. Zacharias was thoughtless enough to send a papal legate to Bavaria without reference to Boniface. The refusal of the latter to be nettled over this unworthy action is a measure of his greatness. He did not waver in his loyalty to Rome. In the event the situation was restored politically by the victory of Pippin over Odilo, who became a feudal dependant of the Frankish crown.

Zacharias apparently realised his initial error, and he hereafter continued the support of Boniface which had been the policy of the two Gregories. But personal relations between him and the archbishop were never warm. In his preliminary letter of loyalty to the pope,[35] in 742, Boniface declares his intention to maintain unswervingly the Catholic faith and the unity of the Roman Church, and to urge obedience to the Holy See upon all his disciples. He requests papal approval of the recently established bishoprics of Wurzburg, Buraburg, and Erfurt, and of a proposed synod which will deal with the reform of the Frankish Church. Such a council, he writes, has not been held for over eighty years. Boniface is particularly anxious for the papal support in this important undertaking. The letter indicates that Boniface will shortly launch a resolute campaign against evil-living bishops, priests, and deacons. It is chiefly notable, however, for its frank condemnation of abuses and pagan survivals in Rome, which continue beneath the very shadow of St Peter's basilica. In language which is almost that of master to pupil, Boniface calls on Zacharias to suppress these heathen customs; it is virtually a piece of advice to the pope to govern his own diocese more thoroughly. It is futile, however, to argue on the strength of this epistle that Boniface had reservations in his attitude to papal supremacy. He was simply expressing in forthright language his concern for the good name of the Holy See, in whose service he had staked his life.

Nevertheless, by this time in his career he was feeling more confident of his own powers, and it is significant that he did not wait for the pope's reply before going ahead with the proposed synod. Indeed, he probably grew tired of waiting. It was more than a year before Zacharias dispatched his reply, which is dated 1 April 743.[36] In a somewhat critical tone the pope confirmed the establishment of the three new sees—he is not certain, he said, whether the sites chosen and the number of inhabitants really justified the archbishop's action. It almost has the air of a peevish hint that Boniface's missionary progress in Germany has not really been so outstanding. The pope had made his countercharge, and his honour was satisfied.

Pippin had inherited something of the martial spirit of his father, but Carloman was devout and ecclesiastical in his tastes. This was fortunate for Boniface, as it was in the latter's territory (which included the Germanic lands east of the Rhine) that the area of the archbishop's mission lay. The synod, under Carloman's auspices, was duly held in the spring of 742. For the next few years Boniface concentrated his attention on the Frankish Church, and left the care of the German Church to his suffragans and assistants. Further synods followed in 743 and 744, and were again held in the springtime, which is not without significance. They took place, that is to say, in connection with the *campus Martius*, or annual meeting of the army held in the spring.[37] The Frankish reform synods from the outset therefore were closely associated with the secular power. Their decrees acquired the force of state law. Boniface himself presided over the synods, his metropolitical authority over the Frankish Church thus being acknowledged. Pippin followed his brother's example, and convened a synod at Soissons in March 744, though this does not seem to have been attended by Boniface himself. In the following year came a joint synod of the whole Frankish Church, with representatives (clerical and lay) from both Neustria and Austrasia, Boniface presiding. Boniface, however, had enemies amongst the Frankish episcopate, and when it was proposed to make him archbishop of Cologne, which would have been a convenient base for his cherished but never realised project to evangelise the Saxons, there was such strong opposition to the proposal that it was dropped, though the pope had approved it.

Amongst those who troubled Boniface were two schismatic heretics, one a Frank by the name of Aldebert and the other an Irishman Clement. The two men worked separately, and had little in common except an undisciplined imagination. Aldebert appears to have been a religious maniac with a fondness for talking with angels. Reporting them to Rome through his trusted priest Denehard, Boniface asked the pope to condemn these heretics, as 'one diseased sheep will infect the whole flock'. On 25 October 745 the matter was considered at a synod in Rome. The two men were deprived of their episcopal orders and imprisoned in Gaul, but they managed to escape and resume their activities. In 747 Zacharias ordered Pippin to restrain them and send them to Rome unless they desisted. They apparently did so, as nothing further is heard of them.[38]

In 747 a second general council of the Frankish Church was held. Its decrees do not survive, though Boniface has summarised them in a letter to Cuthbert, archbishop of Canterbury, which he wrote later in the same year.[39] He says that the council has determined to maintain the Catholic faith and obedience to the Roman see. A synod will in future be held every year in the Frankish Church. The clergy are forbidden to waste their time hunting and hawking, to bear arms, or to wear colourful dress. The terms of the declaration of loyalty to Rome are very emphatic, and indeed suggest that hitherto the Frankish Church had been lax in the matter of papal obedience. Every priest is to make a report concerning his ministry to his bishop during Lent. Bishops are to visit their dioceses annually, instructing and confirming the people, and extirpating pagan rites and customs. In this letter Boniface advised Cuthbert to discourage Englishwomen from making too many journeys to Rome, on the ground of the great moral danger involved. There are towns in Lombardy and Gaul where all the harlots are of English race. This state of affairs is a disgrace to the English Church.

The 747 synod marked the practical conclusion of Boniface's reforming work on behalf of the Frankish Church. It was a work which brought discipline and order into that Church's life, and cemented its bonds with Rome. The Frankish rulers, Carloman and Pippin, were taken into a relationship with the papacy which their father had never known, and which was to have immeasurable consequences for the future history of Europe. After this synod Carloman, always the more pious of the two brothers, abdicated to become a monk.

In 751 there occurred an event of considerable interest, when Childeric III, puppet king and last of the Merovingian house, was deposed and replaced by Pippin. This action had papal approval,[40] and Boniface officiated at Pippin's coronation.[41] Boniface, however, seems to have had no part in the proceedings which led up to this act. Indeed, though his personal ascendancy over the Carolingian rulers was undoubtedly great, his political influence in their territories must not be exaggerated.

Boniface was much hampered in his work for the Frankish Church by constant opposition, both from bishops and heretics. It was probably episcopal obstruction which caused the abandonment of a scheme, after its approval by Zacharias, to grant metropolitan status to the sees of Rheims, Sens, and Rouen. The scheme arose out of the Soissons synod of 744. In the event only the bishop of Rouen secured the pallium. Besides the heretics Aldebert and Clement, who despite their glaring deviation from the Catholic faith were suppressed only with difficulty, Boniface had to contend with a priest Samson, who believed in the sufficiency of confirmation itself without baptism. His main worry, however, was an Irish priest Ferghil, better known as Virgilius, a man of considerable charm, impressing duke Odilo, who made him abbot of St Peter's, Salzburg. After the death of John, whom Boniface had installed as bishop of Salzburg, Odilo made Virgilius his successor as ruler of the diocese. He governed this diocese as abbot, in the Celtic manner, from 745, employing a bishop named Dobdagree for episcopal functions.[42] He was eventually himself consecrated bishop, and held the see until 784. But Boniface for the rest of his own life had to bear in his flesh the excruciating thorn of an abbot in priest's orders ruling a diocese within his province.[43] Virgilius held views concerning the universe which Boniface considered heretical. He believed in the existence of another world besides our own, inhabited by men.[44] However, he was highly regarded, and centuries later canonised. The pope upheld him against the attacks of Boniface, and in general it seems that Zacharias was becoming somewhat wearied with the zeal of his arch-bishop. Thus when Boniface in some cases insisted on a second baptism, the pope found it necessary to remind him of the validity of baptism by a heretic, provided it was performed in the name of the Trinity. In a pointed rebuke, he said that Boniface must try in this connection 'to comply with the doctrine and preaching of the Fathers of the Church'.[45] In other words, let the arch-hunter of heresy beware lest in his enthusiasm he comes perilously near to an unsound viewpoint himself.

The coronation of Pippin as king of the Franks marked the virtual completion of Boniface's work in the field of public affairs. He was now over seventy, and would have been justified in retiring to his monastery of Fulda. But he resolved to make yet another attempt at the conversion of the Frisians amongst whom he had worked years before. He would go to those Frisians who were still heathen, and outside the area of Frankish rule. Some three years previously he had already asked to be relieved of his archiepiscopal duties in Germany. Zacharias had refused the request, though he had agreed to the appointment of a coadjutor-bishop, Boniface choosing for this post Lull, whom he had marked to succeed him as leader of the German mission.

In March 752 Zacharias died, and was succeeded by Stephen II.[46] Several months elapsed before Boniface sent to him, the fourth pope under whom he had served, the customary letter of congratulation. The delay, as the archbishop explains in his letter, was due to his preoccupation in restoring the damage caused by a heathen raid. In this affair, carried out in Thuringia by marauding Saxons, more than thirty churches had been pillaged and burnt.

A missionary advance into Frisia would require Utrecht as a base. But the claim of the bishops of Cologne to jurisdiction over this see complicated the situation. The claim was based on the grant in 639 by Dagobert I to the then bishop of Cologne of the castle and chapel of Utrecht, on condition that the bishop undertook evangelistic work amongst the Frisians. The condition had never been fulfilled, and the Frankish ecclesiastics in general had neglected their missionary responsibilities. In 753 Boniface wrote to Stephen objecting to the bishop of Cologne's claim, and requesting his judgment in favour of Utrecht's independence.[47] The pope's reply is unknown. But Boniface also made an approach to Pippin, who declared him administrator of the Utrecht see.

His farewell with Lull is one of the most moving scenes of his life.[48] Convinced apparently of the imminence of death, he gave Lull instructions relating to the building of new churches in Thuringia and the completion of the abbey of Fulda. During the interview Lull was unable to contain his emotions, and broke down. But Boniface quietly proceeded with his preparations, and in the early summer of 753 boarded ship with his company and sailed down the Rhine. Arriving at Utrecht, he crossed the Zuyder Zee and commenced amongst the heathen Frisians the last act of his apostolate.

The mission prospered. Temples were overthrown, and churches built. Thousands were baptised. In all this Boniface was faithfully assisted by Leoban, whom he had appointed bishop of Utrecht. The chronology of the last year or two of Boniface's life is uncertain, but it seems that after this successful summer of preaching in Frisia in 753 he may have retired to Utrecht for the winter, returning in the following year. Pitching his camp one day on the banks of the river Boorne, at Dokkum some ten miles inland, he prepared to confirm a group of newly baptised converts. It was the feast of Pentecost. But at dawn on the appointed day, 5 June, before the candidates arrived, a troop of heathen soldiers attacked the camp. The companions of Boniface promptly took up arms, but their leader forbade resistance. Thirty of them,[49] probably the entire company, including Leoban, perished with him. Boniface himself was butchered in his tent, making an involuntary movement to shield his head from the death-blow with the book in which he was reading. After the massacre, the heathens quarrelled amongst themselves, and littered the fields with the books which they found in place of the expected treasure. Some of these books were afterwards picked up and taken to Fulda, where three of them are still to be seen, the *Codices Bonifatiani*, including a damaged gospel manuscript which is traditionally identified with the book with which the great martyr tried to protect his head.

After three days, relates Willibald,[50] divine vengeance overtook the murderers. As news of Boniface's death spread through the villages, a Christian host assembled, and advanced on the heathen territory. Pagans were slaughtered in great numbers. The Christians seized their wives and children as spoil, and the non-Christians of the surrounding districts, awed by such retribution, 'opened their minds and hearts to the glory of the faith'.

The bodies of the martyrs were conveyed across the Zuyder Zee to Utrecht, and thence in a voyage of solemn triumph up the Rhine to Mainz. There was no small dispute between the citizens of Utrecht and Mainz over the question of the retention of the archbishop's body. But Lull, mindful of an expressed wish of Boniface, brought the body to Fulda, where it found its final resting-place.

Not long afterwards Cuthbert, archbishop of Canterbury, wrote to his compatriot Lull, expressing the pride of the English in the achievements of Boniface.[51] They count it an honour that it was their nation which sent forth so great a soldier of Christ, to wage battle in distant lands for the praise of God. Like a true champion he has borne the standard of victory into remote regions, and has brought barbarians into the light of Jesus. A synod of the English Church has fixed 5 June as an annual commemoration, declares Cuthbert, and Boniface has taken his place along with Gregory I and Augustine as a patron of the English Church.[52] Milret, bishop of Worcester, who had seen Boniface not long before his death, also wrote from England to Lull. His letter[53] is an indication of the sadness which filled the hearts of Englishmen when the news from Germany reached them. But like Cuthbert's, it glows with a pride which is as patriotic as it is Christian. Boniface is 'the glory and crown of all those whom the Motherland has sent forth', and 'his pilgrimage completed by a supreme effort, he has attained a splendid death as Christ's martyr, and sits now in glory in the heavenly Jerusalem'.

In the great achievement of which Willibrord and Boniface were the main executors three features stand out. In the first place we find an astonishing loyalty to Rome. It is this characteristic, in all its clarity, which has been the main cause of the neglect of Boniface by his fellow-countrymen of modern times. Protestant Englishmen have found it hard to be enthusiastic over a man who was nothing if not a papist. In the spirit of the comitatus Boniface never swerved from the service of his papal masters, who on the whole well supported him. In the dedication of Boniface to Rome the triumph of the Whitby conference bore its ripest fruit. Willibrord, a monastic son of Wilfred, was missionary mentor to Boniface, and the theme of papal allegiance runs through the careers of all three men. The foresight of pope Gregory in making England the special child of the papacy was fully vindicated. A young and vigorous people, unhampered by any traditions save those of heroism, had made Rome the ultimate standard of its loyalties. And now with remarkable persistence this people was conducting a campaign to establish the Church in the heart of Europe. The labours of Boniface and his companions are an important landmark in the foundation of western Christendom, and a contribution of unparalleled significance to the development of papal supremacy.

It is, however, ironical that this contribution might never have been made had the Anglo-Saxon Church lacked its Celtic strain. Willibrord had years of residence in Ireland as part of his training, and Boniface was a native of a region where the Saxons may well have been a minority surrounded by a much larger native population. It was surely from the Celts that the English missionaries took their evangelistic zeal, their devotion to the cause of learning and scholarship, and much of their love of wandering in strange lands. So pronounced are these features in the lives of English missionaries at this time, that we would be justified in entitling the Church which reared them as the Celto-Saxon Church.

And yet the English themselves seem to have had no sense of indebtedness to the Celts, though they were not slow to make use of the Irish schools. Racially their affinities lay with the continental Germans, and it is their eagerness, combined perhaps with a sense of obligation, to convert the latter which constitutes the third feature of the mission. The English wished to lead into the way of salvation the Germans not only because the latter were children of Christ for whom He died, but also because they were their next of kin. It is possible that the Anglo-Saxons regarded the Germans with somewhat the same feelings shown by Australians and New Zealanders towards the British in our own day. To the conquerors and immigrants now settled for some generations in the land beyond the North Sea, Germany was 'the old country'. Boniface wrote of the Saxons of the Continent that they claimed to be 'of one blood and one bone' with the Saxons of England, and to him his native land was 'Saxony across the waters'.[54] At home, Torhthelm, bishop of Leicester, expressed his joy that the Saxons abroad, men of 'our own race', might be brought to believe in Christ.[55] It has been pointed out that the term 'Anglo-Saxon' actually originated on the Continent to distinguish the Anglian from the continental Saxons.[56] It was not coined, as is commonly assumed, to designate the two main branches of the English people. The affinity in race between the English and Germans must be accounted a major reason for the successes and enduring character of the work of Willibrord and Boniface. The Anglo-Saxons really knew their fellow Teutons, possessing a psychological understanding of them, and also it seems having little or no difficulty in practical details such as language. Before Hadrian could take over the abbey at Canterbury he first had to spend a considerable period of time in learning the native tongue. Augustine had needed interpreters, and Aidan had been compelled to make use of the services of Oswald in this capacity. Wilfred, by contrast, on arriving in Frisia was able to begin preaching at once. Such differences as existed linguistically were probably only those of dialect.[57] So close were Old English and Frisian that we are almost justified in regarding them as the same language, and it seems too that the Thuringians in the basin of the Saale, amongst whom Boniface worked, spoke this language.

The policy of reform and centralisation associated with Boniface was continued after his death. Synods were held, and such irregularities as Celtic nomadism were steadily eradicated. The reverence for Rome and the order and discipline which were part of her heritage, inculcated by the missionaries, took firm root in the Frankish and German Churches. From about the middle of the eighth century there was a strong movement to Romanise the liturgy. On the Continent Pippin ordered the adoption of Roman usages, not many years after the synod of Cloveshoe in England (747) removed any vestiges of liturgical eclecticism that may have survived by demanding the general use of the Roman rite. In other ways, too, the influence of the English missionaries continued. Thus the beautiful system of 'confraternities', introduced from England, long endured amongst the Franks.[58] These formal societies of associate members, often widely separated from each other geographically, were a potent means in keeping the missionaries within the memory and the prayers of their compatriots at home. These associations were purely guilds of prayer, with no other object than that the members should consider one another before the altar of the Lord. They undoubtedly played a considerable part in helping to ascribe to the German mission the character of a national undertaking. Yet another important contribution of the English missionaries was their fostering of the system of private penance, which they themselves had learned from the Celts in the British Isles, and which Irishmen had already introduced to the Continent. It was admirably suited to the Germanic peoples, whose pride and reserve would scarcely have permitted them to humiliate themselves publicly after the manner of the Latins. The Penitential code became a regular part of the ecclesiastical system; in the ninth-century Frankish Church it actually got out of hand, so many and various were the manifestations of this disciplinary exercise.

In the modern expression, Boniface was a difficult man to follow, and Lull, who succeeded him at Mainz, could hope to emulate neither his influence nor his achievements. Boniface himself towards the end of his life had become apprehensive about the future position of his missionaries in Germany, as is clear from a letter which he wrote to Fulrad, abbot of St Denis, in 752.[59] Lull maintained the practice of regular correspondence with England, and was a faithful prelate, but did not impress his personality upon ecclesiastical and secular affairs in the manner of his predecessor. Chrodegang of Metz, a continental churchman who succeeded Boniface as archbishop of the Germans following the great man's death, was a more forceful figure, well known for his initiative in compiling a Rule for his cathedral canons, an important point of departure in the history of collegiate institutions.[60]

The later stages of the Anglo-Saxon mission were chiefly notable for final efforts at the conversion of the heathen Frisians and the Old Saxons. On the death of Boniface the diocese of Utrecht was placed in the care of Gregory, an abbot in priest's orders, who employed an Englishman Albert as chorepiscopus. Gregory himself was a Frank and a pupil of Boniface. He died c. 775. Amongst the pupils of Gregory was Liudger, a Frisian, the first bishop of Munster .[61] In fact it is clear that native Christians were increasingly taking over the direction of affairs, though Anglo-Saxon missionaries continued to arrive in Frisia. Amongst the latter was Lebuin, who worked amongst the heathens on the east side of the Yssel, his base being Deventer.[62]

The greatest of these later Anglo-Saxon missionaries, and the last of the entire line, was Willehad.[63] A Northumbrian, he was sent across the North Sea as a missionary by a formal synodal decision of the Church of the north, with the approval of king Alhred. Arriving on the Continent c. 770, he spent some ten years preaching to the heathen Frisians. Then Charlemagne, determined to subdue the Saxons once for all and realising that Christianisation of these peoples was a necessary complement to their military conquest, ordered Willehad to proceed to the region between the Weser and the Elbe. Charles had already for some years been conducting a campaign of conversion at the point of the sword amongst the Saxons, who found a patriotic leader in Widukind. For a while Willehad had success, but in 782 the anger of the Saxons was aroused by a series of harsh regulations against paganism, which amongst other things prescribed death for the eating of flesh in Lent and for the practice of cremation. In such prescriptions Charlemagne overreached himself, and the result was a serious revolt which included the massacre of priests and religious. Willehad made his escape and journeyed to Rome, where he was received by Hadrian I. He next spent two years in the abbey of Echternach. In 785 Widukind submitted and was baptised, with Charles himself as godfather. Two years later Willehad was consecrated the first bishop of Bremen, having been busily engaged meanwhile in restoring the ravages of the insurrection. His death in 789 marks the virtual end of the Anglo-Saxon mission.

Since Willibrord arrived in Frisia in 690, almost a century had elapsed. It was fitting that this heroic mission should conclude with the establishment of the Church Militant amongst the very people on whose conversion the English Saxons had most set their hearts. The end in Saxony, however, did not come for several years. In 792 there was a further rising, in which the Church (the sign and token of enslavement) especially suffered. Charlemagne conducted a series of annual campaigns, and adopted an extreme policy of transporting whole bodies of Saxons and replacing them with Franks. So wearied eventually was the king with the unending resistance that he even, in 804, deported the Saxons of Holstein into Frankland, and put the heathen Obodrites, a Slav tribe, in their place. The final outpost of independent Germany had at last fallen to Rome, and in the sarcastic words of a Quaker historian, 'Christianity, or a religion which believed itself to be Christianity, was triumphant from the Rhine to the Elbe, and three fat bishoprics, Bremen, Munster, and Paderborn, divided between themselves the conquered land '.[64] Certainly the conversion of the Old Saxons reads a sordid tale. But most Anglo-Saxons probably did not regard it in this light, though Alcuin had his misgivings. It must have seemed enough to at least many Englishmen that those whom they regarded affectionately as their blood-brothers were worshipping the one true God and had been baptised in the waters of eternal life.

CHAPTER XVI

THE EIGHTH CENTURY: COUNCILS AND REFORM

There is every reason to believe that the outstanding characteristic of the English missionaries, their loyalty to the papacy, was shared by the whole Anglo-Saxon Church.[1] Eighth-century Englishmen in general were devoted to the Holy See, regarding Rome as the begetter and the final security of their faith, and the centre of all that was majestic and sacred. The Anglo-Saxons seem to have been the first of the northern peoples to establish a military colony in Rome to help in the papacy's defence. Hither came a steady stream of pilgrims from England, to pray at the tombs of the apostles and to fall beneath the spell of a city which had never lost contact with the ancient world.[2] Thus, about the time that Benedict Biscop died, the ferocious heathen Wessex king Caedwalla suddenly repented of his misdeeds, abdicated his throne, and made the pilgrimage to Rome. Here he was baptised, and on his death buried in St Peter's.[3]

He was succeeded in 688 by Ine, during whose reign of thirty-seven years notable advances in English Christianity were made. He was the first king of the West Saxons to issue written laws, a work which he could not have accomplished without the help of churchmen.[4] About the same time Wihtred, king of Kent, also published a written code of laws with the co-operation of archbishop Berhtwald; these laws declare the freedom of the Church from taxation, make provision against heathen practices, and also insist on a faithful standard of duty on the part of the clergy.[5] A primary object of Ine's laws also was the protection of the Church and the furtherance of her work. In this way, Sunday work was forbidden, and the delaying of the baptism of a newly-born child for more than thirty days. The payment of church scot was ordered. The privilege of sanctuary was upheld.

Ine was a supporter of monks, as indeed any propagandist of Christianity had to be in those times, and closely associated with the foundation of Abingdon abbey in particular. He was a patron of Aldhelm, who in 705 was entrusted with the task of persuading the Britons of the south-west peninsula to adopt the Roman Easter. In furtherance of this project Aldhelm wrote to Geraint, king of Dyfnaint, who seems to have been stubbornly resisting the steady advance of the West Saxons. In his letter[6] Aldhelm upbraided the British priests for their adherence to Celtic customs, as well as for their quarrelsome nature and their hatred of the Saxons. He called on them to obey the decrees of St Peter and not to spurn the tradition of the Roman Church. This letter was an important landmark in the victory of Romanism over the Celtic Churches.

Ine's realms undoubtedly contained many British, and indeed his laws implicitly recognise this. The native people are accorded their appropriate value in society, which though only half that of the Saxons, is precise and formal. In the more westerly regions of West Saxony the English must have been colonisers rather than conquerors, slowly and with difficulty making their way and establishing outposts amongst a largely Celtic population. In our own day, after a lapse of some forty generations, a careful observer in the more secluded villages of Wiltshire, Dorset, and Somerset, will see amongst the indigenous, long-established families numerous examples of a distinct Iberian type, small-boned and dark-haired. Ine would be extending his kingdom amongst a people which had long been Christian. There would be Christian centres in many places, such as Glastonbury, where a monastery existed, and where Ine himself raised a church.

Shortly after Aldhelm's letter, the West Saxon diocese, which had been left untouched by Theodore's reorganisation, was divided by order of archbishop Berhtwald. On the death of bishop Hedda in 705, Wessex east of Selwood Forest (that is, Hampshire, Berkshire, much of Wiltshire, together with Surrey and Sussex) remained the territory of the bishopric of Winchester. The new diocese of Sherborne was to consist of Dorset, some of Wiltshire, and such parts of Somerset and Devon as had come under Ine's rule. Aldhelm was consecrated first bishop of Sherborne, and held the see until his death at Doulting, Somerset, in 709. Not long after this, the South Saxons were assigned a diocese of their own, and Eadbert became the first bishop of Selsey.[7]

In the same year, 709, king Coenred of Mercia abdicated and went with Offa, king of the East Saxons, to Rome, where they spent their final days as monks. In 725 Ine also relinquished his throne and departed for Rome, accompanied by his queen, to live humbly and simply until their deaths.[8]

The first bishop of the reduced diocese of Winchester was Daniel, an interesting and attractive figure. It was during his episcopate that the Isle of Wight became part of the diocese. He was of much help to Bede in the compilation of the *Ecclesiastical History* by supplying information relating to the Wessex Church. He visited Rome in 721. He is best known, however, as a supporter and adviser of Boniface. At the time of Daniel's consecration Winfrith was a young monk at Nursling, in the Winchester diocese, whose new bishop discerned in him a man of promise. In his old age Daniel became blind. Resigning his see in 744, he retired to Malmesbury, where he had studied in his youth, to spend his remaining days.

Berhtwald archbishop of Canterbury died in 731, to be succeeded by Tatwine, a scholarly priest from the monastery of Breedon. He in turn was followed in 735 by a London priest Nothelm, who had been one of Bede's principal informants. On this archbishop's death four years later, Cuthbert became primate, reigning for more than twenty years. None of these prelates in any way approached Theodore in stature.

Of northern bishops at this time one of the best was St John of Beverley, a saint who came to be held in a reverence surpassed in the north only by that accorded to St Cuthbert. Educated first in the school of Canterbury, where Theodore was amongst his teachers, he later studied under Hild at Whitby. At the latter place he was one of the group of five who subsequently became bishops, he himself ruling the diocese of Hexham from 686 to 705 and York from 705 to 718. Bede writes affectionately of his work and records that it was from John that he received holy orders.[9] In the forest land of Deira John established a monastery—apparently the beginning of the famous church of Beverley. During his episcopate at Hexham, he built a retreat for private devotional retirement a mile and a half away, on the opposite bank of the Tyne, whither he was wont to repair from time to time, particularly in Lent. The place is associated in local tradition with the present parish of St John Lee. It was John's practice to keep here with him during Lent some poor and infirm person for charity's sake. On one occasion the recipient of this loving care was a certain youth from a neighbouring village, who suffered from baldness of the head, and also, more seriously, from dumbness, never having been known to speak a word. The interesting account which Bede gives is the earliest record in our history of specialised treatment of the dumb.[10] John healed the sufferer by teaching him in stages to articulate simple sounds such as A and B. Overjoyed at the cure, the bishop offered a permanent place in his *familia* to the young man, who, however, chose to return home.

In John of Beverley we see a man who seems to have had the genuine gift of divine healing. Bede records a number of cures, which he regarded as miracles, his chief informant being Berethum, abbot of the monastery in Deirawood. Thus on one occasion, during a visit of John to the nunnery of Watton, in the East Riding, the abbess requested him to minister to a sick nun, whom she believed would be better if he touched and blessed her. He prayed over her, and she recovered. Again, he healed the sick wife of a nobleman by giving her some holy water to drink. Another nobleman begged him to heal a well-loved servant who was at the point of death, by laying hands upon him and giving him his blessing. There is nothing ludicrous or improbable in all this—it is simply the Church's normal ministry of healing in the hands of a man with a special vocation for his work.

One of Bede's most pleasing stories is that of a young man, a cleric of John's *familia*, named Herebald, who in the company of some young laymen was travelling one day with the bishop. On coming to an open stretch of road, the young men galloped their horses. Herebald was thrown and fractured his skull. The bishop prayed all night for him, and on coming to him in the morning, asked him, 'Do you know who is speaking to you?' The young man replied, 'I do, you are my beloved bishop.' John asked, 'Can you live?' The answer was, 'I may do so, through your prayers, if it please the Lord.' The bishop laid hands on him, and blessed him. On the youth showing signs of marked recovery, his master placed him under the care of a medical man, with instructions to bind up his head. John seems in fact to have made a point of co-operating closely with physicians; thus after teaching the dumb youth to speak, he handed him over to a man of medicine for treatment to his bald head.

In 718 John resigned his episcopal duties because of age. He retired to his monastic foundation in Deirawood, where he passed his declining years in pious conversation. He died in 721.[11]

John was succeeded at York by Wilfred II, a worthy and much loved prelate who did much for the beautifying of churches, and was energetic in charitable work within his diocese.[12] On his resignation in 732 to end his days in retirement, he was followed by Egbert, an outstanding bishop who was nevertheless helped by the useful circumstance that he was the brother of the Northumbrian king Eadbert.[13] The two brothers worked together harmoniously for the good of the Northumbrian kingdom, until Eadbert resigned his throne in 758 to become a member of his brother's episcopal *familia*. In 735 York was raised to metropolitical rank,[14] and Egbert was an excellent ruler of the northern province for thirty-one years. He is remembered chiefly as the virtual founder of the school of York. He also worked hard on behalf of Christian discipline and moral behaviour. Theodore had already in the previous century tried to curb the evil habits of the Anglo-Saxons by an elaborate penitentiary system. Egbert in his *Penitentiale* likewise prescribed a system of penalties for specific faults.[15] In such codes we see the operation of practical minds, not content with mere exhortation to good conduct in general, but insistent on grappling with particular current sins. The Penitentials starkly reveal the grossness which existed in Anglo-Saxon life. Drunkenness especially was a besetting sin amongst all classes, from which it appears that even prelates could not be assumed to be free. The value of the Penitentials for the study of social habits during this period must not be exaggerated, but they do suggest an earnestness on the part of the Church authorities to mitigate the incidence of wrongdoing.

Amongst the bishops of Hexham, Acca deserves honourable mention (709–32). A pupil of Bosa, bishop of York, he became a disciple of St Wilfred, and an enthusiastic devotee of his brand of Christianity. He did much for church architecture, and loved to furnish the house of God with relics and vessels. A collector of books,[16] he also encouraged church music, he himself being a skilful singer. He gave much help to Bede in his literary work, and the great scholar speaks highly of him, praising his learning, his orthodoxy, his scrupulous obedience to ecclesiastical rules.[17] In retrospect he seems to us one of the fathers of Roman Christianity in England. In 732 he was, however, deposed from his see, in obscure circumstances, and succeeded by Frithbert, an undistinguished prelate who enjoyed the bishopric of Hexham for over thirty years. Acca died in 740[18] and was buried outside the east end of Hexham abbey church.

The task would be tedious to enumerate the names and what is known of the many bishops of this century.[19] It would, moreover, be largely pointless, as it was not only under the leadership of the episcopate that the fortunes of the Church rose and fell. There was always a close partnership of the Church with the royal houses, and for good or ill the influence of the kings was great.

Politically, the eighth century was the age of Mercian ascendancy. During two lengthy reigns, those of Aethelbald and Offa, Mercia rose to the leading position amongst English kingdoms. It is a period in Anglo-Saxon history whose importance has been insufficiently appreciated. It is, as it were, the water-shed, connecting the golden period of the Conversion and cultural flowering with the age of Wessex dominance, which in turn led to the English State as generally understood.

From a Christian viewpoint, the influence of Aethelbald (716–57) may be seen in the circumstance that the three archbishops of Canterbury appointed during his reign—Tatwine, Nothelm, and Cuthbert —were all drawn from the Mercian territory. But though he had been reared and trained under religious auspices, Aethalbald himself never attained the stature of a Christian monarch. He had reservations in his acceptance of the Church's teachings, while his personal life displayed failings which were castigated by Boniface in an important letter of 746–7.[20]

Boniface begins by praising the king for his generosity and his vigour in suppressing crime. But there follows at once the accusation of fornication and adultery committed in various religious houses with dedicated nuns. Even the heathen, says Boniface, will not countenance adultery. The savage customs of the Old Saxons towards their adulteresses are quoted with an evident approval. The letter goes on to mention a report common on the Continent, even as far afield as Italy, that the English have become a race of adulterers. In Boniface's view a deterioration in national character will surely set in. The English will cease to be strong in war, and the honour in which they are held will decline. This has been the fate of the peoples of Spain, Provence, and Burgundy, upon whom God has unleashed the Saracens as a punishment for their immorality. It is further reported that Aethelbald has confiscated ecclesiastical revenues, a crime as heinous as murder. In fairness to Aethelbald, however, it should be stated that he was not the initiator of this policy. The Church had remained secure in its privileges from the time of the Conversion until Ceolred (Aethelbald's predecessor as king of Mercia), and Osred king of Northumbria, committed the crimes of violation of nuns and destruction of monasteries. The letter ends with a stern call to repentance on Aethelbald's part.

It might be asked whence Boniface had derived his authority to write so bold a letter to a king who was not of his flock. The answer lies, implicitly, in another of his letters—to Egbert archbishop of York.[21] Here he states that his dispatch to Germany by the pope was included within a wider commission to convert all who had been led astray. It was in agreement with this obligation, and with the approval of his fellow-bishops, that he had sent a letter of reproof to Aethelbald. The letter was to be shown first to Egbert. Boniface goes to some pains, in writing to Egbert, to justify his letter to the king of Mercia, and he also urges the archbishop to root out the crimes of adultery and seduction of veiled women from amongst his own people.

Boniface entrusted a certain priest Herefrith with the task of delivering the letter to Aethelbald and reading it out to him and interpreting it. He was assured of Herefrith's courage, and had been given to understand, moreover, that he had a certain amount of moral influence over the king. Herefrith doubtless needed all his courage and moral influence for the thankless errand of personally bearing to a forceful and undevout king a stinging rebuke.[22]

Boniface's letter to Aethelbald is one of our strongest pieces of evidence for the view, frequently expressed, that the eighth century was a time of decadence for the English Church. It is tempting to believe that such decadence, if it existed, was largely due to the creaming-off of the best talent in favour of the continental missions. If there is any truth in the aphorism that there are no bad soldiers but only bad officers, it must lie in the fact that leadership sets the tone of any institution. If an unduly high proportion of potential leadership is taken away, a fall in general standards is almost inevitable. The foundation of splendid monasteries in Germany such as Fulda was followed, with an almost remorseless logic, by a greater worldliness amongst monks at home. It need not surprise us that many English nuns succumbed to temptation, when we consider that the women who as strong abbesses would have kept them in order felt called to serve in the Church overseas.

The forebodings and complaints concerning the state of affairs in the English Church of the eighth century, which we find in the correspondence of Boniface, as also in that of Bede and Alcuin, are confirmed by the considerable conciliar activity of the century, which suggests that not all was well. During Aethelbald's reign one of the greatest of English ecclesiastical councils was held (in 747) at Cloveshoe[23] in the province of Canterbury. It is possible that this council was a direct consequence of the letter of Boniface in 747 to archbishop Cuthbert to which reference has already been made.[24] In this letter

Map 2. Anglo-Saxon dioceses, c. 750.

he pointed out that the English, including their bishops, were addicted to luxury and drunkenness, that monastic lands were being appropriated by the kings—and something which was thoroughly disgraceful, that English women undertaking the pilgrimage to Rome were falling into prostitution on the way. He urged the primate to set measures of reform in motion. Boniface was at the time in a reforming mood, and for some years past had been promoting his reform synods in the Frankish Church. We should therefore not exaggerate the importance to English Church history of his strictures. They may mean little more than that towards the close of his life he was in a particularly stern and prophetical frame of mind.

Our immediate reaction is to suppose that Boniface's letter was the cause of convening the 747 synod at Cloveshoe. Actually, however, the main impetus was a letter of pope Zacharias demanding a reformation. Aethelbald himself attended the council, along with Cuthbert and eleven bishops.[25] Thirty canons were issued. They stipulate that the bishops are to be diligent in their pastoral duties rather than become embroiled in secular business, and must perambulate their dioceses each year, teaching the Word of God and suppressing heathen practices. So far as possible, priests must avoid worldly affairs, devoting their lives to reading and prayer and the care of their churches. It is essential that the clergy understand the meaning of the sacraments and offices which it is their duty to administer.[26] They should be more thoroughly examined before ordination. They are forbidden to declaim in church like secular poets, spoiling the sacred message by striving after dramatic effects, but to keep to the plain and sacred melody of the Church.[27] If plainsong is beyond the capacity of the priest, let him read the service in his natural voice. The canonical hours—according to the monastic office—are to be observed by all. If a cleric does not know Latin, he may still apply to the office the intentions of his heart.

The rogation days must be observed, not with games, horse-racing, and feasting, but by fasting and prayer. Ecclesiastics are to avoid over-drinking, lest the reverence with which laymen regard them be turned into contempt. There is here a distinct hint that the high esteem in which the clergy were held in the age of the Conversion, mentioned by Bede, is beginning to wane.

The bishops are instructed to admonish all abbots and abbesses to live according to rule. A thoroughly satisfactory reformation of the monasteries is asking too much, so greatly are they under the influence of secular persons, yet the bishops should visit them for their spiritual good. The religious must pay attention to study, which in these days is sadly neglected (Boniface also, in his letter to the archbishop, had referred to the prevailing distaste for reading and prayer). Schools for the young are to be maintained by the monasteries. Let monks and nuns avoid gorgeous apparel, and monasteries cease to be the homes of poets, harpists, and comedians. Every monastery should have a priest.

Thus far, the evidence indicates that at least the monasteries had fallen in standards and were lacking in spirituality, a conclusion suggested by Boniface's later correspondence, the canons of Cloveshoé, as well as by the letter of Bede to Egbert some years before. The bishops were not what they might be. The hand of the layman rested heavily upon religion. Moreover, complained Boniface, monks were being enslaved in England for work on royal buildings. This complaint apparently entailed nothing more than that land given to the Church was not being exempted from the customary *trinoda necessitas*—the furnishing of men for the fyrd and contributing to the repair of bridges and strongholds. Bede also had been of the opinion that Church lands should not be charged with these burdens, though he had on the other hand been gravely perturbed lest the nation should be weakened by an excessive donation of land to monasteries. In 749 Aethelbald seems to have given way to ecclesiastical pressure—perhaps on the understanding that as a result of Cloveshoe sham monasteries would be suppressed—to the extent of freeing churches and religious houses from the burdens of taxation and secular service, with the exception of bridge-building and the defence of fortified places.[28]

Aethelbald's lengthy reign prepared the way for that of his cousin Offa (757–96), under whom Mercia attained its greatest influence. The first Anglo-Saxon ruler to adopt the style of 'King of the English', which he did in charters of 774, he was also the first to have political relations with kings on the Continent. From the ecclesiastical point of view, the two great events of his reign were the visit of the papal legates and the creation of an archbishopric of Lichfield.

In 786 two legates from Hadrian I arrived in England. These were George,[29] bishop of Ostia, a trusted servant of the papacy who had already conducted missions on behalf of a number of popes, and Theophylact, bishop of Todi, who a few years later was to take part in the council of Frankfurt at which image worship was discussed. The mission is important and interesting as practically the only legatine visit to this country during Anglo-Saxon times. On the whole, the papacy left the Anglo-Saxon Church very much alone. It was, after all, its most distant dependency, and its loyalty and orthodoxy rendered close attention unnecessary. Hadrian I appears to have had some doubt about Offa's loyalty to him personally, and some time before the legatine visit wrote to Charlemagne mentioning a story which had come to his ears that Offa had proposed to the Frankish king his deposition and the election of a new pope.[30] Not that he really believed the rumour, commented Hadrian. In any case, there was no suggestion of Offa's disloyalty to Rome as such, and there is not the slightest evidence that the English regarded the legatine visit as vexatious, which indeed according to the Chronicle brought a renewal of the blessings which Augustine had introduced. The legates were received on their arrival by Jaenbert, archbishop of Canterbury, after which they presented themselves at Offa's hall, where according to the legates' own subsequent report they had a joyful welcome. A council followed, at which not only Offa was present, but also Cynewulf king of Wessex. The legates first laid before the council the specific articles which the pope thought should be looked into, and then went on a progress of enquiry through the country. The legate George, who investigated Northumbria, procured the adoption of twenty canons at a synod convened in that kingdom. This was clearly a provincial synod for York. These canons were signed by king Aelfweald, archbishop Eanbald, Tilbert bishop of Hexham, and others. Next, the canons were presented before a council of the southern province, where they were read in Latin, with an explanation in the vernacular. The council, attended by Offa and archbishop Jaenbert, duly accepted the canons.[31]

These canons, of which we have a detailed account in the report sent by the legates to the pope,[32] are an impressive landmark in the history of conciliar activity in England. The third canon itself decrees that there shall henceforth be two councils a year, and it does in fact seem that from this time there was a significant increase in the frequency of councils. At any rate, an exceptionally large number of conciliar documents survive for the forty years following. The canons insist on a higher standard of duty from the clergy. Thus the bishops are to visit their dioceses annually, teaching their flocks and co-operating in the appointment of abbots and abbesses. It might be remarked that a feature of the eighth-century reforming activity is that the bishops are made to take their share of the strictures, which are not solely appropriated (as commonly in our own day) to the lower clergy. To care for his people and visit them regularly is the bishop's main function, the neglect of which may imperil the sheep. Bishops must take care that those whom they ordain priests are suitable for the office. The offices are to be said publicly in church, and priests celebrating mass properly vested.[33] There is a tendency to insist on the communal life as the one most fitted for the clergy. Canons should live canonically, and ecclesiastics are not to take their meals privately except during sickness.[34] All Christian folk must know the Lord's Prayer and Creed, which godparents are to teach their charges so soon as they are of age.

The decrees emphasise the importance of legitimate birth. Persons born outside wedlock may not become kings or be ordained priests. Neither may they inherit property—sons of nuns are specifically included in this prohibition. Illicit unions with 'the Lord's handmaids' are altogether forbidden.

Honour is to be paid to kings, whom we now find being described as the Lord's anointed, and prayers are to be said on their behalf. Let no man lay violent hands upon them, exhort the legislators, conceivably having in mind the death of Cynewulf, king of Wessex, who was killed in a broil about this time, and the murder of Aethelbald by his bodyguards thirty years previously. Rulers, however, are enjoined to administer their realms with due deference to the bishops, and not to impose taxes on the Church other than those permitted by Roman Law and the custom of former kings. Payment of tithes is commanded, as well as the faithful performance of vows, and the extirpation of heathen customs such as eating horseflesh and the settlement of disputes by resort to sorcery.

From Offa's point of view as a ruler, the visit of the legates was chiefly important for the encouragement it gave to his project of a Mercian archbishopric. Though he had urged on Hadrian I the vastness of his dominions in justification of the scheme, his real motive was animosity towards the kingdom of Kent. It was galling to his pride that his Mercian dioceses should be subject to the archbishopric of Canterbury. The question was discussed heatedly in synod at Chelsea. Archbishop Jaenbert gave way, probably because he had no option in the matter, and consented, at least by his silence, to the partition of his province. The see of Lichfield was raised to the dignity of an archbishopric in 788, and its bishop Higebert awarded the pallium, though Jaenbert retained the precedence.

Before the legates left England, Offa promised the annual payment of 365 mancuses for poor relief and the upkeep of lights in Rome,[35] perhaps as an act of gratitude for his success as a ruler and more especially for the support of the papacy in the matter of the Lichfield archbishopric. This latter project seems to the historian a hasty and ill-considered one, but the rapid decline of the Mercian kingdom after Offa's death, with the consequent collapse of the scheme, would not have been foreseen at the time.

In 787 Offa caused his son Ecgfrith to be anointed king by anticipation, doubtless to ensure his succession. This is the first known instance of the consecration of an English king, the introduction of the sacred element into the inaugural ceremonies of a new ruler which has remained the English custom to our own day. Offa was following the example of Charlemagne, who in 781 had caused his sons Pippin and Louis to be anointed.

Relations between Offa and the Frankish king were close,[36] and their respective Churches had contacts, notably in connection with the problem of image worship. In 787, as we have observed, the Second Council of Nicaea[37] reaffirmed the reverence due to sacred images. Pope Hadrian confirmed this decision. But Charlemagne misinterpreted the Council's decrees and strongly disapproved, expressing his indignation in the *Caroline Books*. In 792 he wrote to enlist English support, and English prelates duly attended the Frankfurt council which condemned the Nicene canons. This is a rare, and possibly a unique example of the Anglo-Saxon Church being officially out of step with the Catholic Church on an important issue.

A notable event towards the close of Offa's reign was the foundation of St Alban's abbey. About the same time as this pious act, Offa put to death in treacherous circumstances an East Anglian king Ethelbert, who in course of time came to be venerated as a martyr, and over whose relics the cathedral church of Hereford was reared. Offa was succeeded by his son, as he had arranged, but who reigned for a few months only and was followed by Coenwulf, a kinsman of Offa.

During the reign of Coenwulf (796–821), Canterbury was restored to its full and traditional metropolitical rights. In 798 the king wrote to Leo III[38] voicing the concern of English churchmen that the original arrangement of Gregory I for two provinces only had been disregarded. It is reasonably certain, however, that Coenwulf had it in mind that the southern archbishopric should be finally settled neither in Canterbury nor Lichfield, but in London. This would have been in agreement with the exact terms of Gregory's plan, and also would have kept the primatial see inside Coenwulf's own kingdom, which was the real point after which the ascendant Mercian kings were striving. But Leo did not sanction this bold move. This was perhaps the only moment in the entire history of the English Church, with the exception of the Commonwealth period in the seventeenth century, when the very existence of the Canterbury archbishopric has been endangered.[39]

Following the king's letter to the pope, Aethelheard archbishop of Canterbury visited Rome. Alcuin helped to ease his passage across the Continent, by arranging an interview for him with Charlemagne. He was somewhat afraid, however, that the archbishop's splendid retinue might unfavourably surprise the latter, and he advised Aethelheard to travel as simply as possible. All went well, and on 18 January 802 the archbishop of Canterbury was confirmed by the pope in his position as primate over all the dioceses traditionally subject to the see.[40] A council was held at Cloveshoe on 12 October 803 which finally established this situation. It was declared how Offa had obtained the division of the province through false pretences,[41] representing the change as one supported unanimously by the English clergy. At Rome Aethelheard had laid the whole matter before the pope, who agreed that an injustice had been done and ordered a complete restitution of honour to the Canterbury see. Higebert, who so far as we know was a pious and blameless man, apparently made no protest. It seems indeed more than likely that his increased responsibilities had wearied him of episcopal office altogether. At the 803 synod, an act forbidding laymen to be elected as lords of monastic property included amongst its signatories Ealdwulf, bishop of Lichfield, and an abbot Higebert. It is reasonably certain that the latter was the erstwhile archbishop of Lichfield, who must have been either deprived of his see or had voluntarily resigned it.

It is not merely that there had been a lack of unanimity over the question of splitting the southern province; some bishops were positively devoted to the see of St Augustine, which by now had two centuries of tradition behind it. In 798 or thereabouts Eadwulf bishop of Lindsey made a written profession of obedience to the archbishop of Canterbury which is more than formal in its tone.[42] This is the first known example of many such documents. From about this time it became the practice for a new bishop to make a profession of faith and obedience to his metropolitan. The considerable number of such documents, confined to the southern province, which have been preserved suggests that they were guarded carefully as evidence of the supremacy of Canterbury in any future dispute.[43]

The last of the great ecclesiastical councils which characterise the period of Mercian ascendancy took place on 27 July 816 at Chelsea, in the presence of Wulfred, archbishop of Canterbury and formerly Aethelheard's archdeacon—he had succeeded his master as primate on the latter's death on 12 May 805. King Coenwulf also attended, and all the bishops of the southern province. The decrees of this council are not of outstanding interest, largely because most of the needful reform legislation had been already dealt with in preceding councils. But it is significant for a ban which it placed on the ministration of Celtic priests in the province.[44] The Irish schism was a long time dying, and in England as on the Continent wandering ecclesiastics had become a nuisance.

The most important episode of Wulfred's primacy (805–32) was a quarrel between himself and the king, the existence of which is clear from the fact that no charters of Coenwulf for several years after 817 are attested by the archbishop, though in that year itself and for several years before Wulfred's name appears on royal charters. The quarrel undoubtedly had its roots further back. Thus a letter of Leo III in 808 to Charlemagne refers to the bad relations existing between Coenwulf and his archbishop.[45] Wulfred was a man of considerable property in Kent, and it seems that the cause of the quarrel was jealousy on the king's part. The effective control of the Kentish kingdom lay in the hands of the Mercian king, who ruled as overlord of Baldred, the nominal king of Kent. It must therefore have been a serious aggravation to the Mercian king when Wulfred ceased to stamp the archiepiscopal coinage with the name of Coenwulf, and issued his coins entirely in his own name.

In 817 Coenwulf seized the archbishop's monasteries of Minster-in-Thanet and Reculver, and followed up this tactical stroke by a strategic design, bringing accusations against Wulfred before pope Paschal I. It is not known what the charges were, but as a result the archbishop was deprived of the exercise of his primatial functions for some years. The case seems to have lain dormant until 821, when the king convened his witan in London and cited Wulfred to appear. The archbishop was promised the restoration of his authority and the dropping of the charges, in return for a fine of 120 pounds and the surrender of an estate of 300 hides. He agreed, and the quarrel was to some extent patched up. Wulfred did not recover his estates of Minster and Reculver for at least another three or four years. These had been bequeathed by Coenwulf—who fortunately for Wulfred died soon after the settlement—to his daughter, an abbess.

The basic cause of the quarrel was essentially the same as that beneath the foundation of the abortive archbishopric of Lichfield, namely, the jealousy of the Mercian kings towards the archbishops of Canterbury, who were far too influential for their liking. With the rapid decline of the Mercian power which followed the death of Coenwulf in 821, a generally happier period set in for the primates, from the point of view of their relationship with the kings. But the rather clumsy manoeuvres of Offa and Coenwulf at least prove that by the second half of the eighth century the Church was firmly established in the land as a great power, not only a source of help to the crown but also on occasion a cause of embarrassment and annoyance. The degree with which the various monarchs from this time onwards recognised this fact and accommodated themselves to it was to be a test of their capability as rulers. For England as a whole, the failure of the Lichfield archbishopric was probably fortunate. If the scheme had succeeded it must surely have become a disruptive influence in the life of the English Church, at a time when the latter was increasingly a bond of unity between all Englishmen. With three archbishoprics, two of them (Lichfield and Canterbury) of equal strength, the role of the Church in leading the way towards national union could not fail to have been impaired.

In connection with the succession to Coenwulf we have one of those pretty legends which add romantic interest to the study of the Dark Ages. He is said to have been succeeded by his seven year old son Coenhelm. The child's sister, Coenthryth the abbess who had obtained the estates of Minster and Reculver, connived his murder in a forest. A dove flew to St Peter's, Rome, and laid a letter on the high altar. An Anglo-Saxon who was in the church at the time interpreted the letter, reporting the death of the boy, whose body lay hidden in the wood. The pope wrote informing the English kings of the crime. The body was recovered and buried with that of the child's father in the great monastery which had been founded at Winchcombe c. 798. The day of the little child, St Kenelm, king and martyr, was long observed on 17 July.

The real successor to Coenwulf was his brother Ceolwulf, who reigned for two years until his deposition in favour of a certain Beorn-wulf. For a short time this king effectively ruled Mercia and its south-eastern dependencies. It was under him that archbishop Wulfred in 825 secured full restoration to his former position. In the same year Beornwulf was defeated by Egbert of Wessex at the decisive battle of Ellendun, on the north Wiltshire downs near Wroughton. The victory marked the transition of political supremacy from Mercia to Wessex, and the end of an age in Anglo-Saxon history.

The eighth century saw the final decline of Northumbria. From the death of Aldfrith in 705 until the end of the century there were no fewer than fourteen kings, nearly all of whom came to violent ends.[46] Osred, son of Aldfrith, was the first to be murdered, a deed which set the tone of Northumbrian history for many years to come. It is a tale of bloodshed and bitter feuds, one family after another competing for a futile supremacy. In the general circumstances of Anglo-Saxon life political instability entailed an all-round decay, in which the Church was bound to share. The fine old Northumbrian learning and culture slowly withered away, until by the close of the century it was a shadow of its former self.

It was the weakened Northumbrian kingdom which was to bear the initial blows of a scourge destined to effect a revolution in Anglo-Saxon life, though it was actually Wessex where the first blood was apparently shed. It may have been a year or two before 790 that the reeve of Portland, in the course of a visit to the nearby town of Dor-chester, in Dorset, received news that three ships of strangers had landed on the peninsula for which he was responsible. Thinking they must be traders, he rode with a few men to meet them and inquire their business. They turned out to be Scandinavian pirates, who made short work of the unsuspecting reeve and his companions.[47]

Calamities really began, however, on 8 June 793.[48] After a period of alarming portents in the shape of unusually severe thunderstorms, when it seemed that fiery dragons rode the sky, followed by a great famine in the land, heathens (according to the Chronicle) destroyed the church at Lindisfarne on that day. The annals attributed to the twelfth-century writer Simeon of Durham enlarge the story. Some of the Lindisfarne brothers were slain, some drowned in the sea, some taken away as captives, by heathens from the regions of the north. The raid on the island monastery was apparently part of a widespread attack, in which nuns as well as monks suffered.

Amongst those who were distressed at this state of affairs was Alcuin, who saw in the Lindisfarne disaster a fearful foreboding. He alludes to the raid in a number of letters,[49] particularly one to the Northumbrian king Aethelred and another to the Lindisfarne monks, both written as soon as the terrible news reached him. In the former he remarks that it is three hundred and fifty years since the English first inhabited their 'most lovely country', and this is the very worst thing which has happened. The church of St Cuthbert is spattered with the blood of priests and robbed of its ornaments. The most sacred place in Britain has been despoiled by the heathens. The calamity must surely be a divine punishment for sin. He refers to a rain of blood which had been seen in Lent, at a time when the sky was clear and calm, falling from the roof of St Peter's church at York. What else could this have meant save that carnage was approaching? Let the king and his nobles turn from their sinful ways. Let them think less of such frivolities as the careful trimming of hair and beard. They are too fond of luxury, which, says this schoolmaster turned prophet (in the modern spirit of social justice), entails the poverty of the people. Some Englishmen are overfed and overclothed—others die of starvation and cold.

In his letter to the Lindisfarne brothers (with its implicit information that some of them survived the attack, including their bishop Higebald) Alcuin inquired how it was that the remains of St Cuthbert, interred within their church, had not preserved them from assault. The disaster must certainly be a divine judgment. And indeed this sort of thing had happened in history before. God's own city Jerusalem, along with its temple, had perished in flames. Rome, the city of the apostles, had known the ravages of heathens. All Europe had been desolated by Goths and Huns, and yet now was brilliant with churches. Punishment for worldliness and wrongdoing must assuredly come, but let not the brethren be disheartened.

Alcuin wrote also to the monks of Jarrow, warning them of their exposed coastal position. He called on them to emulate their predecessors in that famous house. Let the example of Bede arouse them from their sloth, and their fine library be used again. In 794, indeed, the pirates returned to the north-east coast, and plundered Jarrow.[50] But this time preparations had been made, and the marauders did not go away unscathed. One of their leaders was killed, and a violent storm wrecked some of their ships.

In 800 the raiders were back again, this time to plunder the churches

271

of Tynemouth and Hartness.[51] The year was one of portent and trouble. There was an eclipse of the moon, and a disastrous flood, with a gale which destroyed many villages and uprooted numerous trees. There was a general uneasiness abroad, and there may well have been a good many more Scandinavian raids along the east coasts than the records indicate. By a grant of 804 from Coenwulf, king of Mercia, and Cuthred king of Kent, the abbess and community of Lyminge were given some land in Canterbury to serve as a refuge in case of need.[52] The time was one of insecurity, and though Alcuin, from his detached position on the Continent, saw the threatening dangers with exceptional clarity, it is probable that the English of the coastal regions were alive to what was happening, and were in no mood to regard the raids as merely a temporary nuisance.

Fortunately for the decadent Northumbrians, the north-eastern raids petered out at the end of the eighth century. For England as a whole, these sporadic attacks were a blessing in disguise. The Anglo-Saxons had been warned. Meanwhile the viking raiders turned their attention to Ireland, and the English had some decades of peace before the next generation of Northmen returned in greater strength and with more clearly defined aims. By then there had been a decisive shift of power to Wessex, and though many Englishmen were not to be spared a long period of terror and calamity, a new line of Saxon rulers, devout, capable, and brave, would save the situation and accomplish one of the most remarkable victories in the history of Christendom. Anglo-Saxon society would continue, though great damage caused in various departments was to necessitate a virtually new departure in religion and culture. The viking wars of the ninth century mark a clear line between two phases of Anglo-Saxon history.

CHAPTER XVII

THE DANES AND KING ALFRED

In 802 Egbert became king of Wessex, where he maintained his rule for thirty-seven years, laying the foundations of a dynasty of supreme importance in the history of England. He had to fight hard for his position. Indeed, his reign was preceded by a period of exile on the Continent, where he obtained refuge at Charlemagne's court. During the earlier years of his reign he had trouble with the Celts of Cornwall, who resisted the westward advance of the Saxons. In thanksgiving for his success over them, Egbert gave a tenth of the Cornishmen's land to the West Saxon Church.

After his victory over Beornwulf in 825, Egbert continued his aggressive policy towards Mercia, and by his military success over Wiglaf four years later secured a definite predominance over the midland kingdom. On his death in 839 he was succeeded by his son Aethelwulf (839–58), during whose reign the vikings molested the English kingdoms in strength, bringing terror to their inhabitants and devastation to the land.

Fundamentally, the vikings who emerged early in the ninth century to become the most significant factor in west European history for many decades to come were of the same Nordic stock as the Anglo-Saxons and the other Germanic peoples.[1] The Scandinavians, from whom the viking raiders were drawn, inhabited the northern peninsulas where they have always remained a relatively pure race. In modern Norway, Sweden, and Denmark, one may still see the physical type in exceptionally large numbers—tall and blonde. These are surely the handsomest folk in the world today. But they have for long been men of peace. It is those two very mixed peoples, the British and the Germans, who have in modern times most strongly maintained the old martial and warlike spirit of the north. There is little about the mild and polite men of modern Scandinavia to suggest the character of the vikings—brave indeed, but pitiless, cruel, and treacherous, and in many respects one of the most beastly peoples in human history.

At the time of the breaking of the storm c. 800, the predominant activity of the Scandinavians was farming, and the family estates were growing in size and importance. But there were many disappointed young men, of whom there might be a considerable number in a single family owing to the widespread practice of polygamy. Seafaring as well as the cultivation of the soil was in their blood, and it became a popular practice for those denied a share in the land or in the absorbing duties of political administration to join together in war-bands which raided far and wide across the Baltic and North Seas. At first a summer pastime, the raids became a highly organised profession. Their participants were the 'vikings', a term (derived alternatively from 'vik', a creek or fiord, or 'wic', an armed camp) which denotes members of a raiding-party and should not be used indiscriminately of the Scandinavian people as a whole. By the opening of the ninth century the Scandinavians were already organised in three main national groups. The Swedes do not concern the student of early English history; the activities of their vikings lay eastwards across the Baltic. The Norwegians were less closely welded as a people than the Danes, who moreover were more accessible to the Christian and civilising influences of the Carolingian empire than were the other northern peoples.

After the coastal raids on Northumbria during the closing years of the eighth century, the vikings turned their attention to Ireland and the western islands. They had indeed already sacked Iona, as well as Lambey island near Dublin, in 795. In the early years of the ninth century they raided Inishmurray, off the coast of Sligo. They landed in the Shetlands, the Orkneys, and the Hebrides, which had already for some years been a receiving ground for immigrants from over-populated Norway. Famous Irish religious houses like Bangor, Clonmacnois, and Moville, were pillaged. The Irish, with the English, were amongst the most cultured of western peoples at this time, and in the monasteries were rich stores of wealth in a tangible form—gold and silver vessels, splendid vestments and altar hangings. The vikings could wish for nothing better. Here indeed was wealth simply waiting to be picked up and taken away. There can be little doubt that these raids on exposed coastal monasteries, during the years immediately before and after 800, were in the nature of an appetiser. Not only rich spoil was carried back to the fiords and villages of Norway and Denmark, but something more significant—the tale of a people served by a Church which patronised wealth and at the same time preached a doctrine of humility and resignation. To the English themselves the doctrine was no doubt theoretical, but to the vikings a direct encitement and encouragement.

Meanwhile, as raiders from Norway molested Ireland, parties from Denmark devoted their attention to the Frankish empire. In 799 some islands in the Bay of Biscay were visited. The island monastery of Rhé was attacked in 814, besides that of Noirmoutier off the Loire mouth. This was the year of the death of Charlemagne, under whose rule the empire was too well guarded to fear much from the Danes, with whom indeed it had many commercial contacts. The emperor's successful operations against the Frisians and Saxons had brought his realm face to face with Denmark. It has sometimes been thought that the latter country commenced warlike operations against the empire almost in the role of self-appointed champion of Teutonic heathenism. Be this as it may, Charlemagne fully realised that a new and dreadful threat had come to life on his borders. He had no fear of it while he lived, but was apprehensive of what might happen to his successors. He was succeeded by his son Louis the Pious, who was at first successful in containing the Danish menace, but whose later years saw a weakening of the empire through internal dissension. Enthusiasm for war grew amongst the Danes, and in 834 we find them operating against the empire as an army. At the time of the death of Louis in 840 the floodgates were virtually wide open.

The generation of immunity enjoyed by the English ended in 835, when the Danes overran the Isle of Sheppey. In the following year a force of vikings defeated Egbert in Somerset. In 838 he managed to defeat a combined force of vikings and local Celts from Cornwall in the battle of Hingston Down. But the menace could not now be contained, and Aethelwulf his successor had to contend with a growing Danish threat. Dorset, Somerset, Kent, East Anglia, and Lincolnshire, all suffered. In 842 London was sacked, and a few years later a fleet of three hundred and fifty ships sailed up the Thames, plundering the countryside.[2]

In 849 Aethelwulf's wife Osburh gave birth to her fifth child, Alfred,[3] at Wantage in Berkshire, a region which was now firmly settled, after some hesitation, as part of the kingdom of Wessex. It was not long after this that the viking peril entered upon a new phase. A force spent the whole winter of 850–51 in the Isle of Thanet. The implications of this could not have been lost upon the English. The period of desultory raiding was clearly past, and the invaders had their thoughts not only on temporary spoil, but on the possibility of conquest and settlement. In 851 London was stormed again, along with Canterbury, and the Mercian king put to flight, though the heathen army shortly afterwards suffered a severe defeat at Aclea at the hands of Aethelwulf and his son Aethelbald.[4] In the following year the Wessex king received a begging letter in connection with some church-roof repairs from Lupus, abbot of Ferrières, in which his endeavours against the enemies of Christ were praised.[5] But Aethelwulf appears to have been depressed and alarmed, and saw in greater religious devotion the only answer to the threat. Of Aethelwulf's piety there can indeed be no doubt, and it is clear that his heart lay in the religious rather than the military life. In 853 he sent his infant son Alfred to visit Rome; the child was kindly received by pope Leo IV, and invested with the external array and trappings of a Roman consul.[6]

The Danish menace grew, and the invaders passed the winter of 854–5 on Sheppey. Aethelwulf in 855 decided on a personal visit to Rome, taking his six-year-old son Alfred with him. Before leaving he made over by charter some estates amounting to a tenth of his land to the Church.[7] He stayed for a year in Rome, obtaining audience of the pope, now Benedict III, to whom he presented valuable gifts, including silver *gabatae* or hanging lamps, the work of English craftsmen. Like Offa he promised the payment of an annual tribute. On his way home Aethelwulf, whose wife Osburh had died, married a thirteen-year-old child Judith, the daughter of Charles the Bald. The ceremony was performed by Hincmar, archbishop of Rheims, one of the leading prelates and scholars of the time.

Meanwhile Athelstan, the king's eldest son, had died, and the position of honour held by him had passed to the next son in point of age, Aethelbald, an ambitious young man with a strong following. His supporters included Eahlstan, bishop of Sherborne,[8] a secular-minded prelate who on at least one occasion personally led a force against the Danes. An ecclesiastical neighbour and contemporary of Eahlstan who might be mentioned here was Swithun, bishop of Winchester from 852 to 862. A prelate of the best type, spiritually-minded and caring only for his people, his outstanding characteristic was his humility. Aethelwulf appears to have greatly admired him, and leaned on him heavily for advice.[9] Later, on his death-bed, Swithun asked that he might be buried not inside the cathedral but outside beneath the turf, where the rain would fall upon him and the feet of common men pass over his head.

Aethelwulf, who had no heart for dissension, averted a possible civil strife by handing over to Aethelbald the main governance of Wessex and contenting himself with Essex, Kent, Surrey, and Sussex. Aethelbald was perhaps the leader of a party resenting the piety which moved a king to dally a whole year at the tombs of the Apostles at a time when his subjects were in danger. Aethelwulf, however, did not live much longer. He died in 858, and was buried at Winchester.

Aethelbald created widespread horror in his kingdom by marrying the child widow Judith, after the old Teutonic custom. He died two years later, in 860, and was buried at Sherborne. He was succeeded by his brother Ethelbert, while in the meantime Judith returned to the Continent. Before long she eloped with Baldwin, count of Flanders. From this marriage was ultimately descended Matilda, wife of William the Conqueror. During the reign of Ethelbert (860–66) the Danes were troublesome in England, where their activities included an attack on Winchester, defeated by the ealdormen of Hampshire and Berkshire, and a devastation of Kent, which the inhabitants tried to prevent by recourse to the fatal practice of money bribery. Ethelbert on his death was interred like his elder brother in Sherborne, and succeeded by his younger brother Aethelred. Only two of Aethelwulf's sons now survived; the youngest, Alfred, was a lad about seventeen years old. The two young men, their parents and elder brothers all dead, were left together to face the greatest peril Wessex had so far met.

Alfred now seriously emerges into the world of public life, as the lieutenant and assistant of his elder brother. The age of viking raids was past, and it is more correct to speak from henceforth of a serious and large-scale Danish attempt to exploit English land and resources to the full. It was led by Halfdan and Ivar, two sons of Ragnar Lothbrok, greatest of ninth-century Norse pirates. Their army settled down in East Anglia for the winter of 865–6, where they passed the time in warlike preparations in which the acquisition of horses from the surrounding countryside played a prominent part. In 866 they struck northwards, and occupied York on the Feast of All Saints (1 November).[10] In the following year the Northumbrians fought back fiercely under two rival kings who joined forces in face of a common peril. These were Osbert and Aelle, both of whom were slain in this unsuccessful counter-attack.

There can be little doubt that this storming of York and the harrying of the countryside which followed is one of the decisive events in the history of the north of England. Simeon of Durham says of the destruction wrought in Northumbria at this time that even in his day (*c.* 1104) many places had not recovered.[11] It seems certain that a break in Northumbrian history occurred about this time and that the region henceforth took upon a new character. During these troubles the famous library at York probably perished. The last we actually hear of it is in 852, in a letter of Lupus, abbot of Ferrières, to Ealdsige, abbot of York.[12] Lupus asks for the loan of books by Bede, Quintilian, and Jerome, promising that they will be returned as soon as they have been copied. Obviously the York library was still intact in 852, or regarded as likely to be so by a continental house which had traditional associations with York. From 866, however, there was a process of virtual annihilation of churches and monasteries in Deira. Amongst those which surely perished at this time was Streoneshalh; when later rebuilt it appears under the Danish name of Whitby. The see of York, however, seems to have survived, though it continued in a much impoverished state.

The Danes turned southwards, marched into Mercia and made camp at Nottingham. The Mercian king Burgred called to Wessex for help. The two brothers marched to his aid, and about the same time Alfred married a Mercian lady Ealhswith. It is said that during the wedding festivities the bridegroom was seized by acute pain, an attack of that ill-health which was to trouble Alfred throughout his life.[13]

The help brought from Wessex was of little avail. The Danes, secure behind ramparts, refused battle. Burgred made peace, and Aethelred with his brother marched home.

The Danish army returned to York for another year, and then in the autumn of 869 proceeded to East Anglia, where it came to a halt at Thetford. It is to this moment that we turn for the famous episode of St Edmund, king and martyr. Much legend has gathered round the story of the 'English St Sebastian', who was king of East Anglia from 855 to 869. It is possible that he was by national origin not an Englishman at all, but an Old Saxon born at Nuremberg. What is certain is that with his fighting-men he resisted the Danes under Ivar, who prevailed and slew the king. The fact that before many years were past Edmund was being revered as a martyr and miracle-worker[14] strongly suggests that he did not die a normal soldier's death in battle, but was taken captive and executed, perhaps for refusing to surrender his land and people to a heathen conqueror. The Chronicle does not take much notice of the episode, simply stating that the king was defeated and slain by the Danes,[15] who then proceeded to harry the land and destroy any monasteries in their path, including the wealthy house of Mede-hamstede, where the abbot and monks were put to the sword. The late tenth-century writer Abbo of Fleury elaborates the tale, including the celebrated information that Edmund was bound to a tree and shot at with arrows. St Edmund's day, 20 November, was long popular amongst the English, and his cult was to be a favourite one with the converted Scandinavians.

The next objective of the invaders was Wessex, and by the end of 870 we find them encamped at Reading. They were no longer commanded by Ivar, who it seems may have gone over to Ireland, but by his brother Halfdan and a Dane called Bagsecg. In January 871 Aethelred and Alfred arrived on the scene with the Wessex army, and defeated the Danes at the important battle of Ashdown in Berkshire, though they suffered a reverse at Basing a few days later. The Ashdown battle gives us an interesting insight into the undoubted piety of many of the Anglo-Saxon kings. At the opening of the fight Aethelred refused to move from his tent until the priest saying mass had finished, and Alfred had to open up on his own.

In the spring of 871 the Danes at Reading were reinforced by a force from the Continent. About the same time Aethelred died, possibly from wounds received in battle, and was reverently interred at Wimborne in the presence of his younger brother.[16] Alfred was now left alone, a young man of twenty-two, to face a powerful hostile army encamped well within the bounds of Wessex. It was the immediate presence of this grave menace which ensured the succession of Alfred to the kingship. Aethelred indeed had children, but the urgency of the situation required an adult king.

During 871 the Wessex fyrd fought no fewer than nine battles with the invaders, and inflicted heavy losses upon them. But there were reverses, including a defeat of Alfred near Wilton. The Saxons became weary of the fight, and Alfred had no alternative but to make peace with the Danes. It seems that he paid them to leave his kingdom, which they duly did, offering him a valuable respite (871–5) to consider his position and organise his forces. The Danish host now moved to London, which was within Mercian territory, and wintered there before marching north to Northumbria in the spring of 872. In the same year they returned southwards, settling in Lindsey for almost a year, and then in the autumn of 873 encamped at Repton, Derbyshire, where they remained for the winter. The trail of murder and destruction which they left behind them [17] proved too much for the spirit of Burgred the Mercian king. In 874 he forsook his kingdom and departed to end his days in holy quiet at Rome. His wife Aethelswith, Alfred's sister, apparently declined to accompany him. She did not set out for Rome until some years later, when she died on the way at Pavia.

The host now divided into two forces. The one, under Halfdan, moved northwards to complete the subjugation of Northumbria and settle down there as permanent conquerors, though Halfdan himself seems to have remained in the region a short time only. The north-east now became a Scandinavian kingdom (with York as its capital) which was to endure for some eighty years. Halfdan began his reign with terror. The inhabitants found continued residence in their ancestral homes almost intolerable, and it is likely that a good many of them departed with their wives and children. The exodus was led by the monks of Lindisfarne, under their bishop Eardulf and their abbot Eadred.[18] In 875 the monks left Holy Island, crossing the sands to the mainland, bearing with them the body of St Cuthbert, along with the bones of St Aidan and the head of St Oswald. For seven years they wandered from place to place seeking safety. Once they tried to cross over to Ireland, but were driven back by a storm. In 883, with the coming of more settled conditions, they found a resting-place at Chester-le-Street in county Durham. The romantic nature of this famous episode has obscured what may well be its real significance, namely a displacement of many of the Anglian population in favour of Danes. From approximately this time the north-east assumed the air of a region distinct from the rest of England which remains with it until the present day.

The second Danish force left Repton for Cambridge, under three leaders, Guthrum, Oskytel, and Anund. There it was watched by an English force but managed to slip away and got across Mercia and Wessex into the Dorset town of Wareham. This was the most serious situation Alfred had been confronted with so far. For the first time, a powerful Danish army was encamped in the very heart of his realm. Alfred was compelled to pay them money, though he extracted from them not only hostages but also a solemn oath, sworn upon the holy ring or bracelet which on sacrificial occasions was placed upon the heathen altar, that they would go away. They did indeed leave Wareham, but proceeded instead to Exeter, where their threat to Alfred was as great as ever. He pursued them with all speed and besieged them in their Devonshire fortress. Meanwhile, elsewhere, the invaders suffered their greatest setback so far. A fleet of ships sailing westwards to reinforce the host at Exeter was wrecked by a storm off Swanage, in which a hundred and twenty vessels were lost.

It was now the turn of the Danes to seek peace, and Alfred allowed them to go on condition that they left Wessex. They did so, but settled in Gloucester, not far outside the Wessex borders. During this phase they partitioned Mercia, taking to themselves the region corresponding to the counties of Lincoln, Nottingham, Derby, and Leicester. Then in January 878 they broke loose again and were back in West Saxony, this time at the Wiltshire town of Chippenham. It was clear surely to all Englishmen that the crisis was now at hand, and that the heathen Danes were making a serious bid for the whole of English soil.

The situation, aggravated by numerous raids of the Danes from their Chippenham base, became so bad that in the spring of 878 Alfred was compelled to flee temporarily with his comitatus to await events and think out his future course of action. Life in Wessex was so difficult that many Saxons fled overseas.[19] Alfred chose as his place of refuge the Isle of Athelney, in the Somerset marshes, where he stayed several weeks, supporting himself by frequent raids into the surrounding countryside. Then in May he came out of the swamp with his faithful followers, and riding eastwards set up his standard at a spot referred to in the Chronicle as 'Egbert's Stone'. The exact identity of this place has been much debated. The village of Stourton (where stands the well-known landmark 'King Alfred's Tower', the erection of an eighteenth-century antiquary) in Wiltshire has been claimed, as also Brixton Deverill a few miles away. It is certainly probable that the historic gathering took place in this locality which lies a little to the east of Penselwood, a small village in Somerset close to the Wilts border. A likely location would be the large open tract of land, in the neighbouring parish of Zeals, which was used as an airfield in the Second World War. At the appointed place there gathered the fighting-men of Somerset and Wiltshire, with such Hampshire men as had not fled overseas, rejoicing to see their king again. After a single night's rest, the army moved off, and in a day or two reached Edington, where it came up with the Danish host.

There followed what deserves to rank as one of the decisive victories not only of English history but of Christendom as a whole. As these few thousand men faced each other on this Wiltshire chalk downland there can have been no thought in their minds of great and dramatic issues. The immediate issue was simply the defence, or the conquest, of a small kingdom. The average visitor to Edington today is probably similarly impervious to the strategic significance of what happened in the place on a single summer's day nearly eleven hundred years ago. The main attraction of the village in modern times is the splendid fourteenth-century church, unique in the history of English architecture; its most oft-told story is that recounting the murder of a bishop of Salisbury by the parishioners in later medieval times. Edington, however, should be a household name in England, and indeed in western Europe, as standing for a true victory of right over wrong, a meeting-place of forces which by no stretch of accommodation could be brought to live together. Here the White Christ challenged and overcame his contemporary rival, Odin the Wise, the cynical, deceitful, and ruthless Father of Norse warriors. Edington was a great victory for Christianity and its derivative culture and ways of thought.

There is no need here to discuss the tactics and movements which may have attended the battle. Suffice it to say that the Danes, now under the sole leadership of Guthrum, were defeated and fled for refuge to their base at Chippenham fifteen miles distant. After a short siege they surrendered, and once again swore to leave Wessex. It is important to remember that in the record of all these forays and battles with the Danes Alfred had a strictly limited objective, which was simply to drive the invaders off his own soil. He never envisaged the possibility of subduing them or forcing them to leave England. He fought throughout as king of the West Saxons. This time the promise was kept. Moreover, Guthrum agreed to accept baptism. The ceremony took place at Aller, near Athelney, Guthrum receiving the Christian name of Athelstan and Alfred himself serving as godfather. To Alfred himself the occasion was doubtless a solemn one, but to Guthrum and his followers expediency was surely the leading motive, tempered perhaps with a certain cynical amusement.

The Danes departed, and must have caused Alfred some apprehension by proceeding to settle down for a whole year at Cirencester, which though within Mercia was within convenient striking distance of Wessex. But in the autumn of 879 they marched away to East Anglia, where they established themselves as permanent conquerors.

The peace lasted until 885, in which year Rochester was assailed by a viking fleet from the Continent. Guthrum joined them, probably happy to be back at the old game. But without hesitation Alfred took up the challenge, now fully sure of himself, and forced peace upon the aggressors. He strengthened his position by occupying London, which so far had been left to the Danes. In the treaty which was concluded probably in 886, the boundaries were defined between the Saxon and Danish territories. The Danish land-settlements ensured that the invaders held Northumbria, Essex, East Anglia, and the East Midlands. Alfred remained ruler of the south, from Cornwall to Kent, with a delegated authority over such of Mercia as had not passed within the new Danish realms.

It is clear that the Danish wars left Northumbria, Mercia, and Wessex in an unenviable position from the point of view of ecclesiastical prosperity and efficiency. The monasteries had suffered exceptionally severely, and the schools had virtually disappeared. The stream of culture and learning which had continued since 597 was now dry. Possibly the parish churches, at this time for the most part simple wooden buildings housing little in the way of treasures, had come off comparatively lightly, at any rate in Wessex and western Mercia. So far as we know, the regular Sunday worship of the ordinary folk continued. But the effective centres of the Christian Faith were still the monasteries and the minster churches, with their substantial buildings, their wealth, and their relatively educated clergy. Without these, the Faith could not have long survived. There is evidence enough that something approaching a catastrophe overtook them in the wars which in this chapter have been narrated at a length perhaps unmerited in a work of ecclesiastical history. Moreover, apart from this negative work of destruction, an impetus had been given to the revival of Teutonic heathenism in many parts of England. There are a few place-names to indicate this, such as the early medieval name (Othenesberg) for Roseberry Topping, a high eminence in the Cleveland district.[20] The Danish occupation of the north and the east made necessary what was virtually the third Conversion associated with the Christianisation of Britain.

The beginning of this Conversion was marked by the baptism of Guthrum. The conversion of the Danes in general steadily followed, but the means by which it was accomplished are not clear.[21] There are no great missionary names associated with the movement. The Danes rather surprisingly made ready converts, and the process of assimilation between Englishman and Scandinavian was not difficult. The poet Robert Southey neatly summed up the situation when he remarked that 'the Danes who settled in England became Christians by position and contact'.[22] That the Conversion was carried out almost informally and not as part of a concerted movement on the part of the English Church is indeed suggested by a letter of pope Formosus (891–6) to the English bishops.[23] He complains of the complacence of the English bishops at the revival of heathenism in their land. So indignant is he, in fact, that he has considered excommunicating them for their neglect, though he will not proceed with this extreme measure owing to archbishop Plegmund's assurances that they are beginning to bestir themselves to a sense of their missionary responsibilities. Formosus himself had in his early career been a missionary, and as pope he maintained a keen interest in missionary work from Hamburg amongst the continental Danes.[24]

Alfred was now able to devote himself to the rule and government of his people, and utilise in the service of religion and education energies which hitherto had been perforce directed towards military operations. He did not embark on any large schemes for the restoration of monasteries, though there was plenty of scope for him in this field. Of the decay of the monastic institute his biographer Asser wrote that for many years the desire for the religious life had died out in England, as indeed in many other countries.[25] There were still monasteries in various places, but they no longer observed the rule. Asser is not sure in his own mind whether this decline is due to the Danish invasions or to the corrupting influence of wealth, though he is inclined to think that the latter may be the real cause. Only two new foundations can certainly be attributed to the king. Over the nunnery of Shaftesbury he placed as abbess his own daughter Aethelgifu.[26] Of Athelney a little more will be said in a moment. Let it here be noted that its chief interest is in the known design of its church. It was planned on the model of those round churches of which we possess a famous example at Aachen. It was built around a circular space, and based on four pillars. For its construction Alfred imported foreign craftsmen.

More important was the king's encouragement of learning and scholarship. This department of the national life had suffered grievously from the Danish ravages, and Alfred was wont to lament the lack of opportunity for schooling prevailing in his youth. As a man he tried hard to make up the deficiency by studying in such spare moments as came his way. He was resolved that learning on a broad scale should be reintroduced to Wessex, and to this end he brought in foreign scholars.

Amongst these was Asser. Alfred met this Welshman (who was a priest of St David's) at Dean, in Sussex, c. 885.[27] He invited him to take up residence at his court for six months of each year; in this, as in other details, we find the example of Charlemagne exerting itself in the practice of the West Saxon king. Asser hesitated about the offer, and went home to consult his brethren. They placed no obstacles in Asser's way, and indeed probably saw here the possibility of a connection invaluable for their house. By 887 Alfred was hard at work in the study of the Vulgate, making his way through the Latin with the help of Asser, who was a competent teacher if not a genuine scholar. The tedious work was well rewarded. The king gave a really worthwhile Christmas present to his teacher at the close of 887, making over to him the properties of Congresbury and Banwell, two Somerset monasteries which were apparently no longer serving any useful purpose. Asser's most important work was his Life of the king, written in 893. It is the earliest biography of an English layman. This work has often been adversely criticised, but its authenticity was convincingly demonstrated by W. H. Stevenson in his critical edition. The book is made up of two elements, a strictly biographical narrative being broken up with annals ranging from 851 to 887. Though rhetorical in style, and left uncompleted, the Life is a valuable authority for Alfred and his times.

In due course Asser was promoted to the episcopate. He became associated with the rule of the diocese of Sherborne, first perhaps only of the westerly and more Celtic parts of it, later of the whole diocese. His death as bishop of Sherborne is included in the Chronicle entry for 910.

About the same time as Asser's arrival from Wales, two men came from the Continent. These were Grimbald and John. The former, now a man of seventy, had been for most of his life a monk at St Bertin in northern France but at the time was at Rheims. Alfred wrote to Fulk, archbishop of that see (883–900) in succession to Hincmar, his letter accompanying a gift of wolf-hounds and requesting the services of Grimbald. Fulk acceded to the request, with a patronising letter almost insolent in its tone.[28] The lack of learning, worldly living, and marriage of the English clergy are deplored. Indeed, the ignorance of the clergy and the neglect of the bishops, Fulk implies, are as much responsible for the decadent state of the English Church as are the heathen invasions. In consideration for the pitiable condition of Alfred's kingdom he will do what he can to help. A distasteful letter indeed, though a solid piece of evidence for the condition of religion in ninth-century England. Of Grimbald himself, all that is known is good. He was an accomplished musician, learned in ecclesiastical discipline and the Scriptures, and of a high moral character. Lacking ecclesiastical ambition, he declined the archbishopric of Canterbury. His simple vocation was that of a priest and teacher, with its life of direct service to the souls and minds of men. He took up his abode at Winchester, where in the company of some other clergy he lived in a *monasteriolum* or clergy-house. Here his reputation for sheer goodness of life increased. After his death on 8 July 901 he came to be honoured as a saint, and his cult was widely known in the tenth and eleventh centuries.

John was an Old Saxon, described by Asser as monk and priest and an acute scholar. He possibly came from the abbey of New Corbie, near Paderborn. It was John whom the king chose as first abbot of his Athelney monastery. This foundation was not a success, owing to the difficulty of finding monks willing to settle in so secluded a spot. To the Anglo-Saxons it appears to have made no appeal, and its first monks were drawn from the Continent, supplemented by oblate-children.[29] The house was an unhappy one, and John on occasion had difficulty in restraining his unruly subjects, two of whom were once prepared to resort to murder in an attempt to get rid of their abbot. The further career of John and the year of his death are unknown.

But it was to Mercia that Alfred turned for his most substantial scholarly help. This is not surprising; Mercia had been the most recent of the English kingdoms to enjoy prosperity, and Offa had encouraged scholarship and education. Alfred is known to have introduced four scholars from Mercia to his court. Of two of these, Athelstan and Werwulf, little is known. Plegmund and Werferth were more important; the former became archbishop of Canterbury in 890, while the latter had been bishop of Worcester since 873—an able episcopal ruler who had maintained the Church of the west midlands in comparative security during those troublous times. A public-spirited man, his name occurs constantly in connection with Mercian charters.

During the years 892–6 Alfred again had to take up his sword against the Danes. They had been causing terror on the Continent, but a decisive defeat inflicted upon them in 891 by king Arnulf caused them to look again towards England, and in 892 two large viking fleets arrived in Kent. In the following year they were joined by their brethren of East Anglia and Northumbria, wearied by the peaceful life of land-settlement and farming. But though fighting continued for some three years, it became plain to the invaders that there were no new fields to be conquered in England, and in the summer of 896 the Danish army broke up. The Danes of England returned to their farms, the rest sailed back across the Channel. About this time Alfred ordered the construction of large warships, destined to play an important part in the work of excluding Danish raiders from English shores. They formed, however, only part of a wider scheme of national defence, which included a reorganisation of the army and the establishment of a system of fortified burhs manned by local men.

Something must now be said of the intellectual programme with which the king during the last decade or so of his life was deeply engrossed. Alfred had a very strong sense of the weakness sure to overtake a nation which neglects education, and of the degradation which will inevitably be the fate of a Church whose clergy are allowed to lapse into ignorance. The ninth-century wars and depredations had left the English to a great extent bereft of books or at any rate of the knowledge and scholarship necessary to read them in the Latin in which they were written. Alfred did what he could to revive the tradition of education, though it was principally by turning a number of the more important Latin Christian classics into the vernacular that he hoped to bring his subjects back to a love of learning. The programme was a bold one, well ahead of the times. The really interesting thing about it is the king's refusal to believe that the knowledge of letters should be a preserve of clerics. His leading laymen also must be intellectually trained.

The programme of translation was begun by Werferth c. 891, at the king's command, with a rendering of pope Gregory's *Dialogues* into Old English.[30] This was a book of imaginative tales concerning saints, demons, and spiritual wonders. The translation was not a literal one, but executed on the 'sense for sense' principle. Two or three years later the king himself undertook the translation of a far more important work by the same Gregory, the *Pastoral Care*,[31] with the help of Plegmund, Asser, Grimbald, and John, as he himself acknowledges.

This book was originally a manual of instruction for bishops, in which the great pope portrayed in terms valid for all ages the character which should appertain to the episcopal office. The true bishop is a lover of prayer and devout seclusion, and yet busily devoted to the immortal souls who are his prime responsibility. The work was already a classic. It had been brought by Augustine to this country.[32] Bede in his letter of 734 to bishop Egbert of York had recommended its perusal. Alcuin had written in 796 to Eadbald II, archbishop of York, advising him to carry a copy with him wherever he went. On the Continent, archbishop Hincmar of Rheims insisted on each bishop in his province holding a copy in his hands at his consecration.

In his preface[33] to the Old English rendering of this work which he now made, Alfred states the general purpose underlying his literary and educational schemes. He recalls the happy times formerly prevailing in England, with its abundance of scholars. Then, men came hither from abroad to seek knowledge; now, we must send abroad to obtain it. At the beginning of his reign, Alfred states, there were very few men south of the Humber who knew enough Latin even for such practical purposes as reading the office-books or writing letters, and, so far as he knows, very few in Northumbria. Of the land of which he has particular knowledge, namely, the territory south of the Thames, he cannot recall a single instance. He recalls the time before the invasions when the churches of England were stocked with books and treasures. There had been numerous clerics too, though sadly illiterate; in full view of the tracks of their predecessors they were yet unable to follow them.

The obvious thing to do now is to turn Latin books into English. Fortunately, there are still many people who can read the vernacular. It is for their benefit that Alfred has translated the *Pastoral Care*, in parts literally but sometimes content to render the general sense. He intends to send a copy to every bishop in his kingdom, to help them in the 'art of arts', the cure of souls. Moreover, provided peaceful conditions can be maintained, his policy will be for such young men as are of free birth, of sufficient skill or means, and not earmarked by particular abilities for other work, to be taught to read their mother tongue. Those with a special aptitude for holy orders will then be taught Latin. In implementing this programme, the king formed a school, attached to his household, where his own youngest sons were taught alongside nobly born children and many from humbler families. The boys were taught to read both Latin and the vernacular.[34] In his anxiety that learning should not be a clerical monopoly, the king brought pressure even on adults—ealdormen, reeves, and thegns—to learn to read, on pain of demotion.[35]

Alfred also translated or caused to be translated Bede's *Historia Ecclesiastica*.[36] Modern Old English scholarship tends to deny the Alfredian authorship of this translation, which is in the Mercian rather than the Wessex dialect.[37] It may be that one of the imported Mercian scholars, such as Werferth, was the translator. The work omits much of the original, particularly the papal letters, poems in honour of the saints, and the controversial matter relating to the Easter date.

It is safe, on the other hand, to attribute to Alfred's own hand the translation of Orosius.[38] Early in the fifth century Augustine of Hippo had asked this writer to produce a general History, which he duly did in seven books. This work, specifically directed against the heathen, contains a narrative running from the earliest times to Orosius' own day. It is in the nature of a historical companion to Augustine's *City of God*, and written to refute the pagan argument that the fall of Rome was the fault of the Christians. It points out that there were greater evils in pre-Christian times. The work is an early example of history written from a Christian angle, a tendentious production which became highly popular in the early middle ages. Alfred translated according to the sense rather than literally, and in general was very free in his treatment. The most interesting section from our point of view, as doubtless also to many of Alfred's own readers, is the addition which he inserted describing the geography of northern Europe. He obtained this information from two explorers, one a Norwegian named Ohthere and the other an Anglo-Saxon, Wulfstan. From the former Alfred learnt of the region in the far north of his country, in the Arctic Circle, barren and of limited use for agriculture. Ohthere told of the profitable whale-hunting, of the Lapps who lived by fishing and hunting. He went in for the reindeer trade on a large scale, and dealt in furs and skins. His explorations took him as far as the White Sea, and in another direction into the Skagerrak. Wulfstan had sailed into the Baltic, reaching the Gulf of Danzig, and had interesting things to say of the social customs practised on the mainland known recently in our own day as East Prussia.

Towards the end of his life Alfred became more reflective, and turned to authors of a different type from Orosius. Of such was Boethius, an early sixth-century senator who fell foul of the Ostrogoth king Theodoric. While in his prison cell awaiting death he wrote the *Consolation of Philosophy*, a work in Platonic vein, dwelling on the strength to be found in the contemplation and vision of the one and only Good. In the free rendering which Alfred made of this work,[39] the Christian God appears as the strength and stay of oppressed souls.

Alfred also translated the *Soliloquies* of St Augustine of Hippo,[40] in which the great Latin thinker argues in dialogue form with Reason. In his rendering of this work, Alfred again shows his love of philosophy, of the seeking after truth and the one Reality which gives meaning and purpose to life. Let the soul, says Alfred in his free rendering of this work, be anchored in God—thus will it be safe, no matter how stormy the seas of life.

An event of the highest importance was the commencement of the *Anglo-Saxon Chronicle*. Seven manuscripts survive of this work, the oldest (now at Corpus Christi College, Cambridge) being written to a great extent in a late ninth or early tenth-century hand. The view was long held that the undertaking began in the reign of Alfred and at his direct instigation.[41] This is no longer confidently held, and it seems more likely that the *Chronicle* may have been initiated at an earlier date. It was surely a common undertaking of many minds, drawing on various sources, though it is impossible to believe that it did not receive a powerful stimulus from Alfred, in the course of his encouragement of letters and learning.

Always devout, Alfred attended daily mass and observed the canonical Hours. He kept a 'handbook' which he carried about with him wherever he went, containing the Hours and various psalms and prayers, to which he added extra material from time to time.[42] It is also said that he commenced the translation of the Psalter, though he did not live to complete it.[43]

Alfred had the true Christian sense of the responsible use of time and money. In his rule of life he endeavoured to devote half his income and half his time to the service of religion. Thus, his annual revenue was equally divided into two parts, for secular and religious purposes respectively. The first half was subdivided into three parts, apportioned to the army and court officials, to craftsmen and others introduced from abroad to help restore the ruined buildings of the land, and to strangers and pilgrims. The second half was subdivided into four parts. The first was for the deserving poor. Alfred's two religious foundations, Athelney and Shaftesbury, benefited from the second. The third went to the support of the court school. From the fourth part distribution was made to sundry churches in which the king was specially interested, not only in Wessex and Mercia, but overseas also, in Ireland, Brittany, and France. It was the king's passion for orderly division and arrangement of available resources, not only of money but of time, which led to his famous device of candle-clocks.

Alfred maintained the traditional Anglo-Saxon loyalty to Rome, and indeed his visit thither at the age of four may well have been the earliest recollection of his life. He continued to send alms to the pope,[44] doubtless a resumption of the gift promised by Offa and Aethelwulf. At his plea the Saxon School in Rome was exempted from taxes by pope Marinus (882–4), who also honoured the king by sending to him valuable gifts, including a fragment of the cross, which was in later ages preserved at Canterbury. Alfred also received gifts and communications from Elias, patriarch of Jerusalem.[45] The gifts seem to have been in the nature of a sprat to catch a mackerel, and indeed the patriarch was a good and experienced ecclesiastical beggar. He is known certainly to have written appealing for money to Charles the Fat, and there is no reason for believing that his letters to Alfred had any other object. According to late versions of the *Chronicle*,[46] and William of Malmesbury, Alfred sent alms to St Thomas in India, and to St Bartholomew. The exact meaning of this information, even if accepted as authentic, is uncertain, and it may be that by 'India' is meant Syria and Palestine.

There is some evidence, however, that this pious king was not prepared to render an unqualified obedience to the Church. In a letter which he addressed to Aethelred, archbishop of Canterbury, c. 878, pope John VIII praises the primate for his ready recourse to Rome, 'after the custom of his predecessors', for advice and instruction.[47] But the most interesting part of the letter is the exhortation to the archbishop to resist strenuously the king and others who wish to harm the Church. He must protect priests and religious. The pope says that he has written separately to Alfred, calling on him to show due deference to Canterbury. This latter letter has not survived. We have no indication as to the nature of Alfred's opposition to the Church. The most likely view is that he refused to grant unreasonable exemption from public burdens to ecclesiastics and their churches. At the time of the letter, the struggle between Alfred and the Danes was at its most crucial point. There would be no excuse for preferential treatment, and everyone, whether priest or layman, must pull his weight.

It seems indeed that, though Alfred was a true son of the Church, he was no uncritical admirer of the ecclesiastical order. It was for this reason that he refused to allow learning to become a clerical preserve. He wished his laymen to be instructed members, not docile subjects, of the Church. And the Church itself must be the servant of the people —not merely a claimant of privilege, wealth, and power.

Probably about the middle of his reign, when he was able to draw on the experience of many years, Alfred issued his legal code.[48] This law was based at least theoretically on the Mosaic, and was to be interpreted in the Christian spirit of compassion. The king drew for his actual subject-matter, however, on previous Anglo-Saxon codes, those of Ine, Offa, and Ethelbert. The code fully recognised the position of the Church and accorded to it due dignity. Traditional Christian duties were to be fulfilled by all. Cessation from work was prescribed on the great feasts. Indeed, the amount of holiday ordered in the course of the year seems to a modern reader more than generous. The twelve days of Christmas, Holy Week and Easter Week, a whole week in connection with the Feast of the Assumption, and many single days, are listed as unsuitable for all but the most necessary labour, though slaves must carry on with their work as usual. Lent must be strictly observed, on pain of a fine. Sorcery was proscribed, and the penalty of death ordered for magicians and witches. Emphasis was placed on the sanctity of oaths and contracts, of great importance in a disordered society lacking the legal formality characteristic of modern times. Above all, the principle of a lord's authority over his man was enunciated; treason to one's lord is unforgivable, and must be visited with the direst penalties.

So far as we know, Alfred lived quietly after the final peace with the Danes in 896. He died on 26 October 899,[49] and was buried in the Old Minster, Winchester. Little is known about his wife Ealhswith, who outlived him by three years, during which interval she founded a house for nuns in Winchester, the Nunnaminster. The eldest of Alfred's children was Aethelflaed, who married Aethelred the ealdorman of Mercia and after her husband's death took the government and defence of the midlands into her own hands. Alfred was succeeded by his son Edward, who before long removed his father's body, along with that of his mother Ealhswith, to the New Minster, also in the West Saxon capital. This monastery, dedicated in 903 to the Holy Trinity, the Virgin, and SS. Peter and Paul, was built under the guidance and with the encouragement of Grimbald, who became the first abbot. Early in the twelfth century the relics were again removed, to the new foundation of Hyde abbey a short distance outside the city, which replaced the New Minster. At the Dissolution this abbey suffered a particularly thorough demolition, which was carried a stage further towards the end of the eighteenth century, when the site was cleared to make way for a prison. Nothing now survives of the monastery save a few fragments, and the whereabouts of what still exists, if anything, of the mortal body of England's greatest king are quite unknown.

CHAPTER XVIII

THE MONASTIC REVIVAL

Despite the labours of Alfred, the Church in England at the beginning of the tenth century was in a parlous condition. The repeated Danish harryings and invasions, the main targets of which naturally were the religious centres, where most of the wealth was to be found, had virtually annihilated monasticism—at any rate in eastern England. Alfred's foundation of Athelney had come to little, while the fame of that of Shaftesbury lay in the future. Such centres of religion as existed were mostly of the secular type. Not a great deal is known about the parochial clergy of this time, but few will imagine that their religious ideals and practice were any higher than those of the inhabitants of the religious houses.

As a result of the ninth-century disturbances many well-established sees had come to an end.[1] The bishopric of Dunwich, whose episcopal line began with Felix c. 630, ended with Aethelwald in 870, and was never revived. Elmham was a little more fortunate. This see, which began in 673 with Beaduwine as its first bishop, had its line interrupted in 836, though it was resumed about a century later and lasted into Norman times. Lindsey maintained a steady succession of bishops from c. 678 until the mid-ninth century. After that it seems to have become fitful, and there is evidence for only four bishops between that time and the end of the tenth century, following which there appear to have been no more holders of the see. The north-east naturally suffered much. The see of York continued, but in such an impoverished condition that many of its bishops found it necessary to hold it in plurality with Worcester, from the time of the accession of Oswald in 961 onwards. The famous sees of Lindisfarne and Hexham, which had meant so much for the life of the Church during the days of the Conversion, became permanent victims of the North-men. The last bishop of Hexham was Tidfrith, who died in 821. Lindisfarne was in far too exposed a position to survive an onslaught from across the Northern seas. It repeatedly suffered, and its end came before the ninth century had run its course. Abandoning the island, as we have seen, the bishop embarked on a wandering life for seven years, with some of his monks, carrying with them their precious treasure, the earthly remains of St Cuthbert. In 883 they settled at Chester-le-Street, a few miles from Durham. The fact that they were thus able to settle down, in a still exposed neighbourhood, and found a new line of episcopal rulers which would endure for a century, is significant that the peril was passing, and that securer conditions would before long pave the way for a new religious advance. The see of Whithorn in Galloway was a permanent casualty; its last bishop was Heathured, who acceded there in 821. In the midlands, the Leicester bishopric gave place to a renewed one at Dorchester-on-Thames, a safer place, in the middle of the ninth century, but it was apparently a good many years before this new see really settled down. The other midland see, that of Lichfield, was more fortunate, and maintained a succession to become one of the great sees of the later medieval English Church.

The violent interruption accorded to many sees in regions easily accessible to the invaders indicates the grave damage which had been inflicted upon the Church. In the safer parts of the country the tale is of course less gloomy, at any rate from the point of view of the continuity of ecclesiastical organisation. The least molested dioceses had been Worcester and Hereford, which both had bishops at the beginnng of the tenth century. In Wessex the dioceses of Winchester and Sherborne had maintained their lines, but early in the tenth century they were reorganised, five dioceses taking the place of two. This might suggest that Christianity had actually strengthened there during the times of peril. In 908 Denewulf, bishop of Winchester, died, and the following year or two saw the demise of Asser, bishop of Sherborne and Alfred's biographer. It was a convenient opportunity for a Wessex reorganisation, which Edward the Elder was not slow to seize. Hampshire and Surrey were left to the diocese of Winchester, while Wiltshire and Berkshire became a new diocese centred on Ramsbury. The Sherborne diocese was now to consist only of Dorset; Devon and Cornwall became the territory of the diocese of Crediton; while Somerset went to Wells, a new diocese which would endure. In the next reign a further subdivision took place, St German's becoming a see for Cornwall.

Eastwards along the south coast, the Selsey diocese still existed in the early part of the tenth century, and was destined to endure into the reign of William I. Canterbury, Rochester, and London kept their successions undisturbed, and in general the south-east was relatively unharmed.

Such was the ecclesiastical framework of the English Church during a period which was to be characterised, as we shall now see, mainly by monastic revival. For this new movement, the political conditions were on the whole promising. Alfred was succeeded in October 899 by his son Edward the Elder, a noteworthy feature of whose reign of a quarter of a century was a steady reversal of the tables upon the Danes. Edward moved from the defensive, so ably maintained by his great father, to an offensive policy, in which he was aided by his sister Aethelflaed, the 'Lady of the Mercians'—a warrior indeed. She was widow of the Mercian ruler Aethelred. The Danish menace was steadily pushed further north, and the victory of Tettenhall, Staffordshire, in 910, was decisive. Fortified burhs erected in the midlands ensured the permanence of the gains. Edward himself actually made no outstanding contribution to Church renewal, apart from the increase in the number of the Wessex dioceses noted above. The reforming tendencies of his father's reign were not continued; but by carrying aggressive war into the Danish invader's camp, he was helping to create the conditions which would make later reformation possible.

He was succeeded as king of the West Saxons in 925 by his son Athelstan, who was crowned at Kingston-on-Thames by Athelm, archbishop of Canterbury. The fourteen-year reign of this king is a tantalising one. Comparatively little is known of it, though such as we do know gives us ground for believing that here was one of England's greatest kings. He was indefatigable alike as military conqueror and as a connoisseur in Church affairs. He was no mere island kinglet, and his name was respected on the Continent. It was during his time that the influences leading to the revival of Church life began to take concrete form.

It was above all in the monastic life that the movement towards the revival of Church life during this century was manifested. This is remarkable, and must have been unexpected by those who hoped for revival, because at the very beginning of the century the monastic life was virtually non-existent in England. It had perished partly through inner decay, partly through the invasions. Alfred's attempt at its revival came to little, and indeed he himself does not seem to have had much realisation of the inner spirit of monasticism, and probably not even of its real possibilities as a civilising force. Edward the Elder founded New Minster, Winchester, in the early years of his reign, and Alfred's widow Ealhswith followed this up with a house for women in the same city. But religious life at this time was lacking in austerity and discipline, and the secular canon rather than the monk was the important instrument in maintaining the worship of the greater churches.

The monastic revival of the tenth century is inseparably connected, so far as England is concerned, with the name of Dunstan.[2] This great man was born near Glastonbury c. 909,[3] which was in fact a significant year in English Church history, marking the opening of a new and more hopeful chapter. It was in this year that Edward established his new West Saxon sees. One of the new bishops was Athelm, the first occupant of the see of Wells. He was uncle to the child born about this time, and Dunstan was in fact well connected altogether, being related to the king, who spent much of his time in Somerset. In due course the boy was sent to school at Glastonbury abbey, a religious house which like others fortunate enough to escape destruction had nevertheless fallen below Benedictine strictness.

When Athelm succeeded Plegmund as archbishop of Canterbury in 923 he took his nephew with him to Kent, and there followed a period at Athelstan's court, which ended about 935 with the young man's dismissal, brought about by the complaints of his companions, who found him bookish and dull. He sought the advice of Aelfheah, bishop of Winchester, in response to which he embraced the monastic life at Glastonbury. In 939 Athelstan was succeeded by the eighteen-year-old Edmund, another son of Edward the Elder, who brought Dunstan back into favour at court. But again the old charges of reserve and stand-offishness were brought against the young monk, and again he was expelled from court. Not long afterwards, however, it happened that Edmund was one day hunting near Cheddar, where the royal court was customarily kept. He was intent on pursuing a stag, which he followed furiously. Suddenly he saw that the terrified animal had reached a precipice, over which it took a leap. The king's horse was out of control. Edmund made a momentary vow that if God would spare him he would recall Dunstan. The horse came to a halt by the edge of the precipice.

On returning to Cheddar, the king sent for Dunstan. He conducted him personally to Glastonbury, where he installed him as abbot, promising him every material assistance in the running of the house.

For some thirteen years Dunstan ruled Glastonbury, gradually leading its semi-secular, semi-monastic body of clerks nearer to the Benedictine norm. Both Edmund and his queen, Aethelflaed, kept him well supplied with gifts. But Dunstan, always an idealist and a visionary, could not bear the business of property management, and he put this department of his rule into the hands of his own brother Wulfric.

In 946 his royal patron Edmund was murdered in a brawl at a feast. His two sons, Eadwig and Edgar, of a former marriage, were minors, and Edmund was succeeded by his brother Eadred, who continued in happy co-operation with the abbot of Glastonbury. Though a sick man, Eadred ruled energetically for nine years. On his death in 955 he was followed by Eadwig. So far had the power of the rulers of Wessex grown during the first half of the century, owing to a run of very able monarchs, that the young man held sway over Mercia and the north as well as his native West Saxony. But the new king, though not without ability, showed little inclination to follow the path of duty. He was, moreover, under the influence of his mother, and of the young Aelfgifu, his destined wife. After Eadwig had been crowned at Kingston by Oda, archbishop of Canterbury, he gave offence to the assembled nobles by forsaking their company during the coronation banquet. Dunstan, along with Cynesige, bishop of Lichfield, was assigned the unpleasant task of bringing him back—which he accomplished, at the cost of the lasting hostility of the new king. In 956 Dunstan was again in disfavour. Forced into exile, he took refuge across the Channel.[4]

During the next few months Dunstan was to be brought directly in touch with the monastic reform movement of the Continent, and it may be convenient at this juncture to mention some of the ideals and achievements of those reformers who during this century and beyond strove to rescue the monasteries from the ineffectiveness into which they had fallen. The movement is connected above all with the name of Cluny.[5] It was in 910 that duke William of Aquitaine, in expiation for the misdeeds of his youth, founded this celebrated house. Its first abbot was Berno, who was succeeded in 927 by Odo, to whom was really due the commanding place which the abbey acquired in the West. A characteristic of Cluny was its independence of secular authority, and it was to ensure this that by the foundation charter obtained in 927 from Rudolf king of the Franks, the abbey was made directly dependent on the papacy. A tendency developed for the daughter-houses, which were founded in profusion throughout the century, to remain dependent to a great extent on the mother-house. In course of time a vast monastic organisation was built up in Europe, wielding immense influence. Later on, notably under Odilo, who became abbot c. 994, Cluny became famous for its devotion to liturgical worship and church art. During the abbacy of Hugh, who succeeded Odilo in 1049, and ruled the house for sixty years, a splendid church was built, one of the glories of Christendom, of which a single transept has survived until the present day. This church made a stately setting for the Gregorian music of which the Cluniacs were expert exponents. It was also rich in sculpture, some small portions of this surviving in the sculptured capitals of the choir. These artistic adornments were to be condemned by St Bernard as a needless extravagance, but there was a spirituality inherent in them of deep import for the soul of man, while their significance in the history of art need hardly be emphasised.

A name associated to some extent with Cluny was that of Fleury-on-the-Loire. This monastery, founded in the seventh century, had fallen into evil ways. But its lay owner, count Elisiern, overcome with remorse, invited Cluny to undertake its reformation, which it did c. 930. Both Cluny and Fleury were of course known to English reforming churchmen of this period, and it was at the latter house that Oda, archbishop of Canterbury (940–58),[6] received the Benedictine habit, later thither sending his nephew Oswald—a great figure in the monastic revival subsequently—to study the Benedictine way of life.

But from the point of view of the English reform, it was the parallel movement in Lotharingia which was really significant. This land, lying between Neustria and Austrasia, had suffered more in the ninth-century disturbances than had Burgundy. Many religious houses had been destroyed, and the surviving ones had fallen into the hands of lay owners, who appropriated their revenues, and at the best provided them with secular clerks to maintain a minimum of devotion. Some of these laymen, however, allowed their consciences to be roused. They included Gilbert, the duke of Lotharingia. He was stirred into contrition with regard to his church properties by Gerard, one of the great reformers of the tenth century.[7] Gerard himself rebuilt a ruined church at Brogne, where he established the monastic life in the strict

Benedictine sense, and helped duke Gilbert to restore Benedictinism to some of his ruined abbeys. The duke was also assisted in this work by the reformed abbey of Gorze, under its abbot John. In the Lotharingian reformation many monasteries were restored, but on rather more austere lines than was the case with the Cluniac houses. It was a feature too of Lotharingia that the reformed houses remained individually independent of their mother-house.

In Flanders, a region closely associated with Lotharingia, one of the greatest lay rulers was the count Arnulf, who owned the abbeys of St Bavo and St Peter at Ghent. These had suffered miserably at the hands of the Northmen, and Arnulf invited Gerard of Brogne to undertake the work of restoration. Gerard accordingly arrived in Ghent c. 941. He stayed there some twelve years, establishing Benedictine monasticism at the two abbeys. But his commission was to some extent a roving one, and amongst other houses which he reformed was St Bertin's, where he expelled the secular clerks in favour of Benedictine monks. The ousted canons took refuge in England, where in 944 they were given the abbey of Bath by king Edmund, in recognition of their kindness in burying the body of his brother, drowned in the Channel some time previously. The abbot placed in charge of St Bertin was one Womar, who in 953 became abbot of St Peter's, Ghent, Gerard returning to his own monastery of Brogne.

It was to St Peter's, Ghent, during the abbacy of Womar, that Dunstan came during his exile. Nothing is certainly known of his life there. But we can be sure that he was observant of the monastic revival going on around him, and that he brought the memory of his experiences back with him when he returned to England in 957, in which year king Eadwig was deposed by the Northumbrians and Mercians in favour of his younger brother Edgar.

Edgar became ruler of all England in 959, and the Chronicler sings his praises very highly in the poem which is inserted as the annal for that year. No attempt is made to hide his faults,[8] but these were outbalanced by his virtues. He loved God's law and under him the land prospered. In the history of ecclesiastical reform the reign of this king (959–75) is highly important, and the reformers really had in him a ruler who was ready to support them at every turn. Dunstan, recalled by Edgar, was never again to go into exile. He remained in power, the leading ecclesiastic in England, until his death in 988. On his return from Ghent he was first made bishop of Worcester in 957, and then in

959 bishop of London (retaining the west midland see in plurality). Next year he was translated to Canterbury, Oswald succeeding him at Worcester. He remained Edgar's close adviser throughout the latter's reign, and was doubtless the moving spirit behind the current legislation dealing with church-scot and tithe and the observance of fasts and festivals. Rules and regulations were issued for the guidance of the parochial clergy, who amongst much else are enjoined to teach the manual arts to their people. But it is a point often remarked that from this juncture, though Dunstan certainly maintained his commanding position in Church and State, he does not seem to have played a large part in the monastic reform which now gathered strength. He earned his place in monastic history through his abbacy of Glastonbury earlier on, where he did not carry through any aggressive or violent reforms, but rather in a wise and patient way showed what the monastic life might be. During his latter years, following Edgar's death, he seems to have devoted himself increasingly to contemplation, prayer, and the performance of good works.

By far the most energetic promoters of the Benedictine revival which distinguished these years were Aethelwold[9] and Oswald. The former was a tempestuous, somewhat forbidding character, accustomed to strive towards the end he had in view with drive and not always with scruples. He sacrificed his own health and comfort, and demanded much of others also. Like Dunstan a West Saxon, he was almost his exact contemporary. Born at about the same time as Dunstan, he was his fellow-pupil, and ordained priest with him on the same day. When Dunstan was abbot of Glastonbury, Aethelwold became one of his monks. But the rather moderate monasticism which, apparently, was practised at Glastonbury at this time, did not satisfy Aethelwold's thorough-going temperament, and he asked leave to go to Fleury. This was refused by Eadred, king at this time, on the prompting of his mother Eadgifu, who thought that such an able man as Aethelwold should not be allowed to leave the country. He was offered instead the abbey of Abingdon, in Berkshire, and thither he went with five clerks, Osgar, Foldbricht, and Frithegar from Glastonbury, Ordbricht from Winchester, and Eadric from London.

Abingdon was an old-established monastery fallen on ill days.[10] Under Aethelwold's rule (954–63) its discipline was now restored. The buildings were improved and clerks from Glastonbury introduced.[11] Benedictinism was not immediately established, for the simple reason that Aethelwold was not sure what Benedictinism really was. It was to study the Benedictine Rule at first hand that he had planned to go to Fleury himself, and he now sent thither one of his leading pupils, Osgar. He also sought advice on liturgical matters from the abbot of Corbie in France, who sent a deputation of monks skilled in the Gregorian chant, always so marked and attractive a feature of the Benedictine monastic life. King Eadred died soon after Aethelwold became abbot of Abingdon, and little help could be expected from the unsatisfactory Eadwig. But with the accession of Edgar to the Wessex throne in 959 there was more encouragement for monastic reformers.

By 963 the fame of Abingdon as a centre of monastic revival was at its height, and in that year its abbot was consecrated bishop of the highly important diocese of Winchester.

To Aethelwold's eye, the scene at Winchester must have been a melancholy one: 'At that time there were in the Old Minster, the seat of the bishop, clerks of bad habits, so given over to pride, arrogance, and self-indulgence, that some of them even refused to take their share in the celebration of masses. They broke the law by marrying, and then cast off their wives for other women. They were given over to a constant round of gluttony and drunkenness.'[12] It may be that this was an exaggeration, but the kernel of truth which it certainly contained was more than a Benedictine reformer of uncompromising temperament would tolerate. For a short while Aethelwold tried to persuade the clerks to accept a more disciplined mode of life. Then, tired of their dithering promises which came to nothing, he appeared in the cathedral church at the close of mass on the eve of the first Sunday in Lent, 964. He was accompanied by some of his monks from Abingdon, under the zealous Osgar, and also by Wulfstan, a royal officer. The bishop peremptorily offered the clerks the choice between the monastic habit and way of life, or the surrender of their stalls. The upshot was that three of them submitted, and the remainder lodged an appeal with the king, perhaps remembering the kindly reception given previously by king Edmund to the clerks driven out of St Bertin by a monastic enthusiast. But Edgar was firmly on the side of ecclesiastical reform. He referred the matter to archbishop Dunstan—a politic move. The king saw the whole affair as one for churchmen to fight out amongst themselves, and was confident in the wisdom of Dunstan, a reformer but not a violent one. At the archbishop's request Edgar

ummoned a council at Winchester, and here Dunstan announced his
verdict, that the cathedral clergy should be monks, on the grounds
that its revenues had been originally given for this purpose.
Having accomplished his immediate purpose at the cathedral or
Old Minster, the new bishop proceeded to expel seculars in favour of
monks at the New Minster also. He insisted too on stricter discipline
at Nunnaminster, the Winchester house for women. These three
houses were close to each other and constantly quarrelling over boundaries. They also found the proximity of citizens' houses an annoyance, and the bishop pulled some of these down, so that the monastic
devotions should not be disturbed. Aethelwold was nothing if not
drastic. In all this the king was firmly behind him.

Aethelwold's greatest work, however, was probably the rebuilding
of the cathedral. It was during this work that the body of St Swithun,
a former bishop of Winchester, was brought from outside the cathedral
to a splendid shrine within, on St Swithun's day (15 July) 971. Thus
the ecclesiastical push and drive of Aethelwold overcame even the
humility of Swithun, who had counted himself unworthy of a grave
within the sacred walls.

Aethelwold's vigour was not confined to Abingdon and Winchester.
He acquired by purchase the ruined abbey of Medeshamstede (the later
Peterborough), determined on its restoration. This house, founded
some three centuries before, had come to grief at the hands of the
Danes. Aethelwold built a church—foundations of which exist under
the present cathedral[13]—established a community of monks under
abbot Aldulf, who in 992 became bishop of Worcester. Aethelwold
also bought the site and ruins of the former double monastery of Ely,
placing monks there under the charge of Brihtnoth, who came from
Abingdon. The new church at Ely was consecrated by Dunstan himself, and gifts came in such profusion that the foundations were quickly
laid of what became eventually one of the wealthiest of medieval
abbeys. Another fenland monastery brought to ruin by the Danes,
that of Thorney, was also bought and restored by Aethelwold. He
probably had a hand too in the replacement of seculars by religious at
Chertsey in Surrey and Milton in Dorset.

Oswald[14] was a more attractive character than Aethelwold. Trained
by his uncle, archbishop Oda, he was ordained priest and spent some
time at a small, lax monastery in Winchester before he asked leave
to study monasticism overseas. Making his way to Fleury, he spent

some six years there. He was not the only Englishman at Fleury during this time engaged on the task of observing the reformed Benedictinism at first hand. There was Osgar, who had been sent by Aethelwold from Abingdon, and a certain Germanus from Winchester. The news of his uncle's grave illness brought Oswald home, though not in time to see him before he died. This was in 961. Dunstan succeeded Oda as archbishop of Canterbury, and Oswald followed Dunstan in the see of Worcester.

It would appear that Dunstan had already made progress in introducing the Benedictine way of life at Worcester, and that Oswald continued his work of quiet transformation. The tactics of Aethelwold at Winchester were not followed. It is true that Wulfstan, bishop of Worcester later on, in describing a synod held there in 1092, states that Oswald replaced clerks by regulars in 969.[15] Dr J. Armitage Robinson, however, thought that all we can be sure of is that there were some monks at Worcester by 977, sixteen years after Oswald's consecration.[16] What is certain is that as soon as he was consecrated and settled in, Oswald sent to Fleury for Germanus, who came to teach the Benedictine Rule at Worcester. This does not imply that any attempt was made to enforce its observance generally. A certain tension apparently arose, and the bishop transferred Germanus, along with a priest and a number of novices, to a temporary house at Westbury-on-Trym, near Bristol. It was not many years after that he also acquired the site of Ramsey, in the fens, and there he established a monastery on fully Benedictine lines, to which he transferred the monks who had been in training at Westbury. This new house was kept in close touch with the continental movement, and Abbo, one of Fleury's leading monks, taught in it for two years.

The establishment of Ramsey abbey illustrates Oswald's character and method of work. He was a convinced Benedictine no less than was bishop Aethelwold. Yet he was not prepared to overturn the tables violently at Worcester. He preferred in the first instance to establish an entirely new foundation, from which in time he would hope to draw recruits to his cathedral. The process was one of infiltration. The cathedral chapter was by degrees transformed from one of clerks into a community with a predominantly monastic character, though it does not seem that the seculars had been entirely supplanted by even the close of Oswald's episcopacy.

Oswald founded or reformed other monasteries also, including very likely Deerhurst, Gloucestershire, where the well-known surviving Saxon church probably dates from about this time.[17] He restored Winchcombe, near Cheltenham, putting in Germanus as abbot. Pershore was refounded, Oswald installing as abbot Foldbricht, a monk who had been trained at Glastonbury and Abingdon. Another famous Worcestershire foundation, Evesham, was revived about the same time (c. 970), possibly by Aethelwold acting outside his own diocese.

In 972 Oswald was appointed archbishop of York, continuing to hold the Worcester see in plurality. The diocese of York had suffered much from the Danes, and its resultant poverty made it necessary or at least desirable that the holder of its see should have supplementary revenues. Oswald continued to spend much of his time at Worcester. He displayed considerable business acumen in the management of the property of both sees.[18]

It is clear that the age was pre-eminently one of monastic revival. Monasteries, whether entirely new ones or old houses refounded, sprung up in the southern half of England—nearly forty in all by the end of the century, including half-a-dozen for women.[19] To a large extent the growth was an unregulated one, each house following its own customs, and it became clear to the leaders of the movement that some sort of general direction was necessary. At their request therefore, king Edgar summoned a council at Winchester, with the purpose of co-ordinating the revival.[20] It was attended by many bishops, abbots, and abbesses; there were also monks from Fleury and Ghent, and the results of the council were to show the important influence which the continental reform movement exerted on England during Edgar's reign, though it is probably the case that the original impulse towards reform, as evidenced at Glastonbury under Dunstan, was a native one. The council approved a book of monastic customs, the *Regularis Concordia*, which sets out in detail the liturgical routine to be followed in future by all houses of monks and nuns in England. This famous document has long been accessible, and can now be read in a critical edition.[21] It is fruitless and indeed pointless to try to assign definite authorship to a work of this nature, eclectic and discriminatory as it is, and the most that can be said is that Aethelwold probably had a larger hand in it than anyone else. What is more important is the clear evidence which the book affords that the English religious had decided to align themselves with those of Fleury, Ghent, and Lorraine.

The general reformation, long operative in Europe, had at last taken root in England.

Hitherto the reformed English houses had apparently been purely Benedictine in their simplicity and austerity. That is to say, they were in the tradition of Benedict of Nursia himself. But on the Continent, the work of the second Benedict (of Aniane) had much elaborated the original way of life, especially in regard to the liturgical observances. This was especially so at Cluny, and in varying degrees the multiplication of church services characterised the continental reform. The great father of the Benedictines had never meant his monks to spend a disproportionate amount of time in church, upsetting the balance which should characterise the truly devoted life. But from the tenth century onwards, a system of elaborate ritual and ceremonial held the field—or at least was the ideal—amongst Western monks until the Cistercians reacted to it some two centuries later.

Thus the *Regularis Concordia* is not satisfied with the Hours of Prayer unsupplemented by other devotional forms. Before they were even begun each day, a large block of psalms had to be sung, including the fifteen gradual psalms, a feature of the tenth-century movement which has retained a considerable popularity as an optional devotion down to the present day.[22] After matins and lauds of the day, matins of All Saints and matins of the dead were sung before prime. All this entailed some five hours of psalm singing and prayers and lections before daybreak. There was a morrow mass as well as a conventual mass, and the usual lesser offices. The latter of course in the Monastic Office are comparatively short. After vespers of the day came vespers of All Saints and vespers of the dead. This formidable round of worship was completed in the usual way by compline. Besides the Hours, there were numerous lesser psalms and prayers prescribed for use, notably for the king and the royal family. This was a distinctive feature of the English reform, and the *Regularis Concordia* emphasises that the prayers for the royal house are to be said properly, and not 'chanted at excessive speed'. The 'royal prayers' emphasise the close connection between Church and State, or rather their close intermingling, characteristic of later Saxon England.[23] Moreover, the religious of this country owed much to the support of kings and queens, and this was their own and natural way of repaying the debt. Prayer and psalmody were in fact the special work of monks, their *raison d'être* in society. There was perhaps never a time in English religious history when there was so strong a sense of liturgical worship as in itself an efficacious work. The 'praying man' was just as useful to the nation as was the artificer and the 'fighting man'. It must not be supposed that the religious would be exhausting themselves physically with so many psalms and prayers. They had their full quota of sleep like other men and women. They should not be regarded as self-sacrificing martyrs, and indeed the lot of the Saxon peasant, alternately in his log cabin and the sodden fields, was probably harsher. Apart from liturgical worship the monks did little else. The conventual church was their workshop. Most of the menial duties were performed by hired servants. The majority of the monks were not scholars, and spent little time in intellectual labour.

We do not know whether the *Regularis Concordia* was actually fully practised in all houses, or was regarded rather as an ideal at which to aim. But there is evidence that not all houses managed to fulfil the requirements. About a generation afterwards, the abbot of Eynsham (Aelfric, a former pupil of Aethelwold) made an abridged edition for his house; in his preface, however, he points out that his monks are newcomers to the religious life. The concession that he makes may therefore be merely temporary and something unusual, and one may concede that in fully established and well-trained communities the customal promulged at Winchester was fully followed.

With the death of Edgar in 975 there was, it seems, a certain amount of anti-monastic reaction.[24] The revival and growth in power of the monasteries had not been without its critics. Resentment was felt alike by heirs who had seen much of their future estates given to abbeys by devout fathers, and also by dispossessed secular clergy, many of whom were of aristocratic and influential families. The monks had become landlords on a big scale, and this did not tend to make them popular. The situation was particularly aggravated by a dispute in the succession. Edgar left two sons of tender years; Edward, the son of his first wife Aethelflaed, and Aethelred, son of his later wife Aelfthryth. The nobles were divided, but Dunstan favoured Edward. His decisive intervention proves that the archbishop's influence was still great, though now rather in the background. Edward was duly crowned king of England.

But the wave of anti-monastic feeling was not arrested by this assertion of Dunstan's authority. The ealdorman of Mercia, Aelfhere, evicted the monks from Evesham and distributed their lands amongst his supporters and kinsfolk; Winchcombe and Deerhurst also came to grief. The Chronicler, in recording the accession of the young Edward, breaks into verse as he gives vent to his indignation against the enemies of the monastic order:

> In his days, on account of his youth,
> The opponents of God broke through God's laws;
> Aelfhere the ealdorman and many others;
> And marred monastic rules;
> Minsters they razed,
> And drove the monks away,
> And put God's laws to flight.

In 978 the rivalry of the two royal brothers came to an end with the murder of Edward at Corfe Castle. Hastily buried at Wareham, his uncorrupted body was before long removed to Shaftesbury, where on its windy cliff overlooking the Dorset countryside it became the centre of one of the most popular cults of the middle ages. There is no real evidence for the story that queen Aelfthryth, mother of the younger brother, was responsible for Edward's death, though she was at Corfe Castle at the time, and a tradition—not earlier than the twelfth century —makes her the foundress, in expiation for this crime, of the nunneries of Wherwell and Amesbury. It is a fact, however, that her son Aethelred was now crowned at Kingston, to begin one of the longest, and one of the least satisfactory, reigns in English history (979–1016).[25]

The anti-monastic outbreak, though sharp, was not serious, and broke down with the death in 983 of its leader Aelfhere. In any case it was only the Mercian monasteries which had been really affected. The tide was still running in favour of religion, and the veneration felt by the mass of the population in this country towards monks was not abated. Religious foundations continued to be made in Aethelred's reign, including such notable places as Cerne and Eynsham. By the close of the century flourishing abbeys were fairly numerous in England, though concentrated most thickly in the south, with large numbers in the Severn valley and neighbouring regions, and in the fen country.[26] Two more cathedrals had their secular clergy ousted in favour of religious. These were Sherborne c. 992, and Canterbury c. 997. The creation of the monastic cathedral chapter, a characteristic of the medieval English Church, though not entirely unknown elsewhere, may be regarded as one of the most interesting results of the tenth-century reformation in this country.[27]

Unlike the monastic movement of the Golden Age period and beyond, which was interrupted and destroyed by the ravages of the Northmen, the monastic renaissance of the tenth century set in motion a stream which would continue to flow for several centuries, until the advent of an entirely novel interpretation of Christianity accomplished a revolution more lasting than that effected by the terror of the sword. During the tenth century we see the firm foundations being laid of famous Benedictine monasteries which would maintain their lines unbroken until the Dissolution. This revival, as we have seen, centred very largely around three outstanding men. They died within a few years of each other—Aethelwold first in 984, Dunstan in 988, while Oswald survived until 992. Dunstan in the past has been harshly treated by historians, who mistakenly saw in him a narrow-minded and monkish fanatic. On the other hand, it may be that modern scholars are tending to be too lenient in their judgment on Aethelwold, a ruthless man who placed the efficiency of the institution before the happiness of the individual. Oswald is beloved by all. 'The Spirit of the fear of the Lord was gloriously displayed in him.'[28] The debt which the English Church owed to these three men was immense. They never wavered from the purpose before them, which was the re-establishment of discipline. Though they unhesitatingly sought the aid of foreign reformers when the need required, they remained distinctively English. They trained many disciples in their tradition, though none of these reached their masters' eminence. So great were the masters. Yet so strong was the tradition which they imparted, that the spirit of monasticism permeated the whole history of the later Anglo-Saxon Church, and in the two or three generations preceding the coming of William the Conqueror most of the diocesan bishops were monks.

CHAPTER XIX

THE ORIGIN AND DEVELOPMENT
OF THE PAROCHIAL SYSTEM

The system by which the entire English countryside is mapped out into parishes, and is largely taken for granted in the life of the Church today, was a long time maturing. There were probably local churches with their priests and congregations, here and there, even in the earliest years of the Conversion; four centuries afterwards there were doubtless many districts still without their parish churches and settled priests. The lines are very blurred throughout. It cannot be said of any particular ecclesiastic, such as archbishop Honorius (Canterbury 627–53) or Theodore (668–90), both of whom have been credited with the system, that here is the founder of the parochial organisation of the English Church. Neither can it be dated, even approximately, to any single generation or century. All that can be certainly said is that by the twelfth century the system was an accomplished fact. Since then it has been pruned or modified from time to time, and become the subject of an extensive body of canon law. Any suggestion of severely tampering with it is bound to arouse strong feelings in our own day.[1]

The subject cannot be considered in isolation from similar developments abroad, and the parochial system has been evolved, along somewhat varying lines, in every European country. Rome and southern Italy are usually taken as the starting point. After the 'peace of the Church' early in the fourth century, the number of Christians rapidly increased, as much from motives of respectability as of conviction, and the Church's influence was increasingly felt in country districts. Hitherto the Church had been essentially urban. The first local ecclesiastical units were city parishes, and their incumbents were the bishops. In an average city of the late Roman Empire in the West there might be only a single church, in which the bishop as father of his flock celebrated the Eucharist, baptised and confirmed, and preached the Word. He would have around him his *familia*, a company of priests, deacons, and clerks in lesser orders, who assisted him generally in pastoral and administrative work.

Consequently, in the population-centres where the Christian religion took earliest root, the dioceses were both small and numerous. Thus in the south of Italy there were numerous bishoprics, whereas in the northern half of the same country, a predominantly rural region, there were probably only four or five by c. 300. Three centuries later there were 53 bishoprics in the north, and 197 in the centre and south.[2] Generally, in the great rural and Germanic lands north of the Alps, bishoprics would be large, unwieldy, and comparatively few; in England, the total number reached before the Reformation was seventeen.

It should be noted that the term 'diocese', now universally used to designate the area within the jurisdiction of the bishop, came into ecclesiastical use, at any rate in its present sense, comparatively late. It was taken over from the nomenclature of the civil administration of the later Empire. The word 'parish', or 'parochia', had an earlier use, indicating a local Christian community, which in the first two or three centuries of the history of the Church was normally found in a city and presided over by its bishop. In the seventh century, in England, we find the bishop's area still being called his parish, though here it would be rural and of vast extent. When in 679 Theodore divided Mercia into the five dioceses of Worcester, Lichfield, Leicester, Lindsey, and Dorchester, they were referred to as 'parochiae'.[3]

It cannot be too strongly emphasised that Christianity in its origin was an urban religion, flourishing in trading centres, in seaports, and wherever there was much coming and going of men with a consequent and steady interchange of ideas. This is clear enough in the New Testament, and it remained true of the pre-Nicene Church. But by c. 300 the Church was beginning to penetrate into the rural areas, the *pagi* of the Roman *civitates*, where the country-dwellers or *pagani* clung tenaciously to the traditional beliefs and customs. It was a significant development, illustrating the growth of confidence and missionary enterprise, after the Church had for generations been content merely to hold its ground in the face of persecution. This outward movement was doubtless for a long time led by itinerant preachers, who had no thought of establishing permanent rural churches. In Italy, for example, it was not until the fifth century that the definite establishment of country parishes with resident clergy seems to have been begun.

By the close of the fifth century, however, the founding of country parishes had proceeded far enough in Italy to call for papal legislation, and Gelasius I (492–6) issued a set of instructions for the benefit of private individuals who wished to build churches on their estates or elsewhere.[4] Nothing was to be taken in hand, he laid down, without the cognisance of Rome and the local bishop. The founder of a church, nevertheless, along with his heirs, was allowed the right of nominating the parish priest.

The system which eventually emerged in Italy during the Lombard period (that is, roughly from the entry of the Lombards into Italy in 568 until their conquest by Charlemagne in 774) was one grouped round 'baptisteries', central rural churches ministered by a staff of clergy led by a rector or archpriest. Some of these baptismal churches were probably collegiate institutions, and might be known as *monasteria* and their clergy designated *monachi* without necessarily being monks in the commonly accepted sense. Dependent on the baptisteries were smaller churches, or chapels, in the surrounding villages, some of them of private foundation. As indeed the nomenclature of the system suggests, baptism could be administered only at the central churches, and the possession of a font was a highly regarded privilege.

Contemporaneously in Gaul, much the same sort of development took place. There were first of all the city churches, under the personal and direct pastoral oversight of the bishop; if there should be more than one church in a city, the bishop ministered in each church by turns. Secondly, there were central country churches, cared for in the first instance by clergy who came out from the cathedral city, but by the sixth century possessing their own staffs. It is unnecessary to assume that these churches were large and imposing, though some no doubt had architectural dignity at an early date. But each was the Christian centre for a whole district. As in Italy, it was to such centres that parents were required to bring their children for baptism, and it was from these centres that clergy went out to celebrate mass and preach in the villages of the surrounding countryside.

The process may be detected in Gregory of Tours' *History of the Franks*. Here it is recorded how St Martin of Tours built the first church of that city, and also in many villages destroyed the pagan places of worship, baptising the inhabitants and providing them with churches.[5] It is probable that the great period for the founding of these country churches or mission stations ran from the fourth to the sixth centuries. It is likely too that parallel with this movement many of the city churches were being consolidated into distinctively cathedral foundations—thus Gregory says that Agricola, bishop of Chalon-sur-Saône, who died in 580, built the cathedral there, and indeed did so with distinction, enriching it with mosaics and marbles.[6] In the Auxerre diocese by the close of the sixth century there were thirty-seven country churches. A body of law relating to them is contained in the canons of Gallic councils held during the sixth century. Extensive legislation in connection with an aspect of the Church's life is a certain sign of its rising importance.

The third line of evolution in Gaul was the foundation of chapels, or oratories, though to a much greater extent than in Lombardic Italy these were the work of private landowners building on their estates. The purpose of these local proprietary churches is quite obvious. Though for baptisms, and great ecclesiastical functions, resort must be made to the central country church, it was convenient for the landowner to have actually on the spot a church where he and his family, his tenants, and his slaves, could hear mass. Such a church might at first in many cases be served by a visiting priest from the central church, if only at intervals. But it would be more practical to manumit some comparatively intelligent and pious serf and send him to the bishop for ordination. In Gaul as elsewhere the first village parish priests were undoubtedly sons of the soil. Steadily these private oratories rose in importance and status. Though in an exact sense the property of the landowners, they were the spiritual homes of the peasant population and the ancestors of most of the parish churches of medieval France.

It was from these two Christianised countries, Lombardic Italy and Merovingian Gaul, whence came many of the missionaries who converted England. We might reasonably expect the pastoral system with which they were no doubt familiar to follow in the wake of their preaching. It must be remembered too that the parochial system was in operation or at least known in the Christian East. As early as the time of Athanasius priests were appointed to specified districts in the city of Alexandria. Justinian in 541 encouraged landowners to erect oratories on their estates by promising them the right of presenting the priest.[7] Theodore of Tarsus must have been conversant with the system, and he seems to have made preliminary moves towards its eventual adoption and development in England. Parishes and parish priests in the Celtic West, on the other hand, simply did not exist. The organisation of the Church there was monastic and tribal. The

Celtic missionaries would seem to have made no contribution as such to parochial development in Anglo-Saxon England.

Theodore's achievement was the establishment of a diocesan arrangement, within whose lines the parochial organisation would in course of time develop. Meanwhile, nothing is known about parish churches in the early days of the Conversion and beyond, though it is probable that there were many local churches, albeit without a regular endowment for the maintenance of a resident clergy. By the early part of the eighth century it seems that local churches were becoming more common,[8] though not yet in the smaller villages. This is the inference we draw from a passage in Bede's letter to Egbert, bishop of York, in 734, describing conditions in the Northumbrian Church. Bede says that there are small villages and estates in Egbert's diocese which are without pastoral ministrations. The bishop should ordain and delegate priests to preach the Word of God on his behalf in these remote places, to celebrate the heavenly mysteries, to baptise, and to teach the Creed and Lord's Prayer.[9] Bede is not necessarily proposing the erection of places of worship in such places, much less parish churches with endowed, resident priests. The words do seem to imply, on the other hand, that churches did exist in the larger centres of population; Bede is suggesting, in effect, an increase in their staffs, so that more visits may be paid to outlying hamlets.

Soon afterwards, in 747, the council of Cloveshoe was held, under the presidency of archbishop Cuthbert. Its canons relating to priests are a little confusing, as they appear to suggest that the monasteries had a large measure of pastoral and evangelistic responsibility towards the people, while at the same time it was the bishops who assigned priests to their respective districts. Priests are to recite the canonical hours according to the monastic office. They are apparently attached to conventual bodies, and are ordered to be faithful 'to their abbots and abbesses'. Yet the ninth canon states that priests are to preach diligently, to baptise, teach, and visit, in those places and districts which have been suggested or assigned to them by the bishop.[10] One thing, however, is clear—there is nothing to indicate a settled parochial system in the enactments of this council. Neither is there anything else of a similar nature for the eighth century, a period notable for its conciliar activity. It is almost certain that the clergy who ministered to village folk during this time came from central churches, monastic or secular.

314

We are told how Willibrord, some time previously, established churches in Frisia.[11] The reference is valuable as an indication of the process which was likely in England, and which the missionaries would take with them overseas. Willibrord traversed the Frisian countryside in the course of his evangelistic work, preaching in towns and villages. As the number of the faithful increased, and in particular with the growth of church land following the acquisition of hereditary estates from zealous converts, churches were built and priests and deacons appointed to serve them. These were, however, probably rather in the nature of district churches, and indeed it is specifically said of them that they were places in which the faithful could assemble on feast-days, which suggests that they were gathering-centres for Christians from a scattered area on important occasions in the ecclesiastical year, and whose clergy (conversely) itinerated on normal Sundays.

It is in such mission centres, corresponding somewhat closely to the Italian baptisteries and the central country churches of Gaul, that the true beginning of the English parochial system is to be found. In Anglo-Saxon charters such a church is called a minster, or *monasterium*. Some of them no doubt actually were small monasteries, served by monks living according to rule. But many, and as time went on an increasing proportion, of these *monasteria* were staffed by secular clerks living in community. We may compare them with the baptisteries of Italy, some at least of which were collegiate and known as *monasteria* and their clergy as *fratres* or *monachi* though not necessarily monks. The Anglo-Saxon minsters varied in size and importance, from the 'head' minster or cathedral where the bishop had his seat, to small foundations with perhaps two or three priests assisted by minor clerks. They were mostly of royal, episcopal, or monastic foundation, and their functions partly pastoral, partly missionary. They were an admirable and indeed obvious institution for a people midway between heathenism and Christianity.

In the earlier stages, a minster would serve as a base essential for the peregrinations of missionaries. The work of these evangelisers, almost countless in number, working steadily from the minsters through many decades and generations towards the conversion of the English people, has been underestimated. We allow our attention to be riveted too much on the great names, on Augustine, Paulinus, Aidan, and Birinus. But these were the leaders, the generals, of a large army, of which most have left no name behind them. In his account of Cuthbert, Bede tells how the great man was accustomed to undertake preaching tours in villages neighbouring his monastery, and comments that 'in those days the English people were accustomed to gather together whenever a clerk or priest came into their village, at his call, to hear the Word'.[12] It was to such travelling preachers that Boniface, greatest of all English missionaries, owed the fostering of his vocation. Whenever clergymen, on preaching tour according to their custom, arrived at his native village, the young boy would converse with them on spiritual matters and seek their advice.[13] This was nearly a century after the coming of Augustine of Kent. So long was the Christian gospel in really taking root in England.

In some of the villages to which the minster-clergy went they might possibly find small wooden churches already there, but as likely as not they would preach and say mass in the open before a tall cross erected to serve as a Christian focal-point.

Many of our present parish churches began as minsters, and in a few cases a great deal of the Anglo-Saxon structure remains. At Britford, near Salisbury, we have a very good example of such a church. The pre-Conquest nave, though not very large, conveys a sense of dignity and security. Not many miles away, just off the main road from Salisbury to Bournemouth, is an even more impressive example, the tenth-century church of Breamore. Both of these churches are in an accessible position, situated deep in a low-lying valley. Such buildings must have made a strong impression on the minds of the countryfolk for miles around. The fine inscription, 'In this place the Word is revealed unto thee',[14] cut in Old English over the arch in the south wall of the tower at Breamore, emphasises the evangelistic spirit in which such churches were founded.

In the midlands, the foundation of the church of Breedon, Leicestershire, is documented almost precisely. It was between 675 and 691 that a Mercian ealdorman, Friduric, gave some land here to the abbey of Medeshamstede, to provide for a minster and a priest. At about the same time Medeshamstede also founded the minster of Brixworth, Northamptonshire, where the nave of the seventh-century church survives, a splendid example of the dignified proportions which it was possible for a minster church to assume.

Further north we have Corbridge, Northumberland, a minster serving a royal estate. An imposing eighth-century arch remains, incorporating (as at Brixworth) much re-used Roman material.

It must be remembered of course that a minster was not merely an architectural piece, but a community, secular or monastic, of which the church was the essential centre. Around were gathered the living-quarters of the clergy, together with the various buildings needed for the corporate life, the whole grouped together within some kind of enclosure. When we picture an England garrisoned with spiritual *burhs* of this kind, it is not difficult to understand the triumph of Christianity over a half-hearted heathenism. For a missionary Church it was the sensible answer to the problems of organisation.

It is possible today in some parts of England to detect the geographical distribution of minsters, from the study of charters and place-name evidence. Thus in the diocese of Canterbury, it is thought, church life centred round the seven minsters of Reculver, Minster-in-Thanet, Dover, Folkestone, Lyminge, Minster-in-Sheppey, and Hoo.[15] In south-western counties such as Dorset many of the present villages and country towns may well have begun their history as minster-centres. At any rate the considerable number of place-names compounded with 'minster' suggests the importance of the central church in Wessex. Sturminster, Beaminster, Axminster, Warminster, Charminster, Iwerne Minster, Ilminster, and many other places with similarly compounded names, must once have been the centres of ecclesiastical activity extending into the surrounding countryside. Such places are invariably situated in valleys of rich pasture, and frequently the church stands on the banks of a stream. Minster churches long had a virtual prerogative of baptisms, and it was a primitive custom, practised in the early English Church, to baptise converts in running water. Indeed, the name of many of these places is simply the old Celtic river name with 'minster' added.

The founding of village churches followed naturally that of the minsters, as the missionary stage in the Christianisation of England was succeeded by the pastoral. Thus, John of Beverley, bishop of York from 705 to 718, consecrated village churches for two thegns, Puch and Addi, at Bishop Burton and Cherry Burton respectively.[16] It was in fact probably in the eighth century that the establishment of local churches here and there really began to get under way.[17]

During the period when the inhabitants of villages and hamlets were dependent for their ministrations on the visits of neighbouring minster clergy, the least that they could do, in lieu of possessing a church, was to erect a timber or stone cross on some convenient spot, around which they might gather for divine worship and the hearing of sermons. The most likely explanation of the general origin of the numerous standing crosses is that they were the predecessors of the parish churches. The Anglo-Saxon nun, Huneberc of Heidenheim, in a valuable reference in her Life of Willibald,[18] explicitly states that 'on the estates of the nobles and good men of the Saxon race it is a custom to have a cross, which is dedicated to our Lord and held in great reverence, erected on some prominent spot for the convenience of those who wish to pray daily before it'. It was at the foot of such a cross that the parents of Willibald offered their sick son, promising that in return for his health they would dedicate him to the monastic life.

Theodore in his Penitential allows a bishop to confirm and a priest to say mass in a field, should this be necessary.[19] The saving clause suggests that the primate did not regard such open-air services as a good thing in themselves, and the sooner everyone was within reach of a church the better. In any case, practical considerations would dictate to a landowner the general desirability of a church, if only a simple wooden one, on his estate, where he and his family, his servants and his serfs could attend mass. It would also be far preferable from a pastoral point of view to have a priest on the spot, rather than be dependent on the occasional and uncertain visits of a member of the nearest minster community. It is possible that in some cases the thegn himself may have taken priest's orders and ministered personally. A favourite thesis of German historians such as Ulrich Stütz has been that the parish church in Germanic countries is a logical development from the heathen private temple, in which the head of the household was the officiating priest. But though it is certainly known that landowners in some Scandinavian countries had their private temples, as in Sweden for example, where the builder of a temple might act as its *godi* or priest, there is no evidence at present available to suggest that this was so in England, apart from the place-names Peper Harow (the 'sanctuary of Peper') and Cusanweoh (the 'shrine of Cusa') in Surrey, and Patchway (the 'shrine of Paeccel') in Sussex.

Perhaps the normal practice was for a serf or ceorl to be selected by the landowner and sent to the bishop to obtain priest's orders. On his return he would serve as parish priest, in return for certain advantages and emoluments. He does not seem to have been in the abject position of his counterpart on the Continent. But he was emphatically his lord's man, and the church which he served was his lord's property.

The thegn or nobleman founding a church could virtually do what he liked with it, though here Theodore found it necessary to impose some restrictions. The timbers of a church, he decreed, must not be used for any other purpose, and if a church is removed elsewhere a cross must be erected on the site of the vanished altar.[20] It is explicitly forbidden that the timbers be used for firewood. Theodore's decree incidentally is a clear indication that the average church was in his day being made of wood.

From about the middle of the eighth century, efforts were made in Western Europe to lessen the hold of lay lords on their churches. Carolingian legislation attempted to improve the position of the parochial clergy (in their relationships with the laity), while at the same time to bring them into closer subordination to the episcopate. The parish priest was not to be appointed without the bishop's approval; neither could the manorial lord dismiss him. He must render an annual account of his ministry to the bishop, and attend diocesan synods. An attempt was in fact made under Louis the Pious and Lothair I (813–40 and 840–55) to abolish the proprietary or private church system altogether, but this was found impossible, so strong was the influence of the territorial and manorial lords. It is evident that the local priest, if driven to a choice, would be more likely in those turbulent times to obey the instructions of his lay lord on the spot than those of a king or bishop at a distance.

The general insecurity of the times favoured the growth of the proprietary system. Men wanted protection, prompt and immediate, in days of emergency. The dread aroused by the viking raids was a greater force in encouraging the consolidation of private ownership of churches than any lingering sentiment about local heathen temples managed by landowners. It has been suggested too that the destruction of so many religious houses by the Danes made laymen generally more dependent than formerly on ministrations provided by private churches, and that bishops in consequence had to enlarge the powers of rural priests.[21]

But well before the coming of the Northmen, private ownership of churches and ecclesiastical property was normal in England. By c. 900, that is, at the time of Alfred's death, it was a universal and accomplished fact. In the tenth century every church in England had its proprietor, in most cases a magnate or manorial lord, though often a bishop or monastery and sometimes the king himself. The owner was responsible for his church as he was for any other piece of property, with similar rights in it. The priest said mass, baptised the children, and buried the dead, just as the miller ground corn and the serf ploughed the fields. The proprietor could sell his church, give it away, bequeath it, or divide it into portions. It was from these portions that there developed in course of time the medieval system of medieties. In Domesday Book we find the division of churches often carried to a seemingly ludicrous point, and there are references to one-sixth or even one-twelfth of a church.

In return for his sacerdotal services, the priest received a material reward. In this respect he was decidedly better off than his fellow-priest on the Continent, where lay proprietors were more unscrupulous in diverting to themselves the revenues of the church, which steadily increased as tithes became a legalised charge. Ulrich Stütz remarks that 'the foundation of churches was probably the most profitable investment of the early Middle Ages, and innumerable churches were built as much from motives of speculation as of piety'.[22] In return for his living the Anglo-Saxon priest, besides performing his priestly duties and caring for the souls of the people generally, paid a lump sum of money to the owner on entrance into his office, and an annual rent. The latter might be in money or in the rendering of specific services. Thus the priests of some Herefordshire churches in return for their office were required to act as royal messengers in Wales. After the Norman Conquest, the new landowners introduced the system with which they were familiar on their continental manors, to the financial and social detriment of the Anglo-Saxon parish priests, though Lanfranc unsuccessfully tried to keep the rapacity of the new owners of the English manors and churches in check.

The growing importance of the parish priest is illustrated by a canon of the council of Grateley, Hampshire, in 928, during the reign of Athelstan and the primacy of Wulfhelm. The local priest (*sacerdos loci illius*) is to inform the bishop of the penitent's behaviour, in cases of penance for perjury. The implication is that by this time there was a resident priest in most villages, acquainted at first hand with the people. Meanwhile the foundation of churches was proceeding apace, and Athelstan allowed the status of thegn to any ceorl who prospered to the extent of possessing four hides of his own land complete with church. By the close of the tenth century the English shires were studded with churches. It is from these foundations that most of our present-day village churches are descended. Apart from the fact that in some cases portions of the original fabric remain, it is probable that in a very high proportion of our ancient parishes the spot on which the church now stands is the original one set aside by an Anglo-Saxon thegn for the worship of God.

By the close of the tenth century, parish churches were sufficiently numerous and established to call for a body of canon law dealing specifically with their problems. This was issued during the reigns of Aethelred the Unready and Cnut, and it is likely that Wulfstan, archbishop of York 1002–23, had much to do with it. This legislation promoted the independence of the parish priest by forbidding the proprietor of his church from dismissing the incumbent once he had appointed him. There are four types of churches, classified according to the penalties prescribed for violation of their rights of sanctuary. These were the head minster, or seat of the bishop; the 'medemra mynster', the class of church which during the missionary age served as an evangelistic centre; the lesser minster, that is, the village church; and the field church, or chapel without rights of burial.

Previously, Edgar and his witan, meeting at Andover in 970, had made a three-fold division, consisting of senior churches, churches with burial-grounds, and those without them. This had marked a distinct step away from the old system of minster churches towards a parish church organisation as we know it. William I was to return to this threefold classification, when he prescribed penalties of a hundred shillings for the violation of a cathedral or monastic church, twenty shillings for a 'mother parish church' (*matrix ecclesia parochialis*), and ten shillings for a chapel.

The eleventh century marks the high tide of Anglo-Saxon England, and we are fortunate in possessing Domesday Book, with its numerous references to local churches and their priests. The Conqueror's great compilation is a useful aid in any attempt to estimate the extent to which the parochial system had grown by 1086, though its incompleteness in this respect must be taken account of, and it should be used with caution. Professor H. C. Darby has summarised the evidence for six counties, giving some valuable and interesting statistical information.[23]

Thus for Lincolnshire 755 places of population are noted and 245 churches in connection with them, besides those of the towns Lincoln, Stamford, and Grantham. In Norfolk there are 726 places, with 217 churches; in addition there are the churches of Norwich, Thetford, and

Yarmouth. Suffolk has 639 places, with 345 churches, besides those of the towns. But according to H. C. Darby it is practically certain that there were more churches in these counties than here indicated. For example, there is no church recorded for Holt, a Norfolk market-town. There are a number of hundred-districts with only one church each. On the other hand, there are some villages which are said to have two churches. Occasionally, priests are recorded in connection with places which are not stated to have a church. Thus at Heveningham, Norfolk, the priest, who has 40 acres of land, says mass three times a week, though there is no mention of a church.

In Cambridgeshire churches are recorded at only three of the 141 places listed. In Essex there are seventeen churches for 440 centres of population, though there are a further twenty places mentioned as possessing a priest without any specific reference to a church. In Huntingdonshire there are churches in fifty-two out of eighty-three villages, and two more in Huntingdon itself; the usual form of entry runs 'there is a priest and a church', but some entries omit any reference to a priest, and in one entry it is said specifically that there is a priest though no church.

It is probable that in all these eastern counties, certainly in Cambridgeshire and Essex, there were in fact more village churches than we should be led to believe from Domesday Book. The explanation of course is that Domesday only records a church when it is significant from a revenue point of view. On the other hand, it must be remembered that the villages and hamlets of Domesday were very small places. Thus Lincolnshire had 755 such places for a total rural population of about 21,500, the average for each village being twenty-nine. The average populations for the villages of the other eastern counties were—Norfolk 35, Essex 31, Suffolk 29, Cambridgeshire 34, and Huntingdonshire 28. It is hardly likely that the provision of a church and priest for all of such places has ever been contemplated in the history of Christianity in this country. Nevertheless, we have a general picture of a countryside, towards the close of the eleventh century, peopled by a predominantly rural population, served by a profusion of local village churches. Such an expression as *ecclesia huius villae*, found in some entries, suggests the idea of the parish church. The idea is also implicit in the case of the twelve sokemen of the Suffolk village of Combs, who, it is said, 'used to be parishioners' of the neighbouring village of Stow.

For Kent, with its dioceses of Canterbury and Rochester, there is specific information for the same period.[24] The churches of the arch-diocese are arranged in twelve groups for the purpose of collecting ecclesiastical dues. At the head of each group is a senior church, whose pre-eminence is confined mostly to the issue of the holy oils and the collection of archiepiscopal dues. One sees in the arrangement a move towards the later ruri-decanal system, rather than a continuance or revival of the old minsters. The relevant document is of the time of Lanfranc. The documentary evidence for the other south-eastern diocese is a little later, c. 1100. It lists all the places of worship in the parishes, with the amounts payable for their chrism fees. There are 124 parish churches and 28 chapels.

In the north of England and in many parts of the west the parochial system does not seem to have been so far advanced as in the east and south-east, and to a far greater extent the minster system continued. In the west it was quite common for a hundred-district to be served from a central church.[25]

Much of the foregoing has been concerned with village churches, but it is clear that the urban inhabitants were also well supplied with places of worship. The incidence of church building in the towns, however, was very uneven, and there was nothing in the nature of a doctrinaire attempt to determine how many souls a church should serve. There was a total lack of planning in this respect, and the founders of the town churches appear simply to have pressed on with the task confronting them without argument or delay. Lincoln with a popula-tion of between four thousand and five thousand seems to have had six churches; Norwich with a similar population had at least forty-three churches, some of whose titles are known, such as All Saints, St Michael, and St Lawrence, which still exist. Stamford had four churches for its two thousand to three thousand people. For four thousand souls Thetford had twelve churches. York at the end of the eleventh century had at least fourteen parish churches for about eight thousand people. Ipswich had no fewer than twelve churches for thirteen hundred people. To the modern mind some of the late Anglo-Saxon towns appear to have been ludicrously over-supplied with churches. But we must bear in view the high level of piety which prevailed everywhere in Western Europe during the eleventh century.[26]

Though most of the churches in the country were the work of the manorial lords, it is likely that in the Danish areas, where the free peasantry (freemen and sokemen) were proportionately more numerous than elsewhere in England, many churches were founded by the co-operative action of such men. An example of this occurs at Thorney, where four freemen built a chapel on their own land, the parish church being too small for all the parishioners. In the towns such action would be more common. The church of St Mary Castlegate, York, was founded jointly by three citizens, probably in the late tenth or early eleventh century. The names of the founders, Efrard, Grim, and Aese, are recorded on the dedication stone inside the church. Domesday Book records a very interesting case of a Lincoln builder Colsuen, who built thirty-six houses and two churches to go with them, on some waste land outside the city walls which he had acquired.

One clear fact which emerges from these statistics is that Anglo-Saxon churches were for the most part small buildings, a conclusion which is supported by archeological study. We have a pleasing impression of homely, even family worship, still a long way removed from the grand services of the middle ages and the stately village churches which astonish the traveller today in such regions as East Anglia.

Closely bound up with the history of parochial development is that of ecclesiastical revenues, though it must of course be remembered that the endowment of parish churches was only one amongst various objects of Christian charity.[27] Indeed, the parochial clergy by the close of our period were still a poor class, scarcely raised above the level of the villagers to whom they ministered. The greater part of the Church's undoubted wealth was concentrated in the monasteries and minsters, institutions upon which the learning and devotion of the times were based. By the eleventh century the often ill-afforded contributions of Englishmen to the Church's treasury were being rigorously enforced. The poverty and squalor of the peasantry were part of the price which had to be paid for the culture and faith of the early middle ages.

There were four main sources of revenue. Plough-alms were a small charge payable at Easter, levied on the farmer's plough. Soul-scot was the equivalent of the modern burial fee, and may well have been in the nature of a continuation in Christian form of the heathen custom of depositing some of the belongings of the deceased in his grave.[28] It survived through the middle ages as the mortuary present, the compulsory offering of the second best chattel to the Church. A more important charge was church-scot,[29] payable at Martinmas by all men possessed of an agricultural holding, and usually consisting of grain. Though this charge never died out in Anglo-Saxon times, it was gradually replaced in importance by tithe.

From at least the time of Gelasius I (492–6) the Roman custom was for the general diocesan revenues to be divided, not necessarily equally, into four portions—for the bishop, clergy, poor, and church fabrics respectively.[30] This did not become the universal custom, and there is evidence in Spain of a threefold division, the bishop taking a one-third share though being responsible for the repairs of churches in his diocese. Generally, the bishop's share of revenues was intended to support him and his *familia*, and enable him to fulfil his duty of hospitality. The clergy were to receive their shares according to the bishop's discretion. The fabric fund covered the building and repair of the minster or baptismal churches, and also the provision of their lights, vestments, and vessels—proprietary churches would have no claim on this fund. The poor-fund would include amongst its disbursements help given to widows and orphans, the sick, pilgrims, and captives (whose redemption was a recognised Christian act of charity), distributed according to the bishop's discretion. In due course the monks cashed in on this department of ecclesiastical revenue, on the grounds of their theoretical poverty. The rule about four-fold division was a very general one, and cannot be regarded anywhere as a precise guide. Gregory I, in his replies to Augustine, refers to it but does not approve any contemplated adoption of it by the archbishop.[31]

It is with tithe that the development of church endowment in England is primarily concerned. The belief that Christians should pay tithes of all their possessions, though primitive, is not as old as Christianity itself.[32] It is not mentioned in the canons of the great councils from Nicaea to Chalcedon. But late in the fourth century Jerome and Augustine urged the desirability of Christians dedicating a tenth of their substance to the work of God.[33] There was still no mention of tithe in the ancient canon law of the Roman Church, collected towards the end of the fifth century by Dionysius Exiguus. At the second council of Tours (567) the canons do not refer to tithes, but some of the bishops present subsequently wrote to their flocks urging them to follow the example of Abraham by paying tithes of their means.[34] The payment of tithes became increasingly recognised as a moral and religious duty, which the council of Rouen in 630 sought to enforce by ecclesiastical penalties.[35] In these early centuries, it should be noted, tithe was understood as the tenth of all gains, though it steadily came to be applied more specifically to the produce of the land.

In 765 king Pippin the Short, perhaps attempting to compensate the Church for the spoliation of her land effected by his father Charles Martel, issued legislation making the tithe compulsory.[36] Later on Charlemagne, and Louis the Pious in 829, ordered the recovery of tithes from defaulters.

In England secular enactments of this sort came much more slowly, and there was a preliminary but lengthy process whereby the payment of tithes was first urged as a Christian duty and then encouraged by ecclesiastical penalties. Theodore, in his canons, was the first to take notice of tithe, ruling that it should be paid to strangers and the poor and by laymen to their own churches.[37] Priests are exempt from the payment of tithe, and the poor should be treated with leniency and consideration. In a passage relating to tithe,[38] Bede includes amongst the virtues of Eadbert, Cuthbert's successor at Lindisfarne, the gift of a tithe of his animals, corn, and fruits, as also of his clothes, to the poor. Boniface, in his letter to archbishop Cuthbert in 746–7, refers to the bishops as receiving the offerings and tithes of the people.[39] Bede's letter to Egbert does not mention tithes, but alludes to the bishop as the receiver of obligatory church dues, even from remote districts devoid of direct spiritual ministrations.[40] The legatine councils held towards the close of the eighth century, perhaps influenced by the example of Pippin, ordered the payment of tithes. But this enactment was rather in the nature of a strongly worded pastoral precept. The secular power appears to have made no attempt to enforce it.[41]

Alfred was an active legislator, but though amongst earlier laws which he reissued were the enactments of Ine ordering the payment of church-scot, he did not compel the payment of tithes. This is strong presumptive evidence against there being any previous secular legislation relating to tithe, as if this had existed it is almost certain that Alfred would have confirmed it in his own laws. His approval of tithe in principle is clear from the inclusion of the offering of tithes and first-fruits in the summary of the Levitical laws which forms part of the preface to his code.[42]

Definite action on the part of an English ruler could not now be long delayed. In a treaty between Alfred's successor Edward and the Danes, penalties were prescribed for those who neglected to pay their tithes or other church dues, whether in Wessex or the Danelaw.[43] We have an enactment relating to tithe, as well as to church-scot, soul-scot, and plough-alms, in the laws of Athelstan, acting with the concurrence of the bishops but not of his witan as a whole. The next king, Edmund (939–46), made the non-payment of tithes and church dues in general an offence punishable by excommunication. Tithe is enjoined on every man, as also is church-scot, besides Peter's pence and plough-alms. Edmund ordered the bishops to keep in repair the churches (that is, probably, the minster churches) of their dioceses; the significance of this order is that it was still the practice for the principal churches to be maintained out of central funds, controlled by the bishops.

Finally, Edgar, in his laws issued at Andover in 970, ordered the enforcement of tithes throughout his kingdom.[44] This move marks the definite assumption by the secular authority of responsibility for seeing that the Church received the revenues which first pious inclination, and then a sense of religious obligation fostered by exhortation and conciliar enactments, had brought to her treasury. Edgar's law was certainly not a tax in the modern sense, and indeed the days of taxation proper had not yet arrived. On the other hand, the fact that legal enforcement was necessary is indication enough that there was a widespread unwillingness to pay church dues. It is on the Andover enactment of 970, issued with the full authority and force of the English State, that the right of the Church of England, almost a thousand years later, to hold ancient endowments is ultimately based. To maintain that the modern investments of the Church are the result of the 'generosity and free-will offerings' of our ancestors is in fact an oversimplification.

Edgar ordered the enforcement of his laws with heavy penalties. The reeves were to seize, on behalf of the local church, a tenth of any defaultor's entire tithable property; four-fifths were to be divided between the bishop and the local lord, while the culprit was to be left with the remaining tenth. Normally, the actual recipients of the tithe were the minsters; but Edgar's laws introduced the important exception that the proprietor of a private church, provided this was complete with a burial-ground, should give to it a third of his tithes, the remaining two-thirds going to the minster. We find in this allocation of tithes to the ordinary village church the germ of the later practice, which in the middle ages led to the system of appropriations and vicarages, when the vicar was most commonly awarded a third of the tithes.

The laws of Edgar were repeated and confirmed in those issued in the name of Cnut, a legislation noteworthy in also placing the responsibility for the maintenance of the church fabric upon the parishioners.[45]

It is possible that with the increase of secular intervention there was a certain amount of anxiety amongst churchmen that there might be a lessening of the sense of religious duty in the matter of Christian alms-giving. It was about the time of the Andover council, or shortly after, that the Blickling homilist wrote: 'Let the man who desires to obtain the heavenly blissfulness, ever rightly give the tenth of his goods to God', and again, 'O thou covetous and rich man, what wilt thou do if the Lord taketh from thee nine parts of thy wealth, and letteth thee have only the tenth? For it is right that nine parts should be taken from the man that refuses God the tenth part.'[46] To the homilist the heavy penalties of Edgar were spiritually justified, as gifts withheld from the Church would imperil a man's soul.

Besides enforced contributions of this sort, there was also the direct donation of land and other properties, which throughout the Anglo-Saxon period continued to form an important addition to the Church's wealth. At the very beginning of the Roman mission Ethelbert had granted to Augustine material possessions.[47] The young Saxon adventurer Caedwalla, after conquering the Isle of Wight (to the accompaniment of great cruelty), bestowed a quarter of the island upon Wilfred.[48] Similarly king Egbert, in the ninth century, made over to the Church a tenth of his conquests in Cornwall.[49] Of a more ordinary nature were the numerous individual donations, usually to monasteries or episcopal sees, in connection with which arose the practice of 'book-land', or land guaranteed to its owner by charter. In this matter of the permanent acquisition of land ecclesiastics left nothing to chance. They introduced the practice of written deeds to ensure their newly-acquired possessions against the claims of dispossessed heirs.

Many such grants are instanced by Miss Dorothy Whitelock in the first volume of *English Historical Documents*.[50] Thus c. 692 Nothelm, king of the South Saxons, gives to his sister Nothgyth land for the foundation of a monastery and a church, the latter to be devoted 'to the divine praises and honouring of the saints'. Early in the eighth century Offa, king of Essex, grants land at Hemel Hempstead to Wald-here bishop of London. In 732 Ethelbert II, king of Kent, grants to abbot Dunn and his church at Lyminge some land which was valuable for the production of salt, specifically exempting the land from royal dues.

Of a different kind of gift were the remission of toll on one ship, granted in 734 by Aethelbald, the Mercian king, to St Andrew's church, Rochester; and the grant in 857 by Burgred, also king of Mercia, to the bishop of Worcester of a house in London with commercial rights. By the tenth century ecclesiastics must have been a highly skilled and experienced body in the business of estate transactions. In a deed of 963–75 it is recorded how Aethelwold bishop of Winchester exchanged with one Wulfstan a parcel of land at Washington, Sussex, for some land at Yaxley, Huntingdonshire, and Ailsworth, Northants. After the exchange the bishop proceeded to give the Yaxley land to Thorney abbey, and that of Ailsworth to Peterborough. The Ailsworth land had originally belonged to a certain widow and her son who forfeited it for the sorcerous practice of driving pins into the waxen image of Wulfstan's father Aelfsige. The woman was drowned at London Bridge and her son became an outlaw.[51]

The duties of the office of parish priest could be summed up in the conception of government or rule of souls, expressed in the title of 'rector'. It is not clear when this title was first generally used in England. Gregory the Great in his *Pastoral Care* speaks of the bishop in his pastoral office as 'rector', and it was in Italy that the expression was most used for the parish priest prior to the twelfth century.

The material reward which the priest received in return for his pastoral work was known as his 'benefice'. This term is rooted in the history of feudalism. Feudal holdings held on very favourable terms, with little or no rent and no labour dues, gave rise to the idea of a *beneficium*. Holdings of this nature were widespread by about the middle of the eighth century. Not all vassals would be 'beneficed', but from this time onwards the practice steadily grew. Sometimes a ruler would grant an estate to a vassal along with full rights of ownership in it, but it was more usual to bestow a benefice. The ecclesiastical benefice is essentially a variant of this side of feudalistic practice.[52]

The feudal benefice implied of course the existence of the lord or seigneur, and throughout the later Anglo-Saxon period the parish priest received his church at the hands of its owner, normally a layman. But the Gregorian reform movement was strongly opposed to all forms of lay investiture, and from the middle of the eleventh century increasing efforts were made to wrest the control of churches from the manorial lords and hand it over to the bishops.[53] Through the enactments of the great Lateran Councils, culminating in the Fourth (1215), lay investiture of parish priests was displaced in favour of institution by the bishops. The former proprietor retains his rights in a different and attenuated form. Previously the seigneur in relation to the church, he is now the patron. From now on he does not grant a benefice to a priest; he presents the priest to the bishop. He no longer owns the church, but the patronage, or right of nomination of its rector. The bishop of the diocese admits the nominee to the spiritual office involving the cure of souls, and the archdeacon inducts him to the temporalities. The patron has no legal power over the rector, and he cannot dismiss him, let alone sell his church, bequeath it, or divide it into portions. This system, codified in the canon law of the latter half of the twelfth century, continued in the Western Church throughout the middle ages, and is in force in the Church of England to this day.

CHAPTER XX

HOMILISTS AND WRITERS

A disappointment in store for the student of culture in later Anglo-Saxon England is the small amount of surviving poetry. This is particularly unfortunate, as poetry is of great value in assessing the contemporary climate of religious opinion, far more valuable in this respect than the enactments of canon law, which are often attempts to impose a viewpoint upon minds not yet ready to receive it. Poetry on the other hand is spontaneous, and in the case of the Anglo-Saxons doubtless expressed the sentiments which lay behind the common talk of the intervals between hunting, fighting, and farming during the day, and around the fire by night.

Such verse of the tenth and eleventh centuries as we possess seems to be inspired chiefly by contemporary political or military events, and bears small relation to the life and doctrine of the Church. The poem 'Judith' may be ascribed to the early tenth century; it has been conjectured that it commemorates the victories of Aethelflaed, 'Lady of the Mercians', over the Danes. 'The Battle of Brunanburh', inserted in the *Chronicle*, celebrates the victory of Athelstan in 937 over a combined force of Danes, Welshmen, and Scots. In 'The Battle of Maldon', which describes the defeat of the Essex levy, led by Byrhtnoth, in 991 at the hands of the Danes, we find the traditional Nordic virtue of loyalty to one's lord. Indeed, it is remarkable to find this last notable Anglo-Saxon poem, in its closing lines, expressing the heroic spirit so explicitly. When the old companion Byrhtwold sees all is lost he grasps his shield and spear, and calls on the surviving warriors: 'Thought shall be the harder, heart the keener, courage the greater, as our might lessens. Here lies our leader all hewn down, the valiant man in the dust. ... I am old in age; I will not hence, but I purpose to lie by the side of my lord.' So well did the fine Germanic virtues of heroism and comradeship survive after four centuries of Christian teaching. The acceptance of Christianity certainly did not weaken the character of the English people.

But though later Anglo-Saxon England has left us little poetry, it produced a substantial amount of vernacular prose, in the form of homilies written by monks and intended probably for the use of the parochial clergy. This homiletical literature, a veritable monument of early English prose, has received its due mead of praise from linguists and technical Old English students. Its importance to the student of English Church history has in general been overlooked. Yet in these sermons we have an exposition of Catholic doctrine as it was currently accepted, and a reflection of the Christian way of life from many angles which is of the greatest value and interest.[1]

In the library of Blickling Hall, Norfolk, a mansion now in the possession of the National Trust, are preserved the manuscripts of nineteen homilies, whose strong and homely style places them somewhere in the second half of the tenth century, one of them being actually dated by an internal reference to the year 971. Some of them are scarcely more than fragmentary, and there is nothing to suggest that they are necessarily the work of the same writer or homilist.

The theology of these homilies is sober, and less prone to the miraculous than that of many other early medieval writers. The thought of Doomsday hangs heavily over them, but on the other hand there is here and there a lyrical element, as when the heavenly messenger says to the Blessed Virgin: 'The redness of the rose glitters in thee, and the whiteness of the lily shines in thee; let Christ's bride-bower be adorned with every variety of flowers that are produced.'[2]

The well-known eschatological tendency of the writers of this period mingles with the poetical in a passage which has been sometimes quoted: 'As St Paul was looking towards the northern region of the earth, from whence all waters pass down, he saw above the water a hoary stone; and north of the stone had grown woods very rimy. And there were dark mists; and under the stone was the dwelling-place of monsters and execrable creatures. And he saw hanging on the cliff opposite to the woods, many black souls with their hands bound; and the devils in likeness of monsters were seizing them like greedy wolves; and the water under the cliff beneath was black. And between the cliff and the water were about twelve miles, and when the twigs brake, then down went the souls who hung on the twigs and the monsters seized them.'[3]

By far the greatest in importance in the history of late Anglo-Saxon religious literature, however, is Aelfric, a notable Benedictine who like Bede took no part in the administrative work of the Church, but so far as we know devoted his life entirely to reading, writing, and teaching.

Born about the middle of the tenth century, he became in due course a monk at the Old Minster, Winchester, where he studied under Aethelwold. In 987 he went as novice-master to the new foundation of Cerne, in Dorset, and it was in this secluded place that he commenced the career of authorship which was to give him an honoured position in the history of English literature. Between 990 and 995 he wrote the *Catholic Homilies*, to cover the Sundays and festivals of the ecclesiastical year. Of two series, each consisting of a course of some forty sermons in the vernacular, they were intended for the use of parish priests in their office of teaching. The first series is predominantly doctrinal and didactic, the second more historical in its scope. Soon afterwards, in 996 or the year following, there came the *Lives of the Saints*, written to a great extent in an easy, flowing alliterative verse. The *Catholic Homilies* are dedicated to Sigeric, archbishop of Canterbury; the *Lives* to the ealdorman Aethelweard, who was father of the founder of Cerne abbey, and much interested in Aelfric's literary work.

It was at the request of Aethelweard that Aelfric also attempted biblical translation. His work in this field lay mostly amongst the first seven books of the Old Testament, and his method was that of paraphrase. As with the *Homilies* and *Lives*, he had in mind in the first place the unlettered people attending the church services, and the translations were apparently intended for public reading in church. Genealogies and difficult passages were omitted.

Later works of Aelfric include pastoral letters composed on behalf of Wulfsige, bishop of Sherborne, and Wulfstan, archbishop of York. The letter written at Wulfsige's request is intended for eventual delivery to the rural or 'upland' clergy of Dorset, and includes within its scope such practical topics as celibacy, attendance at synods, and the reservation of the sacrament; it also makes reference to the 'spiritual' character of Our Lord's presence in the Blessed Sacrament, which the writer expounds more fully in the *Catholic Homilies*, notably in his sermon for Easter Day.

In 1005 Aelfric became abbot of Eynsham, and it was here that his last works were written. They include an edition of the *Regularis Concordia* abridged for the use of his monks, a Latin Life of his old teacher Aethelwold, and the *De Veteri et de Novo Testamento*. This last-named work was composed for Sigferth, a thegn living a few miles from Eynsham, and eager for knowledge. The book is really a popular introduction to the Bible, but also enumerates the duties of the three orders of society—the workmen, fighting-men, and praying-men. Aelfric had earlier expounded the doctrine of the 'three orders' in the *Lives of the Saints*.[4] Men of religion, he says, are as valuable to society by virtue of their prayers as are the soldiers in repelling foreign foes. It would seem that in the course of the Danish invasions which were being renewed at this time there was pressure on priests and monks, or a desire on the part of some of them, to take up arms. Aelfric will have none of this. The true servant of God will not defile his hand by fighting; he will not 'even put to death a bird'.

In the *De Veteri* Aelfric warns Sigferth against the evils of over-conviviality. Drunkenness was a characteristic vice of the Anglo-Saxons. To Sigferth, Aelfric also addressed a letter on the necessity of clerical celibacy—always a warm subject with him.

School text-books came from his pen; a Latin Grammar based on Priscian, a Latin-English vocabulary, and the *Colloquy*[5]—a work recording a conversation between a number of persons in everyday occupations, who answer questions put to them by a teacher concerning their respective trades. The whole piece was probably intended as a sort of play for acting by the children of the cloister, who would thus obtain practice in Latin conversation.

Aelfric's final work was a second pastoral letter on behalf of Wulfstan, in which he returns to the subject of celibacy, gives the clergy advice on the manner of celebrating mass (which, he maintains, is their great and characteristic function), and treats of the ministry to the sick and dying. He himself died probably *c.* 1020.

Aelfric was not a speculative philosopher or theologian, but a teacher of wide knowledge who aimed at making available to country priests, and through them to their flocks, the received truths of the Catholic Church, he himself drawing freely on the works of such Fathers as Gregory, Bede, and Augustine of Hippo. He had a genuine horror of doctrinal errors, and was perturbed at the amount of misleading literature in circulation, though he commends the translations of Alfred for their reliability. He was cautious over committing himself in doctrinal questions which were still controversial. His essential role as a teacher is shown by his text-books for boys in the monastic schools. He was at his best expressing the accepted doctrines of the Faith in good and straightforward prose, as when in the sermon for the Epiphany he writes:

'This day is called the Epiphany of the Lord, that is the day of

God's manifestation. On this day Christ was manifested to the three kings, who, with three-fold offerings, sought him from the eastern part of the world. Again, after a course of years, he was, at his baptism, manifested to the world, when the Holy Ghost, in likeness of a dove, rested upon him, and the voice of the Father sounded loudly from heaven, thus saying, "This is my beloved Son who well pleaseth me; obey him". On this day also he turned water to noble wine, and thereby manifested that he is the true Creator who could change his creatures. For these three reasons this festival is called the Manifestation of God.'[6]

He makes occasional shrewd points, as when he says that if Jesus had chosen for his first disciples educated men, it would have appeared as if the true faith had come not through God's might, but from worldly eloquence.[7] But what most characterises his work is its straightforward simplicity; unadorned sayings and expressions abound, quite devoid of sophistication, and yet of the kind that impress themselves on the mind of the reader. 'Whatsoever a man gets easily is not so precious as that which is gotten with difficulty.' 'The Son of God was crowded in his inn, that he might give us a spacious dwelling in the kingdom of heaven.' 'He believes in God, who by works practises that which he believes.' He uses language which would come home to his Anglo-Saxon audience, with its tradition of heroism, when in describing the joy in heaven over the conversion of a sinner he praises the 'greater love which a general feels in battle for the soldier who after flight boldly overcomes his adversary, than for him who never took to flight, nor yet in any conflict performed any deed of valour'.[8] This great master of English prose reveals his skill in the elusive art of making a definition, when he says that 'verily a gathering of righteous men is called the kingdom of heaven'.[9]

One listens in vain to the outpourings of modern egalitarians for such clear teaching on human equality as Aelfric's: 'If a rich woman and a poor one bring forth together, let them go away; thou knowest not which is the rich woman's child, which is the poor one's. Again, if we open the graves of dead men, thou knowest not which are the rich man's bones, which are the poor one's.'[10]

He is thoroughly practical in his realisation that the Faith has to be lived in a mundane context by ordinary people: 'My brothers, behold your conduct, and see if ye yet are God's workmen. Let everyone consider what he does, and behold whether he labours in God's vineyard. . . . They truly toil for God who seek not their own gain through covetousness but meditate on God's tillage, how they may suppress unrighteousness and further righteousness, and benefit other men with the diligence of true love, and they who care with watchful mind how they may gain the souls of other men to God.'[11]

It is clear from Aelfric's writings that the besetting sins of the Anglo-Saxon people were gluttony, drunkenness, and incontinence, which he constantly condemns. And yet his practical, realist turn of mind in dealing with popular sins is evident when he says that even as the Israelites allowed some of the heathen to stay with them, as hewers of wood and drawers of water, so also we cannot wholly eradicate every vice from our bodies. We should conquer the greatest, and in the smaller 'learn humility', 'not however'—he judiciously adds—'in approval of perverse deeds'.[12]

The broad impression which one obtains from a reading of the Homilies is of the importance of right belief, especially concerning the Holy Trinity, which is expounded carefully. Christ taught 'that no man might be saved, except he rightly believe in God, and be baptised, and adorn his faith with good works'. One is left with a feeling that baptism held a higher place in the esteem of Christian men than it does in our own day.[13] There is only one reference to confirmation.[14] There is great emphasis on fasting and abstinence from carnal relationships during Lent, though Aelfric condemns those who fast beyond their strength.[15] The fast most pleasing to God, he says, is the avoidance of sin. There is not a great deal of reference to the sacrament of penance in Aelfric's writings, though he makes the need for it explicit when he declares, in an Ash Wednesday homily, that 'no man gets forgiveness of his sins from God, unless he confess them to some man of God, and by his judgement make satisfaction'.[16] It is usual for confession to be made during Lent.[17] A priest is a ghostly leech.[18]

The Homilies have a biblical and evangelical tone, and are filled with scriptural quotations, with comments thereon, the allegorical method being much used. Thus Joshua is a type of Our Lord; as Joshua led the old Israel to the promised Land, so Jesus leads his people to the eternal country.[19] In the fine Homily on the Dedication of a Church,[20] Aelfric tells the story of Solomon and his visitor the queen of Sheba. Of the latter he writes:

'The queen was a type of the holy Church of all Christian folk, that came to the peaceful Christ, to hear his wisdom and the evangelical doctrine which he established, and of the enlightening of the true belief, and of the doom to come, of our soul's immortality, and the hope and glory of the common resurrection. The queen came to Solomon with great gifts of gold, and of precious gems and perfumes; and camels bare these. The believing church, which comes from every country to Christ, brings him the aforesaid gifts in a ghostly sense. She offers him gold through true belief, and perfumes through prayers, and precious gems through fairness of good morals and holy virtues.'

Aelfric's sermons are saturated with belief in the miraculous; this is especially the case in the *Lives*, where the power to work miracles is the *sine qua non* of sainthood, as for example with St Swithun, the walls of whose church at Winchester were hung from end to end with the crutches and stools of cripples made whole.[21] The miracle as such, moreover, seems to be great for its own sake and for the glory which it bestows on its performer, quite as much as for the benefit it renders to the recipient. Only thus is it possible for us to understand why God sends thunder and rain to save the body of St Mark from fire, though many innocent persons die in the resulting thunderstorm.[22]

It seems to Aelfric and his contemporaries, however, that miracles are for the most part a manifestation of the past. The miracles which the apostles wrought bodily are now performed by the Church spiritually.[23] Each time a priest baptises a child, he performs a miracle by casting out a devil. Spiritual miracles are in fact greater than the bodily ones were, for these latter-day miracles heal a man's soul, which is greater than the body. The former miracles were wrought not only by good but also by evil men, such as Judas. In this somewhat contradictory depreciation of miracle, Aelfric says that though Enoch and Elijah were lifted up to heaven without death, they will not escape death at the last. They are taken to the aërial heaven, not to the ethereal.[24] Meanwhile they are in a secret dwelling-place, and will return at the end of the world, when they will receive death.[25]

In his primary concern for the welfare of the soul, Aelfric is apprehensive about the influence of evil spirits, which to him as to his fellowcountrymen in general were a terrible reality. One of the best of remedies is the sign of the cross, the efficacy of which is frequently emphasised. The holy sign, made with three fingers,[26] repels evil dreams and is a sovereign remedy against the devil and his works.

Along with drunkenness and over-eating, sexual excess was a

besetting sin of the Anglo-Saxons, but Aelfric was not content merely to urge moderation in the last respect. He leaves us in no doubt whatsoever as to where he stands in the matter of clerical celibacy. A very high proportion of the parish priests, possibly most of them, were married, and the rightfulness of this was not probably in doubt amongst the Anglo-Saxon public. In the house of Sigferth the thegn, to whom, as we have seen, Aelfric wrote concerning the importance of clerical celibacy, there was an anchorite who maintained the lawfulness of clerical marriage. This was unthinkable to Aelfric. Marriage, far from being lawful for priests, he says, is a regrettable necessity even for laymen. When he causes the Roman general Gallicanus to say at the time of his conversion, 'I myself am so much a Christian that I have said in a vow, that I henceforth will not have the company of a wife',[27] he is only pointing out the way which he believes any really devout man will follow if possible, at least as soon as he has produced the quota of offspring which the continuance of society requires.

There is something tainted, even inherently sinful, in carnal relationships. St Luke serves God without any sin, 'ever without a wife'.[28] St Peter was married and had a daughter Petronilla, but he renounced his wife on his conversion to the family of Christ.[29] It is true that under the Mosaic law the bishop was allowed to marry, that he might have a son to succeed him in the priesthood; but, says Aelfric, it is different now that priests have to say mass, and handle the mysteries of Christ's body and blood. There are three lawful states for lay-people—maidenhood, widowhood (as with Anna), and matrimony. The first will receive a hundredfold mead in heaven, the second sixty-fold, while members of the third class can hope for thirty-fold provided they restrict carnal relations to the purposes of procreation.[30] It is quite true that Enoch ascended into heaven without death, though he had a wife. Elijah, who was a bachelor, went up in a chariot.[31]

It is by his teaching on the Real Presence in the Eucharist that Aelfric has been best known in modern times, and it is ironical that the Easter homily[32] of this unquestioned Catholic, in which he sets out this teaching, was much quoted by the sixteenth-century Reformers in support of their views.[33] Certain men have inquired, he says, how the bread and wine can be changed into Christ's body and blood. His reply is that some things are said of Christ typically, some literally. It is true literally that Christ was born of a maiden, and rose from the grave. He is bread typically. The bread and wine in the mass appear as one thing to human minds without, but another thing to believing minds within. Externally they appear bread and wine, in aspect and taste, but after consecration they are truly Christ's body and blood through a ghostly mystery. Similarly a baptised child looks the same after baptism, but is changed within. There is a great difference between the invisible power of the holy housel and the visible appearance of its own nature. By nature it is bread and wine; but by the power of the Divine word it is truly Our Lord's body and blood—not, however, bodily, but spiritually.[34] Aelfric brings out this distinction time and again, not only in this Easter sermon but elsewhere, as though anxious to press it home against other teachers, who were expounding the corporeal presence. 'The holy housel is spiritually Christ's body.'[35] 'The bread is truly his body spiritually.'[36] In like manner, the stone from which water flowed in the wilderness was 'ghostly'. The stone was not Christ bodily, but was a type of Christ. The Real Presence is a mystery. 'Ye are not to enquire how it is done, but to hold in your belief that it is done.' In a fine phrase he reaches the heart of all Eucharistical doctrine: 'Christ hallowed on his table the mystery of our peace and our unity.'

Aelfric was not an original teacher, whether in Eucharistical or other doctrine. In the question of the Real Presence he had placed himself in a tradition which was at least a century and a half old by the time he wrote. It was in the mid-ninth century that Paschasius Radbertus (c. 785–c. 860), a Benedictine of Corbie, wrote the first complete treatise to deal specifically with the Eucharist, and thus started a controversy which endured intermittently for some two centuries or more. Paschasius upheld the carnal view—maintaining that the consecrated host is identical with the very flesh born of Mary. The substance is changed, according to his treatise *Liber de Corpore et Sanguine Domine*, though at the same time he makes no attempt to develop a doctrine of transubstantiation by using the metaphysical terms 'substance' and 'accidence'. This material view was at once challenged by another Corbie monk, Ratramnus (d. 868). He held that the Eucharist was a mystery, that it was absurd to identify the bread with the actual body of the historic Christ. The bread and wine really constitute a symbol, though a dynamic one, containing in itself the power and virtue of Christ's body. Rabanus Maurus (784–856), abbot of Fulda and archbishop of Mainz, also wrote against the realist view expounded by Paschasius. One of the greatest scholars and theologians of his time, he maintained that the bread and wine remain after consecration, though with a mystical value.

After the controversy had remained fairly dormant for a considerable time, it revived towards the close of the tenth century. Heriger of Lobbes (d. 1007) attempted a synthesis between realism and symbolism. Fulbert of Chartres (d. 1028) tried to prove that the elements of bread and wine remain, while at the same time being changed into the substance of Christ's body. It is altogether clear that there was a fluid situation, and at the time Aelfric wrote those who held the symbolic or mystical view would not be regarded as heretical. Indeed, the essential respectability of this view is proved by its adoption on the part of a homilist and writer to whom false doctrine was exceptionally abhorrent. In the event, the realist conception triumphed not long after this time. As a result of the Berengarian controversy (which will be discussed in a later chapter), Ratramnus was condemned at the synod of Vercelli in 1050, and the doctrine of transubstantiation had come to stay.

The dependence of Aelfric on Ratramnus has been proved,[37] and there can be no doubt that to him the materialist view of the Lord's Supper was less reasonable than the spiritual. We must beware, however, of deducing too much from this conclusion. The inadequacy of Old English in the expression of abstract ideas must be kept in mind. It is more than doubtful what exact meaning can be attached to the word 'spiritual' (*gastlice*) in the context of Aelfric's writings. It is impossible to square Aelfric's teaching with that defined later by the Roman Church; yet it would be hazardous to draw any parallel between his doctrine, and that, for example, of the Anglican 28th Article, which states that the 'Body of Christ is given, taken, and eaten, in the supper, only after an heavenly and spiritual manner'.

Though the theology of Aelfric is firmly based on the Trinity, he does not restrain his love for the saints and his belief in the efficacy of their prayers. His devotion to Our Lady is manifest in passages which, though not particularly frequent, glow with fervour, as when he speaks of her as being 'void of no holy virtue, nor any beauty, nor any brightness'.[38] She is 'queen of the whole world'.[39] In language instinct with reverence he bids his readers 'be mindful of how great dignity is the holy maiden Mary, the mother of Christ: she is blessed above all women; she is the heavenly queen, and the comfort and support of all Christian men. Our old mother Eve shut to us the gate of heaven's kingdom, and the holy Mary opened it again to us, if we ourselves by evil works shut it not against us. Much may she obtain of her Child, if she be fervently thereof reminded. Let us, therefore, with great fervour pray to her, that she may mediate for us to her own Child.'[40]

Such language is a reminder that extravagance in devotion to the Blessed Virgin is not a peculiar growth of the post-Tridentine Roman Church, as some wishful thinkers in our day are tempted to suppose. On the other hand Aelfric is cautious in his approach to the doctrines of the Conception and the Assumption. Concerning the former he asks: 'What shall we say of the birth-tide of Mary, save that she was begotten by father and by mother as other persons, and was born on the day that we call the eighth of September? Her father was named Joachim, and her mother Anna, pious persons according to the old law; but we will not write further concerning them, lest we fall into any error.'[41]

Of the Assumption he writes: 'What more shall we say to you of this feast-day, but that Mary, the mother of Christ, was on this day, from this world of toil, taken up to the kingdom of heaven to her dear Son, whom she had borne in life, with whom she rejoices in eternal mirth to all eternity.'[42] He declines to discuss the matter further, though mentions heretics who in their own imagination, or from dreams, have recorded false traditions. He asserts that heretical books exist, both in Latin and English, and that ignorant men read them. He certainly hopes that the Assumption is true, but will not rashly assert that of which he is uncertain, and about which doctors disagree.[43]

The homilies of Aelfric are on the whole very readable, even in the century-old translation of Benjamin Thorpe, and some of them—or at least whole passages from them—could still be delivered to an average congregation. A good example of Aelfric's power of narrative is the 'Passion of St Eustace and his Companions', which is an interesting story told well.[44]

Extracts from this great writer have been given at some length, as in spite of a tardy recognition given him in our own day by students of early English literature, his works are less well known than they deserve. He wrote for the parish clergy and their people, and studiously avoided the temptation to indulge in speculative thought. His task, as he understood it, was to hand on the teachings of the Church as he himself had received them; and it is probable that his writings reflect faithfully the broad doctrine of the Church as it was held at the beginning of the eleventh century. Some of this has been discussed or mentioned above. One may note also the reality of the bliss of heaven, and the tortures of hell, where 'the eyes will smart with the powerful smoke, and the teeth quake with the great chill'.[45] The Saxon thegn or ceorl, sitting a winter's night in the smoky, draughty hall, would understand the simile. The heroism inherent in Aelfric's writings would also come home to him; Aelfric doubtless well expressed his reader's thoughts when he called the Holy Innocents 'Christ's young champions', and saw in the Rood the 'standard of victory'. The same heroic note is discernible in the earlier writer or writers responsible for the Blickling Homilies, where John the Baptist is splendidly called 'the trumpet, Christ's crier in this world, and the messenger of God's Son, the standard-bearer of the Supreme King'.[46]

Second only in importance to Aelfric as a vernacular writer in the late Anglo-Saxon period is Wulfstan, who is considered here since it is as a preacher and homilist that he is best known, though unlike Aelfric he took an active part in the external life, political and ecclesiastical, of his day. A statesman, he was the guide and counsellor of kings Aethelred and Cnut. Unfortunately only one medieval account of him exists, and that not earlier than the twelfth century.[47]

It is practically certain that he was a Benedictine. It is claimed that he was probably a monk of Ely.[48] But neither the *Historia Eliensis* nor the Ely Calendar claims him as a brother. He does not appear in any monastery's list of abbots, and though he signs many charters he never uses this title. But it seems that he may well have been a member of one of the Fenland monastic communities, such as Ely, Peterborough, Thorney, and Ramsey, where his name was held in honour. The fact that he was buried at Ely does not prove that he was actually a member of that particular house, though it is a presumption in its favour.

Our first definite notice of him occurs in 996, when he became bishop of London;[49] during his tenure of this see he issued penitential letters, witnessed many charters, while his reputation as a preacher became well established.

In 1002 or the following year he was translated to the sees, held in plurality as usual during this period, of York and Worcester, relinquishing the latter in 1016. There has been some speculation over the significance of this move. The late A. Hamilton Thompson suggested that it was due to the division of England between Edmund and Cnut.[50]

Miss D. Whitelock thinks that Leofsige, abbot of Thorney, who succeeded him at Worcester, may have really been his suffragan.[51] It is in any case possible that Wulfstan retained some influence in the Worcester diocese, as in 1017 we find him issuing two leases of land in Worcestershire. He remained archbishop of York until his death in 1023.

He was an active bishop in many ways. During his tenure of Worcester he reformed the abbey of St Peter at Gloucester, installing monks in place of secular clergy. He understood the importance of law in the right ordering of the Church's life, and was the moving spirit behind a great deal of contemporary legislation. He issued the 'Laws of Edward and Guthrum', which were an attempt to impose Church law on the heathen Danes. His civilising influence on the young Cnut was great. Perhaps his activity extended even further, and both in secular and ecclesiastical affairs he was one of the considerable public men of his day. In his legislative work he was the English counterpart of the celebrated canonist Burchard, bishop of Worms (1000–23),[52] compiler of the *Decretals*. Wulfstan did not compile a collection of canons—to do this would have been pointless in England at this time, secular and ecclesiastical laws existing largely as one body of legislation. But like Burchard he treated in his own way of such subjects as the duties of the clergy, the sacraments, and priestly orders. Wulfstan would have ample opportunity for church reform, in which he was warmly interested, when he went to York, as the monastic reform movement had been confined to the south and midlands. He was an executor of the will of Aelfric, archbishop of Canterbury,[53] and consecrated his successor Aethelnoth, in 1020.

Though of less wide intellectual interests than many of his contemporaries, he encouraged manuscript collection, and was himself a reader familiar with early English writers, such as Bede, Aldhelm, and Alcuin, besides such continental scholars as Theodulf of Orleans and Rabanus Maurus. As a legalist he issued rules of conduct for his parish priests, but his care for them went deeper, and he preached and distributed pastoral letters to them. Like other diocesan bishops he would have an opportunity of addressing his clergy at the annual synod which according to the so-called Canons of Edgar, for which he was himself responsible, all parochial clergy were required to attend. On his behalf, as we have seen, Aelfric composed two pastoral letters, one of which he himself rewrote as being insufficiently vigorous for his liking. Of his other works, there are the *Institutes of Polity*, which deals with the duties of the various social classes; and an Old English text of the Benedictine Office,[54] which he seems to have compiled in collaboration with Aelfric. The latter is an abridgement of the monastic office, with a commentary, probably for the use of the parochial clergy in the public services. It is interesting as an early attempt to bring the essence of the Hours home to the ordinary folk of the Church.

There was something of the prophet in Wulfstan, lawyer-minded though he was, and there is a distinct eschatological flavour about his writings. This may have been encouraged by the not uncommon belief around 1000 that the end of the world was imminent. Of his homilies, the best known is the *Sermo Lupi ad Anglos*, written in 1014, in which he declares in impassioned language that the renewed invasions of the Danes are a judgement of God upon the English for their sins. Because of the war king Aethelred had been forced to abandon his throne temporarily in 1014, and for some months Swegn Forkbeard, king of Denmark and father of Cnut, was uncrowned king of England. In all this Wulfstan saw nothing but evil and foreboding, and yet only such as could be expected.

Another Benedictine who excelled as a scholar and writer was Byrhtferth. Born c. 960, he became a monk at Oswald's foundation of Ramsey, where he studied under Abbo of Fleury, who taught there 985–7. A versatile scholar, he became especially skilled in the physical sciences and mathematics. Though he wrote some theological tracts and homilies, including the *Ages of the World*, the *Loosing of Satan*, and the *Seven Sins*, it is by his *Manual*, written 1011, that he is best known.[55] An amusing half-hour may still be spent over this curious work. Partly in Latin, partly in English, its main object is to explain for the benefit of young priests the reckonings of time and seasons.

It is probable that most of the *Manual* was rather over the heads of the Saxon parochial clergy, and indeed the writer in his opening paragraph does not assume a high level of intelligence on their part. 'In the name of Christ I will begin this work. . . . It begins, that is to say it commences, or takes its beginning, or has its origin.' Perhaps, however, this was a preliminary bout of verbosity. The author mentions the ignorance of many rustic clerks, though he will be indulgent to their slothfulness.[56] He makes reference to some priests who are disloyal to their orders.[57] Some are lazy, and addicted to dice-playing.[58]

To the young clerk, maintains Byrhtferth, the calendar and its necessary calculations, along with the mystical meanings attached to numbers, are important subjects. The book, however, ends on a sombre, theological note. After enumerating the capital sins, Byrhtferth declares that 'whosoever practises any of these vices until his dying day, shall be tortured along with the devil for ever and ever, unless he repent'.

Byrhtferth's interest in mathematics is also evinced by his commentaries on Bede's mathematical works. It is possible too that he was the author of a Latin *Life of Oswald*, written anonymously.

Other writers who are known to have flourished in the late Anglo-Saxon era include an Aelfric, monk of Bath, who translated the gospels into the West Saxon vernacular; and Aldred of Chester-le-Street, who in the second half of the tenth century was responsible for the interlinear gloss, in the Latin text of the Lindisfarne Gospels, which is a valuable example of the Northumbrian dialect. During the same period the eighth-century Rushworth Gospels were also interlineated, partly in the north Mercian dialect, and partly in south Northumbrian. There are thus three English versions of the gospels of tenth-century date. A Winchester monk Wulfstan wrote on music, Aelfward, abbot of Glastonbury, wrote a letter to archbishop Sigeric, and all the while literary monks at Winchester and elsewhere were making their contributions to the *Chronicle*.

We may sum up in this way. While the later Old English Church was not a learned body in the sense of numbering amongst its scholars original thinkers, it seems to have had no lack of sound, competent teachers. The corpus of vernacular literature available to parish priests for help in their duties must have been considerable, greater than that of any other nation in the tenth or eleventh century. It is not until the twelfth century that we find such a body of vernacular homiletical literature on the Continent. When Leofric, bishop of Exeter 1050–72, endowed his cathedral church with sixty books, no fewer than twenty-eight of these were in the vernacular. We have an impression of a steady circulation of the fundamental Christian truths amongst the people. The ecclesiastical machinery necessary for the efficient performance of this evangelistic work, and for the pastoral care which perforce goes hand in hand with it, had not yet become a virtual end in itself, as it was to become in the high tide of the middle ages. The speech which the author of the Blickling Homilies ascribes to St Paul

345

standing before Nero is probably an authentic summary of the heart of the Church's teaching to the Saxon people:

'I taught that men should love one another, and that each should show respect to another. I taught rich and illustrious men that they should not be exalted in pride, nor trust too much in transitory riches, but that they should put their trust in God alone. I taught also the moderate men that they should be frugal in their living, and moderate in their dress; and the poor I have taught to have joy of their poverty and to be thankful to God. I taught the fathers that they should teach their sons the law of the Lord's fear; and I taught the sons to be obedient to their elders and parents. And I taught the landowners to pay their taxes carefully. I taught wives to love their husbands, and regard them with fear. And I taught husbands that they should remain faithful to them alone. . . . And because God is the Creator and Ruler of all his creatures, I taught lords that they should faithfully be obedient to God as to their lords, and should minister to God's churches. And I taught all men that they should serve one almighty, incomprehensible, and invisible God.'[59]

It is in connection with the Homilists that we may best approach the subject of Our Lord's Second Coming, which was expected by many towards the close of the tenth century and later. It is actually in a reference to the end of the world that the author of the Blickling Homilies unwittingly gives us the information enabling us to date his work with precision. He says that no man knows the time of Doomsday. Nevertheless we know that it cannot be far off, because all the signs which Our Lord said would precede Doomsday are now accomplished, save one, which is that the Anti-Christ has not yet appeared. That time cannot be long delayed, says the homilist, for 971 years of this present Age have elapsed.[60] He points out, however, that the different Ages are of varying lengths, and no man knows how long the Lord will take to accomplish this present Age. The somewhat later writer Byrhtferth says that the Sixth Age, now in progress, is not fixed by any period of time; but it is decrepit and must be consummated by the end of the whole world, though the actual date is very uncertain.[61] It is true, he says, that, according to St John, Satan would be let loose after a thousand years; the thousand years are now accomplished, but when the end actually will come rests entirely with the Saviour.

The end, says the Blickling homilist, cannot be far off, as is clear from plagues and strange deaths, nation rising against nation, diseases and famine. Christ himself declared that these things would come before the end. When the day arrives, all will pass away, and the Rood of Christ shall be raised in the course of the stars, and heaven be rolled up like a book.

On the six days preceding this dread event, marvellous tokens will befall. Thus on the first day, men will hear a great noise in heaven as of an army being assembled in order of battle. Next day, battle preparations will continue, the heavens will open on the east, and at the eleventh hour the earth will be overwhelmed with darkness. On the third day, the deeps will rage, and earthquakes occur. On the fourth day the heavens will sound with thunder, and darkness will continue to cover the earth. Next day the heavens will burst asunder from east to west, and the angels will gaze through the opening onto mankind, who will flee to the mountains in terror. Finally, the world shall be filled with accursed spirits, who will try to capture men's souls, but St Michael will come with his angels and drive them to hell. And then he will cause the trumpets to be blown, and the bodies of the dead will arise, and go forth to the Doom.[62]

The moral, says the homilist, is that we should repent while there is time; that we be humble, merciful, and charitable, and put away from our hearts all deceit, leasings, and envy, and have a right mind towards other men. It is all very modern in its evangelical fervour, and reminiscent of a certain type of religious enthusiast in our own day.

On the whole, Aelfric is less eschatological, but he speaks of this Age as the last time, and of himself and his contemporaries as the 'endmen of this world'.[63] In emphatic language he points out that no man knows the actual time of Our Lord's coming.[64] If he did, many a man would spend most of his life gratifying his lusts and turn to repentance at the end. Nevertheless, 'the world which ye see cannot long exist', and 'it is with age oppressed'.[65] The end of the world is imminent.[66] The reality of Doomsday is strongly emphasised throughout the *Catholic Homilies*, though it is hard to decide whether or not Aelfric was so obsessed with it as were some of his contemporaries.

The universality of this belief in a fast-approaching End is in fact disputable, but it is clear that the thought of Doomsday as such—as something which one day must come and for which all Christians must be prepared—greatly occupied the minds of these later Anglo-Saxon writers. It was no innovation, and had been a frequent subject in the religious verse of pre-Danish times, when it was not unusual for a poet to conclude his composition with a picture of the Last Judgment, as in the 'Elene'. One of the finest of Old English apocalyptic poems is the 'Last Judgment', found in the Exeter Book. The opening lines have a grandeur worthy of the subject, telling how the angels

> Shall blow their trumpets in a great blast.
> The earth shall tremble, the mould under men.
> Loud shall resound the strains of the trumpets
> Swelling clear to the course of the stars.
> They shall peal and sing from south to north,
> From east and west over all creation.[67]

The same theme of Doomsday is found in the later verse. One of the most beautiful of Anglo-Saxon poems, apparently of the tenth century, is the 'Doomsday',[68] an expanded translation of a Latin poem, 'De Die Judicii', ascribed variously to Bede or Alcuin. The translation is finer, as poetry, than the original. Like the Blickling Homilies it is lyrical and yet steeped in eschatological fears. The translator begins with a fine piece of descriptive verse. He is sitting in a shady wood, where the streams murmur and the plants bloom; but his mind is disturbed by the rustling in the trees and the roaring of the winds, which cause him to think of his sins and coming death. Doomsday will come, with its award to all of unspeakable misery in hell, where will be found nothing but fire, cold, and loathsome filth, or the bliss of heaven in the presence of the Eternal God, whose 'kind son, Lord of victory, gives to each one everlasting meed, heavenly glories—a splendid gift', and where the blessed Mary leads her maiden throng, garlanded with blossoms, through a garden of red roses. It is the hope and vision of an eternity of delight in the blessed mansions of heaven, says the poet, which enable us to surmount the hardships of this present life.

Of less poetic merit is the short poem entitled 'The Grave', expressing the current Christian preoccupation with death, and given here in Longfellow's translation:

> For thee was a house built
> Ere thou wast born. . . .
> Doorless is that house,
> And dark it is within;
> There thou art fast detained
> And Death hath the key. . . .

The late Anglo-Saxon period was one in which men were greatly impressed by the sterner side of Christianity, in England as elsewhere. One result of this eschatological obsession was an undoubted growth of piety. The eleventh century became a great age of faith, when the Church increased its influence to an unprecedented extent, and men became readier to sacrifice all in the service of Christ. The Age of the Crusades was a natural sequel to this gloomy preoccupation with the Day of Doom.[69] Enthusiasm for the Christian religion reached its highest point in European history. The Church fully consolidated its position at home, and there was an important revival of missionary activity abroad.

CHAPTER XXI

ENGLISH CONTRIBUTIONS TO THE CONVERSION OF SCANDINAVIA

Towards the close of the tenth century a missionary connection was established between England and the lands of the far north which has hitherto been little studied by English historians. This is not surprising, since though the subject is an attractive one, the materials for its study are slender and scattered.[1] Even the chief figures in the story are often shadowy. It is clear, however, that Englishmen and men trained in English monasteries played a prominent part in the conversion of the Scandinavians, the last European peoples to accept the Christian Faith. Thus the Anglo-Saxons continued the noble missionary tradition which had been begun late in the seventh century, and which will always be particularly associated with the memory of Boniface and his companions. The great Apostle of Germany, however, stands out as a distinct historical figure, dominating the ecclesiastical scene in Central Europe during the middle years of the eighth century. He was one of the great men of the Dark Ages. Of his fellow-countrymen who preached further north in a later age, comparatively little is known.

Though Charlemagne was an enthusiastic supporter of Christianity, and compelled the heathen Saxons to accept baptism, he made no effort to spread the Faith outside the bounds of his own dominions. It is even said that he actively discouraged missionary work. Thus the Frisian bishop Liudger, who wished to preach to the Danes, was refused permission.

The next emperor, Louis the Pious, was more eager, though his motives in promoting missions were mixed. Sorely tried by Danish piratical incursions, he thought he saw in the conversion of the Danes an efficient means of curing the trouble at its source. In 823 he gave his support to an evangelising mission amongst the Danes conducted by Ebo, bishop of Rheims.[2]

Three years later the Frankish ruler was approached by Harold, king of Denmark, who was looking for allies in his struggle with internal rivals. With four hundred followers he agreed to receive baptism, and it was arranged that missionaries should enter his country. The emperor himself was godfather to Harold.[3]

The missionary party was led by Anskar, 'Apostle of the North', a Frank born c. 801.[4] He had received his training as a Benedictine in the Westphalian abbey of New Corbie, whence also came Autbert, who accompanied Anskar to Denmark but subsequently returned to New Corbie for health reasons. Anskar had some success in Denmark, and also in Sweden, whither he went for a time on the emperor's instructions.[5] In 829 Louis had received requests from Sweden for Christian teachers. A monk Gislemar was meanwhile appointed to replace Anskar in Denmark. The Swedish king Björn received Anskar favourably, though did not himself become a Christian. Encouraged by the progress made, which though modest held promise of future success, Louis the Pious established an archbishopric at Hamburg, with a general and loosely defined oversight for the lands of the north. Anskar was consecrated first holder of the see in 831, receiving the pallium from Gregory IV. He was also nominated papal legate for all the northern peoples, though this honour was to be held jointly with his predecessor Ebo of Rheims.

But any notions which the Franks may have entertained of Christian missions transforming the vikings into men of peace were without foundation, as indeed the record of Danish ravages throughout this century would show. In 840 the death of Louis placed the missionaries, working under his patronage, in a dangerous position. Five years later the Danish king Horik sailed with a pirate fleet up the Elbe and destroyed Hamburg, Anskar himself narrowly escaping with his life. The destruction was so complete that a union of the see with that of Bremen became necessary. Pope Nicholas I approved the union, though at the same time confirming the archbishop in his position of authority over the northern peoples. Horik was a bitter opponent of the Church, but his attitude was gradually softened by the gentle powers of persuasion in which Anskar trusted. Though not himself accepting Christianity, the Danish king came to tolerate it, and allowed the erection of a church at Schleswig. His successor and namesake Horik was hostile, and persecuted the Danish converts, but Anskar succeeded in winning him round.

Anskar died at Bremen in 865, and was canonised soon afterwards. He was succeeded in the archbishopric by his biographer Rimbert, like him a Frank, and the see maintained its succession. But though Anskar had maintained an interest in Sweden and sent Danish priests thither as missionaries, the Hamburg-Bremen mission never really made much impression in the more northerly country. Until the coming of the English missionaries more than a century later there was only a tiny minority of Christians in Sweden, at the thriving trading port of Birka on the shores of Lake Mälar. Here there was a colony of foreign merchants, and here Anskar had established a congregation.

Considerably later, in 935, archbishop Unni of Hamburg-Bremen went to resume missionary work in Denmark, where king Gorm was an inveterate heathen but his son Harold Bluetooth well disposed to the new religion. Proceeding to Sweden, Unni died at Birka in 936. On his arrival thither he found that the Swedish Christians had relapsed into heathenism. It is likely that the impact of Anskar upon the Swedes had been negligible, and it may be that the Christian community established at Birka was recruited largely from foreigners resident there for commercial purposes. After Unni's death, Harold Bluetooth became a Christian, under pressure from the emperor Otto I, and was in a high degree responsible for the eventual success of the Church in his country. During Harold's final years, his son Swegn Forkbeard rose against him and ousted him from the throne. Harold died c. 986. Swegn was eventually uncrowned king of England for a brief period (autumn 1013–February 1014), and his son Cnut king from 1016 to 1035.

Meanwhile Christian influence and ideas were gradually finding their way into Norway. Haakon the Good, son of the Norwegian king Harold Fairhair, had been brought up in England at Athelstan's court, where he was educated as a Christian. On hearing of his father's death in 945 he returned to Norway and ousted his brother Eric Blood-Axe. Eric made his way to England, where he became the last ruler of the Scandinavian kingdom of York. Haakon attempted, with little success, to introduce Christianity into Norway, sending for missionaries from England and providing them with churches. His attempt to Christianise the country was opposed by his people. They insisted, moreover, on his joining them in the traditional heathen feasts, which included the ceremonial eating of horseflesh. He did so, and though he protested, he was apparently half pagan at heart. He remained nominally a Christian, but after his death in battle his followers gave him the full honours of a pagan funeral.

Haakon the Good was succeeded by the five sons of Eric Blood-Axe, who ruled jointly. They also had been taught the Christian religion in England, and now attempted a conversion of Norway, but with even less success than that which had attended the efforts of their predecessor. Haakon had been tolerant enough to leave the heathen temples alone when he realised the unwillingness of the Norwegians to forsake their ancestral faith, which they regarded as closely bound up with the fertility of the soil. Consequently, Haakon had been held in reverence and esteem by his people. The sons of Eric, to their own undoing, rashly tried to suppress the heathen sacrifices by force.

They were succeeded by another Haakon, a pagan, who rebuilt the temples. A contemporary poet sings of the magnificent harvests that resulted. He ruled on the whole successfully, but grew unpopular towards the end of his life, which came with his murder in 995.

It was from about this time that the English contribution to the conversion of Scandinavia seriously commenced. But before these activities are considered, a brief glance at the heathen religion which prevailed in the north is necessary.

According to Scandinavian religion (our knowledge of which is largely derived from the skaldic songs),[6] the gods were divided into two main groups, the Æsir and the Vanir. The chief gods themselves were Odin, Thor, and Frey. At the head of the pantheon was Odin, the god of war and wisdom, the All-Father on whom men chiefly relied in the perplexities of life. In practical everyday affairs Frey held prime place, as the giver of good weather and harvests. Thor was perhaps the oldest of Scandinavian gods, and favoured especially by the peasants.

Worship seems to have been originally in the open air—in groves or on hill-tops. But in course of time temples were erected, the most famous of them at Uppsala. A Scandinavian temple was a square or rectangular structure, with seats around the walls. It contained an altar of wood or stone, to which was attached a ring on which solemn oaths were sworn. There were images of various deities grouped by the altar or placed in niches, and adorned with jewellery. In the Uppsala temple were three such images, representing Thor, Odin, and Frey.[7]

Temple worship centred around the sacrifice of animals, ceremonially slaughtered before the altar, the blood being sprinkled over the worshippers and the flesh cooked and eaten. Human sacrifice was not unknown. On one occasion a certain king Domald was sacrificed by his subjects after a succession of poor crops. There were three great annual festivals, held in October, January, and April respectively, the mid-winter feast at Uppsala being attended from all parts of Sweden. Neither the holy places nor holy seasons lacked their devotees, and the Scandinavians undoubtedly showed more enthusiasm over the performance of their religious duties than did the heathen Anglo-Saxons of an earlier period. A hard and long struggle awaited the missionaries, especially in Sweden, and there would be many martyrdoms.

It will be clear from the above account, on the other hand, that in some details of ritual observance the heathen Scandinavians would not find the transition to Catholic worship difficult. Indeed no religion other than Catholicism could probably ever have accomplished the conversion at all, whether in Scandinavia or any heathen European country. One important difference between the Catholic Church and the Scandinavian religion, however, was the apparent lack of a professional priesthood in the latter. It would seem to have been customary for the founder of a temple to serve as its *godi* or priest.[8] On great occasions it was the duty of the king himself to offer the sacrifices.

It was under Olav Trygvason that Christianity took root in Norway.[9] Born *c.* 969, a great-grandson of Harold Fairhair, Olav seems to have lived his boyhood in exile, part of the time in Russia. He then became a viking, plundering in Germany, the Low Countries, and the British Isles. In 994 he was with Swegn Forkbeard, raiding in England. A bold attempt of the Northmen to conquer England in that year was defeated, and Olav Trygvason was confirmed by bishop Aelfheah of Winchester at Andover, having it seems been baptised some time previously.

Returning to Norway in 995, Olav succeeded Haakon. He at once announced his attention of Christianising Norway, and threw the whole of his energetic personality into this task. Like his predecessors he met with opposition, and chieftains and peasants clung tenaciously to the old religion. The contrast with the comparative ease of the English Conversion four centuries previously is remarkable. But Olav would brook no opposition, and did not hesitate to use torture on the most recalcitrant. He took as his text Christ's words, 'Compel them to come in'.[10] It is probable indeed that without coercive treatment Scandinavia might never have become Christian at all. On one occasion the king invited a party of heathen magicians to a feast, and set fire to the hall in which they were seated. His vigorous policy, however, made him many enemies, and in the end proved his undoing. A princess named Sigrid whom he was proposing to marry refused to renounce her heathenism at his behest, whereupon he personally insulted her, in his rage striking her with his glove. He would have done better to have held his temper. She revenged herself by forming a coalition of Scandinavian princes against Olav Trygvason, who was defeated and drowned at the battle of the Svolder in 1000, after a brave fight against hopeless odds.

In spite of his cruelty and violence, Olav Trygvason was undoubtedly a member of the Church by conviction. We see in him the viking dedicating his peculiar characteristics to the service of Christ. He was an enthusiastic propagandist, and wherever he journeyed in his kingdom he took missionaries with him. Not only Norway, but also Iceland, the Faroes, the Orkneys, and Greenland, were Christianised by him. Among the many missionaries whom he imported was Sigfrid (or Sigurd), probably an Englishman of the Danelaw but trained as a monk at Glastonbury. Sigfrid brought with him three nephews, Benedictines like himself, who obtained the reward of martyrdom. His movements after the battle of the Svolder are obscure, but it seems that he arrived as a missionary in Sweden, whither he was invited by Olav Ericson, king of Sweden and a member of the alliance which had prevailed in 1000. According to one account, Olav had heard of Sigfrid's work and sent a messenger to report on it. The messenger on his return described unarmed men who wore robes like those of women and performed ceremonies in front of an altar. Sigfrid visited Sweden, and as a result Olav was baptised, though he had already been interested in Christianity for some years. He was the first Christian king of Sweden, and a real help to Sigfrid in his work, making over property to him in expiation of the murder of the missionary's three nephews. Using Växjö as his centre, Sigfrid preached, baptised, and established churches. In his teaching he stressed the love of God, the need for repentance, and the importance of baptism. He made many missionary journeys in Sweden, during the course of one of which he preached to a multitude of people at the important trading town of Sigtuna on the shores of Lake Mälar. He reproved them for their sins, and called for amendment of life. This emphasis on the Christian ethic, involving amongst much else monogamy and sobriety in food and drink, was the real stumbling block with most Scandinavians in the way towards Christianity.

Sigfrid himself was essentially an evangelist, and the first settled diocesan bishop in Sweden was Thurgot, who became bishop of

Skara *c.* 1020. He appears to have worked independently of Sigfrid. Many English bishops are known to have laboured in Sweden during these years. About 1022 Olav Ericson died, and was succeeded by his son Anund Jacob, who was a Christian but did not attempt to promote the fortunes of the Church by forcible means. This was in contrast to the policy of his father, who had aroused the opposition of his people by proposing to suppress the great heathen temple of Uppsala. Anund Jacob was succeeded in 1052 by his half-brother Emund, who tried to make his country ecclesiastically independent of the archbishop of Bremen.

Other missionaries who have been described as Englishmen were also working in the Scandinavian peninsula at this time. Such were Grimkel, Bernard, and Rudolf, but their nationality in the final analysis must remain a matter of doubt. Grimkel has the strongest case for being regarded as an Englishman, though he may have come from the Danelaw. It is likely that a high proportion of the so-called English missionaries were in fact not Anglo-Saxons proper, but Christianised Danes from the eastern counties. They took the enthusiasm of a newly-found faith across the seas to their fellow Northmen. Rudolf was probably a Norman, though he certainly came to England after his Scandinavian missionary labours, settling down as abbot of Abingdon, where he died in 1052. Possibly he should be identified with a Rudolf described as working in Iceland from *c.* 1030 to 1049.[11]

Others who may be mentioned are Gotebald, Eskil, David, and Botvid. The first-named worked in Sweden, and also in Denmark at the request of the Danish king Svend, one of the coalition that had defeated Olav Trygvason. Eskil was another Englishman who helped to evangelise Sweden. His name survives in the Swedish town of Eskiltuna. He was chaplain for a time to Sigfrid. He built a church at Fors, near the southern shores of Lake Mälar, from which he conducted missionary tours in the surrounding district. He was martyred during a period of heathen reaction. Though never formally canonised, he came to be held in wide veneration.

David was an Englishman who on hearing of the martyrdom of Sigfrid's nephews was so stirred that he left his native land for Sweden, where he worked under Sigfrid. He fixed his centre at Munktorp, where he preached and baptised, and evangelised the neighbouring districts. He became the first bishop of Vasteras, and is said to have founded at Munktorp the first Swedish monastery. He seems to have died by natural causes at an advanced age. Though never formally canonised, his name is included in nearly all the Swedish diocesan calendars of the middle ages.

Botvid, an important missionary in the conversion of Sweden, was himself a Swede. He visited England, where he came in touch with the Church and was baptised, returning as a missionary to his fellow-countrymen.

After Olav Trygvason's death in 1000 there was a heathen reaction in Norway—not a surprising development in view of the violence of his methods. Sigfrid, helping in the restoration of Christianity in that country, encountered a doughty champion of the heathen religion in the chieftain Dale Gudbrand. But after the destruction of the idol of Thor, the chieftain declared that since his god was helpless, he would henceforth serve the Christian God. Whereupon he and his son were baptised.

Sigfrid died at Växjö sometime between 1060 and 1070, after playing what appears to have been the leading part in Sweden's conversion.[12] Anskar, by establishing a Christian community at Birka, had prepared the way, but Sigfrid and his contemporaries were the main agents in the general establishment of the Swedish Church. In 1070 the great heathen temple at Uppsala, traditional centre of Swedish religion, was still standing, and most Swedes were as yet unbaptised. But by this time it was clear that the future of religion in this country lay with Christianity.

The conversion of Sweden, however, was a long-drawn-out process.[13] The missionary figures concerned in it often have English connections, such as Osmund, who tried to shake off the Swedish ecclesiastical dependence on Bremen. A nephew of Sigfrid, he eventually came first to the court of Edward the Confessor, and then to Ely abbey, where he died and was buried. His inscription may be seen in the chapel of bishop West. An indication of the undoubted influence of Englishmen in the conversion of Sweden is the large number of English saints commemorated in Swedish pre-Reformation diocesan calendars. The earliest known calendar, of 1198, lists many English saints' days, including those of king Edward the Martyr, Cuthbert, Wilfred, John of Beverley, and Boniface. Sigfrid, who appears to have been canonised formally, was commemorated on 15 February. It is curious to find, on the other hand, that none of the English missionaries to Sweden are commemorated in the English calendars. Throughout the middle ages the English seem to have been largely unaware of the part played by their countrymen in the conversion of Scandinavia. Even in our own day recognition comes tardily; the revised Anglican calendar of 1928 omits Sigfrid, though it includes the Frankish Anskar. We must not, however, allow a new and exaggerated enthusiasm to compensate for a previous neglect. A comprehensive and balanced survey of the conversion of Scandinavia might well reveal that the honours should be fairly evenly divided between the English and the Germans.

Three more indications of English participation in the establishment of Scandinavian Christianity may be noticed.

Firstly, there were many Englishmen (besides other foreigners) amongst the earlier occupants of the Swedish sees, in addition to the missionary bishops mentioned above. Thus three Englishmen in succession held the see of Skara. When Uppsala was raised to metropolitical status by the papacy in 1164, an English Cistercian, Stephen, became the first archbishop. He was consecrated in the presence of Alexander III, who conferred the pallium upon him. Stephen died in 1185. The tradition of English bishops in Sweden ended with Egidius, bishop of Vasteras for more than thirty years, who died in 1213. The fully developed medieval Church in Sweden was organised in seven dioceses, the number existing at the Reformation.

Secondly, the English monastic orders exerted an influence in Scandinavia, where the Cistercian houses of Fountains and Kirkstead had offshoots at Lysekloster and Hovedö in Norway. During the reign of William Rufus the Benedictine abbey of Evesham sent a family of twelve monks to found a house at Odensee, in Denmark; a connection was long maintained by Odensee not only with Evesham, but also with St Mary's York.[14]

Thirdly, it is clear that in details of organisation and liturgical practice the Churches of Norway and Sweden had close affinities with England, though in this respect the Church of Denmark was indebted rather to Germany. The eleventh-century church of St Peter, at Sigtuna on the shores of Lake Mälar, along with several other churches in the neighbourhood, has Anglo-Saxon architectural characteristics.[15]

Even a brief sketch of the conversion of Scandinavia such as that here attempted must make mention of St Olav (to be distinguished from Olav Trygvason), hero-saint of the north. Born *c.* 995, the son of a Norwegian chieftain, he spent his youth in viking adventures, and was apparently associated with the Kentish raids conducted by the Danish Thorkil, during which the primate Aelfheah met his death in a drunken brawl in 1012. At about the age of eighteen Olav was baptised at Rouen, and there is no doubt that he accepted Christianity by conviction. On becoming king of Norway he pursued the familiar policy of compulsory conversion. He organised the Church of Norway on the model of that of England, and among the missionaries whom he brought over from England was Grimkel. Olav showed a particular interest in legal affairs, and a regular church law was established. The Norwegian Church, however, was subject ecclesiastically not to the English Church, but to the archbishop of Hamburg-Bremen. The German ecclesiastics always regarded Scandinavia as their sphere of influence, and there can be no doubt that many German missionaries worked there.

Under Cnut, England became part of a great Nordic maritime Empire ruled from Winchester, and Canterbury bade fair to replace Hamburg-Bremen as its ecclesiastical capital. If this Empire had survived, the course of north-western European history might well have been different. During his reign Cnut stood out as a successful seaking, extending his sway over vast areas of sea and land. He was the enemy and rival of Olav, whom he defeated and slew at the battle of Stiklestad, in 1030. It is related how in the hour of Olav's defeat the sun was darkened in eclipse, and men saw in the ruin of the Norwegian king a type of the death of Christ.[16]

Though Olav, like other Scandinavian rulers, could be treacherous and licentious, he was just and generous on the whole, and a protagonist of Christian civilisation. He came to be regarded not long after his death as the patron saint of the north. To the Scandinavians he was the true Hero, fighting to the end against hopeless odds. In him we see the Christian Faith and the old heroic northern spirit joining hands.

The latest considerable addition to the fold of Western Christendom was Finland, and it is gratifying to find Englishmen here again playing a notable part in the work of missions. It was an exceptionally difficult sphere of work, and Innocent III in a letter to the archbishop of Lund said that he who accepted a bishopric in Finland was almost certain to find a martyr's death. The severity of the climate also was a factor to discourage missionaries.

The heathenism of Finland was animistic in character, and its mythology distinct from that of the Scandinavian. It included the worship of departed spirits, while all nature was peopled by diverse divinities. There were spirits of the land and of the waters. There was a god of the air called the Aged One, upon whom depended the harvest. In this land of forests there were numerous divinities of the woods, the chief being Tapio, who with his wife gave success to the huntsman. There was the familiar host of elves, gnomes, and dwarves.

The little that is known of Finnish heathen worship suggests a sparing use of idols. There was no priestly caste, and worship for the most part took place in the open. Offerings were placed alongside sacred groves and trees, and horses were sacrificed.

It was to this remote territory and forbidding people that an English missionary Henry came early in the second half of the twelfth century. He had previously been consecrated bishop of Uppsala by the papal legate Nicholas Breakspear, himself an Englishman and subsequently pope as Adrian IV. Following a crusade against the heathen Finns by Eric IX of Sweden in 1157 or soon afterwards, Henry, who has been called the Apostle of Finland, preached the Gospel to them. He journeyed throughout the country, paying especial attention to places where there was a concentration of people, such as trading centres. His career was short, and he met a violent death before he was able to accomplish much. His formal canonisation appears doubtful, but subsequent papal bulls referred to him as St Henry the Martyr.

Another Englishman, Thomas, did more lasting work. He became bishop to the Finns c. 1220, about which time he also seems to have become a Dominican. Though a vigorous propagandist of the Faith, his methods were occasionally not above reproach. He was himself affected by remorse towards the close of his life, and sought permission of Innocent IV to retire. He passed his final years peacefully in a Dominican friary in Gottland. The papacy, now at its zenith, took an exceptionally keen interest in Finland, doubtless anxious lest the Orthodox Church should secure a firm footing in the territory first. The success of Thomas in laying the firm foundations of the Finnish Church was due in no small measure to papal support.

The Finns did not make good converts, and were at the best grudging members of the Church. It was common practice for them to accept Christianity when threatened, and then relapse into heathenism with the passing of the danger. The final stage in the Christianisation of their country came about the middle of the thirteenth century. The Swedish king Eric Ericson, at the urging of the papacy, undertook a crusade against the heathen Tavastians, the lake-dwellers of central Finland. The people were offered a choice between baptism and the sword. A fortress was built on the shores of a lake to prevent any heathen uprising. It was the final triumph of the Church in the Scandinavian lands.

CHAPTER XXII

ARCHITECTURE AND ART:
THE LATER STAGES

In England today there are about two hundred churches still in use, mostly as parish churches, which wholly or in part consist of late Anglo-Saxon work. They are generally in villages or out-of-the-way places, where there has been little need or temptation through the centuries to replace the original structures with larger buildings. Though scattered, they form a homogeneous group, members of which can usually be distinguished by certain well-defined characteristics.[1]

In architecture, as in so much else, the Danish wars marked a clear break, and when church building was resumed late in the ninth century it was along lines verging somewhat from those previously prevailing, and under different auspices and influences. During the tenth century, the more settled conditions, together with the ecclesiastical revival and the development of the parochial system which was part of it, led to an increased demand for local centres of worship. It is probable too that there was a considerable move towards building in stone.

At any period in Anglo-Saxon times masonry was an ambitious undertaking. The English were an out-door people, pre-eminently men of the fields and woods. Timber was their natural material for all sorts of construction, and it is a matter for regret that in the nature of things nothing (or virtually nothing) survives of what must have been an experienced and expert tradition of wood carving. All domestic buildings and most churches of the pre-Danish period were undoubtedly of wood, and in the later phase also the craft continued. But the existence of two belts of land in England with suitable building material gave the mason his opportunity, and a high proportion of the surviving remains of stone churches are in fact to be found, as might be expected, in the chalk regions which stretch in a line south-westwards from East Anglia and then south-eastwards into Sussex, and in the limestone country of Yorkshire, Lincolnshire, and the east midlands. Many stone churches, however, were also built elsewhere, and it is clear that the English Saxons were increasingly attracted to this civilised and enduring form of construction.

The wooden church of Greenstead in Essex is commonly taken to be a surviving Saxon church, and it may well be so. In any case it represents a type of building which must have been common in pre-Conquest times. It consists of sections of tree trunks set vertically, a method of construction suitable to the native English tree, which would not have lent itself to horizontal building in the manner of the Scandinavians, with their tall straight pine trees. Our best idea of the interior of the early English churches, and of the more ambitious domestic architecture, can probably be obtained from standing inside any one of the numerous traditional wooden barns which continued to be built in England until quite recent times.

Some of the wooden churches, however, appear to have been half-timbered structures, in the manner of the 'Tudor' style. This style shows a tendency to crop up at varying periods in architectural history, and can be seen today at its best, as is well known, in the west midlands. The two half-timbered churches of Pirton and Warndon, both in Worcestershire, though of a later medieval date, may as far as their style is concerned represent an unbroken line from Anglo-Saxon times. A strong presumption in favour of the use of such work by the Anglo-Saxons is the pilaster-strip style of external decoration, of which Earls Barton and Barton-on-Humber are outstanding examples. These stone strips may not be purely decorative, and perhaps were intended to serve a functional purpose in helping to hold the walling together. But the character of their design surely suggests a copying of half-timbered work, or at least the existence of a picture of such in the builder's mind obtained at second or third hand. It is possible of course that the pilaster-strip style may have been obtained from continental models, which were themselves based on wooden prototypes. Certainly, half-timbered work is part of the established architectural tradition amongst the Germanic peoples, and many examples may still be seen in wooded regions like the Teutoburger Wald in Western Germany.

Little is known directly of the greater English churches of the century and a half preceding the Conquest.[2] This is not surprising, as almost without exception they were cleared away by the Normans to make way for their own distinctive, though not necessarily superior, edifices. It was a policy which had been foreshadowed at Westminster by Edward the Confessor. Many of the churches which were swept away must have been almost brand-new, and indeed there is nothing whatever to suggest that in the middle of the eleventh century Anglo-Saxon architecture was in decline. The great age of the later Anglo-Saxon building programme was the second half of the tenth century, and there are known to have been important edifices at Winchester, Durham, Glastonbury, Worcester, Ely, Ramsey, and elsewhere. These churches would certainly be in the Romanesque style. The ecclesiastical reformers of the monastic revival, such as Dunstan and Aethelwold, were willing pupils of continental churchmen, and would not be slow to notice and reproduce overseas characteristics. Sir A. W. Clapham[3] thought that the great church of St Riquier, in Picardy, whose general character before 1090 is known, was the type of building to which the Anglo-Saxon cathedral churches may have approximated. Its features included a double transept (at the west and east ends respectively), round towers with spiral staircases, and a choir gallery at the west end.

The only greater English church of the late period whose plan is clear beyond doubt is that of North Elmham, Norfolk,[4] where there was a bishopric until the close of the eleventh century. William's policy of transferring Saxon village sees to more important centres of population ruled out the building of a Norman cathedral in this place, with the result that considerable portions of the Saxon cathedral remain. It appears to have been built c. 1000. It consisted of an aisleless nave, with a transept, apse, and two small towers at the east end, and a larger tower at the west end. The building was not a large one, its total length being 123 feet, but the fact that the construction of a new cathedral was undertaken only two generations before the Norman Conquest does not suggest, in East Anglia at any rate, a decadent Anglo-Saxon Church.

A little is known, from written evidence and archeological investigation, of other great churches. Thus the Saxon cathedral built at Durham in 999 had two stone towers, at the east and west ends respectively. There was an imposing tower, in five stages, at Winchester, dedicated in 980. The aisled nave of the cathedral at Canterbury, which was destroyed by fire in 1067, was flanked by north and south towers. Of the important coronation church at Kingston-on-Thames nothing unfortunately is known.[5]

From the many surviving examples of village churches it is possible to form a convincing impression of late Anglo-Saxon ecclesiastical architecture. These churches were not usually aisled, though there are aisles here and there, as at Wing, in Buckinghamshire. The average church apparently comprised a square or rectangular chancel, with a nave. As a rule the chancel-arch is narrow, though wider in the more important churches, as at Worth and Bosham, where it probably indicates the presence of a minster community of clergy. Minor altars were generally accommodated in porticus communicating with the church by doorways, as in the earlier period. The churches were commonly of lofty height, though it is perhaps somewhat far-fetched to suggest that this was to enable the draught from the unglazed windows to be kept away from the worshippers' heads. The Anglo-Saxons were inured to hardship and discomfort, and would hardly have gone to the expenditure of large masses of extra masonry merely for this particular convenience.

Usually the walling is of rubble, ashlar masonry being little used—though there is a fine instance of the latter in the intact church of Bradford-on-Avon, Wilts. The famous 'long-and-short' work (as in the tower of St Bene't's, Cambridge) was very popular in later Anglo-Saxon England, and is a distinctively English characteristic. The most attractive feature, the pilaster-strip, is often combined with an embellishment of round-headed or triangular blind-arcading. Arches and doorways generally have a stone framework, broken by a horizontal strip at the impost level. Towards the middle of the eleventh century Norman influence is often here noticeable, with a more or less elaborate scheme of shafts, as at Hadstock, Essex, and Great Paxton, Huntingdonshire. There are several instances of the triangular-headed doorway, as at Holy Trinity, Colchester, and Barton-on-Humber.

A very widely-spread feature of late Saxon architecture was the double-splayed window. Windows themselves were mostly round-headed, though some were completely circular in form. As a rule the windows were of a single light, though they sometimes consisted of two lights, divided by a baluster shaft. In the earlier period windows had been glazed, as at Wearmouth and Jarrow, and York, but it seems that in the period with which we are now concerned the use of glass was much less frequent (if indeed it existed at all) than that of thin stone slabs or wooden boards. There are surviving stone slabs, pierced with an interlace design, in some of the windows at Barnack, a notable Saxon church in more than one way, and traces of what appear to be wooden boards exist at Birstall.

It is to the tenth century that we may attribute the general introduction of that familiar feature of the English landscape, the square tower. Towers were used for bell-ringing,[6] and as flimsily built structures would never stand up to the vibration caused by large bells, a solidity was required which has ensured the preservation of a high proportion of these buildings. Some towers were used also, or alternatively, for purposes now hard to determine. Thus the Deerhurst tower is divided into compartments at various levels, of which those facing the east communicate with the interior of the church by door or window, and may conceivably have been used by the custodian or some such official. Some towers, however, have external doorways high above the ground, apparently opening into empty space. It is sometimes thought that they were approached by ladders, and that they existed for the convenience of builders engaged in repair work. But this suggests a refinement of foresight of which few builders or architects, in any age, have been capable. It is more likely that there were external annexes to some towers, and indeed this is indicated by structural fragments on the outside walls of the tower at Netheravon, Wilts. Throughout their architectural history the Anglo-Saxons appear to have been fond of small, cosy, apartments attached to their churches in various ways—porticus leading from the nave, upstairs chapels, underground crypts, and rooms in the tower.

One other characteristic may be mentioned. This is the informal, often rather careless, planning of many churches. The Anglo-Saxon builders were not obsessed with the attainment of tidiness and regularity. Barton-on-Humber, Kirkdale in Yorkshire, and most strikingly Chickney in Essex, show this contempt for the cult of the right angle. This feature is one of the earliest manifestations of that casual, unmethodical spirit which has characterised the English people to the present day.

English ecclesiastical architecture during the tenth century was plainly influenced by that of the Carolingian Empire and the Ottonian Empire which followed it. Thus the feature of round towers, which is known to have existed at the old Carolingian cathedral of Cologne, appears on a thirteenth-century seal of the dean and chapter of Chichester, from which it may be inferred that this was a feature also of the Saxon cathedral at either Selsey or Chichester. In course of time the small round tower became an established characteristic of the Rhineland, where it may still be seen in such noble churches as those of Worms and Maria Laach. There is a great deal to be said for the view[7] that if the development of Saxon architecture had been left to itself, without interruption by the intrusion of the Normans, this same kind of Romanesque would have become part of the English tradition. Of other Carolingian features we find the double transept (that is to say, transepts at both the east and west ends) at Ely, and the western gallery at Deerhurst. The Romanesque double-apse plan, however, does not seem to have been favoured by English builders, who preferred the square east end, though there are some round or polygonal eastern apses, as at Wing and Worth, and there were apparently altars at both ends at Canterbury and Thorney. The English pilaster-strip was probably based on Rhineland models. The triangular-headed doorway is also Carolingian, as is the double-splayed window. The planning of some of the churches suggests German influence—at Barton-on-Humber, for example, the round tower formed the centre of a three-sectioned edifice, an arrangement found at Werden in western Germany.

German influence is strikingly indicated at Sompting, Sussex, where stands the only Anglo-Saxon church to retain its original roof. The ridges of the roof rise from the gables which crown the walls of the tower. This pleasing and ingenious design is almost identical with that of the Church of the Apostles in Cologne, which was commenced in the eleventh century, and the central east tower of the abbey church at Maria Laach. It is difficult to see how so idiosyncratic a design could have been produced with such exactness in two widely separated regions without direct contact or borrowing. The plan is so competent, moreover, that we can scarcely believe it to have been confined to a single obscure Sussex village. It may well have been common in England and a feature of some of the greater churches, as at Winchester, where it is known that the tower was capped with pointed roofs.

In general, relations between England and Germany in the tenth century were close, and it is in the interchange of clerics that we find our clue for the introduction of Rhineland Romanesque ideas into this country. Thus in 929 Cenwald, bishop of Worcester, paid a series of visits to German churches; conversely, Godescalc, whom Athelstan placed over the monastery of Abingdon, was a German.

Alfred had married one of his daughters to Baldwin II, count of Flanders, and for some decades following there was a close friendship between the Anglo-Saxon and Flemish royal houses. But the crucial Germanic connection came after the rise of the Ottonian rulers. The death of Louis the Child in 911 brought to an end the direct Carolingian line, which was succeeded after a few years by the Saxon kingdom of Henry I (the Fowler), who ruled from 919 to 936. The empire which he founded is known as the Ottonian, from his son and successor Otto I (936–73), one of the greatest rulers in western European history. Whereas Henry the Fowler was distrustful of ecclesiastics, his son was a champion of the Church and its culture. Otto's defeat of the Magyars was a triumph for Christendom, and the battle of Lechfeld (955) ranks with Alfred's victory at Edington and Charles Martel's at Tours as landmarks in the defence of western civilisation. Otto I married as his first wife an Anglo-Saxon princess Edith, sister of Athelstan, and undoubtedly this marriage helped to establish the close community of interest which seems to have existed between the two Saxon realms in the middle years of the century. From this marriage the later Hohenstaufen dynasty was directly descended, and it is also worthy of note that a greatgrandson of Otto and Edith became pope as Gregory V.

The English-German connection had one particular result of great interest. It appears to have given a powerful stimulus to those Byzantine influences which according to modern research were operative in Anglo-Saxon art. In 972 Otto's son (by a second marriage) married Theophano, a Byzantine princess and a woman of brilliant personality, who was responsible for the introduction into Germany of the refined culture of her homeland. Her husband succeeded to the Saxon throne in 973 as Otto II, to be followed by their son Otto III (983–94), who inherited his mother's love of Byzantine culture and art and was educated under such auspices.

In Anglo-Saxon sculptures from the late ninth century onwards there is constant evidence of Byzantine influence, especially in the closing decades of the tenth century. This was the very period when Byzantine culture was being imported into the Ottonian kingdom, and it is reasonable to believe that the strongly marked Byzantinism of English art at this time was largely due to Anglo-Saxon contacts with Germany.

However, Eastern influence was no new thing in England, and is to be seen in two sculptured figures at Breedon, attributed to the ninth century. In one of these an angel is giving the blessing in the Greek manner, with the fourth finger touching the thumb; in the other, the drapery of the Virgin is Byzantine. In the justly famous carving of a dancing man in the church of Codford St Peter, in the Wylye valley,

Wiltshire, we have a wholly native art. This piece conveys an impression of remarkable freshness and liveliness. It seems almost of yesterday, and yet it is probably ninth-century work. Of about the same time, or perhaps some years earlier, is the vine-scroll ornamentation in the arches at Britford.

The tenth century, however, was the flourishing period for post-Danish stone-carving. Byzantine influence is clear in a number of carved angels, as at Deerhurst, and particularly at Bradford-on-Avon, where we see the Byzantine motive of draped veils over the arms. At Winterbourne Steepleton, Dorset, the 'flying angel' is a very vigorous carving with clearly-cut facial features, and of a decidedly Byzantine flavour. At Stinsford (Thomas Hardy's 'Mellstock') there is a carved angel on an exterior wall of the tower which has been attributed to the twelfth century,[8] though the scholarly study of D. Talbot Rice assigns it more probably to c. 1000. A late rendering of the angel theme (which is a very old Christian one, derived ultimately from the pagan motive of the 'winged victory'), it is delicate with fluttering draperies. Talbot Rice also writes that a 'fragment of sculpture recently discovered at Maiden Newton in Dorset may also represent an angel'.[9] Nothing is known locally of any such discovery, though there are three or four fragments incorporated into the west wall of the south porch of the church, which could possibly (though not very probably) represent an angel. Of more interest in this church is a seated cleric with right arm raised in blessing in the Byzantine manner, in a blocked doorway in the north wall.

There are several examples of the Crucifixion—a popular subject with Anglo-Saxon carvers as with poets. The best is a rood of early eleventh-century date in the cloister at Romsey abbey. A monumental work, its dignity is enhanced by the fact that Christ is here alone, and not accompanied, as usual, by subsidiary figures. So close is the figure to Byzantine types that Talbot Rice concludes (as in many cases) that the Saxon sculptor must have been using an imported model.[10] Of about the same date is a small crucifixion slab inside Romsey church; it is in flat relief, and seems in its original condition to have been coloured.

In contrast with the dignified Romsey cloister rood, is a group of other Crucifixion compositions which stress the human rather than the celestial aspect. Thus at Langford in Oxfordshire there are two roods in one of which the limbs of the suffering Christ are contorted—

a non-Byzantine conception, but characteristic of Syria and Palestine. The rood at Wormington, Worcestershire, shows Our Lord with a sadly dejected head. The same note of human agony is discernible in two roods, now badly defaced, at Headbourne Worthy and Breamore, both in Hampshire. The former, which may be seen in what serves today as the vestry, was undoubtedly an imposing sculpture in its first state. It is high up on the east wall, and apparently in medieval times a ceiling was put over the lower part of the chamber, making of the upper storey a chapel, of which the rood was the reredos. The piscina is still in place. At Breamore, the surface outlines of the rood in the porch emphasise the agonies of the dying Saviour, whose limbs are twisted in pain.

Whereas the winged angel group of carvings are probably of the tenth century, the crucifixions are assigned to the earlier decades of the eleventh century. One more rood may be mentioned, that of Dagling-worth, Gloucestershire, a roughly carved sculpture which is perhaps not untypical of the work which was done by local craftsmen in country districts.

There are two impressive pieces of carving which, if they could be ascribed with confidence to pre-Conquest times, would be an important testimony to the high standards attainable by the late Anglo-Saxon Church. The first consists of the sculptured panels in the choir of Chichester cathedral, representing the Raising of Lazarus, and Mary and Martha greeting Christ. These monumental carvings are ascribed by Talbot Rice to c. 1080.[11] But there is much about them—the draperies, the facial expressions, the posture of the figures—which seems Saxon. Moreover, the panels had clearly been at some time dismantled and reassembled, and it may well be that they were originally in the cathedral of Selsey and later brought to Chichester. Secondly, there is the beautiful Virgin and Child in York Minster, which evinces an absolute mastery of design and is Byzantine in its refinement. So accomplished is it that some students think it must be of the twelfth century. But its closeness to Byzantine work and its dissimilarity from any English post-Conquest work together suggest a date in the first half of the eleventh century. If this latter view be accepted, the Virgin and Child may (along with the Chichester panels) be regarded as the crowning-point of Anglo-Saxon sculpture.

The indebtedness of later Anglo-Saxon art to Byzantium has in general been convincingly demonstrated by Talbot Rice, though at the same time, in view of the specifically historical evidence, it may be believed that the influence came by way of the Rhineland and adjacent regions rather than directly from Constantinople. Indeed, the danger at the present time is that the northern and Germanic influences over English art and culture should come to be underestimated.

Throughout the post-Danish period the hand of the Scandinavian is visible in much English work, especially in the north, where animal carvings in the flat and attenuated ribbon-shape which characterise the Jellinge style (so called after objects found at Jellinge in Denmark) are found in conjunction with specifically Anglian work. The Northmen were fond of animals, and this love showed itself in non-figural sculpture. The dragon is as favourite a motive in the north as the angel is in the south. There are also instances early in the eleventh century, as with the carved lintel in the north transept of Southwell cathedral, of the style known as Ringerike (from the Norwegian quarry which produced the stone for the best-known examples).

There is much memorial sculpture, and to this class belong most of the numerous cross-shafts of this age. They are on a smaller scale than the imposing shafts of earlier Anglo-Saxon art. Distributed especially thickly in the Celtic regions of the west, they are sculpturally undistinguished. On shafts in Northumbria we find the interlace in a degraded form. We also come across the vine-scroll, though this died out before the end of Anglo-Saxon times. A fine wheel-headed cross is to be seen at Gosforth in Cumberland, carved with the crucifixion and scenes from the Scandinavian legend of Ragna Rok. Of the numerous fragmentary crosses may be mentioned at random those of Yetminster in Dorset and Broadchalke, Wiltshire; of complete or nearly complete examples, the cross in the parish church of Leeds and the cylindrical shaft at Wolverhampton. One of the most attractive of crosses, though somewhat earlier than the above, is that which formerly stood at Easby, near Richmond in Yorkshire, and is now exhibited in a fragmentary state in the Victoria and Albert Museum. Its scroll ornament with birds and beasts eating grapes off a vine is of a high artistic order, while the other side shows the heads of the apostles and Christ in Majesty.

To the class of memorial sculpture also belongs the so-called 'hogback' type of grave-slab, found in the north. It is derived from Scandinavia, and consists of a slab of stone carved at the ends in the form of a beast. Of greater dignity is the headstone type, of which there is a good example at Whitchurch, Hampshire, commemorating an unknown woman Frithburga, whose name is included in the inscription. Here the figure of Our Lord is carved in deep relief, one hand holding a book, the other raised in blessing.

In later Saxon times fonts must have been very generally used in churches, but little survives. In the earliest days of Christianity baptism was performed whenever possible in running water by total immersion,[12] and this was the practice of Augustine of Canterbury, and Paulinus, both of whom made use of rivers for mass baptisms.[13] That the more individual method of baptism was also practised, however, is clear from Bede's statement that Augustine and his companions used St Martin's, Canterbury, for mass, preaching, and baptising.[14] The early English Church followed the primitive custom whereby baptisms were generally confined to great festivals.[15] Such a custom emphasised the solemnity of the sacrament and its corporate character. Nothing remains, however, in England of the early system of separate baptisteries, built in conjuction with the more important churches, and regarded as possessing the monopoly of baptisms, which in theory at least should be administered only by the bishop, the father of all his people. On the Continent there are many surviving traces of baptisteries, especially in Italy, where the practice continued well down into the middle ages.[16]

The general development of the parochial system which arose out of the more settled conditions of the tenth century entailed an increased delegation of powers and authority from the bishop to his parish priests, and one form which this took was probably the widespread erection of fonts in the village churches. It is often hard to determine whether a particular surviving font is post-Conquest work or late Saxon, and the problem is further complicated when it appears that indubitably Saxon carving has been incorporated into a font by a later builder or craftsman. A section of a stout circular cross-shaft (like that of Wolverhampton) was turned upside down and hollowed out to form a font possibly at Deerhurst, and certainly at Melbury Bubb, Dorset. In the spirited design of the latter, animals are depicted fighting—perhaps hounds chasing deer. But more typical of what most Anglo-Saxon fonts probably looked like is that at Potterne, Wiltshire. Its form suggests a wooden prototype, a tub in fact, which we may believe served for local, individual baptisms in most English village churches until well into the tenth century.

On the whole, Anglo-Saxon churches had plain interiors, the stone-carver reserving most of his talent for sculptured work on cross-shafts and other individual pieces. There does not seem to have been much expenditure of effort on elaborate decoration of such architectural features as the capitals, and it was left to the Norman builder to introduce motives like the chevron, zigzag, and dog-tooth.

In other art-forms, the Anglo-Saxons excelled in ivory carving, particularly in the second half of the tenth century. Ottonian influences are very evident in the surviving work, and naturally ivories were art-objects specially liable to be transported and copied. An outstanding example is the ivory crucifix now in the Victoria and Albert Museum, which has a distinctly German look about it. An ivory at Winchester with two elegantly carved censing angels is dated c. 970. Two splendid ivories, the Alcester Tau in the British Museum and a crozier head in the Victoria and Albert, are later. Though they look forward to Norman art, they display Saxon characteristics. They are a warning against any tendency to separate too precisely the Saxon and Norman periods. The Alcester ivory, which apparently may have been one of the treasures of Evesham abbey, is an elaborately carved, T-shaped head of a staff. The Victoria and Albert crozier has scenes from the Nativity and Passion carved around the crook, and in its sensitivity and expression is a work of genius.

Little has survived of the precious metal-work objects which the English certainly produced in great profusion towards the close of the tenth century and beyond. The Church in England c. 1000 must have been one of the wealthiest in western Christendom, and Anglo-Saxon craftsmen in precious metals are known to have held a continental reputation. Material wealth in a nation must always be an open temptation to an aggressively minded neighbour, and it may be that the riches of the Anglo-Saxon greater churches were an important element in the amalgam of motives which brought first the Danes back to this country, and then produced the Norman Conquest. These two invasions, carried out within a couple of generations, made havoc of the cathedral and monastic treasuries, and the Protestant Reformation practically completed the pillage.

One of the earliest examples is a chalice, now in the British Museum, found in a hoard at Trewhiddle, Cornwall, and of late ninth-century date. This particular object is of Byzantine type, but Scandinavian influence on metal-work, especially weapons, was marked all through the tenth century. On the whole Ottonian (and therefore Byzantine) influence was not so strong in the craft of the smith as it was on stone-carving. But nearer towards 1000 German and Byzantine influences are important, and indeed the medieval word for bronze, 'cullen', was derived from Cologne, the great continental metal-working centre. Amongst isolated surviving objects are some thuribles, one of them from Pershore and of late tenth or early eleventh-century date, with a gabled roof like the church towers at Sompting and the Holy Apostles, Cologne. An important outlet for the goldsmith's craft lay in finger-rings, which were of course not necessarily ecclesiastical in their significance. The two best known, though of comparatively early date, are that of Aethelwulf, king of Wessex (836–58) and Alfred's father, which was found at Laverstock, and one which belonged to Alfred's sister Aethelswith, queen of Mercia (855–89), discovered in the West Riding. They are both in the British Museum.

The enthusiasm for metal-working was considerable, and ecclesiastics are known to have been not merely patrons of the craft but actually practised it with their own hands, as did Dunstan and Aethelwold. In this they maintained the tradition of the Lindisfarne bishops Eadfrith and Aethelwald, who had a personal share in the production of the Lindisfarne Gospels. The Norman ecclesiastics were men of narrower culture, and lacked the love of beauty for its own sake which was innate in the Anglo-Saxons. The inevitable result after 1066 was a decline in those minor arts which bring grace and pleasure into everyday life. Amongst the casualties was the craft of enamelling, of which there had been a flourishing school in England, an early example being the Alfred Jewel, now in the Ashmolean, and too well known to call for description or comment here.

In the great art of textiles there was no immediate break at the Conquest, though unfortunately little now remains. As embroiderers, Englishwomen were highly thought of across the Channel. There was a large demand for vestments and frontals in the services of the Church, and it is certain that nuns would have a share in their production. The Anglo-Saxons all through their history were fond of fine clothing, and what we know from contemporary illustrations is sufficient to assure us of its pleasing character and design. Amongst royal ladies who practised the art were Edith, queen of the Confessor, and the saintly Margaret, who married Malcolm king of Scotland.

The so-called vestments of St Cuthbert, at Durham, are the only specimens of this art still surviving in England. They consist of fragments of a stole and maniple, along with a few odd pieces, found in the saint's tomb when it was opened in 1827. An inscription which is part of the design dates them fairly precisely to 910–5. The stole is embroidered in silk in a most delicate way with figures of saints and prophets, and though the work is unquestionably that of Englishwomen, the iconography and style once again, as so often in Anglo-Saxon art, suggest Byzantine influence.

Far more celebrated is the great work which has always been associated with Bayeux, where it is still to be seen. Though known as a 'tapestry' it consists in fact of embroidered linen. With its scenes from the life of Harold and the battle of Hastings, it is a valuable historical document as well as a work of art. There is every reason to believe that it was made by English artists and needlewomen at the behest of Odo for his cathedral at Bayeux, which was founded in 1077. It contains a mixture of artistic motives, English, Scandinavian, and Byzantine.

If it is a tragedy that so little remains of embroidery, we happily have much from the great school of manuscript illumination which was one of the glories of the Old English Church. In this field of art, which had a close connection with the Church and its worship, the Danish ravages of the ninth century had played havoc, causing a complete break. When book-production was seriously resumed later on, its main centres were in the south, and it is with the beautiful Winchester school, flourishing from c. 960, that it is above all associated. The pre-Danish school, centred in Northumbria, had been decorative and instinctive with imagination; the illuminations of Wessex are essentially figural and humanistic. The art of the Wessex manuscript school is at once graceful and lively. Amongst its characteristics are delicacy of line-drawing, and a fluttering of the draperies which conveys an impression of youthful freshness.

The Winchester school of illumination was a direct product of the monastic revival, its first clear manifestation being the Foundation Charter produced and illuminated for the New Minster, Winchester, in 966. This was followed after some ten or twelve years by the Benedictional of St Aethelwold, formerly at Chatsworth, now in the British Museum and the most sumptuous of later Anglo-Saxon books, containing no fewer than forty-nine decorated pages. It is written in the Carolingian minuscule, and the style of the illustrations is often Byzantine, but the work in the final analysis must be judged thoroughly

English. It was probably produced at Winchester, and by a team of illuminators rather than by a single individual.

Other notable manuscripts are a Benedictional and a Sacramentary, now at Rouen, both connected with Robert of Jumièges, who became archbishop of Canterbury in 1051 for a short while before he was expelled from England. There are other books also in continental libraries, and in fact the wide diffusion of late Anglo-Saxon manuscripts is a testimony to the esteem in which they were held.

By *c.* 1000 the Winchester style was becoming well known in the south of England as a whole, and subsidiary schools developed, notably at Canterbury. There are many fine specimens, offshoots of the Wessex school, still to be seen, particularly at Trinity College, Cambridge, and the British Museum. Manuscripts were produced at Bury St Edmunds, Crowland, and elsewhere. A west country example is the late tenth-century psalter which is the most venerable possession of the dean and chapter of Salisbury, though this is a less accomplished work than most of the Winchester manuscripts. So fine and influential was the Winchester school that we find manuscripts being produced in its style in the north of France during the eleventh century. A notable Winchester manuscript of the later period is the *Liber Vitae*, produced at the New Minster between 1016 and 1020, with a well-known line-drawing of the Last Judgement. At the time of the Conquest there was no break in the tradition, and English artists, now under Norman patronage, continued to produce their exquisite books.

This artistic beauty provided a worthy setting for the public worship of God, in its two main divisions of the Divine Office and the Mass. Indeed, the importance of worship not only in the life of the Church and the Christian community as such, but also as an influence in the development of culture can scarcely be exaggerated.

In the monasteries of late Saxon England, the Monastic Office was observed, an arrangement of the psalmody in all its essentials identical with that followed by the Benedictines in our own day, and representing the most venerable and enduring form of the Western canonical hours. Its chief peculiarity consisted in the greater number of psalms assigned to Nocturns (the modern Matins), in the singing of psalm 3 at the beginning of the night office before the Venite, and in the use of four psalms only at Vespers instead of five as elsewhere. A variety of psalms was used at Prime and the lesser hours, instead (except on

Sundays) of psalm 119 as in the Roman usage. At Compline the Nunc Dimittis was omitted.

There is evidence to suggest that in some at least of the parish churches the Monastic, rather than the secular, Office was followed, in a simplified and shortened form. In an Old English text which was probably the work of Aelfric supplemented by Wulfstan, we have a vernacular commentary on the Office as used in religious houses, and intended for the use, apparently, of the parochial clergy.[17] Here Matins and Lauds are omitted, and the Office begins with Prime. It enables us to see the priest in his church (accompanied at any rate on Sundays by many of his people) in the early hours of the morning, raising the hymn *Iam lucis orto sidere*, and on behalf of the worshippers beseeching God to 'direct, sanctify, and govern their hearts and bodies in the ways of His laws and the works of His commandments'; we see him offering his simple prayers at Terce, Sext, None, and Vespers; and again at the close of day chanting (in the months of summer) his *Te lucis ante terminum*, or (in the winter) the *Christe qui lux est et dies*, and as the shades of night envelop the church in which gleams a solitary light before the Blessed Sacrament, commending his parish to God, that He may visit it and drive from it all the snares of the evil one.[18]

It was, however, in the Holy Sacrifice that the main worship of the Church consisted, sung on Sundays probably about nine in the morning,[19] and differing in its main outlines but little from the familiar Roman mass of today. In at least the more important churches there would be a daily celebration,[20] often offered with special intention, as appears from the *Leofric Missal* (associated with Leofric, bishop of the Devon see from 1046 to 1072), in which such masses as 'missa pro familiaribus', 'missa in honore Sanctae Crucis', find their place.[21]

Communion, when taken at the public mass, was generally in both kinds, though it was customary for the faithful to receive the consecrated wine through a reed from the chalice. In the early middle ages such reeds formed a regular part of the furniture or treasure of a church.[22] The sacrament was reserved under one species, from which the sick were communicated, as also the whole body of the faithful on Good Friday. It reposed in a pyx, often bowl- or saucer-shaped, suspended from the roof or a beam over the high altar.[23]

Catholic worship is in itself one of the greatest forms of artistic expression, in which all the traditional forms combine—architecture, sculpture, painting, drama, poetry, and music. The earliest influences in the music of the Church came from the synagogue, with its ordered and dignified cycle of psalms, lessons, and prayer. Christians were from the first suspicious of contemporary secular music, and there was a reluctance to utilise musical instruments, despite the obvious Old Testament precedent, where David the sweet psalm-singer was an adept at the harp. Church music originated in a musical improvisation of the sacred text of the Liturgy, its simplest form being the intonation on a single line of such readings as the Epistle and Gospel. From this there early developed the chants of the Sursum Corda, Preface, and Paternoster, still in use and the most venerable of Christian music. Recitative psalm-singing followed naturally, becoming the basis of the plain-chant tradition, to which an important impetus was accorded by the encouragement and patronage of pope Gregory. Plainsong became an accomplished art, and there was a steady growth in that peculiar beauty which one associates with its pure and well-defined melodies. The simpler, more primitive chants were supplemented by the comparatively ornamented music of such forms as the introits, offertories, and psalm-antiphons, of which numerous specimens were composed between 400 and 600. There is often an unconscious though entirely mistaken tendency to assume that such forms were a natural development, spontaneously arising out of the Christian soil. One should rather give due credit to countless anonymous composers, monks of creative ability, making their contributions to a repertory of extraordinary richness, which has survived (unlike the music of the classical world) to constitute one of the supreme artistic treasures of mankind.

The golden age of Gregorian music was probably the seventh century, which was also the time of its introduction to England. Mention has already been made of the influence in this country of such experts as James, Eddius, bishop Putta, and abbot John from Rome. But the absence of musical notation at this time entailed the extensive use of the memory in the maintenance of a musical tradition, and it is virtually certain that during the troubles of the ninth century the art in England would be lost. It was brought back by Alfred, who called in the services of the St Bertin monk Grimbald, and John, both skilled in music, while the monastic revival of succeeding decades ensured its general reintroduction. Dunstan himself was a competent musician, to whom is traditionally ascribed the *Kyrie Rex Splendens*, one of the most haunting plainsong melodies. The 'Worcester Antiphoner',[24] at present preserved at Worcester cathedral, though in itself of early thirteenth-century date is a faithful copy of the chant introduced by Aethelwold to Abingdon and Winchester, which in its turn had been imported from the Continent.

Although by the time of Gregory the proper of the mass was probably fixed into the form which it has ever since held, in following centuries there were many additions to the repertory of the ordinary, and some beautiful examples of the Kyrie, Gloria, Sanctus, and Agnus Dei, are probably of tenth- or eleventh-century date. The traditional melody of the Credo may, however, be referred back to at least the sixth century; the tendency was always against its elaboration or variation, and indeed the Credo was strictly speaking not an integral part of the mass at all. When used it had a congregational character, and was especially associated with the principal Sunday mass.

An attractive feature of Gregorian music has always been the melismatic chant. This consists of the melodic elaboration of the final syllable, and is associated above all with the Alleluia following the Gradual. It offered scope and opportunity to gifted singers, and Gregory had to utter strictures against those who delighted the people in church with their solo performances yet lived lives of dubious morality. A further development, which gathered momentum in the course of the ninth century, was the trope, a kind of embellishment or artistic commentary to the authorised text or chant. It is closely connected with folksong, and marks the earliest attempt to bring the 'popular' into church music and liturgy. The trope composers tried to introduce the contemporary idiom into the services of the Church, very successfully on the whole, and many additions were made to the text and chant of the Liturgy. Troping continued to be popular throughout the eleventh century, and there survive in England two collections of tropes, the 'Winchester Tropers', now at Corpus Christi College, Cambridge, and the Bodleian, which are attributed to the late Saxon period. From the trope there developed the sequence, at first in free rhythmical prose, but by the twelfth century an independent poetic form. In the middle ages the development ran riot, until the Council of Trent c. 1550 banished from the mass all tropes and all sequences save four, the much loved *Victimae Paschali* of Eastertide, the *Veni Sancte Spiritus* and *Lauda Sion Salvatorem*, and the superb *Dies Irae*.[25] Of these only the first-named is of comparatively early date, but amongst sequences which may well have been heard in monastic and minster churches of the late Old English and Anglo-Norman

379

periods, though long since banished from any authorised Liturgy, are such exquisite examples as the Advent *Salus aeterna*, and the Christmas *Laetabundus*, both of which are included in the English Hymnal.

To the same popularising movement which produced the trope and sequence may also be ascribed the liturgical drama, instrumental music, and polyphony, from which forms the modern drama and opera are ultimately descended. Of the first-named of these artistic manifestations the 'Quem quaeritis' is the best known, and it is clear from the *Regularis Concordia* that it was known, or intended to be known, in England. From this account[26] we learn that at the close of the third lesson at Nocturns of Easter Day, a monk attired in an alb was to proceed to the 'sepulcre' and sit there holding a palm in his hand. Three other brethren, in copes and bearing thuribles, were to enter separately and in turn, as though looking for something. On seeing their approach the seated monk was to sing 'Whom seek ye?', to which the three would answer, 'Jesus of Nazareth'. The reply was, 'He is not here, but is risen as he promised. Go, and announce his resurrection from the dead.' The three were then to turn to the choir, singing, 'Alleluia. The Lord is risen.' But he that was seated replied, 'Come and see the place', and rising and unveiling the 'sepulcre' showed them the place void of the cross and containing only the linen in which it had been wrapped. Taking up the linen and placing it on the altar the three then sang, 'The Lord is risen from the sepulcre'.

With regard to musical instruments, it is known that organs were in considerable use in the late Anglo-Saxon Church, though probably for processions and such-like occasions rather than the accompaniment of the Liturgy. Dunstan caused a fine organ to be installed at Malmesbury in honour of St Aldhelm, and the organ of St Swithun's, Winchester, was particularly impressive, requiring the services of seventy men as blowers and possessing four hundred pipes. The thunder of its music, it was said, could be heard throughout the city. It is unlikely, however, that these troublesome and expensive machines had yet been inflicted upon the ordinary parochial clergy and their congregations.

Of greater interest was polyphony. This was at first in the two-part form where note answers to note in parallel motion, known as 'organum', of which there are over a hundred and fifty examples in one of the 'Winchester Tropers'. But there was bound to be much resulting discord in this scheme, and musicians experimented with intervals other than strictly parallel ones. Thus there came about that independence of musical parts which produces 'harmony'. In this way, in the Church's service and based on the Gregorian melodies, the Western tradition of polyphony was born.

The great age of plainsong was now past, but the Gregorian chant continued to be the basis of all polyphonic composition. During the tenth and eleventh centuries the cathedrals and greater monasteries of England resounded with a sacred song of increasing complexity, in which the harmonic strains of solo voices alternated with the gentle rise and fall of the choir's traditional plain chant. It was a pleasing and cultured combination, representing a true feeling for the past along with purely creative aspirations and a love of beauty for its own sake. With the coming of the less cultivated Normans there appears to have been some decline in polyphonic singing, and a temporary return to more primitive and severe standards of ecclesiastical music.[27]

CHAPTER XXIII

THE CLOSING STAGES

On Whitsunday 973, at Bath, there occurred an event of the greatest interest both for those who witnessed it and for Englishmen of the present day. This was the coronation of an Anglo-Saxon king according to a carefully prepared liturgical order which ensured that the ceremony was spiritual rather than political in its significance. English kings had been consecrated before, the earliest instance known to us being that of Ecgfrith, who was anointed in 787 during the lifetime of his father Offa. In 796 Eadwulf was consecrated king of Northumbria in St Peter's, York. During the tenth century the church of Kingston-on-Thames, in Surrey, became particularly associated with the ceremony, and Athelstan was consecrated there in 925. But the religious rites of coronation were long somewhat informal in character, and it was not until 973 that they assumed a dignity fully liturgical in its scope. This was through the instrumentality of archbishop Dunstan.

There are three points about the 973 coronation order which especially impress our minds.[1] Firstly, it was clearly a fruit of the rich liturgical activity of the time, the work of reformed Benedictines who found interest and pleasure in the composition of forms of devotion and worship. Secondly, it expressed the concern of religious men that the increased and highly centralised power of the king, characteristic of this time, should have a spiritual sanction. Thirdly, the circumstance that the coronation of Edgar came fourteen years after the beginning of his reign, and at what appears to have been a chosen period of his life, ensured that the form was the result of a careful and scholarly preparation. Edgar was not consecrated until he was thirty years old (the canonical age for ordination to the priesthood), and it seems almost certain that the ceremony was deliberately deferred in order to emphasise its sacred character. By virtue of his anointing, in fact, the king ceased to be a layman, and became in a sense a member of the ecclesiastical order. This has been the view very commonly accepted by students of the period, but there is another possible reason, more sordid and prosaic, for the long delay in Edgar's anointing. According

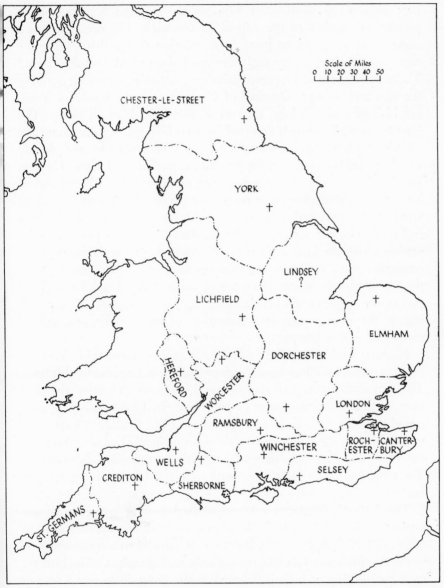

Map 3. Anglo-Saxon dioceses, *c.* 950.

to a strong tradition, his private life was immoral, and Dunstan may have hesitated to hallow him on this score.

We not only have the order itself, but a description of the proceedings by a monk of Ramsey who appears to have been personally present, the author of the *Life of St Oswald*.[2] The occasion was a magnificent one, and no hasty improvisation designed to ensure the succession such as many such services hitherto had probably been.[3] There was a great and representative congregation, including not only the two archbishops, Dunstan of Canterbury and Oswald of York, but bishops and religious, ealdormen, and officials of all kinds. The king entered the church escorted by two bishops. On reaching the altar he took off his crown which (it will be noted) he was already wearing, and lay prone on the ground during the Te Deum. He then arose and made before Dunstan a solemn oath that the Church and all his subjects should keep true peace, that greed and violence in society would be suppressed and justice and mercy maintained. Prayers followed, with the anthem 'Zadok the Priest', and the popular acclamation, 'May the king live for ever'. After this came the heart of the ceremony, the Anointing, and then the Investiture—the girding with the sword, the crowning, the grant of the sceptre. A solemn declaration of the meaning of Christian kingship followed. Next, the anointing of the queen, and the celebration of mass. The proceedings concluded with a banquet.

Nothing could more clearly illustrate than this memorable occasion the close union of Church and State prevailing in England by this time. The remarkable words of the solemn declaration, exhorting the king to stand fast in the place now given to him 'by God's authority, conferred through the bishops and other servants of God', can leave us in no doubt as to the influence of bishops in national counsels. To them the office of king appeared as something fundamentally spiritual. The king was God's vicar upon earth. He ruled by divine grace and favour.

The bishop's importance is emphasised by the insistence of the secular power in being closely associated with his appointment to office. There does not seem, however, to have been a consistent rule in the Anglo-Saxon Church, through the various stages of its history, over the election of bishops, and while the theory was that a bishop should be elected by the clergy of the church concerned, we find varying elements in the process.

At an early point in the history of the English Church we have a clear instance of direct royal action, when Cenwalh, king of Wessex, appointed Agilbert to succeed Birinus as his bishop, and then favoured

Wini, who subsequently purchased from the king of Mercia the see of London.[4] Later, after the synod of Whitby, Wilfred was elected to the northern see by the counsellors of the two Northumbrian kings, with the approval of the kings themselves and all the people; but the actual initiative came from the kings, who had asked for 'a man of worthy character, acceptable to God, and beloved by men'.[5] Next we find Oswy of Northumbria and Egbert of Kent, after conferring together on the state of ecclesiastical affairs, jointly approving the appointment of the priest Wighard to the Canterbury archbishopric, 'with the choice and assent of the English Church'.[6]

Cuthbert was elected to the bishopric of Hexham by a 'whole company', a synod held under the presidency of Theodore. But king Ecgfrith was present. He was a ruler whose character is sufficiently well known for us to be assured that his will would dominate in any matter affecting his subjects. He clearly played a prominent part in the proceedings—he seems to have personally led the deputation which sailed over to Cuthbert on his island retreat to persuade his acceptance of the appointment.[7]

Bede, in his letter to Egbert of York, with its recommendation for more bishoprics, seems to imply that king Ceolwulf will be the effective agent in bringing this to pass. The actual choice, however, of the bishop of a new see is to be left to the religious of the monastery out of which it will be formed.[8]

In short, throughout the entire Anglo-Saxon Christian period the kings, in varying manner, were very much in the picture in the matter of episcopal appointments. This was indeed inevitable, as the bishops were highly important persons socially as great landowners and as rulers of extensive dioceses. And with the growth and consolidation of the royal power in the later decades of Anglo-Saxon history, the interest of the kings in episcopal elections became more exacting and clearly defined. By the time of Cnut and Edward the Confessor the choice of bishops was a royal prerogative, and there is no evidence that this was in the least resented by even the strictest churchmen. The increasing complexities of government led to a keen appreciation of the services of clerics on the part of these two rulers. Cnut began the practice of introducing secular clergy into the court as advisers, and this was the commencement of the decline of the monks from their long history of ascendancy in the counsels of the Church. Cnut continued, however, to appoint monks to the episcopate with a single certain exception, that of the secular priest Duduc, whom he preferred to the see of Wells. During the later years of the tenth century and the earlier part of the eleventh, the episcopate consisted for the most part of men of monastic training and profession, and there was no other period when Benedictines were so prominent in the leadership of the English Church. This is a powerful testimony to the strength of the reforming tradition established by Dunstan and his colleagues.

Between 960 and 1066 there were 116 occupants of the eighteen English sees. Of these no fewer than sixty-seven are certainly known to have been monks, and only about fourteen to have been seculars, most of the latter being appointed during the reign of Edward the Confessor. It may seem paradoxical that the great lover of monks who expended such care on the building of Westminster abbey, should show this tendency to favour secular clergy, but actually he was but developing the useful and practical policy inaugurated by Cnut. About a third of the 116 bishops are unaccounted for, but Professor Knowles thinks it extremely probable that they were nearly all monks.[9] An analysis of the provenance of the monastic bishops reveals that Glastonbury and Winchester were the principal nurseries—that is, where the influence of Dunstan and Aethelwold was particularly great.

It is not difficult to understand why most of the leaders of the English Church were monks during these years. The reforming movement had been of such vigour, that although the actual number of houses founded or refounded was not large compared with the enormous proportions to which the monastic institute was to grow before many generations were passed, almost all that was intellectually best in the life of the nation had been attracted within their walls. These were the only places where anything that might be called an education was to be acquired, and they were the homes of a fine artistic activity. The court of Aethelred II was not such as to produce ecclesiastical leaders, still less the type needed to guide the people in troubled times. But in the religious houses were many potential leaders, who when promoted to sees seem to have acquitted themselves well.

Such was Aethelgar, a Glastonbury monk, who succeeded Dunstan at Canterbury. Of the seven archbishops of Canterbury between Dunstan's death in 988 and the promotion of Robert of Jumièges in 1051, all are definitely known to have been monks, five of them from Glastonbury. Other worthy examples were Aelfstan, a monk of Abingdon, who became bishop of Ramsbury in 970; and Sigegar, bishop of Wells 975–97, who had been a religious at the Old Minster in Winchester and later abbot of Glastonbury. An outstanding bishop of Sherborne was Wulfsige (992–1001), a monk of Glastonbury and abbot of Westminster, who, like other contemporary prelates, tried hard to raise the standard of the parochial clergy—now assuming a position of greater importance in the life of the nation. Amongst the great and patriotic Englishmen who were appointed to the episcopate in pre-Conquest times was Ealdred, trained at Winchester and subsequently abbot of Tavistock. He became in turn bishop of Worcester (1044) and archbishop of York (1061). He inspired and encouraged the people of his borderland diocese, suffering much from the marauding Welsh. He was of considerable help to the Confessor in the quarrel with earl Godwine which occupied so prominent a place in the latter's reign. A great traveller, he twice made the pilgrimage to Rome, and once journeyed to Jerusalem. An accomplished diplomat, he visited Germany in his country's service. A connoisseur of the fine arts, it was he who caused a pulpitum and crucifix, of German workmanship, to be erected at Beverley.[10]

The tendency of modern scholarship is towards clearing the later Old English bishops of the indifferent character formerly attributed to them. Stubbs could write that 'amongst the prelates of this era there are very few except S. Wulfstan who are spoken of with honour', and besides accepting their supposed pluralism almost as a commonplace actually attributed it to the difficulty of finding suitable candidates for episcopal office.[11] It was long taken for granted that their standards were low, and that they were in particular much addicted to pluralism and simony.[12] But although unworthy prelates undoubtedly existed, the Anglo-Saxon episcopate as a whole has been vindicated.[13] Pluralism there certainly was, but nearly always for a legitimate cause. The frequency with which the sees of Worcester and York were held together is an obvious instance; but York was a poor see, having suffered much from Danish harryings, and it was necessary to supplement its revenues by those of the small but wealthy see of the relatively untroubled west midlands. Even the blameless Dunstan had no compunction in holding two sees in conjunction for a while (Worcester and London 959–60). More than a century previously, in Germany, after the sack of Hamburg in 845 by the Danes, the see of that city was in such poor straits that it came to be united with Bremen. The plan had been opposed by the more scrupulous churchmen, including the bishop concerned, St Anskar, but it had the papal approval. At the close of the Anglo-Saxon period Stigand retained his bishopric of Winchester on becoming primate in 1052. Admittedly he was a dubious character. But Alexander II and his successors also held on to their previous sees after attaining the papacy. In 1066 Stigand was actually the only pluralist holding episcopal office in the English Church. Exact scholarship has also revealed little evidence of simony, and in the year of the Conquest England was free of it.

Another important subject concerning which misconceptions have been held is the relationship in later Anglo-Saxon England between the English Church and Rome. It was once almost assumed in some circles that in some sort of way, never clearly specified, this country was independent of the papacy, which reimposed its unwelcome yoke with the coming of William and his Norman churchmen. If anything, the very opposite is closer to the truth. Whereas, as we shall see in the following chapter, William and Lanfranc did to some extent pursue a path free of papal interference, the ties in pre-Conquest days were especially close. Peter's pence was strictly enforced by English monarchs. There was a constant traffic between England and Rome. The archbishops of Canterbury regularly went to collect the pallium.

In the eighth century it had been the practice for the pallium to be sent direct from Rome, but by 927 the custom was established whereby the archbishops of Canterbury went for it in person.[14] This involved long, expensive, and even dangerous journeys. Aelfsige, archbishop-elect of Canterbury, died crossing the Alps in 959. Most of the tenth-and early eleventh-century primates are, however, known to have made the journey, though not (it may be) without protest. It is possible that Wulfstan was the author of a letter from the English bishops complaining to the pope about the immense labour of the journey, and demanding the non-payment of fees in connection with it.[15]

We need not suppose that such protests stood alone, and there was doubtless considerable annoyance from time to time over the requirements of Rome. But a fundamental loyalty existed, and no English churchmen would have denied their communion with the Roman Church, presided over by the pope. Indeed, there is precise evidence, though for the final decade or two when continental connections were unusually strong, that the higher English clergy took an active part in the councils of the Western Church. The council of Rheims in 1049 convened by Leo IX was attended by Duduc, bishop of Wells, Wulfric, abbot of St Augustine's, and Aelfwine, abbot of Ramsey. The council of Rome in the following year had as English delegates Herman, bishop of Ramsbury and Ealdred, bishop of Worcester. In the same year Ulf, bishop of Dorchester, went to the council of Vercelli. And when in 1049–50 the see of Crediton was removed to Exeter, bishop Leofric and king Edward thought it necessary first to obtain papal consent.

The bishops played a prominent part in the work of secular government, and it was by virtue of their office that they sat in the witenagemot. In the legal and administrative fields, the boundaries between Church and State were vaguely drawn. The Church was not allowed to become an ecclesiastical preserve, whilst on the other hand the advice and guidance of churchmen were welcome in the management of worldly affairs. Both the shire and hundred courts dealt with ecclesiastical as well as secular business, while the Old English State, particularly in its later stages, was active in promoting ecclesiastical legislation.

At no point in Anglo-Saxon history would it have been possible to speak of two distinct spheres, secular and ecclesiastical, in the matter of deliberative assemblies. Ethelbert promulgated his law-code, which included provision for the protection of the Church, with the advice of his counsellors.[16] Edwin convened his witan to discuss the abandonment of paganism and the adoption of Christianity.[17] Wulfhere, son of Penda, endowed the monastery of Medeshamstede with the counsel of his nobles.[18] Here we have what appear to be secular assemblies treating of matters which concern the Church.

From about the middle of the seventh century a distinctively ecclesiastical type of assembly makes its appearance in England. Thus, the Whitby conference consisted only of churchmen, though it was presided over by the king.[19] The Hertford synod was purely ecclesiastical—'a council of bishops and many other Church teachers' gathered to discuss the necessary business of the Church, in accordance with the ancient canons.[20] The Hatfield assembly a few years later was also one which consisted of bishops and teachers, met to refute the heresy of Eutyches.[21] But a general witenagemot was held at Hatfield at about the same time,[22] and it may be that the theological discussion was part of a wider assembly. The West Saxon synod referred to in Willibald's *Life of St Boniface* in connection with the saint's early career is purely ecclesiastical.[23]

In the eighth and early ninth centuries, during the period of Mercian ascendancy, there was a series of ecclesiastical councils in which laymen played some part. Thus in 781 a synod was held at Brentford under the presidency of Jaenbert, archbishop of Canterbury and Heathured, bishop of Worcester, to consider a dispute with king Offa concerning some estates. It was attended not only by several bishops, but by the king himself and a number of ealdormen.[24] In 798 Aethelheard, archbishop of Canterbury, summoned to a Cloveshoe synod all the provincial bishops, abbots, and ealdormen, to discuss the belief and practice of the Catholic religion.[25] Again, at the councils of Cloveshoe 747 and Chelsea 816 the clergy of the Canterbury province dealt with matters of ecclesiastical significance, though on both occasions in the presence of the king of Mercia and his chief nobles.[26]

Thus far it is clear that though there was never a clear line between church synods and meetings of the witan, or king's council, there were occasions when the spiritual interest was dominant and at times even exclusive. But the Danish wars of the ninth century led to a new departure. In the tenth and eleventh centuries the meetings of the witan were larger, more comprehensive, and more formal affairs than previously. The higher clergy and principal nobles always attended. There was no need for distinctively ecclesiastical councils, as the king's council was now fully competent and prepared to deal with any kind of business, spiritual or secular. Certainly there was nothing in the last decades of the Old English Church to compare with the great ecclesiastical synods to be held by Lanfranc. But the idea that the absence of national ecclesiastical synods is a sign of decadence, or episcopal laziness, in the Old English Church fails to take account of that close interdependence of Church and State, of that intermingling of their interests, which was highly characteristic of this time, and which has much to commend it.

Diocesan synods, however, were apparently a feature of later Anglo-Saxon church life, and were important as the only practical means by which a bishop could declare his policy at regular intervals to the clergy of his diocese. According to the collection of ecclesiastical rules known as the 'Canons of Edgar', which was the work of archbishop Wulfstan, a parish priest was required to attend the diocesan synod, taking with him his clerk and servant, along with provisions enough for three days.[27]

The now familiar arrangement by which a diocese, for purposes of administrative convenience, is divided into archdeaconries and subdivided into rural deaneries, was really a development of post-Conquest times. There is little evidence of it in the Anglo-Saxon Church.

The office of archdeacon in itself is ancient, and indeed can be traced back to 311, when Caecilianus, archdeacon of Carthage, was promoted to the bishopric of the same church. In these early times the archdeacon appears as the bishop's chief administrative officer, with a close knowledge of the affairs of the diocese. But it was only gradually that the office acquired a territorial connotation. Towards the close of the ninth century, in the metropolitical diocese of Rheims, we find Hincmar addressing diocesan regulations to two archdeacons, who apparently have specified areas. About the mid-tenth century we find three archdeacons in the diocese of Tours. From then onwards in France until the thirteenth century there was a steady development of the archidiaconal system.

In England the office of archdeacon was known at least as early as the beginning of the ninth century.[28] Thus Wulfred, who became archbishop of Canterbury in 805, was archdeacon to his predecessor Aethelheard. He is the first known English archdeacon. Canterbury charters of 830 and c. 850 contain the names of two archdeacons Cyneheard and Dunning, and archbishop Ceolnoth (833–70) apparently had a group of four to help him in the administration of his diocese. There is also evidence of an archdeacon of Rochester in 889.[29] After this there seems to be little trace of the archidiaconal office until the primacy of Aelfheah (1005–12). The homilist Aelfric, moreover, who was writing about this time, was familiar with the office—at least so it would appear from the way he describes St Lawrence as archdeacon to pope Sixtus.[30] A few years earlier the Blickling Homilies referred to those in 'exalted positions subject to God, as bishops, kings, mass-priests, and archdeacons'.[31] Towards the middle of the eleventh century, in the York diocese, priests who are defiant of the archdeacon's summons are fined.[32] Canterbury and York, of course, were wholly exceptional in that their bishops, as metropolitans, would be more likely than others to need assistance in the management of their dioceses.[33]

There is no evidence of rural deans in the Anglo-Saxon Church, but in view of the importance which the office acquired later in this country, it is interesting to notice Hincmar, archbishop of Rheims, addressing his archdeacons in 877 about vacant deaneries. In Italy the office of archpriest was important, and in France we find the metropolitical diocese of Lyons divided into twenty-four *archiprêtrés*, though it is likely that this office was something between those of archdeacon and rural dean as understood subsequently in England.

Probably the office of rural dean had originally some connection with the early monastic use of the term *decanus* to denote a monk set over a group of ten. It would be natural enough for a local group of parish priests to have one of their number as administrative leader or at any rate to represent them in dealings with the bishop. In later centuries it was a characteristic function of the rural dean to visit the cathedral church during Holy Week, and there collect the holy oils for his clergy. We find Raoul, archbishop of Bourges, as early as the mid-ninth century ordering that a priest should be selected out of every ten for this purpose. Naturally, a local group of parishes might consist in practice of anything from half a dozen to about twenty.

In 889 Ricou, bishop of Soissons, ordered the holding of ruridecanal *kalends*, early in each month, for general discussion on matters of common concern to parish priests. We can see in such provisions the germ of the ruridecanal chapter, or its equivalent, as it has probably existed in the Church of almost any country, and it may be confidently believed that the Old English clergy had their arrangements for meeting together locally.[34]

Our knowledge of cathedral capitular bodies and their development in Anglo-Saxon England is slight. At Hippo, St Augustine had introduced a communal life for his clergy at the end of the fourth century, though his austere discipline and time-table was found by experience to be unsuitable for the rigorous conditions of northern Europe. None the less, the uncertainty of life in the sixth and seventh centuries made an amount of corporate living a practical necessity, and this was the usual arrangement in Gaul and Spain. There were two types of communal life for clerks, the 'canonical' and the 'regular', and in 755 at Verne an attempt was made to compel all clergy to adopt either one or the other, that is, life as a member of an extended episcopal *familia* under rule or life in a monastery. Quite shortly afterwards, Chrodegang, bishop of Metz and a former pupil of Boniface, followed the practice of many contemporary bishops by compiling a rule for his clergy.

To make his rule a practical possibility Chrodegang built near his cathedral of St Stephen the various offices required for a life in common, such as the dormitory, refectory, and cloister. The cathedral clergy were to be regular at the Hours and obedient to the bishop. They were normally to sleep in the dormitory, and after compline there must be silence. All clergy were required to attend daily chapter, and to confess at least twice a year to the bishop. There were two meals taken daily in the refectory, the canons serving the tables in turn.

Benedictine influence is apparent in these provisions, but there is a significant, a monk would say a fatal, divergence. A canon may retain the offerings made to him in respect of his priestly services, unless earmarked for the community. On his death his property must pass to the church or to the poor.

This rule became widely popular in Lorraine and elsewhere, and was endorsed and reinforced by the decrees of the council of Aachen in 817. From this time onwards a strong effort was made to enforce the common life upon cathedral clergy, but there was a tendency for the canons, taking advantage of Chrodegang's important saving clause, to live in their own houses and acquire property. In the course of the tenth and eleventh centuries much of the common endowment came to be divided up into separate portions or prebends, whose owners were styled 'secular' canons. There is little evidence, however, to show that this separate prebendal system was adopted in England before the Conquest. It was the constitutional reforms of St Osmund c. 1090 which marked the true beginnings of the English secular cathedral system, with which the saint's church of Old Sarum was associated in the earlier stages, along with the cathedrals of York and Lincoln.

Augustine had introduced the communal life for his clerks at Christchurch, Canterbury, though whether this was monastic or not remains uncertain. When sees were founded in 601 and 604 at London and Rochester respectively, arrangements were made for a common dormitory and refectory. Throughout the years which followed,[35] the common life was considered the proper one for cathedral clergy, though by the close of the eighth century private property for the senior clergy was known at many English greater churches. It was doubtless in reaction to this tendency that archbishop Wulfred introduced at Canterbury the communal life c. 813, trying to enforce upon his *familia* the legatine decree of 786. His clergy were made to promise to eat and sleep in common. They were not deprived altogether of their private houses, of which, however, they can clearly have made but little use.

It appears that during the reign of the Confessor there may have been a strong movement towards the establishment of collegiate churches in England, and at the time of the Conquest there were several secular 'colleges'. The three outstanding examples of this class of church were Beverley, Ripon, and Southwell, which came to assume a quasi-cathedral status within the diocese of York. At Durham the cathedral was served by secular canons from its foundation in 995 until they were replaced by Benedictines in 1083. Earl Harold founded a collegiate church at Waltham, Essex, dedicated to the Holy Cross in 1060 and intended primarily as a centre of education. A number of houses previously monastic were collegiate in 1066. Of such were Wimborne, Taunton, South Malling, and Launceston. St Guthlac, Hereford, was a pre-Conquest college of canons, and Stafford St Mary had thirteen canons at the time of the Domesday survey. St Martin-le-Grand, London, became collegiate in 1068. At St German's, Cornwall, which had been the centre of a bishopric for several years until it became a joint-see with Crediton in 1042, the collegiate system was introduced c. 1050. About the same time bishop Leofric removed the see from Crediton to Exeter, where he built a refectory and dormitory and presented a copy of the rule of Chrodegang to the canons. Ten years later bishop Giso introduced the common life at Wells, though when Bath became the cathedral after the Conquest the prebendal system was adopted at Wells.

We have a general impression of the Church as it existed c. 1000 prominent in the leadership of the nation, and well equipped to perform its tasks. Its organisation was flexible, and still far removed from that machine-like efficiency which in the long run was to contribute to the downfall of the medieval Church in this country. The prestige of the monasteries was high, though they had by this time handed over many of their former functions to the local secular clergy. The monasteries were an increasingly wealthy institution, and great houses such as Ramsey, Ely, and Abingdon were in a flourishing state. But the parish priest and his church had become the backbone of Christian life and worship amongst the ordinary folk. The English Church was firmly established wherever there were people to be served. The diffusion and localisation of the Church had the important result that the second great wave of Danish assaults could not shake its position, as it had done to a dangerous degree when in an earlier period the forces of Christianity tended to be concentrated in monastic centres. The monasteries had been effective strongholds against a spiritual enemy, the old Germanic heathenism, but they were an easy prey for a hostile plunderer. But in the tenth century, largely because of the parochial system, the Church was much closer to the people, and its teachings were interwoven with the national life. The Church in England was by this time a venerable institution. The missionary phase had long since passed. Englishmen had themselves taken the Faith to the Continent, and were now contributing or about to contribute powerfully to the conversion of Scandinavia.

But though by 1000 Christianity in England had become a great tradition, such as to evoke the admiration of many contemporaries abroad, there was a continued survival of heathen ideas and practices, which four centuries of Christian teaching had failed to eradicate completely. These ideas received a reinforcement with the coming of the Northmen, the most stubbornly heathen of all European peoples. The task of the Christian priest must often have been a hard one, as he tried to enforce the precepts of the Gospel against the immemorial traditions and thought-forms of a Teutonic people.

Heathen practice and mentality never entirely died out, and indeed Gregory in his instructions to Augustine had advised him to adapt the pre-Christian customs rather than extirpate them. It has been argued that heathenism would have died more rapidly if the English had at the outset been ordered to break with it completely.[36] But this is very doubtful. Such a policy would have entailed a large measure of compulsion, and the natural reaction might well have been long and strenuous opposition to the Faith such as was later encountered by missionaries in continental Saxony and in Scandinavia. That such tendencies were latent in England is clear from the grudging reception accorded to the Gospel in Essex. A programme of extirpation, root and branch, of everything pertaining to the old religion, would quite possibly have had the effect of rekindling an enthusiasm for Woden and Thunor which was perceptibly on the decline.

Amongst various forms of popular belief which survived were such as included nightmares, dwarfs who worried the sick, and demons. Witches and wizards had power to raise storms. Thus Bede tells how Germanus and Lupus, bishops of Auxerre and Troyes, on their visit to Britain met a host of demons who stirred up the natural elements; Germanus invoked the name of the Trinity, and there was calm.[37] More than five centuries following this visit, Cnut denounced superstition: 'We forbid earnestly every heathenship . . . that is, that a man reverence heathen gods, and the sun and moon, fire and flood, water-wylls or stones, or trees of the wood of any sort; or love witchcraft, or perform bad underhand work in any wise; either by way of sacrifice or divining. . . .'[38] If it be thought that the Danish king only had in mind heathenism introduced by his own countrymen, and that the native Saxons were free of it, one may turn to the pages of his near contemporary Aelfric, the homilist monk who lived and wrote in Wessex. In an interesting sermon on Auguries,[39] he condemns those who trust in signs from birds and horses, dogs and sneezings. The Christian should not inquire from witches concerning his health, who teach him to make offerings to trees, stones, and springs. Women are enjoined to stay away from cross-roads, whither they resort to commit themselves and their children to the devil. In his *Catholic Homilies* Aelfric condemns those who resort for their health's sake to enchantments and witchcraft, stones and trees.[40] He warns his audience against what may well have been a common practice, the sin of cursing other folk.

He tells of a woman who connived with the devil to curse her own son. She went to the church, where she let her hair down into the font, and cursed all her children. When she returned home she found them suffering dreadful agonies in every limb. Overcome with terror, she went and hanged herself.[41]

Aelfric also refers to an idea which was apparently abroad in excuse of evil-doing, that this can be attributed to 'destiny' (*gewyrd*). On the contrary, he protests, nothing takes place by destiny, but by the doom of God.[42]

In connection with Aelfric's references to superstition, a glance at the region where the *Homilies* and *Lives* were written, or any rate begun, may be helpful. No one familiar with the remote upland country around Cerne in Dorset, with its brooding and mysterious hills south of the Blackmoor Vale, will doubt that many of the old practices lingered here. It is a conservative region. There is too the Cerne giant, in his unspeakable crudity, carved in the chalk of Trendle hill overlooking the abbey. His presence may postulate the existence of a thriving heathen cult in the Cerne district; or perhaps he was put there by those loath to part with their heathenism—an aggressive defiance of the new religion, with its insistence on sexual moderation (a hard gospel for the Saxons). How this beastly creature survived centuries of Christian domination in the neighbourhood is a mystery.

Either he is really post-medieval, or paganism must have lingered here stubbornly despite the proximity of the abbey.

To a great extent the Church had to come to terms with the old heathenism, and this is very apparent in connection with charms and the prescriptions of the healing art.[43] Thus to cure your cattle sing the Tersanctus over them every evening; take four two-edged sticks, and write on each edge of either stick the paternoster, then let the sticks fall to the floor.[44] To recover stolen cattle say: 'Bethlehem was hight the borough, wherein Christ was born: it is famed over all earth. So may this deed be in sight of men notorious, per crucem Christi.' Then pray three times to the east, and say thrice, 'May the cross of Christ bring it back from the east'; and turn to the west, and say, 'May the cross of Christ bring it back from the west'; and to the south, and say thrice, 'May the cross of Christ bring it back from the south'; and to the north, and say, 'The cross of Christ was hidden and has been found. The Jews hanged Christ, they did to him the worst of deeds; they concealed what they were not able to conceal. So never may this deed become concealed. Per crucem Christi.'[45]

Again, a lengthy charm against bewitched land includes the singing of four masses on the land itself, and the recitation of the Tersanctus, Benedicite, and Magnificat, that the land may be fortified against fiends and sorceries. After the elaborate ceremonies, a plough shall be driven forward, to the accompaniment of the verses:

> Hail to thee, mother earth
> Mortals maintaining;
> Be growing and fertile
> By the goodness of God,
> Filled with fodder
> Our folk to feed.[46]

Some of the cures prescribed for sundry ailments are a mixture of what may well be good natural remedies, and plain superstition. For ulcers on the face, a ram's lung should be carved up in small pieces and applied to the sores. In the *Leech Book*[47] we have a compendious effort to prescribe something for every type of complaint. The magical element of Christianity is evident, for example, in a complicated cure prescribed for a man possessed by a devil; the compounded drink is to be consumed by the patient from a church bell, and masses and prayers are to be said.[48] A useful precaution against an evil rune or a man full of elvish tricks is to make a compound of blackberry, lupins, and pulegium, and place it beneath the altar where nine masses will be sung; the dust is to be placed into milk, into which holy water will be dripped, and the resultant medicine administered at intervals during the day.[49]

For a fever, one will write upon the eucharistic paten the name of God, wash it with holy water into the patient's drink, and say the creed, paternoster, and Beati immaculati.[50] A laconic cure is laid down for a lunatic. Make a whip of porpoise skin, and flog the man. 'Soon he will be well. Amen.'[51]

In all this there is a mingling of crude common sense, such medical science as existed at the time, Christian belief, and heathen superstition. We see a people slowly groping its way to a solution of the manifold problems which face men in daily life. The Church tries to make its impact. No doubt the priests are at heart as superstitious and credulous as their parishioners. But despite all, a lofty element has been brought into men's lives such as their heathen forefathers had not known. There is no denying the pure Christianity of such verses as the following:

> Holy prayer, and pure love
> Of God and man, and almsgiving, and great trust
> In thy Saviour, that will erase
> Thy sins, and likewise many other
> Good works adorn and bring
> The upright soul to rest
> In heavenly happiness.[52]

There were two ways by which it might be possible to diminish and perhaps finally overcome heathen belief and custom—education, and the pastoral ministrations of parochial clergy. Of the first in later Anglo-Saxon England little is known, though it is clear that efforts were made in at least some places to bring up children in the fear and nurture of the Lord by means of schools. Dunstan had scholars around him at Glastonbury, and Aethelwold himself joined in the teaching work of the school in his abbey at Winchester. The curriculum of these monastic schools of the tenth century would include Latin; it was probably for young pupils that Aelfric wrote a *Latin Grammar* and *Colloquy*. Arithmetic and astronomy would be taught, if only for practical purposes in connection with the Church's calendar, along with the principles of music. The value of monastic schools was publicly recognised, and when Cnut visited any notable monastery or town it was his practice to pay for boys to be educated there for the priesthood, including promising boys from the poorer classes.[53]

But the only education available for most young scholars was such as might be obtained from the parish clergy. On the Continent Theodulf, bishop of Orleans, had decreed that every mass-priest must keep a school, and all priests in England were expected to be diligent in the instruction of the young.[54] The teaching office of priests is emphasised in the laws of Edgar, where it is enacted that priests must instruct young people, both in the fundamental beliefs of Christianity and in handicrafts.[55] Later, c. 994, it was enjoined in council that priests should keep schools in their villages, and teach small boys without fee.[56]

It is doubtful whether the parochial clergy were ever really able to offer much to their parishioners in the way of letters and education. But it was not only to them in their teaching and preaching capacity, but as dispensers of the sacraments, that the people now looked for guidance and help in their daily perplexities. It was the noble vocation of this class of men 'through the innocence of their lives to set a good example'.[57] The influence which must have been exerted upon the English people in the course of the tenth and eleventh centuries by these unchronicled men was surely immense. Little is known about them, but without their ill-rewarded labours there could scarcely have been a Church to offer a glittering field of opportunity to the ambitious and famous, prelates and the like, with whose doings history has been much occupied.

In 978 Aethelred became king, shortly after the murder of his brother Edward at Corfe. His reign covered a calamitous period in Anglo-Saxon history. Within a year or two of his accession Scandinavian raiders were again troubling England, the south-western counties especially suffering. After a few years' respite, these counties were again the object of attack in 988. The situation was not serious, however, and the Danes met with a brave and effective resistance.

But in 991 calamities began. An organised army invaded England, and the king bought them off with a large sum of money, the beginning of the practice of Danegeld which was to prove so fatal during the next few years. Some of the king's subjects refused to submit so tamely, and in the summer of the same year the men of Essex resisted the invaders in the battle of Maldon, the subject of a memorable Old

English poem. The attacks continued, and gathered in force so alarmingly that many English nobles began to despair of successful resistance, and seemed willing to accept Swegn Forkbeard, the Danish leader, as king.[58] But Swegn fortunately returned to Denmark. The other Scandinavian leader, Olav Trygvason, was made a confirmed Christian by Aelfheah, bishop of Winchester, at Andover, with king Aethelred his sponsor. This young viking, famous in the history of Scandinavia, solemnly promised to depart and trouble England no more. He kept his promise, returned to his native Norway, where he became king in the following year, and devoted the remaining few years of his life to the forcible Christianisation of his subjects.

After two years Danish raiders were back in England, in greater strength than ever before, and there followed several years of misery and devastations for the southern counties. The English fighting-men gave evidence that they were as brave as their ancestors. But they were up against adversaries who now had the reputation of being the finest warriors of Europe. The English, moreover, were led by a king of unparalleled weakness and indecision. Aethelred lost his head, and ordered a general massacre of Danes settled in England, for St Brice's day, 13 November 1002. It is clear that many Danes suffered in this senseless crime, and amongst the victims was Gunnhild, sister of Swegn, who had been left behind as a hostage.[59]

The result was a series of invasions of England by Swegn. In 1003 Exeter was taken and Wessex was overrun. In 1004 Norwich was pillaged. The invaders had a setback in 1005 and returned to Denmark. In 1006 they were back again, creating havoc in Kent, and raiding as far as Wiltshire. After leaving England alone for two years, the Danes returned in 1009 with their most formidable army so far. In little more than a year they ravaged no fewer than fifteen counties. By the end of 1011 they were again devastating Kent, and it is to this phase that we turn for the famous martyrdom of Aelfheah, the prelate who had confirmed Olav Trygvason and was now archbishop of Canterbury. His tragic murder by the Danes in 1012 was a reminder, if any were needed, that the viking spirit in all its bestiality was still alive. Weary of waiting for a promised Danegeld, the Danes captured Canterbury and carried off a number of hostages, including Aelfheah and Godwine bishop of Rochester. Before they could be released, a mob of drunken Danes dragged the primate before them on Palm Sunday, and cudgelled him to death with the bones of the animals on which they had been feasting.

His crime was his refusal to take tribute from his tenants to provide a ransom for himself. It is fair to remember that this deed was done without the knowledge of the Danish leaders, who realised the enormity of the crime and made some atonement by handing back the archbishop's body for Christian burial in London. In due course the remains of Aelfheah (St Alphege) were reverently transferred by Cnut to Canterbury.[60]

By 1013 the capacity of the English for resistance was at an end. Evidently realising that England was his for the asking, Swegn Forkbeard landed in that year and before long was uncrowned king. Aethelred II, the ruler who had so miserably failed his people, fled to Normandy.

Swegn, however, died suddenly at Gainsborough in February 1014, and Aethelred was invited by his nobles to return to England, which he duly did. In 1015 Cnut, Swegn's son, landed, and it was in the midst of a struggle between him and Aethelred's son Edmund that Aethelred died, on 23 April 1016. For some months Edmund fought on bravely, but was completely defeated at Ashingdon in Essex, and died soon afterwards on 30 November 1016. Cnut was now undisputed king.

There can be no doubt about the demoralisation of the English during the first few years of the eleventh century, a process which was helped by the feebleness of the king and the defeatism of many of the nobles. The prevailing fear is plainly mirrored in the contemporary legal codes, which bear the impression of a 'recall to religion'. There were many who seem to have seen in a closer attention to religious duties the answer to the crisis, and who regarded the depredations of the Danes as a divine punishment for national sin. The famous homily of Wulfstan, *Sermo Lupi ad Anglos* written in 1014, proclaims the doctrine of the 'judgement of God' for flagrant neglect of his laws—a doctrine which has been heard from more recent prophets in this country in connection with national disaster. Archbishop Wulfstan saw his people as 'completely defeated and greatly disheartened'. The invaders, he says, are now so strong that one of them is frequently worth ten Englishmen in open fight. But the English have brought it on themselves. Sin and wrongdoing have been rampant throughout the land. Many men are guilty of disloyalty—to Church, to the State, to their lord. The clergy have not received due respect. For many years there has been injustice and treachery amongst men. The slave traffic has got out of hand, many Christian folk being sold out of the country.

Even the father has sold his son for a price, and the son his mother. There is a widespread neglect of fasts and festivals. Things have come to such a pass that men are more ashamed of good works than of evil, so much is sin the fashion. Wulfstan recalls the strictures of Gildas against his fellow-Britons centuries before, and how in those days God in his anger had allowed the English to conquer the land. This had come about through the sin of the people, the tyranny of the ruling class, and the indolence of the clergy. Let the English take warning. Let them turn from wrongdoing and follow God's laws. In particular, let them recover the old sense of loyalty to one another, and turn away from that deceitfulness and oath-breaking which according to the homily was a shocking feature of the time.[61]

There are strong traces of Wulfstan's influence in Aethelred's legal codes, which have a markedly ecclesiastical character. Thus the legislation of 1008[62] orders the cessation of heathen practices, and insists on right living on the part of the clergy. Laymen are not to barter churches like so much property, and a parish priest cannot be dismissed save by the bishop's consent. Church dues are to be maintained, including Peter's pence. Sunday and other holy-days, especially festivals of St Mary and of the apostles, are to be rightly observed. Perhaps the most interesting enactment of this code is that which orders the observance of 18 March as a feast-day in honour of St Edward the Martyr. This looks very much like an act of contrition on Aethelred's part. The military disasters of his reign perhaps stirred him to a sense of guilt for the murder of his half-brother. The code also decrees that a widow remain unmarried for at least a year, that every Christian cultivate the habit of frequent confession and communion, and that sin in all its varieties (with the familiar warning against gluttony and drunkenness) be avoided.

The 1008 code, however, is not solely ecclesiastical in its scope. There are secular enactments relating to the equipment of ships, along with warnings against desertion from the army. This double emphasis on religious and military measures is interesting and significant, a clear pointer to the state of affairs in England at the time, when in their desperation men turned alternately to the sword and the altar.[63]

In the following year another code was issued, prescribing a distinctly spiritual remedy for the national troubles.[64] The whole of the English people must come as one man before God in prayer and penitence. A national fast of three days is proclaimed. Every man is to make his confession, barefoot in church. Even slaves are freed from work for this period, so that they might join in the act of penitence. In every minster church the whole community are to sing the psalter through in the course of the three days, and they are to celebrate masses with special intention against the heathen. Every priest is to say mass for the king and all the people.

This was in 1009, when the Danes had returned after a respite with their most powerful army so far. If the great call to prayer was faithfully heeded, there can seldom have been a more impressive and concerted move towards God on the part of the English people. But outwardly at least it was to no avail, and it was followed by a wholesale devastation of well-nigh half England. Another code, in 1014, did not repeat the experiment of 'days of prayer', though it was wholly ecclesiastical in its scope. In this legislation,[65] emphasis was laid upon the right of sanctuary of the churches. Clerical marriage was strongly criticised, though apparently not forbidden. Priests were warned against serving as combatants in the army. Monks were enjoined to be stricter than hitherto in the observance of their rule. The most interesting features of this 1014 code are its enunciation of the doctrine that the king is Christ's vicar upon earth, and its pointed praise of former rulers—Athelstan, Edmund, and Edgar. These kings honoured God and observed his law. One seems to see the finger of the moralist Wulfstan in this, now pointing at none other than king Aethelred himself, at this time back amongst his people by sufferance of the nobles and fast approaching the end of his wretched reign.

The prayers of the English were to be answered in a way which they can scarcely have imagined. In the son of Swegn Forkbeard, who was accepted by the West Saxons as their king after the death of Edmund Ironside towards the close of 1016, they found a strong ruler who raised their humiliated country to a position of remarkable respect in the North and who championed the Church to an extent which made him the darling of ecclesiastics.

Cnut, born and reared in heathenism, in the enthusiasm of youth adopted Christianity, for which religion he had an undoubted admiration and awe. From the outset of his reign he was fully co-operative with the Church, and set himself to recall the English to that sense of religious duty which they seem largely to have lost during the recent wars. Certainly, the inherent viking died hard in him. At the beginning of his reign he ruthlessly executed without trial a number of Englishmen likely to stand in his way, including Eadwig, a son of Aethelred. He stood lightly to Christian views on marriage, and openly regarded two women as his wives at the same time, Aelfgifu and Emma of Normandy.

His legal code, in many respects representing the greatest piece of Old English legislation, deals both with ecclesiastical and secular matters.[66] It insists on the typically English attitude of respect to the king as God's servant. Ecclesiastical persons must keep their rule, and Christian conduct is to be observed by all. The code is not very original, and draws much on previous legislation. Amongst the new matter, however, is an enactment that 19 May is to be observed as the feast-day of St Dunstan. The ecclesiastical part of the code has a homiletical flavour, and like the legislation issued under the name of Aethelred, bears the impress of archbishop Wulfstan's style.

Of probably greater interest are the two letters of Cnut, written in 1020 and 1027 respectively.[67] Both reveal a genuinely religious tone, and a concern on Cnut's part to rule as a Christian king. The first, addressed from Denmark to the English archbishops and bishops, earls, and all the people, shows considerable respect for the clergy and their admonitions. The king promises to keep God's law faithfully. The Sunday festival is to be observed by cessation from trading activities and secular public gatherings, from Saturday noon until dawn on Monday.[68] All men must attend church. Wizards and sorceresses are to be avoided. The second letter was the result of a pilgrimage which the king made to Rome in 1027,[69] where he was present at the coronation of the emperor Conrad II. Writing to his subjects, Cnut was able to announce two sets of advantages which he had managed to obtain on their behalf. From the emperor and from Rudolf king of Burgundy, who was also present, concessions in the matter of tolls were secured for English and Danish pilgrims and merchants on their way to Rome. From the pope, Cnut obtained an undertaking that English archbishops visiting Rome to collect their pallia would not be oppressed in future by exhorbitant demands for fees. In this second letter Cnut declared his personal resolve to forsake the sins of his youth and amend his life. He closed the letter with a strong warning that those who had not paid all their church dues by the time he arrived home must expect severe punishment.

A feature of the reign was the development of a prosperous commerce between England and Denmark, which together with Norway formed a loosely-knit maritime empire. Church-dedications such as St Clement Danes and St Olave Hart Street[70] indicate the existence, probably from about this time, of Danish parishes in London, now growing into considerable importance as a commercial city, though Cnut continued to use Winchester as his capital.

The young king was a benefactor and supporter of monasteries, such as the abbey of St Bene't at Hulme, Norfolk, a refounded house which had perished at the hands of the Danes in 870. In 1020 some monks were sent from St Bene't to colonise Bury St Edmunds, a house raised in honour of the martyred king, whose cult greatly attracted the converted Danes. Cnut was anxious to atone for his heathen youth and the deeds of his viking forefathers. Visiting Glastonbury, he made an offering at the tomb of his brave adversary Edmund Ironside. The monastic chroniclers were to write well of the Danish king, and doubt-less many of the religious shared the sentiments of the Ely monks, who according to the pleasing and well-loved story rejoiced at his approach.[71] Cnut continued the practice of his predecessors in appointing monks to the episcopate, and Duduc of Wells seems to have been the only secular raised to the episcopate during this reign. On the whole, the monasteries had weathered the storm of the Danish wars very well, and it appears that the only houses which passed out of existence during this troubled time were Exeter and Bedford. On the other hand, there was little founding of new houses during Cnut's reign, apart from Hulme and Bury St Edmunds. Of smaller houses which may have come into existence about this time the most interesting is Abbotsbury on the Dorset coast. Its founder was Orc, one of Cnut's followers. In the course of his reign Cnut leaned heavily for advice on his primate, Aethelnoth, who had been a Glastonbury monk—called 'the Good' by Florence of Worcester.[72]

At the regrettably early age of forty Cnut died in 1035 at Shaftes-bury, and was interred in the Old Minster at Winchester. He was succeeded by two worthless sons whose reigns were mercifully brief, Harold Harefoot (1035–40) and Harthacnut (1040–42). The latter died at Lambeth during a wedding-feast, 'as he stood drinking', and was succeeded by Edward the Confessor, son of Aethelred II.

Edward was consecrated in Winchester cathedral on Easter day 1043. Of mainly foreign upbringing, he had been absent from England for a quarter of a century, and as king he quickened the renewed sense of contact with continental countries which had been evident in the reign of Cnut. The secular priest Duduc favoured by Cnut was a Lotharingian, and three other Lotharingian Germans are known to have been presented to English bishoprics during the two reigns. Edward proceeded to introduce Normans into important offices, though it is wrong to assume that they came to outnumber native Englishmen in the appointments of Church and State. Edward's court was actually more Scandinavian than Norman.

In 1044 Edward appointed Robert, abbot of Jumièges, to the see of London. Five years later another Norman, Ulf, became bishop of Dorchester. In 1051 Robert was promoted to Canterbury, and a Norman William succeeded him at London. But in this year there was a patriotic resurgence led by the most powerful of the nobles, earl Godwine, who challenged the king. As a result, Robert and Ulf were expelled from England. The situation was largely saved for Edward by the intervention of Leofric of Mercia and Siward of Northumbria, Godwine's rival earls. Edward banished Godwine and his family, acting with the ruthlessness which he could assume when aroused. His queen Edith, Godwine's daughter, was not allowed to escape the disgrace of her house. She was dismissed from court to the Hampshire nunnery of Wherwell—a truly vindictive and spiteful deed.

Robert was succeeded at Canterbury by Stigand, bishop of Winchester, which from the viewpoint of canon law was wholly irregular. Stigand was excommunicated by Rome, and though he continued to hold his primacy, his position was utterly intolerable to the Roman reforming party now firmly entrenched in the Church. It is clear that the motive of getting rid of a usurping archbishop was prominent in the mind of Alexander II when he gave his formal blessing as pope to William the Norman's invasion of England in 1066. The feelings of strict canonists can be understood and respected. At the same time, the support given by Rome to the foreign conquest and decisive overthrow of Anglo-Saxon England seems a shabby return for over four centuries of unstinted devotion (unparalleled perhaps in western Europe) on the part of Englishmen to the chair of St Peter.

The discomfiture of Godwine gave Edward his opportunity to rule as king entirely in his own right without the interference of over-powerful laymen. But he unwisely increased that Normanisation of the court which he had already begun. The result was a national reaction which brought back Godwine. Soon after his return Godwine died, and his earldom of Wessex passed to his son Harold. The king from now on seems to have lost interest in much more than the formal duties of his kingship, and became increasingly devout and ascetic in his tastes. With the progress of the years, Harold steadily became the real ruler of England.

Edward the sainted king seems of curiously little importance in the history of the Anglo-Saxon Church. He showed some originality in the manner of his episcopal appointments. He seriously inaugurated the practice of promoting secular rather than monastic clergy to the episcopate.[73] This may seem paradoxical, as we have already remarked, because it is as a lover of monks and their ways that the Confessor has been remembered. But the general influence of the monastic institute was tending to decline during this reign. There appears to have been some falling away from strict standards by the Benedictines in the years preceding the Conquest. Important houses like Winchester and Canterbury were not what they had recently been.[74] The two most vigorous monasteries were Evesham, under its abbot Aethelwig, and Worcester, under Wulfstan.[75] Apart from these two men there were no outstanding figures amongst the monks. Monastic scholarship, whilst not necessarily in the doldrums, had lost the fervour and keenness which it had possessed in men like Aelfric, and was in no way to be compared with that of contemporary France. In 1066, though the English monasteries were assuredly not decadent in the commonly accepted meaning of that word, it could scarcely be said of them that this was their finest hour.

Edward's most cherished project during his declining years was a great abbey which would bear comparison with the splendid new houses of Normandy. It was to be in a peculiar sense dependent on himself, and close to the centre of life in London. On the island of Thorney in the Thames there had been a small monastery since the seventh century until it came to grief at the hands of the Danes. Dunstan refounded it soon after the middle of the tenth century, when he was bishop of London; the first abbot of the new foundation was Wulfsige, with twelve monks.[76] Edward proceeded to rebuild and richly endow this monastery, properties from all over England being annexed and diverted (notably from the Worcestershire abbey of Pershore) to its support. The church was dedicated on Holy Innocents day (28 December) 1065, too late for the king, now on his death-bed, to be present.

Map 4. Benedictine houses on the eve of the Norman Conquest, including cells and doubtful houses. + Monasteries O Nunneries.

Map 5. Colleges of secular canons on the eve of the Conquest. (At Shrewsbury there was a group of at least three, and possibly four or five, collegiate churches.)

A few months later, after his defeat of Harold at Hastings, William I was consecrated in this great abbey church of Westminster, and all subsequent English sovereigns have received their hallowing on the same spot. Under the Normans building operations continued on the abbey. The sanctuary and transepts stood for two hundred and fifty years, and the nave for about a century longer.

CHAPTER XXIV

THE PRIMACY OF LANFRANC

The reign of William I (1066–87) almost coincided with the archbishopric of one of our greatest primates (1070–89), and indeed there can seldom have been a time when the high interests of Church and State were so much at one. Both men were administrators of a high order, strong-willed and astute, and they understood each other well. William was determined that his surveillance should extend over ecclesiastical no less than civil affairs. In this he succeeded well, and yet the Church in his reign could not complain of a secular tyranny. On the other hand, the strong hand of Lanfranc was apparent in the business of secular government, and it is at least arguable that the Conqueror's work of consolidation in England would not have attained its high degree of success without the aid of the man who has with reason been called our first prime minister.

The Church which William found in England in 1066 was an integral part of western Christendom. Insular it certainly was, but for this very reason Anglo-Saxon reverence for the papacy was great—in much the same way as loyalty to the Crown today is often greater in distant parts of the British Commonwealth than it is at home. Far from the Norman Conquest riveting the papal yoke more firmly on an unwilling Saxon neck, if anything William rather slackened it. There was, however, much need for an application of the Hildebrandine reform programme in England. The monasteries had perhaps grown somewhat slack, and the parochial clergy were normally married. The Norman churchmen who were shortly to be appointed to high offices in the English Church have often been called 'spiritual drill-sergeants', and indeed there was scope for this type of prelate in England at this time.

William for his first two or three years was too preoccupied completing the subjugation of the kingdom to devote much time to ecclesiastical problems. When he did so, it seemed to him that the first requisite was a reorganisation of the episcopate. This consisted now of fifteen sees, thirteen in the Canterbury province, and two belonging to York. There now followed a gradual ousting of English in favour of Norman bishops, a process which had already started in Edward's reign. Three of the bishops, Giso of Wells, Remigius of Dorchester, and Walter of Hereford, already ruling their dioceses in 1066, were foreigners. At the Winchester Easter council of 1070, papal legates were present, under the leadership of Ermenfrid, bishop of Sion, and the problem of episcopal personnel was seriously faced. Two sees, York and Winchester, were then vacant, but the business of these important appointments was deferred. Leofwine of Lichfield voluntarily resigned his see before the Winchester council met; a married man, he realised the hopelessness of his position. For the time being, this see also was left unfilled. Aethelmar, who had been bishop of Elmham for nearly a quarter of a century, was deposed, for reasons which we do not know.

The most important act of this council was the deposition of the archbishop of Canterbury, Stigand, Aethelmar's brother. This cleric, bishop of Winchester since 1047, became also archbishop of Canterbury in 1052 (in succession to the Norman Robert), holding the two sees in plurality. Essentially a partisan of Godwine, Stigand came to the primacy on the wave of anti-Norman reaction in the latter year. But it was against all canonical order for a bishop to usurp the see of a predecessor still living. On both sides of the Channel strict churchmen regarded Stigand's position as irregular, whatever brief some of them may have held for Robert of Jumièges. Leo IX had almost immediately excommunicated Stigand, a sentence renewed by his successors. For the last few months of 1058 the archbishop was able to breathe more easily—during the pontificate of Benedict X, from whom he obtained the pallium. It was in this brief period of recognition that Stigand performed his only consecrations of bishops, Aethelric of Selsey and Siward of Rochester. But pope Benedict was himself regarded by the reforming party as holding his office unlawfully, and he was deposed in January 1059. Stigand was again excommunicated, first by Nicholas II and then by Alexander II, who formally supported the 1066 expedition partly in the confidence that William would get rid of the archbishop. Even at home churchmen hesitated to recognise Stigand, so much so that no Anglo-Saxon bishop came to him for consecration, save during his brief period of papal favour. When Harold completed his new church of the Holy Cross at Waltham, it was Cynesige, archbishop of York, whom he asked to perform the ceremony of dedication, and it was Cynesige's successor Ealdred who crowned him king. It is

Scale of Miles
0 10 20 30 40 50

DURHAM +

YORK +

+

CHESTER

LINCOLN

NORWICH +

HEREFORD +

WORCESTER +

BATH & WELLS

SALISBURY (Old Sarum) +

WINCHESTER +

LONDON +

ROCH- ESTER

CANTER- BURY +

CHICHESTER

EXETER +

Map 6. Dioceses of the English Church *c.* 1090. (In 1102 the seat of the bishop of Chester was moved to Coventry. From then until the Reformation one or other of Chester, Coventry and Lichfield gave the bishop his title. In 1109 the diocese of Ely was founded, for the county of Cambridge; and in 1133 that of Carlisle, for Cumberland.)

doubtful whether Stigand was really perturbed over this boycott of himself as archbishop. Primarily a politician, he may also have regarded the reforming popes as troublesome upstarts.[1]

Business was resumed at a Whitsuntide council held at Windsor, again under the leadership of Ermenfrid, though meanwhile the two cardinal priests he had brought with him had returned to Rome. The sees of York and Winchester were filled respectively by Thomas, canon of Bayeux, and Walkelin, a royal chaplain. Aethelric of Selsey was deposed, and his place taken by Stigand (not to be confused with the late archbishop). Elmham was given to Herfast, for several years a domestic chaplain to William. Durham was vacant through the flight and subsequent outlawing of its bishop Aethelwine, who from being at first well disposed to the Normans had reacted with indignation to William's harsh treatment of the north in 1069. By the time the council had done its work, only two Saxon bishops remained—Wulfstan, the able and well-loved bishop of Worcester, and Siward of Rochester. The latter was the least important of English sees, and its proximity to Canterbury placed it in a position almost of dependency on the primate. There was little danger in leaving a native in possession. The vacant see of Canterbury was filled by the appointment of Lanfranc, at the time abbot of Caen.

The year of birth of this great man is unknown, and indeed the whole chronology of his early life is confusing.[2] It is reasonably clear, however, that he was born in Pavia between 1000 and 1020. His father Haribald was a man of standing in a city torn by rival factions. Not caring for strife, his son Lanfranc turned early to an intellectual career, first to Latin studies, and then to law, in which Lombardy excelled. He did not become a cleric, and this was in any case not a practical necessity for a bookish young man in northern Italy, where learning was no monopoly of churchmen as in France and England. The emperor at the time was Conrad II (1024–39), who did much to encourage the revived study of Justinian. In Roman as well as the native Lombard law Lanfranc would become well versed. But though he apparently rose to some eminence locally, it would be unsafe to assume that he became one of the great contemporary lawyers. There were other men bearing the name Lanfranc successfully practising law in Lombardy during this period, and this has perhaps led to credit being given to our Lanfranc to which he is not entitled. Moreover, it was once usual for scholars to place his birth c. 1000 (which would make him die at the age of nearly ninety later on as archbishop, in full possession of his natural powers), a dating which implied that the whole of his youth and early middle age were spent in the reading and practice of law. More recent study reveals that he may well have abandoned the law when quite a young man, in which case the extravagant claims made for him as a jurist must be dropped. Suffice it to say that the study of law appealed to one brought up in a legal environment, and that Lanfranc made a name for himself as a young lecturer and practitioner of the subject, developing a forensic habit of mind which remained with him all his life.

For some unknown reason he abandoned his legal career, probably some time before 1040. The ambitious young man saw Normandy as the land of opportunity. An intellectual revival was there in full swing, and the Norman rulers, though stern and violent to their subjects as a whole, were deferential to scholars. But in Normandy the study of law counted for less than that of theology, and the educated layman was non-existent. To be a scholar meant taking orders. Lanfranc therefore now turned his mind to theological study, and making his way to the cathedral school of Tours, listened to the lectures of archdeacon Berengar, a controversial and learned theologian, of whose fame he had heard. The eucharistic theology of this teacher was opposed to the views gaining ground in influential circles, and Lanfranc soon realised that his advancement would not be served by his becoming too closely associated with Berengar. He therefore disengaged himself from this awkward entanglement. There followed an indeterminate period in which he visited various places, possibly including Paris, and eventually settled at Avranches, where he became a teacher in the cathedral school. But though he had by now abandoned legal studies, he was not yet qualified to lecture in theology. It is likely, therefore, that the subject-matter of his lectures lay in such fields as grammar and rhetoric, required by junior students. He now seems to have reached a crisis in his life where ambition and the love of secular learning gave way to religious fervour. He decided in favour of the religious life, and accompanied by one of his pupils unobtrusively slipped away from Avranches. The story of his waylaying by thieves in some woods by the river Rille has often been told.[3] The upshot of this mishap was that he found his way to the new and insignificant monastery of Bec. We now enter upon the purely monastic phase of his life, but it may be well to trace first the history of the foundation of an abbey destined to supply many leaders to the English Church.

Herluin,[4] the founder of Bec, was born *c.* 994 of a noble family, trained from youth in the practice of arms, and a popular figure in Norman courtly circles. At about the age of thirty-seven he experienced a conversion which turned his attention by degrees to the religious life. He did not at once forsake the court and castle, but privately adopted the life which in our day would be that of an oblate or religious associate. He prayed diligently, and while still frequenting the hall with his brother knights ate sparingly while they feasted. After a while he withdrew from the world, and proceeded to build for himself a chapel on his own estate at Bonneville. Ignorant of the life of religion, he visited various monasteries in search of experience, but found little to encourage him. He was sometimes given an unwelcome, even rough, reception, and the pride of many monks unfavourably impressed him. His fervour might well have evaporated under the influence of this bad example, had not his faith been suddenly confirmed by the effectual fervent prayer of one righteous man. On visiting the chapel of a certain monastery during the night, confident of finding it deserted, he saw there a single monk, who remained in prayer until dawn. A changed man, Herluin returned to Bonneville, becoming abbot of a small community which gathered around him. Its life was simple in the extreme, the brethren spending most of their day clearing the ground, tilling the soil, and erecting their wooden buildings. Meals were prepared by Herluin's own mother. It became apparent, however, that the Bonneville site was a poor one, and the community moved to Bec in the wooded vale of Brionne. Wooden buildings were again put up, soon to be replaced by stone ones, and before long a distinctively monastic routine was being followed. Its outstanding characteristic was its simplicity, akin to that of the earliest Benedictinism. Nothing could be further removed from the splendour of the Cluniac observance. Manual labour formed the staple of the life, punctuated by the regular hours of prayer, with such reading as was necessary. There is no evidence that this way of life was adopted by Herluin consciously, nor that he regarded extreme austerity as a *sine qua non* of the monastic life. The simplicity of the earliest days at Bec was dictated purely by circumstances, liable to change; before the close of Herluin's life, Bec would be one of the grandest and most learned of abbeys.

Herluin missed acutely a good teacher for his monks, and Lanfranc was the answer to his prayers. One day the Italian presented himself at the house, having found his way thither in response to a vow made on his deliverance from the robbers. The abbot pointed out to him the hardness of the life at Bec, but Lanfranc decided to stay. From the outset, however, he was a man apart. When the rest of the community were in the fields⁵ he would be in the cloister, laying the foundations of his theological knowledge. He does not seem at first to have been a teacher, but was content himself to learn. And yet he grew dissatisfied with the conditions at Bec. He was repelled by the ignorance of the monks, who were moreover often men of unsaintly life. He seriously contemplated leaving the place in favour of a hermit's life, but was persuaded by Herluin to remain. Friendship and understanding were growing between the two men, and Herluin did the obvious thing when he appointed Lanfranc prior. This was probably *c.* 1044, when the Italian had been three years in the monastery. He was now at last something of a theologian, and held an authoritative position in the abbey. There opened up an important career for Bec as a centre of theological instruction. Lanfranc was probably at this time in his early thirties—a vigorous young man with the prospect of years of activity before him.

During the next few years Bec attracted students from all over Europe, and indeed it was its schools which made its fortunes. Lanfranc had found his second vocation—as a lecturer and organiser of studies. It is clear from later library catalogues that there was early a comprehensive range of teaching at Bec, including grammar and rhetoric, music, arithmetic, and astronomy, besides theology. Boys were taught the rudiments of letters, while advanced students were guided through the difficult problems of the divine sciences. The transformation from a small unlettered band of brothers spending their days in field-work into a brilliant and fertile centre of learning, all within a decade or less, was phenomenal. Amongst Lanfranc's pupils at Bec were many who eventually rose to great eminence in the Church, including pope Alexander II; Anselm and Theobald, two outstanding archbishops of Canterbury, one of them the most original thinker of his time; Ivo of Chartres, a master of the canon law; Gundulf, bishop of Rochester and builder of the Tower of London; Gilbert Crispin, abbot of Westminster and Herluin's biographer; and many other bishops and abbots. One of the Bec students was Paul, later to become abbot of St Albans; generally said to be Lanfranc's nephew, some men thought he was his son.⁵

By now Lanfranc was a well-established ecclesiastic and known throughout Normandy. In 1049 he attended a council held at Rheims under Leo IX's presidency, at which the reforming policy was propounded and simony and clerical marriage condemned. He was perhaps, however, somewhat taken aback on being told that his presence would be required at a council to be held the following year in Rome. Though he did not know it, his orthodoxy had come under suspicion, through his brief connection with Berengar some years before.

The controversy between the two schools of thought on the nature of the Real Presence in the Eucharist, the realist and the symbolic, was rapidly coming to a head.[6] Berengar was in the line of those teachers, such as Rabanus Maurus, Ratramnus, and Aelfric, who held to the spiritual or symbolical view. It was a tradition which appealed to many intellectuals, to whom it was irrational to assert that the substance of bread and wine disappeared after consecration. It was more reasonable to believe that the consecration gave to the bread and wine the effect and value of Our Lord's body and blood to those recipients who had the faith to perceive it. But the popular trend was in the direction of the materialist view. The Host was the historical Body of the Lord, born of Mary. Some asserted that It could work miracles, and was incapable of corruption. 'Certainly the atmosphere in which the doctrine of transubstantiation grows into a dogma is calculated to send a shiver through one's intellectual and moral being.'[7]

Now though Lanfranc's sojourn at the Tours cathedral school had been brief, he seems to have made definite contacts with Berengar, who was favourably impressed with the young man's ability. In 1049 he wrote to Lanfranc at Bec in cordial terms, saying that he would like to hear from him, though he has received reports that he has not been won over to the symbolic view.

When the letter arrived at Bec, Lanfranc was at Rheims. It was disgracefully opened and read by some monks of the community, who forwarded it to the pope at Rheims. Lanfranc was not told of its existence. The letter seemed to suggest that Lanfranc had been in too close a touch with a prominent teacher of unsound views. There was probably little to worry about, as the letter itself made it clear that Lanfranc was scrupulously orthodox. But there may have been an uneasy feeling that some of Berengar's contagion clung to the prior of Bec. In view of the numerous intelligent young men now passing through his hands, it might be as well to make quite sure about his position. Leo IX gave instructions that the letter should be produced, and an explanation demanded, at the Lent synod to be held in Rome in 1050. The erstwhile lawyer was easily able to clear himself of the imputation of heresy (though it may be that he had his mental reservations concerning the truth, or at least the attractiveness, of Berengar's teaching). Berengar was formally condemned and excommunicated, though he managed to keep the fires of controversy burning for several years.

Meanwhile in 1052 William became duke of Normandy. As such he kept a close eye on all persons of authority in his realm. It was a legal dispute which brought him seriously into contact with Lanfranc, one involving the duke personally. In 1053 he married Matilda, daughter of Baldwin count of Flanders, in defiance of Leo IX, who had prohibited the match at the Rheims council of 1049, apparently on the grounds of affinity. Concerning the marriage the prior of Bec also had some hard things to say, which came to William's ears. The duke sent his chaplain Herfast to Bec to enlist Lanfranc's support. The prior acted tactlessly, if not ungraciously. He was so amused at the intellectual feebleness of Herfast that he presented him with an Abecedarium, or child's spelling-book. Angered by the insult, the chaplain returned, and as a result of his bitter complaints William ordered Lanfranc out of Normandy and devastated one of the Bec abbey farms into the bargain.

According to the story, Lanfranc met William on the road as he was riding away from the abbey. The two men fell into conversation and there was a complete reconciliation. Lanfranc returned to Bec, to which full restitution was made for the devastated property. The prior, moreover, became the duke's adviser in ecclesiastical affairs.

Before long the opportunity came for him to render service to William in the most practical form. The duke and his wife, as pious people, were naturally anxious that their union, though an accomplished fact, should be fully recognised. It was here that Lanfranc's legal experience proved invaluable. The case is, in fact, an interesting illustration of Lanfranc's forensic turn of mind. He had denounced the marriage in the first place as contrary to canon law. But he was quite prepared to seek a dispensation on William's behalf which would put matters right. This legal and mechanical mentality was to become the bane of the medieval Church, and it has continued in the Roman Church to this day. In 1059 Lanfranc proceeded to Rome, this time to attend a synod convened by Nicholas II, intending to raise the marriage question. It is quite possible that he would never have succeeded in obtaining the desired recognition, had he not first been able to help the papacy against a renewed outbreak of Berengarianism. Though condemned several years before, Berengar was again active. At the synod he was forced to recant and burn his works. In return for his support, the pope conceded to Lanfranc full canonical recognition of the marriage. In expiation four hospitals were to be built, and William and Matilda were each to found a religious house.

Berengar was irrepressible, and continued to worry the Church for a further twenty years. Between 1050 and 1079 he was condemned by no fewer than thirteen councils. After the 1059 council Berengar gathered together his Eucharistic views in a book, to which Lanfranc made reply maintaining that the real Body of Christ was present after the consecration. About 1070 Berengar wrote for private circulation amongst his friends and close acquaintances the De Sacra Coena, which refuted the new orthodox doctrine of the mass. At last Hugh, abbot of Cluny, could stand it no longer and requested Gregory VII to end the nuisance once for all. The upshot was a council at Rome in 1079 where Berengar finally recanted. He was kindly treated by the pope, and lived in peace with the Church for the remainder of his days. He died in 1088. It is possible that Gregory VII (the former Hildebrand) had, like Lanfranc, some secret sympathy with Berengar's views. A. J. MacDonald made the interesting suggestion that if Lanfranc had stood up for Berengar in the earlier stages of the controversy, Hildebrand would have supported him. 'An opportunity was missed for carrying the reform movement into the region of theology', and the seed was sown from which many future tragic controversies were to grow.[8]

The final period of Lanfranc's purely monastic career is connected with Caen. William took very seriously the conditions of his marriage dispensation, and it was a worthy abbey which he founded. Begun c. 1060, it was in due course dedicated to St Stephen. The duke stressed the importance of his new foundation by appointing as its first abbot Lanfranc, his trusted ecclesiastical adviser, who moved from Bec to Caen in 1063. Here he continued his teaching of young men, though in addition he now had the responsibility of ruling a great house and he was increasingly engaged on the duke's business. He visited Rome in 1067, where an old pupil was now pope as Alexander II. The purpose of the visit was to obtain the pallium for John, bishop of Avranches, recently appointed archbishop of Rouen. Lanfranc himself had been offered this metropolitan see, but he had declined, and indeed William (now king of England) had something far bigger in store for his most reliable helper.[9]

We must now return to the England of 1070. After the Whitsuntide council at Windsor, the papal legates were sent to Normandy to inform Lanfranc of his appointment to Canterbury. He appears to have been genuinely anxious to decline it, pleading his ignorance of the Saxon tongue and his general incapacity to rule a barbarous people. But his objections were overruled. He crossed the Channel early in August, and was consecrated at the end of the month. Canterbury cathedral had been gutted by fire less than three years previously, and the ceremony was held in a temporary wooden building. Nevertheless most of the bishops were present, and there was a large assembly of nobles, monks from the two Canterbury religious houses, and townspeople.

Many problems awaited the new primate, which we shall now discuss, though not necessarily in their chronological order.

First of all, there was the question of the primacy of Canterbury over York. The York province was relatively unimportant, containing only two dioceses, which served wild and sparsely populated areas. Thomas of Bayeux, though nominated to the York archbishopric a few months before Lanfranc's appointment to Canterbury, was still un-consecrated, and now came to Lanfranc for episcopal orders. Before proceeding with the consecration, the archbishop asked Thomas for a written profession of obedience, which was refused. The assembly dispersed, and Thomas departed still a priest. He appealed to the king, who inclined to sympathise with him. But when Lanfranc met William soon afterwards he easily convinced him that he was not quibbling over a mere point of precedence. William must have been conscious too of the ever-present menace from Scandinavia, and of the dangerous rebellion recently suppressed in the north. While the loyalty of Thomas himself was doubtless beyond suspicion, an independent archbishopric of York might well be an encouragement towards a separate northern kingdom. Moreover, it was essential for the success of contemplated reforms that Lanfranc and William should be able to deal with the English as one nation.

The king at once instructed Thomas to return to Canterbury, where he must unreservedly promise obedience to Lanfranc, though his successors would be exempt from the requirement unless it could be proved in open council that previous archbishops of York had rendered such obedience. Thomas was still stubborn, and it probably peeved him that he should be the first archbishop of York to promise explicit obedience to Canterbury.[10] But the king threatened to banish him if he would not give way. He duly promised obedience to Lanfranc, who raised him to episcopal orders. Meanwhile Lanfranc received professions of obedience from the diocesan bishops also.[11]

But the wider question of the permanent subordination of York to Canterbury was by no means settled, and Thomas had an opportunity for raising it at the highest level the following year. In 1071 the two archbishops went to Rome to receive their pallia. While before Alexander II, Thomas raised the problem, maintaining that while there should certainly be a primate of all England, the honour ought to be held by Canterbury and York alternately. Conscious that the meagreness of his province weakened his case, he also claimed the transference of the bishoprics of Lincoln, Lichfield, and Worcester, besides Durham, to his jurisdiction. But Lanfranc never failed to get the better of an opponent in argument, and adroitly turned the tables on Thomas by informing the pope that Thomas was the son of a priest, and that his position as a prelate was therefore strictly speaking irregular. In any case, the English bishops and abbots were about to deal with the whole question of the precedence in full council.

This council was held at Winchester in 1072. Lanfranc produced two main sets of evidence in support of the Canterbury primacy. Firstly, the support of Bede was on his side. This indicated that from the time of Augustine to the earlier part of the eighth century the archbishop of Canterbury had held the primacy, and indeed for a large portion of this period there had been no bishop of York at all. Secondly, Lanfranc was able to produce a number of letters from various popes, addressed to English bishops and kings, supporting the primacy of Canterbury. The old view that Lanfranc forged these documents in support of his case is no longer tenable.[12] The documentary evidence was overwhelming, and Thomas had to submit. He had badly handled his case all along, for though Lanfranc had proved Canterbury to be the senior bishopric of Britain, he had not really demonstrated any cogent reason why the archbishop of York should render explicit obedience to him in writing. If Thomas had been the equal of Lanfranc in argument and forensic ability the outcome may well have been different.

By the terms of the settlement the Humber was to be the boundary between the two provinces. This meant that the three extra dioceses claimed by Thomas remained to Canterbury. Thomas was left with Durham besides York. Scotland was placed in his province, but York never succeeded in securing the obedience of the Scottish bishops. The archbishop of York was to attend any council summoned by the archbishop of Canterbury, and be bound by its canonical decisions. In his written submission, Thomas promised absolute obedience to Lanfranc and his successors in all things canonically ordered.

Lanfranc reported the result to Alexander II, asking for papal confirmation of the Canterbury primacy. But the pope refused, apparently on the advice of Hildebrand, head of his chancery. The papacy at this time may well have seen a distinct possibility of the archbishop of Canterbury becoming a kind of patriarch of the West. That this was in Alexander's mind is suggested by his remarks to Lanfranc on the occasion of the 1071 visit. On Lanfranc's approach, Alexander had risen to greet him, saying that he did not do so 'because he was archbishop of Canterbury', but as a former pupil to his old tutor. The very words indicate by implication the prestige of the Canterbury see. The fear that the see might become too independent actually came dangerously near fulfilment in the course of the next pontificate (Gregory VII), when Lanfranc and William both adopted a somewhat detached attitude to the papacy. Meanwhile, the way was left open for Thomas to reopen the question of the primacy after Lanfranc's death, which in due course he did, in spite of his oath. At the consecration of Lanfranc's successor Anselm he refused to proceed with the ceremony until it was agreed that the archbishop of Canterbury should be styled metropolitan instead of primate. Thomas' successor at York was Gerard (1101), who was ordered by Pascal II to swear obedience to Anselm. Gerard was followed by Thomas II (1108), who was upheld by the papacy, however, when he refused the oath to Anselm. Next came Thurstan (1114), during whose archiepiscopate the pope continued to support the York interest. To strengthen its case the Canterbury party had recourse to piling up documents which stressed the southern primacy, and it is to this period that the celebrated forgeries really belong. But they were of no avail, as it was in the interest of the papacy itself that York should be directly dependent upon it. The matter was finally settled in 1123, when it was declared that the York province should be free of all control from Canterbury.

From Lanfranc's own immediate view-point the problem was satisfactorily settled by the terms of the 1072 solution. He could set about a reorganisation of the English Church in the knowledge that he was master of the whole house. Most of this work was done through councils, of which we have record of six held under Lanfranc's presidency—Winchester (1072), London (1075), Winchester (1076), London (1078), Gloucester (1081), Gloucester (1085).[13]

It was at the first of these councils that the primacy question was settled. At this council Lanfranc also deposed Wulfric, abbot of New Minster in Winchester. Bishops were ordered to hold synods twice a year, and to appoint archdeacons.

The second council, held in St Paul's, was more important, and we fortunately possess a formal record of its proceedings.[14] All the bishops except those of Durham and Rochester were present, along with twenty-one abbots, an archdeacon, and the bishop of Coutances. The question of episcopal precedence was first settled—the four senior sees were to be Canterbury, York, London, and Winchester. The most important business, however, was the transference of episcopal seats from villages to towns. The Saxons were a predominantly rural people. We have observed how in the first place they had avoided Roman urban centres and established their settlements in rural areas. The Danes had reintroduced an appreciation of the advantages of town-life, but it was still customary in the eleventh century for the bishops to have their see-centres in isolated or sparsely populated places.

The newly appointed Norman prelates had no wish to reside in villages. But as with much else in the Anglo-Norman Church, the process of change had already begun. The see of Chester-le-Street had been moved in 994 to the more easily defended Durham. In 1050 bishop Leofric transferred his see from Crediton, which was comparatively exposed to marauding raiders, to Exeter. Thus two of the most famous English sees found their final home. The motive in both cases was security from the Danes. It is possible also that Herfast removed his East Anglian see from North Elmham to Thetford a few years before the 1075 council. No friend of Lanfranc, he may have decided to act on his own account without waiting for the archbishop's authority. At any rate, in his signature to the 1072 decree concerning the Canterbury primacy he styles himself bishop of Thetford. He continued to get on badly with the primate, whose rebukes he treated with contempt. He seems to have never forgiven Lanfranc for the

ABC insult, which had certainly been a very bad lapse on the part of a great man.

The council formally decreed that any future episcopal see must be set up in an urban centre, in accordance with the canons of the councils of Laodicea (320) and Sardica (343), and existing village sees removed. Selsey must lose its see in favour of Chichester, Lichfield in favour of Chester, Ramsbury—Sherborne in favour of Salisbury (Old Sarum). The Dorchester bishopric was moved to Lincoln, but precisely when is not clear. Before long Chester moved again, to Coventry. In 1085 Gisa, bishop of Wells, removed his seat to Bath, and in 1091 bishop Losinga moved from Thetford to Norwich.

At this council it was ordered that a priest should work only in his own diocese. The clergy were to dissociate themselves from the cruel jurisdiction of the times whereby criminals were punished by death or mutilation. Only bishops and abbots were to be allowed freedom of speech in synods; it went against the grain with Lanfranc, ever contemptuous of ignorance, to grant unlettered rural priests the right of speaking at the Church's deliberations. Decrees were also issued against superstitious practices and marriage within the prohibited degrees.

At his third council (Winchester 1076)[15] Lanfranc dealt with the problem of clerical celibacy. Only three years previously Hildebrand had become pope as Gregory VII, and the campaign of ecclesiastical reform in which enforced celibacy figured so prominently was in full swing all over western Christendom. There had been many papal condemnations of priestly marriage within recent years, reaching their climax in a synod at Rome in 1075, when Gregory ordered all priests to banish their wives. Metropolitans were instructed to carry the campaign into their provinces. In England Aethelred II had already legislated against clerical marriage, and bishop Wulfstan II of Worcester ordered his parish clergy to adopt the celibate life.[16] In northern Europe as a whole clerical marriage was common, and in the archdiocese of Milan and in Germany determined opposition was offered to the celibacy decrees. Peter Damian, a papal messenger sent to Milan, was confronted by archbishop Guido, who maintained the right of the parochial clergy to marry. The reformers felt they had the ultimate well-being of the Church on their side. A married clergy implied parish priests not fully devoted to their priestly functions. It also meant, in many cases, hereditary interests, and indeed it was the practice in some English churches, as on the Continent, for son to succeed father as parish priest. There may have been many parishes in England which like the Lucchese parish of Sesto in the early ninth century were 'appanages of a kind of sacerdotal dynasty'.[17] But the root reason for insistence on clerical celibacy was the idea, never far distant from the early medieval mind, that sexual relations were in themselves unclean and sinful.[18] In spite of this, it was a widespread practice in the eleventh century for parochial clergy to be married, and without fear of public opprobrium.[19]

Lanfranc's way of dealing with the issue again reveals his lawyer-like dexterity. Though canons, both in cathedral and collegiate churches, were to put away their wives, and no man was in future to be ordained deacon or priest without a vow of celibacy, parochial clergy already married were not molested. This went a long way towards meeting the Hildebrandine programme, without undue disturbance to existing conditions. In practice the new decrees do not seem to have been enforced harshly, and there were still married priests in the following century.[20]

This council also attempted legislation aimed at protecting the parochial clergy from their patrons. In Anglo-Saxon England the idea was generally accepted that manorial ownership included that of the parish church. The patron did not only appoint the incumbent, but owned the church and its revenues. In the eleventh century it was quite common for the patron to grant away the tithes—in a later age exclusively the property of the clergy concerned—to some cause which appealed to him. Thus in 1067 queen Matilda's father, count Baldwin of Flanders, gave all the tithes of two villages to the abbey of St Winoc at Bergues.[21] A lord could even grant tithes to his lay relatives, or settle them on his wife.[22] With the Norman Conquest there was a tightening up of feudal relationships in England, and the parish priest became more than ever the man of his lay lord. Lanfranc tried in his council to ensure that the new lords, who had taken such widespread hold of the English manors, should not unduly oppress the priests. Up till now, the English parochial clergy had enjoyed far greater freedom and independence than their brothers on the Continent. The council decreed that no service should be required of the priests other than what they had been accustomed to render during the time of king Edward. But in this respect the council's influence was probably far from efficacious, and the Conquest seems to have brought the Saxon parish clergy into a particularly subdued position.

In thus dealing with celibacy, and trying to limit the control of laymen over church benefices, this third council might be regarded as Lanfranc's contribution to the Hildebrandine reform programme. Amongst the council's legislation was a provision forbidding the celebration of marriage except before a priest.[23] But the most significant measure, from the point of view of subsequent English medieval history, was the confirmation of the separation of civil and church courts. Sometime after 1070 the king had issued an ordinance addressed to the lords of Essex, Middlesex, and Hertfordshire, removing from the hundred courts all ecclesiastical cases. Previously, secular and spiritual cases had been heard together in the same court. Henceforth all 'episcopal laws' and that which pertained to the 'cure of souls' were to be brought directly before the bishop. To William's mind this distinction of two kinds of jurisdiction would help towards a tidier administration of the kingdom; he apparently did not see the inherent danger of clergymen becoming established in a position external to the common law. The separation of the courts was fully endorsed by Lanfranc's council, and excommunication prescribed for those who refused to appear, when summoned, before the new spiritual tribunals.[24]

Little is known about the three other councils which the archbishop is known to have held. At the London council of 1078 Aethelnoth, abbot of Glastonbury, was deposed in favour of the Norman Thurstan. At Gloucester in 1081 archbishop Thomas of York consecrated William of St Carilef to the see of Durham, with the approval of Lanfranc. Thomas tried unsuccessfully to obtain the presence of the Scottish bishops at the consecration. At the next council, also in Gloucester (1085), the abbot of Crowland, Ulfketel, was deposed, and three royal chaplains, Maurice, William, and Robert, were elected bishops of London, Thetford, and Chester respectively.

Lanfranc was not only active in promoting councils, but had many direct dealings with individuals in the Church at large. He maintained a close watch over the bishops, as is revealed in his relations with Herfast, bishop of Elmham. Lanfranc intervened when that prelate quarrelled with the abbot of Ely. He also rebuked him for his worldly manner of life, exhorting him to renounce dice-playing and spend his time rather in the study of theology and canon law. The letters of Lanfranc reveal much evidence of his extra-conciliar activity. The case of a married man who was admitted to deacon's orders was not beneath his notice. As the man remained loyal to his wife, he was to be debarred from exercising diaconal functions, though could continue in minor duties. If he eventually agreed to forsake his wife, he might be readmitted to deacon's functions, though reordination would not be required. Lanfranc's concern for the life of the Church in diocese and parish is evinced by his admonition to bishops to visit their flocks. There are to be fixed times for ordinations, which must be held in cathedral churches only. The normal times for baptisms shall be Easter and Whitsuntide. Altars shall be of stone, and (which is interesting evidence of some of the practices which were going on) mass shall be said by properly ordained priests only, and they shall use wine, not water, for the consecration of the sacred elements.

The separation of the ecclesiastical from the civil courts involved the practical acceptance of a body of canon law, upon which the new courts could base their decisions. Though the influence of the Penitential codes must have been considerable, there was no clear distinction between the two laws in the Old English Church, which shared its legislation with that of the State.

The formation of the Canon Law, to be supreme in the later medieval Church, was a gradual process, and prior to the twelfth century there was in fact no official collection of canons at all. In the early middle ages it was taken for granted that each diocese accepted the canons of Nicaea and subsequent general councils, to which it was free to add its own local legislation. By a process of expansion there came to be various national canonical codes, such as those of Spain, Africa, and Gaul. Perhaps the most important of these was the *Hispana*, or Spanish collection. Caesarius of Arles in the early part of the sixth century made a collection called *Statuta Ecclesiae Antiqua*, which included African canons, as well as some from Eastern churches, and papal letters. But his work was less important than that of his near contemporary Dionysius Exiguus, an Eastern monk who came to Rome. Here he formed a compilation of canons of early councils and decretals of pontiffs from the time of pope Siricius (384–98), which became the official collection of the local Roman Church, and remained so until the eleventh century. It was substantially this collection which Hadrian I sent on request to Charlemagne, and accepted by the Frankish Church at Aachen in 802. But though the collection of Dionysius Exiguus secured a general acceptance in the Western Church, it does not seem to have been adopted in England.

The famous collection known as the False Decretals, or Pseudo-

Isidore, was produced *c.* 850 by an unknown writer in the Frankish empire. He was influenced by the barbarous conditions of life current at the time, which induced every man to look towards some feudal lord as his patron and protector. Consequently feudalism was developing, and even the churches tended to be regarded as within the jurisdiction of lay lords. The underlying aim of the Decretals was to vindicate the independence of the bishops from lay control, and this could only be done by declaring them directly answerable to the pope. It must be remembered that in the Frankish territories respect for the papacy was high. The traditions of Boniface, one of the staunchest upholders of Roman authority, lived on. The compiler took the genuine *Hispana* collection, consisting of canons of various councils besides papal decrees from *c.* 380 onwards, and added to this a series of forged papal decrees purporting to emanate from the earlier popes (prior to Nicaea). The aim of the collection was to bestow the authority of antiquity on later claims of popes, such as those of Nicholas I, and in this the collection was highly successful. When Nicholas came to his throne in 858, he enthusiastically accepted the Pseudo-Isidore.

The next outstanding landmark in Canon Law history was the work of Burchard, bishop of Worms (1006–22), who arranged a corpus of ecclesiastical law systematically according to subject-matter. It became a widely used text-book on the Continent, but does not seem to have attained general circulation in England. The effect of the book was to modify somewhat the papal claims (the pope being regarded as a final court of appeal, not as direct ruler as by extreme papalists), though the authenticity of the False Decretals was not questioned. The collection, known as the *Decretum*, stressed the authority of the diocesan bishops, under the immediate control of their metropolitans, in the government of the Church. Papal authority was not in any sense denied, but it was regarded as something which existed at a far distance and should be exercised sparingly.

This was not a sufficiently advanced opinion for the more radical reformers of the Hildebrandine movement, and the balance was secured by a book known as the *Collection in 74 Titles*, by an unknown compiler. This was a compilation drawn from the False Decretals and the writings of Gregory I, and is on the side of full papal authority. The eleventh century was characterised by the compilation of collections of canons, whose course was definitely set in the direction of papalism. Of this order was the substantial work of Anselm (not to be confused with the great archbishop of Canterbury), bishop of Lucca; arranged according to subject-matter, this work utilised Burchard, the *Collection in 74 Titles*, and the False Decretals—it was very popular with the reform party.

At the end of the eleventh century a truly great canonist appeared, Ivo of Chartres, one of Lanfranc's pupils, whose comprehensive manual on church law, the *Pannormia*, became the standard text-book in the first half of the twelfth century and was still being used in the thirteenth. Ivo's great successor was Gratian, a Bologna monk and lecturer in canon law, whose celebrated *Decretum* appeared in 1140. This work quoted authorities in full, and as such was indispensable to students. It became the universal manual, and teachers commented on it in their turn. In due course it became the first part of the *Corpus Juris Canonici*. The second part of this massive work was the *Decretals* of Gregory IX, gathered together at his order in 1230 by the Dominican, Raymond of Penaforte, who drew on papal letters subsequent to the *Decretum*. The third part was the *Sext* of Boniface VIII, issued in 1298. Eventually some additional matter, the *Extravagantes*, was included. All this constituted the Canon Law of the later medieval Church, and was universally accepted in western Christendom.[25]

Lanfranc with his methodical mind would perceive at once the futility of separate Church courts without a distinct Church law. Characteristically therefore Lanfranc was responsible for the introduction of the Canon Law into England. There being no universally authorised Corpus in the eleventh century, metropolitans had a certain amount of choice in the matter, and indeed Lanfranc was perhaps the first metropolitan to impose a collection by his authority upon all his dioceses. He did not merely adopt an already existing collection, though that of Burchard and the *Collection in 74 Titles* were readily available. He compiled his own, and Z. N. Brooke has argued convincingly that a MS. now in Trinity College, Cambridge, is the original.[26] His collection consisted of two main parts—an abridged version of the False Decretals, together with a complete account of the canons of councils from Nicaea to the second council of Seville. To these were added the chief decrees of the Lateran synod of 1059, the papal decrees against simony, and Berengar's oath in abjuration of his heresy. The collection is based on law books which Lanfranc obtained from Bec.

Lanfranc presented the original copy of his Collection (now in Cambridge) to Canterbury cathedral. No fewer than ten copies of this survive in England, of eleventh or early twelfth-century date, in the British Museum and various college and cathedral libraries.[27] Seven of these were made for cathedrals, and it is clear that the archbishop intended his Collection to be generally adopted in England as the Church Law book. And so it became. Lanfranc's Collection seems to have remained the authoritative corpus of canon law in this country until new material was introduced by Theobald, archbishop of Canterbury (1139–62).

Lanfranc was not an ardent papalist, and yet his Collection, based as it was on the False Decretals, had the eventual effect of enhancing the papal prestige in England. For a generation or two, young men in the cathedral schools were to be steadily imbued with the main principles of the Decretals, and by the middle of the twelfth century the victory of the papacy in England was complete.

The general character of the papal relationships with England during the reign of William is clear. William himself was a loyal son of Rome. He was careful to secure papal support for his invasion in 1066. But in his capacity of secular prince he had no intention of falling into subservience, and in this he was fully supported by his archbishop. Alexander II, who had blessed the expedition, seems subsequently to have written to William demanding fealty. The demand was renewed by his successor Gregory VII, to which William's reply has been preserved. He denied the claim that previous kings of England had done fealty for their kingdom; he promised the payment of Peter's Pence, at the same time carefully dissociating this from any suggestion of fealty. Though William never for one moment questioned the belief that the bishop of Rome was Head of the Catholic Church, from the point of view of daily practical government the Head of the Catholic Church in England was William himself. Neither was any pope to be recognised in England, nor were papal letters to be received, without his permission.[28] He himself must grant the final approval to all acts of ecclesiastical legislation. No baron was to be excommunicated without his consent. He even went to the length of forbidding his bishops to visit Rome without leave, much to Gregory's indignation. Lanfranc himself was peremptorily and urgently summoned to Rome by the latter, on pain of deprivation of his spiritual functions. But he is not known to have gone. Though it is going too far to say that a definite barrier was erected between England and Rome, certainly a curtain was drawn. Moreover, 'any legate that came from Rome would be admitted only as an envoy to the king, not as a plenipotentiary with authority over the English Church'.[29] The attitude of both William and Lanfranc to the papacy was detached. When Wibert of Ravenna was set up as an anti-pope (Clement III) against Gregory VII, neither the king nor the archbishop committed himself to one side or the other, and for a time the English Church in this reign was free of papal authority altogether.

William was a supporter of church reform, and it was because of this, and through preoccupations elsewhere, that Gregory VII did not press his claims against him. It would not have made much difference if he had. It is possible to argue that the English Church carried an air of independence about it at this time, and that in this it was peculiar to western Christendom. It might well be that this was realised by the popes, who had their anxious moments concerning the matter. Though Z. N. Brooke in his important study has clearly demonstrated that the English Church was an integral part of the western Church, being based on the same Canon Law, yet he has made some tacit admissions. Thus the popes recognised England to be somewhat exceptional in the matter of clerical celibacy, and dispensations for marriage were being granted even towards the end of the twelfth century.[30] Again, the councils of Lanfranc were not, 'as was usual elsewhere, provincial councils, but, owing to Lanfranc's position as primate, councils of the whole English Church'.[31] Moreover, Gregory VII was angered by the 'barrier' which William had raised between the English Church and the papacy, a barrier which did not exist elsewhere.[32] William made the English Church an integral part of the Church[33]—was it not then an integral part of the Church before?

At the time of the Conquest there were upwards of thirty-five monasteries in England, concentrated for the most part in the Fen country and in the south-west, and including such famous houses as St Albans, Bury, Ely, Glastonbury, Gloucester, Peterborough, Sherborne, and Westminster. There were also nine principal nunneries, the greatest being Shaftesbury, Wilton, and Romsey. The religious houses, as a body, were wealthy and powerful. It is wrong to assume they were in a state of moral decay, though it may be that the zeal of the monastic revival had slackened somewhat. It is certain that they were still a great influence in the general life of the Church.[34]

The Saxon abbots were in due course replaced by Normans, though not in any drastic way. The few who were implicated in the rebellions which took place at the beginning of William's reign were of course deposed, but on the whole the monastic institute in England was little changed, Norman abbots being appointed to vacancies as they occurred. These abbots brought a quickening of zeal, notably in building activities. They came from a land where a carefully-planned complex of buildings attached to a massive church was the ideal. The plans of monastic sites with which we are so familiar are often the work of Normans; the Anglo-Saxon monasteries were more casual in their layout. Invariably, as soon as a Norman abbot was appointed, he began to utilise the ample revenues of the house in rebuilding schemes, not hesitating (in apparently many cases) to pull down noble buildings but recently erected. The architecture of Normandy, of which the church at Bernay (1017–45) was the earliest example, was transplanted to this country, to become the basis upon which English Gothic would arise.

Lanfranc himself set the example with a new cathedral at Canterbury, though here the pre-Conquest church had been destroyed by fire in 1067. Commenced in 1070, the new church took seven years to complete. It had a short life, and was to be enlarged and remodelled by order of archbishop Anselm. Other great churches begun during Lanfranc's primacy were Lincoln, under bishop Remigius; St Albans, built largely of Roman brick, by abbot Paul; the cathedral at Old Sarum, begun by bishop Herman and finished by his successor Osmund; Rochester, during the episcopate of Gundulf, whose interest in architecture was exceptional[35]; Ely abbey church, later to be elevated to cathedral rank; Bury St Edmunds, under abbot Baldwin; Winchester cathedral, begun by bishop Walkelin in 1079; Gloucester abbey church, begun by abbot Serlo towards the close of Lanfranc's primacy, and surviving almost intact until the present day; St Augustine's Canterbury, under abbot Scotland; Worcester, started in 1084 by the English bishop Wulfstan, who was carried away by the general building enthusiasm; and Tewkesbury, under abbot Robert Fitzhamon, still intact and considered by some to be the most lovely church in England. Other great churches, such as Chichester, Norwich, and Chester, followed in the reign of Rufus, to whose years the first important secular edifice in England, Westminster Hall, is also ascribed.

These Norman churches were characterised by long, aisled naves, with transepts and apse, triforium and clerestory. Edward's new church at Westminster, with its great twelve-bayed nave, had already been built in this style. Though the manner is splendid and monumental, the Normans must not be regarded as super-builders. Many of their early towers in England collapsed through sheer bad construction. The Saxon masonry was often far better. It was not long before Saxon features were reasserting themselves—such as the square east end, which returned to establish itself as a permanent part of the English architectural tradition. But it would be foolish and ungenerous not to acknowledge the grandeur of the Norman achievement. The traveller today, as he stands in the north transept of Winchester, or peruses the chapel of St John in the Tower of London, may be excused a heady romanticism and a feeling of immersion in a distant age.

Most of the Norman abbots appointed to English monasteries proved themselves able and vigorous men. Gilbert Crispin may be taken as an example. Of noble family, he had been brought to Bec as an oblate by his parents, and was well known to Herluin, Lanfranc, and Anselm. He became abbot of Westminster c. 1085, having been already preceded there by two Normans—Geoffrey of Jumièges 1071–5, who was deposed for misrule, and Vitalis, formerly abbot of Bernay, who governed his new house in exemplary fashion. All that is known of Gilbert Crispin is good.[36] An able administrator, he was also a scholar. His *Life of Herluin* is one of our most valuable early medieval sources, with its contemporary insight into life at Bec. His *Disputation of a Jew with a Christian* is a fair and balanced controversial work, highly esteemed in medieval times.

There were of course some who betrayed their trust. The story of Thurstan of Glastonbury is well known.[37] But this over-publicised abbot was by no means typical, and on the whole it would seem that the appointment of Norman abbots heralded an improvement in discipline and scholarship in the English houses.

It must be emphasised that the change-over was gradual. Thus seven years after the Conquest there were still at least twelve English abbots, amongst whom were two outstanding men—Wulfstan of Worcester, and Aethelwig of Evesham. The former ruled his house with considerable efficiency, not disdaining Norman methods, though it is as a good pastoral bishop that he is remembered. The abbot of Evesham, Aethelwig, was a public figure with wide influence in the midlands. Though, like Wulfstan, he was a supporter of the king, he was also a patriot. Evesham under his guidance became a haven for sufferers under the new rule, notably those who had lost their homes in the harrying of the north. He was an excellent ruler of his own monastery, which increased in numbers during his abbacy. He died in 1077.

It was about this time that Lanfranc introduced from Bec a certain monk Henry, to become prior of Canterbury cathedral. The cathedral-monastery was a distinctively English institution, and Lanfranc at first wished to abolish it, placing secular canons in all cathedrals as in Normandy. But the cathedral-monastery system was retained, and thus English cathedral chapters came to be fairly evenly divided between monks and seculars. The bishop of a monastic cathedral was, at least theoretically, the abbot. To such a man as Lanfranc, who was himself a monk by choice, this was acceptable. He now exercised his abbatial authority by compiling a set of monastic constitutions for his Canterbury monks, forwarding it to Henry, the new prior.[38] It was not an original work, and in its compilation Lanfranc drew on the customs of celebrated monasteries of his day, and especially those of Cluny compiled by a monk Bernard in 1067. There was no single uniform use amongst monks, as Lanfranc strongly emphasised in his preface, in which he stated that each house was free to make additions or alterations to its customs as it saw fit. The work is in two main parts. Firstly, the liturgical customs, especially for Holy Week, are set out in detail. Secondly, the general administration of the house is described—we learn of the duties of obedientiaries, of punishments, of oblate children, of the care of the sick, of the last rites. The whole forms a valuable guide to what would be the aim of an observant house about this time. We receive a strong impression of the hardness of the conventual life, governed at every point by detailed regulation. Lanfranc's *Constitutions* were shortly adopted at St Albans by his nephew Paul, and at Westminster and other houses.

Though two new houses of some importance were established in England during the Conqueror's reign, William's own foundation of Battle in Sussex to commemorate the Hastings victory, and the Cluniac priory of Lewes founded by William de Warenne, Lanfranc concentrated his own activities on revitalising the monastic order in England as it already existed. The great period of expansion lay a little way ahead. A notable event, however, during the primacy was the establishment of monks at Durham, which had been served by secular priests since 995. This move was the result of a mission sent to the desolate north by Aethelwig, and consisting of three monks. They gathered disciples together, and reinhabited the ruined monasteries of Jarrow and Wearmouth. In 1083 the two communities united and migrated to Durham, at the invitation of its recently consecrated bishop. An Englishman Aldwin, who led the original mission, now became the first prior. He was succeeded by another Englishman, Turgot, who was still prior when bishop William de St Carilef commenced his great cathedral in 1093. Turgot later became bishop of St Andrews.

Durham cathedral priory long remained an outstanding example of an observant Benedictine community. It was not only St Cuthbert's mortal remains which gave lustre to Durham. It was above all the spirit of austerity, exemplified so well in the life and career of the saint, which lived on in this grandest spot of English Christendom. Here worked and prayed men who were as hard as the stones they trod, men whose personal severity matched that of the northern air which they daily breathed. The note of austere simplicity was strong in the north as a whole, and indeed it has never died away. It can be heard today on the sands of Lindisfarne and in the drab streets of Monkwearmouth. It is a far cry from the easy graciousness of a Salisbury cathedral-close to the splendour which crowns the wooded banks of the Wear. The twenty-three monks who settled in Durham in 1083 may be said to have revived the old Christian steadfastness of the north-east; and yet they were also forward-looking, a symptom of the urge to austerity widespread in Europe at this time. The introduction of the Carthusian order into England belongs to the twelfth century, but it may be noted that at the time Aldwin, with his two companions, was journeying northwards in search of a greater solitude than was to be found in the civilised and highly organised monasteries of the south, Bruno was forsaking his canonry and lectureship at Rheims for the company of forest-dwelling hermits. It was in 1084 that with the approval of Hugh, bishop of Grenoble, he established himself on the site to be known as the Grande Chartreuse. For England, however, the multiplication of religious orders lay in the future, and until the end of the primacy of Lanfranc it was Benedictine monks who held the field.

It is in the great cathedral of Christ and the Blessed Virgin Mary at Durham that we might appropriately take leave of the Anglo-Saxons and their Church. This, the most impressively situated ecclesiastical building in Europe, belongs it is true to the Norman period. But perhaps in no other place do we hear so strongly and clearly the call of the Saxon saint and scholar. The church continued to cast its spell on the English long after their subjugation at Norman hands. A short poem of the twelfth century, in late Old English, sings the praises of Durham and enumerates both its majestic position and its lustre as the final home of many saints. It stands on a steep rock, around which flow the waters of the Wear. It is encompassed by dense forests, the home of wild beasts innumerable. There are relics here not only of Cuthbert and Bede, but of Oswald and Aidan, of Aethelwold bishop of Lindisfarne, of abbot Boisil (Cuthbert's teacher), of numerous saints who await the Judgment.[39] To the author of this present work, no other place is as strangely impressive, save the Lorelei rock in the Rhine, around which legends of a different kind have gathered. Durham is a worthy home of the authentic Christian tradition, exemplified so well in the life of Bede, greatest of Northumbrians and the true Teacher of the West during the centuries of transition from the classical to the middle ages.

This church represents too the commanding position of the religion of Christ in England at the close of the eleventh century. It had been a long journey from the time when merchants or soldiers from Gaul brought the Gospel to these shores, to the day when Lanfranc died in May 1089. It is a period covering almost exactly half of the history of English and British Christianity. During these centuries a Germanic people was brought to see in the Son of God the object of its worship. The broad lines of diocesan organisation were laid, and the parochial system developed. The basis of English culture and civilisation was established. Habits of thought and worship were inculcated into the minds and practice of Anglo-Saxons which have not been seriously challenged until modern times. The broad theme of this book has been the Conversion of the English Teutons. To the agents of this process Englishmen can never fail to be grateful; the results of the process they may abandon at their peril.

NOTES

1 *Bell. Gal.* VI, 13–14. The passages are cited in full and discussed in Sir T. D. Kendrick's *The Druids* (1927).

2 According to Valerius Maximus, who wrote early in the first century, the Gauls were so convinced of the immortality of the soul that they would lend money to each other on the security of a future life.

3 Cf. the article 'The Origin of Druidism', by Julius Pokorny in *Celtic Review* (July 1908), where it is maintained that druidism originated as the religion of the pre-Celtic inhabitants of this island.

4 *Claudius,* 25.

5 Tacitus, *Annals,* XIV, 30.

6 *Natural History,* XVI, 95.

7 See Kendrick (*op. cit.* p. 55), and R. J. C. Atkinson, *Stonehenge* (1956), p.180. It was the late seventeenth-century antiquary John Aubrey who first claimed that Stonehenge was built by the druids, an idea thoroughly popularised by William Stukeley in the following century.

8 *V.C.H. Hants,* I, 336.

9 I. A. Richmond, in *Archaeologia Aeliana,* 4th series, XXI (1943), 206–10.

10 Richmond and I. McIntyre, in *Archaeologia Aeliana,* 4th series, XIV (1937), 103–9.

11 Richmond, *Roman Britain* (1955), pp. 92–4.

12 Richmond, *Archaeologia Aeliana,* 4th series, XIX (1941), 37–9.

13 For the adoption of Celtic deities by the Romans cf. F. G. Collingwood, *Roman Britain* (1936), p. 267.

14 See the article by I. Richmond, J. P. Gillam, and E. Birley, 'The Temple of Mithras at Carrawburh', in *Archaeologia Aeliana,* 4th series, XXIX (1951).

Ch. II

1 H. & S., I, 23. It was not Paul himself, but his writings, which made their way to Britain.

2 *Ep. ad Cor.* I, 5 'καὶ ἐπὶ τὸ τέρμα τῆς δύσεως ἐλθών'. Cf. Lightfoot, *The Epistles of St Clement,* p. 50.

3 *Annals,* XII, 35.

4 Prologue, *De Antiquitate Glastoniensis Ecclesiae,* ed. Gale: *Historiae Britannicae Scriptores,* XV (1691). The article by H. Thurston 'The English Legend of St Joseph of Arimathea', may be consulted (*Month,* CLVIII, 1931).

5 J. Ussher, *Britannicarum Ecclesiarum Antiquitates* (1639), pp. 5–12; E. Stillingfleet, *Origines Britannicae* (1840 ed.), pp. 6–12, 39–49. For a criticism of Stillingfleet's views relating to St Paul see W. L. Alexander, *The Ancient British Church* (1889), pp. 52 ff.

6 The Lucius legend derives ultimately from an error in the biographical list of popes known as the *Liber Pontificalis*. Cf. W. Levison, *Bede, his Life, Times, and Writings*, ed. A. Hamilton Thompson (1935), p. 135 n.

7 *Historia Ecclesiastica*, I, 4; V, 24. In the first reference Bede gives the date of Eleutherus' mission as 156, in the second (in a recapitulary chapter) as 167. Gildas does not mention the story.

8 *Historia Brittonum*, XXI.

9 *Adversus Haereses*, I, 3.

10 *Adversus Judaeos*, VII (*P.L.* 2, col. 650): 'Britannorum inaccessa Romanis loca, Christo vero subdita . . . . Christi nomen regnat.' At the time Tertullian was writing, the Romans were in occupation of Britain from the Kent and Sussex coast northwards to Antoninus' Wall, which reached from the Firth of Clyde to the Firth of Forth.

11 E.g. *In Lucam Homiliae VI* (*P.G.* 13, col. 1816): 'Virtus Domini Salvatoris et cum his est, qui ab orbe nostro in Britannia dividuntur.'

12 *Demonstratio Evangelica*, III, 3.

13 *H.E.* I, 4; V, 24.

14 'Supra dicto ut conicimus persecutionis tempore' (*De Excidio Britanniae*, ed. H. Williams (1899), X, XI).

15 According to Eusebius, *H.E.* VIII, 13, and Lactantius, *Vita Constantii* I, Constantius took no part in the Diocletianic persecution.

16 H. & S. I, 8.

17 Bede (*H.E.* I, 8) says that Arianism infected the Church of the Britons, who were 'ever willing to listen to some new thing, and hold steadfastly to nothing'. But he is here following Gildas, who held a poor opinion of his own country-men.

18 H. & S. I, 8.

19 *Historia Arianorum ad Monachos*, I, 360.

20 *Liber de Synodis*, I, 479 (*P.L.* 10).

21 H. & S. I, 9. Cf. Sulpicius Severus, *Historia Sacra*, II, 41 (*P.L.* 20, col. 152).

22 H. & S. I, 10.

23 For Silchester see F. Haverfield in *V.C.H. Hants*, I, 278; and his paper 'Early British Christianity', *E.H.R.* (July 1896), p. 418.

24 These hanging bowls are found fairly widely distributed in the eastern half of Roman Britain. They are discussed by Sir T. D. Kendrick, 'British Hanging Bowls', *Antiquity*, VI (1932), pp. 161–84; also in his *Anglo-Saxon Art* (1938), p. 93. For more recent discussions of this apparently insoluble problem see Aslak Leistöl, 'The Hanging Bowl, a Liturgical and Domestic Vessel', in *Acta Archaeologica*, 24 (Copenhagen 1953), p. 163; and Maire and Liam de Paor, *Early Christian Ireland* (1958), pp. 44–6.

25 G. W. Meates, E. Greenfield, and E. Birchenough, 'The Lullingstone Roman Villa', *Archaeologia Cantiana*, LXV (1952), pp. 26–78. Cf. Gregory of Tours (*History of the Franks*, X, 31, ed. O. Dalton, II, p. 470) who relates that Litorius, who became bishop of Tours during the first year of the emperor Constans (337–50), converted the house of a certain man of senatorial family into a church. This was the first church erected in Tours, he says, and necessary

because of the growing number of Christians. See also G. W. Meates, *Lullingstone Roman Villa* (London 1955).

26 *H.E.* I, 26: ecclesias fabricandi vel restaurandi licentiam acciperent.

27 F. Haverfield, 'Roman Cirencester', in *Archaeologia*, 69, pp. 188–9.

28 Haverfield, 'Early Northumbrian Christianity and the altars to the Di Veteres'. *Archaeologia Aeliana*, 3rd series, xv, 22–43.

29 The 'Confessio' and 'Coroticus' were edited by N. J. D. White, 'Libri Sancti Patricii', in *Proceedings of the Royal Irish Academy* (1904). They may also be read in H. & S. II, 296–319.

30 J. B. Bury, *The Life of St Patrick and his Place in History* (1905). This sane and balanced account perhaps, however, exaggerates the extent of Patrick's connection with Rome. Prof. Bury's underlying thesis was that Patrick brought Ireland within the Roman fold—'he brought Ireland into connection with the Church of the Empire, and made it formally part of universal Christendom' (p. 213). It was maintained by Heinrich Zimmer (*Celtic Church*, pp. 35–41, translated by A. Meyer, 1902) that Patrick was one and the same person as his predecessor Palladius, an identification rejected not only by Bury (pp. 343–4) but by W. Levison, *Bischof Germanus* (pp. 166 ff.). Zimmer sought to disparage the achievement of Patrick, in whom he saw a religious enthusiast of small culture. Other works on Patrick which may be consulted are J. H. Todd, *Saint Patrick, Apostle of Ireland* (Dublin 1864); B. Robert, *Étude critique sur la vie et l'œuvre de Saint Patrick* (Paris 1883); E. J. Newell, *St Patrick: his Life and Teaching* (S.P.C.K. 1907).

More recent work includes T. F. O'Rahilly, *The Two Patricks* (Dublin 1942), in which the theory is put forward that a first Patrick (identified with Palladius) worked for some thirty years in Ireland and was succeeded on his death in 461 by another Patrick who laboured in the country until he died in 493. Mario Esposito, 'The Patrician Problem and a possible solution', in *Irish Historical Studies*, 10 (1956), reverses the order, but places the death of the first evangelist *c.*430, upon which he was succeeded by Palladius. Nora K. Chadwick, in the volume of essays entitled *Studies in the Early British Church* (Cambridge University Press, 1958), p. 26, thinks that the chronological problems of Patrick's life would disappear if we were to study the genuine canon of his own writings in the light not of later, but of contemporary records, especially those of the Continent, and in the light of continental usages.

31 'Patrem habui Calpornum diaconum, filium quendam Potiti filii Odissi presbyteri,' H. & S. II, 296. The Latin is obscure, and one might be tempted to think that it was Patrick's great-grandfather Odissus who may have been the priest. If this were so, we should have evidence of a clerical family reaching back as far, perhaps, as Milan. But actually the words 'filii Odissi' are merely a marginal reading in the Armagh text of the 'Confessio'. It is clear therefore that it was Potitus who was in priest's orders.

32 Siricius, *Ep. ad Himerium* (*P.L.* 56, col. 558–9). The pope writes to Himerius, bishop of Tarragone, calling on him to insist that his priests and deacons observe the rule of celibacy enjoined by the Council of Elvira (*c.* 300). Writing after 386, St Ambrose said there were priests in the more isolated

countries who continued to marry; *De officiis*, I, 50 (*P.L.* 16, col. 105). For a discussion of celibacy amongst the Celtic clergy from the fifth century onward, see Louis Gougaud, *Christianity in Celtic Lands*, pp. 231 ff.; his conclusions on some points, however, are open to question.

33 For the decurions or 'curiales' of this period see S. Dill's *Roman Society in the Last Century of the Western Empire* (1898), bk. III, ch. 2.

34 The place has often been identified with Dumbarton, on the Clyde. But the serious objection to this view is the fact that Calpurnius was an urban official of the Empire. It is hard to see how there could have been any Roman civic organisation so far north as this, especially during the disturbed years towards the close of the fourth century. There is a Bannaventa near Daventry, but this was probably too far inland for a pirate band to reach. J. B. Bury thought that 'Bannaventa was south of the Wall of Hadrian, somewhere in Western Britain, not very far from the coast' (*St Patrick*, p. 325). He further suggested that the existence of three places named Banwen in Glamorganshire might offer a solution of the problem (Preface, p. x).

35 The evidence for pre-Patrician Christianity in Ireland is summarised in H. & S. II, 289–91.

36 'Chronicle', *sub anno* 431 (*M.G.H. Auctores Antiquissimi. Chronica Minora*, I, 473). 'Ad Scottos in Christum credentes ordinatus a papa Caelestino Palladius primus episcopus mittitur.' It should be noted once for all that at this time and throughout the period covered by this present book, the term 'Scotia' signified Ireland.

37 'Dum Romanam insulam studet servare catholicam, fecit etiam barbaram christianam', Prosper, *Liber contra Collatorem*, XXI, 2 (*P.L.* 51, col. 271).

38 Cf. Mrs C. F. Alexander's translation in *Hymns A. & M. Revised*, 162.

39 There is an interesting note by J. T. Fowler on this subject, in his edition of Adamnan's *Vita S. Columbae*, p. xxxii. Ireland's immunity from serpents had been noticed as early as the third century. Cf. Colomba's effective action against the snakes of Iona: Adamnan, II, 28.

40 *Annals of Ulster*, ed. W. M. Hennessy and B. MacCarthy, 4 vols. (London 1887–1901), *sub anno* 441. Cf. the tradition that Patrick visited Rome in the company of one Sachellus, returning with relics, related by the seventh-century writer Tirechan. The Roman visit is accepted by Bury (pp. 150 ff.), who sees in it the prelude to the founding of the Armagh bishopric; it is considered doubtful by the Benedictine scholar Dom L. Gougaud (*Christianity in Celtic Lands*, p. 47).

41 Maire and Liam de Paor, *Early Christian Ireland* (1958), p. 48.

42 Both Gildas (*De Excidio*, XIX) and Bede (*H.E.* I, 8), it is true, speak slightingly of the orthodoxy of the British Church. But the rhetorical character of Gildas' language lessens its value, and Bede in the main merely reproduced Gildas' passage.

43 Various writers testify to Pelagius as a native of Britain. Cf. Augustine, *Ep. CLXXXVI*, I (*Corpus Scriptorum Ecclesiasticorum Latinorum*, 45; also *P.L.* 33, col. 816); Marius Mercator, *Liber subnot. in verba Juliana*, praef. 2 (*P.L.* 48, col. 111); Prosper of Aquitaine, 'Chronicle', *sub anno* 413 (*M.G.H.*

Auct. ant. Chronica Minora, I, 467), and in *Carmen de ingrat*, I (*P.L.* 51, col. 94).

44 *H.E.* I, 17.

45 See the discussion of John Cassian's thought by Peter Munz in *Jour. Eccl. Hist.* XI No. 1, (April 1960).

46 Fastidius, *De Vita Christiana*, XIV (*P.L.* 50, col. 400). 'Nec quisquam se Christianum judicet, nisi qui Christi et doctrinam sequitur et imitatur exemplum ... Christianus est, qui omnibus misericordiam facit, qui omnino non movetur injuria, qui opprimi pauperem se praesente non patitur, qui miseris subvenit, qui indigentibus succurrit ...' For Fastidius see Germain Morin, Le 'De vita christiana' de l'évêque breton Fastidius et le livre de Pélage ad viduam (*Revue bénédictine*, XV, 1898, pp. 481–93); and R. S. T. Haslehurst, *The Works of Fastidius* (1927).

47 The most reliable authority for St Ninian is the brief notice by Bede, *H.E.* III, 4. His Life, written in the twelfth century by Ailred of Rievaulx, was edited by A. P. Forbes, 'Lives of S. Ninian and S. Kentigern', in the *Historians of Scotland*, V (1874), and is also included by J. Pinkerton in *Lives of the Scottish Saints*, revised by W. M. Metcalfe, I (1889).

48 *H.E.* III, 4, 'qui erat Romae regulariter fidem et mysteria veritatis edoctus'. The trustworthiness of this statement is questioned by Nora K. Chadwick, *Studies in the Early British Church*, p. 27.

49 J. A. Duke, *The Columban Church* (Edinburgh 1957 ed), Appendix I.

50 Letters of Apollinaris Sidonius, IX, 3, p. 152 (*M.G.H. Auct. ant.* VIII). Cf. *The Letters of Sidonius*, trans. O. M. Dalton, II, 181.

51 H. & S. I, 7–11.

52 Earlier, towards the end of the fourth century, Victricius, bishop of Rouen, had come to Britain to restore peace amongst the British bishops, who were in a state of dissension. Victricius, *De laude sanctorum* I, 2 (*P.L.* 20, col. 443). Cf. E. Vacandard, *Saint Victrice évêque de Rouen* (Paris 1909), pp. 126–7).

53 'Ex Britanniis directa legatio Gallicanis episcopis nunciavit Pelagianam perversitatem in suis locis late populos occupasse, et quamprimum fidei Catholicae debere succurri' (*Const. Vit. S. Germ.* I, 19). Cf. Bede, *H. E.* I, 17.

54 According to Nora Chadwick (*Studies in the Early British Church*, p. 23), there was probably only one visit of Germanus to Britain, Constantius duplicating a single historical event by unconsciously following variant traditions. The writer thinks this was a common error, and cites further Bede's account of the two interviews of Augustine with the British bishops.

55 Louis Prunel, *Saint Germain d'Auxerre* (Paris 1929), pp. 93 ff.

56 Sidon. Apoll. *Epistles*, IX, 9, p. 157 (*M.G.H. Auct. ant.* VIII).

Ch. III

1 D. Whitelock, *The Beginnings of English Society* (1956), p. 18.

2 Cf. R. G. Collingwood, *Roman Britain*, 2nd ed. (1937), p. 319 and G. O. Sayles, *Medieval Foundations of England* (1948), pp. 32–5.

3 *De Excidio Britanniae*, ed. H. Williams (1899), pp. 56–61.

4 *The Letters of Sidonius*, ed. O. M. Dalton, I, 17 (*M.G.H. Auct. ant.* VIII, 11).

5 Jordanes, *Getica*, 45 (*M.G.H. Auct. ant.* V, 118–19).

6 For British Christians in Armorica see H. & S. II, 71–80.

7 *History of the Franks*, V, 11. Ed. O. M. Dalton, II, 185.

8 H. Williams, *Christianity in Early Britain* (1912), pp. 277, 287.

9 *History of the Franks*, X, 9. Dalton, II, 436. At the time of the immigrations, of course, Armorica may well have been a largely depopulated wilderness, following depredations by Teutonic raiders.

10 Ed. and trans. A. W. Wade-Evans, *The Life of St David* (1923). Rhigyfarch was a scholarly member of a clerical family which had an hereditary interest at Llanbadarn Fawr; he himself was a son of Sulien, who twice held the see of St David's. The 'Life' was written in the last quarter of the eleventh century to defend the prestige of the Welsh see, threatened by the encroachments of Canterbury. Rhigyfarch died in 1099.

11 His fragmentary Life was edited by A. P. Forbes, 'The Lives of S. Ninian and S. Kentigern' (*Historians of Scotland*, V, 1874). See the elaborate, detailed criticism of this Life by Prof. K. H. Jackson in *Studies in the Early British Church* (ed. Nora K. Chadwick, 1958). He concludes that we may be reasonably certain Kentigern was a real person and founder of the church in Glasgow (p. 341).

12 R. H. Hodgkin, *History of the Anglo-Saxons*, I, 248.

13 As in the well-known 'bee-hive' cells, in which each course of stone is a little within the one below.

14 C. A. Ralegh Radford, 'Tintagel: the Castle and Celtic Monastery' (*Antiquaries Journal*, XV, 1935). Also, by the same author, *Tintagel Castle* (H.M.S.O. 1955).

15 H. & S. II, 292–4. It has been edited by P. Grosjean in *Analecta Bollandiana* (1955), LXXIII.

16 Tírechán (*Book of Armagh*, Tir. 18) says that Patrick consecrated 450 bishops, though he gives the names of only 42 of them. In the fourth and fifth centuries it was normal for all Christian Churches to be organised in a great many dioceses. The originality about the Irish Church was that bishops were appointed to rural districts.

17 Fr. Ryan (*Irish Monasticism*, pp. 189–90) states that in sixth-century Ireland 'about half the leading abbot-rulers were bishops, about half priests, and the more illustrious names were to be found amongst the latter'. In personal dignity a bishop ranked superior to a priest, but it was considered that he should be 'a saint rather than a ruler'.

18 This monastery must not of course be confused with that of Bangor founded late in the sixth century near Chester.

19 On the subject see: A. W. Haddon, 'Scots on the Continent' (*Remains*, ed. A. P. Forbes, 1876); J. von Pflugk-Harttung, 'The Old Irish on the Continent' (*Trans. R.H.S.*, New Series, V, 1891); W. Levison, 'Die Iren und die Fränkische Kirche' (*Historische Zeitschrift*, CIX, 1–22). For Columbanus, Eugene Martin, *Saint Columban* (Paris 1905, 3rd ed. 1921), and the *Vita Columbani* by Jonas (*M.G.H. Scriptores Merovingicarum*, IV).

20   On this debatable topic see G. T. Stokes, 'The Knowledge of Greek in Ireland' (*Proceedings of Royal Irish Academy*, 3rd series, II, 187–202), and on the study of Greek more generally in the early middle ages, M. L. W. Laistner, *Thought and Letters in Western Europe*, ch. x.

21   For the adoption of Latin as the ecclesiastical language of the West see: P. Fredericq, 'Les conséquences de l'evangélisation par Rome et par Byzance sur le développement de la langue maternelle des peuples convertis' (*Bull. de l'Académie royale de Belgique*, Classe des Lettres, 1903, n.11, pp. 738–51); and F. Cumont, 'Pourquoi le Latin fut la seule langue liturgique de l'occident?' (*Mélanges Paul Frédéricq*, 1904, pp. 63–6).

22   The Welsh Church was the most probable source from which the Irish derived their love of learning. The Church of Romano-Britain knew Latin culture at first hand; this knowledge was transmitted, via Wales, to Ireland.

23   *H.E.* III, 27. The Irish provided their visitors with free tuition, lodging, and access to books.

24   The indispensable authority for Columba is Adamnan's *Vita S. Columbae*. J. T. Fowler's convenient edition (1894, 2nd ed. 1920) draws on the larger and more exhaustive work of W. Reeves, the *Life of Columba by Adamnan* (1857). There is a translation by W. Huyshe, *The Life of St Columba* (1906).

25   On this see W. Oakeshott, *The Sequence of English Medieval Art* (1950), p. 8 and Appendix I (p. 36).

26   For the account of Columba's last hours see Adamnan, III, 23, a passage of exceptional beauty.

27   The changing of water into wine, of bitter apples into sweet, the healing of a broken hip-bone by means of holy water, the stilling of a storm, the driving of a demon out of a milk-pail, the curing of a nose-bleed, the blessing of a poor man's cattle, the cursing of sinners, the sentence of death passed on a wild boar encountered by the saint in a dense wood, the tussle with the Loch Ness monster (for all of which see Adamnan, II), in some cases suggest a reading of New Testament miracles into Columba's life, in others the genuine influence of a holy man amongst a poetical and susceptible people. For his angelic visions see III.

28   See genealogical table in Fowler's edition (facing p. xcv).

29   On Celtic monasticism see J. Ryan, *Irish Monasticism: Origins and Early Development* (1931); cf. the same author's paper, 'Irish Learning in the Seventh Century' (*Journal of the Royal Society of Antiquaries of Ireland*, 80, 1950).

30   H. & S. I, 142–3.

31   William of Malmesbury, *De Gestis pontificum* (R.S.), I, 204.

32   It is suggested by M. and L. de Paor, *Early Christian Ireland* (1958), p. 52, that the bishops may have lost their administrative functions partly because of the strictures on bishops by Gildas. This is very improbable. It was above all the tribal and rural nature of Irish society which ensured the predominance of the monastic communities.

33   I.e. it was certainly not worship of the 'protestant' type.

34   According to Cassian, who expounded to the West the principles of Eastern

monasticism, with which he was familiar through many years of residence in Bethlehem, vespers ends the service of the day. *Institutes of the Coenobitic Life*, III. Benedict, however, in his Rule added compline, and he was probably the originator of this office.

35 Jonas, *Vita Columbani*, II, 16; Adamnan, *Vita Columbae*, I, 40.

36 'vespertinalis Dominicae noctis missa' (III, 23). The actual meaning of this is, however, obscure, and it is probable that mass was normally celebrated early in the day.

37 Adamnan, I, 40, 'sacrae oblationis mysteria'; III, 17, 'sacram oblationem'. *Vitae Sanctorum Hiberniae*, ed. Plummer, I, 53, 'invenit sacerdotem stantem ante altare et volentem offerre sacrificium'.

38 Adamnan, I, 44; Jonas, II, 16.

39 The classic work dealing with this subject as a whole is F. E. Warren's *Liturgy and Ritual of the Celtic Church* (1881). There is a useful article by H. Jenner, 'Celtic Rite', in the *Catholic Encyclopaedia*.

40 There is a convenient rendering of the Stowe Liturgy in *Western Liturgies* (1938), a short book of translations by R. C. West.

41 Cf. Adamnan, I, 37: 'nam ipse Sanctus cum paucis fratribus extra regis munitionem dum vespertinales Dei laudes ex more celebraret, quidem magi, ad eos propius accedentes, in quantum poterant, prohibere conabantur, ne de ore ipsorum divinae laudis sonus inter gentiles audiretur populus'.

42 *H.E.* II, 20; IV, 18.

43 Cf. the story of Columba being sent to a certain bishop Etchen, to obtain from him episcopal orders on the spot. J. T. Fowler, lviii.

44 According to Eddius, he was re-ordained to all orders: 'per omnes gradus ecclesiasticos'. *The Life of Wilfred*, XV.

45 Theodore, *Canones*, II, IX, 3.

46 For public confession in the sixth-century Irish Church cf. Adamnan, I, 31: 'coram omnibus qui ibidem inerant, peccantias confitetur suas'.

47 On this see P. Fournier, 'Étude sur les pénitentiels' (*Revue d'histoire et de littérature religieuse*, VI–IX); and Le Bras, 'Penitentiels', in *Dictionnaire de Théologie Catholique*, ed. Vacant and Mangenot, XII, 1160 f. See also O. D. Watkins, *A History of Penance* (2 vols. 1920), especially II, 643 ff.

48 *Geschichte des deutschen Kirchenrechts* (Strasburg 1878), II, 468 ff.

49 Jonas, I, 5; II, 8.

50 *H.E.* IV, 25.

51 Cf. the bold manner in which he wrote to the papacy: *M.G.H. Epistolae Merovingici et Karolini Aevi*, I, 156–60. It is true that boldness of speech does not preclude fundamental loyalty. Columbanus undoubtedly had great respect for Rome, but in the last analysis he refused to abandon the Celtic Easter.

52 *H.E.* II, 20.

53 *M.G.H. Epist.* III, 292.

54 Quoted by Gougaud, *Christianity in Celtic Lands*, p. 46.

Ch. IV

1 *H.E.* I, 15. Cf. H. M. Chadwick, *The Origin of the English Nation* (1924), pp. 51 ff.

2 *Germania*, XL.

3 *English Historical Documents*, I, ed. D. Whitelock, p. 8.

4 *De Bello Gothico*, IV, 19.

5 The Victorians were prone to simplify the whole story of the Saxon conquest: thus J. R. Green, in the well-known comment of Plummer (*Baedae Opera Historica*, II, 28), wrote as 'if he had been present at the landing of the Saxons, and had watched every step of their subsequent progress'.

6 For the political division of England at the end of the sixth century see map facing p. 10, Chadwick, *op. cit.*

7 Cf. Tacitus, *Germania*, XVI. The peoples of Germany never live in cities, and their houses (invariably constructed of wood) are separate from each other. Each man likes to have an open space around him.

8 For an example of the way in which Roman remains later came to be used as quarries see *H.E.* IV, 19.

9 According to the slave-boy story as recorded by Bede (*H.E.* II, 1), the inhabitants of Britain were a fair, handsome people. But it would probably be false to assume that the pure blonde type was universal amongst the Saxons. The two missionaries named Hewald, 'de natione Anglorum', were fair and dark-haired respectively (*H.E.* V, 10).

10 Cf. J. R. Green, *Short History of the English People*, 1.

11 *Germania*, XIV.

12 On this see Bede, *Historia Abbatum*, 1. Benedict Biscop, on becoming a thegn of Oswy, receives a suitable grant of land: 'denique cum esset minister Oswiu regis, et possessionem terrae suo gradui competentem illo donante perciperet'.

13 For an example of the comitatus-principle in action see the Anglo-Saxon Chronicle, *sub anno* 755. Cf. *H.E.* II, 9, where we read how Lilla, loyal thegn of Edwin, saved his king from the assassin's dagger by interposing his own body. It was the same sense of loyalty to one's master that ensured the preservation of a large body of the correspondence of Boniface by his devoted servant Lull, as Miss Whitelock points out: *Eng. Hist. Doc.* I, 574.

14 *Germania*, XL.

15 On the subject of Anglo-Saxon heathenism may be mentioned P. D. C. de la Saussaye, *The Religion of the Teutons* (1902); H. M. Chadwick, *The Origin of the English Nation* (1924); A. E. Philippson, *Germanisches Heidentum bei den Angelsachsen* (1929). J. M. Kemble devoted a lengthy chapter to the subject in the first volume of his *Saxons in England* (1849). The big classical work is J. Grimm, *Teutonic Mythology*, 4 vols., ed. J. E. Stallybrass (1880–8).

16 They were recognised implicitly over a century ago by Kemble, *The Saxons in England*, I, 405: 'the rude rocks and lakes of Norway and Sweden, the volcanoes, hot springs, ice plains and snow-covered mountains of Iceland, readily moulded the Northmen to a different train of thought from that which satisfied the dwellers in the marshlands of the Elbe and the fat plains of

Britain.' He went on to say, however, that 'in the main it cannot be doubted that the heathendom of both races was the same'.

17 *Opera*, ed. J. A. Giles, VI, 139–342.

18 Cf. the list of names given by Kemble, *op. cit.* I, 343–4, 347–8.

19 Bruce Dickins, 'English Names and Old English Heathenism', in *Essays and Studies by members of the English Association*, XIX (1934), should be consulted, and the subject is treated by Sir F. Stenton, *Anglo-Saxon England*, pp. 96–102.

20 Stenton, *op. cit.* p. 102; Hodgkin, *History of the Anglo-Saxons*, I, 239.

21 Cf. Tacitus, *Germania*, IX. The holy places of the Germans are in woods and groves, and it is considered inconsistent with the dignity of a god that he should be imprisoned within walls.

22 *H.E.* I, 30.

23 P. Hunter Blair, *An Introduction to Anglo-Saxon England* (1956), p. 119.

24 Bede has many references to idol-worship. *H.E.* I, 30, 32; II, 5, 10, 11, 13, 20; III, 1, 22, 30; IV, 13; V, 19. In connection with altars, Bede invariably draws a distinction between Christian 'altaria' and heathen 'arae'.

Ch. V

1 For Gregory's life see the *Vita* of John the Deacon, *P.L.* 75, cols. 59–242; for his correspondence the edition of P. Ewald and L. M. Hartmann in *M.G.H. Epistolae*, I–II. The standard English modern life is by F. Homes Dudden, *Gregory the Great* (1905), 2 vols.

2 John the Deacon, *Vita*, I, 9.

3 I.e. an agent or nuncio at the imperial court.

4 See the historical fragment on Edgar's establishment of the monasteries, printed in *Leechdoms, Wortcunning, and Starcraft*, ed. O. Cockayne (R.S.), III, 433 ff.

5 *H.E.* II, 1.

6 Ed. F. A. Gasquet, *A Life of Pope St Gregory the Great* (1904), pp. 13–14. Extracts of this text, which was the work of a Whitby monk, are given by Plummer in Appendix I to his *Baedae Opera Historica* (II, 388–91). The relevant passages are translated by D. Whitelock in *Eng. Hist. Doc.* I, 687–90. A critical edition of this text is, however, still awaited. Of the story itself, R. H. Hodgkin thinks it must have some factual basis, and calls it 'a turning-point in the history of Latin Christianity' (*History of the Anglo-Saxons*, I, 259). According to Stenton, the story 'contains nothing that is improbable, and it belongs to the oldest stratum of tradition about Gregory's life' (*Anglo-Saxon England*, p. 103). Oman regarded it as 'a pretty tale' (*England before the Norman Conquest*, p. 255). In the Whitby text, it should be noted, there is no indication that the English boys whom Gregory noticed in Rome were actually slaves.

7 *H.E.* Preface.

8 The plague was known to Latin writers as 'lues inguinaria'. It broke out periodically from the reign of Justinian onwards. In the sixth and seventh

centuries the plague was undoubtedly a dreadful and potent factor in human existence, with which men had to learn to live. It was this scourge which carried away the inmates of Jarrow monastery during the abbacy of Ceolfrith, leaving only him and a small boy (apparently Bede himself). The plague made serious inroads into the educated and upper classes, creating problems in the supply of leadership. The unique appointment of an Eastern churchman, Theodore, to the see of Canterbury in 669, was due to the virtual annihilation by the plague of all English candidates for the office. Bede discusses the causes of plague in *De Natura Rerum*, XXXVII. He refers to the great plague of 664 in *H.E.* III, 27, apparently the same outbreak mentioned in Adamnan, *Vita Columbae*, II, 46, as devastating the greater part of Europe.

9 *M.G.H. Epistolae*, I, 388–9; *Eng. Hist. Doc.* I, 727. On the sale of Saxon slaves on the Continent see Levison, *England and the Continent*, pp. 8–10, and Pirenne, *Mohammed and Charlemagne*, p. 98. Ine of Wessex (688–726) legislated unsuccessfully against the practice. The Germanic peoples, doubtless on account of their physical beauty, were an important source of the slave-trade, which was conducted largely by Jews.

10 W. E. H. Lecky, *History of European Morals*, ch. IV. Cf. however, H. Pirenne, *op. cit.* p. 96: the Church 'neither condemned nor attacked the institution of slavery on principle'. St Paul, it will be remembered, returned the escaped slave Onesimus to his master Philemon: Philemon, vv. 10–14.

11 Dudden, *Gregory the Great*, II, 181.

12 *H.E.* I, 25.

13 *History of the Franks*, IV, 19; IX, 26. The view, however, of the English editor, O. M. Dalton, that Gaul and England had little in common by way of contracts is open to question. Ingoberg was a devout woman, 'constant in vigils, in prayers, and in the giving of alms'. At her death she left benefactions to churches, and freed many serfs.

14 Stenton, *op. cit.* p. 59.

15 *M.G.H. Epistolae*, I, 423; *Eng. Hist. Doc.* I, 727.

16 H. & S. III, 539: 'syncellus'.

17 *H.E.* I, 23. The documents relevant to the mission are conveniently collected and translated in A. J. Mason's *The Mission of St Augustine* (1897).

18 H. & S. III, 5 ff.

19 *M.G.H. Epistolae*, I, 423: 'atque ideo pervenit ad nos, Anglorum gentem ad fidem Christianam, Deo miserante, desideranter velle converti, sed sacerdotes e vicino negligere'. *Eng. Hist. Doc.* I, 728.

20 See A. S. Cook, 'Augustine's Journey from Rome to Richborough' (*Speculum*, I (1926)), and T. McKenny Hughes, 'The Landing Place of St Augustine' (*The Mission of St Augustine*, pp. 209–34).

21 As St Martin of Tours died c. 400, not long before this church probably fell into disuse, the actual dedication to the Gallic saint would seem to have been the work of Bertha herself, or her chaplain Liudhard.

22 On the complete absence of martyrdom from the history of the Christianisation of England, cf. the observation of J. Lingard, that the success of the missionaries here 'is sufficient to disprove the opinion of those who imagine

that no church can be firmly established, the foundations of which are not cemented with the blood of martyrs' (*History and Antiquities of the Anglo-Saxon Church*, I, 39).

23 *H.E.* IV, 22.

24 *H.E.* I, 25.

25 *Catholic Homilies*, II, 129.

26 Daniel IX, 16. The antiphon was part of the Rogationtide rite.

27 *H.E.* I, 26.

28 Thomas of Elmham, *Historia Monasterii S. Augustini Cantuariensis* (R.S.), p. 78. The text here is doubtful, and it is perhaps more likely that the king's baptism took place at the end of the year along with that of his people in general.

29 *Op. cit.* I, 22.

30 According to Bede (*H.E.* I, 27) the consecrating bishop at Arles was Aetherius, 'archbishop of that city'. But it is known that at this time Aetherius was bishop of Lyons.

31 W. Thorne, *Chronicon S. Augustini Cantuariensis*, translated by A. H. Davis, *William Thorne's Chronicle* (1934): see p. 6. Cf. Thomas of Elmham, pp. 79–81.

32 *M.G.H. Epistolae*, II, 30 f; *Eng. Hist. Doc.* I, 728. It is this letter which tells us of the mass baptism of over ten thousand converts at Christmas.

33 H. & S. III, 33 ff.

34 *M.G.H. Epistolae*, II, 308 ff; *H.E.* I, 32.

35 *M.G.H. Epistolae*, II, 304.

36 *H.E.* I, 30.

37 On this, see the article by M. Deanesly and P. Grosjean, 'The Canterbury Edition of the Answers of Pope Gregory I to St Augustine' (*Journal of Eccles. Hist.* X, i, Apr. 1959). This draws attention to a book published in Munster, 1941, *Die Quellen zur Angelsachsenmission Gregors des Grossen: eine historiographische Studie*, by S. Brechter, which declared the 'responsa' spurious, and the result of circumstances and problems which did not appear in the English Church until after the reorganisation by Theodore (d. 690). Brechter thought that Nothelm (Bede's informant) was the real author of the 'responsa'. Miss Deanesly and Fr. Grosjean, however, conclude that Nothelm was rather the editor of documents which he found at Canterbury, and which in a loose sense are Gregorian, with the exception of the fifth, eighth, and ninth resonsa, which are later. Cf. Levison, *England and the Continent*, p. 17 n., where the genuineness of the responsa is upheld, after some earlier hesitation on the part of that scholar. Cf. also Knowles, *Monastic Order*, p. 619 n.

38 *H.E.* I, 29.

39 Cf. Thomas of Elmham, *op. cit.* p. 95. The metropolitical honour should remain in the city where Augustine was buried.

40 *H.E.* I, 27; *M.G.H. Epistolae*, II, 331–43. The Preface to the Responsa is not in Bede. It is printed in H. & S. III, 18. For similar replies, by Gregory II and Gregory III to questions from Boniface, see *Monumenta Moguntina*, ed. Jaffé, pp. 88–94.

41 'clerici extra sacros ordines constituti'.

42 Miss Deanesly and Fr. Grosjean think this 'answer' may really be based on written instructions given to Augustine before he actually set out for Kent. It deals with problems which Augustine may have foreseen.

43 Cf. M. Deanesly and P. Grosjean, *op. cit.* pp. 40–2.

44 It was suggested by H. H. Howarth, *St Augustine of Canterbury* (1913), pp. 42, 48, on the other hand, that Liudhard was probably dead at the time of Augustine's arrival in Canterbury, 'or Bede would have had something to say about him on that occasion, nor would the missionaries have taken immediate possession of his church as they did'.

45 H. & S. III, 367: 'in baptismi officio, in missarum celebratione, in cantilenae modo celebrantur, iuxta exemplar videlicet quod scriptum de Romana habernus ecclesia': canon 13.

46 In the view of M. Deanesly and P. Grosjean (*op. cit.* pp. 5–9), this reply cannot be the work of Gregory, as prohibition by degrees would not be possible as early as this.

47 The council of Arles had recommended seven bishops as desirable for a consecration, Nicaea not less than three. But this was intended as a precaution against clandestine consecrations, and it was not suggested that a consecration by a single bishop was invalid.

48 At first the pallium was a mark of favour (like a modern 'decoration') granted by the emperor, then by the pope, to distinguished prelates. It was sometimes conferred by patriarchs other than the pope. But it became recognised eventually as the necessary confirmatory sign from Rome of a metropolitan's authority. The pallium itself is a circular band of white wool with pendants behind and before the wearer. The wool has always been made from that of lambs specially reared in the convent of St Agnes, Rome. See Levison, pp. 18–22; Plummer, I, 49–52.

49 *H.E.* I, 28.

50 *The Mission of St Augustine*, p. 79 n.

51 'qualiter debemus cum Galliarum Brittaniarumque episcopis agere?'

52 *Op. cit.* p. 79 n.

53 *H.E.* I, 29.

54 'sed etiam omnes Britanniae sacerdotes'. Gregory hitherto uses the word 'episcopi' for bishops, and his use of 'sacerdotes' here suggests that he was doubtful of the real character of the Celtic bishops. It is possible that having been told something of the monastic character of the Celtic Churches, he may have thought that the bishops would not be the clergy with whom Augustine would have effectively to deal.

55 *Op. cit.* p. 86 n.

56 Deanesly and Grosjean think these were based on moral theology lectures given at Canterbury after Augustine's time: *op. cit.* pp. 10 f., 43.

57 Deanesly and Grosjean think it doubtful that the Easter date was discussed at the conference—the controversy did not become acute in the west until c. 600: *op. cit.* p. 43. But Bede, though he does not make it quite clear (*H.E.* II, 2) that the Easter question was discussed at the first conference, specifically

states that Augustine required conformity in Easter dating from the Britons at the second conference which shortly followed.

58 *H.E.* II, 2.
59 *H.E.* II, 3.
60 *H.E.* II, 3.
61 *H.E.* II, 4; cf. Lightfoot, *Apostolic Fathers*, I, 1, 64, 158.
62 *H.E.* II, 3.

Ch. VI

1 *H.E.* II, 4.
2 This bishop has been identified with bishop Dagan, of Inbher Daeile, Co. Wicklow, who died 639; *Baedae Opera Historica*, ed. Plummer, II, 83. According to Goscelin, an Irish bishop Terenan was attracted to England by the fame of Laurentius, and converted to the true Easter; H. & S. III, 61 n.
3 On the common Teutonic custom of a son marrying his step-mother, cf. Procopius, *De Bello Gothico*, IV, 20, where we learn that Ermengisl, the sixth-century king of the Varni, commanded his son Radiger to marry his step-mother, according to their national custom.
4 The story plainly has a suspicious look, and if genuine probably represents a deliberate stratagem on the part of Laurentius to frighten the king into repentance: *H.E.* II, 6. There were several instances in early Christian tradition of visionary scourgings; Jerome, for example, was thus punished because of his love of the classical writers: Plummer, II, 89. Cf. Fowler, *Adamnani Vita Columbae*, p. 134 n.
5 *H.E.* II, 8.
6 *H.E.* II, 9.
7 *H.E.* II, 13.
8 *H.E.* II, 10.
9 *H.E.* II, 16.
10 *H.E.* II, 16. It occurred near the city of Tiovulfingacestir, identified probably with Littleborough, Notts. *Place-names of Nottinghamshire* (E.P.N.S.), pp. 35–6. There was long a tradition that Southwell was the place.
11 This is the second drowning of an important member of the Augustinian mission. He was drowned off the Italian coast, *H.E.* II, 20. The other casualty was Peter, first abbot of SS. Peter and Paul, who was drowned in the Channel off Ambleteuse and buried in Boulogne, *H.E.* I, 33. The courage of Augustine and his followers in facing natural perils should not be underestimated.
12 *H.E.* III, 8.
13 *H.E.* II, 15.
14 Stenton, *Anglo-Saxon England*, p. 50. Cf. also Stenton in *The Anglo-Saxons* (ed. P. Clemoes), pp. 50–2; and D. Wilson, *The Anglo-Saxons* (1960), who thinks that Sutton Hoo commemorates Aethelhere, who died in 655.
15 Bede calls him 'a thorough Christian, very learned, a good and devout man', *H.E.* II, 15; III, 18.

16 *H.E.* III, 25.
17 *H.E.* III, 19.
18 In Gaul he founded a monastery at Lagny, near Chelles. He died *c.* 650. For Fursa we have a 'Vita Fursei', ed. B. Krusch (*M.G.H. Scr. rer Merov.* IV).
19 A.S. Chronicle, *sub anno*. According to the anonymous Life of Ceolfrith, Botolf's monastery was in East Anglia. This would rule out the common identification with Boston. *Historia Abbatum auctore Anonymo,* IV (ed. Plummer, *Baedae Opera Historica*), translated in *Eng. Hist. Doc.* I, pp. 697 ff.
20 *H.E.* III, 7.
21 Thomas of Elmham, *Historia Monasterii S. Augustini Cantuariensis* (R.S.) p. 192.

Ch. VII

1 Northumbria is early found divided into two sections. Bernicia reached from the Lammermuir Hills to the Tyne or Tees, Deira (roughly the modern Yorkshire) southwards to the Humber.
2 *H.E.* III, 1, 2. Cf. *Adamnani Vita S. Columbae,* I, ch. 1.
3 On this, see J. M. Mackinlay, 'Celtic Relations of St. Oswald of Northumbria' (*Celtic Review,* V, 1909).
4 *H.E.* III, 4.
5 H. & S. III, 493: 'locus cunctis in Britannia venerabilior.'
6 *H.E.* III, 5.
7 *De Gestis Regum Anglorum,* ed. W. Stubbs (R.S.), I, 3.
8 W. Bright wrote that Aidan kept his followers 'aloof from what might be called ecclesiastical civilisation'. *Early English Church History,* p. 168 (3rd ed. 1897).
9 See Plummer, II, 157–60, for a list of the many places in Britain and on the Continent which came to claim possession of relics of St Oswald.
10 Finan also built a church at Lindisfarne, no doubt to replace Aidan's. He did not use stone, but hewn oaks thatched with reeds, 'after the Scottish manner' (*H.E.* III, 25). Eadbert, a later bishop of Lindisfarne, replaced the thatch with lead. How such wooden buildings might be kept windproof, by the use of clay in the crevices and nailing skins to the walls, is shown in Bede's *Life of Cuthbert,* XLVI.
11 *H.E.* III, 21.
12 *H.E.* III, 21.
13 Penda had become the strongest king in England by reason of his own character and military prowess. It does not seem that he set out over-consciously to be a conqueror. His effective career started from the defeat of Edwin in 632, when he was the ally of Cadwallon.
14 Chronicle, *sub anno* 655. Cf. however, W. Hunt, *The English Church from its Foundation to the Norman Conquest* (1899), p. 104.
15 *H.E.* III, 24.
16 Cf. the exceptionally large number of local heathen sites in Essex indicated by the place-name evidence.

17 *H.E.* III, 22.

18 *H.E.* III, 23.

Ch. VIII

1 In particular, Anglican writers have shown a stong tendency to underestimate the achievements of the Roman missionaries. Dean Hook remarked unkindly that 'a desire to die for the truth's sake was not characteristic of the Italian missionaries. . . . Paulinus had an excuse for leaving his flock, and he availed himself of it' (*Lives of the Archbishops of Canterbury*, I, 115). The Italians, as missionaries, were inept, and lacked 'courage, energy, and sound judgment' (p. 120). W. Hunt (*The English Church from its Foundation*, pp. 73–4), however, is balanced in his judgement.

2 P. Hunter Blair, *Introduction to Anglo-Saxon England*, p. 119. The most that can be said is that there may have been lingering memories of Christianity amongst some of the inhabitants encountered by Paulinus. But it is significant that Paulinus had to baptise all his hearers—there is not the slightest evidence of even the rudiments of a Church organisation in the district prior to his arrival.

3 *The Life of Bishop Wilfred by Eddius Stephanus*, ed. and trans. by B. Colgrave (1927). Little is known of Eddius, save that he was a musician, and a priest in Wilfred's entourage. This biography is of exceptional value as based on first-hand knowledge. It has the faults of a partisan work, and has often been criticised (cf. B. W. Wells and R. L. Poole, 'Eddius's Life of Wilfred', *E.H.R.* VI (1891), CXXXIII (1919)). Yet Eddius does not attempt to disguise the failings of his hero. The work was probably written 710–20, and was doubtless one of Bede's sources a few years later. Bede has various notices relating to Wilfred, to whom he was apparently not well disposed (*H.E.* III, 25, 28; IV, 13, 15, 16, 19, 23, and especially V, 19). In matters of detail he is the more reliable authority. Eddius' text is also edited by Levison in *M.G.H. Scr. rer. Merov.* VI, 163 ff., and by Raine, *Historians of York*, I (R.S.).

4 Eddius, V; *H.E.* V, 19. In 1879 a leaden bulla inscribed 'Bonifatii Arceidiac' was found in an old shell heap at Whitby along with a number of finds connected with Wilfred: Colgrave, p. 153. Cf. W. Levison, *England and the Continent*, p. 17, where a photograph of the seal is reproduced.

5 There has been confusion over the identity of Dalfinus, who according to Eddius (IV) was the archbishop. Bede (*H.E.* V, 19) follows Eddius in this. But according to 'Gallia Christiana', ed. P. Piolin, IV (1876), 43, Dalfinus was count of the city, and his brother Annemundus the archbishop. Dalfinus' daughter was offered in marriage to Wilfred as an inducement for him to stay. See Levison, *M.G.H. Scr. rer. Merov.* VI, 197 for the view that Annemundus was also called Dalfinus. Cf. Hunt, *The English Church*, p. 107 n.

6 H. M. Gwatkin, *Early Church History to* A.D. *313*, I, (1912), 157 ff.

7 Eddius, VIII, 'aet Stanforda'. This has been identified with Stamford in Lincolnshire, however, as also with Stainforth near Doncaster and a place of the same name near Giggleswick. Colgrave, pp. 155–6.

8 For a discussion of the date, see Stenton, *Anglo-Saxon England*, p. 129.
9 Those who wish to pursue the subject may be referred to J. F. Kenney, *The Sources for the Early History of Ireland*, I, 210 ff.
10 *H.E.* III, 25, Eddius, x.
11 Eddius, XII.
12 *H.E.* III, 26.
13 H. & S. III, 581.
14 B. Colgrave, *Two Lives of St Cuthbert* (1940), including a prose life by Bede and a life by an anonymous writer.
15 *Anon. Vit.* VI; 'vivens ibi quoque secundum sanctam scripturam contemplativam vitam in actuali agens.'
16 *H.E.* IV, 26; V, 12.
17 Alcuin, *Versus de sanctis Eboricensis Ecclesiae*, v, 843 ff. (*M.G.H. poet. Lat.* I, 188).
18 Cf. Stenton, *Anglo-Saxon England*, p. 88.

Ch. IX

1 *H.E.* III, 30.
2 *H.E.* III, 29; IV, 1. This action marks a clear point in the opening stages of the movement to English unity.
3 The episcopal lines of medieval and modern England (whether Anglican or Roman) are accordingly not derived from the bishops of the Augustinian mission.
4 For a lucid sketch of the great archbishop's career, see the article 'Theodore of Tarsus', by William Stubbs, in *D.C.B.* IV, 926–32. This useful compilation in four volumes, published in 1887, covers the first eight centuries.
5 G. Every, *The Byzantine Patriarchate* (1947), pp. 75–8.
6 Levison, *England and the Continent*, p. 13.
7 Aldhelm, *Ep. ad Eahfridum* (*PL.* 89, col. 95).
8 Theodore's action is somewhat uncertain. According to Eddius (xv), he consecrated Chad 'per omnes gradus ecclesiasticos', which would seem to imply that he regarded Celtic ordinations, as well as consecrations, as dubious. But according to Bede (*H.E.* IV, 2) he simply completed Chad's consecration, after the Catholic rite.
9 *H.E.* IV, 3. The tribute of Eddius also is noteworthy (XIV), coming from one who regarded him as a usurper: he calls him 'servum Dei religiosissimum et admirabilem doctorem'.
10 *H.E.* IV, 2.
11 *H.E.* IV, 12.
12 It is possible that he had resigned, in penitence for his act of simony, about this time (Rudborne, 'Hist. Maj. Wint', *Angl. Sac.* I, 192). But his successor Eorcenwald did not succeed him till 675, and it is unlikely that Theodore would have left the London see vacant for three years.
13 For the Hertford decrees see H. & S. III, 118–21; Gee and Hardy, *Documents* (1896), pp. 10–3. Matrimony is considered under the tenth heading. A man

may not leave his wife, save for fornication. If he dismiss his wife, he must not remarry if he desires to be regarded as a true Christian.

14   Hertford was 'the first constitutional measure of the collective English race'. Stubbs, *D.C.B.* IV, 928.

15   According to Florence of Worcester, the division was a fivefold one, in 679 (*M.H.B.* 622, appendix).

16   *H.E.* IV, 12. Bede's narrative does not suggest, however, that Putta exercised episcopal functions after the Rochester disaster. Florence of Worcester heads the list of the Hereford bishops with Putta, placing his death in 688. W. Bright accepts this as evidence that Putta of Rochester became a kind of acting bishop for Hereford (*Early English Church History*, p. 300), but Plummer is sceptical (II, 222). Cf. G. Hill, *The English Dioceses*, pp. 120–1.

17   Stenton, *Anglo-Saxon England*, p. 44.

18   *H.E.* IV, 6; Malmesbury, *De Gestis Pontificum* (R.S.), p. 144.

19   She entered the double monastery of Coldingham, in Co. Berwick, whose abbess was Aebbe. The latter has left her name in Ebchester, Co. Durham, St Abb's Head three miles from Coldingham, and the dedication of one of the Oxford city churches. The community was visited by Cuthbert. For some reason it deteriorated rapidly in standards, and it seems to be the first known instance of monastic degeneracy in Anglo-Saxon England (*H.E.* IV, 25). The year of St Aebbe's death is uncertain.

20   It is said that after Ecgfrith's death she also took the veil (Eddius, XXIV), and became a perfect abbess. Cf. *De Gestis Pontificum*, pp. 219 f.

21   Eddius, XXIV.

22   Lindsey was reconquered by Aethelred of Mercia in 678, but the new diocesan arrangements remained.

23   As William of Malmesbury thinks (*De Gestis Pont.* p. 220).

24   678–9, according to W. Levison (*England and the Continent*, p. 51).

25   H. & S. III, 141–4; Gee and Hardy, *Documents*, pp. 13–15.

26   Monothelitism was the denial of the two wills, human and divine, in Christ.

27   Eddius, XXXVI, XXXVIII.

28   *H.E.* IV, 13.

29   *H.E.* III, 20. Cf. too G. R. Stephens and W. D. Stephens, 'Cuthman: a neglected Saint' (*Speculum*, XIII (1938), 451). This saint, associated with Steyning, is, however, of eighth- or ninth-century date. He has two short biographical sketches in *Acta Sanctorum*.

30   Eddius, XIII.

31   This story is told by Bede (*H.E.* IV, 13), but omitted by Eddius.

32   *H.E.* IV, 13.

33   The name is British, and suggests a native mother.

34   Eddius, XLIV.

35   Cf. Bright, *Early English Church History*, p. 396; and H. & S. III, 172.

36   *H.E.* V, 19: 'sedem suam et episcopatum . . . recepit'.

37   *H.E.* V, 2.

38   So R. L. Poole, 'St Wilfred and the See of Ripon' (*E.H.R.* XXXIV (1919),

1–22). This article, which includes a full discussion of Wilfred's episcopal career, was reprinted in the same writer's *Studies in Chronology and History* (1933). There is a valuable note on the chronology of Wilfred's life in Plummer, II, 316–20.

39 H. & S. III, 177–203.

40 Kemble (*Saxons in England*, II, 404) wrote in a derogatory, and indeed unjust manner of the Penitentials, which, he maintained, demonstrate 'the folly and wickedness of squaring and shaping the unlimited mercy of God by the rule and measure of mere human intelligence'. With this may be compared Plummer's remark: 'the penitential literature is ... a deplorable feature of the medieval Church ... It is hard to see how anyone could busy himself with such literature and not be the worse for it' (I, clviii).

41 According to the *Dialogue* of Egbert, archbishop of York, not only monks but also laymen with their wives and families (since the time of Theodore) were accustomed to go to private confession in the days preceding Christmas. This appears to be the beginning of the practice of regular sacramental confession in the Western Church. H. & S. III, 413. On confession, see Levison, *England and the Continent*, pp. 98–100.

42 According to Malmesbury (*Gesta Regum*, R.S. I, 29) Berhtwald was first abbot of Glastonbury before being transferred to Reculver against his will; but he seems to have been confused here with a Beortwald of Glastonbury. See Plummer, II, 283.

43 H. & S. III, 274–5; *Eng. Hist. Doc.* I, 729.

44 The diocese of Whithorn was revived in 730, shortly before Berhtwald's death. It appears to have petered out early in the ninth century. W. G. Searle, *Anglo-Saxon Bishops, Kings, and Nobles* (1899), pp. 194–7.

45 *H.E.* V, 8.

46 *De Gestis Pont.* pp. 337–9; *Eng. Hist. Doc.* I, 730. On the practice of followers sharing their master's exile cf. *Eng. Hist. Doc.* I, 780.

47 Eddius, XLV.

48 Leicester as his seat is preferred before Lichfield, the only possible alternative, by Florence of Worcester (*M.H.B.* Appendix, 623); cf. H. & S. III, 127 ff.

49 John VI (701–5) was a Greek by birth, a gently disposed man with a great love of peace.

50 It is possible that on this occasion he also bore with him a letter of John VI addressed to the English bishops and clergy, recommending them to follow the example of their brethren the English clergy in Rome, who had recently abandoned the wearing of lay dress and adopted the Roman cassock. H. & S. III, 264.

51 Eddius, LXVI.

Ch. X

1 A rhetorical Life of Paul was written by Jerome: *P.L.* 23.

2 *Vita Antonii* by Athanasius: *P.G.* 26.

3 *Vita Ant.* x.

4   Cf. Rufinus, *Vit. Pat.* II: 'commanent per eremum dispersi et separati cellulis. Ob hoc autem dirimuntur habitaculis, ut in silentii quiete, et intentione mentis divina sectantes, nec vox aliqua, nec occursus ullus, aut sermo aliquis otiosus obturbet'. For an excellent account of the early stages of monasticism see J. Ryan, *Irish Monasticism* (1931), section I.

5   *Vita Pachomii,* Acta SS T iii Maii.

6   Honoratus, of a Gallic noble family, later became bishop of Arles, where he died in 429.

7   Ps. 119, v. 62.

8   On great fasts of the Church there was a single meal, after vespers. On lesser fasts the single meal was earlier, and on feasts and summer ferias 'prandium' was at noon and 'cena' at about 6.

9   *H.E.* I, 33.

10   D. Knowles, *The Monastic Order in England*, p. 21.

11   Eddius, XLVII.

12   Bede, *Hist. Abb.* I.

13   There has sometimes been confusion over the exact number of these visits. Five were made from Britain, and one (the third) from Lérins.

14   Bede, *Hist. Abb.* V: 'iuxta Romanorum quem semper amabat morem'. Cf. *H.E.* V, 21, where we read that Nechtan, king of the Picts, on his conversion to the Roman usages, sent to abbot Ceolfrith (*c.* 710) a request for architects who would build for him a stone church in the Roman manner. The abbot of the monastery from which Biscop obtained his masons was an old friend bearing the English name of Torhthelm: *Historia Abbatum auctore Anonymo,* VII, and *Eng. Hist. Doc.* I, 699.

15   *Historia Abbatum auctore Anonymo,* VI; Bede, *Hist. Abb.* XI.

16   *H.E.* IV, 18.

17   Cf. however, p. 172 of the present work.

18   On the family and hereditary character of many English monasteries see Levison, *England and the Continent*, pp. 28–9.

19   Knowles, *Monastic Order*, p. 22.

20   1 Samuel 1, vv. 27, 28. A full discussion of the child-oblate system is contained in ch. 14 of G. G. Coulton's *Five Centuries of Religion*, I. Cf. the remarks of D. Knowles on the system, in his edition of Lanfranc's *Monastic Constitutions* (1951), pp. xviii-xix, 110 n.

21   Aelfled was described by Eddius as 'sapientissima virgo' and 'semper totius provinciae consolatrix optimaque consiliatrix', LIX, LX. She was a supporter of Wilfred.

22   On this see Mary Bateson, 'Origin and Early History of Double Monasteries' (*Trans. R. H.S.* New Series, XIII (1899)); Berlière, *Les monastères doubles aux xii et xiii siècles* (Brussels 1923); J. Ryan, *Irish Monasticism*, pp. 141–5.

23   *Codex Just. Novell.* CXXIII, c. 36.

24   J. Ryan, however, thinks that double monasteries were in no sense a characteristic of Celtic Christianity, and that Kildare was the only double house proper in the entire Celtic world (*Irish Monasticism*, pp. 144–5).

25   *H.E.* III, 8.

26 *Anglo-Saxon Missionaries in Germany*, ed. C. H. Talbot (1954), p. 207. Rudolf's 'Vita Leobae' is edited by G. Waitz in *M.G.H. Scriptores*, xv, i, 118 f.

27 *H.E.* iv, 7.

28 Quoted from G. F. Browne, *St Aldhelm* (1903), p. 239.

29 *H.E.* iv, 25.

30 Bishop Lightfoot in his well-known collection of sermons *Leaders in the Northern Church* (1892), p. 66, in discussing the invariable abbacy of a woman over a double monastery, remarked that 'the chivalry of their Christianity and their race gave the precedence to women'. This missed the point altogether, which is surely that a double monastery was really a nunnery, utilising the indispensable services of men.

31 Theodore disliked the institution, but was prepared to tolerate it as an established local custom: 'non licet viris feminas habere monachas, neque feminis viros; tamen nos non destruamus quod consuetudo est in hac terra'. *Penitentiale*, ii, vi, 8 (H. & S. iii, 195).

32 *H.E.* iv, 23.

33 *Germania*, viii. Cf. Bede, *Opera*, ed. Giles, viii, 378.

34 She had reputedly arrived on the Continent as an Anglo-Saxon slave. As a queen her influence was widespread; she served as regent for her son Clothair III on the death of her husband Clovis II in 656.

35 *H.E.* iii, 8.

36 Both these houses were founded by Clothild, wife of Clovis I. Chelles was rebuilt by Bathildis on a larger scale; one of its subsequent abbesses was Gisla, sister of Charlemagne: Plummer, ii, 149.

37 Egwin is not mentioned by Bede. See *Chronicon Monasterii de Evesham* (R.S.), pp. 3 ff. Of aristocratic origin, he early adopted an ecclesiastical career, and was bishop of Worcester *c.* 693–717. He aroused the opposition of his flock by his condemnation of their idolatrous practices.

38 Felix's *Life of St Guthlac*, ed. and trans. by B. Colgrave (1956).

39 The graphic sketch of St Guthlac by Charles Kingsley is still worth reading. '... through the dreary winter's night the whistle of the wind and the wild cries of the waterfowl were translated into the howls of witches and demons; and the delirious fancies of marsh fever made those fiends take hideous shapes before the inner eye.' *The Hermits*, p. 303. There can be little doubt that the minds of the anchorites were often unbalanced as a result of self-inflicted privations. Yet the prestige of these men was high. Elsewhere, Farne was long a home of anchorites. Bede (*H.E.* v, 12) tells of a hermit in Ireland, named Haemgils, who lived on bread and water, and of a Northumbrian monk Drycthelm who recited his prayers standing up to his neck in water so cold that he frequently had to break the ice to get to it. Simeon of Durham (*sub anno* 767) mentions an anchorite Etha, who 'died happily' at Crayke, ten miles from York.

40 It has long been usual to ascribe the foundation of Crowland abbey to Aethelbald, in the year of Guthlac's death. But cf. Colgrave, pp. 7 ff., where the early foundation of the abbey is rejected. Felix does not mention it, though it is recorded by the Anglo-Norman historian Orderic Vitalis.

41 H. & S. III, 314-25; *Eng. Hist. Doc.* I, 735-45, where it is translated in full. It is also printed in Plummer, I, 405-23, with notes, II, 378 ff.

42 According to the third canon of the council of Cloveshoe, to be held in 747, it was the duty of the bishop to visit his diocese each year, addressing his people at convenient centres.

43 On confirmation at this time see Plummer, II, 382-3.

44 In this case the family-community of Little Gidding (1626-37), ruled over by Nicholas Ferrar, was a revival rather than an invention, and J. H. Moorman's description of it as standing for 'something unique in the history of Christian thought and life' is an overstatement: *A History of the Church in England* (1953, reprinted 1958), p. 237.

45 Cuthbert, abbot of Jarrow, was to write to Lull, bishop of Mainz, in 764, complaining that he lacked the services of a harpist: *Eng. Hist. Doc.* I, 766.

46 H. & S. III, 394-6; *Eng. Hist. Doc.* I, 764.

47 Pseudo or secular monasteries were implicitly condemned by the council of Cloveshoe 747 (canon 5). Their reformation was regarded as virtually impossible, but bishops should visit them and see that they at least have the services of a priest: H. & S. III, 364. No more is heard of these monasteries after this, and Lingard may not be far from the truth when he remarks that probably 'in process of time they settled down into parochial churches, whilst the lands remained in the undisturbed possession of the family'. *History and Antiquities of the Anglo-Saxon Church*, I, 209.

Ch. XI

1 See especially A. W. Clapham, *English Romanesque Architecture*, I, 17 ff.; R. H. Hodgkin, *History of the Anglo-Saxons*, I, 270-3; C. R. Peers in *Antiquity*, III (1929), 65-74, and in *Archaeologia*, LXXVII (1927), 201-17; F. Stenton, *Anglo-Saxon England*, p. 111.

2 Thomas of Elmham, *Historia Monasterii S. Augustini Cantuariensis* (R.S.), p. 131.

3 There is a detailed plan of St Augustine's by J. P. G. Meaden, in *Archaeologia Cantiana*, XL (1928), facing p. 65. See also R. U. Potts, 'The Tombs of the Kings and Archbishops in St. Austin's Abbey', in *Archaeologia Cantiana*, XXXVIII (1926).

4 As does Clapham, I, 28.

5 *Early Churches in Syria*, H. C. Butler (ed. E. Baldwin Smith), (Princeton 1929), p. 18. The numerous photographs and plans in this volume are of the highest interest.

6 *Ibid.* p. 59.

7 *Ibid.* pp. 71, 73.

8 *Ibid.* p. 264.

9 *Ibid.* p. 216.

10 *Ibid.* p. 32.

11 Cf. a Gallic epitaph (*ibid.* p. 264) of the third century, which mentions a Syrian 'who left his native country to come into this land to trade'.

12 J. Sparke, *Historiae Anglicanae Scriptores* (1723), p. 9.

13 *Chronicon Monasterii de Abingdon* (R.S.), II, 272.

14 Clapham, I, 37.

15 Cf. Baldwin Brown, *The Arts in Early England (Architecture)*, p. 136.

16 *Historia Abbatum*, v.

17 Clapham, I, 42.

18 So Richard of Hexham; see Raine's *Priory of Hexham* (Surtees Society), I, 18.

19 Eddius, XXII. Not only were imported pictures displayed, but on festivals the walls were also hung with silk. Lights were suspended from the ceiling:

> 'Sanctaque suspendit varias per tecta lucernas,
> Esset ut in templis coeli stellantis imago.'

De SS. Ecc. Ebor. v. 280.

20 Eddius, XVII.

21 Eddius, XVI. On the use of glass cf. Bede. *Hist. Abb.* v: Biscop introduced from Gaul glass-makers to glaze the windows of the church and other parts of his monastery. Abbot Cuthbert in his letter to bishop Lull in 764 asked for a skilled glazier: *Eng. Hist. Doc.* I, 766. Bede refers to architects and glass-makers in a homily: *Opera*, ed. Giles, v, 184, 185.

22 *Priory of Hexham* (Surtees Soc.), I, 14.

23 Later examples were Charlemagne's palace chapel at Aachen, Alfred's church at Athelney, and a round mausoleum built in the tenth century at Bury St Edmunds to enshrine the body of the royal martyr. Just before the Conquest abbot Wulfric at Canterbury embarked on an ambitious scheme to combine the adjacent churches of SS. Peter and Paul and St Mary into one edifice by means of a rotunda, though the general rebuilding of the whole abbey church by the Norman abbot Scotland brought the scheme to nothing.

24 *Historians of the Church at York* (R.S.), ed. J. Raine, I, lxi.

25 Malmesbury, *De Gestis Pontificum* (R.S.): 'basilica pulcherrimi operis.'

26 Stenton, *Anglo-Saxon England*, p. 151.

27 *Northumbrian Crosses* (1927). On the English crosses, see also J. Brøndsted, *Early English Ornament* (1924); Clapham, I, ch. 3; Hodgkin, I, 362 ff., II, 438 ff.; Kendrick, *Anglo-Saxon Art* (1938), ch. 7; G. Baldwin Brown, *Arts in Early England* (1937), VI, pt. 2.

28 *Historia Regum, sub anno* 740.

29 *De Gestis Pontificum*, 383–4. G. F. Browne, *St Aldhelm*, pp. 149–53, attempted to trace the stages of the funeral procession, and suggested as the resting-places Frome, Westbury, Bradford-on-Avon, Bath, Colerne, Littleton Drew, until finally Malmesbury was reached. At all of these places, except Westbury and Malmesbury, crosses survive.

30 *De Gestis Regum* (R.S.), I, 25.

31 The idea of the 'underlying inspiration' should of course be distinguished from that which takes the 'primary cause' of the erection of the crosses to have been the need for a local centre of prayer and worship.

32 In the Breviary, the Feast of the Invention of the Cross is observed on 3 May, when the story of Helena is read in the lessons at Matins; the recovery of the

True Cross by Heraclius is remembered on 14 September, the Feast of the Exaltation of the Cross.

33 The practical effect of an idea can be easily understood by a glance at any English churchyard. The plain gravestones of the eighteenth and early nineteenth centuries are replaced during the latter half of the nineteenth century by the cross, under the influence of the Oxford Movement.

34 Catalogue, *Masterpieces of Byzantine Art*, p. 20.

35 It is, however, often ascribed to later Anglo-Saxon times. Cf. F. Saxl and R. Wittkower, *British Art and the Mediterranean* (1948), p. 20, and especially D. Talbot Rice, *English Art 871–1100* (1952), pp. 96–8. For the seventh-century date see C. R. Peers, 'Reculver: its Saxon Church and Cross', in *Archaeologia*, LXXVII (1928), 255.

36 They correspond to lines 39–41, 44–5, 48–9, 56–9, 62–4.

37 In the Victoria and Albert Museum there are plaster casts of a number of crosses, including those of Bewcastle, Ruthwell, and Acca. On the revival of the Whithorn (Candida Casa) diocese, see Bede, *H.E.* v, 23. The report of the papal legates in 786 includes amongst its signatories the bishops of Whithorn and Mayo: *Eng. Hist. Doc.* I, 772.

38 Twysden, *Decem Scriptores* (1652), I, 3. Cf. Gregory I, writing to Severus, bishop of Marseilles—pictures are placed in churches, he says, so that illiterate people may learn lessons from them which they cannot obtain from books: *M.G.H. Epistolae*, II, 269 ff. For a defence of sacred representations in art see Bede, *De Templo Salomonis*, *Opera*, ed. Giles, VIII, 336–7.

39 Bede, *Hist. Abb.* VI. The central feature of the scheme was a representation of the Blessed Virgin and the Apostles, adorning the nave. The stated purpose of the pictures was to enable all who entered the church, including those who could not read, to be met with the loving countenance of Christ and his saints.

40 A. W. Clapham ascribes them to the late eighth century: 'The Carved Stones at Breedon on the Hill' (*Archaeologia*, LXXVII (1928), 219).

41 Clapham, *English Romanesque Architecture*, I, 74. Cf. the Syrian church of Zebed (Butler, p. 216).

42 Generally regarded as the best manuscript of the Vulgate, it was taken by Wordsworth and White as their most important authority. One of the leaves of the sister manuscript now in the British Museum was found in a Newcastle antique shop in 1909.

43 See plate 2 in W. Oakeshott's *The Sequence of English Medieval Art* (1950).

44 *Anglo-Saxon Art*, pp. 97 ff.

45 For support of the Northumbrian origin of Durrow see Oakeshott (Appendix I) who dates it *c.* 670, and Clapham, in *Antiquity* (1934), VIII, 43. Cf. also F. C. Burkitt, in *Antiquity* (1935), IX, 33.

46 Plate 40 in Kendrick, *Anglo-Saxon Art*.

47 *Ibid.* p. 137.

Ch. XII

1 See H. Gee and W. J. Hardy, *Documents illustrative of English Church History*, p. 21; H. & S. III, 366.

2   *H.E.* IV, 24.

3   *Genesis*, 278–85. See p. 53 of C. W. Kennedy's *Early English Christian Poetry* (1952), from which book the extracts in this chapter are taken.

4   On this see Bright, 'The Relation of the Caedmonian "Exodus" to the Liturgy', in *Modern Language Notes*, XXVII, 97–103.

5   *Ascension*, 773–4.

6   *Ascension*, 783–4.

7   *Elene*, 1287–1302.

8   Kennedy, p. 23.

9   *Andreas*, 1–10.

10   *Andreas*, 371–84.

11   *Andreas*, 1717–22.

12   *Dream of the Rood*, 28–45.

13   Kennedy, pp. 75–78.

14   C. W. Kennedy writes of the 'Advent Lyrics': 'They combine a poet's skill and a Churchman's religious feeling. They clothe with lyric grace the meditations of a devout Christian deeply moved by the spirit of Advent, and trained in the significance of its mysteries', p. 78, *Early English Christian Poetry*.

15   *Homilies on the Gospels*, 29 (*P.L.* 76, cols. 1218–19).

Ch. XIII

1   A. F. Leach, *The Schools of Medieval England* (1915), p. 11.

2   Tacitus, *Agricola*, XXI. Cf. Martial, XI, 3, 5: 'Dicitur et nostros cantare Britannia versus'.

3   R. G. Collingwood and J. N. L. Myres, *Roman Britain and the English Settlements* (1937), p. 274.

4   Leach, *ibid.* p. 28.

5   On pagan learning and the Christian attitude towards it, see further M. L. W. Laistner, *Thought and Letters in Western Europe* (1957 ed.), pp. 34 ff.

6   *H.E.* III, 18: 'instituit scolam, in qua pueri litteris erudirentur.' On this topic as a whole see P. F. Jones, 'The Gregorian Mission and English Education' (*Speculum*, III (1928), 335 ff), where it is maintained that though Augustine introduced education, it was strictly for religious purposes, and did not include humane studies.

7   *H.E.* IV, 2.

8   *H.E.*v, 3. Miss E. Duckett's imagination, however, probably over-reaches itself when she writes of Theodore training 'his students in "first-aid" classes as a most valuable help for their pastoral ministry' (*Anglo-Saxon Saints and Scholars* (1947), p. 36). On the medical studies of Anglo-Saxons see further J. D. A. Ogilvy, *Books known to Anglo-Latin Writers from Aldhelm to Alcuin* (1936), pp. 63–4. Like their modern descendants, the English of the seventh and eighth centuries suffered much from colds in the head, and Mr Ogilvy found several prescriptions of the use of mustard for this ailment.

9   *Ep. ad Eahfridum* (*P.L.* 89, col. 94).

10 A. Hamilton Thompson's pamphlet, *Song Schools in the Middle Ages* (1942), may be consulted.
11 Knowles, *Monastic Order in England*, p. 547.
12 *H.E.* IV, 2.
13 *H.E.* II, 20.
14 *H.E.* IV, 2.
15 For Aldhelm see *De Gestis Pontificum* (R.S.), V, 332–443. Malmesbury made use of a Life of Aldhelm by Faricius, physician to Henry I and abbot of Abingdon, which is in *P.L.* 89. The year of Aldhelm's death according to Bede (*H.E.* V, 18) was 709. On the commonly accepted date of his birth see E. S. Duckett (p. 26); R. H. Hodgkin (I, 321); P. Hunter Blair (p. 326); G. F. Browne (p. 57); M. L.W. Laistner (p. 153). W. Bright, however, is sceptical (pp. 294–5, 493), and thinks Aldhelm was only a youth in 675. Aldhelm in a letter cited by Malmesbury (p. 334) speaks of Hadrian as the teacher of his 'simple childhood' ('rudis meae infantiae praeceptor'). Hadrian became abbot of Canterbury in 671 (Bede, *Hist. Abb.* III). But Aldhelm was a rhetorical writer, and the expression as used by him could be one of feigned humility. Cf. Ebert, *Literatur d. Mittelalters, 2te Auflage*, I, 623 n. 3.
16 *De Gestis Pont.* pp. 333 ff., 345.
17 Kenney, *Sources for the Early History of Ireland* (1929), I, 625 f.
18 See J. Jenkinson, *The Hisperica Famina* (1908).
19 *De Gestis Pont.* pp. 376 ff. As J. D. A. Ogilvy (*op. cit.* p. 100) points out, this story is interesting as showing that French sailors regarded England as a good market for books.
20 The views of A. F. Leach of this subject have not found general acceptance. He maintained (*op. cit.* ch. 3) that Aldhelm never studied at Canterbury, that he should be connected rather with Winchester, and that Maildubh was a mythical figure.
21 *De Gestis Pont.* pp. 341 ff; *M.G.H. Auct. ant.* XV, 475 ff.; Leach, *Educational Charters and Documents*, pp. 9–11.
22 *H.E.* V, 18.
23 *De Gestis Pont.* p. 346.
24 Clapham, *English Romaneque Architecture*, I, 114, 137.
25 G. S. Williams, 'The Site of S. Aldhelm's Church "juxta Werham"' (*Proceedings Dorset N. H. & Archeol. Soc.* LXV (1943)).
26 *De Gestis Pont.* p. 382.
27 *De Gestis Pont.* 428.
28 *De Gestis Pont.* 335 ff. The letter is addressed to 'Acircius', who is taken to be Aldfrith.
29 *M.G.H. Auct. ant.* XV, 228 ff.
30 The council of Cloveshoe in 747 specifically enjoined monks and nuns (particularly the latter) to eschew vainglorious apparel: canons 19 and 20, H. & S. III, 369. But the fashion continued, and we find Alcuin, at the beginning of the ninth century, deploring it. On the general addiction of Anglo-Saxons to fine clothes see C. J. B. Gaskoin, *Alcuin: his Life and his Work*, pp. 43–5.

NOTES

31 The nuns are represented as receiving it in an illumination at the beginning of an early MS. of the letter: this is reproduced in H. D. Traill and J. S. Mann, *Social England*, illus. ed. (1901), I, 307.

32 *M.G.H. Auct. ant.* XV; *P.L.* 89.

33 For a discussion of the identity of this personage see G. F. Browne, *St. Aldhelm*, p. 81 n.

34 See J. P. Fuhrmann, *Irish Medieval Monasteries on the Continent* (1927), pp. 19 ff. For the text of Cellanus' letter see *M.G.H. Auct. ant.* XV, 498 ff.

35 Cf. F. J. E. Raby, *History of Christian Latin Poetry* (1927), 144 ff.

36 *Analecta Hymnica Medii Aevi*, ed. G. M. Dreves, C. Blume, and H. M. Bannister.

37 *Eng. Hist. Doc.* I, 750.

38 Bede, *Hist. Abb.* IX.

39 *Dict. of Christian Biography*, I, 309.

40 Ceolfrith had resigned the abbey with the object of spending his last days in Rome. In the moving story of his departure, we are told how he was in process of giving each of the brethren the kiss of peace, but many were so overcome with emotion that the ceremony had to be abandoned. Then, seated in the boat which was to take him over the river, deacons by his side holding a golden cross and lighted candles, this great abbot, a true father to his monks, finally broke down and could not contain his tears. *Historia Abbatum auctore Anonymo*, XXIII–XXVII.

41 *H.E.* V, 20.

42 Traditionally at Monkton, near Jarrow, but possibly Sunderland: see Plummer, I, ix, and A. H. Thompson, *Bede: his Life and Times*, p. 4.

43 *H.E.* V, 24.

44 *Hist. Anon.* XIV.

45 J. R. Green wrote that 'the quiet grandeur of a life consecrated to knowledge, the tranquil pleasure that lies in learning and teaching and writing dawned in fact for Englishmen in the story of Baeda' (*Making of England*, p. 399). In the opening words of his fourth book to the Commentary on Samuel, Bede remarks that after completing the third book he had paused for a while to regain the delight which came to him in writing and study: *Opera*, ed. Giles, VIII, 162.

46 *H.E.* V, 24.

47 The first critical edition of the *Historia Ecclesiastica* was issued in 1722, the joint work of Canon John Smith of Durham and his son George. Subsequent writers mostly reproduced this text, until the authoritative edition of Charles Plummer (1896) in 2 vols. which includes, besides the *H.E.*, the *Historia Abbatum* of Bede, the anonymous *Historia Abbatum*, and Bede's epistle to Egbert. Mr B. Colgrave with his *Two Lives of St Cuthbert* (1940), including Bede's prose life of the saint as well as that by an anonymous author, is the only English modern scholar to have critically edited anything of Bede, though some work in this direction has been done in America by M. L. W. Laistner and C. W. Jones, and in Germany by W. Jaager. A complete edition of Bede's works by J. A. Giles was published in 1843–4: *Venerabilis Bedae*

Opera (12 vols., London). This edition was described by Laistner (*Trans. R.H.S.*, 4th ser., XVI (1933), p. 79) as a disgrace even for the time when it was published, but it is still indispensable to the general scholar. Migne, *P.L.* 90–5, mainly reproduces this edition. Of the *H.E.*, there are over 160 MSS. extant: see M. L. W. Laistner and H. H. King, *A Hand-List of Bede Manuscripts* (Ithaca 1943). The first printed edition of the *H.E.* appeared in 1475 in Strasburg, and the first to be printed in England was published at Cambridge in 1644. The earliest translation into English was by Thomas Stapleton (Antwerp 1565), his aim being to show that the new Reformed Church was alien to the primitive English Church.

48 The verse life has been edited by W. Jaager, *Bedas metrische Vita Sancti Cuthberti* (Leipzig 1935).

49 His Life of Felix of Nola, a third-century priest, was edited by Giles, IV, 173 ff. His Life of St Athanasius is lost.

50 *De Temporibus* is edited by C. W. Jones, *Bedae Opera de Temporibus* (Medieval Academy of America, XLI (1943)). In this work Bede set forward the six ages of the world, of which the sixth begins with the birth of Christ and will end when God determines. The book involved Bede for a brief moment in an accusation of heresy, made by some Northumbrian monks, who accused him of denying that the Incarnation occurred during the Sixth Age.

51 *De Orthographia* was edited by H. Keil, *Grammatici Latini*, VII (1880), 261 ff.

52 'Bede as a Classical and a Patristic Scholar' (*Trans. R.H.S.*, 4th ser., XVI (1933), 69–94).

53 Bodleian MS. Cod. Laudianus Graecus 35 is thought to be a Greek text of Acts which was at Jarrow in Bede's time.

54 *Trans. R.H.S.*, 4th ser., XVI, p. 92. Cf. J. D. A. Ogilvy's careful catalogue of books which appear to have been available to English scholars (*Books known to Anglo-Latin Writers from Aldhelm to Alcuin*). His main conclusions are the same as Laistner's: that the Anglo-Saxons enjoyed the Latin (especially the Christian) poets, were thoroughly conversant with the Fathers, and largely ignorant of Greek.

55 *H.E.* V, 24. Bede was careful to place the names of the authors against such extracts, though subsequent copyists have omitted them.

56 On Bede's cautious attitude to the use of pagan literature see Plummer, I, liii.

57 Bede's verse Life of Cuthbert is too steeped in the miraculous to be of much value as a biography. The prose Life which followed after several years is more critical, but even so, is a less interesting historical work than that by the anonymous monk.

58 *Studies in the Early British Church* (1958): two papers by Nora K. Chadwick. See pp. 19, 23, 27, 60.

59 Cf. Stenton, *Anglo-Saxon England*, p. 187.

60 Nothelm's researches into the papal archives took place during the pontificate of Gregory II (715–31), who had himself been an archivist and so able to give Nothelm expert help. Nothelm became archbishop of Canterbury in 735, and died in 739.

61 Text and translation in Plummer, I, lxxii ff., clx ff.

62 There has been some disagreement amongst chroniclers over the year of Bede's death, ascribed to various years between 730 and 737. But it could not have been earlier than 734, towards the end of which year Bede wrote his epistle to bishop Egbert (Plummer, II, 388). Good local authorities give 735, e.g. Simeon of Durham (*Historia Regum, sub anno*).

63 Passages from his works were used for lessons in the Hours. Cf. the York Breviary (ed. Lawley, Surtees Soc. II, 286 ff.). His name was commemorated in later editions of the Sarum Breviary: see also the *Second Recension of the Quignon Breviary*, I, ed. J. Wickham Legg (Henry Bradshaw Soc. XXXV, 88, 301). In 1662 his name was included in the calendar of the English Prayer Book, and in 1899 Leo XIII declared him a Doctor of the Universal Church.

64 One must beware, however, of such over-simplification as that of C. J. B. Gaskoin (*Alcuin: his Life and his Work* (1904)), who stated that 'at the death of Bede York supplanted Jarrow as the home of English letters' (p. 33).

65 Besides the good book by Gaskoin on Alcuin, we have W. Levison's discussion in his Ford Lectures, *England and the Continent in the Eighth Century* (1946); a more recent work is *Alcuin, Friend of Charlemagne* (1951), by Eleanor Duckett, which, as usual with that author's writings, combines readability with thorough documentation. Alcuin's *Vita* is in *M.G.H. Scriptores*, XV. His letters are edited by E. Dümmler in *M.G.H. Epist. Karol. Aevi*, II, to which must be added a newly-discovered letter included by Levison in *England and the Continent*, Appendix XI.

66 The question is discussed by Gaskoin, Appendix I. Levison inclines to think that Alcuin may have been a monk who, however, fell short of the full exercise of his profession (pp. 153–4).

67 Raine, *Historians of York* (R.S.), I, 349 ff., and Leach, *Educational Charters*, 11 ff. In addition to the Bible, Liudger (one of Alcuin's most prominent pupils at York) read 'nonnullos saecularis litteraturae libros': *Vita Liudgeri*, quoted by Gaskoin, p. 39 n.

68 *Educational Charters*, p. 18. H. & S. III, 503: 'praevideat sancta solertia tua magistros pueris, clero segregentur, separati more illorum, qui libros legant, qui cantilenae inserviant, qui scribendi studio deputentur. Habeas et singulis his ordinibus magistros suos ....'

69 *Educational Charters*, p. 20: 'multitudo sapientium, sanitas est orbis'.

70 Cf. Einhard's *Life of Charlemagne*, ed. H. W. Garrod and R. B. Mowat (1925), XXV. In connection with the palace school Einhard only mentions Peter, as a grammar teacher, and Alcuin, who taught 'in ceteris disciplinis'. Paul is well known for his History of the Lombards. Theodulf in his poem 'Ad Karolum Regem' (*M.G.H. Poet. Aev. Kar.* I, 483 ff.) describes Charlemagne's literary circle.

71 His numerous poems are edited in *M.G.H. Poet. Aev. Kar.* I.

72 On this see the comments of C. Dawson, *Religion and the Rise of Western Culture* (1950), pp. 227–8.

73 See E. K. Rand, *A Survey of the MSS. of Tours* (Cambridge, Mass. 1929), and the same author's 'Preliminary Study of Alcuin's Bible' (*Harvard Theological Review*), XXIV (1931).

74 F. Cabrol, *Dictionnaire d'archéol. chrét. et de liturgie*, I, 1, col. 1072 ff.
75 *M.G.H. Epistolae*, IV, 84, 89
76 Levison, *England and the Continent*, p. 159.
77 *Libri Carolini*, ed. H. Bastgen, *M.G.H. Concilia*, II, Supplementum (1924) 1 ff.
78 Simeon of Durham, *Hist. Regum, sub anno* 792 (*Eng. Hist. Doc.* I, 247).
79 At Tours Alcuin found the shortage of books a handicap, and he wrote to the king asking permission to send some of his pupils to Britain to obtain books: *Eng. Hist. Doc.* I, 786.
80 Levison, *England and the Continent*, pp. 168–9.

Ch. XIV

1 On the missionaries see S. J. Crawford, *Anglo-Saxon Influence on Western Christendom*, 600–800, and W. Levison, *England and the Continent in the Eighth Century*.
2 *H.E.* V, 9. On the appellation of 'Garmani' by the Celts to the English cf. however, Plummer, II, 285–6.
3 *H.E.* III, 27; V, 9, 22. See Hauck, *Kirchengeschichte Deutschlands* (5 vols. 1887–1920), I, 432 f. The date was 716 according to the *Chronicle*, but 715 according to Bede, *H.E.* III, 4.
4 Willibrord was the true Apostle of Friesland. 'The Frisians were pagans until the pontiff of the Roman see, Sergius, sent Willibrord as their bishop and teacher. It was he who converted them to the faith of Christ' (Boniface, *Epistles*, ed. Tangl, 109). An early Life of Willibrord by an Irishman has disappeared. Alcuin wrote a Life some fifty years after the subject's death, the text of which is edited by W. Levison, in *M.G.H. Scriptores Rerum Merovingicarum*, VII, 81–141. It is translated by C. H. Talbot in *Anglo-Saxon Missionaries in Germany* (1954). Unfortunately, this Life is largely preoccupied with miracles, and as moreover Willibrord's correspondence has been lost, the personality of the saint eludes us. There is another translation of Alcuin's 'Life' in A. Grieve, *Willibrord* (1923), with a bibliography. See also G. H. Verbist, *Saint Willibrord* (1939).
5 Radbod made his famous declaration in 718, a year before his death, refusing baptism at the last moment, 'dicens se non posse carere consortio praedecessorum suorum, et cum parvo numero sedere in caelesti regno.' H. & S. III, 225. Not long after Radbod's death, Eadburga (Bugga), abbess of Minster-in-Thanet, wrote to Boniface, referring to the late Frisian king as 'inimicus catholicae ecclesiae' (Tangl, 15; Talbot, p. 69).
6 *H.E.* V, 11; Hauck, I, 437 n.
7 *H.E.* V, 10.
8 *H.E.* V, 11.
9 Bede gives the date as 696 (*H.E.* V, 11), but according to the Bedan indiction this would be 695.
10 Eddius, XXVI.
11 *H.E.* III, 13.
12 Willibrord was apparently succeeded in the Utrecht see by Wera, who was in

turn followed by Eoba. Both men were Anglo-Saxons: see Levison, *England and the Continent*, p. 82 n. Eoba was to be amongst those martyred with Boniface in 754. After this event the Frisian Church was ruled by a Frank, an abbot in priest's orders named Gregory, who had as chorepiscopus an Englishman Albert, consecrated at York in 767 for this purpose: *Eng. Hist. Doc.* I, 243, 725. Gregory, after his death *c.* 775, was succeeded by his nephew Alberic, who was consecrated at Cologne, which now assumed metropolitan oversight of the Utrecht diocese.

13 Alcuin, *Vita*, IX; Talbot, p. 9.
14 Pertz (*M.G.H. Diplomata*, I, 93 f., 173) disputes the tradition of Irmina. Cf. however, Levison, *M.G.H. Script. Rer. Merov.* VII, 88 f.
15 For Willibrord's Calendar see H. A. Wilson, *The Calendar of St Willibrord* (Henry Bradshaw Soc.) LV, which contains a complete reproduction. A facsimile of the page on which Willibrord's entry occurs is in Cabrol and Leclerq, *Dictionnaire d'archéologie Chrétienne et de liturgie*, III, 2, after cols. 2603–4. Cf. also W. H. Frere, 'A Relic of St Willibrord' (*Church Quarterly Review*, XCI (1921), pp. 356–62).
16 *H.E.* V, 11.
17 Boniface, *Epistles*, ed. Tangl, 109; Talbot, p. 146, cf. Talbot, p. 41.

Ch. XV

1 *Ordinale Exon.* (Henry Bradshaw Soc.), XXXVIII (1909), p. 407: 'ex civitate Criditonie iuxta Exoniam.'
2 *Vita Bonifatii auctore Willibaldo*, ed. W. Levison, in *M.G.H. Scriptores Rerum Germanicarum* (1905). It is translated by C. H. Talbot, *Anglo-Saxon Missionaries in Germany*. There are accounts of Boniface in A. Hauck, *Kirchengeschichte Deutschlands*, I; G. Kurth, *Saint Boniface*; G. F. Browne, *Boniface of Crediton and his Companions* (1910); G. W. Greenaway, *Saint Boniface* (1955). But a full, critical biography of this great Anglo-Saxon, in English, is long overdue.
3 Tangl, 63. For the correspondence of Boniface see the edition of M. Tangl in *M.G.H. Epistolae Selectae*, I. Much of it is translated by C. H. Talbot in *Anglo-Saxon Missionaries in Germany*, and by E. Emerton in *The Letters of Saint Boniface* (1940).
4 He wrote a Latin grammar, for which see Angelo Mai, *M.G.H. Auctores Classici*, VII (1835), 475 ff, and G. J. Gebauer, *Prolegomena to the Ars Grammatica Bonifatii* (1942). For an example of his verse see *M.G.H. Poetae Aevi Karolini*, I, 16 ff.
5 J. Armitage Robinson, *Somerset Historical Essays*, p. 31. This is the earliest Wessex synod of which we have any record: *Vita*, IV, Talbot, p. 33.
6 Tangl, 33.
7 Or possibly 717. Hauck, I, 443 n.; Levison ed. *Vita*, 17 n.
8 Tangl, 11; *Vita*, V; H. & S. III, 302.
9 Levison, *England and the Continent*, p. 72; Tangl, 12; Talbot, pp. 68–9.
10 *Vita*, V; Talbot, p. 39.

11 There are dedications to St Kilian in Germany, as at Lügde and Höxter in the Teutoburger Wald.

12 Hefele-Leclerq, *Histoire des Conciles* (1909–10), III, II, 836 f.

13 O. Fischer, *Bonifatius, der Apostel der Deutschen* (1881), p. 35.

14 W. Levison has a valuable discussion concerning the 'chorepiscopi' in *England and the Continent*, pp. 65–8.

15 Tangl, 15; Talbot, pp. 69–70.

16 *Vita*, V; cf. Talbot, p. 41.

17 Probably 722, as accepted by most scholars, but perhaps the following year. Levison leaves it an open question: ed. *Vita*, 29, note 1.

18 *Vita*, VI. There are several places of this name in Hesse. See Levison, *Vita* 31, note 1.

19 Tangl, 23; Talbot, pp. 75–8.

20 Tangl, 24; Talbot, pp. 78–9. Written in December 723.

21 Tangl, 26; Talbot, pp. 80–3. Gregory's letter is dated November 726. Cf. Gratian, *Decreta*, pt. ii, ch. 32, q. 7, can. 18.

22 *Vita*, VI; Talbot, p. 47.

23 Lupus Servatus, *Vita Wigberti*, ed. Holder-Egger, *M.G.H. Scriptores*, XV, 1, 36 f. Wigbert was a monk of Nursling before coming to Germany. There was another monk of the same name, from Glastonbury, who joined the mission. Tangl, 101. See Hahn, *Bonifaʒ und Lul* (1833), 141 ff., for the Wigberts.

24 His *Vita* was written by Lambert of Hersfeld in the eleventh century: ed. Holder-Egger, *M.G.H. Scriptores*, XV, i, 132 ff. There are discussions of Lull in Hauck, I, 486 ff., and Hahn, 236 ff.

25 Tangl, 29; Talbot, pp. 87–8. Leoba's Life was written by Rudolf, a monk of Fulda, in 836: ed. Waitz, *M.G.H. Scriptores*, XV, i, 127–31, and translated by Talbot, pp. 205 ff.

26 Tangl, 30 and 35; Talbot, pp. 88 and 91. For women in the scriptoria see Lina Eckenstein, *Women under Monasticism* (1896), p. 122, and for the significance of women in general, G. F. Browne, *The Importance of Women in Anglo-Saxon Times* (1919).

27 Tangl, 32. Pecthelm was one of Bede's informants: *H.E.*, V, 13, 18, 23. Boniface at this time did not know Bede's writings, though some years later wrote to Egbert of York and Huetbert abbot of Wearmouth with a request for books by Bede, that 'luminary of the Church' of whom he has heard: Tangl, 75, 76, and Talbot, pp. 127, 128.

28 Tangl, 28; Talbot, pp. 84–7.

29 Bede refers to the Islamic invasion of Gaul and its defeat: *H.E.* V, 23. There are many references to the Arabs in his theological works: cf. Plummer, II, 339.

30 Tangl, 46; Talbot, p. 96.

31 *Vitae Willibaldi et Wynnebaldi*, ed. Holder-Egger, *M.G.H. Scriptores*, XV, 80 ff. These Lives were written c. 778. For a translation of Willibald's travels see Talbot, pp. 153 ff.

32 Pirmin evangelised the Alemanni in the modern Alsace and Switzerland,

though his work had already been prepared by an Irishman, St Gall. The *Vita S. Pirminii* (*M.G.H. Scriptores*, XV, 17 ff.) is a ninth-century production.

33 Tangl, 45; Talbot, p. 93–5.

34 Eigil, *Vita Sturmi* (*M.G.H. Scriptores*, II, 365 ff.). Eigil was abbot of Fulda, 818–22.

35 Tangl, 50; Talbot, pp. 98–102. The statement that a synod had not met for over eighty years was probably the exaggeration of a reformer. According to Levison (*England and the Continent*, p. 47), there had been a synod in 696.

36 Tangl, 51; Talbot, pp. 102–6.

37 Levison, *England and the Continent*, p. 85.

38 For the 745 synod, see Tangl, 59; Talbot, pp. 107–16.

39 Tangl, 78; Talbot, pp. 129–34.

40 *Annales Lauriss. min.* (*M.G.H. Scriptores*, II, 116).

41 *Annales regni Francorum*, ed. F. Kurze (*Scriptores Rerum Germanicarum in usum scholarum* (1891), 8 and 10). See J. P. Whitney, 'The Earlier Growth of Papal Jurisdiction' (*Camb. Hist. Journal*, IV (1932) 22 f.).

42 J. F. Kenney, *The Sources for the Early History of Ireland*, I, 523 f.

43 Virgilius was not consecrated bishop until 755 (according to Krusch, *M.G.H. Scriptores Rer. Merov.* VI, 519), and according to the *Annales Salisburgenses* (*M.G.H. Scriptores*, I, 89) not until 767. In any case it was after the death of Boniface.

44 See H. van der Linden, 'Virgile de Salzburg et les théories cosmographiques au VIIIe siècle' (*Bulletins de l'Académie royale de Belgique, Classe des Lettres* (1914), pp. 163–87).

45 Tangl, 68; Talbot, pp. 119–20.

46 Stephen died a few days after his election, and was succeeded by another churchman of the same name, who is generally reckoned as Stephen II. The short-lived pope was not included in medieval papal lists, but in more recent lists he is sometimes included as Stephen II, in which case the pope with whom Boniface corresponded would be known as Stephen III. He is referred to above as Stephen II. (*Handbook of Dates*, ed. C. R. Cheney, Royal Hist. Soc. (1948), p. 35.)

47 Tangl, 109; Talbot, pp. 146–7.

48 *Vita*, VIII; Talbot, p. 54. On the same occasion he bade farewell to Leoba, exhorting her to be faithful to the country of her adoption, and commending her to Lull. He expressed the wish that after her death she might be buried beside him in the same tomb: *Vita Leobae*, XVII; Talbot, pp. 221–2.

49 According to a later tradition, fifty-two. Cf. *Baedae Continuatio*.

50 *Vita*, VIII; Talbot, p. 58.

51 Tangl, 111; *Eng. Hist. Doc.* I, 761–4.

52 June 5 has never been disputed as the day of martyrdom, though there is doubt about the actual year. According to Willibald, it was 755 (VIII), but the tradition of Fulda is in favour of 754. Tangl argued strongly in behalf of the latter ('Das Todesjahr des Bonifatius', in *Zeitschrift des Vereins f. hess. Geschichte und Landesbunde*, N.F. XXVII, Kassel 1903, 223 f.), and he was followed by Hauck, I, 590 n. 7, and Levison ed. *Vita*, 55, n. 2. The weight of

scholarly opinion is clearly now in favour of the earlier year, though G. W. Greenaway (*Saint Boniface*, which he wrote at the request of the Exeter Diocesan Festival of 1955 for the Twelfth Centenary) guardedly accepts 755 (82 n.).

53 Tangl, 112; Talbot, pp. 147–9.

54 Cf. the Celtic application of the term 'Saxonia' to the Teutonic parts of Britain. Thus Fursa came 'per Britanniam in Saxoniam' : *Vita*, XXVI. Adamnan calls England 'Saxonia': *Vita S. Columbae*, I. On the other hand, to Bede the island as a whole is always 'Britannia', though in the letter of Hwaetbert to Gregory II which he includes in *Hist. Abb.* XIX, Northumbria is called Saxony.

55 Tangl, 47.

56 Levison, *England and the Continent*, p. 92 n. He also points out (p. 126) that the term which was to be used generally for the German language and people, 'theodisc' (deutsch), is actually first known to have been used in England, though probably introduced thither from Frankland (p. 128). Its original application was to the Germanic dialects, in contrast with the Latin of ecclesiastics. Both Aldhelm and Boniface described themselves as born members of a German race (p. 129 n.). There was clearly a sense of unity amongst the Teutonic peoples, a conception of 'Germania' to which the Anglo-Saxons were proud to belong.

57 Even two centuries after the time of Wilfred it is probable that 'the differences between the two languages were comparatively slight—not very much greater than those observable between the various English dialects themselves'. H. M. Chadwick, *The Origin of the English Nation*, p. 91.

58 On confraternities see Levison, *England and the Continent*, pp. 101–3; J. Duhr, 'La confrérie dans la vie de l'Eglise' (*Revue d'histoire ecclésiastique*, XXXV, 1939). Somewhat more informally, the system existed in Northumbria in Bede's day. Bede asked the Lindisfarne monks to include his name in their intercession-book, or 'album': *Two Lives of St Cuthbert*, ed. Colgrave, p. 146. For a formal intercessory bond between Ferrières and York see *M.G.H. Epistolae*, VI, 61. Cf. A. Wilmart, 'Le règlement ecclésiastique de Berne' (*Rev. Bén.* LI, 1939, pp. 37–52), which contains some confraternity rules, attributed by the editor to the influence of Britain.

59 Tangl, 93; Talbot, pp. 139–40; *Eng. Hist. Doc.* I, 759.

60 On the death of Boniface the see of Mainz lost its metropolitical status, and Lull did not receive the pallium until *c.* 781. The profession of faith (printed in Levison, *England and the Continent*, pp. 238–40) made by Lull to the papacy on this occasion is the only surviving one of its kind for the eighth century.

61 The *Vita Liudgeri* by Altfrid is in *M.G.H. Scriptores*, II, 403–19. Extracts are printed in *Eng. Hist. Doc.* I, 724–6.

62 For Lebuin (whose English name was Liafwine) see *Vita Liudgeri*, I, and his own *Vita* in *M.G.H. Scriptores*, XXX, 2, pp. 789–95.

63 *Vita Willehadi*: *M.G.H. Scriptores*, II.

64 Thomas Hodgkin, *Charles the Great* (1897), p. 124.

Ch. XVI

1 One evidence of this is the high proportion of English dedications to St Peter. From a list of seventh- and eighth-century dedications compiled by Levison (*England and the Continent*, Appendix V) we arrive at the following statistics: S. Peter 22, S. Mary 19, S. Andrew 7, SS. Peter and Paul 6, S. Martin 6, S. Paul 5, S. Michael 4, S. Lawrence 3, S. Gregory 3, S. John Baptist 2, and seven others with one each. Cf. the dedicatory lines prefixed by Ceolfrith to the *Codex Amiatinus* which he took with him on his journey to Rome, addressed to Peter, whom 'faith of old declares to be head of the Church'. *Hist. Abb. Anon.* XXXVII.

2 On Anglo-Saxon connections with Rome see Levison, *England and the Continent*, ch. II.

3 *H.E.* v, 7. Aldhelm celebrates the king's pilgrimage and death in verse:

'... regni possessor et haeres.
Sed mox imperium mundi sceptrumque reliquit.'

Opp. Aldh. ed. Giles, p. 115.

4 Cf. the preamble to Ine's laws, in which he acknowledges his debt to ecclesiastics, *Eng. Hist. Doc.* I, 364.

5 Priests who are so drunk that they cannot perform their functions are singled out for censure. Wihtred 6: *Eng. Hist. Doc.* I, 362.

6 H. & S. III, 268–73.

7 Wilfred had been bishop of the South Saxons 680–6, with his seat at Selsey, but this was a more or less informal arrangement, and it would not be correct to speak of a diocese of Selsey as existing at this time. At the time of his consecration Eadbert was abbot of Selsey: *H.E.* v, 18. He was succeeded in the bishopric by Eolla, but at the time Bede wrote (731), the see had been vacant for some years and was being administered by the bishop of the West Saxons: *H.E.* v, 23. Cf. G. Hill, *The English Dioceses* (1900), pp. 140–1; W. G. Searle, *Anglo-Saxon Bishops, Kings, and Nobles* (1899), pp. 54–5.

8 Ine founded the Saxon School at Rome: *Flores Historiae* (ed. R. Smith, Paris 1654), p. 137. The year of his death is unknown.

9 *H.E.* v, 24.

10 *H.E.* v, 2.

11 He was canonised in 1037, and in the same year his relics moved to a splendid shrine in Beverley Minster.

12 Alcuin warmly praises Wilfred II in his poem on the saints of York: lines 1215 ff. Wilfred's death is recorded in the Chronicle, *sub anno* 744.

13 There seems, however, some doubt as to whether it was in 732 or 734 that Egbert became bishop of York: Searle, *Anglo-Saxon Bishops*, p. 164. When Egbert became bishop his cousin Ceolwulf (to whom Bede dedicated his *H.E.*) was king of Northumbria; the latter resigned his kingdom in 737 to become a monk at Lindisfarne—he was then succeeded as king by Egbert's brother Eadbert, who had a long reign of twenty-one years. On Egbert see Alcuin, *De Sanct. Ebor. Eccles.* lines 1247 ff.

14 Plummer calls Egbert 'the first archbishop of York, "de iure" and "de facto"': II, 378.

15 H. & S. III, 416–31.

16 Bede mentions the 'very fine and complete library' gathered together by Acca: *H.E.* v, 20. Levison has some valuable pages (*England and the Continent*, ch. vi) on the Anglo-Saxon 'pride in the possession of beautiful volumes'.

17 *H.E.* v, 20. Bede dedicated most of his theological works to Acca, at whose request some of them were written. Acca was one of those by whose encouragement Eddius undertook his biography of Wilfred: Eddius, preface.

18 Simeon of Durham, *Historia Regum, sub anno: Eng. Hist. Doc.* I, 240.

19 During the course of the eighth century there were 120 occupants of the seventeen sees. W. G. Searle may be consulted, supplemented by *D.C.B.*

20 Tangl, 73; Talbot, pp. 120–7, *Eng. Hist. Doc.* I, 751-6. This letter was in the name not only of Boniface himself, but of seven other bishops, all Anglo-Saxons—Wera, Burchard, Werberht, Abel, Willibald, Hwita, Leofwine.

21 Tangl, 75; Talbot, pp. 126–7, *Eng. Hist. Doc.* I, 757–8. With this letter were two gifts useful liturgically—a corporas and a towel for drying the brethren's feet. C. H. Talbot renders 'corporale pallium' as 'cloak', but it more probably signifies the corporal cloth used to cover the sacred elements at mass. In early times this cloth was much larger than it is today, though the conservative Carthusians retain the ancient form (*Liturgies of the Religious Orders* (1955), A. A. King, p. 46). Cf. D. Rock, *Church of our Fathers*, I, 32–3, and H. & S. III, 359.

22 It is possible, however, that the actual letter which reached Aethelbald was a modified and shortened version—as given by William of Malmesbury, *De Gestis Regum* (R.S.) I, 81–2. The Malmesbury version accuses the Mercian nobility as a whole of immorality, with nuns and adulteresses.

23 This unidentified place was a favourite centre for councils, which had already been held there in 716 and 742, and would be frequently held in the future.

24 See previous chapter, p. 244.

25 All that we know of Cuthbert is to his credit as archbishop. On his death in 758 he was succeeded by Bregwin, a friend of Lull. Bregwin died in 765, the next archbishop being Jaenbert, abbot of St Augustine's, whose long primacy carried him to the closing decade of the century. For the 747 synod see H. & S. III, 362–76, and Gee and Hardy, pp. 15–32.

26 In July 746 pope Zacharias had written to Boniface in Germany concerning reports that the archbishop was insisting on a second baptism in some cases. Zacharias, who was less friendly disposed than his predecessor Gregory III to Boniface, rebuked the latter for his punctiliousness. He has been told of a priest in Bavaria who knew no Latin, and who baptised with the formula: 'baptizo te in nomine patria et filia et spiritus sancti'. Boniface thought that this grammatical error made rebaptism necessary, but the pope cannot agree. He further reminded his zealous archbishop that even baptism by a heretic was valid, and should not be repeated: Tangl, 68; Talbot, p. 119.

27 'ut presbyteri saecularium poetarum modo in ecclesia non garriant, ne tragico sono sacrorum verborum compositionem ac distinctinem corrumpant vel

confundant, sed simplicem sanctamque melodiam secundum morem Ecclesiae sectentur': canon 12.

28 H. & S. III, 286.

29 Simeon of Durham, *sub anno: Eng. Hist. Doc.* I, 245. For George's ecclesiastical career see Levison, *England and the Continent*, pp. 127–8. Shortly before the Norman Conquest there was a visit of two papal legates to England in connection with an appointment to the see of Worcester. See Malmesbury, *Vita Wulfstani*, ed. R. R. Darlington, pp. 16–18.

30 H. & S. III, 441.

31 It has usually been held that these synods are identical with two known to have been held at Pincahala and Celcyth respectively about this time, but this view is questioned by Stenton, *Anglo-Saxon England*, p. 216 n. Pincahala is probably Finchale, near Durham; Celcyth is identified with Chelsea, which was within the Mercian kingdom.

32 H. & S. III, 447–61; *Eng. Hist. Doc.* I, 770–4. The report of the legates was first printed by the Magdeburg Centuriators, and their edition used by Haddon and Stubbs. The manuscript which the former used was long thought to be lost, but has come to light since the edition of H. & S. A correct version is now available in *M.G.H. Epp. Karolini Aevi*, II, 20 ff. The report, according to H. & S., was read to the assembled company in Latin and the vernacular— 'tam Latine quam Teutonice', but the true reading in place of 'Teutonice' is 'theodisce', the earliest known instance of this word (deutsch).

33 I.e., not with bare legs showing. This would seem to suggest that some clergy had been celebrating mass without wearing alb or cassock: canon 10.

34 In his letter to England asking prayers for his project of missionary work amongst the continental Saxons in 738, Boniface included 'canons' amongst the clerics to whom he addressed himself: Tangl, 46; Talbot, p. 96.

35 On the supposed connection of Offa's gift with the origin of Peter's pence see Stenton, *Anglo-Saxon England*, p. 215 n.

36 For a dispute leading to a cessation of commercial relations between the two kings cf. however a letter of Alcuin to an Irishman Colcu: *Eng. Hist. Doc.* I, 774–5.

37 For a discussion of this Council see E. J. Martin, *A History of the Iconoclastic Controversy* (S.P.C.K., no date), pp. 92–109.

38 H. & S. III, 521 ff. On the subject of the Lichfield archbishopric see the letters included by Miss D. Whitelock in *Eng. Hist. Doc.* I, 788 ff.

39 The Roman Catholic historian J. Lingard magnanimously remarked that as a result of these proceedings 'the authority of the see of Canterbury' was so firmly established 'that it has since borne without material injury the revolutions of ten centuries'. *History and Antiquities of the Anglo-Saxon Church*, I, 77.

40 H. & S. III, 536–7.

41 'cum maxime fraude': H. & S. III, 542; *Eng. Hist. Doc.* I, 799.

42 H. & S. III, 506.

43 For further examples see H. & S. III, 511, 525 (bishop Denebert of Worcester to Aethelheard, a document of interest in connection with the introduction of the Athanasian Creed into England), 528, 529, *passim*.

44 H. & S. III, 581.

45 H. & S. III, 563.

46 See list in Stubbs, *Constitutional History*, I, 137.

47 Chronicle, 789. According to some versions of this work, these first viking raiders to England came from Norway. The raid has usually been assigned to 789, but the Chronicle entry states that it occurred during the reign of Beorhtric, king of Wessex 786–802.

48 Chronicle, 793; Simeon of Durham (see *Eng. Hist. Doc.* I, 247).

49 *Eng. Hist. Doc.* I, 775 ff.; H. & S. III, 472–3 and 492–5.

50 Chronicle, 794; Simeon of Durham (*Eng. Hist. Doc.* I, 247).

51 Roger of Wendover, *Flores Historiarum, sub anno* (*Eng. Hist. Doc.* I, 255).

52 *Eng. Hist. Doc.* I, 473.

Ch. XVII

1 For a general account of the vikings see J. Brøndsted, *The Vikings* (1960: trans. by E. Bannister-Good); also G. Turville-Petre, *The Heroic Age of Scandinavia* (1951).

2 It was as sailors that the vikings primarily excelled, and under equal conditions they do not seem to have been superior to the other Germanic peoples as soldiers. On the size of the ninth-century Danish armies see Stenton, *Anglo-Saxon England*, p. 241 n.

3 Asser, I. The Chronicle has no entries between 845 and 851. For Alfred see *Asser's Life of King Alfred*, ed. W. H. Stevenson (1904), selections of which are translated by Miss D. Whitelock in *Eng. Hist. Doc.* I, 264–76. C. Plummer, *The Life and Times of Alfred the Great* (1902), is valuable. The best modern life is by Beatrice A. Lees, *Alfred the Great: the Truth Teller* (1915), the most recent by Eleanor S. Duckett, *Alfred the Great and his England* (1957).

4 Chronicle, *sub anno.*

5 *Eng. Hist. Doc.* I, 809. From about this time we have the conception of a sacred war against the foes of Christ. It is perhaps here that we find the germ of the crusading idea, to exercise so profound an influence in the history of Christendom. Cf. the homilist Aelfric, who refers to English kings who won victories through God's aid, as did Alfred against the Danes: *Eng. Hist. Doc.* I, 854.

6 Asser, VIII. Cf. Stevenson's note, pp. 180–5.

7 'To the praise of God and his own eternal salvation': Chronicle. According to Asser (XI), Aethelwulf freed a tenth of his realm from royal dues and service and offered it to God, 'for the redemption of his own soul and those of his ancestors'.

8 Asser, XII. Asser speaks well of his episcopate, saying that it was 'honourably' fulfilled (XXVIII).

9 See the Life of St Swithun by the eleventh-century Goscelin (*Acta Sanctorum,* Julii, I, 327), though the detail that Swithun ordained Aethelwulf to the diaconate is unlikely. The enthusiasm of still later writers for this pious king made him into a bishop.

10 Roger of Wendover, *Flores Historiarum, s.a.*

NOTES

11 *Historia Regum*, ed. T. Arnold (R.S.), I, 55.

12 *Eng. Hist. Doc.* I, 807–9.

13 Asser, LXXIV.

14 Coins inscribed 'Sc. Eadmund' were being struck by the converted Danes in East Anglia late in the ninth century or early in the tenth. The church of St Edmund is mentioned in the will of Theodred, bishop of London (942–51): *Eng. Hist. Doc.* I, 510.

15 Asser also (XXXIII) simply speaks of him as slain by the Danes.

16 A seventeenth-century inscription preserves his memory: 'Here lies the body of St Ethelred, king of the West Saxons, Martyr, who fell by the hands of heathen Danes.'

17 It is probable, for example, that the important monastery of Breedon (seven miles from Repton) perished at this time. It was not restored in the tenth-century monastic revival. See A. W. Clapham, 'The Carved Stones at Breedon on the Hill', *Archaeologia*, LXXVII (1928), p. 220.

18 Simeon of Durham, *Historia Regum*, *sub anno* 875.

19 Probably with a large ecclesiastical element. See B. A. Lees, *Alfred the Great*, p. 160.

20 Stenton, *Anglo-Saxon England*, p. 428.

21 On this subject see D. Whitelock, 'The Conversion of the Eastern Danelaw', *Saga book of the Viking Society*, XII.

22 *The Book of the Church* (1824), I, 77.

23 *Eng. Hist. Doc.* I, 820–1. On the lamentable state of affairs in Rome itself at this time and the grisly fate of Formosus see Hodgkin, *History of the Anglo-Saxons*, II, 638.

24 *M.G.H. Epist. Karol. Aevi*, V, 366 ff.

25 Asser, XCIII.

26 Asser, XCVIII.—Cf A. J. Robertson, *Anglo-Saxon Charters*, p. 25. Alfred's daughter was in ill-health. Shaftesbury is still noted for its air, which has been compared with that of Switzerland.

27 Asser, LXXIX.

28 *Eng. Hist. Doc.* I, 813–17.

29 Asser, XCII–XCIV. The monastery also included amongst its inmates a heathen youth (i.e. a Dane).

30 Asser, LXXVII.

31 Ed. H. Sweet (E.E.T.S. 1871–2).

32 As Alfred himself says: see Sweet's ed. pp. 8–9.

33 See translation by D. Whitelock: *Eng. Hist. Doc.* I, 818–19.

34 Cf. Asser, LXXV.

35 Asser, CVI.

36 Ed. T. Miller (E.E.T.S. 1890–8).

37 Aelfric maintained that Alfred was the author of the Bede translation: *Cath. Homilies* II, 116–18. He also said that until he himself wrote vernacular works, the translations of Alfred were the only vernacular writings available: *ibid.* I, 2.

38 Ed. H. Sweet (E.E.T.S. 1883).

39 Ed. W. J. Sedgefield (1899), and translated by him in the following year.
40 Ed. H. L. Hargrove, *Yale Studies in English*, XIII (1902), and translated by him *ibid*. XXII (1904).
41 Cf. Lees, *op. cit.* p. 334. The oldest MS. 'may safely be attributed to the direct initiative of King Alfred'. For discussions of the Chronicle see Hodgkin, *History of the Anglo-Saxons*, II, 706–8, and D. Whitelock in *Eng. Hist. Doc.* I, 114–15.
42 Asser, XXIV, LXXXVIII.
43 William of Malmesbury, *De Gestis Regum* (R.S.), II, 123.
44 Chronicle, 883, 887, 888, 890. In 889 there was no actual mission to Rome, but Alfred sent two messengers with letters.
45 Asser, XCI.
46 *Sub anno* 883.
47 *Eng. Hist. Doc.* I, 811–13.
48 *Eng. Hist. Doc.* I, 372–80.
49 The oldest version of the Chronicle places the death of Alfred in 901, though Simeon of Durham and other writers are in favour of 899. W. H. Stevenson argued for 899, and this date was also accepted by Beatrice Lees. See also M. L. R. Beaven, *E.H.R.* XXXLI.

Concerning the ultimate significance of this man who died while still within his prime, however, few will disagree. Lawgiver, warrior, and administrator, he also realised the necessity for religion and education, the twin pillars upon which any civilised community must be built. The concluding words of his last work (*The Soliloquies*) are his abiding testimony to his fellow-countrymen: 'he is a very foolish man, who will not increase his understanding while he is still in this world, and long to reach that endless life where all shall be made clear'.

Ch. XVIII

1 For the history of dioceses W. G. Searle's *Anglo-Saxon Bishops, Kings, and Nobles* (1899) and G. Hill's *English Dioceses* (1900) are useful. From *c.* 1880 S.P.C.K. published a readable series under the general title 'Diocesan Histories', which must sometimes be used cautiously.
2 The best authority for Dunstan is the *Vita Sancti Dunstani*, written *c.* 1000 by an anonymous Saxon priest, who probably knew his subject personally. This, and other materials for the saint's life, were gathered together by Stubbs in *Memorials of St Dunstan* (R.S.). Good modern works are *The Times of St Dunstan* (1923), by J. Armitage Robinson, and Miss E. S. Duckett's *Saint Dunstan of Canterbury* (1955), the latter work also containing accounts of Aethelwold and Oswald. There is an account of the monastic revival in *Regularis Concordia*, ed. T. Symons, pp. ix–xxviii.
3 Duckett, p. 28. Edgarley and Baltonsborough in Somerset are each claimed as his birthplace.
4 On this famous incident see Duckett, pp. 57–8.
5 J. Evans, *Monastic Life at Cluny* (1931); *Vita S. Odonis*, by John of Salerno (*Acta Sanctorum Ordinis S. Benedicti*, ed. Mabillon, v).

6 Oda was a Dane, the son (it was believed) of a viking; *Vita Odonis, Anglia Sacra*, II, 78 ff. Before becoming archbishop of Canterbury he held the see of Ramsbury. He was held in high regard by Dunstan, and long known by the English as Oda the Good.

7 For Gerard see A. Hauck, *Kirchengeschichte Deutschlands*, III, 345 ff.

8 He favoured the heathen Danes, to the annoyance of monastic chroniclers. He was father by an irregular union of St Edith of Wilton. Duckett, p. 83; cf. Aelfric, *Lives of the Saints* (ed. Skeat, E.E.T.S.) I, 2, 468.

9 We are fortunate in possessing two nearly contemporary lives of Aethelwold: a *Vita* written *c.* 1004–5 by Aelfric, his former pupil and subsequently abbot of Eynsham (*Chronicon Monasterii de Abingdon* (R.S. 1858, ed. J. Stevenson), II), and a 'Vita' possibly the work of Wulfstan, precentor of Winchester cathedral, *c.* 1000 (*Acta Sanctorum Ordinis S. Benedicti*, V, 594 ff.). See D. J. V. Fisher, 'The Early Biographers of St. Ethelwold' (*E.H.R.* 1952).

10 Stenton, *The Early History of the Abbey of Abingdon* (1913).

11 Aethelwold's church at Abingdon was round, after the model of Charlemagne's church at Aachen. Clapham, *English Romanesque Architecture*, I, 148; *Chron. Abing.* II, 277.

12 *Chron. Abing.* II, 260.

13 Clapham, I, 91.

14 Oswald's *Vita* was written *c.* 1000 by an anonymous author. It is in *Historians of the Church of York*, I, ed. J. Raine (R.S.).

15 *Eng. Hist. Doc.* II, ed. D. C. Douglas and G. W. Greenaway, 1953, pp. 624 ff.

16 *The Times of St Dunstan*, p. 129.

17 There seems to have been a monastery in Deerhurst from *c.* 804. Its history was to be exceptionally varied, including probably destruction by the Danes and subsequent refounding, and then a long period from the time of Edward the Confessor as an alien priory under the French abbey of St Denis. There was a short spell of independence in the fifteenth century, and then the monastery was granted to Eton College. Finally, before the Dissolution, it became a cell of the neighbouring abbey of Tewkesbury (*Medieval Religious Houses*, D. Knowles and R. N. Hadcock, 1953, p. 64; *Abbeys*, M. R. James, 1925, p. 52). Since the Reformation the monastic church has served for the parishioners, but close by, as part of a group of farm buildings, is a pre-Conquest structure now known as 'Odda's chapel'; about 40 ft. long and consisting of rectangular chancel and nave, this was probably the original parish church. For a full architectural account of Deerhurst priory church see W. H. Knowles, in *Archaeologia*, LXXVII (1928).

18 See Duckett, pp. 154 ff.

19 These monasteries are reviewed by Knowles, *Monastic Order*, pp. 49–52.

20 Miss Duckett (p. 159) suggests that Oswald, with his practical turn of mind, was the original force behind the inception of the council.

21 *Regularis Concordia*, ed. and trans. Dom Thomas Symons (1953).

22 Psalms 120–134 (Book of Common Prayer numeration). This devotion goes back to Benedict of Aniane, who took a leading part in the reforms of Charlemagne. Cf. Symons, p. 13 n.

23 See ed. Symons, XLVI, 5, 13.
24 But see D. J. V. Fisher, 'The Anti-Monastic Reaction in the Reign of Edward the Martyr' (*Camb. Hist. Journ.* X (1952), pp. 254–70).
25 On the circumstances of Edward's death see Duckett, pp. 189–91, and Stenton, *Anglo-Saxon England*, p. 368. The story making Aelfthryth a murderess is not found until a century after the actual deed: *Memorials of St. Dunstan* (R.S.), p. 114. In the present ruins of Shaftesbury abbey some bones are preserved which according to a local tradition are those of the murdered Edward. But Wulfstan, in *Sermo Lupi ad Anglos*, says that after the murder the body was burnt: *Eng. Hist. Doc.* I, 857
26 See map facing p. 449, Stenton, *Anglo-Saxon England.*
27 The only medieval monastic cathedrals outside England were apparently the Benedictine Monreale in Sicily, which became the cathedral in 1176: and Downpatrick in Ireland, 1188, which was founded directly from Chester (K. Edwards, *English Secular Cathedrals*, p. 10 n.).
28 Byrhtferth, *Manual* (E.E.T.S. 1929), p. 213.

Ch. XIX

1 The origins and development of the English parochial system are lucidly summarised by Canon G. W. O. Addleshaw in two pamphlets, *The Beginnings of the Parochial System*, and *The Development of the Parochial System from Charlemagne to Urban II* (1954), which also include useful bibliographies. The same author continues his studies further in *Rectors, Vicars, and Patrons in the Twelfth and early Thirteenth Century Canon Law* (1956).
2 Catherine E. Boyd, *Tithes and Parishes in Medieval Italy* (1952), p. 49.
3 H. & S. III, 127.
4 Boyd, *Tithes and Parishes*, p. 51.
5 Gregory of Tours, *History of the Franks*, ed. O. Dalton (1927), II, 470.
6 *Ibid.* II, 218.
7 E. L. Cutts, *Parish Priests and their People* (1898), p. 44.
8 Cf. *H.E.* I, 33; II, 14, 16; III, 7. Local lords would imitate the example of the kings in promoting the foundation of churches.
9 H. & S. III 316; *Eng. Hist. Doc.* I, 737.
10 'Ut presbyteri per loca . . . studeant explere'; H. & S. III, 365. Such districts would be known as priestshires rather than parishes, as at this time the term 'parochia' signified the territory of the bishop. It is best, however, not to dogmatise either way, and the truth probably is that a 'parochia' was essentially a geographical area, great or small (as distinct from a diocese, which was a unit of administration). So far, the local village districts had not secured sufficient status to warrant the description of 'parochiae'.
11 Alcuin's *Life of Willibrord*, ed. and trans. C. H. Talbot, *Anglo-Saxon Missionaries in Germany*, p. 11.
12 *H.E.* IV, 27.
13 Willibald's *Life of Boniface*, ed. Talbot, p. 27.
14 'Her swvtelad seo gecwydraednes de.'

15 Addleshaw, *Beginnings of the Parochial System*, p. 14.

16 *H.E.* v, 4, 5.

17 That not all villages had churches early in the eighth century is implied by a comment of Bede on Our Lord's entry into the Temple, to the effect that the custom of his contemporaries, on visiting a village, was first to enter the church if there was one there, to offer prayer to God. *Opera*, ed. Giles, x, 173.

18 Talbot, p. 155.

19 'si necesse sit'; H. & S. iii, 191.

20 H. & S. iii, 190.

21 Selborne, *Ancient Facts and Fictions concerning Churches and Tithes* (1888), p. 173.

22 'The Proprietary Church as an element of Medieval Germanic Ecclesiastical Law', in *Medieval Germany*, 911–1250, ed. and trans. G. Barraclough (1948), p. 68.

23 *The Domesday Geography of Eastern England* (1952).

24 See the 'List of Saxon Churches in the Domesday Monachorum' (*Archaeologia Cantiana*, XLV, 60–89), and the 'List of Saxon Churches in the Textus Roffensis' (*Archaeologia Cantiana*, XLIV, 35–59).

25 W. Page, 'Some Remarks on the Churches of the Domesday Survey' (*Archaeologia*, LXVI, 61–102).

26 There are of course many examples in our own day of a similarly liberal supply of churches in country towns. Thus the town of Shaftesbury, with a little over 3,000 people, has four parish churches still in use, besides four Dissenting places of worship.

27 On the subject of endowments see Stenton, *Anglo-Saxon England*, pp. 152–6; E. W. Watson, *Cambridge Medieval History*, VI, 534 ff.; and Selborne, *Ancient Facts and Fictions concerning Churches and Tithes*, a book of wider usefulness than is indicated by its title.

28 Plough-alms and soul-scot are both first mentioned in the laws of Athelstan (925–39).

29 Enforced by the laws of Ine, issued early in his reign (688–726).

30 Mansi, *Sacrorum Conciliorum*, VIII, 12.

31 *H.E.* I, 27.

32 Although it has strong Old Testament precedent. Thus, Abraham gave tithes to Melchizedek, king of Salem (Gen. xiv. 20); Jacob vowed to the Lord the tithe of all his substance which he might acquire in Mesopotamia (Gen. xxviii. 22). According to Lev. xxvii. 30–32, all the tithe of the land, including fruit-trees, and of herds and flocks, is devoted to the Lord. But in the New Testament there is no mention of Our Lord or his apostles recommending the payment of tithes; Jesus refers to the punctilious payment of tithes on the part of the scribes and pharisees, who omit the weightier matters of the law (Matt. xxiii. 23).

33 Jerome, *Comm. on Malachi*, cap. iii; Augustine, *Sermo* 85 (on Matt. xix. 17).

34 Mansi, IX, 809.

35 Grat. Decretum, causa xvi, quaest 7, cap. 5.

36 Boniface, *Epistles* (Tangl, 118).

37 H. & S. III, 191, 203.

38 *H.E.* IV, 29. Cf. Eddius. *Vita Wilfridi*, LXV (ed. Colgrave, pp. 140-1), where we read of an abbot's share in the tithes of herds and flocks, in 709.

39 The reference is merely incidental. Tangl, 78. It is omitted by Talbot in his translation (*Anglo-Saxon Missionaries*, p. 133).

40 *Eng. Hist. Doc.* I, 738.

41 Selborne, *op. cit.* pp. 144-5.

42 Cf. Asser, XCIX.

43 Selborne, *op. cit.* p. 180.

44 *Eng. Hist. Doc.* I, 395. Miss Whitelock dates the Andover enactments to the period 959-63.

45 *Eng. Hist. Doc.* I, 428. The enactment formed part of the secular, not the ecclesiastical, code.

46 *Blickling Homilies of the Tenth Century* (E.E.T.S.), pp. 50, 52.

47 *H.E.* I, 26.

48 *H.E.* IV, 16.

49 *Eng. Hist. Doc.* I, 822.

50 See pp. 440 ff.

51 *Ibid.* p. 519.

52 For the development of the benefice conception in general, see F. L. Ganshof's study, *Feudalism*, trans. P. Grierson (1952). Cf. Alfons Dopsch, *The Economic and Social Foundations of European Civilisation* (1937), chaps. VIII and IX.

53 Thus Aelfric remarked: 'never let a layman hold authority over the ordained servants of God; but if anyone do so, be it known to him that he sets against the ordinance of Christ and all his saints' (*Cath. Homilies*, II, 595).

Ch. XX

1 See the Homilies of Aelfric, printed with translation in *Liber Sermonum Catholicorum* ed. B. Thorpe (2 vols., 1844, Aelfric Society); Aelfric's *Lives of the Saints*, ed. W. W. Skeat (E.E.T.S. 2 vols. 1881 & 1900); the *Blickling Homilies of the Tenth Century*, ed. R. Morris (E.E.T.S. 1880).

2 *Blickling Homilies*, p. 6.

3 *Blickling Homilies*, p. 208.

4 II, 121-5.

5 Ed. G. N. Garmonsway (Methuen's Old English Library, 1938).

6 *Catholic Homilies*, I, 105.

7 *Catholic Homilies*, I, 579.

8 *Catholic Homilies*, I, 343.

9 *Catholic Homilies*, I, 521.

10 *Catholic Homilies*, I, 257.

11 *Catholic Homilies*, II, 77.

12 *Catholic Homilies*, II, 223.

13 In the *Blickling Homilies* (p. 214), baptism is distinguished from christening. It is said that when St Martin had completed his eighteenth year he was

baptised according to the ordinances of the Church, but was christened three years previously.

14 *Catholic Homilies*, I, 329.

15 *Lives of the Saints*, I, 291.

16 *Lives of the Saints*, I, 275.

17 *Catholic Homilies*, II, 99.

18 *Catholic Homilies*, I, 125. According to the *Blickling Homilies* (p. 42), to hide your sins from your confessor is devil's treasure. A priest who is tardy in driving out the devil from a man will be assigned to the fiery river and the iron hook.

19 *Catholic Homilies*, II, 215.

20 *Catholic Homilies*, II, 575 ff.

21 *Lives of the Saints*, I, 469.

22 *Lives of the Saints*, I, 327.

23 *Catholic Homilies*, I, 305.

24 'Hi sind gerumene to lyftenre heofenan na to rodor-licere.'

25 *Catholic Homilies*, I, 309.

26 *Lives of the Saints*, II, 155.

27 *Lives of the Saints*, I, 191.

28 *Lives of the Saints*, I, 331.

29 *Lives of the Saints*, I, 233.

30 *Catholic Homilies*, I, 149; II, 71, 94.

31 *Catholic Homilies*, I, 309. Cf. *Blickling Homilies*, p. 172. Nero's wife Livia and Agrippina wife of Agrippa became such convinced Christians that they renounced normal relations in marriage.

32 *Catholic Homilies*, II, 263 ff.

33 It was reprinted in 1566 under the auspices of archbishop Parker and other bishops. A. J. Macdonald, *Berengar and the Reform of Sacramental Doctrine*, p. 410 (London 1930).

34 'na swa-deah lichamlice, ac gastlice.'

35 *Catholic Homilies*, I, 35; cf. I, 267.

36 *Catholic Homilies*, II, 203.

37 See A. J. Macdonald, p. 249.

38 *Catholic Homilies*, I, 445.

39 *Catholic Homilies*, I, 439.

40 *Catholic Homilies*, II, 23.

41 *Catholic Homilies*, II, 467.

42 *Catholic Homilies*, II, 445.

43 *Catholic Homilies*, I, 441. The *Blickling Homilies* come out on the side of the bodily Assumption; see the homily on the Assumption, pp. 136–59.

44 *Lives of the Saints*, II, 191 ff.

45 *Catholic Homilies*, I, 531.

46 *Blickling Homilies*, p. 162.

47 The *Historia Eliensis* (ed. D. J. Stewart, 1848, for the Anglia Christiana Society) contains this Life. There has been a great deal of research on Wulfstan recently, notably by Miss Dorothy Whitelock, whose article in *Trans.*

R.H. Soc. 1942, XXIV, Fourth Series, is of special value, by Dr K. Jost (*Wulfstanstudien*, 1950), and by Professor Dorothy Bethurum, whose critical edition (*The Homilies of Wulfstan*, Oxford 1957) is indispensable.

48 D. Knowles, *The Monastic Order in England*, p. 494.
49 The *Oxford Dictionary of the Christian Church* (p. 1479) describes his tenure of this see as 'probable', but its certainty was clearly demonstrated by Miss Whitelock. See 'A Note on Wulfstan the Homilist', *E.H.R.* LII (1937), pp. 460–5.
50 'The Jurisdiction of the Archbishops of York in Gloucestershire' (*Trans. Bristol and Glos. Archeol. Soc.* 1921, XLIII, 86 n.).
51 *Sermo Lupi ad Anglos* (1952 ed.), p. 30.
52 For Burchard see Paul Fournier, *Études critiques sur le décret de Burchard de Worms* (Paris 1910).
53 This ecclesiastic was often confused in the past with the homilist, as by Dean Hook in his *Lives of the Archbishops of Canterbury*.
54 Recently edited by J. H. Ure, *The Benedictine Office: an Old English Text* (Edinburgh 1957).
55 *Byrhtferth's Manual*, ed. S. J. Crawford (E.E.T.S. 1929).
56 *Ibid.* p. 17.
57 *Ibid.* p. 41.
58 *Ibid.* p. 59.
59 *Blickling Homilies*, p. 184.
60 *Blickling Homilies*, p. 116.
61 *Byrhtferth's Manual*, pp. 239, 241.
62 *Blickling Homilies*, pp. 90–95.
63 *Catholic Homilies*, I, 299, 477; II, 371; *Lives of the Saints*, I, 305, 353.
64 *Catholic Homilies*, II, 569, 575.
65 *Catholic Homilies*, I, 615.
66 *Catholic Homilies*, I, 3.
67 C. W. Kennedy, *Early English Christian Poetry*, p. 268.
68 *Be Domes Daege*, ed. J. R. Lumby (E.E.T.S. 1876). For a translation into modern alliterative verse see C. W. Kennedy, *Early English Christian Poetry* (1952), pp. 259–67.
69 See further G. L. Burr, 'The Year 1000 and the Antecedents of the Crusades' (*American Hist. Review*, 1901, VI, 429–39). The subject is most recently discussed by D. Bethurum, *The Homilies of Wulfstan*, pp. 278 ff.

Ch. XXI

1 The subject is treated briefly by J. R. H. Moorman, *History of the Church in England*, pp. 44–6; and, from a monastic standpoint, by D. Knowles, *Monastic Order*, pp. 67–9. The only full treatment in English appears to be in *English Missionaries in Sweden and Finland* (1937), by C. J. A. Oppermann. For Norway there is useful information in Hjalmar H. Boyesen's *History of Norway* (Story of the Nations Series, 1900). Scandinavian modern works on the subject remain untranslated, including the important book by A. Taranger,

Den Angelsaksiske Kirkes Indflydelse paa den Norske (Christiana 1890). On the wider aspects, G. Turville-Petre, *The Heroic Age of Scandinavia* (1951), is helpful. There is little to be gleaned from early medieval chroniclers, only Adam of Bremen, *Gesta Hannaburgensis Ecclesiae Pontificum* (*M.G.H. Scriptores*, 7), being of much value.

2   *M.G.H. Annales Xantenses, sub anno.*

3   Oppermann, p. 37.

4   For Anskar, the authority is *Vita S. Anscharii*, by Rimbert (*Scriptores Rerum Suecicarum*, II, Uppsala (1818–76)).

5   For the story that the first Christian missionary in Sweden was not Anskar but a certain Herbert, sent thither by Charlemagne, see Oppermann, p. 39 n. with its references.

6   On this see Turville-Petre, ch. xv.

7   The Uppsala temple is described by Adam of Bremen, IV, cc. 26, 27.

8   Cf. Hrafnkels Saga, c. I, iii: 'Hrafnkell settled the whole of the valley, bestowing lands on other people, on condition of being their chief; and thus he assumed priesthood over them.' Quoted by Oppermann, p. 22.

9   Olav's career is fully discussed by Turville-Petre, ch. XIII.

10 Luke xiv. 23.

11 Cf. Stenton, *Anglo-Saxon England*, p. 457.

12 There is difference of opinion over Sigfrid's identity. See the full note by Oppermann, p. 61.

13 The struggle did not end until 1138, when the materials of the temple at Uppsala were re-used to build a cathedral there.

14 Knowles, *Monastic Order*, pp. 164, 248. As Knowles remarks, these monastic colonising activities marked the virtual end of the English missionary tradition in the northern lands.

15 There are many fonts of twelfth-century date in Västergötland which are clearly based on English prototypes of the early Norman period. See D. Talbot Rice, *English Art, 871–1100*, p. 45; J. Roosval, 'Swedish and English Fonts', in *Burlington*, XXXII (1918), 85.

16 The blood still warms at the rhythm of the war-cry chanted by Olav's men at the great battle:

'Fram, fram, Kristmenn, Krossmenn, Konungsmenn'.

(Forward, forward, Christ's men, Crossmen, Kingsmen.)

Ch. XXII

1   For the later churches see A. W. Clapham, *English Romanesque Architecture*, and G. Baldwin Brown, *The Arts in Early England*. For late Anglo-Saxon art the standard book is now *English Art, 871–1100* (1952), by D. Talbot Rice. T. D. Kendrick's *Late Saxon and Viking Art* (1949) is also valuable. Much of the work in this field lies in articles, whose scattered nature may be gathered from Talbot Rice's bibliography; besides the few full-length works, he lists no fewer than 172 separate articles in various English, and ten in continental, journals.

2   The evidence is summarised by Clapham, I, 85 ff.

3　I, 79 ff.

4　Clapham, I, 88–9; A. W. Clapham and W. H. Godfrey, 'The Saxon Cathedral at Elmham' (*Antiq. Journal*, VI, 402).

5　Cf. the two articles by W. E. St Lawrence Finny: 'The Saxon Church at Kingston-upon-Thames' (*Journ. Brit. Arch. Assoc.* XXXII (1926)), and 'The Church of the Saxon coronation at Kingston' (*Surrey Archeological Collections*, XLVIII (1943)).

6　There are several references in the *Regularis Concordia* to the 'pealing of all the bells'. See pp. 28, 30, 48, 50, in T. Symons' edition. Cf. further Knowles, *Monastic Order*, pp. 543–4. An impetus had probably also been given to the building of square towers by the Danish invasions. These towers would form local strongholds, and the bells give warning of impending danger.

7　Clapham, I, 77.

8　F. C. Eeles, *Report on behalf of the Central Council for the Care of Churches*; Talbot Rice, p. 94.

9　*Op. cit.* p. 95.

10　*Ibid.* p. 98.

11　*Ibid.* p. 112. For a still later dating of the Chichester slabs see Evelyn Hardy, 'The Chichester Reliefs' (*History Today*, February 1956), based on the researches of Dr G. Zarnecki, who places them c. 1140.

12　The Ethiopian eunuch was baptised in this manner by the apostle Philip: Acts viii. 38. This was the only practical way by which could be realised St Paul's words: 'we are buried with him by baptism into death': Romans vi. 4.

13　Gregory informed Eulogius of Alexandria of Augustine's baptism of 10,000 converts in the river Swale, Kent, on Christmas Day, 597. Paulinus made use of the little river Glen (the modern Bowment, in Glendale), while preaching and baptising at the royal country-seat of Yeavering, and also (on other occasions) the Yorkshire Swale, which flows near Catterick. *H.E.* II, 14.

14　*H.E.* I, 26.

15　According to Tertullian (*De Baptismo*, c. XIX), baptism was normally confined to Easter and Pentecost. Christmas and Epiphany were also favourite times, but this was discouraged by the early Roman Church (Plummer, II, 95). Of early English kings, Edwin (*H.E.* II, 14), Caedwalla (*H.E.* V, 7), and Ethelbert (*Thomas of Elmham*, p. 78) were baptised on great festivals, the first two at Easter, the third at Pentecost.

16　In France there are surviving examples at Frejus, Aix-en-Provence, Strasbourg, and elsewhere; in Germany at such places as Mainz, Worms, and Aachen; in Italy at Bologna, Pisa, Florence, Ravenna, and other early Christian centres. Baptisteries were usually dedicated to St John Baptist. The only baptistery known to have been built in England was the work of archbishop Cuthbert, in the mid-eighth century; it stood at the east end of his cathedral of Canterbury, almost adjoining it.

17　*The Benedictine Office: an Old English Text*, ed. J. M. Ure (1957).

18　According to the *Law of the Northumbrian Priests*, the priest is to sing the Hours at the appointed times, giving warning by ringing the bell, c. 36.

19 *H.E.* IV, 22: 'a tertia autem hora, quando missae fieri solebant'.

20 The clergy must 'minister daily to God's people, or at least once a week sing mass', *Blickling Homilies*, p. 44.

21 Alcuin, whose interest in liturgical matters we have already noticed, forwarded a list of such masses to the monks of Fulda (Alcuin, *Ad Fuldenses*, *P.L.* 100, col. 385); see further the 'Law of the Northumbrian Priests' (*Eng. Hist. Doc.* I, 434 ff.). A priest may not celebrate more than three times a day. He must not use a wooden chalice, nor celebrate without wine.

22 The reed, or 'fistula', is still used at Rome for solemn papal masses: A. A. King, *Liturgies of the Religious Orders*, p. 11.

23 In monasteries the Eucharist was possibly reserved also in the infirmary, as appears from Bede, *H.E.* IV, 24.

24 Concerning this book, very important in the early history of English music, see Knowles, *Monastic Order*, p. 553.

25 The *Stabat Mater*, itself a thirteenth-century composition, was admitted into the Liturgy in 1727.

26 *Regularis Concordia*, ed. Symons, pp. 49-50.

27 For examples of the possessions of greater churches, in vestments, service-books and liturgical objects, see the lists in A. J. Robertson, *Anglo-Saxon Charters*, pp. 73 (Peterborough), 195 (Bury St Edmunds), 227 (Exeter), 249-51 (Sherburn-in-Elmet, Durham, Worcester). Cf. Miss Robertson's notes, pp. 476-7.

Ch. XXIII

1 On the coronation ritual see P. E. Schramm, *A History of the English Coronation* (1937, trans. L. G. Wickham Legg); E. S. Duckett, *Saint Dunstan of Canterbury* (1955), pp. 99 ff.

2 *Historians of the Church of York* (R.S.), I, 436 ff.

3 Later, king Harold was to be consecrated on the very day following the death of Edward the Confessor.

4 *H.E.* III, 7.

5 Eddius, XI.

6 *H.E.* III, 29.

7 *H.E.* IV, 28.

8 *Eng. Hist. Doc.* I, 739-40.

9 *Monastic Order in England*, Appendix IV.

10 *Historians of the Church of York* (R.S.), II, 354. This would seem to be the earliest known instance of the practice of separating the choir from the nave by a 'pulpitum' or screen which was to exert so strong an influence on English church architecture. It need perhaps hardly be said that a pulpitum was not a pulpit in the modern sense.

11 *Constitutional History*, I, 243.

12 Cf. W. Hunt, who wrote that the 'bishops were busy in intrigue and greedy for wealth and power; they treated their bishoprics like temporal lordships, were eager for plurality . . .' Again, '. . . spirituality and learning decayed, and

the prelates are as a rule men of whom our authorities say little that is to their honour.' *History of the English Church*, pp. 390–1.

13 See especially R. R. Darlington, 'Ecclesiastical Reform in the late Old English Period', *E.H.R.* (1936), LI.

14 The first archbishop of York known to have gone to Rome for this purpose was Aelfric, Wulfstan's successor, in 1026.

15 Cf. Miss D. Bethurum, 'A Letter of Protest from the English Bishops to the Pope' (*Philologia*, Malone Anniversary Studies, 97–104). The letter was formerly ascribed to 805 by scholars including R. H. Hodgkin, R. R. Darlington, and W. E. Lunt, but W. Levison (*England and the Continent*, pp. 241–8) demonstrated that the custom of archbishops going to Rome for their pallia was not in force as early as this.

16 *H.E.* II, 5.

17 *H.E.* II, 13.

18 Chronicle, 656.

19 *H.E.* III, 25.

20 *H.E.* IV, 5.

21 *H.E.* IV, 17.

22 Chronicle, 675, 680.

23 *Eng. Hist. Doc.* I, 715.

24 *Eng. Hist. Doc.* I, 466–7.

25 *Eng. Hist. Doc.* I, 468–9.

26 H. & S. III, 362, 579.

27 Cf. the 'Law of the Northumbrian Priests', a document of great value for the history of the Church in the northern province, assigned by Miss Whitelock to c. 1020–3 (*Eng. Hist. Doc.* I, 434 ff.). Here it is stated to be an offence for a priest to absent himself from a synod: c. 44.

28 M. Deanesly, 'The Archdeacons of Canterbury under Archbishop Ceolnoth', *E.H.R.* (1927), XLII.

29 W. de Gray Birch, *Cartularium Saxonicum*, II, no. 562.

30 *Catholic Homilies*, I, 417.

31 *Blickling Homilies of the Tenth Century*, ed. R. Morris (E.E.T.S. 1880), p. 108. The context of the passage suggests that the archdeacons were ecclesiastics of some authority.

32 *Law of the Northumbrian Priests*, c. 6. An archdeacon, moreover, has authority to prohibit an erring priest from saying mass.

33 For much of the above, see A. Hamilton Thompson, *Diocesan Organisation in the Middle Ages*, and Sir Frank Stenton, *Anglo-Saxon England*, p. 434. Cf. W. Levison, *England and the Continent*, p. 107. On archdeacons see further MacDonald, *Lanfranc*, pp. 122–3. By c. 1100 there were five archdeacons in the York diocese, seven in Lincoln, four in Salisbury, one in Wells, and a number in Chichester. By 1116 the number in Wells had risen to three, and by 1125–7 there were three in Norwich.

34 The classic book on the origin of the office of rural dean is *Horae Decanicae Rurales* (1835), by William Dansey, who thought that the office developed from the early country bishop, or 'choepiscopus', a conclusion which in the

NOTES

opinion of the late A. H. Thompson should be treated with caution (*Diocesan Organisation*, p. 19). The *Horae* appears to have been largely inspired by an earlier work, a paper entitled *The Nature, Use, and End of the Office of Dean Rural*, written by Dr John Priaulx, rector of Berwick St John and archdeacon of Salisbury, in 1666. This lay in the church chest at Berwick until discovered by Dansey (rector of the neighbouring parish of Donhead St Andrew) and published by him with notes of his own in 1832.

35 Cf. the report of the legatine synods in 787. Canons are to live canonically, and ecclesiastics are not to eat their meals in private. H. & S. III, 450–1.
36 Hunt, *History of the English Church*, p. 33.
37 *H.E.* I, 17.
38 Cnut's Laws (Secular), 5.
39 *Lives of the Saints*, I, 364 ff.
40 *Catholic Homilies*, I, 475.
41 *Catholic Homilies*, II, 31, 35.   Such practices explain why fonts in medieval times came to have locked covers.
42 *Catholic Homilies*, I, 3.
43 Cf. O. Cockayne, *Leechdoms, Wortcunning, and Starcraft* (R.S.), I, p. xxix, who justly remarks in connection with the centuries 500–1000: 'so strong was the general acceptance of magic influence, so general was the fashion set in that direction, that every candidate for the confidence of the public must fall in with it.' No one will dispute that in the process of the Conversion of England there was much expediency, both in one direction and the other. But it is impossible to accept such a sweeping statement, made of one class of Englishmen, in connection with the continuance of the craft of jewellery after the Conversion: 'the metalworker merely changed his religion because he considered it politic' (David Wilson, *The Anglo-Saxons* (1960), p. 142). In the final analysis the Conversion was based on a deep spiritual conviction, amply borne out by the Lives of saints and the notices of devout men and women.
44 *Leechdoms*, I, 387.
45 *Ibid.* I, 391.
46 *Ibid.* I, 399 ff.
47 *Leechdoms*, II.
48 *Ibid.* II, 137.
49 *Ibid.* II, 139.
50 *Ibid.* II, 137.
51 *Ibid.* II, 335.
52 From an 'Exhortation' in the same MS. as the 'Be Domes Daege' ed. J. R. Lumby (E.E.T.S. 1876). For further evidence of heathen practice see the 'Law of the Northumbrian Priests' (*Eng. Hist. Doc.* I, 437–8, and Miss Whitelock's introduction, p. 75).
53 *Memorials of Bury St Edmunds* (R.S.), I, 46–7.
54 Wilkins, *Concilia*, I, 228.
55 Leach, *Charters*, p. 34.
56 Leach, *Charters*, p. 36; Wilkins, *Concilia*, I, 270.

NOTES

57 Aelfric, *Catholic Homilies*, II, 533.

58 Cf. *Eng. Hist. Doc.* I, 535.

59 William of Malmesbury, *De Gestis Regum* (R.S.), I, 207.

60 For the murder of Aelfheah see the contemporary account by Thietmar of Merseburg. 'Chronicle', VII, 42, 43 (*Eng. Hist. Doc.* I, 320–1.)

61 *Sermo Lupi ad Anglos*, ed. Dorothy Whitelock (Methuen's Old English Library, 2nd ed. 1952), with translation by the same author in *Eng. Hist. Doc.* I, 854–9. For confirmation of the demoralised state of the English at this time cf. Thietmar of Merseburg, VII, 36.

62 *Eng. Hist. Doc.* I, 405–9.

63 For an example of the type of burden which was now falling heavily on Englishmen, and which engrossed much of their thoughts, cf. the will of archbishop Aelfric, in 1005 (*Eng. Hist. Doc.* I, 544). He bequeaths to the king his best ship and armour for sixty men, besides a ship to the men of Kent and another to those of Wiltshire.

64 *Eng. Hist. Doc.* I, 409–11.

65 *Eng. Hist. Doc.* I, 411–14. According to c. 30 a priest 'has no concern with a wife'. Cf. the *Law of the Northumbrian Priests*, c. 35, issued a few years later; a grudging tolerance is accorded to priestly marriage—the legislator refers to the priest's wife as his 'woman'.

66 Liebermann, *Gesetze*, I, 278 ff. In the extracts given in *Eng. Hist. Doc.* I, 419–30, the ecclesiastical section is for the most part omitted.

67 Both letters are included in *Eng. Hist. Doc.* I, 414 ff.

68 Cf. the *Law of the Northumbrian Priests*, c. 55. Sunday markets are forbidden, all public meetings, and transportation of goods, whether by wagon or horse or on one's back.

69 Cnut made the journey in the spirit of a true pilgrim, visiting churches which lay in his way. Cf. the work *Enconium Emmae Reginae*, written c. 1040 at St Omer, II, c. 20 (ed. A. Campbell for R. Hist. Soc. 1949).

70 St Olave Old Jewry, burnt in 1666, was rebuilt by Wren but demolished (except the tower) in 1888. St Olave Silver Street was not rebuilt after the Great Fire.

71 *Liber Eliensis*, 202–3. Cnut was accustomed to spend Candlemas of each year at Ely abbey, for which he appears to have had a particular fondness.

72 *Sub anno* 1020. Aethelnoth died in 1038. The Chronicle, in recording his death, refers to him as 'the good archbishop'. The bishop of Selsey, Aethelric, was so overcome at the death of the archbishop, 'his beloved father', that he lost the desire to live, and himself died within a week.

73 See D. Knowles, *Monastic Order*, p. 71 n. for a list of the Confessor's episcopal appointments. William I in his turn continued Edward's policy, and of his eighteen episcopal appointments only five are known with certainty to have been of monks.

74 William of Malmesbury, *De Gestis Pont.* p. 70, writes of the Canterbury monks' worldly and luxurious manner of life. Cf. Eadmer, 'Vita S. Dunstani' (*Memorials of St Dunstan*), p. 236.

75 Knowles, pp. 74–8.

76 Concerning the foundation of Westminster abbey see H. F. Westlake, *Westminster Abbey* (1923), pp. 5 ff. Much uncertainty surrounds the history of the earlier house, whose reputed founder was king Saebert, Ethelbert's nephew. The true history of the Abbey begins *c.* 959, and its practical founder was Dunstan.

Ch. XXIV

1 Stenton, *Anglo-Saxon England*, p. 460. It is uncertain what happened to Stigand after his deposition. It was often thought that he was imprisoned, but Stenton points out (p. 652 n.) that he was holding an important manor at the time of his death, which seems to have occurred soon after the holding of the council.

2 We possess a very satisfactory account of Lanfranc in the late Dr A. J. MacDonald's *Lanfranc: a Study of his Life, Work, and Writing* (1944 ed.). His works were edited by J. A. Giles, *Lanfranci Opera* (2 vols., 1844), which also includes Lanfranc's *Vita* by Milo. There is valuable information relating to his earlier career in Gilbert Crispin's *Life of Herluin* (1911), edited by J. Armitage Robinson. A learned, though somewhat biased work on the Church in England at this time is *Kirche und Staat in England und in der Normandie* (Leipzig 1899), by H. Boehmer.

3 MacDonald, *Lanfranc*, p. 13.

4 J. Armitage Robinson's edition of Crispin's *Vita Herluini* was included as part of his work, *Gilbert Crispin: Abbot of Westminster*, pp. 87 ff.

5 So a tradition at St Albans (*Gesta Abbat. Monast. S. Alb.* I, 52), though it was refuted by the St Albans chroniclers Matthew Paris (*Hist. Ang.* III, 172) and Roger of Wendover (*Flores Historiarum* II, 5, 21). The suggestion of Dean Hook (*Lives of the Archbishops of Canterbury*, I, 80), that Lanfranc was married and turned to religion on the death of his wife, is plausible enough though there is no authority for it.

6 On this controversy see A. J. MacDonald, *Berengar and the Reform of Sacramental Doctrine* (1930).

7 C. Gore, *The Body of Christ* (1909), p. 118.

8 *Lanfranc*, p. 55. Dr MacDonald considered the failure of Berengar's views to be a disaster (*Berengar*, pp. 223–5). Cf. his remarks (*Berengar*, p. 214): 'the story of Berengarianism illustrates the fate which overtakes ideas when unsupported by a dominant personality for their publication. Berengar was not a Luther. His temperament was not qualified for the rough-and-tumble of life among ambitious churchmen, who place expediency before principle.'

9 William of Poitiers, *Gesta Willelmi Ducis* (ed. J. A. Giles, 1845), p. 147.

10 *Historians of York* (R.S.), II, 357. There were of course many instances of written professions of obedience from the ordinary diocesans.

11 Malmesbury, *De Gestis Pont.* p. 40.

12 The view was put forward by Heinrich Boehmer (*Die Fälschungen Erzbischof Lanfranks von Canterbury*, Leipzig 1902) and succeeded in convincing most

English students; but the charge of dishonesty has been convincingly refuted by MacDonald (*Lanfranc*, Appendix I).

13 For the councils see Wilkins, *Concilia* I, 362–8.

14 Wilkins, I, 363–4.

15 For the decrees of this council see especially Matthew Parker, *De antiquitate Britannicae Ecclesiae* (Hanau 1605).

16 *Vita Wulfstani*, ed. R. R. Darlington, pp. 53–4. A priest must choose between his wife or his church. This second (and sainted) Wulfstan was more thorough-going in his attitude to the problem than his namesake and predecessor, who with his lawyer-like mind was realistic and accommodating.

17 Catherine Boyd, *Tithes and Parishes in Medieval Italy*, p. 67.

18 Cf. St Augustine, *The City of God*, XIV, ch. xviii.

19 Thus Ailred of Rievaulx, born in 1110, 'came of a long line of married priests, learned, respectable, conscientious' (F. M. Powicke, p. xxxiv, *Life of Ailred of Rievaulx, by Walter Daniel*, 1950).

20 The Winchester council is the only one known in the Western Church at this time to modify the papal decrees on clerical marriage (cf. MacDonald, *Lanfranc*, pp. 105–6). A synod at Westminster in 1102, under Anselm, legis-lated against clerical marriage, without immediate success (Eadmer, *Historia Novorum* (R.S.), p. 142). The practice was again prohibited in 1108 (*ibid.* p. 174). Councils in 1125 and 1127 returned to the assault. The church of St Denis Walmgate, York, was hereditary until *c.* 1170 (G. W. O. Addleshaw, *The Development of the Parochial System*, p. 14). Clerical marriage seems to have survived longer in the north than elsewhere in England. By the thirteenth century many parochial clergy were still undoubtedly married. See further J. R. H. Moorman, *Church Life in England in the Thirteenth Century* (1945), pp. 63–7, and, on the whole subject, H. C. Lea, *History of Sacerdotal Celibacy* (3rd ed. 1907).

21 H. A. R. Hartridge, *History of Vicarages in the Middle Ages* (1930), p. 3.

22 *Ibid.* p. 4.

23 See Stenton's note in *Anglo-Saxon England*, p. 662.

24 See Stubbs, *Constitutional History*, I, 283–4 (1874), and for William's ordinance separating the two courts, the same scholar's *Select Charters* (9th edition, 1921), p. 99.

25 The *Corpus Juris Canonici*, ed. Aemilius Friedberg, 2 vols. (Leipzig 1879–81) has recently been reprinted (1955). There is a full and lucid summary of Canon Law history in the Report to *The Canon Law of the Church of England* (1947), pp. 3 ff.

26 *The English Church and the Papacy from the Conquest to the Reign of John* (1952), pp. 59 ff.

27 *Ibid.* pp. 63, 231.

28 Eadmer, *Historia Novorum* (R.S.), p. 9.

29 Brooke, *ibid.* p. 138.

30 *Ibid.* p. 128.

31 *Ibid.* p. 137.

32 *Ibid.* p. 139.

33 *Ibid.* p. 136.
34 Cf. the observations of D. Knowles, *Monastic Order*, pp. 81–2.
35 The authority for Gundulf's work in connection with the Tower is *Textus Roffensis* ed. T. Hearne, p. 212.
36 J. A. Robinson, *Gilbert Crispin*, p. x.
37 See Knowles, pp. 114–15.
38 Trans. and ed. by Knowles, *The Monastic Constitutions of Lanfranc* (1951). Cf. MacDonald, *Lanfranc*, ch. XI.
39 The text is included in Simeon of Durham, *Historia ecclesiae Dunelmensis* (R.S.), I, 221–2.

BIBLIOGRAPHY

The following is intended as a guide to some of the more important and useful sources and authorities for the study of the first Christian centuries in England. It is not in any sense exhaustive, and may be supplemented both by my notes to the chapters, and by the bibliographies in many of the books listed.

GENERAL REFERENCE BOOKS AND COLLECTIONS

OF SOURCES, ETC.

Dorothy Whitelock (ed.), *Eng. Hist. Doc. c.* 500–1042 (Lond. 1955). This is now the indispensable starting point to the whole subject.

D. C. Douglas and G. W. Greenaway (ed.), *Eng. Hist. Doc.* 1042–1189 (Lond. 1953).

A. W. Haddon and W. Stubbs (ed.), *Councils and Ecclesiastical Documents*, 3 vols. (Oxf. 1871). This great collection unfortunately was only taken as far as 870. For the period beyond we have D. Wilkins, *Concilia Magnae Britanniae et Hiberniae* (Lond. 1737), a much less satisfactory work. Wilkins, a German who was Lambeth Librarian 1715–18 (his real name was Wilke), gathered together a large miscellany of documents, but treated them in a very cavalier fashion.

W. Dugdale, *Monasticon Anglicanum*, 6 vols. in 8 (2nd ed. revised, Lond. 1817–30). A general book of sources for monastic history.

W. Smith and H. Wace (ed.), *Dictionary of Christian Biography*, 4 vols. (Lond. 1887). Still useful, especially for its articles by W. Stubbs, of which those on Theodore and Offa may be here mentioned.

W. Smith and S. Cheetham (ed.), *Dictionary of Christian Antiquities*, 2 vols. (Lond. 1875–80).

F. Cabrol and H. Leclercq (ed.), *Dictionnaire d'Archéologie Chrétienne et de Liturgie* (Paris 1903 ff.).

Cambridge Medieval History.

Publications of the English Place-Name Society.

W. G. Searle, *Anglo-Saxon Bishops, Kings, and Nobles* (Camb. 1899). The dates of the bishops given by Searle are largely followed by the *Handbook of British Chronology* (R. Hist. Soc. 1939).

W. Stubbs, *Registrum Sacrum Anglicanum* (Oxf., 2nd ed., 1897). A register of episcopal consecrations.

F. L. Cross (ed.), *Oxford Dictionary of the Christian Church* (1957).

H. Gee and W. J. Hardy (ed.), *Documents Illustrative of English Church History* (Lond. 1896). A handy book of translations.

B. Thorpe, *Ancient Laws and Institutes of England* (Lond. 1840).

R. W. Chambers, *England before the Norman Conquest* (Lond. 1928).

D. Whitelock, *Anglo-Saxon Wills* (Camb. 1930).

493

A. J. Robertson, *Anglo-Saxon Charters* (Camb. 1956 ed.).

F. E. Harmer, *Anglo-Saxon Writs* (Manchester 1952).

J. P. Migne, *Patrologia Latina*, 221 vols. (Paris 1844–64); *Patrologia Graeca*, 161 vols. (Paris 1857–1904). Reference to this great collection of the works of fathers and historians up to the year 1215 is often essential.

G. H. Pertz and others (ed.), *Monumenta Germaniae Historica*, in process since 1826. The English counterpart to this, the Rolls Series, has many valuable volumes, but the series was discontinued *c*. 1886.

The two fullest collections of charters are *Codex Diplomaticus Aevi Saxonici* (Lond., 6 vols., 1839–48), ed. by J. M. Kemble, and covering the entire Anglo-Saxon period; and the much more critical edition, *Cartularium Saxonicum*, by W. de Gray Birch (Lond., 3 vols., 1885–93), which, however, went no further than the death of king Edgar.

CHRONICLES, BIOGRAPHIES, AND OTHER ORIGINAL SOURCES

The two fundamental authorities are the *Anglo-Saxon Chronicle*, and Bede's *Historia Ecclesiastica*. The former was edited by B. Thorpe for the Rolls Series (2 vols. 1861), while the A and E texts are in *Two of the Saxon Chronicles Parallel*, ed. C. Plummer (Oxf. 1952 ed.). The Chronicle has often been translated, and recently by G. N. Garmonsway (Everyman 1953). The *Historia Ecclesiastica*, along with *Historia Abbatum* and the Letter to Egbert, was edited by C. Plummer, *Venerabilis Baedae Opera Historica*, 2 vols. (Oxf. 1896). Of the many translations may be mentioned that by L. Shirley-Price (Penguin 1955).

For the Augustinian mission the two great authorities are Bede, and the correspondence of Gregory I. The latter was edited by P. Ewald and L. M. Hartmann in *M.G.H. Epistolae*, I–II. An early Life of Gregory by a Whitby monk was found by P. Ewald at St Gall, and partly published by him in *Historische Aufsätze dem Andenken an G. Waitz gewidmet* (1886). It was edited by F. A. Gasquet (Westminster 1904).

Later authorities for the mission are the late eleventh-century Gocelin, whose Life of Augustine is in the *Acta Sanctorum* (under 26 May). It is too steeped in the miraculous to be of much value. William Thorne's *Chronicle* of St Augustine's abbey is more helpful. It is printed in Twysden and Selden, *Hist. Angl. Scriptores Decem* (Oxf. 1652), and was translated by A. H. Davis, *William Thorne's Chronicle*, in 1934. Thomas of Elmham, *Historia Monasterii S. Augustini Cantuariensis*, ed. C. Hardwick (R.S. 1858), has little to add to Thorne.

A handy collection of relevant documents, with translation, was edited by A. J. Mason, *The Mission of St Augustine to England* (Camb. 1897).

Three editions by B. Colgrave: *Eddius's Life of Bishop Wilfrid* (Camb. 1927); *Two Lives of St Cuthbert* (Camb. 1940); *Felix's Life of St Guthlac* (Camb. 1956). All of these have text, translation, and commentary.

W. H. Stevenson (ed.), *Asser's Life of King Alfred* (Oxf. 1904).

The *Historia Regum*, based on Bede and other materials, and attributed to Simeon of Durham, is in *Symeonis Monachi Opera*, ed. T. Arnold (R.S. 1885). Two other useful sources are Roger of Wendover's *Flores Historiarum*, ed. H. O. Coxe (Lond. 1841), and Florence of Worcester in *Florentii Wigorniensis Monachi Chronicon ex Chronicis*, ed. B. Thorpe (Lond. 1848).

A large and somewhat unwieldy, though very useful, volume was edited by H. Petrie and T. Sharpe, *Monumenta Historica Britannica* (Lond. 1848). It contains many of the texts necessary for the study of Anglo-Saxon history, and is still particularly useful as including the otherwise almost inaccessible Chronicle of Aethelweard.

William of Malmesbury:

De Antiquitate Ecclesiae Glastoniensis, ed. Gale, *Historiae Britannicae Scriptores* xv (Oxf. 1691).

De Gestis Pontificum Anglorum, ed. N. E. S. A. Hamilton (R.S. 1870).

De Gestis Regum Anglorum, ed. W. Stubbs (R.S. 1887–9).

Valuable sources for the later period are:

Memorials of St Dunstan, ed. W. Stubbs (R.S. 1874).

Regularis Concordia, ed. T. Symons (Nelson's Medieval Classics, 1953).

Enconium Emmae Reginae, ed. A. Campbell (Camden Third Series, LXXII, Lond. 1949).

Lanfranc's Monastic Constitutions, ed. D. Knowles (Nelson's Medieval Classics, 1951).

For the continental missions the correspondence of Boniface and Lull is fundamental. It was edited by M. Tangl in *M.G.H. Epistolae Selectae*, I (1916). Translations have been made by E. Kylie, *The English Correspondence of Saint Boniface* (Lond. 1911); E. Emerton, *The Letters of Saint Boniface* (Columbia 1940); and C. H. Talbot, in *The Anglo-Saxon Missionaries in Germany* (Lond. 1954).

The following are important biographies for the missions:

Alcuin's Life of Willibrord, ed. W. Levison, *M.G.H. Scriptores Rerum Merovingicarum*, VII, pt. I (1920).

Willibald's Life of Boniface, ed. Levison, *M.G.H. Scriptores Rerum Germanicarum* (1905).

Lives of Willibald and Winnebald by Huneberc of Heidenheim, ed. O. Holder-Egger, *M.G.H. Scriptores*, xv, pt. I (1887).

Life of Leoba by Rudolf, ed. G. Waitz, *M.G.H. Scriptores*, xv, pt. I (1887).

Life of Sturm by Eigil, ed. G. H. Pertz, *M.G.H. Scriptores*, II (1829).

Life of Lebuin, ed. A. Hofmeister, *M.G.H. Scriptores*, xxx, pt. II (1934).

Translations of the above are in Talbot. Cf. his bibliography of these sources, pp. xix–xx. See further D. Whitelock, *Eng. Hist. Doc.* I, 582.

O. Cockayne, *Leechdoms, Wortcunning, and Starcraft in Early England*, 3 vols. (R.S. 1866), is valuable for the survival of heathen and superstitious practices.

SECONDARY WORKS

Of older books may be mentioned:

J. M. Kemble, *The Saxons in England*, 2 vols. (Lond. 1849).

A. P. Stanley, 'The Landing of Augustine and Conversion of Ethelbert', in *Historical Memorials of Canterbury* (first published Lond. 1854).

J. Lingard, *History and Antiquities of the Anglo-Saxon Church*, 2 vols. (Lond. 1858).

W. Stubbs, *Constitutional History of England*, 1, ch. 8 (Oxf. 1874).

W. Bright, *Chapters of Early English Church History* (Oxf. 3rd ed, 1897).

J. A. Ramsay, *The Foundations of England*, 1 (Lond. 1898).

General works:

R. G. Collingwood and J. N. L. Myres, *Roman Britain and the English Settlements* (Oxf., 2nd ed., 1937).

Sir Frank Stenton, *Anglo-Saxon England* (Oxf., 2nd ed., 1947).

T. Hodgkin, *History of England from the Earliest Times to the Norman Conquest* (Lond. 1906).

C. Oman, *England before the Norman Conquest* (Lond., 8th ed., 1937).

R. H. Hodgkin, *History of the Anglo-Saxons*, 2 vols. (Oxf., 3rd ed., 1952).

W. Hunt, *The English Church from its Foundation to the Norman Conquest* (Lond. 1907).

G. O. Sayles, *The Medieval Foundations of England* (Lond., 2nd ed., 1950).

P. Hunter Blair, *Introduction to Anglo-Saxon England* (Camb. 1956).

D. Whitelock, *The Beginnings of English Society* (Pelican 1952).

A. Plummer, *The Churches in England before A.D. 1000*, 2 vols. (Lond. 1912).

J. R. H. Moorman, *A History of the Church in England* (Lond. 1958 ed.).

M. Deanesly, *A History of the Medieval Church* (Lond. 1925).

H. von Schubert, *Geschichte der Christlichen Kirche im Frühmittelalter* (Tubingen 1917–21).

A. Hauck, *Kirchengeschichte Deutschlands* (Leipzig 1887–1920).

M. Deanesly, *The Pre-conquest Church in England* (Lond. 1961).

Books of interest on various topics:

Sir Henry H. Howarth, *Saint Augustine of Canterbury* (Lond. 1913).

A. H. Thompson (ed.), *Bede: his Life, Times, and Writings* (Oxf. 1935).

D. Whitelock, *The Audience of Beowulf* (Oxf. 1951).

C. J. B. Gaskoin, *Alcuin: his Life and his Work* (Camb. 1904).

J. Armitage Robinson, *Somerset Historical Essays* (Oxf. 1921). Valuable for Glastonbury.

D. M. Wilson, *The Anglo-Saxons* (Lond. 1960). From the archeological standpoint.

D. Rock, *The Church of our Fathers* (ed. G. W. Hart and W. H. Frere, Lond. 1905, 4 vols.).

D. Knowles, *The Monastic Order in England* (Camb. 1950 ed.).

K. Edwards, *The English Secular Cathedrals in the Middle Ages* (Manchester 1949).

D. Knowles and R. N. Hadcock, *Medieval Religious Houses, England and Wales* (Lond. 1953).

L. M. Smith, *The Early History of the Monastery of Cluny* (Lond. 1920).

Joan Evans, *Monastic Life at Cluny, 910–1157* (Lond. 1931).

A. H. Thompson, *Diocesan Organisation in the Middle Ages* (Raleigh Lecture, 1943).

G. Hill, *The English Dioceses* (Lond. 1900).

J. M. Ure (ed.), *The Benedictine Office: an Old English Text* (Edinburgh 1957).

J. Armitage Robinson, *The Times of St Dunstan* (Oxf. 1923).

T. J. Oleson, *The Witenagemot in the Reign of Edward the Confessor* (Oxf. 1955).

J. Armitage Robinson, *Gilbert Crispin, Abbot of Westminster* (Camb. 1911).

Z. N. Brooke, *The English Church and the Papacy from the Conquest to John* (Camb. 1952 ed.).

P. Clemoes (ed.), *The Anglo-Saxons* (Lond. 1959). Especially for paper by H. M. Taylor, 'Some Little Known Aspects of English pre-Conquest Churches'.

A. J. MacDonald, *Lanfranc: a Study of his Life, Work, and Writing* (Oxf. 1926, republished S.P.C.K. 1944).

——*Berengar and the Reform of Sacramental Doctrine* (Lond. 1930).

H. Böhmer, *Die Fälschungen Erzbischof Lanfrancs von Canterbury* (Leipzig 1902).

——*Kirche und Staat in England und in der Normandie* (Leipzig 1899).

F. A. Gasquet and E. Bishop, *The Bosworth Psalter* (Lond. 1908). Useful for the study of saints' days.

F. Wormald, *English Kalendars before A.D. 1000* (Henry Bradshaw Soc., LXXII, 1934).

H. Pirenne, *Mohammed and Charlemagne* (trans. B. Miall, 1954 ed., Lond.).

Alfons Dopsch, *The Economic and Social Foundations of European Civilisation* (trans. M. G. Beard and N. Marshall, Lond. 1953 ed.).

C. Dawson, *The Making of Europe* (Lond. 1946).

——*Religion and the Rise of Western Culture* (Lond. 1950).

P. E. Schramm, *A History of the English Coronation* (trans. L. G. Wickham Legg, Oxf. 1937).

C. Creighton, *A History of Epidemics in Britain*, 2 vols. (Camb. 1891). Valuable for a knowledge of the plagues.

A series of books by Bishop G. F. Browne, based largely on lecture notes and therefore discursive in character, but still reliable and useful on the whole:

The Church in these Islands before Augustine (Lond. 1894).
Augustine and his Companions (1895).
The Conversion of the Heptarchy (1896).
Theodore and Wilfrith (1897).
St Aldhelm (1903).
Boniface of Crediton and his Companions (1910).
The Importance of Women in Anglo-Saxon Times, with other addresses. (1919).
The Venerable Bede: His Life and Writings (1930).

Eleanor S. Duckett, *Anglo-Saxon Saints and Scholars* (N.Y. 1947).
——*Alcuin, Friend of Charlemagne* (N.Y. 1951).
——*Saint Dunstan of Canterbury* (Lond. 1955).
——*Alfred the Great and his England* (Lond. 1957).

On the German missions:

H. Hahn, *Bonifaz und Lul* (Leipzig 1883).
S. J. Crawford, *Anglo-Saxon Influence on Western Christendom, 600–800* (Oxf. 1933).
W. Levison, *England and the Continent in the Eighth Century* (Oxf. 1946).
G. W. Greenaway, *Saint Boniface* (Lond. 1955).

On the Scandinavian missions:

K. Maurer, *Die Bekehrung des norwegischen Stammes zum Christenthume* (Munich 1855).
A. Taranger, *Den Angelsaksiske Kirkes Indflydelse paa den Norske* (Christiana 1890).
C. J. A. Oppermann, *The English Missionaries in Sweden and Finland* (Lond. 1937).
G. Turville-Petre, *The Heroic Age in Scandinavia* (Lond. 1951).

ARTICLES, PAPERS, ETC.

M. Deanesly, 'The Familia at Christchurch, Canterbury', in *Essays in Medieval History presented to T. F. Tout* (Manchester 1925).
——'The Archdeacons of Canterbury under Archbishop Ceolnoth' (*E.H.R.* XLII, 1927).
——'Early English and Gallic Minsters' (*Trans. R.H.S.*, 4th series, 1941).
——'Canterbury and Paris in the Reign of Ethelbert' (*History*, XXVI, 1941).
——'The Court of King Ethelbert of Kent' (*Camb. Hist. Journ.* VII 1942).
M. Deanesly and P. Grosjean, 'The Canterbury Edition of the Answers of Pope Gregory I to St. Augustine' (*J.E.H.* x, i, 1959).
D. Knowles, 'The Early Community at Christchurch, Canterbury' (*J.T.S.* XXXIX, 1938).
R. A. L. Smith, 'The Early Community of St Andrew at Rochester, 604–c. 1080'. (*E.H.R.* LX, 1945).
A. S. Cook, 'Augustine's Journey from Rome to Richborough' (*Speculum*, I, 1926).
P. F. Jones, 'The Gregorian Mission and English Education' (*Speculum*, III, 1928).
R. L. Poole, 'St Wilfred and the See of Ripon' (*E.H.R.* XXXIV, 1919, reprinted in *Studies in Chronology and History*, Oxf. 1934).
M. L. W. Laistner, 'Bede as a Classical and a Patristic Scholar' (*Trans. R.H.S.*, 4th series, XVI, 1933).
W. Levison, 'St. Willibrord and his Place in History' (*Durham Univ. Journ.* XXXII, 1940).
Sir Ivor Atkins, 'The Church of Worcester from the Eighth to the Twelfth Century' (*Antiq. Journ.* XVII, 1937).
P. Grierson, 'Grimbald of St. Bertin's' (*E.H.R.* LV, 1940).

Sir Frank Stenton, 'The Historical Bearing of Place-Name Studies: Anglo-Saxon Heathenism' (*Trans. R.H.S.*, 4th series, 1941). With map of heathen place-names facing p. 24.

——'The Early History of the Abbot of Abingdon' (*Reading Studies in Local History*, O.U.P. 1913).

——'St Frideswide and her Times' (*Oxoniensa*, I, 1936).

H. P. R. Finberg, 'The House of Ordgar and the Foundation of Tavistock Abbey, (*E.H.R.* LVIII, 1943).

——'Sherborne, Glastonbury, and the Expansion of Wessex' (*Trans. R.H.S.*, 5th series, 1953).

D. J. V. Fisher, 'The Church in England between the Death of Bede and the Danish Invasions' (*Trans. R.H.S.*, 5th series, 1952).

——'The Anti-Monastic Reaction in the Reign of Edward the Martyr' (*Camb. Hist. Journ.* X, pt. III, 1952).

Mary Bateson, 'Rules for Monks and Secular Canons after the Revival under King Edgar' (*E.H.R.* IX, 1894).

——'Origin and Early History of Double Monasteries' (*Trans. R.H.S.*, new series, XIII, 1899).

D. Whitelock, 'The Conversion of the Eastern Danelaw' (*Saga-Book of the Viking Society*, XII, pt. III, 1941).

——'Archbishop Wulfstan, Homilist and Statesman' (*Trans. R.H.S.*, 4th series, 1942).

R. R. Darlington, 'Ecclesiastical Reform in the late Old English Period' (*E.H.R.* LI, 1936). An article which has had considerable influence in swinging historians away from the old view of late Anglo-Saxon ecclesiastical decadence.

T. Symons, 'The English Monastic Reform of the Tenth Century' (*Downside Review*, LX, 1942).

Rose Graham, 'The Intellectual Influence of English Monasticism between the Tenth and Twelfth Centuries', in *English Ecclesiastical Studies* (Lond. 1929).

E. John, 'St Oswald and the Tenth Century Reformation' (*J.E.H.* IX, 1958).

P. G. Caraman, 'The Character of the late Saxon clergy' (*Downside Review*, LXIII, 1945).

J. Armitage Robinson, 'The Early Community of Christchurch, Canterbury' (*J.T.S.* XXVII, 1926).

——'The Saxon Bishops of Wells' (*British Academy Supplementary Papers*, No. 4, 1918).

——'St Oswald and the Church of Worcester' (*British Academy Supplementary Papers*, No. 4, 1919).

——'Byrhtferth and the Life of St. Oswald' (*J.T.S.* XXXI, 1930).

——'Lanfranc's Monastic Constitutions' (*J.T.S.* X, 1909).

CHRISTIANITY IN EARLY BRITAIN

H. Williams, *Christianity in Early Britain* (Oxf. 1912). A valuable book which contains extracts from early Christian writers relating to the British Church, and an excursus on British hagiographic literature.

H. Williams (ed.), *De Excidio Britanniae* (Lond. 1899, with trans.). On the historical value of Gildas see F. Lot, 'De la valeur du "De Excidio"' in *Medieval Studies in memory of Gertrude Schoepperle* (Paris and N.Y. 1927).

On St. Patrick:

Whitley Stokes, *The Tripartite Life of St Patrick* (R.S. 1887).
J. B. Bury, *The Life of St Patrick and his Place in History* (Lond. and N.Y. 1905).
E. J. Newell, *St Patrick: his Life and Teaching* (Lond. 1907).
N. J. D. White, *St Patrick, his Writings and Life* (Lond. 1920).
——*The Writings of St Patrick* (translations, Lond. 1932).

T. D. Kendrick, *The Druids* (Lond. 1927).
I. A. Richmond, *Roman Britain* (Pelican 1955).
G. T. Stokes, *Ireland and the Celtic Church* (Lond. 1886).
J. Ryan, *Irish Monasticism: Origins and Early Development* (Lond. 1931).
F. E. Warren, *Liturgy and Ritual of the Celtic Church* (Oxf. 1881).
L. Gougaud, *Christianity in Celtic Lands* (trans. Maud Joynt, Lond. 1932). Extensive bibliographies.
J. F. Kenney, *Sources for the Early History of Ireland, Vol. I: Ecclesiastical* (Columbia 1929). Especially valuable for its survey of editions of texts.
W. A. Philips (ed.), *History of the Church of Ireland*, 1 (Oxf. 1933).
J. A. Duke, *The Columban Church* (Oxf. 1932, reprinted Edinburgh 1957). Full bibliography.
M. and L. de Paor, *Early Christian Ireland* (Lond. 1958). The illustrations are an excellent feature of this book.
Nora K. Chadwick and others (ed.), *Studies in the Early British Church* (Camb. 1958). Highly critical and technical.
J. T. Fowler (ed.), *Adamnani Vita S. Columbae* (Oxf. 1894, 2nd ed. 1920).

Articles:

F. Haverfield, 'Early Northumbrian Christianity and the Altars to the "Di Veteres"' (*Archeologia Aeliana*, 3rd series, xv).
——'Early British Christianity' (*E.H.R.* xi, 1896).
S. N. Miller, 'The British Bishops at the Council of Arles' (*E.H.R.* XLII, 1927).
C. R. Peers, 'The Earliest Christian Churches in Britain' (*Antiquity*, III, 1929).
W. J. Watson, 'The Celtic Church and its Relations with Paganism' (*Celtic Review*, Nov. 1915).

LITERATURE AND LEARNING

Two books which contain translations of Christian poetry are:
C. W. Kennedy, *Early English Christian Poetry* (Lond. 1952).
R. K. Gordon, *Anglo–Saxon Poetry* (Everyman 1926).

For prose literature see:
Aelfric's Homilies in *Liber Sermonum Catholicorum*, ed. B. Thorpe, 2 vols. (Lond. 1844).

Aelfric's *Lives of the Saints*, ed. W. W. Skeat (E.E.T.S. 1881–1900). For bibliography of works relating to Aelfric see D. Whitelock, *Eng. Hist. Doc.* I, 584.

The Blickling Homilies of the Tenth Century, ed. R. Morris (E.E.T.S. 1880).

Byrhtferth's Manual, ed. S. J. Crawford (E.E.T.S. 1928).

Be Domes Daege, ed. J. R. Lumby (E.E.T.S. 1876).

The Homilies of Wulfstan, ed. Dorothy Bethurum (Oxf. 1957).

Sermo Lupi ad Anglos, ed. D. Whitelock (Methuen Old English Library, 2nd ed., 1952, containing a summary of recent work on Wulfstan).

The letters of Aldhelm are edited by R. Ehwald in *M.G.H. Auct. Ant.* XV (1919), those of Alcuin by E. Dümmler in *M.G.H. Epist. Karol. Aevi*, II (1895). Alcuin's poem on the saints of York may be read in *Historians of the Church of York*, ed. J. Raine, I (R.S. 1879).

H. M. Chadwick, *Early National Poetry* (Camb. Hist. of English Literature, 1907).

M. Bentinck Smith, *Old English Christian Poetry (ibid.)*.

A. F. Leach, *Educational Charters and Documents, 598–1909)* (Camb. 1911).

——*The Schools of Medieval England* (Lond. 1915).

M. L. W. Laistner, *Thought and Letters in Western Europe* (Lond. 1931, new ed. 1957).

R. W. Chambers, *The Exeter Book of Old English Poetry* (Lond. 1933).

——'Bede' (Proceedings Brit. Acad. XXII, 1936).

J. D. A. Ogilvy, *Books known to Anglo-Latin writers from Aldhelm to Alcuin* (Camb., Mass., 1936).

F. E. Harmer, 'The Intellectual Background', in her book *Anglo-Saxon Writs* (Manchester 1952).

N. K. Chadwick, *Poetry and Letters in Early Christian Gaul* (Lond. 1955).

ART AND ARCHITECTURE

Out of the many books the following are amongst the most important for the student of Anglo-Saxon Church history:

T. D. Kendrick, *Anglo-Saxon Art to A.D. 900* (Lond. 1938).

——*Late Saxon and Viking Art* (Lond. 1949).

D. Talbot Rice, *English Art 871–1100* (Oxf. 1952).

G. Baldwin Brown, *The Arts in Early England*, 6 vols. (Lond. 1903–37). The second volume contains a list of churches with recognisable Saxon work.

A. W. Clapham, *English Romanesque Architecture*, 2 vols. (Oxf. 1930 and 1934).

——*Romanesque Architecture in Western Europe* (Oxf. 1936).

Studies in various departments include:

W. Oakeshott, *The Sequence of English Medieval Art* (Lond. 1950).

F. Masai, *Essai sur les Origines de la Miniature Dite Irlandaise* (Brussels 1947).

F. Wormald, *English Drawings of the Tenth and Eleventh Centuries* (Lond. 1952).

O. E. Saunders, *English Illumination*, I (Florence and Paris 1928).

E. G. Millar, *English Illuminated Manuscripts from the Xth to the XIIIth Centuries* (Paris and Brussels 1926).

W. G. Collingwood, *Northumbrian Crosses of the Pre-Norman Age* (Lond. 1927).

A. Gardner, *English Medieval Sculpture* (Camb. 1951).

A. R. Green and P. M. Green, *Saxon Architecture and Sculpture in Hampshire* (Winchester 1951).

M. H. Longhurst, *English Ivories* (Lond. 1926).

R. Jessup, *Anglo-Saxon Jewellery* (Lond. 1950).

H. C. Butler, *Early Churches in Syria* (ed. E. Baldwin Smith, Princetown 1929).

C. Peers and C. A. Ralegh Radford, *The Saxon Monastery of Whitby* (*Archaeologia*, LXXXIX, 1943).

For Augustine's churches see C. R. Peers, in *Antiquity*, III (1929), and in *Archaeologia*, LXXVII (1927).

F. Henry, *Irish Art in the Early Christian Period* (Lond. 1940).

F. Wormald, *The Benedictional of St Ethelwold* (Lond. 1959).

HISTORY OF PAROCHIAL DEVELOPMENT

Two old books which are still valuable are:

J. Selden, *The History of Tithes* (Lond. 1618).

H. Wharton, *A Defence of Pluralities* (Lond. 1692).

For France the important book is Imbart de la Tour, *Les Paroisses Rurales du ive au xie Siecle* (Paris 1900). A recent work is that by H. G. J. Beck, *The Pastoral Care of Souls in South-East France during the Sixth Century* (Rome 1950).

For Italy see Catherine E. Boyd, *Tithes and Parishes in Medieval Italy* (Ithaca, N.Y. 1952).

In Germany, Ulrich Stutz led the field in the study of the proprietary church. See his essay 'The Proprietary Church as an Element of Medieval Germanic Ecclesiastical Law', in *Medieval Germany, 911–1250. Essays by German Historians* II (trans. G. Barraclough Blackwell, 1948).

   See also his *Benefizialwesens von seinen Anfängen bis auf die Zeit Alexanders III: Geschichte des Kirchlichen*, I (Berlin 1895), and H. Böhmer, 'Das Eigenkirchentum in England', in *Texte und Forschungen zur Englischen Kulturgeschichte: Festgabe fur Felix Liebermann* (Halle 1921).

The theories of Stutz were criticised by Paul Fournier, 'La propriété des églises dans les premiers siècles du moyen âge' (*Nouvelle revue historique de droit français et étranger*, XXI, 1897).

The whole subject of the private church, though much studied on the Continent, has been neglected in England. For bibliographies see Catherine Boyd, Appendix I; the note by D. Knowles in *Monastic Order*, p. 562; and especially G. W. O. Addleshaw in his valuable papers published for St Anthony's Hall, York: *The Beginnings of the Parochial System* (1954), *The Development of the Parochial System* (1954), and *Rectors, Vicars, and Patrons* (1956).

For the feudal background see F. L. Ganshof, *Feudalism* (trans. P. Grierson, Lond. 1952, from the French of *Qu'est-ce que la féodalité?* first published Brussels 1944).

Amongst valuable studies may be mentioned:

P. Thomas, *Le Droit de propriété des laïques sur les églises* (Paris 1906).

D. C. Douglas, *The Domesday Monachorum of Christchurch, Canterbury* (R.H.S. 1944).

G. Ward, 'The List of Saxon Churches in the Textus Roffensis (*Archaeologia Cantiana*, XLIV).

——'The List of Saxon Churches in the Domesday Monachorum and White Book of St. Augustine' (*Archaeologia Cantiana*, XLV).

J. W. F. Hill, *Medieval Lincoln* (Camb. 1948). Valuable for the rise of the parish in an urban area.

H. C. Darby, *The Domesday Geography of Eastern England* (Camb. 1952).

Roundell, Earl of Selborne, *Ancient Facts and Fictions concerning Churches and Tithes* (Lond. 1888).

D. Knowles, *Monastic Order*, pp. 562 ff. and 592 ff.

W. Page, 'Some Remarks on the Churches of the Domesday Survey' (*Archaeologia*, LXVI, 1914).

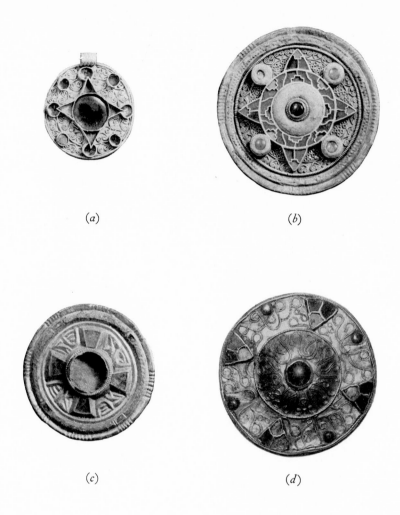

(a)   (b)

(c)   (d)

1   Germanic jewellery of the pagan period. (a) Gold pendant with filigree and garnet inlay. (b) Jewelled brooch of silver and gold with garnet cloisonné. (c) Keystone brooch set with garnets, and ornamented with chip-carving designs. [These brooches, found at Faversham, Kent, are now in the Pitt-Rivers Museum, Farnham, Dorset.] (d) Gold brooch from Liège [now in the collection of Mr Mark Dineley, Berwick St John, Wilts.]

All four brooches are reproduced life-size.

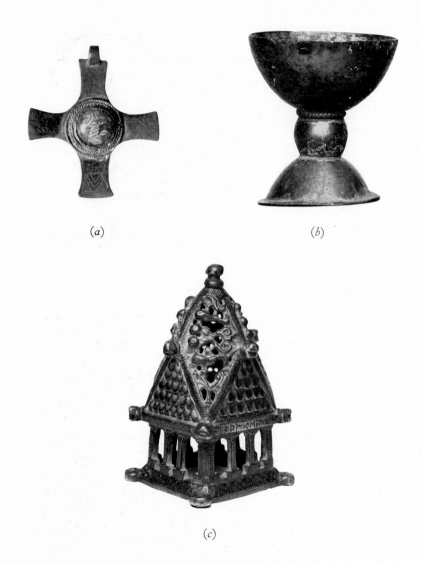

(a)

(b)

(c)

2 (a) Silver pendant cross, from Gravesend. Late ninth century. (B.M.) (b) Gilt-bronze chalice (probably portable), from Hexham. $2\frac{1}{2}$ in. high. One of the two surviving Anglo-Saxon chalices. The other (also in B.M.) was found as part of a hoard at Trewhiddle, Cornwall. (B.M.) (c) Gilt-bronze censer-cover from Pershore. Early eleventh century. (B.M.)

3   Ninth-century cross from Easby, Yorks, in Victoria and Albert Museum since 1930. Carved with the Twelve Apostles and Christ in Majesty. (V. & A.)

(b)

(a)

4 (a) Part of a ninth-century cross from Sheffield, with vine-scroll ornament containing the figure of
an archer. (B.M.) (b) Cross-fragment at Shaftesbury. Tenth century. (Shaftesbury Abbey Museum.)

5 Shrine of the Hewald martyrs in St Cunibert church, Cologne.

6 The Rupert Cross, from Bischofshofen, near Salzburg. The only surviving Anglo-Saxon altar cross. [Cf. the well-known frontispiece to the *Liber Vitae* of the New Minster, now in B.M., showing king Cnut placing such a cross on an altar.] Anglo-Saxon work *c.* 800. Height 5 ft. 1½ in., width 3 ft. 1¾ in. (Bayerisches Nationalmuseum, Munich.)

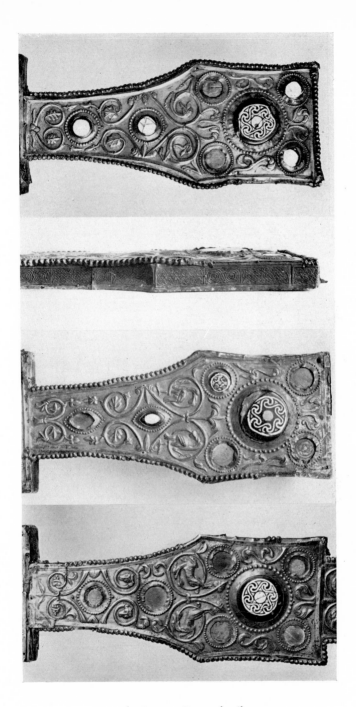

7 The Rupert Cross: details.

8 (*a*) Bronze Celtic crozier-head from Ekerö, Uppland. Eighth century. Height 3¾ in. See W. Holmqvist, 'An Irish crozier-head found near Stockholm' (*Antiquaries Journal*, 1955, pp. 46–51). (Statens Historiska Museum, Stockholm.)

(*b*) English crozier-head, with scenes from Life of Christ and Life of St Nicholas. Date disputed, but possibly late Anglo-Saxon. (V. & A.)

(*a*) Christ in Majesty. Height 3¾ in.

(*b*) Virgin and Child. Height 3⅞ in.
(Both V. & A.)

9   Ivory carvings, probably originally part of a book-cover. Anglo-Saxon work
of early eleventh century.

10 A late Anglo-Saxon ivory, on a German cross of gold filigree and cloisonné enamel. The edge is inscribed with a list of relics formerly enclosed in the cross. The back is embossed with the Agnus Dei and symbols of the Evangelists. Height of cross 7·4 in. (V. & A.)

Clamaui et exau ... diui me

TRIBVLARER CLAMA

VI ET EX AUDIVIT

ME :-

11   Late tenth-century psalter at Salisbury; f. 122 of MS. 150, with opening words
of Psalm 120. The colouring is mainly a dusky red. The psalms and canticles have
large initial letters formed of dragons or birds. The interlinear gloss is of importance
for the study of Old English. (Salisbury Cathedral Library.)

tamen emuloru uefaniæ cœdenfquicontra uirtu
di zelantef rancida liuorif inuidia cōrqueban
tur pfugur longe pficifcenf exulat adeo utfe
annorum intercapedine marida cifterne late
bra delitefcenf nequaquā limphido folif radio
potiretur; Sed menf dō dedita coce durior ferro
fortior adamante rigidior omnef calamicatū
Infeccationefquafclandeftina liuidorum confpi
ratio hoftiliter inrogabat inflexicordif conftan
cia æqua nimiter perferebat;

QVIDBEATVM BABILLVM LOQVAR
quidominici gregif excubiaf & mandraf
aecclefiæ aduerfufcruculencam tyran
norum rabiem uelut contra ferinam
luporum ferocicacem nonmore mercen
narii fedfolercia paftorali tuebatur; Cumeffet
summi pontificatuf infula prædicuf numeria
num auguftum interfectorū cruore concam
natum nonpmifit bafilice facrarium intran
do pullutif pedibuf profanare fedacerrimæ
caftigationif cenfura afacrif aecclefiæ liminibu
funefti regif incroitum arcebat nequaquam

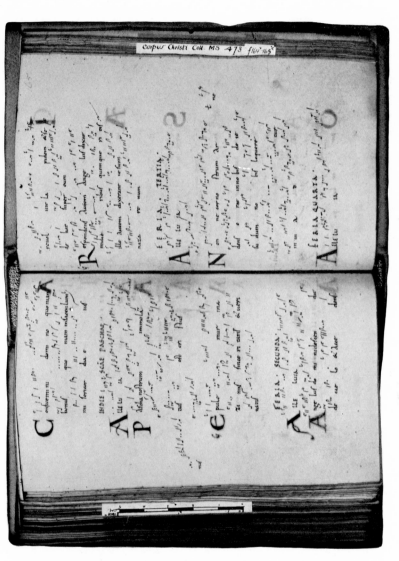

13   Winchester Troper; f. 164b–165a of MS. 473.   Early eleventh century.   (Corpus Christi College, Cambridge.)

14 (*a*) Church of the Apostles, Cologne. Commenced eleventh century. A fine example of Rhineland Romanesque architecture.

(*b*) Sompting church, Sussex. Eleventh century. [Cf. censer-cover, Plate 2.]

(a)

(b)

15 (a) An impressive early minster interior, at Brixworth, Northants. Seventh century. Not originally aisled, as once supposed, but with separate 'porticus' on each side opening out from the arches. See H. M. Taylor, in *The Anglo-Saxons* (ed. P. Clemoes), p. 143. (b) Interior of Escomb church, Co. Durham, a seventh or eighth-century village church, with sanctuary and nave.

16 Kirk Hammerton, Yorks. A typical village church of about the time of the Norman Conquest.

INDEX